T0368343

Lecture Notes in Computer Science

# Lecture Notes in Artificial Intelligence     **15208**

Founding Editor

Jörg Siekmann

Series Editors

Randy Goebel, *University of Alberta, Edmonton, Canada*
Wolfgang Wahlster, *DFKI, Berlin, Germany*
Zhi-Hua Zhou, *Nanjing University, Nanjing, China*

The series Lecture Notes in Artificial Intelligence (LNAI) was established in 1988 as a topical subseries of LNCS devoted to artificial intelligence.

The series publishes state-of-the-art research results at a high level. As with the LNCS mother series, the mission of the series is to serve the international R & D community by providing an invaluable service, mainly focused on the publication of conference and workshop proceedings and postproceedings.

Xuguang Lan · Xuesong Mei · Caigui Jiang ·
Fei Zhao · Zhiqiang Tian
Editors

# Intelligent Robotics
# and Applications

17th International Conference, ICIRA 2024
Xi'an, China, July 31 – August 2, 2024
Proceedings, Part VIII

 Springer

*Editors*
Xuguang Lan
Xi'an Jiaotong University
Xi'an, China

Xuesong Mei
Xi'an Jiaotong University
Xi'an, China

Caigui Jiang
Xi'an Jiaotong University
Xi'an, China

Fei Zhao
Xi'an Jiaotong University
Xi'an, China

Zhiqiang Tian
Xi'an Jiaotong University
Xi'an, China

ISSN 0302-9743          ISSN 1611-3349 (electronic)
Lecture Notes in Artificial Intelligence
ISBN 978-981-96-0782-2          ISBN 978-981-96-0783-9 (eBook)
https://doi.org/10.1007/978-981-96-0783-9

LNCS Sublibrary: SL7 – Artificial Intelligence

This Springer imprint is published by the registered company Springer Nature Singapore Pte Ltd.
The registered company address is: 152 Beach Road, #21-01/04 Gateway East, Singapore 189721, Singapore

If disposing of this product, please recycle the paper.

# Preface

With the theme "AI & Robotics for Smart Society", the 17th International Conference on Intelligent Robotics and Applications (ICIRA 2024) was held in Xi'an, China, July 31 – August 2, 2024, and designed to encourage advancement in the field of robotics, automation, mechatronics, and applications. It aimed to promote top-level research and globalize quality research in general, making discussions and presentations more internationally competitive and focusing on the latest outstanding achievements, future trends, and demands.

ICIRA 2024 was organized and hosted by Xi'an Jiaotong University, co-hosted by Zhejiang University, Harbin Institute of Technology, Shenyang Institute of Automation Chinese Academy of Sciences, and Huazhong University of Science and Technology. Also, ICIRA 2024 was technically co-sponsored by Springer. ICIRA 2024 was a successful event. It attracted more than 490 submissions, of which 489 were sent for peer review, and the Program Committee undertook a rigorous review process to select the most deserving research for publication. The Advisory Committee gave advice for the conference program. Also, they helped to organize special sections for ICIRA 2024. Finally, a total of 321 papers were selected for publication in 10 volumes of Springer's Lecture Note in Computer Science. For the review process, single-blind peer review was used. Each review took around 2–3 weeks, and each submission received at least 2 reviews and 1 meta-review.

In ICIRA 2024, 12 distinguished plenary speakers delivered their outstanding research works in various fields of robotics. Participants gave a total of 180 oral presentations and 142 poster presentations, enjoying this excellent opportunity to share their latest research findings. Here, we would like to express our sincere appreciation to all the authors, participants, and distinguished plenary and keynote speakers. Special thanks are also extended to all members of the Organizing Committee, all reviewers for peer review, all staff of the conference affairs group, and all volunteers for their diligent work.

August 2024

Xuguang Lan
Xuesong Mei
Caigui Jiang
Fei Zhao
Zhiqiang Tian

# Organization

## Conference Chair

Xuguang Lan                 Xi'an Jiaotong University, China

## Program Chairs

| | |
|---|---|
| Xuesong Mei | Xi'an Jiaotong University, China |
| Xinjun Liu | Tsinghua University, China |
| Heping Chen | Texas State University, USA |
| Bo Tao | Huazhong University of Science and Technology, China |
| Lianqing Liu | Chinese Academy of Sciences, China |
| Geng Yang | Zhejiang University, China |

## Organizing Chairs

| | |
|---|---|
| Honghai Liu | Harbin Institute of Technology, China |
| Jun Zou | Zhejiang University, China |

## Award Committee Chairs

| | |
|---|---|
| Fei Zhao | Xi'an Jiaotong University, China |
| Xuetao Zhang | Xi'an Jiaotong University, China |

## Publication Chairs

| | |
|---|---|
| Caigui Jiang | Xi'an Jiaotong University, China |
| Zhiyong Wang | Harbin Institute of Technology, China |

## Local Arrangement Chairs

Zhiqiang Tian                  Xi'an Jiaotong University, China
Jianyi Liu                     Xi'an Jiaotong University, China

## Registration Chair

Liangjun Chen                  Xi'an Jiaotong University, China

## Regional Chairs

Zhiyong Chen                   University of Newcastle, Australia
Naoyuki Kubota                 Tokyo Metropolitan University, Japan
Zhaojie Ju                     University of Portsmouth, UK
Eric Perreault                 Northeastern University, USA
Peter Xu                       University of Auckland, New Zealand
Simon Yang                     University of Guelph, Canada
Houxiang Zhang                 Norwegian University of Science and Technology,
                                 Norway
Imad Elhajj                    American University of Beirut, Lebanon
Yaguo Lei                      Xi'an Jiaotong University, China

## Program Committee Members

Yuwen Sun                      Dalian University of Technology, China
Zeyang Xia                     Shanghai Jiao Tong University, China
Guimin Chen                    Xi'an Jiaotong University, China
Weijun Tian                    Jilin University, China
Lei Jiang                      Shanghai Humanoid Robot Manufacturing
                                 Innovation Center, China
Xiaofeng Liu                   Hohai University, China
Daqi Zhu                       University of Shanghai for Science and
                                 Technology, China
Duanling Li                    Beijing University of Posts and
                                 Telecommunications, China
Baiquan Su                     Beijing University of Posts and
                                 Telecommunications, China
Jihua Zhu                      Xi'an Jiaotong University, China
Ning Sun                       Nankai University, China

| | |
|---|---|
| Yang Gao | Chang'an University, China |
| Xing Liu | Northwestern Polytechnical University, China |
| Jiyu Cheng | Shandong University, China |
| Yanfeng Lv | Chinese Academy of Sciences, China |
| Liang Zhao | Henan University of Technology, China |
| Anzhu Gao | Shanghai Jiao Tong University, China |
| Yixing Gao | Jilin University, China |
| Laihao Yang | Xi'an Jiaotong University, China |
| Yuquan Leng | South University of Science and Technology, China |
| Honghao Lv | Zhejiang University, China |
| Weiliang Zuo | Xi'an Jiaotong University, China |

# Contents – Part VIII

**Robot Skill Learning and Transfer**

## AI-Driven Smart Industrial Systems

## Natural Interaction and Coordinated Collaboration of Robots in Dynamic Unstructured Environments

# Robot Skill Learning and Transfer

# Utilizing Large Language Models for Robot Skill Reward Shaping in Reinforcement Learning

Qi Guo[1], Xing Liu[1(✉)], Jianjiang Hui[2], Zhengxiong Liu[1], and Panfeng Huang[1]

[1] Research Center for Intelligent Robotics, School of Astronautics,
Northwestern Polytechnical University, Xi'an 710072, China
`qiguo@mail.nwpu.edu.cn`, {`xingliu,liuzhengxiong,pfhuang`}`@nwpu.edu.cn`
[2] Beijing Institute of Tracking and Telecommunication Technology,
Beijing 100094, China

**Abstract.** In this paper, we examines the integration of LLMs in designing reward functions for reinforcement learning (RL) to enhance robotic applications with minimal human input. In RL, the reward function is pivotal, guiding the agent's learning trajectory by evaluating the desirability of behaviors within specific environments. Traditional reward functions, often sparse, lead to slow convergence as agents require extensive interactions to learn effectively. By leveraging LLM's ability to generate code from task semantics, we propose a new method that reduces the complexity of reward design, allowing even non-experts to create effective reward policies using semantic prompts. We utilize the Soft Actor-Critic (SAC) algorithm, known for its efficiency and stability, to train agents under these conditions. To validate the efficacy of our method, we compare it with traditional techniques like Trajectory-ranked reward extrapolation (T-REX). Our findings indicate that the LLM-generated rewards enable quicker convergence and are as effective as those crafted through conventional methods, demonstrating the potential of LLMs to revolutionize reward shaping in RL. Furthermore, we transferred the robot door-opening task from the real-world simulation environment to a real robot, achieving sim-to-real.This approach allows for the rapid deployment of robotic systems, making sophisticated robotics technology more accessible and feasible for a wider range of applications. This study underscores the transformative impact of integrating advanced language models into the realm of robotics and RL, opening up new avenues for future research and application.

**Keywords:** Large language model(LLMs) · reward shaping · reinforcement learning

## 1 Introduction

In the domain of robotic skill acquisition, researchers and engineers have developed various methods to accelerate the learning process in order to enhance efficiency and quality. These methods address the challenges of slow learning rates and suboptimal outcomes from diverse perspectives and are typically applied to complex robotic tasks. One approach involves the direct transfer of human knowledge and policies to robots through human-machine interaction, thereby accelerating the learning process [1–3]. Human operators can directly influence the robots' learning trajectories by demonstrating tasks or providing feedback, enabling robots to rapidly acquire core skills for complex tasks. This method is particularly suited to tasks requiring intricate decision-making and precision manipulation. Imitation learning allows robots to learn tasks by observing the actions of human experts [4,5]. By directly imitating effective policies, robots can avoid aimless exploration in the initial stages, significantly increasing the speed of learning. This approach is especially effective for tasks involving complex manipulations or motion patterns.

In reinforcement learning (RL), the reward function is a crucial component that guides the agent's learning trajectory by quantifying the desirability of its behaviors within a given environment. Essentially serving as a guiding signal, this function encourages the agent to adopt behaviors that maximize cumulative rewards. The ability to design accurate and effective reward functions that aptly describe tasks is critical for the practical application of reinforcement learning to complex robotic manipulations. Providing positive rewards when the target state is reached, and none otherwise, exemplifies the sparsity of rewards. It is well-known that sparse reward functions can lead to slow convergence. Agents need to interact with the environment multiple times and learn from extensive samples to converge to an optimal solution. If agents only receive rewards at the endpoint of a predetermined trajectory, they may spend considerable time exploring the environment to learn appropriate behaviors. Offering intermediate rewards that encourage progress towards the goal can reduce unnecessary exploration, a concept known as reward shaping [6,7]. However, designing intermediate rewards is challenging, especially for non-experts, as it involves numerous factors such as task complexity, environmental dynamics, and the feasibility of policies. Designing an appropriate reward function to guide robots quickly in mastering tasks requires extensive expertise and is challenging in practice. Therefore, how to shape rewards with fewer trials and errors is key to accelerating the learning of robotic skills.

Recently, the emergence of large language models (LLMs) such as LLaMa2, GPT-3, and GPT-4 has fundamentally transformed the capability to interpret and process user inputs using natural language. Extensively pre-trained on vast text datasets, these models have developed a nuanced understanding of language and acquired comprehensive semantic knowledge. This profound understanding of language enables them to generate detailed, text-based operational sequences that accurately reflect complex linguistic descriptions and effectively translate subtle instructions into executable tasks. This capability significantly reduces the reliance on human programmers to manually write complex code for various applications, simplifying the software development process. Particularly transformative in the field of robotics, this technological advance reduces the traditional reliance on extensive labeled data required in conventional reinforcement learning setups for training models to learn policies or optimize existing reward functions.

Large language models can leverage their pre-trained knowledge to generate initial reward designs, thus diminishing the need for exhaustive labeled datasets. This makes deploying RL solutions more feasible in domains where data is scarce or data collection is costly. Designing effective reward functions is one of the most challenging aspects of RL. Reward functions need to precisely reflect task objectives while considering potential unknown outcomes and behaviors during their design. Large language models, by understanding complex task descriptions and objectives, can automatically generate detailed and intricate reward logic [8–10], simplifying the manual design process and reducing design errors. Traditionally, reinforcement learning projects required experienced researchers to meticulously design reward mechanisms. The use of large language models lowers this barrier, enabling non-experts to generate reasonable reward schemes [11–13]. This simplifies interaction with systems through natural language processing interfaces, allowing more researchers and developers to participate in the design and optimization of RL systems. Manually designed reward functions may be imperfect due to the designer's biases or limitations in understanding the problem. Large language models, with their extensive knowledge and data learning, can provide more objective and comprehensive reward design solutions, reducing the impact of human errors.

In this work, our goal is to answer the question: Is there a method that allows us to design more effectively learning rewards with reduced human involvement? We propose a new prompt paradigm to code-writing using GPT-4, designed to transform task semantics into reward functions.

## 2   Related Work

The integration of LLMs into various aspects of reinforcement learning marks a pivotal advancement in the interaction between artificial intelligence and human input [14,15]. As we delve into the related work, it is crucial to understand how these technologies have not only revolutionized the field but also addressed the nuanced challenges of translating complex human instructions into actionable machine tasks. This exploration spans several key areas: the direct generation of executable code for robotics, the enhancement of machine learning models through human feedback, and the sophisticated incorporation of human preferences into the learning algorithms.

**Learning from LLMs.** LLMs have demonstrated proficiency in code generation, and numerous code productivity tools, such as Copilot, have been developed leveraging this capability. LLMs can also be utilized for generating control code for robotics. In the PromptCraft project [16], the skill function interfaces of robots are described to LLMs, after which human language feedback enables the models to combine these skills into policies. This paper investigates the application of large models for generating code for reward functions, aiming to reduce the reliance on real-time feedback.

**Reinforcement Learning from Human Feedback.** Reinforcement Learning from Human Feedback (RLHF) is an influential method used to enhance the performance of LLMs like GPT-4 by integrating human evaluations into their training process. This approach helps refine the output of these models to align more closely with human preferences and expectations. RLHF leverages human feedback to construct a reward model that the learning algorithm uses to optimize the model's outputs for quality and relevance [17–19].

**Learning from Human Preference.** Trajectory-ranked reward extrapolation (T-REX) [20] is an algorithm that infers the users implicit intent to surpass the optimal demonstration, even when all available demonstrations are suboptimal. This inference enables RL agents to optimize an extrapolated reward function, potentially exceeding the performance of the demonstrators. Specifically, the algorithm utilizes ranked demonstrations to learn a state-based reward function that allocates greater total returns to higher-ranked trajectories. Consequently, while standard inverse reinforcement learning approaches aim to derive a reward function that justifies the rationality of the demonstrations, T-REX seeks to formulate a reward function that explains the ranking of the demonstrations, thereby potentially achieving superior performance. This solution can be considered both a demonstration-based inverse reinforcement learning method and a preference-based RL algorithm. However, a significant limitation of this algorithm is its dependency on suboptimal data. We circumvent the challenge of data collection by effectively utilizing LLMs to generate reward function code.

## 3   Reward Shaping Method Using the LLM

The development of a reward shaping methodology using LLMs represents a significant advancement in the field of RL for robotics. By integrating sophisticated natural language processing capabilities with structured logical reasoning, we have formulated a method that significantly simplifies the design of complex reward functions. Moreover, the inclusion of human feedback in the refining process ensures that our models remain adaptable and relevant, ultimately enhancing the autonomy and efficiency of robotic systems in performing intricate tasks (Fig. 1).

### 3.1   Design of Prompt Paradigm for Reward Generation

Due to the high cost of fine-tuning LLMs, prompt-based methods using natural language have become the primary approach for utilizing LLMs to address downstream tasks. Since the quality of the prompts significantly influences the performance of large language models in specific tasks, we generate suitable prompts through manually designed paradigms.To utilize LLMs for generating reward functions, we employ the Chain-of-Thought (CoT) technique [21], which

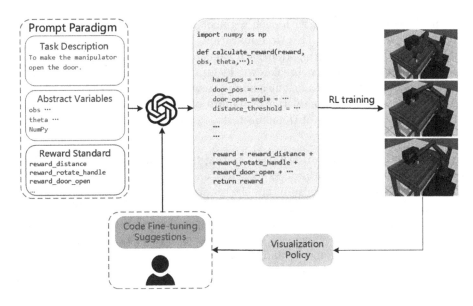

**Fig. 1.** The framework of our method.

enhances the capability of LLMs to solve complex reasoning tasks. This technique involves structuring the prompt to include a series of intermediate reasoning steps, thereby facilitating a more comprehensive analysis and better solution generation. The design process comprises four distinct stages:

**Task Description.** Initially, the task is succinctly described to set a clear and focused context for the LLM. For example, stating "To make the manipulator open the door" provides a direct and unambiguous objective. Variations in phrasing, such as "Ensure the door is opened by the manipulator," might lead the LLM to prioritize different aspects of the task, demonstrating the critical nature of precise language in prompt design.

**Definition of Task-Related Abstract Variables.** According to the task description, it is crucial to define the key variables that generate rewards in a specific environment. This includes specifying the states of relevant objects, such as the positions of a robotic arm and a door, and determining the Python libraries (such as NumPy) that the LLM needs to utilize. The precise definition of these variables enables the LLM to accurately assess the environment and the interactions required to complete the task. The accuracy of these definitions is vital, as inaccuracies can lead to ineffective reward functions, thereby misguiding the learning process of the agent.

**Reward Standard.** The LLM is prompted to deconstruct the main task into simpler, detailed subtasks. This step is designed to simplify a complex problem into manageable segments, with each segment focusing on a specific aspect or step of the original task. This decomposition allows the LLM to tackle each subtask sequentially, ensuring that each element is thoroughly considered and addressed. This systematic breakdown facilitates the creation of a nuanced reward system, where specific, measurable rewards or penalties are assigned based on the successful completion or failure of each subtask, aligning closely with the overall objectives of the main task.

**Reward Code Validation.** After generating the initial reward code, it undergoes a rigorous verification process to detect and rectify any syntax or runtime errors. This step is vital to ensure that the reward functions are not only theoretically correct but also practically functional. If errors are identified, the code is meticulously fine-tuned, enhancing the accuracy and effectiveness of the reward function. This iterative refinement ensures that the final reward function fully satisfies the task requirements and aligns seamlessly with the environmental dynamics and the robotic system's capabilities.

## 3.2   Improve Reward Codes Based on Human Feedback

The fundamental principle of integrating human feedback into the development of reward functions lies in its capacity to refine and adjust the learning process based on nuanced human evaluations that automated systems may not fully capture. Humans can provide subjective assessments that aid in fine-tuning the reward functions beyond just relying on traditional, objective performance metrics.

In initial interactions, humans often provide instructions lacking precise details, which presents challenges in creating optimal reward functions. At best, the initially designed reward functions may be syntactically correct but not ideally suited to the subtleties of the task. For example, when instructing a robot to open a door, users may not specify whether to pull the handle or the door itself. While both actions achieve the objective, pulling the handle is generally preferable as it reduces the risk of damaging the furniture and the robot.

To address the issue of imprecise instructions leading to suboptimal reward functions, we enhance the generated rewards by seeking human feedback. After each RL training cycle, users are shown videos demonstrating how the current strategy executes the task. From these observations, users provide valuable feedback, which is code fine-tuning suggestions, highlighting the strengths and weaknesses in task execution. For instance, when a manipulator gets stuck in a local optimum near the door handle, appropriately increasing the penalties guides the manipulator to approach correctly, or if getting too close results in collisions with the door handle, appropriately increasing safety rewards ensures the completeness of task accomplishment. These inputs are integrated into future prompts, resulting in more precise and effective reward functions. This iterative process ensures the continuous improvement and optimization of the reward system based on direct user evaluations.

## 4    Experiment Setup

In the experimental setup, the Soft Actor-Critic (SAC) algorithm was utilized to train agents within a "door-open-v2" scenario. The SAC algorithm, renowned for its stability and efficiency, was specifically chosen to evaluate the efficacy of reward functions generated by GPT-4. Our method employs a multi-faceted approach for the reward generation: initially providing a baseline reward when the robot's manipulator approaches the door handle, further when the handle is turned, and finally when the door is opened. Such structured reward generation aims to incrementally guide the agents through the necessary steps of the task.

The learning rate for the experiments was set at 0.0003 to ensure smooth convergence without overshooting optimal policy thresholds. Each training session ran for 1,000,000 steps across various seeds to ensure a comprehensive exploration of the policy space. The batch size was maintained at 512 to provide a balance between computational demand and the stability of the learning updates. Furthermore, both the critic and actor networks within the SAC setup were configured with 256 hidden dimensions and three layers, designed to effectively process complex decision-making scenarios within the environment (Fig. 2).

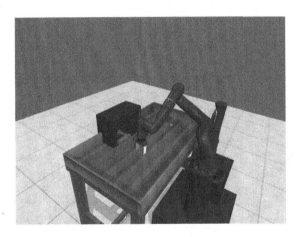

**Fig. 2.** Metaworld door-open-v2 scenatio.

### 4.1    Comparison with the Ground Truth Reward Function

The concept of a ground truth reward function refers to a densely populated, expert-authored reward function that the environment explicitly supplies. In our research, we utilized LLMs to generate reward functions to train agents. Notably, the performance of agents trained with these LLM-generated reward functions did not significantly differ in success rates when compared to those trained with the ground truth reward functions. Importantly, the network parameters trained with the ground truth reward and those trained with the LLM-generated reward functions were consistent, indicating that the LLMs are capable of producing reward functions that closely mirror the expert-written versions in terms of their effectiveness in guiding agent behaviors. During the experimental phase, we employed a systematic approach for evaluating the behavior and effectiveness of the trained agents. Specifically, trajectory segments were captured and compiled into 1-second video clips. These clips were then presented to human evaluators every 20 episodes, providing a consistent and manageable method for assessing the agent's actions and the appropriateness of the reward functions over time. This frequent evaluation helped ensure that the agents' performance remained aligned with the expectations set by both the LLM-generated and ground truth reward functions throughout the course of the experiments (Fig. 3).

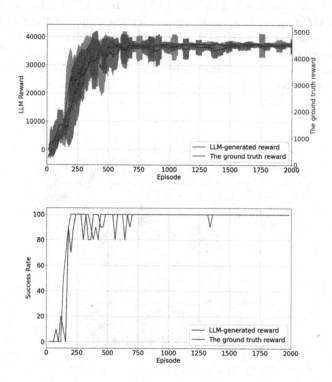

**Fig. 3.** Comparison of LLM-generated reward and the ground truth reward

## 4.2   Comparison with T-REX

The learning of robot door-opening skills using the T-REX approach begins with the application of the Proximal Policy Optimization (PPO) algorithm to acquire complete demonstration data for the door-opening task. The state includes the position and velocity of each joint, the position of the door handle, and the position of the end effector in world coordinates. The policy action consists of controller inputs. During training, a baseline reward is used as the reward function. At the start of each episode, the robot's position and orientation are randomly initialized. Each episode lasts for 512 time steps (10.2 s), with training conducted over eight episodes in a multi-process setting. The learning rate used in this study is 0.0001. The training process involves 1000 episodes (1 million steps). Reward function learning utilizes suboptimal demonstrations from the demonstration data. In the reward learning phase, we collect preference data sets based on the first 200 episodes of demonstration data, and the reward function is inferred based on the constructed preference data set. To evaluate the quality of the rewards learned through T-REX, we maximize the inferred reward function using PPO to learn the reward-based task. The effectiveness of the learning is compared to rewards generated by LLMs as shown in Fig. 4.

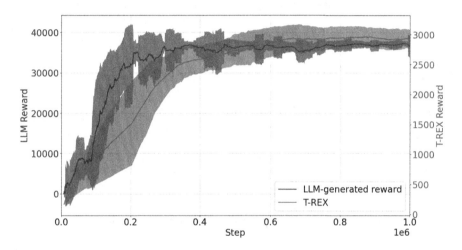

**Fig. 4.** Comparison of LLM-generated reward and T-REX.

## 4.3 Sim-To-Real

This experiment aims to transfer the robot door-opening task from the Meta-world simulation environment to the KUKA LBR iiwa 14 R820 robot, achieving the transition from simulation to reality (sim-to-real).

Firstly, we set up a door-opening task in the meatworld simulation environment and generated the trajectory data for the robot's end effector. The purpose of this simulation phase is to ensure that the robot can successfully complete the door-opening operation and record the motion trajectory of the end effector throughout the process.

Next, we processed the trajectory data from the simulation environment through coordinate transformation to adapt it to the coordinate system of the KUKA robot in the physical environment. Specifically, we carried out the following steps:

**Coordinate Transformation.** The trajectory data from the simulation environment was transformed from its original coordinate system to the KUKA robot's coordinate system. This process includes translations, rotations, and other geometric transformations to ensure the trajectory data has accurate spatial references in the physical environment.

**Time Calibration.** Based on the motion characteristics of the actual robot, the trajectory data was adjusted in terms of time to ensure the robot can execute the task at an appropriate speed and rhythm in actual operation. The trajectory points were fed to the KUKA robot at a frequency of 10 Hz.

Finally, we input the processed trajectory data into the KUKA robot for actual operation verification. During this process, we focused on the following aspects:

**Trajectory Tracking Accuracy.** Whether the robot's end effector can accurately follow the predetermined trajectory.

**Motion Smoothness.** Whether the robot's motion is smooth while executing the trajectory, and if there are any noticeable vibrations or discontinuities.

**Task Completion.** Whether the robot can successfully complete the door-opening task and how the actual operation performance compares with the simulation results.

Through the above steps, we successfully achieved the trajectory transfer from simulation to reality, providing a reliable experimental foundation for further research and applications (Fig. 5).

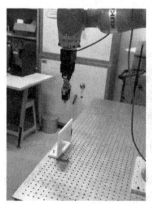

**Fig. 5.** Door opening task

# 5    Experiment Results Discussion

**Reward Function Performance and Convergence.** The experimental results show that training with three kinds of rewards can complete the task goal, which are LLM-generated reward, the ground truth reward and T-REX reward. It is feasible to use LLMs like GPT-4 to generate complex reward functions that facilitate efficient learning of robotic tasks. Agents trained with these LLM-generated rewards not only met the success metrics comparable to those trained with ground truth rewards but also showed a faster convergence rate in many instances. This suggests that the intricate understanding of task semantics that GPT-4 brings can significantly enhance the learning process, reducing the number of episodes required to achieve optimal performance. The use of video clips for real-time human evaluation every 20 episodes has provided continuous feedback, ensuring that the reward functions are consistently aligned with the desired task outcomes. This method of iterative feedback and adjustment has proven essential for maintaining the quality and relevance of the reward functions throughout the training process.

**Comparative Study with T-REX.** During the experiments, we noted that while T-REX effectively guides the learning process by inferring complex reward functions from demonstrator preferences, it inherently relies on the availability and quality of these demonstrations. In contrast, our LLM-based approach frees the training process from these dependencies by generating reward functions that do not require pre-existing demonstrations. This aspect was particularly advantageous in scenarios where prior expert demonstrations were scarce or difficult to perform accurately. Moreover, our findings indicated that agents trained with rewards generated by GPT-4 achieved optimal performance metrics more rapidly than those trained with T-REX. Specifically, the agents using GPT-4 generated rewards required fewer episodes to reach a predefined performance threshold, demonstrating an approximate 60% improvement in convergence speed over the T-REX method. This efficiency is attributable to the direct and precise nature of reward functions generated by GPT-4, which are tailored specifically to the task at hand without the need for intermediary interpretation of human-ranked demonstrations. These results underscore the potential of using LLMs to enhance the flexibility and efficiency of reward generation in RL, particularly in complex or poorly understood domains where generating high-quality demonstrations is challenging. The use of GPT-4 to directly translate task descriptions into functional reward codes not only simplifies the training process but also provides a more scalable and adaptable approach compared to traditional methods reliant on human feedback and demonstration ranking.

**Visualization of Learning Progress.** Visualizations of the learning progress, represented in the learning curves, show a steady and consistent improvement in agent performance with GPT-4 rewards, without the fluctuations typically observed with manually coded or T-REX generated reward functions. This steadiness suggests that the GPT-4 model provides a more stable learning trajectory for the agents.

# 6 Conclusion

In conclusion, this study demonstrates the significant potential of integrating GPT-4, a sophisticated LLM, into the design of reward functions for reinforcement learning applications in robotics. By leveraging GPT-4's ability to interpret and process complex natural language inputs, we have successfully developed a method that automates the generation of nuanced reward functions, thus reducing reliance on human expertise and manual coding efforts.

Our approach utilizes the CoT technique to guide the LLM through structured reasoning processes, enabling the generation of effective reward functions that align with specific task requirements. The detailed method involves stages of task description, variable extraction, reward standard formulation, and rigorous verification, which collectively ensure that the reward functions not only achieve technical accuracy but also practical applicability.

The experimental results indicate that the LLM-generated rewards facilitate faster convergence and comparable performance to agents trained with traditional ground truth reward functions. This efficiency in learning underscores the utility of LLMs in streamlining the development and deployment phases of robotic systems, making advanced robotic capabilities more accessible across various industries.

Comparative analysis with the T-REX method further emphasizes the advantages of our LLM-based approach, particularly in environments where rapid adaptability and deployment are crucial. The findings advocate for broader adoption of LLMs in reward shaping, suggesting a shift towards more intelligent, flexible, and user-friendly RL frameworks.

The sim-to-real experiment successfully transferred a robot door-opening task from the Metaworld simulation environment to the KUKA LBR iiwa 14 R820 robot. This process involved coordinate transformation and time calibration to adapt simulation data to the physical robot, ensuring accurate trajectory tracking, smooth motion, and successful task completion. This demonstrates the feasibility of sim-to-real transitions, providing a robust foundation for future research and applications.

Looking ahead, the integration of LLMs into RL poses exciting opportunities for further research and development. Future studies could explore the adaptation of LLMs across a broader range of applications, including those in unpredictable environments where adaptive learning and decision-making are critical. Additionally, the exploration of hybrid models that combine the strengths of multiple LLMs could lead to even more robust and versatile systems. Another promising direction involves enhancing the interpretability and transparency of the LLM-generated reward functions, which is crucial for trust and scalability in practical applications. This could involve developing methods that allow users to understand and modify the LLM reasoning process more intuitively.

Overall, this research not only enriches the dialogue on enhancing autonomous learning capabilities in robotics but also paves the way for future innovations in integrating language understanding into dynamic reward policies, potentially revolutionizing how machines learn and interact with their environments. The continued evolution of LLM capabilities, combined with advances in other areas of artificial intelligence, promises to further transform the landscape of robotics and automation.

**Acknowledgement.** This work was supported by the National Natural Science Foundation of China under Grant 92370123, 62103334, 62103337 and 62273280.

# Appendix

The following provides an illustrative example of how a reward function is constructed within the Metaworld door-open-v2 scenario.

```
Q:
1. Python function for reward shaping in a reinforcement learning task
2. The task involves a robot with an articulated arm tasked with opening
a hinged door in a simulated environment.
3. The observation is a numerical array where:
- The first three values represent the robot's hand position.
- The next three values represent the door's position, which requires
adding a fixed offset to be calculated.
- 'theta' is the angle of the door in radians, where 0 is closed and
pi/2 is fully open, provided in an 'info' dictionary.
4. The reward function, named 'reward_shaping', should take an 'info'
dictionary containing 'obs' and 'theta' as arguments.
5. The 'obs' includes the full observation array and 'theta' is the
current angle of the door.
6. Criteria for the reward:
- A higher reward for when the robot's hand is close to the door, with a
specified 'distance_threshold' for this proximity reward.
- Incremental positive rewards as the door opens wider, with a bonus
when the angle is less than a 'door_open_angle' threshold.
- Efficiency is encouraged with a small reward for each timestep taken,
promoting the robot to open the door promptly.
7. Please provide the implementation of the 'calculate_reward' function
based on the above description, using numpy for any mathematical
operations.


A:
import numpy as np

def reward_shaping(info):
obs = info['obs']
theta = info['theta']

# Constants and thresholds
distance_threshold = 0.1
```

```
door_open_angle = np.pi / 4
time_penalty = -0.01

# Extract positions from observation
hand_pos = np.array(obs[0:3])
door_pos = np.array(obs[3:6])
door_offset = np.array([0.5, 0, 0])

# Calculate the actual door interaction point
door_interaction_point = door_pos + door_offset

# Calculate distance between hand and door interaction point
distance = np.linalg.norm(hand_pos - door_interaction_point)

# Reward based on distance
if distance < distance_threshold:
proximity_reward = 1.0  # Positive reward if within threshold
else:
proximity_reward = 0.0  # No reward if outside threshold

# Reward based on door angle
angle_reward = (theta / (np.pi / 2))

# Bonus for reaching a sufficient angle threshold
if theta > door_open_angle:
bonus_reward = 0.5
else:
bonus_reward = 0.0

# Total reward calculation
total_reward = proximity_reward + angle_reward + bonus_reward +
time_penalty

return total_reward

# Example usage
info = {
'obs': [1.2, 0.5, 0.3, 1.5, 0.5, 0.3],  # Example observation array
'theta': np.pi / 3  # Example door angle
}

reward = reward_shaping(info)
print("Calculated Reward:", reward)
```

# References

1. Li, B., Liu, X., Liu, Z., et al.: Episode-Fuzzy-COACH method for fast robot skill learning. IEEE Trans. Ind. Electron. **71**(6), 5931–5940 (2024)
2. Bıyık, E., et al.: Learning reward functions from diverse sources of human feedback: optimally integrating demonstrations and preferences. Int. J. Robot. Res. **41**(1), 45–67 (2022)

3. Celemin, C., et al.: An interactive framework for learning continuous actions policies based on corrective feedback. J. Intell. Robot. Syst. **95**, 77–97 (2019)
4. Nguyen, K.: Imitation learning with recurrent neural networks. arXiv preprint arXiv:1607.05241 (2016)
5. Rahmatizadeh, R., et al.: Learning real manipulation tasks from virtual demonstrations using LSTM. arXiv preprint arXiv:1603.03833 (2016)
6. Ng, A.Y.: Policy invariance under reward transformations: theory and application to reward shaping. In: Proceedings of the ICML, vol. 99, pp. 278–287 (1999)
7. Wiewiora, E.: Potential-based shaping and Q-value initialization are equivalent. J. Artif. Intell. Res. **19**, 205–208 (2003)
8. Goyal, P., Niekum, S., Mooney, R.J.: Policy invariance under reward transformations: using natural language for reward shaping in reinforcement learning. arXiv preprint arXiv:1903.02020 (2019)
9. Yu, W., Gileadi, N., Fu, C., et al.: Language to rewards for robotic skill synthesis. arXiv preprint arXiv:2306.08647 (2023)
10. Ma, Yecheng Jason, et al.: Eureka: Human-level reward design via coding large language models. arXiv preprint arXiv:2310.12931 (2023)
11. Xie, T., Zhao, S., Wu, C.H., et al.: Text2Reward: automated dense reward function generation for reinforcement learning. arXiv preprint arXiv:2309.11489 (2023)
12. Zeng, Y., Yao M., Lin, S.: Learning Reward for robot skills using large language models via self-alignment. arXiv preprint arXiv:2405.07162 (2024)
13. Wang, B., et al.: Secrets of RLHF in large language models part II: reward modeling. arXiv preprint arXiv:2401.06080 (2024)
14. Liang, J., et al.: Code as policies: language model programs for embodied control. IEEE International Conference on Robotics and Automation, pp. 9493–9500 (2023)
15. Wu, Y., et al.: Read and reap the rewards: Learning to play Atari with the help of instruction manuals. In: Advances in Neural Information Processing Systems, vol. 36 (2024)
16. Vemprala, S.H., Bonatti, R., Bucker, A., Kapoor, A.: ChatGPT for robotics: design principles and model abilities. IEEE Access **12**, 55682–55696 (2024)
17. Christiano, P.F., Leike, J., Brown, T., Martic, M., Legg, S., Amodei, D.: Deep reinforcement learning from human preferences. In: Advances in Neural Information Processing Systems, vol. 30 (2017)
18. Daniel, M.Z., et al.: Fine-tuning language models from human preferences. arXiv preprint arXiv:1909.08593 (2019)
19. Yuntao, B., et al.: Training a helpful and harmless assistant with reinforcement learning from human feedback. arXiv preprint arXiv:2204.05862 (2022a)
20. Brown, D., Wonjoon, G., Prabhat, N., Scott, N.: Extrapolating beyond suboptimal demonstrations via inverse reinforcement learning from observations. In: International Conference on Machine Learning, pp. 783–792 (2019)
21. Wei, J., Wang, X., Schuurmans, D., et al.: Chain-of-thought prompting elicits reasoning in large language models. Adv. Neural. Inf. Process. Syst. **35**, 24824–24837 (2022)

# Research on Intelligent Dynamic Obstacle Avoidance Strategy for Space Collaborative Robots

Yaobing Wang[1], Fanglin Xie[1(✉)], Yahang Zhang[1], and Lingxin Wang[1,2]

[1] China Academy of Space Technology, Beijing 100094, China
xfl18@tsinghua.org.cn
[2] Harbin Institute of Technology, Harbin 150001, China

**Abstract.** To achieve the great safety requirements for space collaborative robots and astronauts working in remote, unknown and complex space environment, the robots should be clever enough to avoid moving human or obstacles in a quite short time to keep both safe. In this paper, Deep Reinforcement Learning (DRL) techniques were applied to robot manipulators with a grasping workspace invaded by unpredictable moving obstacles. By introducing a hierarchical curriculum learning framework, a multidimensional agent was trained in a high-precision virtual environment. The dynamic obstacle avoidance success rate of strategy trained by Soft Actor-Critic (SAC) achieves 94.6%, higher than 68.4% by Deep Deterministic Policy Gradient (DDPG). Then the Actor network's weight and bias matrices were copied and successfully implanted in a real RM63-6F anthropomorphic robot manipulator. The robot manipulator's end clamp can reach about 0.02 m near the target site, which verifies that using DRL to obtain the motion planning strategy of space robot manipulator with limited computing resources is feasible.

**Keywords:** space collaborative robots · deep reinforcement learning · motion planning · dynamic obstacle avoidance strategy · sim-to-real

## 1 Introduction

In remote, random, and non-deterministic space environments, the random movement of dynamic obstacles greatly impacts the safe operation of collaborative robotic arms. This is particularly challenging in 'space human-robot collaboration' scenarios, where human astronauts are in a low-gravity space environment and wearing space suits, making it difficult to coordinate their own postures. This increases the risk of dangerous collisions while collaborating with robotic arms on tasks. Hence, real-time autonomous motion planning capabilities for obstacle avoidance in space robotic arms pose a significant challenge.

Currently, classical algorithms for robotic motion planning mainly approach from two perspectives: sampling-based and optimization-based, and they are applied in quasi-static scenarios. However, the sampling-based approach is prone to dimensional explosion in high-dimensional spaces, consuming significant computational resources in the high-dimensional space of multi-degree-of-freedom robotic arms, resulting in lower computational efficiency. Representative algorithms include Rapidly-exploring Random Trees (RRT) [5] and Probabilistic Road-maps (PRM) [3].At the same time, the sampling-based approach struggles to effectively address dynamic random scenarios. Constructing trajectory optimization functions using the optimization-based approach is challenging, often leading to local optima in application and lacking adaptability to more complex operating conditions. Representative algorithms include artificial potential field methods [4] and covariant Hamiltonian optimization methods [12].

In recent years, algorithms combining the strengths of both approaches have been proposed. The Russ's team introduced the Convex Set Graph Trajectory Planning algorithm [1,7,10], which segments the obstacle avoidance planning space through sampling and then uses integer optimization to find the shortest path for obstacle avoidance. This solves the problem of robotic arm trajectory planning in convex envelope spaces. However, the computation time cannot achieve real-time performance while considering the random movement of dynamic obstacles. Merckaert and others combined the RRT-Connect [11] and Explicit Reference Governor (ERG) methods [8]. The former drives the robotic arm's end effector to the target position in scenarios with static obstacles, while the latter detects and avoids human collaborators entering the operational scene during the task to ensure the safety of human collaborators.

In addition to sampling-based and optimization-based methods, emerging Deep Reinforcement Learning (DRL) methods have gradually been introduced into motion planning and obstacle avoidance grasp tasks for robotic arms, acquiring planning and control strategies through training. Bianca first applied Deep Reinforcement Learning methods to robot obstacle avoidance control in a virtual environment, but did not conduct real-world transfer experiments, and the training time was relatively long [13]. Lars trained the robotic arm's static obstacle avoidance ability gradually by designing progressively difficult scenarios and experimentally transferred the strategy to a real-world scenario, but did not conduct sufficient experimental validation [15]. Given the need for transferring trained strategies to real-world applications, challenges still exist, such as significant differences between simulated and real-world scenarios and inefficient search for learning samples during training leading to long training times [16].

In this article, we analyze and model the obstacle avoidance and end-effector reachability tasks of robotic arms based on deep reinforcement learning algorithms, by introducing a hierarchical curriculum learning framework. We set progressively challenging scenarios and reward functions to guide the robotic arm in exploring obstacle avoidance strategies in a simulated environment with dynamic obstacles. This approach enables the creation of highly accurate simulated environments for robotic arm dynamics, effectively improving the search efficiency for high-quality samples. It allows the strategy to quickly converge in dynamic and complex scenarios with high-dimensional planning problems, and enables the transfer of neural network parameters from simulation to reality under limited computational resources. This validates the technical feasibility of using machine learning methods to train and obtain dynamic obstacle avoidance and grasping strategies for space collaborative robots.

## 2   Deep Reinforcement Learning Framework

Based on the Markov decision process, the two main elements of reinforcement learning are the agent and the environment. The Deep Deterministic Policy Gradient (DDPG) [6] and the Soft Actor-Critic (SAC) [2] are two of the most representative deep reinforcement learning framework. Compared to online policy, these two offline policy have higher sampling efficiency and sample utilization rates, making them suitable for training environments with continuous action space.

### 2.1   Deep Determination Policy Gradient (DDPG)

DDPG is a framework for deep reinforcement learning that uses a deep neural network in an Actor-Critic structure to approximate the state-action value $Q_\omega^\mu(\mathbf{s}, \mathbf{a})$ and deterministic policy $\mu_\theta(\mathbf{s})$ . Here, $\mathbf{s}$ and $\mathbf{a}$ belong to the state space $\mathcal{S}$ and action space $\mathcal{A}$, respectively. The goal of this framework is to adjust $\omega$ and $\theta$ to maximize the expected cumulative reward within each episode. After multiple episodes of learning, the framework can obtain a policy $\mu^*$ that meets the requirements of the task.

   after each interaction between the agent and the environment within a single time step, $(\mathbf{s}_t, \mathbf{a}_t, r_t, \mathbf{s}_{t+1})$ is stored as a set of data in the experience buffer $\mathcal{M}$. The framework randomly samples data from $\mathcal{M}$ as samples for learning and training. First, it uses gradient descent to minimize the error of the value estimate of the current time step. The loss function is given by

$$L = \frac{1}{N} \sum_{i=1}^{N} \left( y_i - Q_\omega(\mathbf{s}_i, \mathbf{a}_i) \right)^2 \tag{1}$$

where $N$ is the number of random samples. $y_t = r_t + \gamma Q_{\omega^-}(\mathbf{s}_{t+1}, \mu_{\theta^-}(\mathbf{s}_{t+1}))$ is the discounted value estimate calculated from the target value network $\omega^-$ and the target policy network $\theta^-$. Leveraging the Deterministic Policy Gradient theorem and the chain rule of gradients, framework uses gradient descent to maximize the state value estimate according to

$$\nabla_\theta J_\mu = -\frac{1}{N} \sum_{i=1}^{N} \nabla_\theta \mu_\theta(\mathbf{s}_i) \nabla_\mathbf{a} Q_\omega(\mathbf{s}_i, \mathbf{a}) \mid_{\mathbf{a}=\mu_\theta(\mathbf{s}_i)} \tag{2}$$

where $\mathbf{a}$ is the regenerated action with gradients.

## 2.2   Soft Actor-Critic (SAC)

Different from DDPG, while SAC also employs the actor-critic approach, it intro-duces an entropy regularization term. The optimal policy is defined by

$$\pi^* = \arg \max_{\pi} \mathbf{E}_{\pi} \left[ \sum_{t} R(\mathbf{s}_t, \mathbf{a}_t) + \alpha H \big( \pi(\cdot | \mathbf{s}_t) \big) \right] \tag{3}$$

where $\alpha$ is a regularization coefficient used to control the importance of entropy, where a higher $\alpha$ leads to stronger exploration. The error in the sample value estimate is given by

$$L = \frac{1}{N} \sum_{i=1}^{N} \big( y_i - Q_{\omega_j}(\mathbf{s}_i, \mathbf{a}_i) \big)^2 \tag{4}$$

where $j = 1$ or 2. To alleviate overestimation of values, SAC selects the network with smaller value estimates according to

$$y_t = r_t + \gamma \min_{j=1,2} Q_{\omega_j^-}(\mathbf{s}_{t+1}, \mathbf{a}_{t+1}) - \alpha \log \pi_\theta(\mathbf{a}_{t+1}, \mathbf{s}_{t+1}) \tag{5}$$

where $\mathbf{a}_{t+1} = \pi_\theta(\mathbf{s}_{t+1})$. Then, it uses gradient descent to maximize the state value estimate of the current time step according to

$$J_\pi(\theta) = -\frac{1}{N} \sum_{i=1}^{N} \alpha \log \pi_\theta(\tilde{\mathbf{a}} | \mathbf{s}_i) - \min Q_{\omega_j}(\mathbf{s}_i, \pi_\theta(\mathbf{s}_i)) \tag{6}$$

# 3   Virtual Environment for Obstacle Avoidance Task

The agent and environment are the two major elements in reinforcement learn-ing. After using a neural network as the agent, an interactive environment that evaluates the agent's behavior and provides feedback according to task require-ments is needed. Additionally, in this virtual training environment, the sample distribution should be consistent with the real environment, meaning the posi-tions of targets and obstacles are randomly distributed in space. We created a simulated training environment for the obstacle avoidance task of a robotic arm in MuJoCo. The work includes analyzing and modeling the task, designing cor-responding reward functions $\mathcal{R}$, and defining the state space $\mathcal{S}$ and action space $\mathcal{A}$.

## 3.1   Analysis of Task and Reward Function

The end-effector reachability and obstacle avoidance of the robotic arm in three-dimensional space essentially involve the continuous changes in spatial distances. the end-effector of the robotic arm should gradually approach the target, reach-ing within a designated graspable range while avoiding collisions with the arm

and obstacles. The reward function is established based on this principle to evaluate the policy, distinguishing between good and bad strategies based on the
score's magnitude.

To adapt to obstacles of various shapes, when modeling obstacle avoidance
problems, multiple spherical surfaces are used to fit the envelopes of obstacles
and the robotic arm. During single-step planning, the spatial distance $\{d_o(t)\}$
between the center of each obstacle envelope sphere and the center of each robotic
arm envelope sphere is calculated. The policy only focuses on the obstacle envelope sphere closest to the robotic arm for obstacle avoidance planning, which
means min$\{d_o(t)\}$. This can be explained as follows: regardless of how complex
the scene is, from the perspective of the machine, there is always only one obstacle envelope sphere with randomly distributed positions. Thus, this improves
the adaptability of the policy to random unknown scenarios. Additionally, the
target object is abstracted as a target grasp point at the end-effector in space,
and the spatial distance $d(t)$ between the center of the gripper and the target
point is the evaluation metric for end-effector reachability.

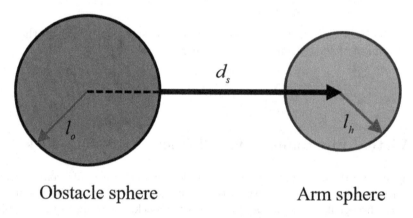

**Fig. 1.** Diagram of safe distance. The obstacle avoidance strategy should minimize $d(t)$
as much as possible while maximizing $d_s(t)$ as much as possible.

To obtain the position coordinates of the centers of the spherical envelopes on
the robotic arm and the center point of the end-effector, a rigid body coordinate
transformation method is used to model the kinematics of the six-degree-of-
freedom RM63-6F robotic arm. Through physical measurements, the radius $l_h$ of
the robotic arm's envelope sphere is determined to be 0.05 m. To ensure accurate
fitting of different obstacle envelope surfaces, the radius of the obstacle envelope
sphere used during training varies randomly. The evaluation metric for obstacle
avoidance consequently changes to the safety distance $d_s(t) = \min\{d_o(t)\} - l_o$.
where the obstacle avoidance strategy should minimize $d(t)$ as much as possible
while maximizing $d_s(t)$ as much as possible. (See Fig. 1)

So, the reward function includes at least two parts as follows:

$$R(t) = R_d(t) + R_o(t) \tag{7}$$

where $R_d(t)$ and $R_o(t)$ are given by

$$R_d(t) = \begin{cases} 50 & d(t) \leq \delta \\ 3000 * (d(t-1) - d(t)) - d(t) & d(t) < \delta \end{cases} \tag{8}$$

$$R_o(t) = \begin{cases} -2000 & d_s(t) \leq l_h \\ \frac{-0.50420}{d_s(t) - 0.04958} & l_h < d_s(t) \leq l_h + \max l_o \\ 0 & d_s(t) > l_h + \max l_o \end{cases} \tag{9}$$

When the robotic arm's end-effector does not reach the specified grasping range $\delta$, if the end-effector is closer to the target at the current time compared to the previous time, a positive reward is given; otherwise, a negative penalty is given. When the safety distance $d_s(t)$ enters the truncation interval, the reward function imposes a negative penalty. In addition to $R_d(t)$ and $R_o(t)$, the reward function also includes a collision detection term. Collision detection values are extracted from Mujoco, and if there is a collision within the robotic arm model or a scrape against the base platform plane, the reward function will provide a negative penalty, which is $R_c(t) = -200$.

## 3.2   Action Space $\mathcal{A}$

Action space $\mathcal{A}$ is defined by

$$\mathcal{A} = \{[\Delta q_1, \Delta q_2, \Delta q_3, \Delta q_4, \Delta q_5, \Delta q_6]\} \tag{10}$$

where $\Delta q$ is the change in angle of the six joints of the robotic arm within a single time step.

## 3.3   State Space $\mathcal{S}$

State space $\mathcal{S}$ is defined by

$$\mathcal{S} = \{[\mathbf{q}, \dot{\mathbf{q}}, d(t), \mathbf{p}_e, \mathbf{p}_t, \mathbf{p}_o, d_s(t), \min\{d_o(t)\}]\} \tag{11}$$

where $\mathbf{q}$ and $\dot{\mathbf{q}}$ respectively refer to the absolute angle values and rotational speeds of each joint of the robotic arm at the current time step; $\mathbf{p}_e$, $\mathbf{p}_t$, $\mathbf{p}_o$ represent the spatial coordinates of the end-effector center, target, and obstacle.

## 3.4   Virtual PD Controller

In actual control, the RM63-6F robotic arm joint motors are directly controlled using a pass-through function for position-loop control, with a minimum feedback command cycle of 10ms.

**Joint Control Performance Test.** To determine the actual operating speed and model parameters for the PD controller in the simulation environment, we tested the maximum command step that the pass-through frame can accept. Ultimately, we selected a maximum angle of $0.11°$ per frame for the pass-through, corresponding to a maximum joint speed limit of $11°/s$. (See Table 1)

**Table 1.** Test of transparent transmission following performance.

| Numbers | Maximum frame angle/° | Mean error/° |
|---------|----------------------|--------------|
| 1 | 0.04 | 0.11 |
| 2 | 0.11 | 0.75 |
| 3 | 0.16 | 3.26 |
| 4 | 0.22 | 6.77 |

**Table 2.** Table of PD Control Parameters.

| Parameter | Value |
|-----------|-------|
| $k$ | 6500 |
| $\xi$ | 0.32 |

**Modeling of Virtual Controller.** Based on the test results from the previous section, a virtual PD controller is modeled to facilitate interaction between the agent and the environment. The Actor policy network outputs joint angle change values, while the joint controller in Mujoco [14] only accepts joint torque signals. Therefore, the robotic arm joints are equivalent to a spring-damping system according to

$$M\ddot{q} + c\dot{q} + kq = F \tag{12}$$

where $M$ represents the mass matrix; $c$ is the viscous friction coefficient; $k$ is the spring coefficient. The damping ratio of the system can be solved as

$$\xi = \frac{1}{2} \cdot \frac{c}{\sqrt{mk}} \tag{13}$$

We adjust the damping ratio to make the joint control behavior in the simulation environment consistent with the tracking behavior of the actual robotic arm. We maintain the actual robotic arm control period of 10ms and automatically tune the parameters as shown in Table 2. Additionally, the robotic arm control period will serve as the time interval for single-step updates of the policy.

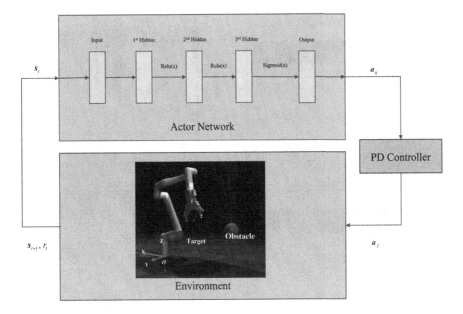

**Fig. 2.** Complete interactive process between Agent and Environment.

## 4   Training and Testing

### 4.1   Training: Hierarchical Curriculum Learning Framework

In the simulated training environment, the target grasp point and obstacles are placed within a cubic space of 0.4 m side length in front of the robotic arm. To leverage the Markov Decision Process's property of current decisions being independent of past states, each training round begins with a random reset and remains static throughout the training process. To reduce the exploration difficulty of high-dimensional policies and accelerate convergence, a Hierarchical Curriculum Learning Framework is utilized. The target task is decomposed into an end-effector reaching task without obstacles and an end-effector reaching task with obstacles. After multiple rounds of training, two source task policy networks, Actor-1 and Actor-2, are obtained sequentially. During the training of Actor-2, the neural network inherits relevant parameters from the Actor-1 network. After gaining experience in end-effector reaching without obstacles, it then interacts with an environment containing obstacles, reducing ineffective exploration time in the initial stages (Figs. 2 and 3).

The two framework use the same parameter settings, as shown in Table 3. $\sigma$ represents the noise standard deviation, which increases the exploration of the action space by the Actor policy network. Training with both framework took 14 h.

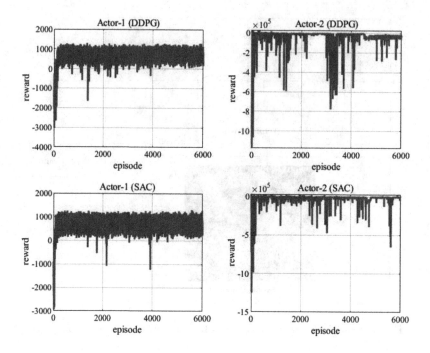

**Fig. 3.** The figure shows the reward curves during the training of Actor-1 and Actor-2, with the DDPG framework on the top and the SAC framework at the bottom.

**Table 3.** Training Details of SAC or DDPG Framework

| Parameter | Value |
|---|---|
| Learning rate of Actor network | 3e-5 |
| Learning rate of Actor network | 3e-4 |
| Discounted factor $\gamma$ | 0.98 |
| Soft updating rate $\tau$ | 0.005 |
| Noise standard deviation $\sigma$ | 0.005 |
| Timesteps $T$ | 600 |
| Batch size $N$ | 128 |
| Memory Capacity | 10000 |

## 4.2 Simulation Test Results

Two networks together constitute the final obstacle avoidance strategy. When the safety distance is larger than 0.15 m, Actor-1 guides the movement of the robotic arm. When the safety distance is less than 0.15 m, Actor-2 outputs obstacle avoidance actions to ensure the safety of the robotic arm, as shown in Fig. 4.

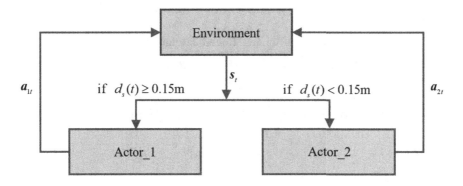

**Fig. 4.** Strategy allocation according to safe distance.

**Arrival Accuracy Test.** Testing the Actor-1 strategy for end-effector arrival accuracy in obstacle-free environments. The test consists of 5 rounds, each with 100 episodes. At the beginning of each episode, the target is randomly initialized within a cubic space and remains stationary during the test. An accuracy threshold Delta is set, and successful arrival is recorded when the end-effector distance is less than Delta. The number of successful arrivals is recorded for each round, as shown in Table 4 and Table 5. The strategy trained using the SAC framework exhibits higher search accuracy for the target, achieving 0.015 m, which is higher than the DDPG framework's test result of 0.026 m.

**Table 4.** Arrival Accuracy Test (DDPG)

| $\delta$ | Round 1 | Round 2 | Round 3 | Round 4 | Round 5 |
|---|---|---|---|---|---|
| 0.005 m | 46 | 64 | 54 | 53 | 38 |
| 0.010 m | 74 | 74 | 79 | 92 | 79 |
| 0.015 m | 93 | 95 | 94 | 96 | 92 |
| 0.020 m | 100 | 100 | 99 | 99 | 99 |
| 0.026 m | 100 | 100 | 100 | 100 | 100 |

**Dynamic Obstacle Avoidance Test.** Testing the complete obstacle avoidance strategy in an environment with dynamic obstacles. At the beginning of each episode, the target is randomly initialized within a cubic space, and the initial position of the obstacles is randomized. The obstacles move at unknown and random speeds in three different patterns: back and forth along the x-axis, back and forth along the y-axis, and random movement. When the obstacles move along the x-axis or y-axis, there are small random speed components in the other two directions, causing the obstacles to move linearly while also fluctuating. In this scenario, the target remains stationary. In the case of random

Table 5. Arrival Accuracy Test (SAC)

| δ | Round 1 | Round 2 | Round 3 | Round 4 | Round 5 |
|---|---|---|---|---|---|
| 0.005 m | 87 | 83 | 80 | 84 | 76 |
| 0.010 m | 98 | 98 | 99 | 98 | 98 |
| 0.015 m | 100 | 100 | 100 | 100 | 100 |
| 0.020 m | 100 | 100 | 100 | 100 | 100 |
| 0.025 m | 100 | 100 | 100 | 100 | 100 |

movement, the obstacles move randomly back and forth in space, and the target also moves randomly in direction and speed within the cubic space.

Table 6. Dynamic Obstacle Avoidance Test (DDPG)

| Types of Obstacle | Round 1 | Round 2 | Round 3 | Round 4 | Round 5 |
|---|---|---|---|---|---|
| y direction | 83 | 78 | 77 | 78 | 75 |
| x direction | 75 | 74 | 78 | 75 | 81 |
| random | 68 | 68 | 74 | 75 | 57 |

Table 7. Dynamic Obstacle Avoidance Test (SAC)

| Types of Obstacle | Round 1 | Round 2 | Round 3 | Round 4 | Round 5 |
|---|---|---|---|---|---|
| y direction | 89 | 88 | 82 | 88 | 88 |
| x direction | 97 | 96 | 96 | 96 | 92 |
| random | 96 | 96 | 94 | 93 | 94 |

Similarly, the test is conducted in 5 rounds, each with 100 episodes. Each episode lasts for 30 s, and if the robotic arm successfully avoids collisions with obstacles throughout the episode, it is considered a successful episode. The number of successful episodes is recorded for each round, as shown in Table 6 and Table 7. Through simulation testing, the SAC strategy demonstrates better obstacle avoidance performance, with a success rate of 94.6%, higher than the DDPG strategy's 68.4% (Fig. 5).

## 4.3  Deployment on Real Hardware

Copying the weights $\mathbf{W}$, biases $\mathbf{b}$ and the corresponding activation functions, we successfully deployed the SAC strategy from the virtual environment to the

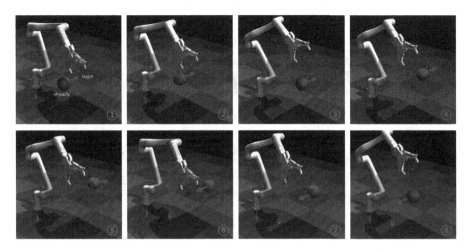

**Fig. 5.** In the simulated virtual environment, the SAC strategy guides the RM63-6F robotic arm in avoiding dynamic obstacle.

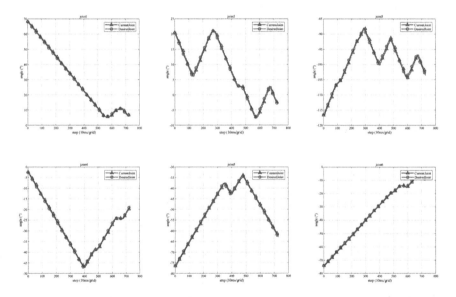

**Fig. 6.** After deployment on actual hardware, we tested the joint angle tracking performance of the SAC strategy in real-world scenarios with obstacle interference and found that the test yielded good results.

real robotic arm. Figure 6 shows the joint angle tracking test results of the real RM63-6F robotic arm after deploying the SAC strategy in a scene with obstacle interference, while Fig. 7 depicts the obstacle avoidance effect. During testing, frequent policy switching can cause arm trembling, so we have implemented

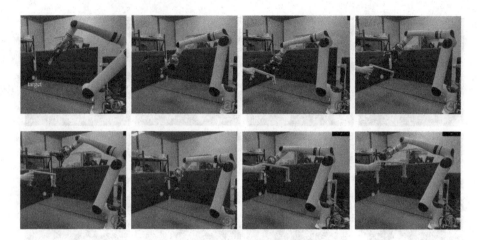

**Fig. 7.** The figure demonstrates the actual obstacle avoidance effect. When there is no interference, Actor-1 guides the robotic arm towards the pre-defined target point. However, in the presence of random disturbances, it switches to Actor-2 to maneuver the arm away from obstacles. Once the obstacles are removed, Actor-1 regains control of the robotic arm, guiding it back towards the target point. The coordinate output of point clouds from the visual camera serves as the center coordinate of obstacle spheres. Due to obstacles appearing in the virtual environment in the form of enveloping spheres, we have reduced the resolution of the point cloud.

a delay switching mechanism where the response from Actor-2 to Actor-1 is delayed to reduce the switching frequency and alleviate trembling.

## 5   Conclusion

In this research, we modeled the obstacle avoidance task and designed a hierarchical curriculum learning framework, trained neural networks to learn obstacle avoidance strategies under dynamic obstacle interference, and successfully deployed the strategy to the real RM63-6F robotic arm.

For the high-dimensional and complex problem of the robotic arm avoiding randomly moving obstacles during operation, training with the SAC framework can yield well-performing strategies. Abstract analysis and modeling of the obstacle avoidance task help improve the adaptability of strategies to random scenarios. The introduction of a hierarchical curriculum learning framework improves the efficiency of exploring high-quality learning samples during training, significantly reducing training time. However, the performance of strategies is greatly influenced by the strength of algorithmic exploration.

By rewriting the weights and biases of the strategy's neural network for real deployment, the search accuracy for target points in space can reach 0.02 m. This verifies the feasibility of training and obtaining obstacle avoidance and grasping motion planning strategies for spatial collaborative robots through machine learning methods under conditions of limited computational resources in spatial environments.

Real-time state observation and sample collection platforms can be provided by highly accurate simulated environments for supervised and guided training tasks involving human participation. This can provide expert data support for the subsequent introduction of generative adversarial imitation learning and inverse reinforcement learning methods.

# References

1. Cohn, T., Petersen, M.E., Simchowitz, M., Tedrake, R.: Non-Euclidean motion planning with graphs of geodesically-convex sets. arXiv preprint arXiv:2305.06341 (2023)
2. Haarnoja, T., Zhou, A., Abbeel, P., Levine, S.: Soft actor-critic: off-policy maximum entropy deep reinforcement learning with a stochastic actor. arXiv preprint arXiv:1801.01290 (2018)
3. Kavraki, L., Svestka, P., Latombe, J.C., Overmars, M.: Probabilistic roadmaps for path planning in high-dimensional configuration spaces. IEEE Trans. Robot. Autom. **12**(4), 566–580 (1996)
4. Khatib, O.: Real-time obstacle avoidance for manipulators and mobile robots. Int. J. Rob. Res. **5**, 90–98 (1985)
5. LaValle, S.M.: Rapidly-exploring random trees : a new tool for path planning. The Annual Research Report (1998)
6. Lillicrap, T.P., et al.: Continuous control with deep reinforcement learning. arXiv preprint arXiv:1509.02971 (2015)
7. Marcucci, T., Petersen, M., von Wrangel, D., Tedrake, R.: Motion planning around obstacles with convex optimization. Sci. Rob. **8**(84), eadf7843 (2023)
8. Nicotra, M.M., Garone, E.: The explicit reference governor: a general framework for the closed-form control of constrained nonlinear systems. IEEE Control Syst. Mag. **38**(4), 89–107 (2018)
9. Owen, T.: The complexity of robot motion planning. Robotica **8**(3), 259–260 (1990)
10. Petersen, M.E., Tedrake, R.: Growing convex collision-free regions in configuration space using nonlinear programming. arXiv preprint arXiv:2303.14737 (2023)
11. Pupa, A., Arrfou, M., Andreoni, G., Secchi, C.: A safety-aware kinodynamic architecture for human-robot collaboration. IEEE Rob. Autom. Lett. **6**(3), 4465–4471 (2021)
12. Ratliff, N.D., Zucker, M., Bagnell, J.A., Srinivasa, S.S.: CHOMP: gradient optimization techniques for efficient motion planning. In: 2009 IEEE International Conference on Robotics and Automation, pp. 489–494 (2009). https://api.semanticscholar.org/CorpusID:6327672
13. Sangiovanni, B., Rendiniello, A., Incremona, G.P., Ferrara, A., Piastra, M.: Deep reinforcement learning for collision avoidance of robotic manipulators. In: 2018 European Control Conference (ECC), pp. 2063–2068 (2018). https://doi.org/10.23919/ECC.2018.8550363
14. Tunyasuvunakool, S., et al.: dm-control: software and tasks for continuous control. Softw. Impacts **6**, 100022 (2020)

15. Væhrens, L., Álvarez, D.D., Berger, U., Bøgh, S.: Learning task-independent joint control for robotic manipulators with reinforcement learning and curriculum learning. In: 2022 21st IEEE International Conference on Machine Learning and Applications (ICMLA), pp. 1250–1257 (2022). https://doi.org/10.1109/ICMLA55696.2022.00201
16. Zhao, W., Queralta, J.P., Westerlund, T.: Sim-to-real transfer in deep reinforcement learning for robotics: a survey. In: 2020 IEEE Symposium Series on Computational Intelligence (SSCI), pp. 737–744 (2020)

# An Adaptive Five-Axis Sweep Scanning Path Planning Method for Variable Curvature Parts

Zherun Li, Yijun Shen, Limin Zhu, and Yang Zhang(✉)

School of Mechanical Engineering, Shanghai Jiao Tong University,
No. 800 Dongchuan Road, Minhang District, Shanghai 200240, China
meyzhang@sjtu.edu.cn

**Abstract.** The inspection of the variable curvature parts lacks efficiency using the traditional three-axis inspection method. The five-axis sweep scanning method can efficiently inspect free form surfaces. However, a uniform period planning of the sweeping path can lead to the waste of measurement resources and a decrease in measurement efficiency. Traditional five-axis sweep scanning methods typically consider only a fixed sweeping period when planning the sweeping path, which neglects the relationship between the surface curvature and the sweeping period. For parts with variable curvature, such as the blade cross-section, more sampling points are often required in the edge areas than in the other areas, or it would result in inspection precision decrease. This paper proposes an adaptive five-axis sweep scanning path planning method that transforms the adaptive allocation of the sweeping period into a sampling planning issue. The sampling process is conducted along the guiding curve based on its curvature, with the resulting points serving as the basis for generating the sweeping period. Finally, to address the issue of abrupt stylus orientation changes at the transition between the parts of the path with different sweeping density, a Non-Uniform Rational B-Splines (NURBS) smoothing method is applied to smooth the probe orientations at the transition part. In experiment, compared to the uniform period method, the proposed method reduces the path length by 27.4%. The proposed method and the uniform period method are equivalent in inspection accuracy, which validates our proposed method.

**Keywords:** Five-axis Sweep Scanning · Coordinate Measurement Machine · Adaptive Period Path Planning · Aero-blade

## 1 Introduction

The parts with variable curvature are commonly found in industrial products such as the aero-blade. However, these products have complex geometrical surfaces, which increases the inspection planning difficulty. In surface inspection, the coordinate measurement machine (CMM) is most frequently used [1]. The three-axis inspection method and the five-axis inspection method are two representative inspection methods using CMM [2].

For the three-axis inspection method, Gao et al. [3] introduced a sampling method for blade cross-section inspection using point by point inspection manner. This approach optimized the inspection time by reducing the density of inspection points. Jiang et al. [4] proposed an adaptive sampling method based maximum chordal deviation, alongside an inspection point sampling technique for sectional curves to enhance measurement accuracy and minimize deviations. Bowen Yi et al. [5] introduced an 3+2 axis CMM path planning method considering the probe posture. The inspection points are classified into several clusters and in each cluster the probe can inspection those points without change orientation. C.-Y. Hwang et al. [6] proposed a three-axis CMM inspection scheme that based on a greedy algorithm to minimize the number of parts setup and the stylus orientation changes. Bowen Yi et al. [7] proposed an on-machine adaptive sampling method, which takes the surface curvature, sampling density and approximation error into account. This method can reduce the sampling error compared to other sampling methods.

The point-by-point inspection manner is not efficient, i.e., 2–3 points/s, because its approach and withdraw process consumes the majority of the inspection time. Hence, an advanced technology called the five-axis sweep scanning technology is introduce to improve the inspection efficiency. As shown in Fig. 1 the typical layout of a five-axis CMM composes of a three-axis CMM and a two-axis rotary probe head. The probe head can move continuously with a carbon-fiber stylus that can swing quit swiftly i.e., 250mm/s, mounted on it. As an emerging technology, there is a limited amount of researches on the five-axis sweep scanning method. Zhou Zi et al. [8] proposed a five-axis sweep scanning algorithm for free-form surfaces, allowing automatic inspection path generation from pre-segmented surface patches. Zhang et al. [9] devised a five-axis sweep scanning path planning method to simplify inspection by decomposing free-form surfaces into basic shapes which can be inspected in one go. Shen et al. [10] proposed a five-axis sweep scanning path generation method for blade inspections, dividing the blade surface into four distinct areas according to their curvature for individual examination. Shen et al. [11] presented a two-step algorithm for creating smooth, collision-free five-axis scanning paths. Zhang et al. [12] developed an adaptive five-axis inspection algorithm capable of automatically generating scanning paths for deformed surfaces.

The prior works has developed a complete process of inspecting a free-form surface. However, for curvature variable surfaces, e.g., the blade cross-section, the sampling adaptability in five-axis sweep scanning is overlooked by the prior works. Traditional five-axis sweep scanning methods planned the path using the uniform period. For a surface with curvature variation, the uniform period path may result in insufficient digitization data in the area with high curvature region.

This paper concentrates on the sampling adaptability issue in five-axis sweeping scanning of the curvature variable parts. An adaptive five-axis sweeping scanning path generation method based on curvature is proposed. First, the basic

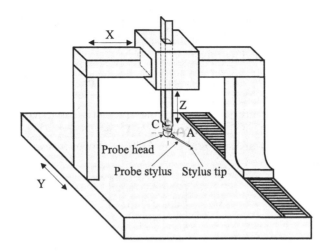

**Fig. 1.** The typical layout of a five-axis CMM.

element of a five-axis sweep scanning path is defined. The period distribution issue is settled by using an adaptive sampling method which conducts the sampling process according to curvature. Then the stylus orientation abrupt changes problem is solved by a NURBS smoothing method. Compared to existing methods, the proposed approach has the following advantages:

1. A sampling period calculation algorithm based on curvature is proposed to acquire a reasonable distribution of sweeping path on the blade cross-section
2. The sharp corner of the transition part is smoothed by using the NURBS smoothing method.

The remainder of this paper is organized as follows. Section 2 introduces some necessary knowledge concerning five-axis scanning path planning. In Sect. 3, the adaptive sampling algorithm based on curvature information and a transition corner smoothing method are described in detail. The effectiveness of the proposed method is elaborated in Sect. 4. Conclusions are drawn in Sect. 5.

## 2   Preliminary

In this section, the overview of the five-axis sweep scanning path planning process is provided. A five-axis sweeping path consists of three basic curves, i.g., the guiding curve, the reference curve, the probe head trajectory and probe tip trajectory. The guiding curve is a parametric curve representing the surface topological feature. The reference curve is an auxiliary curve which is used to help the generation of probe tip point.

The sketch of the five-axis sweep scanning path generation is shown in Fig. 2. A guiding curve $G(t)$ is firstly defined in the inspection surface, then a sampling process is conducted to acquire a guiding curve point sequence

$G_i, (i = 0, 1, 2, ..., n)$ with $n$ sampling points. For a specific point $G_i$, a local coordinate system(LCS) can be established and its corresponding probe head point $HT_i$ can be obtained as follows:

$$HT_i = Rt_i^{3\times3} \cdot SV_i \cdot l_{stylus} + T_i^{3\times1} \tag{1}$$

where $Rt_i^{3\times3}$ and $T_i^{3\times1}$ are the rotation and translation matrices from LCS to PCS. $l_{stylus}$ is the length of the probe stylus. $SV_i$ is the stylus orientation which is represented by a yaw angle $\varphi$ and $\omega$ in LCS as shown in Fig. 3. The $SV_i$ in the LCS can be calculated as

$$SV_i = \begin{bmatrix} \cos\varphi \cdot \cos\omega \\ \cos\varphi \cdot \sin\omega \\ \sin\varphi \end{bmatrix} \tag{2}$$

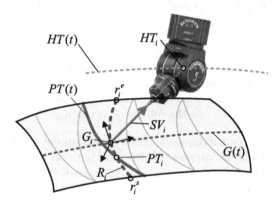

**Fig. 2.** The sketch of the five-axis sweep scanning path planning.

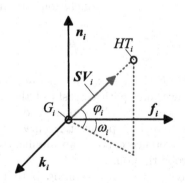

**Fig. 3.** The local coordinate system at $G_i$.

Once all $HT_i$ points are determined, they are used to define the probe head trajectory, $HT(t)$. To create the reference curve, a sphere is constructed with its center at $HT_i$ and a radius equal to the stylus length. The sphere intersects the surface, forming the reference curve $R_i$. The points $PT_i$ are then obtained by sampling on $R_i$ using the following formula,

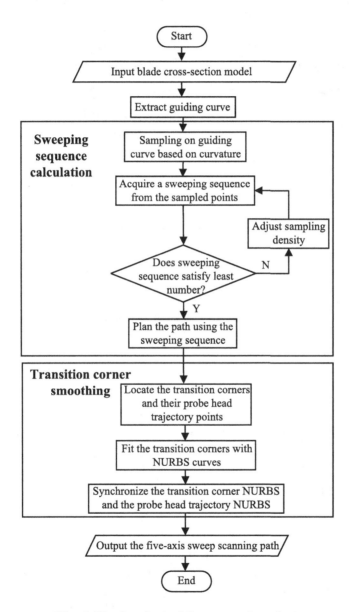

**Fig. 4.** The flowchart of the proposed method.

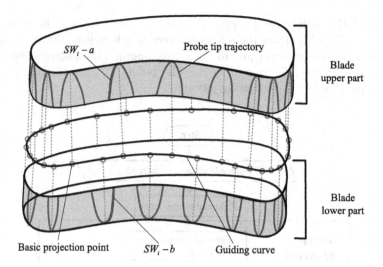

**Fig. 5.** Basic segments projected on the guiding curve.

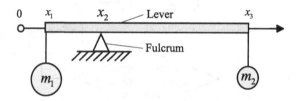

**Fig. 6.** A balanced lever system.

$$\widehat{r_i^s PT_i} = \widehat{r_i^s r_i^e} \cdot \frac{(1 + \sin 2\pi n_s t_i)}{2} \tag{3}$$

where $r_i^s$ and $r_i^e$ are the start point and end point of a reference curve. $n_s$ stands for the number of the sweeping cycle. $t_i$ is the $i-th$ parametric value. The ultimate sweeping scan curve $PT(t)$ is derived by linking together all the $PT_i$ points.

## 3 The Adaptive and Smooth Sweep Scanning Path Generation

In this section the adaptive period five-axis sweep scanning path is generated for a rapid curvature variation part (the blade cross-section). Firstly, the sweeping period of a five-axis sweep scanning path is calculated by implementing a curvature based sampling method [13]. Secondly, In order to avoid sudden changes of the stylus orientations at the transition corner between sweeping paths with different sweeping periods, the transition corner is smoothed using a NURBS smoothing algorithm. The flowchart of the proposed method is shown in Fig. 4.

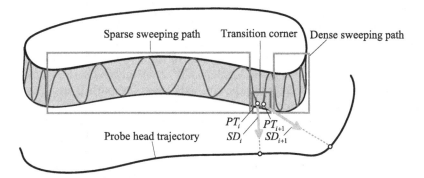

**Fig. 7.** The sudden change of stylus orientations at the transition corner.

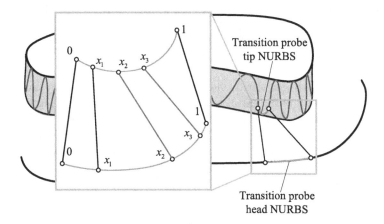

**Fig. 8.** Corresponding points mismatching on two NURBS curves.

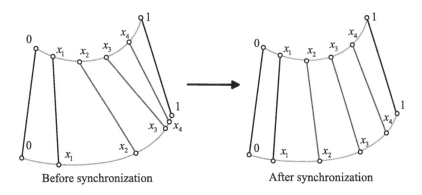

**Fig. 9.** Parameter synchronization on NURBS curves.

## 3.1   Adaptive Period Algorithm Based on Curvature

In a five-axis sweeping curve, the curve swings from one boundary of the surface to another. At this point, this small segment of the five-axis sweeping scanning path can be referred to as a basic segment $SW_i$ that makes up the whole path. The adaptive period planning for the five-axis sweeping path is essentially the planning of the distribution of basic segments on the surface to be measured. Although the distribution of basic segments can reflect the density of the sweeping path, it is difficult to quantify the distribution location of the basic segments during path planning.

In this paper, the adaptive distribution of basic segments is done by transforming it into an adaptive sampling problem. The endpoints of the basic segments are extracted and projected onto the surface's guiding curve $G(t)$ as shown in Fig. 5. The probe tip trajectory is separated into two parts(the upper part and the lower part). Each part has basic segments and a basic segment($SW_i - a$ and $SW_i - b$) contributes two projection points on the $G(t)$. The distribution of projection points on $G(t)$ can be utilized to represent the sweeping periods of the sweeping path.

The adaptive path generation method is now transferred into an adaptive sampling method on a parametric curve. That is to say, by adjusting the density of the endpoints of the basic segments, the adaptive distribution of the five-axis sweeping path can be achieved. The adaptive sampling method applied in this paper is based on a balanced lever theory. As illustrated in Fig. 6, the balanced system is can be expressed using the following formula:

$$m_1 \cdot (x_2 - x_1) = m_2 \cdot (x_3 - x_2), \tag{4}$$

where $m_1$ and $m_2$ are the weight of the objects. $x_1$, $x_3$, and $x_2$ are the position of lever endpoint and the fulcrum. For the adaptive sampling on a guiding curve, which is often represented as a NURBS curve, the curvature can be deemed as the weight. The parameter difference between sampling points would be the distance. However, it is not adequate to directly use the curvature of a sampling point as its weight. Therefore, the degree of curvature of a sampling point is calculated using a curvature representative function,

$$cp(t) = \lambda + \frac{k(t) - k_{min}}{k_{max} - k_{min}} \tag{5}$$

where $\lambda$ is an coefficient for controlling the impact of curvature on the distribution of sampling points, with a larger $\lambda$ reducing curvature's influence and promoting a more uniform parameter domain distribution. $k(t)$ is the curvature function of the sampling curve.

According to the balanced lever system in Fig. 6, the $i - th$ sampling point should satisfy the following equation,

$$\sum_{j \in N_i} cp(t_j)(t_i - t_j) = 0 \tag{6}$$

where $N_i$ is the $i - th$ sampling point's neighboring set. Obviously this is a nonlinear equation and it can be solved using an iterative method.

$$t_i^{k+1} = \sum_{j \in N_i} (\frac{cp(t_j^k)t_j^k}{\sum_{j \in N_i} cp(t_j^k)}) \tag{7}$$

where, $k$ is the number of iteration. The criterion for convergence is as follows,

$$\sum_{i=1}^{n} |t_i^{k+1} - t_i^k| < \varepsilon \tag{8}$$

where $n$ is the total sampling number, $\varepsilon$ is a user defined convergence parameter.

However, sometimes the sampling parameter $\lambda$ can not be decided directly. An adjustment process must be included in case the sweeping density is insufficient at high curvature region. For a pre-set basic segment number $m$ at the high curvature region. If the basic segments of the sampling result does not satisfy the least basic segment number, the $\lambda$ would be adjusted. The bigger the $\lambda$ is, the more uniform the sampling result would be. The smaller the $\lambda$ is, the more basic segments would be in the high curvature region. This process would go on until the least basic segment number is reached.

The adaptive sampling points on the guiding curve $G(t)$ can be calculated using the above-mentioned method and the distribution of $SW_i$ along the five-axis sweep scanning path can be determined accordingly. Nevertheless, the issue of sudden stylus orientation changes would happen at the transition corner between the dense sweeping region and the sparse sweeping region, which might cause the inspection process to abort because of significant acceleration.

## 3.2   Transition Corner Smoothing Method

During the sweep scanning inspection process, the stylus passes through the transition corner, it may generate a significant acceleration at the probe head due to the drastic change in the angle of the stylus, as shown in Fig. 7. The $SD_i$ and $SD_{i+1}$ change greatly, which requires the probe head to accelerate in a short-time. Corner smoothing methods are commonly used in five-axis machining to smooth the machining trajectory with sudden changes [14,15]. A NURBS curve corner smoothing method is utilized to smooth the probe tip trajectory and probe head trajectory at the transition corner of the adaptive five-axis sweeping path.

**NURBS Smoothing of Transition Corner.** The transition point $TP$ in probe tip path is firstly identified which is a boundary point of the dense sweeping path and the sparse sweeping path. A point set $FP_i = (fp_1, fp_2, ..., TP, ..., fp_{m+1})$, ($m$ is the point number) contains the points at the dense side and sparse side are extracted from the five-axis sweeping path. With $FP_i$ being acquired, this points can be fitted into a NURBS curve according to the NURBS definition [16],

$$TC(u) = \frac{\sum_{i=0}^{n} w_i d_i N_{i,k(u)}}{\sum_{i=0}^{n} w_i N_{i,k(u)}}, 0 \leq u \leq 1 \tag{9}$$

where $k$ is the degree of the NURBS curve, $w_i$ is the weight, $d_i$ is the control point, $N_{i,k}$ is the basic function of a NURBS curve. The NURBS curve fitted in the probe head trajectory is defined in the same way. It can be expressed as follows,

$$PC(v) = \frac{\sum_{i=0}^{n} wp_i dp_i N_{i,k(v)}}{\sum_{i=0}^{n} wp_i N_{i,k(v)}}, 0 \leq v \leq 1 \tag{10}$$

where, $k$ is the degree of the NURBS curve, $wp_i$ is the weight, $dp_i$ is the control point, $N_{i,k}$ is the basic function of a NURBS curve.

Although the NURBS curves at the transition corner for smoothing the probe tip trajectory and probe head trajectory are obtained, the path smoothing process is not finished yet. For a five-axis sweep scanning path, the probe head trajectory and probe tip trajectory they are not synchronized in parameter which would cause the stylus orientations disorder.

**Parametric Synchronization of NURBS Curves.** As shown in Fig. 8 the fitted transition probe tip trajectory and probe head trajectory are not synchronized in parameter. The points on the probe tip NURBS are evenly spaced, but the points on the probe head NURBS are closely spaced at the end of the curve, which causes the point mismatch. The point mismatch might lead to the stylus orientation drastic change and result in collision.

To tackle this issue, a linear parameter synchronization method is proposed in this paper to synchronize the transition probe tip NURBS and the transition probe head NURBS. The knot vectors of the two NURBS curves are utilized to facilitate the synchronization and the synchronization function can be expressed as follows,

$$v = f(u) = \begin{cases} v_i, (u = u_i, u_i \in U, v_i \in V) \\ v_i + \frac{\delta_v(u-u_i)}{\delta_u}(u \in U) \end{cases} \tag{11}$$

where $U$ is the knot vector of the transition probe tip NURBS, $V$ is the knot vector of the transition probe head NURBS, $\delta_u = u_{i+1} - u_i$, $\delta_v = v_{i+1} - v_i$. Then for an exact point in the probe tip NUBRS, its corresponding point on the probe head NURBS can be calculated using the synchronization method. As illustrated in Fig. 9, the synchronized NURBS curves are well matched, and the stylus orientations can change smoothly when compared with the two curves before synchronization.

When the issue of parameter synchronization is settled, the transition corner of the five-axis sweep scanning path can be smoothed. Until now an adaptive period five-axis sweep scanning path can be generated, which considers the distribution of sweep scanning path on the regions with different curvatures.

## 4  Experiment

In this section, we conduct inspection experiments on a blade cross-section which is measured by using the proposed method and the uniform period method. The effectiveness of the proposed method is validated by experiment result analysis.

**Fig. 10.** The five-axis CMM used for inspection experiment.

The inspection setup for the experiments are shown in Fig. 10. The CMM used here is the Renishaw Agility with a two-axis rotary probe head (Renishaw Revo2). The length of the probe head is 250 mm and the radius of the stylus tip is 3 mm. The inspection is conducted under the I++ DME interface using a self-developed inspection platform based on C++ and QT framework.

### 4.1  The Proposed Method and the Uniform Period Method

The proposed five-axis sweeping path is planned on blade cross-section which is acquired by intersecting the blade model at different positions on the stacking axis in the Solid Works. The guiding curve is obtained by slicing the blade cross-section. Then the adaptive distribution of the sweeping periods is completed by using the proposed adaptive sampling method as shown in Fig. 11. The basic segments at curvature variation regions has a number of 3–4. Obviously, the generated five-axis sweeping path on the leading edge and the trailing edge, is denser than that in the suction surface and the pressure surface.

The path generated by using the traditional uniform period method is shown in Fig. 12. There exists only 1–2 basic segments on the curvature variation region(blade edge). Though the path can accomplish the inspection of a blade cross-section, the sweeping density is rather sparse when compared with the proposed method. This may cause issues when executing the inspection accuracy evaluation or the surface reconstruction.

## 4.2  Experiment Result Analysis

For the path generated from the proposed method and the uniform period method, inspection experiments on a blade cross-section was conducted. The error color maps of the proposed method and the uniform period method are shown in Fig. 13 and Fig. 14. It can be seen from Table 1 that the max error of the propose method is 0.308 mm. The max error of uniform period method is -0.712 mm. The RMS error of the proposed method and the uniform period method are 0.149 mm and 0.155 mm. The length of the proposed method is 1125 mm and the length of the uniform period method is 1550 mm. The proposed method has achieve a 27.4% reduction in total length. It means that the proposed method can have a shorter inspection time compared with the uniform period method under the same speed parameters. Thus, the proposed method can achieve a better inspection performance than the uniform period method.

### 4.3  Discussion

The experiment results has demonstrated the effectiveness of the proposed method. The five-axis sweep scanning path generated by the proposed method has a higher sweeping density in the region with large curvature and a lower sweeping density in the region with small curvature. The inspection accuracy of the proposed method and the uniform period method is basically the same. While the path length of the proposed method is reduced by 27.4% compared with the uniform period method. Analysing the reason, the uniform period method does not consider the geometric feature of the inspected surface and simply applies the same sweeping period in the path generation. It may result in insufficient points at high curvature region and inspection resources waste at low curvature region.

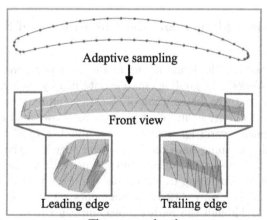

**Fig. 11.** The path planning result using the proposed method.

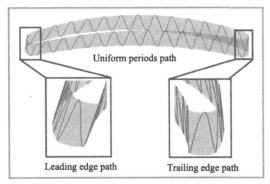

Fig. 12. The path planning result using the uniform period method.

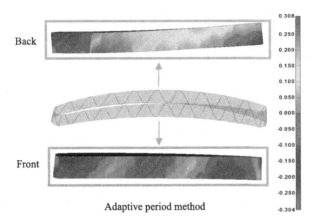

Fig. 13. The error map from the result of the proposed method.

Table 1. Error Analysis of the Proposed and Uniform Period Method

| Method | Max Error (mm) | RMS Error (mm) |
|---|---|---|
| Proposed Method | **0.308** | **0.149** |
| Uniform Period Method | −0.712 | 0.155 |

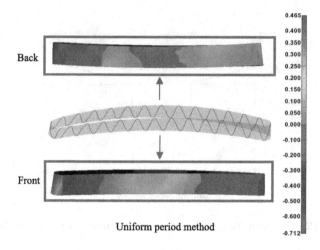

**Fig. 14.** The error map from the result of the uniform period method.

## 5    Conclusion

Conventional five-axis sweep scanning methods, which employ a uniform sweeping period, often overlook the surface feature in path planning. This paper introduced an adaptive approach in five-axis sweep scanning path planning that settles the period adaptive distribution issue by implementing a guiding curve adaptive sampling strategy. The method involves sampling along the guide curve in accordance with its curvature, utilizing the obtained points to determine the sweeping periods. The sudden change of stylus orientations at the transition path between different sweeping density is mitigated by a NURBS smooth method to avoid inspection failure. Experimental results demonstrate that the proposed method doubles the number of basic segments compared to the uniform period method. For the path length, there is a 27.4% reduction in path length with the proposed method versus the uniform period method. The proposed technique maintains the same level of inspection accuracy compared to the uniform period method. Though the proposed method can achieve a short and accurate inspection result, the generation of the sweeping period heavily relies on the guiding curve. For parts with complex geometries and variable curvature, the guiding curve may fail to adequately represent the surface curvature, preventing the creation of paths that adapt to the curvature. Therefore, future work could focus on developing adaptive sweeping paths without the need for guiding curve.

**Acknowledgments.** This work was partially supported by the National Natural Science Foundation of China (Grant No. 52375505) and partially supported by the Natural Science Foundation of Shanghai Municipality (Grant No. 22ZR1435200) and partially supported by the National Natural Science Foundation of China (Grant No. 52305546).

# References

1. Dhanish, P., Mathew, J.: Effect of CMM point coordinate uncertainty on uncertainties in determination of circular features. Measurement **39**(6), 522–531 (2006). https://doi.org/10.1016/j.measurement.2005.12.005
2. Shen, Y., Ren, J., Huang, N., Zhang, Y., Zhang, X., Zhu, L.: Surface form inspection with contact coordinate measurement: a review. Int. J. Extreme Manuf. **5**(2), 022006 (2023). https://doi.org/10.1088/2631-7990/acc76e
3. Feng, G., Ziyue, P., Xutao, Z., Yan, L., Jihao, D.: An adaptive sampling method for accurate measurement of aeroengine blades. Measurement **173**, 108531 (2021). https://doi.org/10.1016/j.measurement.2020.108531
4. Jiang, R.S., Wang, W.H., Zhang, D.H., Wang, Z.Q.: A practical sampling method for profile measurement of complex blades. Measurement **81**, 57–65 (2016). https://doi.org/10.1016/j.measurement.2015.11.039
5. Yi, B., Qiao, F., Hua, L., Wang, X., Wu, S., Huang, N.: Touch trigger probe-based interference-free inspection path planning for free-form surfaces by optimizing the probe posture. IEEE Trans. Instrum. Meas. **71**, 1–8 (2022)
6. Hwang, C.Y., Tsai, C.Y., Chang, C.A.: Efficient inspection planning for coordinate measuring machines. Int. J. Adv. Manuf. Technol. **23**(9–10), 732–742 (2004). https://doi.org/10.1007/s00170-003-1642-x
7. Yi, B., Qiao, F., Huang, N., Wang, X., Wu, S., Biermann, D.: Adaptive sampling point planning for free-form surface inspection under multi-geometric constraints. Precis. Eng. **72**, 95–101 (2021)
8. Zhou, Z., Zhang, Y., Tang, K.: Sweep scan path planning for efficient freeform surface inspection on five-axis CMM. Comput. Aided Des. **77**, 1–17 (2016). https://doi.org/10.1016/j.cad.2016.03.003
9. Zhang, Y., Zhou, Z., Tang, K.: Sweep scan path planning for five-axis inspection of free-form surfaces. Rob. Comput. Integr. Manuf. **49**, 335–348 (2018). https://doi.org/10.1016/j.rcim.2017.08.010
10. Shen, Y., Zhang, Y., Zhu, L., Zhang, Y.: Automatic generation of interference-free five-axis sweep scanning paths for inspection of impeller blades. Int. J. Adv. Manuf. Technol. **123**(7–8), 2227–2237 (2022). https://doi.org/10.1007/s00170-022-10300-5
11. Shen, Y., Zhang, W., Zhu, L., Zhang, Y.: An image-based algorithm for generating smooth and interference-free five-axis sweep scanning path. Rob. Comput. Integr. Manuf. **71**, 102159 (2021). https://doi.org/10.1016/j.rcim.2021.102159
12. Zhang, W., Huang, W., Shen, Y., Zhang, Y., Zhu, L., Zhang, Y.: Adaptive five-axis scanning of deformed surfaces based on real-time path planning. IEEE Trans. Instrum. Meas. **72**, 1–13 (2023). https://doi.org/10.1109/TIM.2023.3271007
13. Li, S.Z.: Adaptive sampling and mesh generation. Comput. Aided Des. **27**(3), 235–240 (1995)
14. Bi, Q., Shi, J., Wang, Y., Zhu, L., Ding, H.: Analytical curvature-continuous dual-Bézier corner transition for five-axis linear tool path. Int. J. Mach. Tools Manuf. **91**, 96–108 (2015). https://doi.org/10.1016/j.ijmachtools.2015.02.002
15. Zhao, X., Zhao, H., Li, X., Ding, H.: Path smoothing for five-axis machine tools using dual quaternion approximation with dominant points. Int. J. Precis. Eng. Manuf. **18**(5), 711–720 (2017). https://doi.org/10.1007/s12541-017-0085-5
16. Piegl, L., Tiller, W.: The NURBS Book. Springer Science & Business Media (2012)

# Prediction of Hand Kinematics in Grasping with Mamba-Based Graph Convolutional Networks

Weiting Peng[1], Jing Tang[2], Zeyu Gong[2]([✉]), and Bo Tao[2]

[1] School of Mechanical Science and Engineering, Huazhong University of Science and Technology, Wuhan 430074, Hubei, China
[2] State Key Laboratory of Intelligent Manufacturing Equipment and Technology, School of Mechanical Science and Engineering, Huazhong University of Science and Technology, Wuhan 430074, Hubei, China
gongzeyu@hust.edu.cn

**Abstract.** Prediction of hand kinematics in grasping contributes to accurate and efficient robotic grasping. In existing methods, the topology graph of hands only focuses on local constraints of hand structure, neglecting global coordination by the brain. Also, hand kinematics can be viewed as multivariate time series collected by sensors, so utilizing advanced neural networks can improve prediction accuracy. Therefore, we propose a virtual node-optimized topology graph and design Mamba-based graph convolutional networks (MambaGCN). Our topology graph achieves global coordination using virtual nodes, optimizing the aggregation of multivariate time series. We introduce the advanced Mamba architecture to enhance the modeling of multivariate time series. This study conducts on predicting hand kinematics in grasping using multivariate time series collected by sensors, which can serve as a pretext task for denoising and guiding robotic grasping. On the publicly available HANDdata dataset, results indicate that the proposed method outperforms three advanced models in terms of accuracy. Ablation studies validate the effectiveness of the virtual node-optimized topology graph and the improved Mamba architecture. The framework of MambaGCN is open-sourced at https://github.com/White-oranges/MambaGCN.

**Keywords:** Time series prediction · Neural network · robotic grasping

## 1 Introduction

Robotic grasping has played a significant role in various fields, including intelligent manufacturing [1,2] and medical robots [3,4]. In complex working conditions, accurate and efficient robotic grasping methods are challenging and important problems [5].

To optimize robotic grasping, Sundaram et al. propose learning from the kinematics of human hands, as humans can feel diverse objects and infer material properties [6]. Accurate prediction of hand kinematics in grasping is helpful to understand human grasping [7], involving the rotation of finger joints and the palm. Most existing works focus on indirectly predicting hand kinematics

X. Lan et al. (Eds.): ICIRA 2024, LNAI 15208, pp. 48–59, 2025.
https://doi.org/10.1007/978-981-96-0783-9_4

through electromyography [8,9]. They are usually only used to assist patients in the medical field. Direct prediction using current hand kinematics is relatively scarce but can be applied to various tasks, such as denoising and guiding robotic grasping. Zhou et al. propose the multi-task spatial-temporal graph auto-encoder (Multi-STGAE) for accurately denoising and predicting hand motion, achieving mutual benefits for denoising and prediction [10]. Shi et al. propose a method for predicting grasp poses based on the motion prior field, improving the control of bionic and prosthetic hands [11]. In this study, we focus on directly predicting hand kinematics in grasping.

In predicting hand kinematics, modeling the hand topology is a challenging problem [12]. The signals of hand kinematics are typically collected by sensors located on finger joints and palms. Therefore, the relationship between sensors represents the topology of finger joints and the palm. Convolutional neural network (CNN) is used to aggregate information from sensors [13], but they are not ideal for capturing the topology due to the CNN structure. Human hands can be described as topology graphs based on their structure, while graph neural network (GNN) is suitable for data with the graph structure. In some works about human hands and biomimetic hands, GNN and its improvements are used to understand the hand topology [14]. Multivariate time series as features of nodes are connected into the dense topology for intricate tactile sensor alignments on fingers [15]. Topology and affinity graphs based on the location of sensors are proposed to improve robotic tactile exploration [16]. In summary, topology graphs and GNN are beneficial for modeling hand structure.

While analysing signals collected by sensors using the topology graph, hand kinematics can be viewed as multivariate time series collected by sensors, essentially. Therefore, neural networks for time series are of great significance to predict hand kinematics in grasping. In existing researches, to add time information into the instant state in grasping, spatio-temporal attention-based long short-term memory (LSTM) are used to process haptic signals [17]. In conventional neural networks for time series, recurrent neural network (RNN) [18] and LSTM [19] are constrained by long-term dependencies and sequential computation, leading to slow efficiency. Transformer [20] addresses the issue of long-term dependency using multi-head attention, but it is unfavorable for quantization. In summary, we need improved neural networks to effectively learn multivariate time series of hand kinematics.

Based on existing researches, the topology graph of hands only focuses on local constraints of hand structure, neglecting global coordination by the brain. Also, advanced neural networks are required to analyze multivariate time series collected by sensors in grasping. To address aforementioned problems, we propose a virtual node-optimized topology graph and design Mamba-based graph convolutional networks (MambaGCN). The virtual node-optimized topology graph optimizes the aggregation of multivariate time series using virtual nodes for global coordination. We introduce Mamba architecture to enhance the modeling of multivariate time series.

The contributions of this study can be summarized as follows: (1) We propose a virtual node-optimized topology graph to focus on global coordination by the brain using virtual nodes. (2) We introduce Mamba architecture and design a MambaGCN model to enhance the modeling ability in the spatio-temporal dimension. (3) We predict multivariate time series of hand kinematics, and our results outperform three advanced models in terms of accuracy on the HAND-data dataset.

The rest of this paper is organized as follows. Section 2 is detailed description of the dataset and the proposed method. Section 3 presents our experiments, including parameters, comparisons with advanced models and ablation studies. Finally, Sect. 4 concludes this study.

## 2 Methodology

### 2.1 Preliminary

The architecture of Mamba is mainly based on the state space model (SSM) architecture as shown in Fig. 1 [21], which is suitable for processing continuous data, such as sensor signals. Mamba is composed of gate Multilayer Perceptron (MLP) and SSM. Gate MLP is prepared for SSM. SSM learns how to map input $x_t$ to output $y_t$ through the hidden state $h_t$, which is like RNN. Mamba has an efficient parallel algorithm to train quickly, which makes its complexity lower than Transformer.

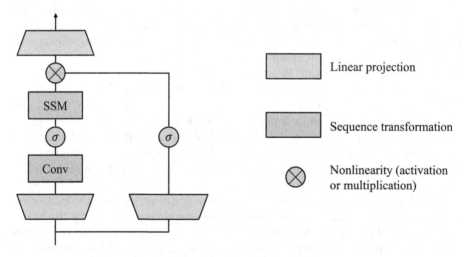

**Fig. 1.** The structure of Mamba.

### 2.2 Dataset

HANDdata provides hand kinematics during reach to grasp actions of objects, specifically designed for autonomous grasping of robotic arms, which an includes inertial measurement unit (IMU), radar, time of flight (TOF) and a glove with sensors [22]. The experimental platform is shown in Fig. 2 (a). In this study, we focus on the dataset of glove. The right hand glove includes 18 strain gauges and data acquisition equipment, which can collect joints angles with a resolution of less than one degree and a frequency of 90 Hz. Their locations are shown in Fig. 3 (a) and their names are shown in Table 1. The process of pick-and-lift is shown in Fig. 2 (b). The right hand extends towards the object and complete actions include grasping, lifting and lowering in sequence. Sensors record the entire process as multivariate time series.

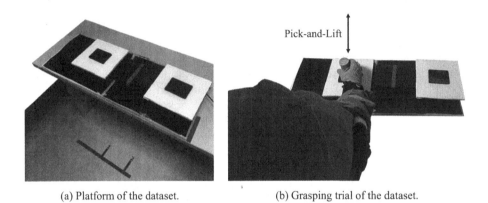

(a) Platform of the dataset.                    (b) Grasping trial of the dataset.

**Fig. 2.** Platform of the dataset and Grasping trial of the dataset [22].

**Table 1.** Names of sensors on glove.

| Number | 1 | 2 | 3 | 4 | 5 | 6 |
|---|---|---|---|---|---|---|
| Function | Thumb-Roll | Thumb-Proximal | Thumb-Distal | Thumb-Index Abd. | Index-Proximal | Index-Distal |
| Number | 7 | 8 | 9 | 10 | 11 | 12 |
| Function | Middle-Proximal | Middle-Distal | Index-Middle Abd. | Ring-Proximal | Ring-Distal | Middle-Ring Abd. |
| Number | 13 | 14 | 15 | 16 | 17 | 18 |
| Function | Pinky-Proximal | Pinky-Distal | Ring-Pinky Abd. | Palm Arch | Wrist Flex | Wrist Abd. |

## 2.3   Problem Definition

This study focuses on predicting hand kinematics which are multivariate time series collected by sensors. Set a time sliding window $W = \{s_1, s_2, \cdots, s_{18}\}$,

$s_n = \{s_{n1}, s_{n2}, \cdots, s_{nt}\} \in \mathbb{R}^t$ is a vector that records signals from a sensor. We predict future series $\{s_{1(t+1)}, s_{2(t+1)}, \cdots, s_{18(t+1)}\} \in \mathbb{R}^{18}$ using time sliding windows $W$.

In Sect. 2.4, we propose virtual node-optimized topology graph for information aggregation between sensors $\{s_1, s_2, \cdots, s_{18}\}$, which achieves global coordination using virtual nodes. In Sect. 2.5, we introduce Mamba and design a MambaGCN model. Improved Mamba contributes to learning the temporal relationships of a sensor $\{s_{n1}, s_{n2}, \cdots, s_{nt}\}$.

## 2.4   Virtual Node-Optimized Topology Graph

The proposed virtual node-optimized topology graph is shown in Fig. 3 (b). We design the topology based on local constraints of hand structure and global coordination in grasping.

For the local constraints of hand structure, orange nodes and black edges imitate the physiological structure of human hands. In grasping action, nodes that require collaborative motion are connected, such as the joints of a finger and the parts of the palm. The connection is obvious because adjacent parts of the hand will affect each other during grasping. For example, it is difficult to bend only the ring finger without affecting other fingers in any way.

However, we observed the correlation matrix of sensor signals in Fig. 4, which is not only affected by local constraints of hand structure. Due to the global coordinating role of the human brain, there are other influencing factors beyond the local constraints.

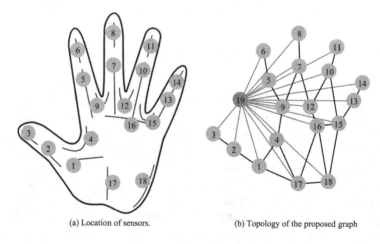

(a) Location of sensors.          (b) Topology of the proposed graph

**Fig. 3.** Location of sensors and topology of the proposed graph.

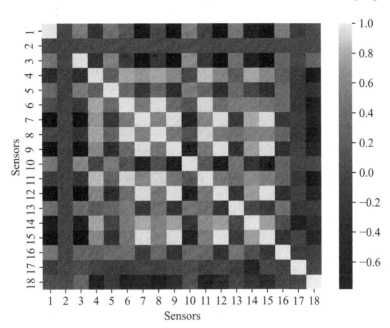

**Fig. 4.** The correlation matrix of sensor signals.

Considering the global coordination by the brain, we imitate the process using virtual nodes in the topology graph. The red virtual node $s_{19} \in \mathbb{R}^t$ connected to all other nodes by gray edges. Virtual nodes can enable nodes on the graph to quickly exchange information. With just one round of information aggregation and propagation, any node can obtain information from all other nodes. Through the process, we can obtain the global features in grasping.

Based on the local and global topology, we set the feature matrix of the graph $X = \{s_1, s_2, \cdots, s_{18}, s_{19}\}$ and the adjacency matrix of the graph $A_0$. To optimize information transmission, the cosine similarity of vectors is added as the weight to edges.

$$C_{ij} = \frac{\langle s_i, s_j \rangle}{|s_i||s_j|} \tag{1}$$

$C$ is the weight matrix of vectors, $\langle s_i, s_j \rangle$ represents the vector inner product.

$$A = C \odot A_0 \tag{2}$$

$A$ is the adjacency matrix with weight, $\odot$ represents Hadamard product.

In summary, we obtain the virtual node-optimized topology graph $\mathcal{G} = \{X, A\}$.

## 2.5   MambaGCN

To extract information from the proposed graph effectively and predict hand kinematics accurately, we design Mamba-based graph convolutional networks (MambaGCN) composed of $L$ MambaGCN blocks, as shown in Fig. 5.

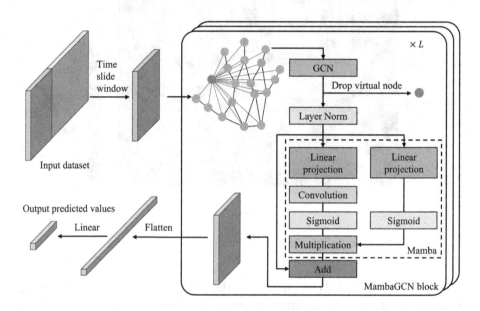

**Fig. 5.** Framework of MambaGCN.

After sliding time windows and constructing the graph, the graph is input into graph convolutional network (GCN) to learn the mutual influence between features based on the virtual node-optimized topology graph.

$$X^{(l')} = \sigma(\tilde{D}^{-\frac{1}{2}} \tilde{A} \tilde{D}^{-\frac{1}{2}} X^{(l)} W) \tag{3}$$

$\tilde{D}_{ii} = \sum_j \tilde{A}_{ij}$, $\tilde{A} = A + I$, $I$ is identity matrix, $W$ is a trainable weight matrix.

To ensure the input and output sizes of MambaGCN blocks, the virtual node is dropped after the GCN layer. Then the features are normalized using layer normalization, which is suitable for time series data. This process helps accelerate model training and alleviate gradient vanishing. As an advanced model, Mamba is used to learn the dependence of time series. The core formulas of Mamba [21]:

$$h_t = \overline{A} h_{t-1} + \overline{B} x_t \tag{4}$$

$$y_t = C h_t \tag{5}$$

$h_t$ and $h_{t-1}$ are vectors in $t$-th and $(t-1)$-th hidden layers, $x_t$ is the $t$-th input vector and $y_t$ is the $t$-th output vector. $\overline{A}$, $\overline{B}$ and $C$ belong to parameter matrix.

Also, residual structure is used to skip Mamba for preventing potential gradient problems.

$$X^{(l+1)} = LayerNorm(X^{(l_1)}) + Mamba(LayerNorm(X^{(l')})) \qquad (6)$$

In the MambaGCN block, the input size and output size are the same, allowing more blocks to address complex problems. After MambaGCN blocks, the output matrix is flattened and passed through the linear layer to obtain predicted results.

We used the mean square error (MSE) loss function.

$$\mathcal{L} = \frac{1}{18n} \sum_{i=1}^{18} \sum_{j=1}^{n} (s_{ij} - \hat{s}_{ij})^2 \qquad (7)$$

$s_{ij}$ is the actual value and $\hat{s}_{ij}$ is the predicted value.

# 3 Experiments

In this section, we demonstrate the performance of the proposed method on the HANDdata dataset and our results outperforms three advanced models in terms of accuracy. Parameters of the proposed framework are set in Sect. 3.1. Experimental results and comparisons with advanced methods are shown in Sect. 3.2, using MSE and MAE to evaluate errors. The ablation studies on virtual node-optimized graph and Mamba are recorded in Sect. 3.3.

## 3.1 Framework Parameters and Training Methods

This study is based on pytorch2.1.1+cu118, torch vision 0.16.1+cu118, python 3.10.9 and NVIDIA GeForce RTX 3060. In the prediction of action, the optimizer is Adam, batch size is 16, max epochs are 150, input size is [18,8], output size is [18,1], early stopping is true. Parameters of layers in MambaGCN are shown in Table 2.

Table 2. Parameters of layers in MambaGCN model.

| Layer | Parameters |
|---|---|
| GCNConv | in_channels = 32, out_channels = 32 |
| LayerNorm | normalized_shape = [18,8] |
| Mamba | d_model = 8, d_state = 4, d_conv = 2, expand = 1 |
| Linear | in_features = 144, out_features = 18 |

To test the performance of the model on small samples, we only select nine grasping trial, recorded as Trial 1–9. The training set includes Trial 1–5 and the testing set includes Trial 6–9.

MSE and MAE are selected as error evaluation indicators:

$$MSE = \frac{1}{18n} \sum_{i=1}^{18} \sum_{j=1}^{n} (s_{ij} - \hat{s}_{ij})^2 \tag{8}$$

$$MAE = \frac{1}{18n} \sum_{i=1}^{18} \sum_{j=1}^{n} |s_{ij} - \hat{s}_{ij}| \tag{9}$$

## 3.2 Experimental Results

On the testing dataset that includes four grasping Trial 6,7,8 and 9, we test the performance of the proposed method. The red and blue curves of the actual values and the predicted values are drawn on Fig. 6, indicating the effectiveness of the prediction.

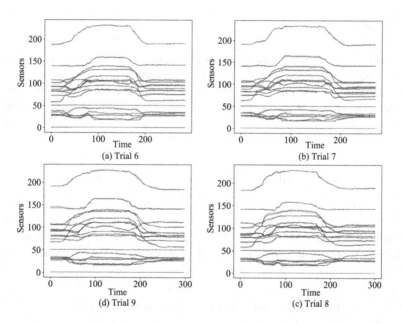

**Fig. 6.** Predicted values of sensors, red curves are actual values and blue curves are predicted values. (Color figure online)

To further demonstrate the performance of the proposed method, our results are compared with advanced multivariate time series models ETSformer [23], TSMixer [24] and Mamba [21] using MSE and MAE error evaluation indicators in Table 3. The comparison shows that the proposed method outperforms them in terms of accuracy. In practical application scenarios, we analyze problems, construct the topology graph and improve neural networks. Therefore, the proposed method achieves better results on the grasping dataset.

**Table 3.** Comparison between proposed method and advanced neural networks.

| Dataset | | Proposed | ETSformer | TSMixer | Mamba |
|---|---|---|---|---|---|
| Trial6 | MSE | **0.673** | 0.717 | 1.163 | 1.075 |
| | MAE | **0.628** | 0.666 | 0.858 | 0.799 |
| Trial7 | MSE | **1.070** | 1.391 | 1.324 | 1.291 |
| | MAE | **0.815** | 0.928 | 0.920 | 0.866 |
| Trial8 | MSE | **0.835** | 1.027 | 1.217 | 1.109 |
| | MAE | **0.708** | 0.790 | 0.886 | 0.840 |
| Trial9 | MSE | **1.033** | 1.259 | 1.329 | 1.215 |
| | MAE | **0.790** | 0.885 | 0.893 | 0.843 |

### 3.3   Ablation Study

To validate the effectiveness of the proposed parts in our method, we set up two ablation studies, including models without topology and without Mamba. Results are shown in Table 4. Without topology and without mamba respectively affect the spatial and temporal dimensions.

**Table 4.** Results of ablation studies.

| Dataset | | Proposed | Without topology | Without Mamba |
|---|---|---|---|---|
| Trial6 | MSE | **0.673** | 1.041 | 1.776 |
| | MAE | **0.628** | 0.793 | 1.051 |
| Trial7 | MSE | **1.070** | 1.249 | 2.148 |
| | MAE | **0.815** | 0.865 | 1.150 |
| Trial8 | MSE | **0.835** | 1.177 | 2.401 |
| | MAE | **0.708** | 0.847 | 1.168 |
| Trial9 | MSE | **1.033** | 1.199 | 2.090 |
| | MAE | **0.790** | 0.834 | 1.124 |

The study of the model without topology uses the full connected graph instead of the virtual node-optimized topology graph. Comparing to the model without topology, the proposed method has significant advantages. The full connected graph may cause unfavorable aggregation between sensors and increase unnecessary complexity. Therefore, the virtual node-optimized topology graph contributes to learning the relationships between features.

The study of the model without Mamba replaces the Mamba layer with the RNN layer. Results without Mamba 1.776, 2.148, 2.401 and 2.090 are weaker than the proposed method in terms of accuracy, which are almost twice as much as our 0.673, 1.070, 0.835 and 1.033. It clearly illustrates the importance of Mamba in accurate prediction.

## 4    Conclusion

In this study, research conducts on predicting hand kinematics in grasping using multivariate time series collected by sensors. We propose a virtual node-optimized topology graph and design Mamba-based graph convolutional networks (MambaGCN). The proposed method achieves global coordination of the topology graph using virtual nodes, optimizing the aggregation of multivariate time series. We introduce Mamba architecture to enhance the modeling of multivariate time series. On the HANDdata dataset, results of MambaGCN outperform three advanced models for multivariate time series in terms of accuracy. Ablation studies demonstrate the effectiveness of the virtual node-optimized graph and the improved Mamba architecture. In the future, we will apply our prediction method to more tasks, including denoising and guiding robotic grasping.

**Acknowledgments.** This work was supported by the National Natural Science Foundation of China under Grant (52188102).

**Disclosure of Interests.** The authors have no competing interests to declare that are relevant to the content of this article.

## References

1. Liu, Z., Liu, Q., Xu, W., Wang, L., Zhou, Z.: Robot learning towards smart robotic manufacturing: a review. Rob. Comput. Integr. Manuf. **77**, 1–21 (2022)
2. Liu, Y., Xu, H., Liu, D., Wang, L.: A digital twin-based sim-to-real transfer for deep reinforcement learning-enabled industrial robot grasping. Rob. Comput. Integr. Manuf. **78**, 1–12 (2022)
3. Mengmeng, S., et al.: Reconfigurable magnetic slime robot: Deformation, adaptability, and multifunction. Adv. Func. Mater. **32**, 03 (2022)
4. Chen, W., et al.: Soft exoskeleton with fully actuated thumb movements for grasping assistance. IEEE Trans. Rob. **38**, 1–14 (2022)
5. Tang, J., Gong, Z., Tao, B., Yin, Z., Ding, H.: Network convergence indicator for efficient robot grasping pose detection under limited computation resource. IEEE Trans. Instrum. Meas. **73**, 1–12 (2024)
6. Sundaram, S., Kellnhofer, P., Li, Y., Zhu, J.Y., Torralba, A., Matusik, W.: Learning the signatures of the human grasp using a scalable tactile glove. Nature **569**, 698–702 (2019)

7. Zheng, K., Liu, S., Yang, J., Al-Selwi, M., Li, J.: SEMG-based continuous hand action prediction by using key state transition and model pruning. Sensors **22**, 9949 (2022)
8. Yang, X., Fu, Z., Li, B., Liu, J.: An sEMG-based human-exoskeleton interface fusing convolutional neural networks with hand-crafted features. Front. Neurorobotics **16**, 938345 (2022)
9. Mahboob, T., Chung, M., Choi, K.: EMG-based 3D hand gesture prediction using transformer-encoder classification. ICT Express **9**, 04 (2023)
10. Zhou, K., Shum, H.P., Li, F.W., Liang, X.: Multi-task spatial-temporal graph autoencoder for hand motion denoising. In: IEEE Transactions on Visualization and Computer Graphics (2023)
11. Shi, X., Guo, W., Xu, W., Sheng, X.: Hand grasp pose prediction based on motion prior field. Biomimetics **8**, 250 (2023)
12. Roda-Sales, A., Sancho-Bru, J.L., Vergara, M.: Problems using data gloves with strain gauges to measure distal interphalangeal joints' kinematics. Sensors **22**, 3757 (2022)
13. Liu, Q., et al.: CNN-based hand grasping prediction and control via postural synergy basis extraction. Sensors **22**, 831 (2022)
14. Krammer, W., Missimer, J., Habegger, S., Pastore-Wapp, M., Wiest, R., Weder, B.: Sensing form - finger gaiting as key to tactile object exploration - a data glove analysis of a prototypical daily task. J. Neuroeng. Rehabil. **17**, 09 (2020)
15. Funabashi, S., et al.: Multi-fingered in-hand manipulation with various object properties using graph convolutional networks and distributed tactile sensors (2022)
16. Liao, J., Xiong, P., Liu, P.X., Li, Z., Song, A.: Enhancing robotic tactile exploration with multireceptive graph convolutional networks. In: IEEE Transactions on Industrial Electronics, pp. 1–12 (2023)
17. Wang, D., Teng, Y., Peng, J., Zhao, J., Wang, P.: Deep-learning-based object classification of tactile robot hand for smart factory. Appl. Intell. **53**, 1–17 (2023)
18. Lipton, Z.C.: A critical review of recurrent neural networks for sequence learning. arXiv preprint arXiv:1506.00019 (2015)
19. Hochreiter, S., Schmidhuber, J.: Long short-term memory. Neural Comput. **9**(8), 1735–1780 (1997)
20. Vaswani, A., et al.: Attention is all you need. In: Proceedings of the 31st International Conference on Neural Information Processing Systems, NIPS'17, pp. 6000–6010 (2017)
21. Gu, A., Dao, T.: Mamba: linear-time sequence modeling with selective state spaces (2023)
22. Mastinu, E., Coletti, A., Mohammad, S., Berg, J., Cipriani, C.: HANDdata - first-person dataset including proximity and kinematics measurements from reach-to-grasp actions. Sci. Data **10**, 06 (2023)
23. Woo, G., Liu, C., Sahoo, D., Kumar, A., Hoi, S.: ETSformer: exponential smoothing transformers for time-series forecasting (2022)
24. Chen, S.A., Li, C.L., Yoder, N., Arik, S.O., Pfister, T.: TSMixer: an all-MLP architecture for time series forecasting (2023)

# Motion Planing of Powered-Caster Vehicle Based on Gaussian Process

Xiao Wang[2] , Fei Zhao[1,2(✉)] , Heyuan Li[1,2] , Baolin Liu[1,2] ,
Chenwei Gong[1,2] , and Xuesong Mei[1,2]

[1] School of Mechanical Engineering, Xi'an Jiaotong University, Xi'an 710049, China
`ztzhao@mail.xjtu.edu.cn`
[2] Shaanxi Key Laboratory of Intelligent Robots and School of Mechanical
Engineering, Xi'an Jiaotong University, Xi'an 710049, Shaanxi, China

**Abstract.** This paper presents a motion planning strategy for powered-caster omnidirectional robots within the ROS framework that is driven by Gaussian Processes and integrates cubic spline interpolation to enhance both navigation precision and motion smoothness. By dynamically adjusting the Gaussian kernel based on trajectory costs and collision risks, the algorithm achieves superior positional tracking accuracy and computational efficiency, operating at up to 1 kHz. Experimental validation on the robot demonstrates improved performance over conventional techniques, especially in accuracy and computational speed.

**Keywords:** ROS · Gaussian Process · Motion Planing ·
Powered-Caste

## 1 Introduction

Motion planning is crucial in robotics as it enables robots to autonomously navigate and perform tasks efficiently and safely in dynamic environments [1]. Robot has various applications in daily life and Industry, such as autonomous vacuum cleaners navigating efficiently through household environments, robotic arms precisely assembling components in manufacturing plants, and service robots safely interacting with humans in public spaces.

Fox [3] introduced the Dynamic Window Approach (DWA) in 1996, a technique tailored for differential-drive robots that employs dynamic windowing to respect kinematic constraints. Its integration into ROS led to prevalent use in commercial robotics. Meanwhile, Quinlan's Timed Elastic Band (TEB) [4] was later incorporated into ROS [8] by Rösmann [5], also advancing the field with refined path planning capabilities. Subsequently, a myriad of refined algorithms based on DWA and TEB have been extensively adopted in autonomous vehicles and service robots. For instance, Zai [6] integrated TEB with the A* algorithm to facilitate navigation for Ackermann steering geometry-based robots. Dobrevski

X. Lan et al. (Eds.): ICIRA 2024, LNAI 15208, pp. 60–74, 2025.
https://doi.org/10.1007/978-981-96-0783-9_5

[7] proposed the Adaptive Dynamic Window Approach (ADWA), an advancement that enhances a robot's capability to evade dynamic obstacles, thereby improving its performance in dynamic environments. Zheng [9] employed reinforcement learning to dynamically adjust TEB parameters in real-time, thereby enhancing the algorithm's capability to avoid dynamic obstacles effectively. Jiang [10] proposed a reinforcement learning-based variant of the DWA algorithm, specifically tailored for operation in scenarios characterized by dense obstacles. Currently, the majority of motion planning algorithms are primarily integrated with differential drive models and Ackermann steering models, with scant few algorithms directly designed to leverage the characteristics of omnidirectional mobile robots. Imamoglu [11] conducted a comparative analysis of the TEB and DWA algorithms when applied to omnidirectional mobile robots, revealing that TEB yields significantly smoother output trajectories compared to DWA. However, TEB's performance is mitigated by an abundance of parameters and constraints, resulting in a lower computational frequency. Moreover, this excess complexity can inadvertently lead to planning maneuvers reminiscent of car-like turning patterns for the omnidirectional robot, an inefficiency not inherent to its full mobility capabilities.

Liu [12] proposed a trajectory planning method for 7-DOF manipulator using Gaussian Processes combined with a time optimizer, which generates collision-free trajectories through a sampling approach, offering excellent real-time performance and stability. For the first time, this paper adapts and applies this methodology to an omnidirectional mobile robot platform, further extending its application scope and exploring its effectiveness in a different robotic domain. This adaptation involves addressing unique challenges presented by the maneuverability and dynamic behavior of omnidirectional robots, potentially enhancing their autonomous navigation capabilities in complex environments. The kinematics algorithm employed in this paper's robot utilizes the control approach for omni-directional mobile robots with active wheels, as proposed by Jia [13,14]. The main contributions are summarized as follows:

1. A software system for a load-carrying robot was designed based on ROS, encompassing localization, navigation, vision, and control systems, and subsequently deployed on an actual robotic platform.
2. A load-carrying robot was designed, and the active wheel kinematics algorithm was implemented on the robot constructed in this paper.
3. An improvement to the Gaussian Process-based motion planning algorithm was made based on the ROS system and applied to the load-carrying robot designed in this paper.

## 2    Robot System Framework Design Based on ROS

This chapter outlines a holistic robot control system based on ROS. As shown in Fig. 1, integrating key functionalities such as navigation, vision, motion control, and simulation. The system architecture consists of localization, planning, control, and vision subsystems. The positioning system, informed by sensor data and control feedback, determines the robot's location within a map, informing the planning system which then makes decisions based on combined localization and vision data. Localization accuracy is achieved through LiDAR, odometry, and IMU fusion under the AMCL algorithm, with static maps managed by ROS's Map Server. Enhanced by EKF of odometry and IMU data, AMCL ensures precise robot localization.

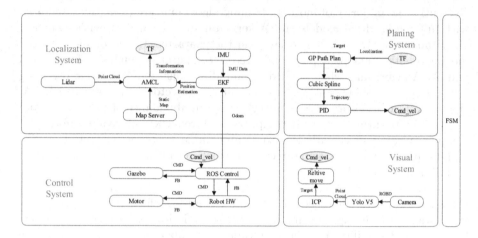

**Fig. 1.** ROS framework

The control aspect relies on ROS Control for actuator command conversion and odometry calculation. Real-world robot control utilizes EtherCAT for motor communication, while Gazebo simulation emulates this process for virtual testing. Planning involves Gaussian Process optimized trajectories, refined with cubic splines, controlled by a PID loop ensuring trajectory adherence. Vision processing with YOLOv5 detects targets, followed by ICP for cylinder fitting to calculate the workpiece's relative position to the robot, directing motion accordingly.

## 3    Kinematics of Powered-Caster Holonomic Robot

This section adopts a scheme with biased Powered-Caster to achieve omnidirectional movement of the robot. This chapter will introduce the forward and inverse kinematics of the active caster omni-directional mobile robot, as well as the calculation of odometry. The implementation of this part of the content is realized in roscontrol.As shown in Fig. 2, the origin of the coordinate axis is set at the origin of the robot coordinate system, denoted as $C$. $A$ represents the projection of the steering axle of the caster wheel onto the coordinate system, while $O$ signifies the projection of the point where the caster wheel touches the ground onto the same coordinate system. The angle $\alpha$ denotes the angular deviation between vector $AO$ and the positive x-axis direction (with a positive value when rotating counterclockwise from the positive x-axis, as depicted in the diagram). The angle $\varphi$ represents the angle between vector $CA$ and the x-axis. The length of segment $CA$ is designated as $l$, and that of segment $AO$ as $b$.

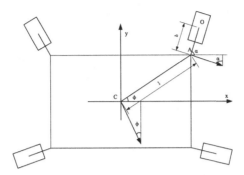

**Fig. 2.** Powered-Caster Holonomic Robotic Vehicle Geometry Diagram

### 3.1   Inverse Kinematics

Let $\dot{\theta}$ represent the rotational speed of the driving wheel. We define the positive direction of wheel rotation as "the direction in which the robot moves along the direction of vector $AO$, corresponding to the wheel's rotation direction at that time." Let $\dot{\alpha}$ represent the rotational speed of the steering actuator, with its positive direction defined as the counterclockwise direction when observed from a top-down perspective on the robot.To analyze the velocity at point $C$, the origin of the robot's coordinate system, the velocity generated by the driving wheels is as follows:

$$v_o = R\dot{\theta}(i\cos\alpha + j\sin\alpha) \tag{1}$$

where $v_o$ denotes the velocity of the point of contact between the wheel and the ground, projected onto the robot's coordinate system. $R$ represents the radius of the driving wheel, and $i, j$ are unit vectors along the $x$ and $y$ axes, respectively. The linear velocity generated due to steering by the steering mechanism is as follows:

$$v_a = \dot{\eta}b(\sin\alpha i - \cos\alpha j) \tag{2}$$

where $v_a$ represents the linear velocity provided to point $A$ by the rotation of the steering mechanism, and $\dot{\eta}$ is the angular velocity of segment $AO$ in the ground coordinate system. Since the rotational speed of the motor does not necessarily equal $\dot{\eta}$ directly, they adhere to the following relationship:

$$\dot{\alpha} + \omega = \dot{\eta} \tag{3}$$

where $\omega$ signifies the angular velocity of the robot's body in the world coordinate system, which is also the angular velocity of segment CA in the world coordinate system, serving as a given condition in the inverse kinematics equation. $\dot{\alpha}$ represents the angular velocity of the steering mechanism, which is the parameter to be solved for.

$$v_\omega = \omega l(\sin\varphi i - \cos\varphi j) \tag{4}$$

where $v_\omega$ denotes the velocity vector contributed to point A when the robot's body rotates with an angular velocity of $\omega$ in the world coordinate system. Additionally, according to kinetics in theoretical mechanics, the equation for the linear velocity of point C is derived as follows:

$$v_c = v_o + v_a + v_\omega \tag{5}$$

By combining Eqs. (1), (2), (4), and (5), we obtain the formulas for linear velocities in the x-direction and y-direction respectively.

$$\begin{aligned} v_{cx} &= R\dot{\theta}\cos\alpha + \dot{\eta}b\sin\alpha + \omega l\sin\varphi \\ v_{cy} &= R\dot{\theta}\sin\alpha - \dot{\eta}b\cos\alpha - \omega l\cos\varphi \end{aligned} \tag{6}$$

Represent $\dot{\eta}$ using $v_{cx}$:

$$\dot{\eta} = \frac{v_{cx} - (R\dot{\theta}\cos\alpha + \omega l\sin\varphi)}{b\sin\alpha} \tag{7}$$

Substitute this into $v_{cy}$ of Eq. (6) and solving for the rotational speed of the driving wheel gives:

$$\dot{\theta} = \frac{1}{R}[v_{cy}\sin\alpha + v_{cx}\cos\alpha + \omega l\sin(\alpha - \varphi)] \tag{8}$$

By combining Eqs. (8),(3) and (7), we get:

$$\dot{\alpha} = \frac{1}{b}(v_{cx}\sin\alpha - v_{cy}\cos\alpha) - \frac{\omega l\cos(\varphi - \alpha)}{b} - \omega \tag{9}$$

With this, the inverse kinematics solution is completed. Each set of steering wheels has distinct parameters, which can be substituted as needed. Next, we proceed to solve the forward kinematics for the omni-directional mobile robot.

## 3.2 Forward Kinematics

The problem in forward kinematics is as follows: Given the rotational speeds $\dot{\alpha}, \dot{\theta}$ of each wheel, we aim to solve for the robot body's angular velocity $v_{cx}, v_{cy}, \omega$. Utilizing Eqs. (3) and (6), resolving three unknown quantities with just a single set of active wheels is not feasible. However, an omni-directional mobile robot with a single active caster wheel configuration consists of at least two sets of active wheels. By substituting the parameters of these two sets of active wheels into the term $v_{cx}$ in Eq. (6), since the $v_{cx}$ values calculated from both sets of steering wheels should be equal, we arrive at:

$$R_1 \dot{\theta}_1 \cos \alpha_1 + l_1 \omega \sin \varphi_1 + B_1 (\omega + \dot{\alpha}_1) \sin \alpha_1 =$$
$$R_2 \dot{\theta}_2 \cos \alpha_2 + l_2 \omega \sin \varphi_2 + B_2 (\omega + \dot{\alpha}_2) \sin \alpha_2 \tag{10}$$

Bringing B to the left side of the equation yields:

$$\omega = \frac{B_2 \dot{\alpha}_2 \sin \alpha_2 - B_1 \dot{\alpha}_1 \sin \alpha_1 + R_2 \dot{\theta}_2 \cos \alpha_2 - R_1 \dot{\theta}_1 \cos \alpha_1}{B_1 \sin \alpha_1 - B_2 \sin \alpha_2 + L_1 \sin \varphi_1 - L_2 \sin \varphi_2} \tag{11}$$

The robot's angular velocity $\omega$ becomes known, substituting into Eq. (6) yields:

$$v_{cx} = R_1 \dot{\theta}_1 c\alpha_1 + B_1 \dot{\alpha}_1 s\alpha_1$$
$$+ \left( \frac{B_2 \dot{\alpha}_2 s\alpha_2 - B_1 \dot{\alpha}_1 s\alpha_1 + R_2 \dot{\theta}_2 c\alpha_2 - R_1 \dot{\theta}_1 c\alpha_1}{B_1 s\alpha_1 - B_2 s\alpha_2 + L_1 s\varphi_1 - L_2 s\varphi_2} \right) (l_1 s\varphi_1 + B_1 s\alpha_1)$$
$$v_{cy} = R_1 \dot{\theta}_1 s\alpha_1 - B_1 \dot{\alpha}_1 c\alpha_1 \tag{12}$$
$$- \left( \frac{B_2 \dot{\alpha}_2 s\alpha_2 - B_1 \dot{\alpha}_1 s\alpha_1 + R_2 \dot{\theta}_2 c\alpha_2 - R_1 \dot{\theta}_1 c\alpha_1}{B_1 s\alpha_1 - B_2 s\alpha_2 + L_1 s\varphi_1 - L_2 s\varphi_2} \right) (l_1 s\varphi_1 + B_1 c\alpha_1)$$

where $s$ and $c$ are abbreviations for sin and cos, respectively. The forward and inverse kinematics for the omni-directional mobile robot with steerable wheels have been fully solved. Using forward kinematics, the robot's odometry can be computed; a general algorithm for odometry is outlined as follows:

$$\begin{bmatrix} x_{t+1} \\ y_{t+1} \\ \theta_{t+1} \end{bmatrix} = \begin{bmatrix} x_t \\ y_t \\ \theta_t \end{bmatrix} + \begin{bmatrix} \cos \theta_t & -\sin \theta_t & 0 \\ \sin \theta_t & \cos \theta_t & 0 \\ 0 & 0 & 1 \end{bmatrix} \begin{bmatrix} v_{xt} \\ v_{yt} \\ \omega_t \end{bmatrix} d\,t \tag{13}$$

where $x_t, y_t, \theta_t$ represents the position in the world coordinate system at time t, $v_{xt}, v_{yt}, \omega_t$ denotes the velocity in the robot's coordinate system at the same instant, and $dt$ is the computation cycle. This section's content is embodied within the ROScontrol controller. Specifically, the velocities obtained from the inverse kinematics are transmitted to the robotHW for communication with the robot's servo motors, while the odometry calculated from forward kinematics contributes to the robot's localization process.

## 4   Motion Planning Based on Gaussian Processes

The motion planning based on GP is a versatile probabilistic framework employed to tackle challenges such as localization, path planning, and state estimation, particularly excelling in scenarios fraught with uncertainty, noise, and incomplete information. Its inherent capability to handle uncertainties renders it highly effective in robotic navigation and state prediction tasks. To incorporate randomness and enhance the exploratory capacity of the trajectory planning algorithm, thereby endowing it with a superior ability to escape local optima, this paper adopts a Gaussian Process distribution as the prior for trajectory variables. The entire motion planning algorithm is bifurcated into two stages: a Gaussian Process-based path planning method followed by cubic spline trajectory planning.

## 4.1 Gaussian Process-Based Path Planning

With the goal and initial points predefined, this section leverages a Gaussian random process to probabilistically generate multiple feasible trajectories connecting the starting point to the target point. Thereafter, the costs associated with these trajectories are meticulously evaluated by employing a cost map derived from obstacle data. The trajectory incurring the least cost is then selected as the pivotal trajectory guiding the subsequent trajectory generation phase. To ascertain potential obstacle infringements, the cost metric serves as an indicator, prompting an expansion of the search space upon detection of penetration and a constriction thereof when navigation remains collision-free. Initially, in the course of this study, a two-dimensional support vector $t_{\text{support}} = [0.0, 1.0]^T$ is introduced, which represents a reference point or datum in the context of the problem under consideration. To construct a model based on Gaussian Process Regression (GPR), an appropriate kernel function must be selected to characterize the inherent relationships among data points. Here, the Radial Basis Function (RBF) kernel, also known as the Gaussian kernel, is employed due to its smooth and globally differentiable properties. The expression for the RBF kernel is given by:

$$K_{\text{suppoot}} \left( t_{\text{suppoot}}, t'_{\text{support}} \right) = \sigma^2 \exp \left( -\frac{\left\| t_{\text{support}} - t'_{\text{suppoot}} \right\|^2}{2\ell^2} \right) \tag{14}$$

In this formula, $\left\| t_{\text{support}} - t'_{\text{suppoot}} \right\|^2$ represents the squared Euclidean distance between two vectors, $\sigma$ is the variance parameter that controls the amplitude of function variations, and $\ell$ is the length scale parameter affecting the breadth of the function's spatial spread. This text first calculates the covariance $K_{\text{support}} \left( t_{\text{support}}, t_{\text{support}} \right)$ between two identical support points, which serves as a fundamental component in constructing the Gaussian process model.

Subsequently, to ensure the positive definiteness and numerical stability of the covariance matrix, a Laplacian regularization term $\epsilon I$ is added to the covariance matrix $K_{\text{support}}$ computed from the support points, with $\epsilon$ being a very small positive real number and $I$ representing the identity matrix. Thereafter, the Cholesky decomposition (LLT decomposition) is employed to solve the covariance matrix after regularization, yielding the lower triangular matrix $L$. This decomposition facilitates efficient computation of predictive distributions and associated statistics. After constructing the model, the focus shifts to the data points to be predicted, namely, the set of test points $t_{test}$, which may be a set of discrete points generated through uniform interpolation from a continuous interval. For each test point, the covariance matrix $K_{support,test}$ is computed between this point and the support points; this matrix encapsulates the similarity between the test point and the unique set of support points.

$$K_{supporttest} \left( t_{suppoot}, t_{test} \right) = \sigma^2 \exp \left( -\frac{\| t_{support} - t_{test} \|^2}{2\ell^2} \right) \quad (15)$$

Then, leveraging the precomputed matrix $L$, this work addresses the covariance matrix between the test points and the support points, facilitating the derivation of the predictive distribution. In acknowledgment of the correlations among the test points, a posterior covariance matrix $K_{test}$ is constructed.

$$K_{test} \left( t_{test}, t'_{test} \right) = \sigma^2 \exp \left( -\frac{\| t_{test} - t'_{test} \|^2}{2\ell^2} \right) \quad (16)$$

Building upon this, to accurately estimate the function values and their uncertainties at the test points, a modified approximation of the posterior covariance matrix in its lower triangular form, denoted as $L_{posterior}$, is established. This is accomplished by introducing yet another small positive regularization term $\epsilon'$ to $K_{test}$, while accounting for the effect of subtracting the diagonal elements of $K_{support,test}$ transformed by some operation $L$.

$$L_{posterior} = \text{chol} \left( K_{test} + \epsilon' I - K_{support,test}^\top L^{-\top} L^{-1} K_{support,test} \right) \quad (17)$$

Finally, with the posterior covariance matrix $L_{posterior}$ obtained through the above steps and its Cholesky decomposition (LLT), random paths are generated based on a Gaussian kernel and the mean trajectory. The mean trajectory is given by $\mu(x)$, where $x$ represents an n-dimensional input variable, and each row corresponds to a data point. Meanwhile, $\mu(\mathbf{x}) \in \mathbb{R}^m$ denotes that the generated trajectory has $m$ degrees of freedom; for instance, in the case of trajectory planning within a two-dimensional map space, $m = 2$.

Given a set of $N$ discrete input points $\mathbf{X} = [\mathbf{x}_1, \mathbf{x}_2, \ldots, \mathbf{x}_N]$, the mean path matrix of the corresponding Gaussian process is denoted as $M$, where $\mathbf{M}_{ij} = \mu_j(\mathbf{x}_i)$. To generate $P$ random path samples deviating from this mean path, a stochastic perturbation is defined. For each input point $x_i$, an m-dimensional vector of independent and identically distributed standard normal random variables $\epsilon_i \sim \mathcal{N}(\mathbf{0}, \mathbf{I})$ is generated. For each sample $p(1 \leq p \leq P)$ to be generated, the following procedure is carried out:

$$\mathbf{Y}_p = \mathbf{M} + \mathbf{L} \cdot \epsilon_p \quad (18)$$

All $\mathbf{Y}_p$ together form $P$ random path samples, each of which conducts a random search based on the original path. Following this, the cost of each path is computed using a cost map. This work utilizes the costmap_2d component within ROS to equip mobile robots with the capability to build and update two-dimensional cost maps, thereby facilitating a quantitative evaluation of potential paths by the path planning algorithm. Below, the process of calculating path costs using costmap_2d is elaborated upon.

Initially, costmap_2d constructs a gridded environmental model by fusing sensor data, such as that from lidars, depth cameras, etc. Each grid cell is assigned a cost value, which typically correlates with factors like obstacle proximity, terrain roughness, and dynamical constraints. The cost function can generally be expressed as:

$$C(x, y) = f\left(d_{\text{obs}}, d_{\text{inflated}}\right) \tag{19}$$

wherein, $(x, y)$ signifies the grid coordinates, $d_{\text{obs}}$ denotes the measured distance from the current grid cell to the nearest obstacle, and $d_{\text{inflated}}$ represents the additional inflation distance applied for safety, creating a buffer zone around obstacles. Within costmap_2d, obstacle costs are quantified using non-negative values, escalating as the proximity to obstacles increases, while remaining minimal or zero in unobstructed open spaces. Significantly, the inflation layer bolsters the costs of cells neighboring obstacles to assure a secure clearance for the robot. When evaluating the aggregate cost of a path composed of a series of grid points, a cumulative cost approach is employed:

$$\text{Cost}\left(\mathrm{T}_i\right) = \sum_{i=1}^{n} w_i \cdot C\left(x_i, y_i\right) \tag{20}$$

In this context, $\mathrm{T}_i = [(x_1, y_1), (x_2, y_2), \ldots, (x_n, y_n)]$ represents the path under evaluation, a sequence comprising a series of adjacent grid points; $C\left(x_i, y_i\right)$ denotes the local cost at the i-th point along the path; $w_i$ is a weighting factor that reflects the relative importance of different locations, inversely proportional to factors such as the distance from the start or goal points, thereby prioritizing path segments closer to crucial locations. Consequently, a set $\mathcal{T} = \{T_1, T_2, \ldots, T_N\}$ of candidate trajectories is obtained, with each trajectory $T_i$ associated with a cost function $cost(T_i)$, which gauges its safety, efficiency, or other pertinent criteria. The trajectory with the minimum cost is then selected as the mean path for the next planning iteration, mathematically represented as:

$$T_{\text{min-cost}} = \arg\min_{T_i \in \mathcal{T}} C\left(T_i\right) \tag{21}$$

As shown in Fig. 3, depending on the comparison between the minimum-cost trajectory and a pre-established collision threshold $C_{\text{threshold}}$, the parameters of the Gaussian kernel $\sigma$ are adjusted dynamically. When $C\left(T_{\text{min-cost}}\right) > C_{\text{threshold}}$, indicating that the cost of the optimal trajectory is excessively high and potentially entails significant collision risks, the Gaussian kernel parameter $\sigma$ is increased to broaden the search scope-this adjustment aims to explore a larger solution space, represented as $\sigma \leftarrow \alpha \cdot \sigma$, where $\alpha > 1$ is an expansion factor. Conversely, if the risk is assessed as lower, $\sigma$ is decreased to narrow the search, implementing a strategy denoted as $\sigma \leftarrow \beta \cdot \sigma$, with $0 < \beta < 1$ functioning as a contraction factor.

(a) $C\left(T_{\text{min-cost}}\right) > C_{\text{threshold}}$        (b) $C\left(T_{\text{min-cost}}\right) < C_{\text{threshold}}$

**Fig. 3.** The variation pattern of $\sigma$

## 4.2   Cubic Spline Interpolation

During the path planning stage, the algorithm employed performs a spatial search based on a finite number of key points and successfully generates a continuous path that avoids obstacles. However, this path is represented merely as a series of discrete spatial coordinate points, which are insufficient to accurately depict the requirement for smooth trajectories in complex environments. This section adopts cubic spline interpolation techniques to fit the existing set of discrete path points, thereby achieving a smoother trajectory. Let $S(t)$ represent a cubic spline curve, which is expressed as a piecewise cubic polynomial and possesses continuous second-order derivatives. At the node $t_i$ , let the value of the second derivative be $S''(t_i) = M_i (i = 0, 1, \cdots, n)$, and $M_i$ denotes a specific parameter related to the position. According to [2], the cubic spline curve equation is derived as follows:

$$
S(t) = \frac{(t_i - t)^3}{6h_i} M_{i-1} + \frac{(t - t_{i-1})^3}{6h_i} M_i + \left( y_{i-1} - \frac{h_i^2}{6} M_{i-1} \right) \frac{t_i - t}{h_i}
$$
$$
+ \left( y_i - \frac{h_i^2}{6} M_i \right) \frac{t - t_{i-1}}{h_i}, \quad t_{i-1} \leq t \leq t_i. \tag{22}
$$

Given that the initial and final velocities for the robot trajectory planning are known, the second type of boundary condition is employed, specified as: $y_0' = f'(a), y_n' = f'(b)$. Derive the three bending moment equations:

$$
\begin{pmatrix} 2 & 1 & & & & \\ \mu_1 & 2 & \lambda_1 & & & \\ & \mu_2 & 2 & \lambda_2 & & \\ & & \ddots & \ddots & \ddots & \\ & & & \mu_{n-1} & 2 & \lambda_{n-1} \\ & & & & 1 & 2 \end{pmatrix} \begin{pmatrix} M_0 \\ M_1 \\ M_2 \\ \vdots \\ M_{n-1} \\ M_n \end{pmatrix} = \begin{pmatrix} d_0 \\ d_1 \\ d_2 \\ \vdots \\ d_{n-1} \\ d_n \end{pmatrix} \tag{23}
$$

where:

$$\mu_i = \frac{h_i}{h_i + h_{i+1}}, \quad \lambda_i = \frac{h_{i+1}}{h_i + h_{i+1}} = 1 - \mu_i$$

$$d_0 = \frac{6}{h_1} \left( \frac{y_1 - y_0}{h_1} - y_0' \right) = 6f[x_0, x_0, x_1],$$

$$d_n = \frac{6}{h_n} \left( y_n' - \frac{y_n - y_{n-1}}{h_n} \right) = 6f[x_{n-1}, x_n, x_n].$$   (24)

$$d_i = \frac{6}{h_i + h_{i+1}} \left[ \frac{y_{i+1} - y_i}{h_{i+1}} - \frac{y_i - y_{i-1}}{h_i} \right] = 6f[x_{i-1}, x_i, x_{i+1}].$$

where $i = 1, 2, \cdots, n-1$, parameter $h_i$ needs to be determined, and in this work, it is computed by adopting an average velocity of $v_m$. For any arbitrary pair of consecutive coordinate points $y_{i-1}, y_i$, along the prescribed path, the pertinent formula is expressed as follows:

$$h_i = \frac{\|y_i - y_{i-1}\|_2}{v_m}$$   (25)

Upon completion of the trajectory planning, the generated trajectory is input into a PID controller, which computes the current command velocity for the robot. This command is then transmitted to the lower-level controller, thereby accomplishing the control task.

## 5    Experiments and Results

### 5.1    Experimental Hardware and Platform Construction

The hardware platform of the Powered-Caster holonomic robot used in this experiment is shown in Fig. 4, which consists of Two-Powered-Caster chassis, two TIM-571 LIDARs, Ch140M IMU, Mech-Eye camera and PC, where the CPU of the PC is i5-13600KF with 16 GB memory and RTX4060Ti GPU. The data processing side is the operating system of Ubuntu 20.04.

 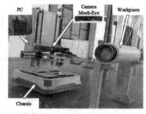 

(a) Robot Chassis          (b) Overall structure          (c) Electric cabinet

**Fig. 4.** Hardware Platform

## 5.2   Experiment of Workpiece Handling

This thesis utilizes a scenario involving the handling of cylindrical workpieces as its experimental context, as depicted in Fig. 5. It outlines a process where a robot commences from an initial point, traverses an environment replete with obstacles, ultimately arriving at the workpiece's location. Furthermore, the study contrasts the efficacy of three distinct methods: A* coupled with TEB (Topology-based Elastic Band), A* combined with DWA (Dynamic Window Approach), and the novel methodology proposed within this paper.

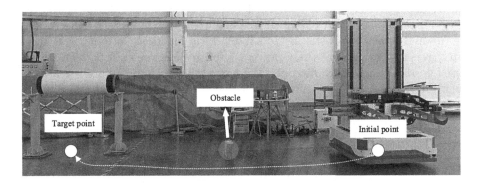

**Fig. 5.** Experiment

Figure 6 compares the sequences of velocity commands produced by three planning algorithms. Subplots a, b, and c respectively depict the velocities in the x-direction, y-direction, and the angular velocity around the z-axis in the robot's coordinate system. Here, the red line represents the performance of A*+DWA, the green line shows the outcome of A*+TEB, while the blue line signifies our proposed method. Our approach achieves the target destination first, with a time of 14.253 s. The DWA and TEB methods, in comparison, take 14.651 s and 17.396 s, respectively.

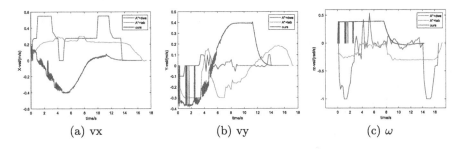

(a) vx          (b) vy          (c) $\omega$

**Fig. 6.** The sequence of velocity commands generated by three planning algorithms (Color figure online)

In this experiment, to ensure stability, we set the frequency of our proposed method to 50 Hz, whereas the other two methods could only operate at a maximum frequency of 30 Hz. If required, our planning algorithm has the capability to reach up to 1kHz to guarantee real-time performance.

During the first three seconds, our algorithm generates plans with moments of zero velocity, a phenomenon arising from the utilization of the costmap_2d package for generating obstacle cost maps. The planning process involves frequent queries for cost values to assess potential paths. Occasionally, under high query loads, the costmap_2d momentarily returns a zero cost for occupied areas, misleading our algorithm into perceiving a straight-line path as the most optimal due to its perceived minimal distance. This misinterpretation narrows the search space for subsequent path planning, focusing exclusively on direct trajectories.

However, when the costmap_2d subsequently functions correctly and accurately reports the costs of these previously misread regions, all paths explored based on the linear assumption and the narrowed search radius are revealed to incur severe collisions. To ensure safety, this detection triggers a safeguard mechanism within our algorithm, promptly reducing the robot's velocity to zero to avert any potential accidents.

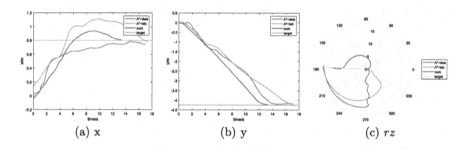

(a) x          (b) y          (c) $rz$

**Fig. 7.** Pose-time curves

Figure 7 illustrates the pose-time curves for the three methodologies, demonstrating that the DWA algorithm maintains a relatively constant heading during the initial half of the traversal, only initiating significant attitude adjustments as it approaches the target, which leads to deviations from the target and an increase in positional errors during the maneuvering phase. Overall, it is evident that the trajectory smoothness produced by our method significantly surpasses that of TEB and DWA. This superiority is attributed to our approach's continuous global path planning, in contrast to the other two algorithms that plan within limited windows only.

As illustrated in Table 1, ours demonstrates superior performance in terms of positional errors along both the x and y axes compared to the other two methods. Furthermore, akin to TEB, ours also achieves an angular error of less than 1°C, showcasing its commendable precision in orientation control. We have uploaded the experimental video and code to the internet.

**Table 1.** The positional error after the robot halts relative to the target point

| Algorithm | x error (mm) | y error (mm) | rz error (°) |
|---|---|---|---|
| A*+DWA | 57.2 | 80.1 | 2.5 |
| A*+TEB | 14.9 | 15.7 | 0.44 |
| Ours | 7.2 | 13.5 | 0.66 |

## 6 Conclusions

This paper integrates Gaussian Process-based path planning with cubic spline interpolation to introduce a novel Gaussian Process-driven trajectory planning approach, which is then implemented on a manipulator robot for object handling tasks. Empirical results affirm that our proposed methodology, when applied to an actively steered holonomic mobile robot, surpasses conventional algorithms, particularly in aspects of positional tracking accuracy, motion smoothness, and computational frequency. Notably, it achieves a significantly higher computational rate, with the upper limit reaching approximately 1kHz, far exceeding those of traditional methods. Additionally, our study has unveiled that the performance of our proposed scheme is constrained by the limitations of the costmap_2d package. Consequently, future work will entail replacing the costmap_2d component to enhance the overall efficiency and effectiveness of the algorithm. We have uploaded the experimental video[1] and code[2] to the internet.

**Acknowledgements.** This work is supported by the National Natural Science Foundation of China (Grant No. 52175029).

## References

1. Latombe, J.-C.: Introduction and overview. In: Latombe, J.-C. (ed.) Robotic Motion Planning, pp. 1–57. Springer, US, Boston, MA (1991)
2. Gautschi, W.: Approximation and interpolation. In: Gautschi, W. (ed.) Numerical Analysis, pp. 55–158. Birkhäuser, Boston (2012)
3. Fox, D., Burgard, W., Thrun, S.: Controlling synchro-drive robots with the dynamic window approach to collision avoidance. In: Proceedings of IEEE/RSJ International Conference on Intelligent Robots and Systems. IROS '96, vol. 3, pp. 1280–1287 (1996)
4. Quinlan, S., Khatib, O.: Elastic bands: connecting path planning and control. In: Proceedings IEEE International Conference on Robotics and Automation, vol. 2, pp. 802–807 (1993)
5. Rösmann, C., Hoffmann, F., Bertram, T.: Kinodynamic trajectory optimization and control for car-like robots. In: 2017 IEEE/RSJ International Conference on Intelligent Robots and Systems (IROS), pp. 5681–5686 (2017)

---

[1] https://www.bilibili.com/video/BV1jD421G7h5.
[2] https://github.com/yeying256/agv_housheng.

6. Zai, W., Lin, Q., Wang, S., Lin, X.: Path planning for wheeled robots based on the fusion of improved A* and TEB algorithms. In: 2023 China Automation Congress (CAC), pp. 3257–3261 (2023)
7. Dobrevski, M., Skočaj, D.: Dynamic adaptive dynamic window approach. IEEE Trans. Rob., 1–14 (2024). https://doi.org/10.1109/TRO.2024.3400932
8. Stanford Artificial Intelligence Laboratory: Robotic operating system. https://www.ros.org
9. Zheng, H., Dai, M., Zhang, Z., Xia, Z., Zhang, G., Jia, F.: The navigation based on hybrid a star and TEB algorithm implemented in obstacles avoidance. In: 2023 29th International Conference on Mechatronics and Machine Vision in Practice (M2VIP), pp. 1–6 (2023)
10. Jiang, D., et al.: An improved dynamic window approach based on reinforcement learning for the trajectory planning of automated guided vehicles. IEEE Access **12**, 36016–36025 (2024). https://doi.org/10.1109/ACCESS.2024.3373446
11. Imamoglu, M.R., Sumer, E., Temeltas, H.: A comparison of local planner algorithms for a ROS-based omnidirectional mobile robot. In: 2023 8th International Conference on Robotics and Automation Engineering (ICRAE), pp. 26–30 (2023)
12. Liu, B., Jiang, G., Zhao, F., Mei, X.: Collision-free motion generation based on stochastic optimization and composite signed distance field networks of articulated robot. IEEE Robot. Autom. Lett. **8**, 7082–7089 (2023). https://doi.org/10.1109/LRA.2023.3311357
13. Jia, W., Yang, G., Gu, L., Zheng, T.: Dynamics modelling of a mobile manipulator with powered castor wheels. In: 2017 IEEE International Conference on Cybernetics and Intelligent Systems (CIS) and IEEE Conference on Robotics, Automation and Mechatronics (RAM), pp. 730–735 (2017)
14. Jia, W., Yang, G., Zhang, C., Chen, G.: Dynamic modeling with nonsqueezing load distribution for omnidirectional mobile robots with powered caster wheels. In: 2018 13th IEEE Conference on Industrial Electronics and Applications (ICIEA), pp. 2327–2332 (2018)

# Enhanced RAMPAGE Framework for Mobile Manipulator Motion Planning

Mengyuan He[1], Yuqiang Yang[2], Zhenyu Lu[1], Zhiquan Fu[3], Wang Ning[1], and Chenguang Yang[4(✉)]

[1] Bristol Robotics Laboratory, the University of the West of England, Bristol, UK
[2] The South China University of Technology, Guangzhou, China
[3] Zhejiang VIE Science and Technology Co. Ltd., Zhuji, China
[4] Department of Computer Science, University of Liverpool, Liverpool, UK
cyang@ieee.org

**Abstract.** The application of mobile manipulators in industrial dynamic cluttered environments is becoming increasingly prevalent. Therefore, a mobile manipulator system that can effectively predict the movement trajectories of dynamic obstacles and perform obstacle avoidance planning in dynamic environments is of great significance. The RAMPAGE framework, as a newly proposed emerging dynamic obstacle avoidance planning framework, possesses efficient and reliable path planning capabilities. However, it cannot predict the movement trajectories of dynamic obstacles. Thus, in this paper, we integrate the Trajectron++ trajectory prediction model with RAMPAGE to enhance its prediction capabilities. Through simulation experiments, it has been verified that the RAMPAGE framework, after integration, gains the ability to predict dynamic obstacles. However, the planning speed and operational success rate have decreased. This integration model still represents a significant challenge in mobile robotics, combining machine learning-based prediction with robust motion planning, enabling more effective navigation in complex dynamic environments.

**Keywords:** Mothion planning · Mobile manipulator · Trajectron++

## 1 Introduction

With the demand for industrial development, mobile robots that assist industrial production are increasingly used in industrial applications. Among them, mobile manipulators (MM), which combine the mobility of a mobile base (MB) with the dexterity of a manipulator arm, have shown remarkable performance in this field. Generally speaking, the current tasks of such robots are mostly concentrated on moving an object from one place to another without conflicting with the surrounding environment. However, since MM's working environment is in an unstructured indoor environment, the main challenge is how to quickly find

X. Lan et al. (Eds.): ICIRA 2024, LNAI 15208, pp. 75–89, 2025.
https://doi.org/10.1007/978-981-96-0783-9_6

and accurately execute a reasonable path in this constrained environment. To solve this problem, the MM needs to address challenges including navigating in dynamic unstructured spaces, avoiding collisions with moving obstacles and performing tasks in real-time [5].

First, navigation and obstacle avoidance in a complex dynamic environment need to overcome the influence of dynamic obstacles in the environment [1]. However, this involves good real-time planning and control to meet the safety requirements of avoiding multiple dynamically moving and deforming three-dimensional obstacles. For this problem, [2] proposed that combining deep neural networks with a sliding window approach can effectively classify each point in a laser scan for people detection and obstacle avoidance, but it relies too much on fixed window parameters and cannot predict the movement trajectories of dynamic obstacles. Another improved Dynamic Window Approach (DWA) introduces innovative heading angle assessment and adaptive dynamic strategies to increase adaptability in dynamic environments [1], but it still often fails to meet the requirements in real-time performance and coping with rapid environmental changes. While some methods, such as Model Predictive Control (MPC), can achieve safe control and maintain stability and manoeuvrability in narrow and complex spaces by generating obstacle avoidance paths and dynamic wheel poses, MPC is too computationally intensive and may not always provide real-time feasible solutions in highly dynamic environments [4].

To effectively solve the above problems, [6] proposed the RAMPAGE framework to achieve real-time agile motion planning and control of MM in cluttered environments. This framework addresses these challenges by integrating perception, planning, and control into a unified system. RAMPAGE first achieves real-time updates of the surrounding environment for collision detection and path planning through occupancy grid maps (OGM) and Euclidean signed distance fields (ESDF). Then, the framework employs hierarchical trajectory search and space-time Rapidly-exploring Random Tree (ST-RRT) to generate initial trajectories and optimises these trajectories using an augmented Lagrangian Differential Dynamic Programming (AL-DDP) method to ensure smoothness and feasibility. However, this framework heavily relies on real-time updates for dynamic obstacle perception and lacks sufficient capability to predict the movement trajectories of moving obstacles, which may increase the sub-optimality of path planning and the risk of collisions. Therefore, accurately predicting the movement trajectories of dynamic obstacles and planning safe and efficient paths become key.

Therefore, we propose to enhance the RAMPAGE framework's capability to predict the movement trajectories of dynamic obstacles by integrating it with Trajectron++ [5]. Trajectron++ is a very advanced trajectory prediction model mainly dealing with multi-agent trajectory prediction problems, adopting a spatiotemporal graph structure. It encodes the historical states of agents through Long Short-Term Memory (LSTM) networks and incorporates interactions between agents using an attention mechanism. The Conditional Variational Autoencoder (CVAE) framework of Trajectron++ will generate multi-modal trajectory predictions to capture the uncertainty and variability of dynamic obstacles in motion. By integrating Trajectron++ into the RAMPAGE framework, our main aim is to leverage its advanced trajectory prediction capabilities to enhance the RAMPAGE framework's ability to predict the movements of dynamic obstacles. This integration will enable the RAMPAGE framework to plan more accurate and safer paths, improving its performance in highly dynamic environments.

In summary, this work addresses the critical challenges of dynamic obstacle avoidance and trajectory prediction in MM motion planning. By enhancing the RAMPAGE framework with Trajectron++, we provide a more robust and efficient solution for real-time navigation in complex and dynamic environments. Our contributions include developing a seamless integration of Trajectron++ with RAMPAGE, evaluating the enhanced framework through quasi-realistic experiments, and demonstrating changes in dynamic obstacle handling and overall path planning.

## 2    Related Works

### 2.1    Dynamic Environment Motion Planning

Motion planning in dynamic environments has always been a major challenge for MM, involving complex and real-time capable motion planning strategies. In recent years, many advanced methods have been developed, each with different advantages and limitations. Among them, [14] demonstrated the Hierarchical Adaptive Mobile Manipulator Planner (HAMP), which integrates adaptive sampling strategies within a hierarchical framework, enabling path optimisation in narrow and cluttered environments. Despite its high computational efficiency, it is primarily suited for static or semi-static environments and faces challenges in fully dynamic environments. The Optimised Hierarchical Mobile Manipulator Planner (OHMP), proposed by [10], has a similar mechanism. OHMP decomposes the planning task into basic 2D path planning and 3D trajectory planning for the manipulator, thereby improving planning efficiency in complex environments. However, OHMP shows insufficient real-time adaptability in dynamic environments and increases computational overhead due to its hierarchical nature. In industrial applications, [9] designed a fully mobile humanoid manipulator that employs omnidirectional motion and Mecanum wheels, providing high manoeuvrability and precise operation. However, its effectiveness is limited by mechanical constraints and the need for detailed environmental maps, making it less adaptable to unpredictable environments.

In summary, although OHMP and HAMP perform excellently in complex static environments, their real-time adaptability to dynamic environments is limited. The fully mobile humanoid manipulator offers high precision but is constrained by its mechanical design. While the RAMPAGE framework does not face the aforementioned issues, it still requires the integration of dynamic obstacle prediction methods like Trajectron++ to enhance performance in dynamic environments, ensuring safer and more efficient path planning.

## 2.2   Trajectory Prediction Techniques

Trajectory prediction for dynamic obstacles is crucial for obstacle avoidance and motion planning in MM dynamic environments. Many deep learning methods have made significant advances in this field by capturing complex temporal sequences and interaction patterns. For instance, Social LSTM uses Long Short-Term Memory (LSTM) networks to model the sequential nature of trajectories and incorporates a social pooling layer to account for interactions between multiple agents [13]. Although it is highly effective in capturing social interactions and improving prediction accuracy, its high computational cost and model training complexity limit its use in real-time planning applications.

On the other hand, Social GAN employs Generative Adversarial Networks (GANs) for trajectory prediction [11]. It generates future trajectories through a generator and then evaluates their realism with a discriminator. While Social GAN handles uncertainty well and excels in generating diverse and realistic trajectories, its training instability and high computational demands pose challenges for real-time applications.

Moreover, [12] proposed Social-STGCNN, which integrates Spatio-Temporal Graph Convolutional Networks (STGCNN) to model spatial and temporal dependencies in trajectories. This method effectively captures complex interactions among agents and shows robust performance in large-scale data processing. Despite this, it still struggles with handling highly irregular and unpredictable movements.

Therefore, compared to these methods, Trajectron++ enhances prediction capabilities through multimodal outputs and efficient computation, improving its feasibility for real-time applications to some extent.

## 3   Methodology

### 3.1   RAMPAGE Framework

The RAMPAGE framework primarily provides robust motion planning and control capabilities for MM in dynamic and complex environments. This section will detail and explain the methods and principles used in the RAMPAGE framework.

**Environment Modelling.** The RAMPAGE framework uses a layered map approach to model the environment surrounding the MM, including the Occupancy Grid Map (OGM) and the Euclidean Signed Distance Field (ESDF). These two methods can provide a real-time display of the environment, crucial for accurate collision detection and path planning.

The OGM represents the environment in a grid form where each cell indicates whether it is occupied, free, or unknown. The OGM updates this grid representation in real time based on sensor data. The probability of occupancy for each cell is updated using a raycasting algorithm that processes point cloud data from onboard sensors.

The ESDF provides a continuous measure of the distance from any point in the environment to the nearest obstacle. This allows efficient collision checking and gradient-based optimisation during trajectory planning. The ESDF is updated at 20 Hz using an O(N) time complexity algorithm.

The collision detection process uses sphere decomposition to approximate the body of the mobile manipulator as several spheres. Collision checking is done by comparing the radii of these spheres with the corresponding ESDF values at their centres. Figure 1 shows an example of a planar ESDF.

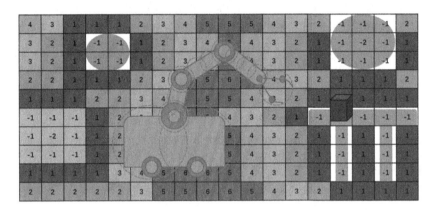

**Fig. 1.** An ESDF example of an MM grasping a cube on a table. The light blue table, square grids and circular represent obstacles. The results of the sphere decomposition approximation of the robot body are represented by dashed circles. The value shown in each grid represents the distance between that grid and its nearest obstacle (Color figure online)

The centre positions of the spheres $c_i$ are calculated using the forward kinematics chain $\mathrm{FK}_i(x)$:

$$c_i = \mathrm{FK}_i(x), \quad i = 1, 2, \ldots, M. \tag{1}$$

The collision checking is performed using the following conditions:

$$d(c_i) - r_i > 0, \quad \forall i, \tag{2}$$

$$\|c_i - c_j\| - r_i - r_j > 0, \quad \forall i, j \in S, \tag{3}$$

where $r_i$ is the radius of the $i$-th sphere, $S$ is the set of spheres, and $d(c_i)$ is the distance to the nearest obstacle, read directly from the ESDF.

The penalty function $o(x)$ to keep the mobile manipulator away from obstacles is formulated as:

$$o(x) = \sum_{i=1}^{M} p(d(c_i) - r_i) + \sum_{i,j \in S} p(\|c_i - c_j\| - r_i - r_j), \tag{4}$$

where:

$$p(y) = \begin{cases} 0 & y > s_d \\ (s_d - y)^3 & 0 < y < s_d \\ 3s_d(s_d - y)^2 - 3s_d^2(s_d - y) + s_d^3 & y < 0 \end{cases} \tag{5}$$

Here, $s_d$ represents the desired clearance between the robot body and obstacles.

**Motion Planning.** In the RAMPAGE framework, MM generates collision-free and smooth trajectories through hierarchical searching and optimisation by the trajectory planning module. This module is divided into two main parts: initial trajectory generation and kinodynamic trajectory planning.

*Initial Path Generation for MB.* The initial path is generated using a hierarchical trajectory search method similar to the A* heuristic algorithm. This method employs different topological paths to guide the search, significantly improving efficiency in handling complex environments with static and dynamic obstacles. The core steps of the algorithm are as follows:

1. **Topological Path Generation**: First, a roadmap is built through random sampling and then pruned based on topological equivalence.
2. **Search Process**: The hybrid A* method is used to search within the graph, employing preset motion primitives and heuristic cost $F$ to guide the search. All explored nodes are pushed into an ordered queue $O$ for reuse in the topological guided search.
3. **State Propagation**: The state and time of nodes are propagated using preset motion primitives. If the trajectory between nodes is collision-free, the cost-from-start $s$ is calculated as follows:

$$s = s_{\text{last}} + \lambda_1 L_b + \lambda_2 \Delta v_b + \lambda_3 \Delta \omega_b + \lambda_4 \Gamma(v \cdot v_{\text{last}}), \tag{6}$$

where $\lambda_i$ $(i = 1, \ldots, 4)$ are positive constants, $L_b$ is the current trajectory length, $\Delta v_b$ is velocity difference between trajectory nodes, $\Delta \omega_b$ is angular velocity difference, and $\Gamma$ is an indicator function.

*Kinodynamic Trajectory Planning for MM.* After determining the MB's trajectory, the RAMPAGE framework uses the ST-RRT algorithm to perform kinodynamic trajectory planning for the MM's whole body. This algorithm extends the tree in the spatial-temporal configuration space to find feasible whole-body trajectories. The specific steps are as follows:

1. **Tree Expansion**: Sample nodes $n_s$ are generated from the root node and the tree is extended in the spatial-temporal state space.
2. **Distance Metric**: The spatial-temporal distance metric is used to find the nearest node $n_n$ to the sample node $n_s$:

$$dst(n_1, n_2) = \begin{cases} \omega_t \Delta t^2 + \|n_1.x - n_2.x\|^2 & n_1.t \leq n_2.t \\ \infty & n_1.t > n_2.t \end{cases}, \tag{7}$$

where $\omega_t$ is the time weight.

3. **Edge Expansion and Collision Checking**: Edges are expanded, and collisions are checked between the new nodes and existing nodes. Feasible edges and nodes are then added to the tree.

*AL-DDP Solver for Integrated Planning and Control.* RAMPAGE solves Integrated Planning and Control (IPC) problems through an AL-DDP solver combined with direct and indirect optimization methods. Traditional DDP has difficulty in dealing with constraints, but it can decompose problems and achieve faster real-time control. Solve constraint processing problems through augmented Lagrange methods to ensure efficient resolution and processing of constraints. Constraints are integrated into the cost function, and after fixing the Lagrange multiplier, DDP is used to recursively solve the optimal control problem. The cost arrival function and Hamiltonian system equations are used for iterative optimization, and the strategy is updated based on constraint violations. Regularization and positive definite matrices ensure that the solver converges. The inner loop converges to a local minimum under certain conditions, and achieves a global minimum under convexity and linearity assumptions to ensure the robustness of real-time control.

By considering both spatial and temporal dimensions, these methods efficiently generate collision-free trajectories, ensuring real-time obstacle avoidance performance for the MM in complex dynamic environments.

## 3.2 Trajectron++ Framework

Trajectron++ is a modular, graph-structured recurrent model that can predict the trajectories of multiple interacting agents by incorporating their dynamics and heterogeneous data (e.g., semantic maps). This section will detail and explain the methods and principles used in Trajectron++.

**Scene Representation.** In Trajectron++, the scene is represented as a directed spatiotemporal graph $G = (V, E)$. Nodes $V$ represent agents (e.g., cars, pedestrians) and edges $E$ represent interactions between agents. Each node in the graph has a semantic class matching the class of its agent. An example of a spatiotemporal graph is shown in Fig. 2.

Formally, an edge is directed from $A_i$ to $A_j$ if:

$$\|p_i - p_j\|_2 \leq d_{S_j}, \tag{8}$$

where $p_i$ and $p_j$ are the 2D positions of agents $A_i$ and $A_j$, and $d_{S_j}$ is a distance that encodes the perception range of agents of semantic class $S_j$.

**Modelling Agent History.** The history of each agent is modelled using a LSTM network with 32 hidden dimensions. The observed history, consisting of the agent's current and previous states, is fed into the LSTM to produce a hidden state representation:

$$h_i(t) = \text{LSTM}(s_i(t-1), h_i(t-1)), \tag{9}$$

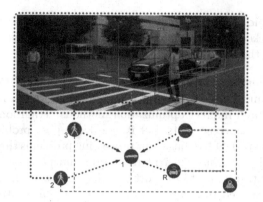

**Fig. 2.** A example of a directed spatiotemporal graph to represent a scene, adapted from [5]

where $h_i(t)$ is the hidden state of agent $i$ at time $t$, and $s_i(t)$ is the state vector (e.g., position, velocity).

**Encoding Agent Interactions.** To model the influence of neighbouring agents, Trajectron++ aggregates edge information using an element-wise sum and then feeds it into another LSTM with 8 hidden dimensions:

$$e_{ij}(t) = \text{LSTM}_{edge}(s_j(t-1), e_{ij}(t-1)), \tag{10}$$

where $e_{ij}(t)$ is the encoded interaction from agent $j$ to agent $i$.

These encodings are aggregated using an attention mechanism to produce a single influence representation:

$$e_i'(t) = \sum_{j \in \text{Neighbours}(i)} \alpha_{ij} e_{ij}(t), \tag{11}$$

where $\alpha_{ij}$ are attention weights.

**Incorporating Heterogeneous Data.** Trajectron++ integrates additional information such as semantic maps using Convolutional Neural Networks (CNNs). For each agent, a local map $M_i(t)$ is encoded and concatenated with the agent's state and influence representation:

$$m_i(t) = \text{CNN}(M_i(t)), \tag{12}$$

$$e_i''(t) = \text{concat}(h_i(t), e_i'(t), m_i(t)). \tag{13}$$

**Future Ego-Agent Motion Plans Encoding.** Trajectron++ uses a bi-directi- onal LSTM to encode the ego-agent's future T timesteps motion plan, which is crucial for robotic decision-making and control. This allows the evaluation of motion primitives based on possible responses from other agents. Then the final hidden states are concatenated into influence representation $e_i''(t)$.

**Explicitly Accounting for Multimodality.** Trajectron++ utilises the Conditional Variational Autoencoder (CVAE) framework to handle multimodality, generating the target distribution $p(y|x)$. The specific formula is as follows:

$$p(y|x) = \sum_{z \in Z} p_{\psi}(y|x, z) p_{\theta}(z|x) \tag{14}$$

where $z$ is the discrete high-level behaviour mode variable, and $|Z| = 25$, and $\psi$ and $\theta$ are the weights of the neural networks.

**Producing Dynamically-Feasible Trajectories.** To ensure the predicted trajectories are dynamically feasible, Trajectron++ incorporates system dynamics into the decoding process. For each agent, a 128-dimensional Gated Recurrent Unit (GRU) use input latent variable z and influence representation $e_i''(t)$ to generate the control actions $u^{(t)}$. Then $u^{(t)}$ integrated with the agent's system dynamics to produce trajectories in position space. For a single integrator (e.g., pedestrians) with control actions $u^{(t)} = \dot{p}^{(t)}$, the position mean at t + 1 is :

$$\mu_p^{(t+1)} = \mu_p^{(t)} + \mu_u^{(t)} \Delta t, \tag{15}$$

where $\mu_u^{(t)}$ is generated by Trajectron++.

Nonlinear dynamics (such as unicycle models) can be handled approximately by linearising them around the agent's current state and control inputs. The output trajectories are generated by sampling control actions and integrating them through the dynamics model, ensuring that all predicted trajectories are feasible given the agents' physical constraints.

**System Integration.** In the initial system integration design, the objective was to place at least five different dynamic obstacles in the scenario to test the optimisation of Trajectron++ for the RAMPAGE framework. However, after completing the training of the Trajectron++ model and attempting to apply Trajectron++ in real-time within the RAMPAGE framework, it was found that the computational power requirements were too high, which often caused the program to crash. Initial trials and tests revealed that due to the computational power limitations of the physical equipment, only one type of dynamic obstacle could be added to the scenario to maintain the normal operation of the integrated system. Therefore, in the final simulation experiment, the environmental scenario included only one type of dynamic obstacle.

Moreover, since trajectron++ is a model only able to carry out 2D trajectory prediction, hence in the model training and experiment part, the dynamic obstacle only has 2D movement. Since the RAMPAGE frame originally is designed for a 3D environment, this still allows the integrated system to work in a 3D environment, but all the dynamic object movements need to have the same 2D axis, for example, only the X and Y axis.

In the final integrated system, after obtaining the real-time predictions of the trajectories of dynamic obstacles from Trajectron++, the RAMPAGE framework will form an obstacle occupancy grid in the OGM along the predicted trajectories of these obstacles, which will be displayed in the ESDF. This approach allows the MM to perform collision detection based on the OGM and ESDF that include the predicted trajectories of dynamic obstacles provided by Trajectron++, ensuring complete avoidance of the predicted paths of dynamic obstacles.

However, in trial tests, it was observed that while only one type of dynamic obstacle was included, the simultaneous inclusion of multiple dynamic obstacles and multiple possible predicted paths in the occupancy grid map resulted in excessive pre-emptively moving obstacle occupancy grids. This caused the RAMPAGE framework to be unable to quickly find the optimal path. Therefore, in the integrated system, only the highest probability predicted path provided by Trajectron++ will be used to form the pre-emptively moving obstacle occupancy grid. Subsequently, the RAMPAGE framework will perform path planning and obstacle avoidance operations based on the existing control planning algorithms.

# 4    Experiments and Results

The integration of Trajectron++ with the RAMPAGE framework was evaluated through a series of simulation experiments designed to test the system's performance in dynamic and complex environments. This section presents the experimental setup, and the results obtained from these experiments.

## 4.1    Experimental Setup

The simulation experiments were conducted using algorithms written in C++ running on the ROS Melodic open-source platform, on a computer equipped with an Intel i7-7700HQ CPU, 32GB RAM, and an NVIDIA GTX 1050TI graphics card. Before MM, obstacles in the environment were completely unknown and were reconstructed in real-time using simulated lidar with 360c irc horizontal fields of view (FOVs). The IPC parameters of the RAMPAGE framework are listed in Table 1. For dynamic obstacles in a dynamic environment, only one type of dynamically operating sphere was designed to ensure the stable operation of the integrated system. The initial parameters modified for Trajectron++ are listed in Table 2, the rest parameters use default value, and the dynamic model parameter selected for the simulation experiments is the Single Integrator Model. For the trajectorn++ predicted trajectories included in OGM the predicted time is 2 s.

**Table 1.** IPC Parameters

| $\lambda_1$ | $\lambda_2$ | $\lambda_3$ | $\lambda_4$ | $s_d$ | $g_b$ | $w_t$ | $\mu$ | R | Q |
|---|---|---|---|---|---|---|---|---|---|
| 1 | 0.1 | 0.1 | 6 | 0.1 | 0.06 | 1 | 0.5 | diag(0.5) | diag(10) |

Table 2. Trajectron++ Model Parameters

| Parameter | Value |
|---|---|
| Node State Dimension $D$ | 4 |
| Perception Range $d_{S_j}$ | 10 |
| History Length $H$ | 8 |

## 4.2    Experimental Procedure

The experiment is conducted in three phases:

- **Baseline Comparison**: Firstly, the performance of using only the RAM-PAGE framework is evaluated to establish a baseline for comparison. MM navigates the environment using only the RAMPAGE framework without integrating Trajectron++.
- **Trajectron++ Model Training**: Based on the scenario established by the RAMPAGE framework baseline, the Trajectron++ model is trained and subsequently integrated into the RAMPAGE framework.
- **Integrated System Evaluation**: The performance of the integrated RAM-PAGE -Trajectron++ system is then evaluated. MM uses the trajectory predictions from Trajectron++ to enhance its path planning and collision avoidance strategies.

Each phase consists of 40 trials in an environment with dynamic obstacles at varying speeds.

## 4.3    Simulation Results

To test the optimisation of the integrated system, whole-body collision avoidance experiments were conducted in different dynamic cluttered environments. The goals were set 45 m away. The average speeds of obstacles in four environments were 0.25 m/s, 0.5 m/s, 0.75 m/s, and 1 m/s. The MM used a simulated 360-degree field of view on-vehicle lidar to perceive obstacles in real-time, then constructed the OGM and ESDF and found the trajectory.

The baseline runs for whole-body collision avoidance experiments are shown in Fig. 3. In Fig. 3, the red line is the found front-end, and the blue line is optimized kinodynamic trajectories by RAMPAGE. In cluttered environments, only spheres are dynamic objects, and cylinders and cubes are static. In the baseline tests of the RAMPAGE framework, when the average obstacle speed was 1 m/s, the success rate of the RAMPAGE framework was 73%. A common issue was the sudden rush of fast-moving obstacles towards the MM from outside the field of view, leading to failure.

As discussed in the system integration part, we directly allow the RAMPAGE framework to form an obstacle occupancy grid in the OGM along the predicted trajectories of these obstacles. This is because Trajectron++ does not provide

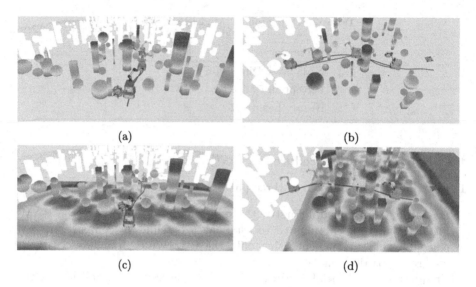

**Fig. 3.** Baseline running for the mobile manipulator in dynamic cluttered environments. (a) Back view. (b) Top view. (c) Back view with ESDF. (d) Top view with ESDF

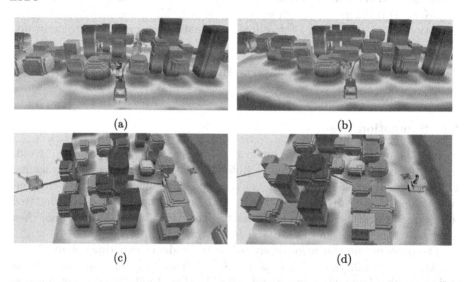

**Fig. 4.** Motion planning results for the mobile manipulator in dynamic cluttered environments. (a) RAMPAGE framework only with ESDF. (b) RAMPAGE framework only with constructed OGM and ESDF. (c) Integrate the system with ESDF. (d) Integrate system-constructed OGM and ESDF

a real-time observation of the predicted trajectory, hence we directly build it into the ESDF map. The baseline running and the integrated system test with constructed OGM and ESDF are shown in Fig. 4. It is clear from Fig. 4c and 4d that in Fig. 4d, there are many more occupied obstacle spheres on the map, these are the predicted moving obstacles formed based on the trajectories predicted by Trajectron++.

However, during the operation, the integrated system still faced situations where the RAMPAGE framework could not find an executable path due to excessive occupancy of the OGM map by predicted dynamic obstacles. There were also instances of program crashes due to excessive computational load. Therefore, the success rate of the integrated system was only 55%.

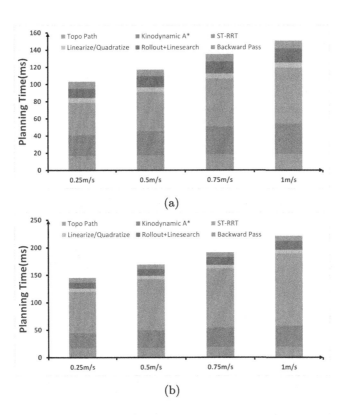

(a)

(b)

**Fig. 5.** Running time for RAMPAGE framework module with and without trajectorn++. (a) without trajectorn++. (b) with trajectorn++

The running times of the modules in the RAMPAGE framework at different average obstacle speeds are shown in Fig. 5. It is clear from Fig. 3 that the heuristic-based initial MB path search algorithm, Kinodynamic A*, and the running time of st-rrt in the RAMPAGE framework during the integrated system's operation vary significantly compared to the running time under the same speeds when only the RAMPAGE framework is running. The running time of st-rrt is nearly twice that of running only the RAMPAGE framework at the same speeds.

Although the running times of other modules have increased, the increase is not significant.

Therefore, based on the results, it can be concluded that attempting to enhance the RAMPAGE framework with Trajectron++ was successful to some extent. The RAMPAGE framework successfully gained the ability to predict the trajectories of dynamic obstacles. However, it reduced the advantage of the original RAMPAGE framework's high-speed path planning and obstacle avoidance capability and also decreased the system's success rate due to the increased computational demand.

## 5   Conclusion

In this work, we integrated Trajectron++ with the RAMPAGE framework to enhance trajectory prediction and obstacle avoidance capabilities in dynamic environments. This integration leverages the predictive power of Trajectron++ to foresee the movement of dynamic obstacles, allowing the mobile manipulator to plan paths more effectively. Although Trajectron++ was successfully integrated with the RAMPAGE framework, the added predicted obstacle trajectories and the high computational demands led to a decrease in the success rate of the integrated framework's operation due to increased computation time.

Future work will explore other integration methods or use different dynamic obstacle trajectory prediction algorithms to optimise the RAMPAGE framework. Additionally, attempts will be made to deploy the system in real-world environments. This integration model represents a significant challenge in mobile robotics, combining machine learning-based prediction with robust motion planning to navigate more effectively in complex dynamic environments.

## References

1. Dastider, A., Lin, M.: DAMON: dynamic amorphous obstacle navigation using topological manifold learning and variational autoencoding (2022)
2. Zheng, K., Wu, F., Chen, X.: Laser-based people detection and obstacle avoidance for a hospital transport robot. Sensors (2021)
3. Lin, C.: An adaptive dynamic window approach for UUV obstacle avoidance planning in 3D environments. J. Phys. Conf. Ser. (2024)
4. Xu, Z., Deng, D., Yang, D., Shimada, K.: DPMPC-planner: a real-time UAV trajectory planning framework for complex static environments with dynamic obstacles (2021)
5. Sandakalum, T., Hang Jr, M. H.: Motion planning for mobile manipulators-a systematic review. Machines (2022)
6. Yang, Y., Meng, F., Meng, Z., Yang, C.: RAMPAGE: toward whole-body, real-time, and agile motion planning in unknown cluttered environments for mobile manipulators. IEEE Trans. Ind. Electron. (2024)
7. Salzmann, T., Ivanovic, B., Chakravarty, P., Pavone, M.: Trajectron++: dynamically-feasible trajectory forecasting with heterogeneous data (2021)

8. Azizi, M.R., Rastegarpanah, A., Stolkin, R.: Motion planning and control of an omnidirectional mobile robot in dynamic environments. Robotics **10**(2021), 48 (2021)
9. Pająk, I., Pająk, G.: Motion planning for a mobile humanoid manipulator working in an industrial environment. Appl. Sci. (2021)
10. Li, Q., Mu, Y., You, Y., Zhang, Z., Feng, C.: A hierarchical motion planning for mobile manipulator. IEEJ Trans. Electr. Electron. Eng. **15** (2020)
11. Yu, B., Yin, H., Zhu, Z.: Spatio-temporal graph convolutional networks: a deep learning framework for traffic forecasting. In: Proceedings of the Twenty-Seventh International Joint Conference on Artificial Intelligence, International Joint Conferences on Artificial Intelligence Organization (2018)
12. Mohamed, A., Qian, K., Elhoseiny, M., Claudel, C.: Social-STGCNN: a social spatio-temporal graph convolutional neural network for human trajectory prediction (2020)
13. Alahi, A., Goel, K., Ramanathan, V., Robicquet, A., Li, F., Savarese, S.: Social LSTM: human trajectory prediction in crowded spaces. In: 2016 IEEE Conference on Computer Vision and Pattern Recognition (CVPR) (2016)
14. Pilania, V.K., Gupta, K.K.: A hierarchical and adaptive mobile manipulator planner with base pose uncertainty. Autonom. Rob. **39**, 65–85 (2014). https://api.semanticscholar.org/CorpusID:28540610

# Motion Control of Single-Degree-of-Freedom Magnetic Suspension System Based on Both Position and Flux Feedback

Pengfei Gao, Xiaochao Sheng[✉], Denghui Zhang, and Chenhao Wang

School of Mechanical and Electrical Engineering, Xi'an Polytechnic University, Xi'an 710048, Shaanxi, China
xchsheng@xpu.edu.cn

**Abstract.** Actuation force precision is important for precision motion control of magnetic suspension system. In order to realize the motion control of magnetic levitation system, it is assumed that the electromagnetic force changes instantaneously with the change of the input current. However, due to the hysteresis effect of the electromagnetic material, the current output from the power amplifier in the traditional control method cannot compensate for this in time. In this paper, a single-degree-of-freedom (SDOF) magnetic suspension motion control system is designed with a Hall sensor to measure the magnetic field strength for flux feedback control. By adding an inner flux feedback loop to the traditional position feedback control, the position-flux feedback control is realized, and the hysteresis effect of electromagnet is compensated to improve the electromagnet force accuracy and position control accuracy. Proportional Integral (PI) control is applied for flux feedback control. Proportional Derivative (PD) control strategies is applied for position feedback control with a Extended state observer (ESO) to reduce the effect of other unknown perturbations and improve the robustness of the system. The results show that the flux feedback control has faster response speed, better control accuracy and dynamic performance than the traditional control methods.

**Keywords:** Magnetic suspension system · Flux feedback control · Extended state observer

## 1 Introduction

Magnetic suspension is a technology that utilizes electromagnetic force to overcome the gravity of an object to make it suspended. With the continuous development of electronic technology and control technology, the magnetic suspension system has been widely used in various fields such as transportation, industry, medicine and so on due to its advantages of no friction, no lubrication, long service life, low noise, low heat loss and so on [1–4]. In the research of magnetic suspension technology, the development of control technology and measurement technology is of great significance to the precise movement of magnetic suspension, so the research on the control of magnetic suspension has a positive impact on the development of magnetic suspension technology [5].

X. Lan et al. (Eds.): ICIRA 2024, LNAI 15208, pp. 90–104, 2025.
https://doi.org/10.1007/978-981-96-0783-9_7

Magnetic suspension technology has also been increasingly used in precision motion of multiple degrees of freedom system. And the SDOF magnetic suspension system, as a typical nonlinear system, is able to visualize the control effect of the controller more intuitively. And the magnetic suspension system as an open-loop unstable system, feedback control is necessary for magnetic suspension system [6]. Traditional closed-loop control of the magnetic suspension system usually adopts the position information measured by photoelectric position sensors [7], eddy current sensors [8] and other sensors as the feedback signals, and the desired voltage or current as the controller output [9]. However, due to magnetic leakage and hysteresis of magnetic suspension system, accurate modeling of the system is more difficult to realize [10]. In order to improve the position accuracy, a variety of control strategies have been applied. Reference [11] applied third-order nonlinear differential equations to model the SDOF magnetic suspension system and designed a global sliding mode controller to achieve system motion control. Reference [12] designed adaptive linear controller and neural network controller for SDOF magnetic suspension system respectively. Reference [13] designed a nonlinear model predictive controller with nonlinear mathematical model of single-degree-of-freedom magnetic suspension system containing the dynamic parameters of electromagnet inductance current. Reference [14] designed a nonlinear motion controller with a disturbance observer to compensate the nonlinear dynamics with velocity feed-forward compensation through the disturbance observer, and verified the advantages of the controller on a single-degree-of-freedom magnetic suspension platform. Reference [15] designed an active damping anti-disturbance control algorithm for a six-degree-of-freedom magnetic levitation stage. However, the references [11–15] only use laser sensors or eddy current sensors to measure the position of the magnetically levitated actuator for feedback control, and there is only a single control loop and no compensation for hysteresis and eddy current. A multi-loop control system with current inner loop and position outer loop for SDOF magnetic suspension stages is proposed in reference [16], in which the infrared sensor is used for the position loop control and the current sensor is used for the inner current loop, which ultimately improves the control accuracy of the system. And among many control methods, the multi-loop control can gradually optimize the control performance according to the control hierarchy to improve the stability and control performance of the system, which has a wide range of applications in motor control [17], quadrotor motion control, and so on.

The SDOF magnetic suspension system controls the position of the floater through the interaction between the electromagnetic force applied to the actuator and the gravity force, and the precision motion control of the floater can be realized by realizing the precise control of the electromagnetic force. This paper proposes to use the magnetic flux in the electromagnet also as the feedback signal of the control system to realize the precise control of the electromagnetic force, and to add the inner loop of magnetic flux control to the traditional position feedback loop, so as to realize the position control of the magnetically levitated ball. In order to verify the effectiveness of the added flux feedback control to the system, it is compared with the position feedback control. The results show that, compared with the traditional position feedback control, the position-flux feedback control has faster response speed, better control accuracy, better dynamic performance.

The organization of this paper is as follows: the principle and experimental setup of SDOF magnetic suspension platform are presented in Sect. 2; the mathematical models of the position feedback control and the flux feedback control are developed in Sect. 3; the design of the control algorithm and the design of the control parameters are presented in Sect. 4; the experimental design is carried out in Sect. 5 and the results are analyzed; and finally, the conclusions are given in Sect. 6.

## 2   Working Principle and Hardware Realization of SDOF Magnetic Suspension System

The working principle of SDOF magnetic suspension system is shown in Fig. 1, the position of the floater is detected by the feedback sensor and compared with the desired input, the controller outputs the control effect to regulated the output current of the power amplifier, the current generates magnetic force to overcome the gravity of the floater and produces the movement of the floater along the expected trajectory [18].

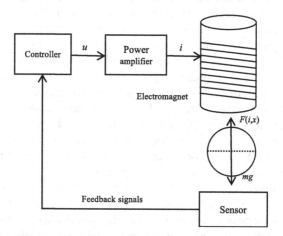

**Fig. 1.** SDOF magnetic suspension system schematic

The structure of the magnetic ball suspension system used in this paper is shown in Fig. 2, which is mainly composed of an electromagnetic coil, a Hall sensor, an eddy current sensor, a steel ball, a ball positioning table, and other parts. Eddy current sensor and Hall sensor are adopted to feedback the position and magnetic flux density through analog-to-digital conversion module. The desired current signal is sent to the power amplifier via digital-to-analog conversion module. The parameters of the magnetic suspension system are shown in Table 1.

## 3   System Model

The establishment of the mathematical model of the magnetic ball suspension system usually requires linearization, but when linearizing the electromagnetic force and current, the nonlinear factors such as magnetic leakage and hysteresis in the actual system will

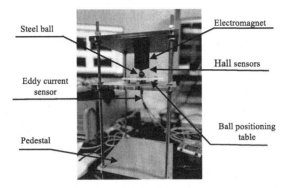

**Fig. 2.** Diagram of the experimental setup

**Table 1.** The parameters of the magnetic ball suspension system

| Description | Parameters | Value |
|---|---|---|
| Ball mass | $m$ | $2.4 \times 10^{-2}$ (kg) |
| Initial air gap | $g_0$ | $10 \times 10^{-3}$ (m) |
| Magnetic-cross-sectional area | $S$ | $7.7 \times 10^{-2}$ (m$^{2)}$) |
| Coil number | $N$ | 984 |
| Vacuum permeability | $\mu_0$ | $4\pi \times 10^{-7}$ (H/m) |
| Gravitational acceleration | $g$ | 9.8 (m/s$^{2)}$) |

be neglected, thus leading to unmodeled uncertainty. However, as shown in Fig. 3, the electromagnetic force applied on the ball is mainly generated by the electromagnet. A flux feedback control loop can be introduced so that the electromagnetic force can be generated more precisely.

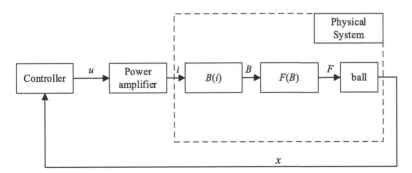

**Fig. 3.** Block diagram of SDOF magnetic suspension system force analysis

### 3.1   System Modeling Only Based on Positional Feedback

According to the working principle of the magnetic suspension system, while ignoring the magnetization of the iron, flux leakage, eddy current losses, and only considering the uniform distribution of magnetic flux in the air gap between the ball and the electromagnet, the equation of motion of the system can be expressed as

$$\begin{cases} m\frac{d^2x}{dt^2} = F(i, x) - mg \\ F(i, x) = K(\frac{i}{g_0 - x})^2 \end{cases} \tag{1}$$

where $K = \mu_0 SN^2/4$, m is the mass of the ball, kg; $t$ is the time, s; $g$ is the acceleration of gravity, m/s$^2$; $g_0$ is the is the initial air gap, m; $x$ is the ball movement, m; $i$ is the current in the magnetic coil, A; $F$ is the electromagnetic force on the ball, N.

The system is linearized at the equilibrium position of the ball, where $F(i_0, x_0) = mg$ and $x_0$, $i_0$ are the air gap and current of the ball at the equilibrium position. The second equation in Eq. (1) is Taylor expanded at $x_0$, $i_0$.

$$F(i, x) = F(i_0, x_0) + \frac{2Ki_0}{(g_0 - x_0)^2}(i - i_0) + \frac{-2Ki_0^2}{(g_0 - x_0)^3}(x - x_0) + o(i, x)$$

Ignoring the higher order terms and substituting the force equation into Eq. (1), the system dynamics can be expressed as

$$m\frac{d^2x}{dt^2} = k_i i + k_x x \tag{2}$$

where $k_i = \mu_0 SN^2 i_0^2 / 2(g_0 - x_0)^2$ represents the current stiffness and $k_x = -\mu_0 SN^2 i_0 / 2(g_0 - x_0)^3$ represents the displacement stiffness of the system. Laplace transform Eq. (2) and write the transfer function from $i$ to $x$ as

$$G_I(s) = \frac{X(s)}{i(s)} = \frac{k_i}{ms^2 - k_x} \tag{3}$$

### 3.2   System Modeling Based on Both Flux and Position Feedback

Considering the same conditions as for the position feedback, the dynamics equation of the ball under flux feedback control and position feedback control can be expressed as

$$\begin{cases} m\frac{d^2x}{dt^2} = F - mg \\ \Phi = BS = \frac{\mu_0 NiS}{2(g_0 - x)} \\ F(i, x) = K(\frac{i}{g_0 - x})^2 \end{cases} \tag{4}$$

The parameters in Eq. (4) are the same as in Eq. (1), $\Phi$ is the magnetic flux, Wb; $B$ is the flux density, T; $\mu_0$ is the vacuum permeability, H/m; $S$ is the cross-sectional area of the flux path, m$^2$; and $N$ is the number of turns of the magnetic coil.

From Eq. (4) the relationship between force and flux can be expressed as

$$F = \frac{1}{2\mu_0 S} \Phi^2 = \frac{B^2 S}{2\mu_0} = k_1 B^2 \tag{5}$$

where $k_1 = \frac{S}{2\mu_0}$.

It can be seen from the Eq. (5) that the force generated by the electromagnet is proportional to the square of the magnetic flux, and under the condition of neglecting the magnetic leakage and magneto resistance, the magnetic flux passing through the ball is equal to the magnetic flux generated by the electromagnet and the feedback control of the electromagnetic force $F$ can be realized by the measurement of the magnetic flux density $B$ through the Hall sensor. By defining $B_1 = B^2$, the magnetic ball suspension system can be modeled as a second-order system [19]. Considering the ball for motion, Eq. (4) can be written as

$$m\frac{d^2x}{dt^2} = F(B_1) - mg \tag{6}$$

The transfer function of Eq. (6) can be written as

$$G_f(s) = \frac{k_1}{ms^2} \tag{7}$$

For system position control, due to the existence of hysteresis, eddy current losses and unmodeled dynamics in the actual physical system, and these nonlinear phenomena and losses generally occur when the current $i$ is converted into the magnetic flux $\Phi$. So, the current signal output through the position feedback controller generally cannot realize the accurate compensation for this, which produces the magnetic flux density and the magnitude of the force may be a certain degree of deviation. Moreover, the current stiffness coefficient $k_i$ in Eq. (3) cannot compensate the position control effect. On the other hand, the proposed flux feedback control, $\Phi$ contains parameters related to system nonlinearity and position, so that the system position and nonlinearity can be compensated by measuring and controlling the magnetic flux density.

## 4 Control Design and Parameters Tunning

### 4.1 Control Design

The essence of the magnetic suspension control system is to control the stabilization of the force, and it can be seen from the mechanical equations that the magnetic flux density is directly related to the electromagnetic force, and there is a univariate quadratic relationship between them. In this paper, the purpose of adding flux feedback control loop in magnetic suspension control is to adjust the flux so that the electromagnetic force can reach the desired amplitude quickly and accurately. Although the ultimate purpose of the position loop is also to achieve the adjustment of the electromagnetic force, it is to achieve the indirect adjustment of the electromagnetic force by adjusting the current [20]. Therefore, in terms of electromagnetic force regulation, the flux feedback control loop takes direct way, while the adjustment of the current takes indirect way.

In this paper, a linear Hall sensor is used to measure the magnetic flux density, and the magnetic flux can be easily obtained from the conversion formula. PID controller as one of the most commonly used control methods in various control systems [21, 22], this paper designs a position loop controller ($C_p(s)$) based on PD control with ESO for position feedback control, and position-flux loop controller ($C_p(s) - C_f(s)$) based on PD and PI control with ESO for position-flux feedback control. The flow charts of traditional position feedback control and position-flux feedback control are shown in Fig. 4 and Fig. 5, respectively.

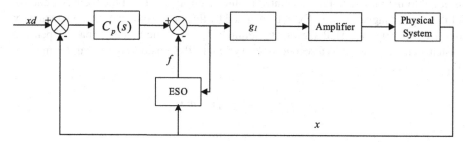

**Fig. 4.** Flow diagram of traditional position feedback control

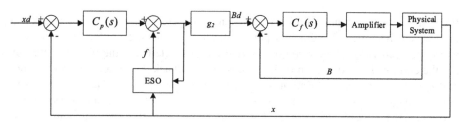

**Fig. 5.** Flow diagram of position-flux feedback control

$g_1$ and $g_2$ in the figures represent the conversion equations. In the traditional position feedback control mode, the output current of the power amplifier is adjusted only according to the position feedback, while the position-flux feedback adds a magnetic flux feedback control loop in the position feedback loop and then output the desired current. The magnetic flux feedback control loop acts as the inner-loop of position loop control in the position-flux feedback control. And as the inner loop of the flux feedback control has a higher control rate can make better compensation for the control effect, in the dynamic effect of the control also has a better performance.

The design of Extended State Observer (ESO) is carried out on this basis. ESO extends the lumped unknown disturbance of the system to a new state variable. The state observer is then designed by the extended state and the observed state variables are used to realize disturbance rejection control [23, 24]. In this paper, the lumped unknown disturbance $f$ is extended as a new state $x_3$, then the extended state space equation can be expressed as

$$\begin{cases} \dot{x}_1 = x_2 \\ \dot{x}_2 = k_x x_1 + k_i i + x_3 \\ \dot{x}_3 = \dot{f} \end{cases} \tag{8}$$

where $x_1$ represents $x$, $x_2$ represents the velocity of the floater.

Define the observer vector $L = [\beta_1, \beta_2, \beta_3]^T$, build the state space observer as

$$\begin{cases} e_1 = z_1 - x_1 \\ \dot{z}_1 = z_2 - \beta_1 e_1 \\ \dot{z}_2 = z_3 + k_x x_1 + k_i i - \beta_2 e_1 \\ \dot{z}_3 = -\beta_3 e_1 \end{cases} \tag{9}$$

where $z_1$, $z_2$, and $z_3$ are the estimates of $x_1$, $x_2$, and $x_3$, respectively. By defining $e_1 = z_1 - x_1$, $e_2 = z_2 - x_2$, $e_3 = z_3 - x_3$, the following error dynamics is obtained.

$$\begin{cases} \dot{e}_1 = e_2 - \beta_1 e_1 \\ \dot{e}_2 = e_3 - \beta_2 e_1 \\ \dot{e}_3 = -\dot{x}_3 - \beta_3 e_1 \end{cases} \tag{10}$$

The above formula can be expressed as

$$\dot{e} = Ae - B\dot{x}_3$$

where $A = \begin{bmatrix} -\beta_1 & 1 & 0 \\ -\beta_2 & 0 & 1 \\ -\beta_3 & 0 & 0 \end{bmatrix}$, $e = \begin{bmatrix} e_1 \\ e_2 \\ e_3 \end{bmatrix}$, $B = \begin{bmatrix} 0 \\ 0 \\ -1 \end{bmatrix}$. In order to place the poles of the observer's characteristic equation at the same location, the eigenvalue needs to satisfy the equation

$$\det(\lambda I - A) = \lambda^3 + \beta_1 \lambda^2 + \beta_2 \lambda + \beta_3 = (\lambda + \omega_0)^3$$

where $\beta_1 = 3\omega_0$, $\beta_2 = 3\omega_0^2$, $\beta_3 = \omega_0^3$, $\omega_0$ is the observer bandwidth, which is chosen taking into account the noise effects and the accuracy of the acquired signal [25].

In position-flux feedback control, the outer loop is the position feedback control loop, and the inner loop is the flux feedback control loop. The position feedback control loop adopts PD control to reduce the excessive cumulative error which may be caused by the integral term of PID controller, and adopts ESO to suppress the lumped disturbance of the system. The inner loop adopts PI control based on flux feedback to prevent the amplification of system noise caused by differential control items.

The flux feedback control loop outputs the desired current to the electromagnet, which generates flux when energized. The relationship from current to magnetic flux density can be described as a first-order delay system, and the system transfer function of the flux feedback control loop can be written as

$$G_{fb}(s) = \frac{B(s)}{i(s)} = \frac{k_3}{Ts+1} \tag{11}$$

where $k_3$ and T are the gain and time constant of the first-order transfer function $G_{fb}(s)$.

The flux feedback control loop controller is denoted as $C_f(s) = k_{fp} + k_{fi}/s$, then the closed-loop transfer function of the overall flux feedback control loop can be written as

$$G_1(s) = \frac{G_{fb}C_f}{(1 + G_{fb}C_f)}$$

where $k_{fp}$ and $k_{fi}$ are the proportional and integral gains of the flux feedback control loop controller $C_f(s)$.

In position-flux feedback control, the output of the position loop is converted to the input of the flux feedback control loop by the gain equation g2, that is, the desired magnetic flux density. The position loop controller is denoted by $C_p(s) = k_{pp} + k_{pd}s$, where $k_{pP}$ and $k_{pD}$ are the proportional and differential gains of the position loop controller $C_p(s)$.

### 4.2 Parameters Tunning

Based on Eq. (11), the transfer function from input current to output magnetic flux density is obtained by system identification. According to this first order transfer function, the PI controller parameters of the flux feedback control loop can be designed. For Eq. (11), a closed-loop PI controller can be designed with proportional control parameters of $k_{fp} = T/k_3 \times \omega_{ic}$ and integral control parameters of $k_{fi} = 1/k_3 \times \omega_{ic}$. The control parameters of PI controller can be determined by selecting the appropriate controller bandwidth $\omega_{ic}$.

By using a PD controller and ESO on the position loop, the controller parameters can be determined by the controller bandwidth $\omega_{oc}$, $k_{pp} = \omega_{oc}^2$, $k_{pd} = 2\omega_{oc}$. And in position-flux feedback control, the inner-loop controller bandwidth needs to be larger than the outer-loop controller bandwidth, so as to ensure the stability of the control effect.

For the determination of the gain formula g2, it can be obtained from Eq. (2), The output of the position feedback loop controller acts as an acceleration signal, which is related to the desired force $F$, and the desired magnetic flux density $B = \sqrt{2\mu_0 m\ddot{x}/S}$ can be obtained from $F = m\ddot{x}$, which is used as the gain formula g2.

## 5 Experiments

### 5.1 Experiments with Different Control Bandwidths

In position-flux feedback control, the inner-loop control bandwidth and parameters usually need to be adjusted first. In this paper, in order to meet the control design requirements and minimize the waste of controller resources, different flux feedback inner-loop control bandwidths are selected for experiments. As shown in Fig. 6, three different inner-loop control bandwidths $\omega_1 = 188.4$ rad/s, $\omega_2 = 219.8$ rad/s, $\omega_3 = 251.2$ rad/s, make the ball step 1.2 mm. $\omega_1$ jitter is more obvious in the rising process and steady state, and $\omega_3$ rises in the smoothest process, but compared to $\omega_2$ the rising time and steady state fluctuation are not significantly improved, so $\omega_2 = \omega_{ic} = 219.8$ rad/s is selected as the control bandwidth of the flux feedback control loop and further experiments.

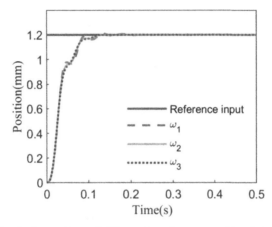

**Fig. 6.** Comparison of different inner loop control bandwidths

After the inner loop control bandwidth is determined, the outer loop control bandwidth needs to be determined. As shown in Fig. 7, three different outer-loop control bandwidths $\omega_{o1} = 50.3$ rad/s, $\omega_{o2} = 62.8$ rad/s, $\omega_{o3} = 69.1$ rad/s, the response speed of the system increases with the increase of the outer loop bandwidth, but the vibration in the rising process will increase, and the time required to reach steady state will also increase. Therefore, $\omega_{o1} = \omega_{oc} = 50.3$ rad/s is selected as the control bandwidth of the position feedback control loop bandwidth. Comparison experiments are carried out on this basis.

In order to verify the control effect of position-flux feedback control, the response speed and dynamic tracking performance of position feedback and position-flux feedback are compared under the same initial conditions. Select flux loop controller bandwidth $\omega_{ic} = 219.8$ rad/s, position loop controller bandwidth $\omega_{oc} = 50.3$ rad/s, and ESO bandwidth $\omega_0 = 314.2$ rad/s are selected. The PD control parameters of the traditional position feedback control are the same as those of position loop control in position-flux feedback control, which are $k_{pp} = 2526.6$ and $k_{pd} = 100.5$; and the PI control parameters of the flux loop are $k_{fp} = 10.6$ and $k_{fi} = 1508.7$.

## 5.2 Position Response

The initial air gap between the ball and the electromagnetic coil is 10 mm, and under the same conditions, the ball is made to make a step of 1.2 mm, so that it is stably levitated at the position where the air gap is 8.8 mm. The traditional position feedback control

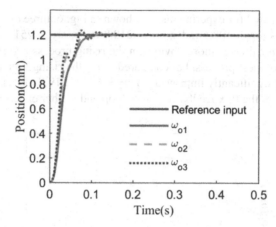

**Fig. 7.** Comparison of different outer loop control bandwidths

and position-flux feedback control position response are shown in Fig. 8. Both control methods can make the system reach a stable suspension state at about 0.15 s. However, compared with traditional position feedback control, the flux feedback control algorithm makes the system respond faster and takes less time to reach steady state.

Figure 9 shows the comparison of the error when the ball reaches the steady state under the two control methods, and it can be seen that the error of both control methods is controlled within 0.005 mm, realizing the micron-level control. But compared with the traditional position feedback control, the position flux feedback control algorithm makes the position fluctuation of the system smaller, the average position error smaller, and the control effect is better.

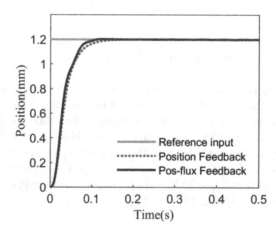

**Fig. 8.** Comparison of step responses of two control methods

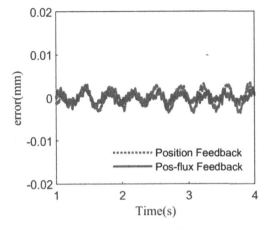

**Fig. 9.** Comparison of steady-state errors of the two control methods

### 5.3 Dynamic Performance

In order to verify the dynamic performance of the control methods, a sinusoidal signal is applied to the control system, and the system is able to track the displacement of the ball well when the magnetically suspended ball moves within a certain range. As shown in Fig. 10 and Fig. 11, the errors of both control methods are controlled within 0.05 mm, but the fluctuation of the position-flux feedback control is smaller and the tracking effect is better. The errors in Fig. 11 show periodic fluctuations, which are due to the dynamic hysteresis exhibited by the ball in its periodic motion and can be reduced by feed-forward control.

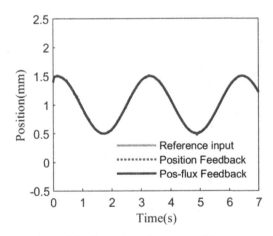

**Fig. 10.** Comparison of the dynamic performance of the two control methods

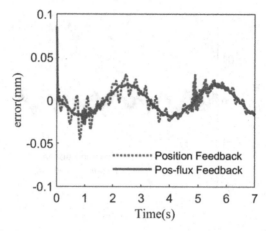

**Fig. 11.** Dynamic response error of the two control methods

## 6   Conclusion

In this paper, a SDOF magnetic ball suspension system is designed based on position feedback control and flux feedback control. By adding flux feedback control loop to the traditional position feedback control loop, the influence of hysteresis nonlinearity on electromagnetic force and position control accuracy is reduced. Firstly, based on the PD and PI control strategies, after selecting the appropriate control bandwidth, the corresponding position loop and flux loop control parameters are calculated, and the comparison experiments with different bandwidths is carried out to select the control parameters that meet the design requirements, and meanwhile, the ESO is designed to estimate the lumped unknown dynamics, and then the comparison experiments of the two control methods is designed. The results show that the position-flux feedback control has faster response speed, better control accuracy and dynamic performance than the traditional position feedback control method.

**Acknowledgments.** This work is supported by the National Natural Science Foundation of China under grant [No. 52105584].

## References

1. Phaenkongngam, T., Chinnawong, K., Patumasuit, N., Techawatcharapaikul, C.: Reviewing propulsion & levitation system for magnetic levitation train. In: 2021 9th International Electrical Engineering Congress (iEECON), Pattaya, Thailand, pp. 185–188 (2021). https://doi.org/10.1109/iEECON51072.2021.9440283
2. Nasiri-Zarandi, R., Hekmati, A.: A review of suspension and traction technologies in maglev trains. In: 2019 International Power System Conference (PSC), Tehran, Iran, pp. 129–135 (2019). https://doi.org/10.1109/PSC49016.2019.9081455
3. Li, P., Wu, T., Hsu, P.L., Wei, X., Dong, N.: 30-day in vivo study of a fully maglev extracorporeal ventricular assist device. Artif. Organs **46**(11), 2171–2178 (2022). https://doi.org/10.1111/aor.14317

4. Moreno, M.M.P., Carlos, J.: Control Lineal y No Lineal de un Levitador Magnético. Estudio Comparativo (2010)
5. Venghi, L.E., González, G.N., Serra, F.M.: Implementation and control of a magnetic levitation system. IEEE Lat. Am. Trans. **14**(6), 2651–2656 (2016). https://doi.org/10.1109/TLA.2016.7555233
6. Wai, R.-J., Lee, J.-D.: Robust levitation control for linear maglev rail system using fuzzy neural network. IEEE Trans. Control Syst. Technol. **17**(1), 4–14 (2009). https://doi.org/10.1109/TCST.2008.908205
7. Zhang, Z., Menq, C.-H.: Six-axis magnetic levitation and motion control. IEEE Trans. Robot. **23**(2), 196–205 (2007). https://doi.org/10.1109/TRO.2007.892232
8. Tang, H., Zhou, J., Jin, C., Xu, Y.: Modeling of axial self-inductive displacement sensor considering fringing effects and eddy current effects. Rev. Sci. Instrum. **94**(12), 125001 (2023). https://doi.org/10.1063/5.0168684
9. Katalenic, A., Butler, H., van den Bosch, P.P.J.: High precision force control of short-stroke reluctance actuators with an air gap observer. IEEE/ASME Trans. Mechatron. **21**(5), 2431–2439 (2016). https://doi.org/10.1109/TMECH.2016.2569023
10. Cigarini, F., Ito, S., Konig, J., Sinn, A., Schitter, G.: Compensation of hysteresis in hybrid reluctance actuator for high-precision motion. IFAC-PapersOnLine **52**(15), 477–482 (2019)
11. Zhang, J., Tao, T., Mei, X., Jiang, G., Zhang, D.: Non-linear robust control of a voltage-controlled magnetic levitation system with a feedback linearization approach. Proc. Inst. Mech. Eng. Part I J. Syst. Control Eng. **225**(1), 85–98 (2011). https://doi.org/10.1243/095965 18JSCE1018
12. Rawat, A., Nigam, M.J.: Comparison between adaptive linear controller and radial basis function neurocontroller with real time implementation on magnetic levitation system. In: 2013 IEEE International Conference on Computational Intelligence and Computing Research, Enathi, India, pp. 1–4 (2013). https://doi.org/10.1109/ICCIC.2013.6724244
13. Bächle, T., Hentzelt, S., Graichen, K.: Nonlinear model predictive control of a magnetic levitation system. Control. Eng. Pract. **21**(9), 1250–1258 (2013). https://doi.org/10.1016/j.conengprac.2013.0
14. Yang, Z.-J., Tsubakihara, H., Kanae, S., Wada, K., Su, C.-Y.: A novel robust nonlinear motion controller with disturbance observer. In: 2006 IEEE Conference on Computer Aided Control System Design, 2006 IEEE International Conference on Control Applications, 2006 IEEE International Symposium on Intelligent Control, Munich, Germany, pp. 320–325 (2006). https://doi.org/10.1109/CACSD-CCA-ISIC.2006.4776666
15. Sheng, X., Menq, C.-H., Tao, T.: Active damping and disturbance rejection control of a six-axis magnetic levitation stage. Rev. Sci. Instrum. **89**(7), 075109 (2018). https://doi.org/10.1063/1.5010432
16. Venghi, L.E., González, G.N., Serra, F.M.: Implementation and control of a magnetic suspension system. IEEE Lat. Am. Trans. **14**(6), 2651–2656 (2016). https://doi.org/10.1109/TLA.2016.7555233
17. Liu, C., Luo, G., Tu, W., Wan, H.: Servo systems with double closed-loops based on active disturbance rejection controllers. In: Proceedings of the Chinese Society of Electrical Engineering. vol. 37, pp. 7032–7039 (2017). https://doi.org/10.13334/j.0258-8013.pcsee.161957
18. Zhang, C., Lu, Y., Liu, G., Ye, Z.: Research on one-dimensional motion control system and method of a magnetic levitation ball. Rev. Sci. Instrum. **90**(11), 115005 (2019). https://doi.org/10.1063/1.5119767
19. Ito, S., Cigarini, F., Schitter, G.: Flux-controlled hybrid reluctance actuator for high-precision scanning motion. IEEE Trans. Ind. Electron. **67**(11), 9593–9600 (2020). https://doi.org/10.1109/TIE.2019.2952829

20. Long, F., Cheng, P., Meng, T.-M., Menq, C.-H.: Optimal current allocation rendering 3-D magnetic force production in hexapole electromagnetic actuation. IEEE/ASME Trans. Mechatron. **26**(5), 2408–2417 (2021). https://doi.org/10.1109/TMECH.2020.3039258

21. Wang, F., Ren, B., Liu, Y., Cui, B.: Tracking moving target for 6 degree-of-freedom robot manipulator with adaptive visual servoing based on deep reinforcement learning PID controller. Rev. Sci. Instrum. **93**(4), 045108 (2022). https://doi.org/10.1063/5.0087561

22. Subrata, R.H., Hardenberg, J.L., Gozali, F.: The use of pid controller to get the stable floating condition of the objects in magnetic levitation system. In: 2017 15th International Conference on Quality in Research (QiR): International Symposium on Electrical and Computer Engineering, Nusa Dua, Bali, Indonesia, pp. 321–324 (2017). https://doi.org/10.1109/QIR.2017.8168504

23. Zheng, Q., Gao, Z.: On practical applications of active disturbance rejection control. In: Proceedings of the 29th Chinese Control Conference, Beijing, China, pp. 6095–6100 (2010)

24. Hua, X., Huang, D., Guo, S.: Extended state observer based on ADRC of linear system with incipient fault. Int. J. Control Autom. Syst. **18**, 1425–1434 (2020). https://doi.org/10.1007/s12555-019-0052-2

25. Tian, G., Gao, Z.: Frequency response analysis of active disturbance rejection based control system. In: 2007 IEEE International Conference on Control Applications, Singapore, pp. 1595–1599 (2007)

# Modeling of Human Throwing Motion from Human Demonstration Using a Hidden Markov Model

Shaowu Li[1,2], Yanjiang Huang[1,2], and Xianmin Zhang[1,2(✉)]

[1] School of Mechanical and Automotive Engineering, South China University of Technology, Guangzhou 510640, China
zhangxm@scut.edu.cn
[2] Guangdong Provincial Key Laboratory of Precision Equipment and Manufacturing Technology, South China University of Technology, Guangzhou 510640, China

**Abstract.** In the human-robot interaction, teaching robots to learn human skills is a challenging work. Throwing is a process of projecting an object to a distant target location, and it is usually considered as one of the skills possessed by humans. To enable robots to perform throwing skills, two steps are required: firstly, modeling and outputting the motion sequences of human throwing motion; secondly, transferring the motion sequences to the robotic arm and realizing the throwing skill on the robotic arm. This paper aims to model the motion of human throwing. First of all, raw datas of human throwing motion are obtained through human demonstration. Afterwards, feature vectors are extracted through the analysis of the raw datas. By applying the HMM to train the feature vectors, the model of human throwing motion $\lambda_{final}$ has ultimately been finalized. The result shows that our model can effectively describe the behavior of human throwing and generate the motion sequences of human throwing motion.

**Keywords:** Human Throwing Motion · Feature Vectors · HMM · Motion Sequences

## 1 Introduction

Robots are becoming an integral part of our daily lives, with the anticipation that they will acquire human skills to facilitate and enhance our ability to perform tasks. However, it is a significant challenge for robots to acquire human skills, and numerous scholars have made substantial efforts in this endeavor [1–5].

Throwing is a fundamental skill for humans. With appropriate training, the average individual can effortlessly propel a variety of objects towards diverse target locations. Nevertheless, it proves to be a formidable challenge for robots to execute such task. Scientists have devoted tremendous efforts to enable robots to master the skill of throwing. Through quality diversity search, Seungsu Kim et al. [6] trained the Baxter robot in high-speed throwing motion. By establishing a physical model, Deng Lin et al. [7] enabled a cable-suspended sling-like parallel robot to achieve throwing motion. Jwu-Sheng Hu

X. Lan et al. (Eds.): ICIRA 2024, LNAI 15208, pp. 105–116, 2025.
https://doi.org/10.1007/978-981-96-0783-9_8

et al. [8] used a visual feedback system to guide the robot in successfully shooting the ball into the basketball hoop. Andy Zeng et al. [9] trained the UR5 robot to throw various objects into different comartments by integrating visual perception and residual physics.

Hidden Markov Model (HMM) is a generative model of the simplest structured dynamic Bayesian network, which is an effective tool for modeling data sequences and can achieve data recognition and generation. It was originally applied in traditional speech recognition technology [10, 11]. Currently, HMM has been increasingly utilized in robotics to facilitate the learning of human skills such as playing the tower of hanoi [12], conducting assisted surgical procedures [13], and assembling 3C products [14]. This paper aims to utilize HMM for the learning of human throwing skills.

The paper is organized as follows. Section 2 describes the process of obtaining and preprocessing raw datas for human throwing motion. Section 3 presents the process of modeling human throwing motion and generating sequences of human throwing motion. Section 4 shows the conclusion and future work.

## 2 Acquisition and Preprocessing of Human Throwing Motion Datas

### 2.1 Acquisition of Raw Data

Considering the precision requirement, we employs the NOKOV optical three-dimensional motion capture system, which designed for high-precision movement tracking, to gather raw datas of human throwing. Firstly, we constructed a 4 * 3 m experimental site (see Fig. 1) by utilizing eight Mars1.3H lenses. Subsequently, the aperture and focal length of each lens were meticulously adjusted to enhance the precision of the collected datas. The calibration results indicated that the system's 2D residual was 0.30 pixels, the 3D residual was 1.44 mm, and the data variance for the calibration bar was 4.05. These results meet the requirements, allowing for the commencement of subsequent phases of data collection.

Next, we applied 6 marker points on the subject's arm (see Fig. 2). Marker A was affixed to the upper arm, marker B was positioned over the elbow joint, and marker C was secured to the forearm. Due to the complexity of hand movements, marker points on the hand can be easily obscured by the thrown object and the hand itself during the throwing process. Therefore we applied marker point D on the wrist joint, marker points E and F were applied on other parts of the palm. These three points formed a rigid body, with a virtual point O as its center of mass. The advantage of arranging marker points in this way was that it facilitated the conversion of marker points from Cartesian coordinate values to joint angles in joint coordinate system (details are provided in the Sect. 2.2). During the experiment, the subject sat on a chair, keeping his upper body motionless except for the right arm, and then threw the provided sandbags into a designated target box. The mass of the experimental sandbags was 150g. The target box was placed 2 m horizontally from the subject.The subject was instructed to throw sandbags into the target box, with the motion capture system meticulously recording datas for each successful attempt. A total of eight sets of data were collected to ensure the subsequent analysis and training process.

**Fig. 1.** The experimental site, including a motion capture system, a sandbag and a tagget box.

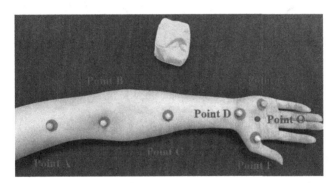

Point D    Point O

**Fig. 2.** The location of the markers.

## 2.2 Feature Extraction

In order to facilitate the subsequent transplantation of human throwing skills to robotic arms, it is necessary to convert the Cartesian space coordinates into joint space angles, and then transform each set of recorded three-dimensional space coordinates into corresponding angles for the shoulder joint, elbow joint, and wrist joint. This will enable the transplantation of human throwing skills onto robotic arms in a more efficient manner.

The angles of the shoulder joint, elbow joint, and wrist joint are denoted as $\theta_s$, $\theta_e$, an $\theta_w$ respectively. Assuming the coordinates of point P at time t is $P_t(x_{P,t}, y_{P,t}, z_{P,t})$, then the joint angles (see Fig. 3) at time t can be obtained as:

$$\theta_{s,t} = arccos\left(\frac{z_{A,t} - z_{B,t}}{\sqrt{(x_{B,t} - x_{A,t})^2 + (y_{B,t} - y_{A,t})^2 + (z_{B,t} - z_{A,t})^2}}\right) \tag{1}$$

$$\theta_{e,t} = arccos\left(\frac{(x_{A,t} - x_{B,t})(x_{C,t} - x_{B,t}) + (y_{A,t} - y_{B,t}) + (y_{C,t} - y_{B,t}) + (z_{A,t} - z_{B,t})(z_{C,t} - z_{B,t})}{\sqrt{(x_{A,t} - x_{B,t})^2 + (y_{A,t} - y_{B,t})^2 + (z_{A,t} - z_{B,t})^2}\sqrt{(x_{C,t} - x_{B,t})^2 + (y_{C,t} - y_{B,t})^2 + (z_{C,t} - z_{B,t})^2}}\right) \tag{2}$$

$$\theta_{w,t} = arccos\left(\frac{(x_{C,t}-x_{D,t})(x_{D,t}-x_{O,t}) + (y_{C,t}-y_{D,t})(y_{D,t}-y_{O,t}) + (z_{C,t}-z_{D,t})(z_{D,t}-z_{O,t})}{\sqrt{(x_{C,t}-x_{D,t})^2 + (y_{C,t}-y_{D,t})^2 + (z_{C,t}-z_{D,t})^2}\sqrt{(x_{D,t}-x_{O,t})^2 + (y_{D,t}-y_{O,t})^2 + (z_{D,t}-z_{O,t})^2}}\right)$$

(3)

For human throwing motion process $l(1 \leq l \leq 8)$, extract the sequences of joint angles at each moment as the feature vectors of the throwing process:

$$x_l(t) = \{\theta_{s,t}, \theta_{e,t}, \theta_{s,t}\}, 1 \leq t \leq T \tag{4}$$

All the training datas can be represented as:

$$X = \{x_l, 1 \leq l \leq 8\} \tag{5}$$

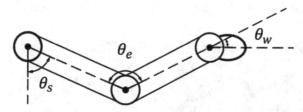

**Fig. 3.** Angles of shoulder joint, elbow joint, and wrist joint.

## 2.3 Analysis and Keyframe Extraction

Now we analyze the human throwing process by combining a set of typical feature vectors of human throwing motion (see Fig. 4).

Upon the curve shown in the Fig. 4, it is apparent that during the human throwing process, the most noticeable change occurs in the angles of shoulder joint, indicating that the shoulder joint contributes the majority of the kinetic energy to the act. Firstly, the angle of the shoulder joint decreases slowly, allowing the subjects to reserve more space for shoulder joint movement. Having more space means that the shoulder joint has more time to accelerate. Afterwards, there is a sharp increase in the angle of the shoulder joint, providing the object with sufficient throwing speed during the process. The object is thrown in these processes, but mainly controlled by the wrist joint. After reaching its maximum value, the angle of the shoulder joint begins to decrease slowly, as gravity starts to take effect after the throwing process ends.

During the throwing process, there is minimal change in the angles of the elbow joint, typically less than $15°$. This is because the elbow joint is not the primary working part in the throwing process, but rather driven by the upper arm. It can be observed that as the angles of the shoulder joint decreases to its minimum value, the angles of the elbow joint slowly increases to its maximum value; when the shoulder joint angle sharply increases, the rapidly rising upper arm begins to drive up the forearm, thereby causing a decrease in the angles of the elbow joint.

Finally, pay attention to the wrist joint. It demonstrates an "Ω" shape during the throwing process. It rapidly rises to a certain peak, then gradually increases to another peak, and finally decreases rapidly. The angle of the thrown object is primarily controlled by the wrist joint in its execution. The throwing moment is situated between the two peaks.

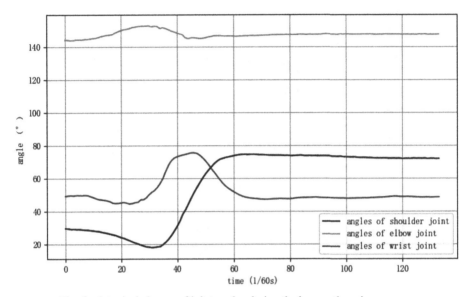

**Fig. 4.** A typical change of joint angles during the human throwing process.

Based on the above analysis, we define a set of key frames that best represent the human throwing motion:

$$\varepsilon = \{\varepsilon_1, \varepsilon_2, \varepsilon_3, \varepsilon_4, \varepsilon_5\} \tag{6}$$

where $\varepsilon_1$ donotes the feature vector at the minimum angle of the shoulder joint, $\varepsilon_2$ donotes the feature vector at the maximum angle of the elbow joint, $\varepsilon_3$ and $\varepsilon_4$ donote the two feature vectors located at the two peaks of the angle curve of the shoulder joint, $\varepsilon_5$ donotes the feature vector at the maximum angle of the shoulder joint.

## 3 Modeling of HMM-Based Human Throwing Motion

### 3.1 Initialization of the HMM

The process of human throwing encompasses a degree of inherent stochasticity, making it challenging to capture with precise deterministic models. However, different throwing processes conceal the same underlying intents to throw. HMM can utilize these hidden intents to model the throwing process and generate the motion sequences of human throwing.

A typical HMM comprises five fundamental components:

1. $N$ Denotes a finite set of state values in the model, $N = (s_1, s_2, \ldots, s_N)$. Assuming that at time t, the observed value (i.e. feature vector) $x_t$ of the model is in state $q_t$, then we have $q_t \in N$.
2. $M$ Denotes a finite set of observed values in the model, $M = (o_1, o_2, \ldots, o_M)$. Assuming that at time t, we are presented with the observed value $x_t$, then we have $x_t \in M$.
3. $\Pi$ Denotes the set of initial state probabilities, $\Pi = (\pi_1, \pi_2, \ldots, \pi_N)$. It represents the probability of being in each state at the beginning:

$$\pi_i = P(q_1 = s_i), 1 \le i \le N \tag{7}$$

4. $A$ Denotes the transition probability matrix of the states, $A = \{a_{ij}\}_{N \times N}$. And $a_{ij}$ represents the transition probability of taking the transition from state $i$ to state $j$:

$$a_{ij} = P(q_{t+1} = s_j | q_t = s_i), 1 \le i, j \le N \tag{8}$$

5. $B$ Denotes the output probability matrix, $B = \{b_{jk}\}_{N \times M}$. $b_{jk}$ is defined as the probability of observed value $o_k$ belonging to state $s_i$:

$$b_{jk} = P(x_t = o_k | q_t = s_j), 1 \le j \le N, 1 \le k \le M \tag{9}$$

Then an HMM can be represented as:

$$\lambda = (\Pi, A, B)$$

The above model is suitable for situations where the observed values are discrete. The observed values $x$ collected in this paper can be considered as continuously joint angles, therefore a corresponding continuous gaussian mixture module HMM (GMMHMM) should be applied. In GMMHMM, B is no longer a matrix but a set of probability density functions for observed values, $B = \{b_j(x), j = 1, 2, \ldots, N\}$. $b_j(x)$ is the probability density function of observed value $x$, represented using the Gaussian probability density function:

$$b_j(x) = (2\pi)^{-\frac{r}{2}} |U_j|^{-\frac{1}{2}} exp\left\{-\frac{1}{2}(x - \mu_j)^T U_j^{-1}(x - \mu_j)\right\} \tag{10}$$

Where $r$ means the dimensions of feature vector $x$, $U_j$ means the covariance matrix of the mixed Gaussian components in state $j$, $\mu_j$ means the mean vector of the mixed Gaussian components in state $j$.

Practically, using a single Gaussian probability density function $N(x; \mu_j, U_j)$ to represent the output probability distribution of observed values is often insufficient. Therefore, it is common to use a multivariate Gaussian density function. Specifically, for each state, a linear combination of several normal Gaussian probability density functions is used to represent the output probability distribution. Therefore we have:

$$b_j(x) = \sum_{m=1}^{M} c_{jm} b_{jm}(x) = \sum_{m=1}^{M} c_{jm} N(x; \mu_{jm}, U_{jm}) \tag{11}$$

Now we initialize the parameters of the human throwing motion GMMHMM. As mentioned previously, in the process of human throwing, there are five keyframes, representing five distinct states. Then the $\Pi$ and the $A$ can be initialized as:

$$\Pi_{init} = (0.2, 0.2, 0.2, 0.2, 0.2) \tag{12}$$

$$A_{init} = \begin{bmatrix} 0.5 & 0.5 & 0 & 0 & 0 \\ 0 & 0.5 & 0.5 & 0 & 0 \\ 0 & 0 & 0.5 & 0.5 & 0 \\ 0 & 0 & 0 & 0.5 & 0.5 \\ 0 & 0 & 0 & 0 & 0.5 \end{bmatrix} \tag{13}$$

The determination of the components of the normal gaussian probability density function is acquired through the utilization of the k-means clustering method (see Fig. 5). For a set of training datas $x_l$, it can be divided into three categories using three clusters, hence $m = 3$. As for each normal gaussian probability density function, the $\mu_j$ and the $U_j$ can be initialized as:

$$\mu_{j,init} = ((1,1,1), (1,1,1), (1,1,1)) \tag{14}$$

$$U_{j,init} = \begin{bmatrix} 1 & 0 & 0 \\ 0 & 1 & 0 \\ 0 & 0 & 1 \end{bmatrix} \tag{15}$$

The combination coefficients for each normal gaussian probability density function $c_j$ can be initialized as:

$$c_{j,init} = (0.3, 0.3, 0.4) \tag{16}$$

It is worth noting that the training process of the model is an iterative process, and the establishment of the final model mainly depends on the training datas. Therefore, the initialization of the parameters will not have a significant impact on the final results.

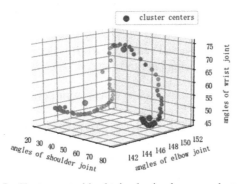

**Fig. 5.** Cluster centroids obtained using k-means clustering.

## 3.2 Model Training

The training process of the GMMHMM is to iteratively update the parameters $\Pi, A, \mu_j$, $U_j$, $c_j$ using training datas until convergence is achieved.

The forward algorithm is applied to define the forward probability $\alpha_t(i)$ as:

$$\alpha_t(i) = P(o_1, o_2, \ldots, o_t, s_t = i|\lambda) \tag{17}$$

It is evident that:

$$\alpha_1(i) = \pi_i b_i(o_1) \tag{18}$$

Then we have:

$$\alpha_{t+1}(i) = \left( \sum_{j=1}^{N} \alpha_t(j) a_{ji} \right) b_i(o_{t+1}) \tag{19}$$

The backward algorithm is applied to define the backward probability $\beta_t(i)$ as:

$$\beta_t(i) = P(o_{t+1}, o_{t+2}, \ldots, o_T, s_t = i|\lambda) \tag{20}$$

It is evident that:

$$\beta_T(i) = 1 \tag{21}$$

Then we have:

$$\beta_{t-1}(i) = \sum_{j=1}^{N} \beta_t(j) b_j(o_t) a_{ij} \tag{22}$$

The Baum-Welch algorithm is then applied to define the probabilities $\gamma_t(i, m)$ and $\xi_t(i, j)$. Given the sequences of observed values $x$, $\gamma_t(i, m)$ is denoted as the probability that the observed value $o_t$ belongs to state i:

$$\gamma_t(i, m) = P(s_t = i, gauss = m|o, \lambda)$$

$$= \left[ \frac{\alpha_t(j)\beta_t(j)}{\sum_{j=1}^{N} \alpha_t(j)\beta_t(j)} \right] \left[ \frac{c_{jm}N(o_t, \mu_{jm}, U_{jm})}{\sum_{m=1}^{M} c_{jm}N(o_t, \mu_{jm}, U_{jm})} \right] \tag{23}$$

Given the sequences of observed values $x$, $\xi_t(i, j)$ is denoted as the probability that the state being i at time t and being j at time $t + 1$:

$$\xi_t(i, j) = P(s_t = i, s_{t+1} = j|o, \lambda)$$

$$= \frac{a_{ij} b_j(o_{t+1}) \alpha_t(i) \beta_{t+1}(j)}{\sum_{i=1}^{N} \sum_{j=1}^{N} a_{ij} b_j(o_{t+1}) \alpha_t(i) \beta_{t+1}(j)} \tag{24}$$

Then the parameters $\Pi, A, \mu_j, U_j, c_m$ can be updated as:

$$\overline{\pi}_i = \frac{\sum_{l=1}^{L} \sum_{m=1}^{M} c_{im} \gamma_1^{(l)}(i, m)}{L} \tag{25}$$

$$\overline{a}_{ij} = \frac{\sum_{l=1}^{L}\sum_{n=1}^{N-1}\xi_t^{(l)}(i,j)}{\sum_{l=1}^{L}\sum_{n}^{N-1}\sum_{m=1}^{M}\gamma_t^{(l)}(i,m)} \tag{26}$$

$$\overline{\mu}_{im} = \frac{\sum_{l=1}^{L}\sum_{t=1}^{T^{(l)}}\gamma_t^{(l)}(i,m)o_t^{(l)}}{\sum_{l=1}^{L}\sum_{t=1}^{T^{(l)}}\gamma_t^{(l)}(i,m)} \tag{27}$$

$$\overline{U}_{jm} = \frac{\sum_{l=1}^{L}\sum_{t=1}^{T^{(l)}}\gamma_t^{(l)}(i,m)(o_t^{(l)}-\mu_{jm})(o_t^{(l)}-\mu_{jm})^T}{\sum_{l=1}^{L}\sum_{t=1}^{T^{(l)}}\gamma_t^{(l)}(i,m)} \tag{28}$$

$$\overline{c}_{im} = \frac{\sum_{l=1}^{L}\sum_{t=1}^{T^{(l)}}\gamma_t^{(l)}(i,m)}{\sum_{l=1}^{L}\sum_{t=1}^{T^{(l)}}\sum_{m=1}^{M}\gamma_t^{(l)}(i,m)} \tag{29}$$

Each iteration yields a new model:

$$\overline{\lambda} = (\overline{\Pi}, \overline{A}, \overline{c}, \overline{\mu}, \overline{U}) \tag{30}$$

Check if the computational model converges:

$$|P(o|\lambda_{i+1}) - P(o|\lambda_i)| < 0.001 \tag{31}$$

If the inequality is met, then we stop the iteration and get the final model $\lambda_{final}$.

### 3.3   Generation of Human Throwing Motion

The parameters of the final model $\lambda_{final}$ are listed below:

$$\Pi_{final} = (1.0, 0.0, 0.0, 0.0, 0.0) \tag{32}$$

$$A_{final} = \begin{bmatrix} 0.97225 & 0 & 0 & 0.02775 & 0 \\ 0 & 0.97956 & 0 & 0 & 0.02044 \\ 0 & 0 & 0.93878 & 0.02042 & 0.04080 \\ 0 & 0.04712 & 0.07071 & 0.88217 & 0 \\ 0 & 0 & 0 & 0 & 1 \end{bmatrix} \tag{33}$$

$$c_{final} = \begin{bmatrix} 0.33534329 & 0.59834755 & 0.06630916 \\ 0.69399211 & 0.07535072 & 0.23065717 \\ 0.19573967 & 0.47475542 & 0.32950491 \\ 0.06866393 & 0.40953196 & 0.52180411 \\ 0.64424014 & 0.04714712 & 0.30861273 \end{bmatrix} \tag{34}$$

$$\mu_{final} = \begin{bmatrix} \begin{bmatrix} 29.63398168 & 143.53124477 & 48.36433418 \\ 23.83200356 & 149.45735866 & 46.63468047 \\ 17.93170278 & 151.12182568 & 50.22372183 \end{bmatrix} \\ \begin{bmatrix} 74.53577012 & 146.98937972 & 47.66162634 \\ 53.51706511 & 147.48265344 & 73.48121836 \\ 72.57265094 & 148.38735181 & 58.33429338 \end{bmatrix} \\ \begin{bmatrix} 63.25661597 & 141.77103898 & 69.22593376 \\ 46.43598216 & 142.84645759 & 76.16575464 \\ 71.66556457 & 143.18185152 & 54.87120856 \end{bmatrix} \\ \begin{bmatrix} 64.27097209 & 146.22159035 & 72.34075074 \\ 30.29669843 & 147.78543633 & 71.39012867 \\ 21.31939259 & 150.68546185 & 57.39698729 \end{bmatrix} \\ \begin{bmatrix} 72.02310335 & 146.60934878 & 48.30019697 \\ 75.15313517 & 143.23819661 & 45.81307546 \\ 65.13850972 & 143.75529157 & 49.25055287 \end{bmatrix} \end{bmatrix} \quad (35)$$

$$U_{final} = \begin{bmatrix} \begin{bmatrix} 4.10094008 & 1.5367435 & 2.5655011 \\ 9.47319997 & 11.54114588 & 3.0290942 \\ 0.23200735 & 1.35164812 & 5.94980606 \end{bmatrix} \\ \begin{bmatrix} 2.61401104 & 0.21950614 & 2.18033971 \\ 44.02411176 & 0.23597679 & 1.06341175 \\ 14.44504767 & 1.54650129 & 36.47838474 \end{bmatrix} \\ \begin{bmatrix} 19.65843076 & 3.49973351 & 15.41387786 \\ 60.79651789 & 3.13542274 & 2.96694497 \\ 18.54064408 & 1.49864658 & 20.33313438 \end{bmatrix} \\ \begin{bmatrix} 6.19616633 & 0.41699636 & 24.73405924 \\ 21.0542246 & 5.08367808 & 5.9335521 \\ 3.89775312 & 10.5031953 & 26.03644019 \end{bmatrix} \\ \begin{bmatrix} 1.25001242 & 3.28822654 & 0.18641129 \\ 1.07111932 & 0.08349702 & 0.43960377 \\ 7.00448857 & 2.900288 & 0.73765848 \end{bmatrix} \end{bmatrix} \quad (36)$$

After obtaining the final model, a motion sequences of human throwing can be generated by probability and outputted after polynomial fitting(see Fig. 6).

As depicted in Fig. 6, the curves of joint angles generated by our model exhibit a strong resemblance to the original curve (see Fig. 4). From the first frame to the thirty-fifth frame (i.e. the main process of human throwing), the curve of shoulder joint angles appears a rapid increase from 25° to 72°, while the original curve shows a same increase from 20° to 70°. Regarding the curve of the wrist joint angles, it also demonstrates an "Ω" shape from 45° to 73°, whereas the original curve ranges from 44° to 75°. As for the curve of elbow joint angles, it shows a gradual change around 145° similar to the original curve. After this stage, all three curves tend to smooth out just like the original curves.

Since the motion sequences are generated by HMM probabilities, it is not possible to achieve a 100% match with the training data. However, it can be observed that both numerically and in terms of trend, the motion sequences generated by our model already possess the characteristics of human throwing. In conclusion, our model effectively describe the behavior of human throwing motion.

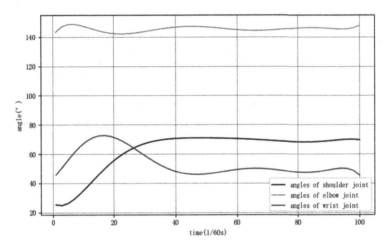

**Fig. 6.** Motion sequences of human throwing generated by the final model.

## 4 Conclusion and Future Work

This paper presents a model for human throwing motion. Firstly, raw datas of human throwing is obtained from the motion capture system. The angles of the shoulder joint, elbow joint, and wrist joint are extracted as the feature vectors of the human throwing. Then the feature vectors is analyzed to obtain the key frames. Subsequently, a model for the human throwing is established by utilizing GMMHMM. Parameter initialization is conducted through analysis, followed by training the model using the training datas and we get the final model $\lambda_{final}$. The output motion sequences of the final model indicate that our model is effective and can generate the motions sequences of human throwing.

In the future, motion sequences generated by the model will be transferred to a UR5 robotic arm, which will have the capability to throw various objects into different designated target boxes.

**Acknowledgements.** This work was supported by the National Natural Science Foundation of China (Grant No. 52075178, 52130508) and the Guangzhou Municipal Scientific and Technological Project under Grant 2024A04J6287.

# References

1. Odesanmi, G.A., Wang, Q., Mai, J.: Skill learning framework for human–robot interaction and manipulation tasks. Robot. Comput. Integr. Manuf. **79**, 102444 (2023). https://doi.org/10.1016/j.rcim.2022.102444
2. Peternel, L., Petrič, T., Oztop, E., Babič, J.: Teaching robots to cooperate with humans in dynamic manipulation tasks based on multi-modal human-in-the-loop approach. Auton. Robot. **36**, 123–136 (2014). https://doi.org/10.1007/s10514-013-9361-0
3. Yu, Z., et al.: Design of a humanoid ping-pong player robot with redundant joints. In: 2013 IEEE International Conference on Robotics and Biomimetics (ROBIO), Shenzhen, China, pp. 911–916. IEEE (2013) https://doi.org/10.1109/ROBIO.2013.6739578
4. Qiang, H., et al.: Planning walking patterns for a biped robot. IEEE Trans. Robot. Autom. **17**, 280–289 (2001). https://doi.org/10.1109/70.938385
5. Ajoudani, A., Tsagarakis, N., Bicchi, A.: Tele-impedance: teleoperation with impedance regulation using a body–machine interface. Int. J. Robot. Res. **31**, 1642–1656 (2012). https://doi.org/10.1177/0278364912464668
6. Kim, S., Doncieux, S.: Learning highly diverse robot throwing movements through quality diversity search. In: Proceedings of the Genetic and Evolutionary Computation Conference Companion, Berlin Germany, pp. 1177–1178. ACM (2017). https://doi.org/10.1145/3067695.3082463
7. Lin, D., Mottola, G., Carricato, M., Jiang, X.: Modeling and control of a cable-suspended sling-like parallel robot for throwing operations. Appl. Sci. **10**, 9067 (2020). https://doi.org/10.3390/app10249067
8. Hu, J.-S., Chien, M.-C., Chang, Y.-J., Su, S.-H., Kai, C.-Y.: A ball-throwing robot with visual feedback. In: 2010 IEEE/RSJ International Conference on Intelligent Robots and Systems, Taipei, pp. 2511–2512. IEEE (2010). https://doi.org/10.1109/IROS.2010.5649335
9. Zeng, A., Song, S., Lee, J., Rodriguez, A., Funkhouser, T.: TossingBot: learning to throw arbitrary objects with residual physics. IEEE Trans. Robot. **36**, 1307–1319 (2020). https://doi.org/10.1109/TRO.2020.2988642
10. Huang, X., Alleva, F., Hwang, M.-Y., Rosenfeld, R.: An overview of the SPHINX-II speech recognition system. In: Proceedings of the Workshop on Human Language Technology - HLT 1993, Princeton, New Jersey, p. 81. Association for Computational Linguistics (1993). https://doi.org/10.3115/1075671.1075690
11. Juang, B.H., Rabiner, L.R.: Hidden Markov models for speech recognition. Technometrics **33**, 251–272 (1991). https://doi.org/10.1080/00401706.1991.10484833
12. Lee, K., Su, Y., Kim, T.-K., Demiris, Y.: A syntactic approach to robot imitation learning using probabilistic activity grammars. Robot. Auton. Syst. **61**, 1323–1334 (2013). https://doi.org/10.1016/j.robot.2013.08.003
13. Yang, D., Lv, Q., Liao, G., Zheng, K., Luo, J., Wei, B.: Learning from demonstration: dynamical movement primitives based reusable suturing skill modelling method. In: 2018 Chinese Automation Congress (CAC), Xi'an, China, pp. 4252–4257. IEEE (2018). https://doi.org/10.1109/CAC.2018.8623781
14. Hu, H., Cao, Z., Yang, X., Xiong, H., Lou, Y.: Performance evaluation of optical motion capture sensors for assembly motion capturing. IEEE Access **9**, 61444–61454 (2021). https://doi.org/10.1109/ACCESS.2021.3074260

# Robot-to-Human Object Handovers Based on Hand Key Points Detection

Zhenguo Shi[1,2], Yanjiang Huang[1,2], and Xianmin Zhang[1,2]([✉])

[1] School of Mechanical and Automotive Engineering, South China University of Technology, Guangzhou 510640, China
zhangxm@scut.edu.cn

[2] Guangdong Provincial Key Laboratory of Precision Equipment and Manufacturing Technology, South China University of Technology, Guangzhou 510640, China

**Abstract.** The object transfer between human and robot is a hot and significant research direction in human-robot interaction. We propose a method for transferring object from a robotic arm to a human. Based on depth filter binarization and object geometry, the robotic arm can grasp the object from the table without knowing the type of object in advance. Different from the methods based on the detection of the body or arm in previous studies, based on the identification of the key points of hand and the singular value decomposition(svd), the hand posture can be determined. So we can drive the robot to pass object to the human in the appropriate posture. Through 200 experiments on 10 kinds of objects, the effectiveness of the method is proved, and the grasp process and the transfer process of the object have a high success rate. This method can be applied in industry and life fields.

**Keywords:** Object grasping · Object transfer · Depth filter binarization · Hand posture

## 1 Introduction

With the continuous progress of robot hardware and machine vision, our need for robots is no longer limited to a single isolated robot system, and human-robot interaction is also constantly developing and improving [1]. The transfer of the object between people and robot is a hot topic in the field of human-robot collaboration.

The transfer of the object from robot to human can improve people's life quality and experience to a certain extent [2, 3], and has great research value. For example: in an assembly task, the operator needs to assemble a chair, when the assembly process requires a tool, the robot should take out it and pass it to the operator. Robots provide drinks to customers and so on [4, 5]. However, the process of object transfer faces challenges such as environmental perception and predicting human behavior [6–9].

The direction of object transfer is divided into human to robot and robot to human. This paper will focus on transferring the object from robot to human, which is mainly divided into two processes: grasping the object and transferring the object. As for the grasping process of the object, this paper studies the grasping process of cuboid objects or approximately cuboid objects from the table. Different from the recognition of grasping points using convolutional neural networks, this paper recognizes grasping points based on depth filter binarization and geometric features, and can successfully grasp the object without knowing the object type in advance. As for the transfer process of the object, previous studies based on the recognition of body or arm to determine the posture, and then complete the object transfer [10, 11]. This paper will be specific to the recognition of human hand [12]. Based on the detection of the key points of the hand and svd method, the hand posture can be determined. We can finally complete the transfer process of the object. The method does not depend on the active motion of human, and robot can transfer object to human in the appropriate posture. Theoretically, this method can accurately determine the handover position and the handover posture of robot.

The content is divided into the following parts:

1. System setup and calibration, calibration part mainly describes the hand-eye calibration and gripper calibration.
2. Object grasping. It is mainly divided into depth filter processing of the depth image and grasp parameters acquisition.
3. Object transfer. The content includes the recognition of the key points of the hand, the determination of hand posture and the motion control of robot.
4. Experiment and analysis. Based on the previous content, the experiment of grasping and transferring the object is finished. The effectiveness of algorithm is proved by calculating success rate.
5. Conclusion and future work. Summarize the research results, and indicate future research directions.

## 2  System Setup and Calibration

For this work an UR5 robotic arm with a fixed base was used. The robot has 6 degrees of freedom, and is equipped with a Robotiq-2F-85 gripper at the end of UR5. Fully open, the gripper has a maximal width of 8.5 cm. An Intel RealSense SR300 camera, is installed to the end of UR5 (See Fig. 1). A laptop equipped with a 4GB NVIDIA GeForce RTX 3050 Ti GPU controls the robotic arm.

Hand-eye calibration is carried out by the eye-in-hand method. It is assumed that the matrix from the end to the base of UR5 before and after motion is respectively expressed as $_{E,1}^{B}T$ and $_{E,2}^{B}T$. The matrix from SR300 to the end of UR5 before and after motion is respectively expressed as $_{C,1}^{E,1}T$ and $_{C,2}^{E,2}T$. The matrix from the plate to SR300 before and after motion is respectively expressed as $_{P}^{C,1}T$ and $_{P}^{C,2}T$. After UR5 moves, the relative position of plate and the base does not change. As a result:

$$_{E,1}^{B}T\,_{C,1}^{E,1}T\,_{P}^{C,1}T = {}_{E,2}^{B}T\,_{C,2}^{E,2}T\,_{P}^{C,2}T \tag{1}$$

$$_{C,1}^{E,1}T = {}_{C,2}^{E,2}T \tag{2}$$

According to the parameters of UR5 and $\theta_i$ values of each joint, $_{E,i}^{B}T$ can be obtained. According to the internal parameters of the depth camera, $_{P}^{C,i}T$ can be obtained. Therefore, $_{C}^{E}T$ can be solved.

**Fig. 1.** System setup diagram

The Robotiq-2F-85 gripper, as an end-effector, describes the distance between the two fingers using a position number from 0 to 255, where the 0 position number corresponds to the fully open state of the gripper and the 255 position number corresponds to the fully closed state of the gripper theoretically. The relationship between the position number *num* and the opening width of the gripper *w* is approximately linear. Function fitting is performed through data acquisition, and the result is:

$$num = 250 - 3.125w \tag{3}$$

In addition, after the gripper is closed, its length in the vertical direction will increase. Assuming that the increased length is $l_{\mathrm{plus}}$, through data acquisition, the result of function fitting between *num* and $l_{\mathrm{plus}}$ is:

$$l_{\mathrm{plus}} = -0.0003num^2 + 0.1291num + 0.8258 \tag{4}$$

## 3 Object Grasping

To grasp the object on the table, the recognition of the grasping point is a key step. At present, the commonly used grasping point recognition methods are mainly based on convolutional neural network model. This chapter takes cuboid objects or approximately cuboid objects as an example, and proposes an object grasping method based on depth filter binarization. This method can successfully grasp the object on the table without knowing the object type in advance.

### 3.1 Depth Filter Binarization

First adjust the robotic arm so that its end is perpendicular to the table top. The Intel RealSense SR300 depth camera takes images and performs a depth filter binarization on the resulting depth image, where positions on the depth image that are less than the filter depth threshold are assigned as 1 and positions that are greater than the threshold are assigned as 0. The initial filter depth threshold can be set to be 1 to 2cm less than the vertical distance between the undersurface of SR300 and the upper surface of object.

The given area threshold is $Area_{th}$ (which is slightly smaller than the projected area of the object to be grasped in the overlooking direction). Calculate the actual area of minimum envelope rectangle of graph in binary image after depth filtering to determine whether it exceeds $Area_{th}$. If not, increase the filter depth and repeat the process of depth filter binarization until it exceeds the threshold.

## 3.2  Determination of Grasp Parameters

Considering that the robotic arm needs to pass the object to the human after grasping it and the maximum grasp width of the gripper is 8.5 cm, the following scheme is adopted in this section to determine the grasp parameters:

1. If the actual length of the minimum external rectangle is less than or equal to 8.5 cm, the robotic arm grasps the midpoints of the two widths of the rectangle. The width of Robotiq-2F-85 $w$ is slightly smaller than the actual length of rectangle [13]. In addition, the rotation angle of the end of UR5 is $\gamma$. It is the angle between the line connected by the midpoints of two widths of rectangle and horizontal direction.
2. If the actual length of envelope rectangle is greater than 8.5 cm and its actual width is less than or equal to 8.5 cm, the robotic arm grasps the midpoints of the two lengths of the rectangle. $w$ is slightly smaller than actual width of the rectangle. In addition, $\gamma$ is the angle between the line connected by the midpoints of two lengths of rectangle and horizontal direction [14, 15].
3. If the length and width of the minimum external rectangle are greater than 8.5 cm, the robotic arm cannot grasp the object.

For case 2, taking a tea box as an example, Fig. 2 shows its minimum external rectangle and grasp width diagram.

**Fig. 2.** Minimum external rectangle and grasp width diagram

For cases 1 and 2, the robotic arm is able to grasp the object. According to formulas (3) and (4), $l_{plus}$ can be calculated. Assuming that the coordinate of the rectangle box's center in camera is $(x_{middle}, y_{middle}, z_{middle})$, according to the height of object $d_{object}$ and the length of the gripper when fully opened $l_{robotiq-2F-85}$, the normal distance that the end of UR5 should move is:

$$z_{move} = z_{middle} - l_{plus} - l_{robotiq-2F-85} + 0.5d_{object} \tag{5}$$

According to the grasp parameters $w$, $\gamma$, $(x_{middle}, y_{middle}, z_{middle})$, $z_{move}$ and hand-eye calibration results, UR5 can move to specified position to grasp the object. After UR5 grasps the object, it is driven away from the table, ready to pass the object to the human [16].

# 4 Object Transfer

After the robotic arm has grasped the object from the table to be transferred, the object needs to be handed over to the human. This chapter will adjust the position and posture of UR5 according to the human hand's position and posture, and then complete the object transfer. This chapter is divided into the following parts: the detection of hand's key points, the determination of hand posture by fitting the three-dimensional points to a plane, and the motion control of the robotic arm.

## 4.1 Hand Key Points Detection

In this section, a hand key points detection network based on deep learning and OpenCV is used, which requires a human hand model to be prepared in advance.

The Intel RealSense SR300 depth camera takes images. The captured RGB images are transmitted to the hand key points detection network, and the network outputs the detected 21 key points and the line chart of key points of each finger, as shown in the Fig. 3.

## 4.2 Determination of Hand Posture

In this section, svd method is used to fit three-dimensional points to a plane, and then the hand posture is approximately determined.

Select 7 key points from the 21 detected hand key points (labeled 0, 1, 2, 5, 9, 13, 17 in the Fig. 3). Their $x$ and $y$ coordinates in camera can be got by the hand key points detection network, and the $z$ coordinate can be got from depth graph. The depth image pixels here should be one-to-one corresponding to the RGB image pixels.

Suppose that the three-dimensional coordinates of these 7 key points in camera are respectively represented as: $p_0 (x_0, y_0, z_0)$, $p_1 (x_1, y_1, z_1)$, $p_2 (x_2, y_2, z_2)$, $p_5 (x_5, y_5, z_5)$, $p_9 (x_9, y_9, z_9)$, $p_{13} (x_{13}, y_{13}, z_{13})$, $p_{17} (x_{17}, y_{17}, z_{17})$.

If the center of these points is $pm$ and the three-dimensional coordinates of $pm$ are expressed as: $pm (xm, ym, zm)$, then:

$$x_m = \frac{1}{7}(x_0 + x_1 + x_2 + x_5 + x_9 + x_{13} + x_{17}) \tag{6}$$

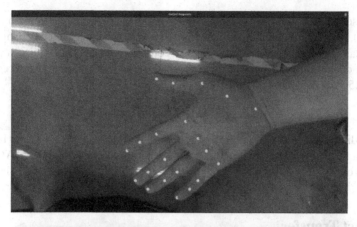

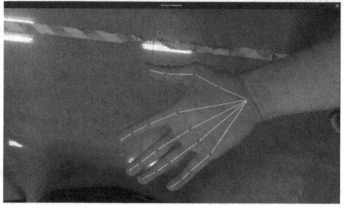

**Fig. 3.** Hand key points identification diagram and its line diagram

$$y_m = \frac{1}{7}(y_0 + y_1 + y_2 + y_5 + y_9 + y_{13} + y_{17}) \tag{7}$$

$$z_m = \frac{1}{7}(z_0 + z_1 + z_2 + z_5 + z_9 + z_{13} + z_{17}) \tag{8}$$

Suppose that the fitted plane equation is:

$$ax + by + cz + d = 0 \tag{9}$$

The constraint condition is:

$$a^2 + b^2 + c^2 = 1 \tag{10}$$

Assuming the plane passes $p_m$, then:

$$ax_m + by_m + cz_m + d = 0 \tag{11}$$

$$\text{Hypothesis matrix: } A = \begin{bmatrix} x_0 - x_m & y_0 - y_m & z_0 - z_m \\ x_1 - x_m & y_1 - y_m & z_1 - z_m \\ x_2 - x_m & y_2 - y_m & z_2 - z_m \\ x_5 - x_m & y_5 - y_m & z_5 - z_m \\ x_9 - x_m & y_9 - y_m & z_9 - z_m \\ x_{13} - x_m & y_{13} - y_m & z_{13} - z_m \\ x_{17} - x_m & y_{17} - y_m & z_{17} - z_m \end{bmatrix}, n = \begin{bmatrix} a \\ b \\ c \end{bmatrix}$$

Formula (11) is subtracted from formula (9), then:

$$An = 0 \tag{12}$$

Ideally, if all points are on the plane, Eq. (12) holds; In fact, some points are outside the plane, so the objective function is:

$$S = \min\|An\| \tag{13}$$

The constraint is:

$$\|n\| = 1 \tag{14}$$

If $A$ can perform singular value decomposition:

$$A = UDV^T \tag{15}$$

Then:

$$\|An\| = \left\|UDV^Tn\right\| = \left\|DV^Tn\right\| \tag{16}$$

$V^Tn$ is the column matrix, and:

$$\left\|V^Tn\right\| = \|n\| = 1 \tag{17}$$

Because the diagonal element of $D$ is a singular value, assuming that the last diagonal element is the least singular value, then if and only if:

$$V^Tn = \begin{bmatrix} 0 \\ 0 \\ 0 \\ 0 \\ 0 \\ 0 \\ 1 \end{bmatrix} \tag{18}$$

$\|An\|$ can take the minimum value, that is, formula (13) is true, then:

$$\boldsymbol{n} = \boldsymbol{V} \begin{bmatrix} 0 \\ 0 \\ 0 \\ 0 \\ 0 \\ 0 \\ 1 \end{bmatrix} = [v_1, v_2, v_3, v_4, v_5, v_6, v_7] \begin{bmatrix} 0 \\ 0 \\ 0 \\ 0 \\ 0 \\ 0 \\ 1 \end{bmatrix} \tag{19}$$

The optimal solution of the objective function (13) under the constraint (14) is:

$$\boldsymbol{n} = \begin{bmatrix} a \\ b \\ c \end{bmatrix} = v_7 \tag{20}$$

According to Eqs. (11) and (20), $d$ can be obtained as:

$$d = -ax_m - by_m - cz_m \tag{21}$$

According to the fitted plane, the posture of the hand can be approximately determined.

## 4.3  Motion Control of the Robot

In this section, the matrix of the fitted plane relative to SR300 is first calculated. The transformation matrix of SR300 relative to the end of UR5 is calculated according to the translation and rotation matrix got from calibration. Then, the matrix of SR300 relative to the base of UR5 can be obtained from the matrix of the end of UR5 relative to the base of UR5. Then the matrix of the fitted plane relative to the base of UR5 is obtained. This transformation matrix is converted to the quaternion, and finally, the robotic arm is driven to make its end posture perpendicular to the fitted plane.

It must be noted that the posture of the robotic arm has changed at this time. Assuming that hand position relative to the ground remains the same, hand position relative to the camera has also changed. The depth camera should reshoot the RGB image and the depth image at this time to drive UR5 to the specified position. Using the RGB image, hand's key points can be recognized again.

If UR5 grasps the midpoints of two widths of the rectangle in the previous chapter, select the key points labeled 5 and 17, assuming that the angle between the line formed by them and horizontal direction in RGB image is $\beta_1$. Suppose that the three-dimensional coordinates of the key points labeled 5 and 17 in the camera coordinate system are expressed as: $p_5 (x_5, y_5, z_5)$, $p_{17} (x_{17}, y_{17}, z_{17})$.

When $x_5$ is equal to $x_{17}$:

$$\beta_1 = 90° \tag{22}$$

When $x_5$ is not equal to $x_{17}$:

$$\beta_1 = \arctan(\frac{y_5 - y_{17}}{x_5 - x_{17}}) \tag{23}$$

At this time, the rotation angle of the end of UR5 is:

$$\alpha = \beta_1 \tag{24}$$

If the robotic arm grasps the midpoints of two lengths of the rectangle in the previous chapter, select the key points labeled 5 and 17, assuming that the angle between the line formed by them and vertical direction in RGB image is $\beta_2$.

When $y_5$ is equal to $y_{17}$:

$$\beta_2 = 90° \tag{25}$$

When $y_5$ is not equal to $y_{17}$:

$$\beta_2 = \arctan(\frac{x_5 - x_{17}}{y_5 - y_{17}}) \tag{26}$$

At this time, the rotation angle of the end of UR5 is:

$$\alpha = \beta_2 \tag{27}$$

Suppose that the point's three-dimensional coordinates (labeled 9) in camera are: $p_9$ $(x_9, y_9, z_9)$. According to the matrix of SR300 relative to the base, its position in the base can be obtained.

Drive the end of UR5 to rotate $\alpha$ and move to the position of key point labeled 9. It must be noted that $l_{robotiq\text{-}2F\text{-}85}$, $l_{plus}$, and $d_{object}$ should be taken into account here. That is, the normal distance of the translation of the end of UR5 $l_{translation}$ is:

$$l_{translation} = -(l_{robotiq\text{-}2F\text{-}85} + l_{plus} + 0.5d_{object}) \tag{28}$$

According to $l_{translation}$ and $p_9$ $(x_9, y_9, z_9)$, UR5 can move to the specified position to transfer object to people in an appropriate posture.

After UR5 moves to the specified position and stays for two seconds, release the gripper and drive the robotic arm away from the human hand [17].

## 5 Experiment and Analysis

Select 10 kinds of objects to carry out the experiments of grasping the object from the table and passing the grasped object to human. Figure 4 shows the grasping experiments. Figure 5 shows the object transfer process.

We calculate the success rate of the experimental process of grasping the object from the table and passing it to the human (See Table 1).

The results of 200 experiments on 10 kinds of objects show that the success rate of the proposed method based on depth filter binarization and object geometry features reaches

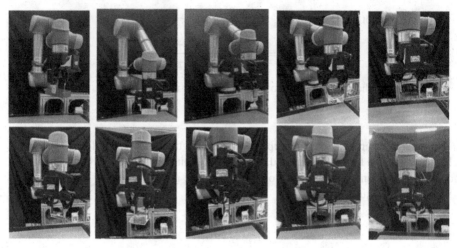

**Fig. 4.** Grasping process diagram

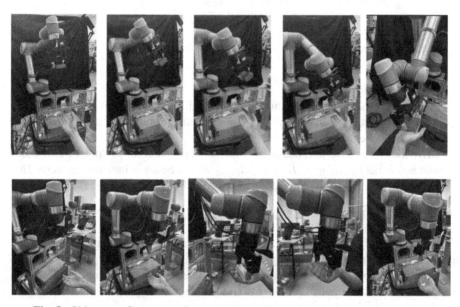

**Fig. 5.** Object transfer process diagram (take tea box and cosmetic box as examples)

96.5%, and it can grasp cuboid objects or approximately cuboid objects well without knowing the object type in advance. The main reason for the failure of the grasping process is that when the grasping width $w$ is less than but close to the maximum open width of the gripper, the grasping failure will be mainly caused by hand-eye calibration error.

In addition, the success rate of the process of transferring the object from the robotic arm to the human based on hand's key points recognition can reach 93.78%. The main

**Table 1.** The success rate of grasping process and object transfer process

| Object type | Grasping success rate | The success rate of object transfer |
|---|---|---|
| Tea box | 20/20 | 18/20 |
| Cosmetic box | 18/20 | 17/18 |
| Medicine box | 20/20 | 19/20 |
| Soy milk | 20/20 | 18/20 |
| Handkerchief paper | 20/20 | 19/20 |
| Milling cutter box | 19/20 | 18/19 |
| Staple | 19/20 | 18/19 |
| Biscuit | 19/20 | 17/19 |
| Eraser | 19/20 | 19/19 |
| Candy | 19/20 | 18/19 |

reason for the failure of the object transfer process is that FOV of the camera is disturbed after grasping a large object.

We prove the effectiveness of algorithm by theoretical analysis and experiments. And the total success rate of the grasping process and object transfer process is 90.5% (multiplication of two processes).

## 6  Conclusion and Future Work

We propose a method to transfer object from UR5 to human in a suitable posture based on hand's key points recognition. By selecting the right key points of human hand, svd method is used to determine the hand posture, and the robotic arm is driven to transfer the object grasped from the table to a human in a suitable pose. This method has a wide application prospect in industry and life. Through 200 experiments of 10 kinds of objects, the results show that the method does not depend on the active movement of human, and has a high success rate. We will add advanced tactile sensors to achieve a more fluent and comfortable handover process. We will also optimize the algorithm to adapt to more object types and human hand poses to complete object handover.

**Acknowledgments.** This work was supported by the National Natural Science Foundation of China (Grant No. 52075178, 52130508) and the Guangzhou Municipal Scientific and Technological Project under Grant 2024A04J6287.

# References

1. Ortenzi, V., Cosgun, A., Pardi, T., Chan, W.P., Croft, E., Kulić, D.: Object handovers: a review for robotics. IEEE Trans. Robot. **36**(7), 1855–1873 (2021)
2. Leal, D., Yihun, Y.: Progress in human-robot collaboration for object handover. In: Proceedings of the 2019 IEEE International Symposium on Measurement and Control in Robotics (ISMCR), pp. C3-2-1–C3-2-6 (2019)
3. Duan, H., Wang, P., Li, Y., Li, D., Wei, W.: Learning human-to-robot dexterous handovers for anthropomorphic hand. IEEE Trans. Cogn. Dev. Syst. **15**(3), 1224–1238 (2022)
4. Gu, Y., Thobbi, A., Sheng, W.: Human-robot collaborative manipulation through imitation and reinforcement learning. In: Proceedings of the 2011 IEEE International Conference on Information and Automation (ICIA), pp. 151–156 (2011)
5. Lin, H.C., Smith, J., Babarahmati, K.K., Dehio, N., Mistry, M.: A projected inverse dynamics approach for multi-arm cartesian impedance control. In: Proceedings of the 2018 IEEE International Conference on Robotics and Automation (ICRA), pp. 5421–5428 (2018)
6. Rosenberger, P., et al.: Object-independent human-to-robot handovers using real time robotic vision. IEEE Robot. Autom. Lett. **37**(6), 1855–1873 (2021)
7. Ford, C.J., et al.: Tactile-driven gentle grasping for human-robot collaborative tasks. In: Proceedings of the 2023 IEEE International Conference on Robotics and Automation (ICRA), pp. 10394–10400 (2023)
8. Pandey, A.K., Alami, R.: Towards human-level semantics understanding of human-centered object manipulation tasks for HRI: reasoning about effect, ability, effort and perspective taking. Int. J. Social Robot. **6**(4), 593–620 (2014)
9. Capozzi, F., Becchio, C., Garbarini, F., Savazzi, S., Pia, L.: Temporal perception in joint action: this is MY action. Consciousness Cogn. **40**, 26–33 (2016)
10. Liu, D., Wang, X., Cong, M., Du, Y., Zou, Q., Zhang, X.: Object transfer point predicting based on human comfort model for human-robot handover. IEEE Trans. Instrum. Meas. **70**, 1–11 (2021)
11. Pan, M.K.X.J., Croft, E.A., Niemeyer, G.: Exploration of geometry and forces occurring within human-to-robot handovers. In: Proceedings of the 2018 IEEE Haptics Symposium (HAPTICS), pp. 327–333 (2018)
12. Feix, T., Romero, J., Schmiedmayer, H.-B., Dollar, A.M., Kragic, D.: The grasp taxonomy of human grasp types. IEEE Trans. Human-Mach. Syst. **46**(1), 66–77 (2016)
13. Ortenzi, V., Controzzi, M., Cini, F., et al.: Robotic manipulation and the role of the task in the metric of success. Nature Mach. Intell. **1**(8), 340–346 (2019)
14. Chan, W.P., Pan, M.K.X.J., Croft, E.A., Inaba, M.: Characterization of handover orientations used by humans for efficient robot to human handovers. In: Proceedings of the 2015 IEEE/RSJ International Conference on Intelligent Robots and Systems (IROS), pp. 1–6 (2015)
15. Chan, W.P., Pan, M.K.X.J., Croft, E.A., Inaba, M.: An affordance and distance minimization based method for computing object orientations for robot human handovers. Int. J. Social Robot. **12**(1), 143–162 (2019)
16. Mahler, J., et al.: Guest editorial open discussion of robot grasping benchmarks, protocols, and metrics. IEEE Trans. Autom. Sci. Eng. **15**(4), 1440–1442 (2018)
17. Aleotti, J., Micelli, V., Caselli, S.: An affordance sensitive system for robot to human object handover. Int. J. Soc. Robot. **6**, 653–666 (2014)

# Learning Fault-Tolerant Quadruped Locomotion with Unknown Motor Failure Using Reliability Reward

Shuhan Wang, Chuanlin Zhao, Letian Qian, and Xin Luo[✉]

Huazhong University of Science and Technology, Wuhan, China
mexinluo@hust.edu.cn

**Abstract.** As the locomotion capabilities of quadruped robots are further developed, they are increasingly deployed in more complex environments, heightening the risk of motor failures and significantly impacting their performance. Autonomous adaptation to such failures is crucial to ensure continued operation or safe return. In this paper, we propose a learning-based framework that enables quadruped robots to adapt to single-motor failure and maintain reliable locomotion. Our approach combines a teacher-student framework with a reliability reward term to learn adaptive and robust control policies. The teacher network, which has access to privileged information about motor failures, guides the learning of the student network, which relies solely on a history of proprioceptive observations. The reliability reward term encourages the robot to lift the weak leg to a safe height, mitigating the risks associated with motor failures. We evaluate our framework through extensive simulation experiments, analyzing the adaptability and reliability of the learned policies. The results demonstrate that our approach effectively enhances the robot's ability to maintain stable locomotion under motor failure conditions.

**Keywords:** Quadruped Robots · Fault-Tolerant Control · Reinforcements Learning

## 1 Introduction

As quadruped robots continue to advance in their locomotion capabilities, they are being deployed in increasingly complex environments to perform tasks such as outdoor inspection [1], exploration [2], and delivery [3]. These applications highlight the robots' potential to operate in diverse and challenging terrains. However, the complexity of these tasks also exposes the robots to higher risks of motor failures. Such failures can severely impact the robots' performance, leading to instability, catastrophic falls, and mission failures. Given the nature of many operational scenarios, which often occur in remote locations without immediate human intervention, it is crucial for these robots to autonomously adjust to motor failures and maintain stable locomotion. Ensuring continued operation or safe return under these conditions is essential for their effective deployment.

© The Author(s), under exclusive license to Springer Nature Singapore Pte Ltd. 2025
X. Lan et al. (Eds.): ICIRA 2024, LNAI 15208, pp. 129–143, 2025.
https://doi.org/10.1007/978-981-96-0783-9_10

**Fig. 1.** Simulation environment for parallel training of multiple quadruped robots with random motor failure.

There are significant challenges in fault-tolerant control for quadruped robots when dealing with motor failures. A leg affected by a motor failure becomes partially uncontrollable, making the overall system less stable and more prone to errors. The unpredictability introduced by such uncontrollable factors increases the difficulty of developing effective fault-tolerant mechanisms.

Existing approaches to fault-tolerant control in quadruped robots primarily fall into two categories: model-based and learning-based methods. Model-based methods often involve intricate modeling [4–7] of the robot's dynamics and require precise knowledge of the failure states to generate compensatory actions. However, these methods are limited by their reliance on accurate models and inability to adapt to unforeseen or dynamic failure conditions. In contrast, learning-based methods mainly leverage reinforcement learning to develop adaptive control policies. These methods [8–12] have shown promise in handling diverse failure scenarios by learning from interactions with the environment. Despite their potential, current learning-based fault-tolerant methods typically do not adequately address the unique challenges posed by the partially uncontrollable leg because they have not specifically treated the weak leg, resulting in unreliable performance when this leg participates in locomotion, especially in complex and unpredictable environments.

Building on the strengths of existing learning-based approaches and addressing their limitations, we propose a novel teacher-student framework enhanced with a reliability reward mechanism. This framework aims to improve the robot's adaptability and reliability in the presence of motor failures by encouraging the weak leg to lift to a safe height, thus mitigating the risks associated with its partial controllability (as shown in Fig. 1). Our approach not only enhances the fault-tolerance of quadruped robots but also ensures more robust and stable locomotion under failure conditions, paving the way for more reliable deployment in challenging operational scenarios. The main contributions of this work can be summarized as:

1) We propose a novel teacher-student learning framework for quadruped robots to achieve adaptive and reliable locomotion under motor failures, by leveraging privileged information during training.
2) We introduce a reliability reward term that encourages safe and proactive failure-mitigation behaviors, enhancing the stability and robustness of the learned controller.
3) We conduct extensive simulation experiments to validate the effectiveness of our approach in handling various motor failure scenarios and challenging terrains.

## 2 Related Works

### 2.1 Reinforcement Learning for Quadruped Locomotion

Reinforcement learning has emerged as a promising approach for developing quadruped control algorithms without the need for laborious and intricate dynamic modeling. Recent research has concentrated on enhancing agile quadrupedal locomotion, expanding the skills of quadruped robots, and minimizing the sim-to-real gap. Several studies have achieved robust or swift locomotion in challenging terrains, including high-speed running extensions [13, 14], crossing various terrains [15–17], and fast movement on deformable surfaces [18]. In addition to agile locomotion, training robots to acquire multiple skills is also a hotspot, including achieving multiple gaits [19, 20], fore-limb manipulating [21], etc. Another important focus has been on reducing the domain gap between simulation and real-world conditions through environmental state adaptation [22], domain randomization [23], teacher-student training methodologies [15], and asymmetric actor-critic framework [24]. These studies have greatly inspired our work.

### 2.2 Learning-Based Method for Fault-Tolerant Control

Current learning-based fault-tolerant control algorithms are primarily categorized into those utilizing teacher-student frameworks [8, 9, 11] and those employing hierarchical architectures [10, 12] with multiple low-level policies. These methods have achieved a degree of adaptive control in quadruped robots facing single-joint or limb failures, demonstrating practical adaptability in real-world scenarios. Compared to traditional control methods, learning-based fault-tolerant control for quadruped robots offers superior performance without the need for exhaustive modeling of various failure conditions. However, existing strategies fail to address the specific handling of the weak leg associated with a damaged motor, leading to residual uncontrollable factors.

To ensure consistency in control policies and streamline the training process, we adopted a teacher-student framework similar to that proposed by Kim et al. [8]. Additionally, we introduced a reliability reward mechanism that encourages the lifting of the weak leg, thereby enhancing locomotion reliability.

## 3 Method

### 3.1 Overview

In this work, we propose a learning-based framework that enables quadruped robots to rapidly adapt their locomotion and maintain reliable and robust mobility when faced with single-motor failure and torque loss. A key challenge in this context is the inability to

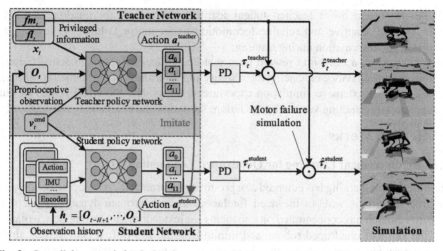

**Fig. 2.** Overall framework for fault-tolerant control in quadruped robots. We propose a Teacher-Student framework for training a quadruped robot to adapt to motor failures. The Teacher Network, equipped with privileged information, generates actions that are mimicked by the Student Network, which relies solely on a history of proprioceptive observations. We evaluate the system's performance in a simulation environment focusing on single-motor failure scenarios to assess the robot's ability to maintain reliability and stability under these conditions.

directly and accurately obtain the motor failure signal in real-world scenarios. To address this, we implement a Teacher-Student framework, as illustrated in Fig. 2, drawing from the approach used in related research [8]. This framework is particularly effective as it employs privileged learning [25], which can mitigate training challenges that arise from the inability to directly obtain certain information. Our teacher policy, trained with access to privileged information such as motor failure flags, learns to generate optimal joint position commands for various failure scenarios. In contrast, we direct the student policy to focus on emulating the teacher's strategies through supervised learning, using only proprioceptive observations without direct access to privileged information. This streamlined and unified control strategy allows the robot to effectively adapt to diverse motor failure scenarios without relying on multiple, separately trained policies.

Compared to existing studies like those discussed in [8], our work introduces the innovation of incorporating a reliability mechanism in the reward function. This aims to enhance the robot's ability to maintain reliable and robust locomotion in the presence of motor failures.

## 3.2    Reinforcement Learning Problem Formulation

We formulate the quadrupedal locomotion control problem under motor failure as a Markov Decision Process (MDP) with discrete-time dynamics, where the environment is completely defined by the state $s_t \in S$ at time step $t$. An MDP is defined by a tuple $(S, A, P, R, \gamma)$, where $S$ is the state space, $A$ is the action space, $P : S \times A \times S \rightarrow [0,1]$ is the transition probability function, $R : S \times A \rightarrow R$ is the reward function, and $\gamma \in (0, 1)$

**Table 1.** Reward function terms

| Term | | Equation | Weight |
|---|---|---|---|
| $r^{\text{task}}$ | x, y velocity tracking | $\exp\left(-|v_{xy} - v_{xy}^{\text{cmd}}|^2/0.25\right)$ | 1.5 |
| | yaw velocity tracking | $\exp\left(-|\omega_z - \omega_z^{\text{cmd}}|^2/0.25\right)$ | 0.5 |
| $r^{\text{stability}}$ | z velocity | $|v_z|^2$ | −1.0 |
| | pitch, yaw velocity | $|\omega_{xy}|^2$ | −0.05 |
| | body height tracking | $|h_z - h_z^{\text{cmd}}|^2/0.01$ | −0.5 |
| | orientation | $|p_{xy}^{\text{gravity}}|^2$ | −1.0 |
| | base collision | $1_{\text{base collision}}$ | −1.0 |
| $r^{\text{smoothness}}$ | joint torques | $|\tau|^2$ | −1 e-5 |
| | action rate | $|a_{t-1} - a_t|$ | −0.1 |
| $r^{\text{reliability}}$ | | (4) | −1.5 |

is the discount factor. The policy $\pi$ performs an action $a_t \in A$, and then the environment transitions to the next state $s_{t+1}$ with probability $P(s_{t+1}|s_t, a_t)$ and returns a reward $r_t = R(s_t, a_t)$. The goal of the reinforcement learning problem is to find an optimal policy $\pi^*$ that maximizes the expected discounted return:

$$\pi^* = \arg\max_{\pi} \mathbb{E}_{\tau \sim \pi} \left[ \sum_{t=0}^{T-1} \gamma^t R(s_t, a_t) \right] \tag{1}$$

where $\tau$ denotes a trajectory under policy $\pi$, $T$ is the episode length.

**State Space.** In our formulation, the robot's state $s_t$ comprises privileged information $x_t$, desired velocity commands $v_t^{\text{cmd}}$, and proprioceptive observations $o_t$, expressed as $s_t = (x_t, v_t^{\text{cmd}}, o_t)$. The privileged information $x_t$ includes motor failure flags $fm_t \in \mathbb{R}^{12}$, , which indicate the operational status of each motor (1 for functional and 0 for failed), and leg weakness indicators $fl_t \in \mathbb{R}^4$ that reflect the functionality of each leg (1 for fully functional and 0 for any motor failure within the leg). The desired velocity commands $v_t^{\text{cmd}} \in \mathbb{R}^3$ specify the target linear velocities in the forward and lateral directions, as well as the target angular velocity for yaw rotation. The proprioceptive observations $o_t \in \mathbb{R}^{49}$ consist of the robot's base linear and angular velocities, orientation of gravity vector in robot's base frame, joint position offsets relative to the initial position, joint velocities, feet contact indication, and the previous action $a_{t-1}$.

**Action Space.** The actions $a_t \in \mathbb{R}^{12}$ represent the offsets to the desired joint positions for each of the robot's 12 degrees of freedom. These offsets are used to calculate the motor torques $\tau_t$ through a PD controller

$$\tau_t = K_p(a_t + q_{init} - q_t) + K_d(0 - \dot{q}_t), \tag{2}$$

with $K_p$ and $K_d$ being the proportional and derivative gain matrices, respectively. $q_{init}$ Denotes the nominal joint angle configuration corresponding to the robot's default upright standing posture at a height of 0.3 m. In our framework, the actions of the teacher policy are denoted by $a_t^{\text{teacher}}$, while the actions of the student policy are represented as $a_t^{\text{student}}$.

### 3.3   Reward Shaping for Reliable Fault-Tolerant Locomotion

To facilitate a unified control policy that enables a quadruped robot to adapt reliably when faced with single-motor failure, our approach incorporates a composite reward function structured into two key components: reliability and general performance. The reward at each time step $t$ is articulated as:

$$
\begin{aligned}
r_t &= r_t^{\text{reliability}} + r_t^{\text{general}} \\
r_t^{\text{general}} &= r_t^{\text{task}} + r_t^{\text{stability}} + r_t^{\text{smoothness}}
\end{aligned}
\tag{3}
$$

The formulations of these reward terms are presented in Table 1.

**Reliability Reward.** The reliability term $r_t^{\text{reliability}}$ is designed to encourage the robot to lift the leg with the failed motor to a predefined safe height $h_{\text{target}}^{\text{weakness}}$ while traversing across the terrain. The motivation is to mitigate risks caused by the reduced controllability of the weak leg, such as hitting obstacles or scuffing along the ground. The value of $r_t^{\text{reliability}}$ is computed as:

$$
\begin{aligned}
r_t^{\text{reliability}} &= -\sum_{i=1}^{4}\left(\max\left(0, h_{\text{target}}^{\text{weakness}} - h_{t,i}\right) \cdot fl_{t,i}^{\text{weakness}}/\sigma\right)^2, \\
fl_t^{\text{weakness}} &= 1 - fl_t
\end{aligned}
\tag{4}
$$

where $h_{t,i}$ is the actual foot height above the ground of leg $i$ at time $t$, $fl_{t,i}^{\text{weakness}}$ denotes the weakness state of leg i, which is the $i$-th element of the leg weakness vector $fl_t^{\text{weakness}}$ calculated as the opposite of the leg weakness indicator $fl_t$ defined earlier. Therefore, $fl_{t,i}^{\text{weakness}} = 0$ for a normal leg and 1 for a weak leg. The scaling factor $\sigma$ is set to 0.05 in our implementation.

This reward term thus only applies a penalty for the weak leg, encouraging it to be lifted to the target height $h_{\text{target}}^{\text{weakness}}$ determined based on empirical evidence and the robot's dimensions, to mitigate risks from reduced controllability.

**General Reward.** The general term $r_t^{\text{general}}$, inspired by the works of Rudin et al. [16] and Margolis and Agrawal [19], consists of three parts: the task reward $r^{\text{task}}$, the stability reward $r_t^{\text{stability}}$, and the smoothness reward $r_t^{\text{smoothness}}$. The specific formulations of these reward components are provided in Table 1, following established practices in quadruped reinforcement learning to promote the accomplishment of locomotion tasks, the maintenance of body stability, and the smoothness of motions.

By adding the reliability reward term, the composite reward function guides the learning of a unified control policy that prioritizes reliable motion and adapts to motor failures by adjusting the robot's behavior to maintain stability and mitigate risks.

## 3.4   Training

**Motor Failure Simulation.** To simulate motor failure during training, we randomly assign the robot to either a normal or failure state where one of the twelve motors outputs zero torque. The motor failure is simulated by setting the torque output of the affected motor to zero throughout the episode, effectively rendering it unresponsive to control commands. This failure simulation can be formally expressed as:

$$\hat{\tau}_t = \tau_t \odot fm_t, \tag{5}$$

where $\hat{\tau}_t$ represents the actual torque input to the simulator, and the operator $\odot$ signifies element-wise multiplication. Notably, in our motor failure simulation, the joint angle and angular velocity feedback from the failed motor can still be accessed normally, as these feedback states may not be directly affected by the loss of torque output and could be obtained through external encoders if needed.

**Training Curriculum.** To facilitate learning and enable adaptation to challenging environments, we employ a curriculum learning strategy [15, 16]. The curriculum introduces three terrain types: flat ground, undulating terrain with noise increasing from $\pm1$ cm to $\pm3$ cm, and terrain with discrete obstacles of heights varying from $\pm1$ cm to $\pm5$ cm. The robot follows velocity commands sampled from ranges of $(-0.5, 1.5)$, $(-0.5, 0.5)$, and $(-1.0, 1.0)$ for forward, lateral, and yaw velocities, respectively. On flat ground, commands are randomly sampled, while on complex terrains, the robot aims to reach a goal point with dynamically adjusted yaw velocity based on its orientation. Advancement through the curriculum depends on consistently reaching the goal points.

**Teacher Policy Training and Architecture.** The teacher policy, which is the optimized strategy we aim to derive within our defined reinforcement learning problem, leverages the complete state $s_t$, including $x_t = (fm_t, fl_t)$. This privileged information, encompassing motor failure flags and leg weakness indicators, plays a crucial role in enhancing the adaptability of the teacher policy to motor failure conditions, enabling stable locomotion under such circumstances. The teacher policy is trained using the Proximal Policy Optimization (PPO) algorithm [26], leveraging the composite reward function we propose that incorporates a reliability term. The architecture of the teacher policy network comprises a multi-layer perceptron (MLP) with three hidden layers, containing 512, 256, and 128 units respectively. Each layer utilizes the Exponential Linear Unit (ELU) as its activation function. The effectiveness and broader implications of integrating such privileged information will be evaluated in subsequent simulation experiments to assess its impact on locomotion performance.

**Student Policy Training and Architecture.** In real-world deployments, motor failure-related information $fm_t$ and $fl_t$ within the privileged information may not be reliably available. To address these practical limitations, we have devised a unified control strategy for the student policy that does not rely on the direct use of privileged information, which is often unavailable or unreliable in actual deployment scenarios. Instead, the student policy inputs desired velocity commands $v_t^{cmd}$ and a history of proprioceptive observations $h_t = (o_{t-H+1}, \ldots, o_t)$, where $H$ represents the length of the history window.

This historical data enables the student policy to adaptively modulate the robot's loco-motion without explicit reliance on motor failure signals. The student policy's training follows a supervised learning framework, with the loss function defined as:

$$\mathcal{L} := \ominus \left( a_t^{\text{teacher}}(s_t) - a_t^{\text{student}} \left( v_t^{\text{cmd}}, h_t \right) \right)^2. \tag{6}$$

We employ the Dataset Aggregation (DAgger) algorithm [27], which iteratively updates training data by alternating between using the student policy to collect new trajectories and querying the teacher policy for optimal actions. The student policy's network architecture mirrors that of the teacher policy, featuring three fully connected hidden layers with 512, 256, and 128 units each, activated by ELU functions.

## 4   Simulation Experiments and Analysis

### 4.1   Implementation and Simulation Setup

**Implementation.** We conduct our simulation experiments using the Isaac Gym sim-ulator [28]. The simulated robot model is based on the Unitree A1 quadruped, which features 12 joints and a mass of approximately 13 kg. Our joint-level PD controller is configured with $K_p$ of 20 and $K_d$ of 0.5. In the teacher-student strategy, the student network processes a history of observations with $H = 16$.

**Simulation.** In our simulation setup, we train 8,192 parallel agents, each engaging in episodes lasting up to 1,500 steps, equivalent to 30 s of real-time interaction. Episodes are terminated early if a trunk-ground collision is detected, improving the training efficiency. The training is conducted at a control frequency of 50 Hz, powered by a single NVIDIA RTX 4090 GPU.

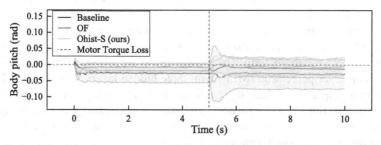

**Fig. 3.** Body pitch angle response to motor failure. The robot walks at 0.5 m/s, with the failure occurring at the 5-s mark. The vertical dashed line separates the normal operation phase (left) from the motor failure phase (right). Solid lines represent mean values, and shaded areas denote standard deviations. Greater variance in the pitch angle indicates less stability.

**Agents and Baselines.** We investigate the performance of five distinct control strategies: **Baseline, OF, OFR-T(ours), Ohist-S(ours)**, and **OhistR**. The Baseline strategy relies solely on proprioceptive state information as input, while the OF strategy incorporates both proprioceptive state information and privileged information, which includes motor failure flags and corresponding leg weakness indicators. Our proposed teacher strategy, OFR-T, builds upon the OF strategy by additionally incorporating a reliability reward term that encourages lifting the weak leg. The corresponding student strategy, Ohist-S, takes a history of proprioceptive state information as input, aiming to inherit the capability of the teacher strategy without direct access to privileged information during deployment. The OhistR strategy, like Ohist-S, also uses a history of proprioceptive state information as input but does not include the privileged information, thereby serving as a baseline to highlight the importance of privileged information in adaptability.

### 4.2   Analysis of Adaptability

In this section, we investigate the adaptability of our proposed framework in comparison to baseline methods, focusing on the robot's ability to maintain stable locomotion when faced with single-motor failure during normal operation. The primary objective is to assess the impact of incorporating privileged information, specifically the motor failure flags and leg weakness indicators, on the robot's adaptability to unexpected motor failure scenarios.

To evaluate the adaptability, we conduct experiments in the simulation environment where the robot experiences a sudden loss of torque in one of its joint motors. We focused on the robot's body stability and its response speed to the failure in such scenarios.

Figure 3 presents the body pitch angle variations of the robot under different control strategies. As shown, upon the occurrence of motor failure, the Baseline strategy exhibits the largest variance in pitch angle, indicating significant body oscillations and instability. In contrast, the OF and Ohist-S strategies demonstrate improved stability, with smaller pitch angle deviations and quicker convergence to a stable state.

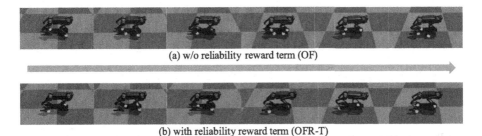

(a) w/o reliability reward term (OF)

(b) with reliability reward term (OFR-T)

**Fig. 4.** Temporal alignment of robot movement sequences demonstrating the effects of different strategies. The green markers indicate foot-ground contact, and red colored links indicate the corresponding motor failure. By comparing the (a) OF strategy versus the (b) OFR-T strategy, we observe that introducing the extra reliability reward term ensures the weak leg is lifted.

To further analyze adaptability, we examined the foot height of the weak leg after motor failure in different joint positions, focusing on the Ohist-S and OhistR strategies, both of which incorporate the reliability reward term, encouraging the weak leg to lift (Fig. 4). The results in Fig. 5 reveal that our Ohist-S strategy achieves faster foot lifting

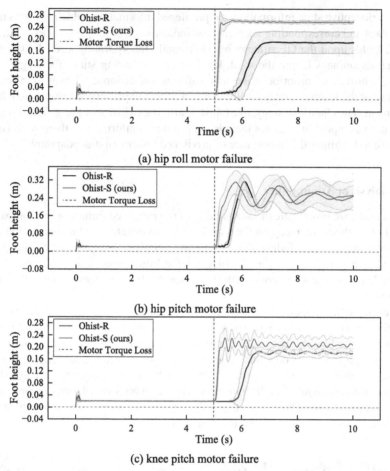

**Fig. 5.** Foot height response to different motor failures. For a fair comparison, we command a stationary position to the robot, ensuring a consistent foot height during normal operation.

responses compared to the OhistR strategy, which also lacks privileged information. However, the teacher policy for Ohist-S had access to privileged information, which may explain its superior performance. This demonstrates the effectiveness of our teacher-student framework in quickly adjusting the weak leg to mitigate the impact of motor failure.

These experimental findings highlight the significance of incorporating privileged information in improving the robot's adaptability to single-motor failure. The OF and Ohist-S strategies, which leverage motor failure flags and leg weakness indicators (directly or indirectly), exhibit superior stability and responsiveness compared to the Baseline approach. Moreover, the Ohist-S strategy, which relies on a history of proprioceptive observations, demonstrates comparable adaptability to the OF strategy, indicating the effectiveness of our framework in extracting relevant information for failure detection.

**Fig. 6.** Step climbing test under motor failure conditions. Steps range from 5.5 cm to 15.5 cm in height. The robot must traverse the step and continue walking forward to a distance of 3 m without falling to be considered successful.

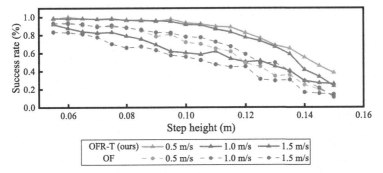

**Fig. 7.** Success rates for different step heights and speeds. Each scenario is sampled 20 times.

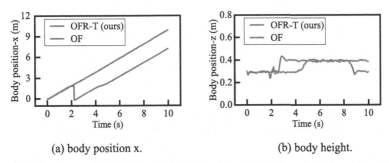

(a) body position x.                    (b) body height.

**Fig. 8.** Sample trajectory of the robot under different strategies. The robot's speed is set to 1 m/s and the step height is 10 cm, which is the maximum obstacle height used in our training process. The x position resetting to zero indicates instances where the robot failed and the simulation was reset. The effectiveness of each strategy is demonstrated by the robot's ability to maintain its trajectory without resets (Color figure online).

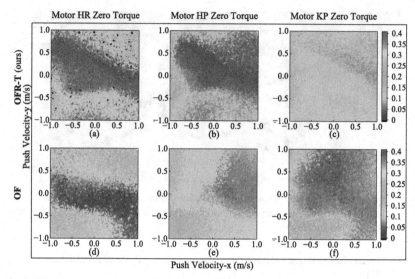

**Fig. 9.** Stability response to external disturbances in motor failure scenarios. The x-axis represents applied speed disturbance in the x direction, and the y-axis in the y direction. Each motor failure scenario is sampled 2000 times. Color coding indicates body angle deviation, with blue signifying stable postures and green indicating instability (Color figure online).

### 4.3 Analysis of Reliability

In this section, we examine the influence of the reliability reward term on the robot's locomotion reliability under motor failure conditions. Figure 4 illustrates the effect of introducing the reliability reward term, which ensures that the weak leg maintains its lifted state. Building upon this observation, we further analyze how this improved leg lifting behavior contributes to the robot's performance in two key aspects: terrain traversal reliability and disturbance rejection.

To assess terrain traversal reliability, we design a step-crossing scenario where the robot encounters steps of varying heights as Fig. 6 illustrates. Figure 7 summarizes the success rates for different step heights and forward velocities. The results consistently show higher success rates for our OFR-T strategy compared to the OF strategy, particularly at higher velocities and step heights. This validates the effectiveness of the reliability reward in improving the robot's reliability to navigate challenging terrains under motor failure conditions. A sample of the robot's body position and height during the step-crossing test is presented in Fig. 8. The red curve in Fig. 8(a) shows a noticeable perturbation around the 2-s mark, indicating the moment the robot crosses the step. The OF strategy requires a reset after falling, while our OFR-T strategy successfully traverses the step in a single attempt.

To evaluate disturbance rejection, we subject the robot to external velocity perturbations in the x and y directions while maintaining a stationary position. The plots in Fig. 9 demonstrate that our OFR-T strategy achieves better disturbance rejection compared to the OF strategy, as evidenced by fewer green dots near the boundaries, indicating better stability under significant perturbations.

These experiments highlight the crucial role of the reliability reward in enhancing the robot's locomotion reliability under motor failure conditions. Motor failure leads to partial uncontrollability of the affected leg, significantly compromising the robot's overall stability. By lifting the weak leg and excluding it from the locomotion cycle, our strategy ensures that only the fully controllable legs contribute to the movement, which minimizes the impact of the uncontrollable factors and could be one of the keys to maintaining the robot's stability and robustness.

The simulation results align with our expectations and validate the design choices made in our methodology. The teacher-student framework, combined with the reliability reward term, enables the robot to learn robust and adaptive behaviors. The comprehensive analysis of adaptability and reliability provides valuable insights into the performance of our proposed framework and it has potential to enhance the fault tolerance of quadruped robots.

## 5   Conclusion and Future Work

In this paper, we introduce a novel learning-based framework that enables quadruped robots to adapt to single-motor failure and maintain reliable locomotion. Combining a teacher-student framework with a reliability reward term that encourages lifting the weak leg to a safe height and mitigating uncontrollable risks, our approach develops adaptive and robust control policies specifically for motor failure scenarios. Simulation experiments validate our framework's effectiveness.

Future work will focus on extending the framework to handle multiple simultaneous motor failures and validating its performance through real-world experiments. Additionally, investigating the integration of sensory feedback and higher-level decision-making strategies could further enhance the robot's adaptability and autonomy in complex scenarios.

**Acknowledgement.** This work was supported by the National Natural Science Foundation of China (Grant No. 52375014).

## References

1. Bellicoso, C.D., et al.: Advances in real-world applications for legged robots. J. Field Robot. **35**, 1311–1326 (2018)
2. Bouman, A., et al.: Autonomous spot: long-range autonomous exploration of extreme environments with legged locomotion. In: Proceedings of the 2020 IEEE/RSJ International Conference on Intelligent Robots and Systems (IROS), pp. 2518–2525 (2020)
3. Hooks, J., et al.: ALPHRED: a multi-modal operations quadruped robot for package delivery applications. IEEE Robot. Autom. Lett. **5**, 5409–5416 (2020)
4. Cui, J., Li, Z., Qiu, J., Li, T.: Fault-tolerant motion planning and generation of quadruped robots synthesised by posture optimization and whole body control. Complex Intell. Syst. **8**, 2991–3003 (2022)
5. Chen, Z., Xi, Q., Gao, F., Zhao, Y.: Fault-tolerant gait design for quadruped robots with one locked leg using the GF set theory. Mech. Mach. Theory **178**, 105069 (2022)

6. Chen, Z., Xi, Q., Qi, C., Chen, X., Gao, Y., Gao, F.: Fault-tolerant gait design for quadruped robots with two locked legs using the GF set theory. Mech. Mach. Theory **195**, 105592 (2024)
7. Lin, C.-M., Chen, C.-H.: Robust fault-tolerant control for a biped robot using a recurrent cerebellar model articulation controller. IEEE Trans. Syst. Man Cybern. Part B Cybern. **37**, 110–123 (2007)
8. Kim, M., Shin, U., Kim, J.-Y.: Learning quadrupedal locomotion with impaired joints using random joint masking. arXiv:2403.00398 (2024)
9. Luo, Z., Xiao, E., Lu, P.: FT-Net: learning failure recovery and fault-tolerant locomotion for quadruped robots. IEEE Robot. Autom. Lett. **8**, 8414–8421 (2023)
10. Hou, T., Tu, J., Gao, X., Dong, Z., Zhai, P., Zhang, L.: Multi-task learning of active fault-tolerant controller for leg failures in quadruped robots. arXiv:2402.08996 (2024)
11. Liu, D., Zhang, T., Yin, J., See, S.: Saving the limping: fault-tolerant quadruped locomotion via reinforcement learning. arXiv:2210.00474 (2023)
12. Wu, X., Dong, W., Lai, H., Yu, Y., Wen, Y.: Adaptive control strategy for quadruped robots in actuator degradation scenarios. In: Proceedings of the Fifth International Conference on Distributed Artificial Intelligence, pp. 1–13. Association for Computing Machinery, New York (2023)
13. Margolis, G.B., Yang, G., Paigwar, K., Chen, T., Agrawal, P.: Rapid locomotion via reinforcement learning. arXiv:2205.02824 (2022)
14. Jin, Y., Liu, X., Shao, Y., Wang, H., Yang, W.: High-speed quadrupedal locomotion by imitation-relaxation reinforcement learning. Nat. Mach. Intell. **4**, 1198–1208 (2022)
15. Lee, J., Hwangbo, J., Wellhausen, L., Koltun, V., Hutter, M.: Learning quadrupedal locomotion over challenging terrain. Sci. Robot. **5**, eabc5986 (2020)
16. Rudin, N., Hoeller, D., Reist, P., Hutter, M.: Learning to walk in minutes using massively parallel deep reinforcement learning. Presented at the 5th Annual Conference on Robot Learning, 19 June 2021
17. Wu, J., Xin, G., Qi, C., Xue, Y.: Learning robust and agile legged locomotion using adversarial motion priors. IEEE Robot. Autom. Lett. **8**, 4975–4982 (2023)
18. Choi, S., Ji, G., Park, J., Kim, H., Mun, J., Lee, J.H., Hwangbo, J.: Learning quadrupedal locomotion on deformable terrain. Sci. Robot. **8**, eade2256 (2023)
19. Margolis, G.B., Agrawal, P.: Walk these ways: tuning robot control for generalization with multiplicity of behavior. In: Proceedings of the 6th Conference on Robot Learning, pp. 22–31. PMLR (2022)
20. Wu, J., Xue, Y., Qi, C.: Learning multiple gaits within latent space for quadruped robots. arXiv:2308.03014 (2023)
21. He, Z., Lei, K., Ze, Y., Sreenath, K., Li, Z., Xu, H.: Learning visual quadrupedal loco-manipulation from demonstrations. arXiv:2403.20328 (2024)
22. Kumar, A., Fu, Z., Pathak, D., Malik, J.: RMA: rapid motor adaptation for legged robots. In: Robotics: Science and Systems XVII. Robotics: Science and Systems Foundation (2021)
23. Tobin, J., Fong, R., Ray, A., Schneider, J., Zaremba, W., Abbeel, P.: Domain randomization for transferring deep neural networks from simulation to the real world. In: Proceedings of the 2017 IEEE/RSJ International Conference on Intelligent Robots and Systems (IROS), pp. 23–30 (2017)
24. Pinto, L., Andrychowicz, M., Welinder, P., Zaremba, W., Abbeel, P.: Asymmetric actor critic for image-based robot learning. In: Robotics: Science and Systems (2018)
25. Chen, D., Zhou, B., Koltun, V., Krähenbühl, P.: Learning by cheating. In: Proceedings of the Conference on Robot Learning, pp. 66–75. PMLR (2020)
26. Schulman, J., Wolski, F., Dhariwal, P., Radford, A., Klimov, O.: Proximal policy optimization algorithms. arXiv:1707.06347 (2017)

27. Ross, S., Gordon, G., Bagnell, D.: A reduction of imitation learning and structured prediction to no-regret online learning. In: Proceedings of the Fourteenth International Conference on Artificial Intelligence and Statistics, JMLR Workshop and Conference Proceedings, pp. 627–635 (2011)
28. Makoviychuk, V., et al.: Isaac Gym: high performance GPU-based physics simulation for robot learning. arXiv:2108.10470 (2021)

# Human-Robot Dynamic System:
# Learning, Modelling and Control

# Identification of Wiener-Hammerstein Model Using Stochastic Variational Bayesian Learning

Junhao Li[1], Fukai Zhang[2], Cong Wang[2], and Yuehu Liu[1(✉)]

[1] The Institute of Artificial Intelligence and Robotics, Xi'an Jiaotong University,
Xi'an, China
44chili@stu.xjtu.edu.cn, liyh@xjtu.edu.cn
[2] School of Control Science and Engineering, Shandong Univeristy, Jinan, China

**Abstract.** The complexity of probability estimation has limited the application of Bayesian learning in nonlinear system identification. This paper addresses Wiener-Hammerstein (WH) nonlinear process identification in the presence of process noise and measurement noise, we propose a Stochastic Variational Inference (SVI) method inspired by stochastic optimization. The SVI method leverages probabilities of intermediate variables to estimate natural gradients of model parameters and updates the posterior probabilities of hidden variables. Compared to the traditional Variational Inference (VI) method, our proposed approach significantly reduces computational complexity. The effectiveness of the SVI method is verified by two numerical simulations and the WH benchmark problem, thereby providing a fresh perspective for efficiently identifying nonlinear systems with large-scale uncertain data.

**Keywords:** Bayesian learning · Stchastic optimization · nonlinear system identification · Wiener-Hammerstein model

## 1 Introduction

Nonlinear system identification, as an important research content in the field of modern control theory and signal processing, has been receiving extensive attention [1]. Due to the complex structure of the actual working environment and the existence of many nonlinear problems such as uncertainty, it has brought great challenges to the research in this direction [2]. The first problem to be considered is how to describe the dynamic process of nonlinear system or how to establish the model of nonlinear system, and the common models to describe the nonlinear process include the following: Nonlinear State Space models [3], Linear Parameter Varying models [4], NARMAX (Nonlinear Autoregressive Moving Average with eXogenous inputs) [5], Neural Network models [6], and Block-oriented models [7]. Among those models, the bock-oriented models has been widely used due to its simple structure, flexible parameters, strong interpretability. The Wiener-Hammerstein(WH) model is a typical block-oriented model, which consists of

X. Lan et al. (Eds.): ICIRA 2024, LNAI 15208, pp. 147–158, 2025.
https://doi.org/10.1007/978-981-96-0783-9_11

two parts, Wiener and Hammerstein [8], and can be used to approximate almost any nonlinear systems, which is chosen in this peper to study the identification of nonlinear processes.

The structure of the Wiener-Hammerstein model is illustrated by Fig. 1 which consists of two dynamic linear links as well as a static nonlinear link in between. Where $x_n$ is the intermediate, unmeasurable variable and $y_n$ is the output of the system affected by the measurement noise(as shown by $e_n$). In addition to the effect of measurement noise on the system, which is taken into account in most methods, the effect of process noise (as shown by $w_n$) on the intermediate variable is also considered in this paper, which improves the accuracy of the description. According to Ljung [9], there are few methods that can better deal with the situation where both of these noises exist. The identification methods of WH model mainly include the Prediction Error Minimization(PEM) method [10] and the Maximization Likelihood Estimation(MLE) method [9]. The PEM method fits the input and output data by minimizing the prediction error to obtain the model parameters. However, when the model has large noise, the parameter estimates obtained by this method are usually biased, and it is difficult to obtain satisfactory parameter estimates; The MLE method deals with the parameter identification problem under strong noise by maximizing the likelihood function. However, for the identification of nonlinear system, a large number of exponential and integral operations are often required, and the likelihood function cannot be directly calculated when there are hidden variables in the system. Therefore, the traditional MLE method cannot be directly used for parameter estimation. Different from the above two methods, The Variational Bayesian method was proposed to identify the WH model [11]. The method uses Variational Inference(VI) combined with the importance sampling technique to approximate the posterior distribution of the hidden variables, and then estimates the model parameters by maximizing the total probability likelihood function, which improves the accuracy of the identification. However, due to the use of importance sampling technique and the need to perform variational inference on all hidden variables in each iteration, which makes the computational amount of this method is too large to be suitable for system identification in the case of large-scale data.

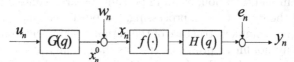

**Fig. 1.** The structure of Wiener-Hammerstein model

Acknowledging the limitations of the above methods, this paper introduces the Stochastic Variational Inference(SVI) method to solve the WH model identification problem in the presence of process noise. According to the idea of stochastic optimization, the natural gradient descent method is used to update the model parameters. By adopting the stochastic gradient descent method, the convergence of gradient descent can be ensured by only obtaining the expectation value of the gradient during the iteration process. Under the assumption that the hidden variables are independent, the system hidden variables are classified into global hidden variables and local hidden variables according to the different updating methods. Only partial local hidden variable information is needed to update the model parameters, which significantly reduces the computational burden of variational inference. Two simulation examples and a WH benchmark problem are used to verify the effectiveness of the method and its great advantages in computational efficiency, This method also provides a new idea for nonlinear system identification under large-scale uncertain data.

## 2  Problem Statement

The WH model considered in this paper is shown in Fig. 1, which can be described as follows

$$x_n^0 = G(q)u_n$$
$$x_n = x_n^0 + w_n$$
$$y_n = \sum_{i=0}^{M} \lambda_i f(x_{n-i}) + e_n \tag{1}$$

where $u_n$ is system input singals, $y_n$ is output signals disturbed by the measurement noise $e_n$, and intermediate variable $x_n$ is unmeasured which disturbed by the process noise $w_n$. $f(\cdot)$ is nonlinear part of the system, and $G(q)$ is the input transfer function and is described by

$$G(q) = \frac{b_0 + b_1 q^{-1} + \cdots + b_{n_b} q^{-n_b}}{1 + a_1 q^{-1} + \cdots + a_{n_a} q^{-n_a}} . \tag{2}$$

For simplicity, converting $G(q)$ into an impluse response model [12], we use $\Theta = [\theta_0, \theta_1, \theta_2, \cdots, \theta_L]^{\mathrm{T}}$ to represent input transfer function. Similarly, using $\Lambda = [\lambda_0, \lambda_1, \lambda_2, \cdots, \lambda_M]^{\mathrm{T}}$ to represent output transfer function $H(q)$ in Fig. 1.

To deal with the parameter uncertainties, The first assumption is that $e_n$ and $w_n$ are independent Gaussian noises with zero means, namely $w_n \sim \mathcal{N}(0, \delta_w^{-1})$ and $e_n \sim \mathcal{N}(0, \delta_e^{-1})$, where $\delta_w$ and $\delta_e$ are precisions. The second assumption is that the prior distributions of $\Theta$ and $\Lambda$ follow a Gaussian gamma distribution and the prior distribution of $\delta_w$ and $\delta_e$ follow a gammma distribution. Then, The joint prior distribution of the parameters is

$$p(\Theta, \Lambda, \delta_w, \delta_e, \alpha) = p(\Theta|\alpha)p(\Lambda|\alpha)p(\delta_w|a_0, b_0)p(\delta_e|a_0, b_0)$$
$$= \mathcal{N}(0, \alpha^{-1}\mathrm{I})\mathcal{G}(\alpha|a_0, b_0)\mathcal{G}(\delta_w|a_0, b_0)\mathcal{G}(\delta_e|a_0, b_0) , \tag{3}$$

where $\alpha^{-1}$ is the variance of each element of $\Theta$ and $\Lambda$. I is identity matrix, $a_0$ and $b_0$ are hyperparameters of the prior distribution which are constants.

Let $u_{1:N} = \{u_1, \cdots, u_N\}$ and $y_{1:N} = \{y_1, \cdots, y_N\}$ in which $N$ is the length of the singals. Let $\Xi = \{\Theta, \Lambda, \delta_w, \delta_e, \alpha\}$ denote the model parameters which can be treated as hidden variables. The parameter estimation is obtained by maximizing the likelihood function, namely

$$\hat{\Xi} = \arg \max_{\Xi} p(y_{1:N}) \,. \tag{4}$$

Due to the nonlinearity of the system and the introduction of hidden variables, it is difficult to directly calculate the likelihood function of the observed data, so this paper uses the Variational Bayesian method to solve the above optimization problem.

## 3    Stochastic Variational Inference of WH Model

### 3.1    Overview of the Variational Inference

For the WH model described in this paper, Let $Y = \{y_1, \cdots, y_N\}$ denote observed data, $H = \{X, \Xi\}$, where $X = \{x_1, \cdots, x_N\}$ denotes the set of local hidden variables and $\Xi = \{\Theta, \Lambda, \delta_w, \delta_e, \alpha\}$ denotes the set of global hidden variables. The log-likelihood function of observed data is given by

$$
\begin{aligned}
\ln p(Y) &= \ln \int q(H)p(Y)dH \\
&= \int q(H) \ln p(Y)dH \\
&= \int q(H) \ln \frac{p(Y, H)}{q(H)}dH + \int q(H) \ln \frac{q(H)}{p(H|Y)}dH \\
&= L(q) + KL(q\|p)
\end{aligned} \tag{5}
$$

where $q(\cdot)$ represents the variational posterior distribution. $L(q)$ denotes the lower bound of $\ln p(Y)$, have $\ln p(Y) \geq L(q)$. $KL(q\|p)$ denotes the Kullback-Leibler divergence of $q(H)$ and $p(H|Y)$, and $KL(q\|p) \geq 0$ always holds. It can be seen that $L(q)$ can take the maximum value when $q(H)$ is equals to $p(H|Y)$, and the value of $KL(q\|p)$ is zero at this time. In the nonlinear cases, the true posterior distribution $p(H|Y)$ is not resolvable and cannot be calculated directly, the VI method makes the $q(H)$ gradually close to the $p(H|Y)$ through iterative updating, and achieves the purpose of maximizing $L(q)$ [13].

Consider the set of hidden variables $H = \{X, \Xi\}$. Without loss of generality, use $\xi$ to denotes arbitrary hidden variable. we have $\xi \in H$, $H_{-\xi} = \{H \backslash \xi\}$. Then, $L(q)$ with respect to $\xi$ is expressed as

$$
\begin{aligned}
L(\xi) &= \int q(H) \ln \frac{p(Y, H)}{q(H)}dH \\
&= \int q(\xi) \ln \frac{\exp\{\int q(H_{-\xi}) \ln p(Y, H)dH_{-\xi}\}}{q(\xi)} + const
\end{aligned} \tag{6}
$$

where $const$ denotes a const value. Based on (6), the maximization of $L(q)$ is obtained if

$$q(\xi) \propto \exp\{\int q(\mathrm{H}_{-\xi}) \ln[p(\mathrm{Y}, \mathrm{H}_{-\xi})p(\xi)]\mathrm{dH}_{-\xi}\}$$
$$\propto \exp\{\mathbb{E}_{q(\mathrm{H}_{-\xi})}[\ln[p(\mathrm{Y}, \mathrm{H}_{-\xi})p(\xi)]]\} \tag{7}$$

$\mathbb{E}_{q(\cdot)}$ denotes the expectation in terms of $q(\cdot)$. This is the result of the optimization of the lower bound based on VI. It can be seen from (7) that all the data samples needed to be used for updating variable, and when the data samples are too large, the computational complexity of the algorithm is too high, which is not suitable for the application under the large-scale sample data.

## 3.2  Stochastic Variational Inference

Equation (7) determines the form of the variational posterior distribution, and consider $\Xi = \{\Theta, \Lambda, \delta_w, \delta_e, \alpha\}$, let $\xi \in \Xi$. Based on the property of the exponential distribution, we can find an appropriate prior distribution of $\xi$, namely a conjugate prior, which can make the form of $q(\xi)$ is same as that of $p(\xi)$ and can be expressed as

$$p(\xi) = h(\xi) \exp\{\Omega^{\mathrm{T}} t(\xi) - a_g(\Omega)\} , \tag{8}$$

where $h(\xi)$ and $a_g(\Omega)$ are respectively the base measure and log-normalizer. $\Omega$ is the natural parameter which is the function of the variables that are being conditioned on, and $t(\xi)$ is called sufficient statistics which is the function of $\xi$ [14]. Due to the conjugation property, the posterior distribution $q(\xi)$ is inherently a member of exponential family, namely

$$q(\xi) = h(\xi) \exp\{\beta^{\mathrm{T}} t(\xi) - a_g(\beta)\} , \tag{9}$$

where $\beta$ is the new natural parameter. Based on (7) and (9), we have

$$\mathbb{E}_{q(\mathrm{H}_{-\xi})}[\ln[p(\mathrm{Y}, \mathrm{H}_{-\xi})p(\xi)]] = g^{\mathrm{T}}(\mathrm{Y}, \mathrm{H}_{-\xi})t(\xi) - a_g[g(\mathrm{Y}, \mathrm{H}_{-\xi})] , \tag{10}$$

where

$$g^{\mathrm{T}}(\mathrm{Y}, \mathrm{H}_{-\xi}) = \mathbb{E}_{q(\mathrm{H}_{-\xi})}[\sum_{n=1}^{N} \ln p(\mathrm{Y}_n|\mathrm{H}_{-\xi}) + \ln p(\mathrm{H}_{-\xi})] . \tag{11}$$

The equation is obtained based on the fact that all the samples are independent. Then, the lower bound function $L(\xi)$ with respect to $\beta$ can be rewritten as

$$L(\beta) = (g(\mathrm{Y}, \mathrm{H}_{-\xi}) - \beta)^{\mathrm{T}} \nabla_\beta a_g(\beta) + a_g(\beta) + const . \tag{12}$$

This equation is another form of the (6), which is a function of $\beta$. we can use gradient ascent method to update the lower bound. Then, the gradient [14] of $L(\xi)$ in terms of $\beta$ is given by

$$\nabla_\beta L(\beta) = (g(\mathrm{Y}, \mathrm{H}_{-\xi}) - \beta)^{\mathrm{T}} \nabla_\beta^2 a_g(\beta) . \tag{13}$$

This is the classical gradient of the $L(\beta)$. However, the amount of change in the probability distribution due to the change in the parameters is not suitable to be characterized by the Euclidean distance, and the convergence rate is slow using the classical gradient descent method. Amari in [15] proposed to use the natural gradient in Riemannian space to characterize the change of probability distribution, expressed as the product of the classical gradient and the inverse of the Fisher information matrix of $q(\xi)$, namely

$$
\begin{aligned}
G(\beta) &= \mathbb{E}_q[(\nabla_\beta \ln q(\xi))(\nabla_\beta \ln q(\xi))^\mathrm{T}] \\
&= \mathbb{E}_q[(t(\xi) - \nabla_\beta a_g(\beta)(t(\xi) - \nabla_\beta a_g \beta)^\mathrm{T}] , \\
&= \nabla_\beta^2 a_g(\beta)
\end{aligned} \tag{14}
$$

Then, the natural gradient of $L(\beta)$ has the following form.

$$
\hat{\nabla}_\beta L(\beta) = G(\beta_m)^{-1} \nabla_\beta L(\beta) = g(\mathrm{Y}, \mathrm{H}_{-\xi}) - \beta . \tag{15}
$$

According to (11) and (15), it can be seen that the natural gradient of $L(\beta)$ consists of a polynomial summation. At this point, the computation of the true gradient information of the parameters is proportional to the number of sampling points. Based on the idea of stochastic optimization, which provides a noisy gradient estimation with respect to the objective function, thus reducing the computational complexity. Specifically, since all the sampling points are independent, the noise estimate of the natural gradient can be obtained by subsampling the sampling points [16]. Therefore, based on (11), the noise estimate about the natural gradient can be expressed as

$$
\hat{\nabla}_\beta \bar{\mathcal{L}}(\beta) = \mathbb{E}_{q(\mathrm{H}_{-\xi})}[\frac{N}{S} \sum_{s=1}^{S} \ln p(\mathrm{Y}_s | \mathrm{H}_{-\xi}) + \ln p(\mathrm{H}_{-\xi})] - \beta , \tag{16}
$$

where $s$ is sampled from $\{1, 2, \cdots, N\}$ uniformly, and has the length of $S$. All the samples are independent and according to the stochastic optimization idea [17] we have

$$
\mathbb{E}_q[\hat{\nabla}_\beta \bar{\mathcal{L}}(\beta)] = \hat{\nabla}_\beta L(\beta) . \tag{17}
$$

According to the gradient descent method and (17), the natural parameter $\beta$ at $k$th iteration is update as

$$
\beta^k = \beta^{k-1} + \rho_k \mathbb{E}_q[\hat{\nabla}_\beta \bar{\mathcal{L}}(\beta^{k-1})] , \tag{18}
$$

where $\rho_k$ denotes step sizes, satisfying $\sum \rho_k = \infty, \sum \rho_k^2 < \infty$. In order to improve the speed of the algorithm, we take $\rho_k = (k + \tau)^{-\gamma} \le 1$, where $\gamma$ represents the forgetting rate, which is used to control the forgetting rate of the old information, and the delay factor is $\tau \ge 0$.

Up to this point, we have obtained a way of updating global hidden variable, which is only related to the information of a number of samples, and the computational complexity of the algorithm is significantly reduced in comparison with the VI method. Specifically, taking updating $q(\Theta)$ as an example, we first compute the natural gradient, namely

$$g^{\mathrm{T}}(\mathrm{Y}, \mathrm{H}_{-\xi}) = \mathbb{E}_q[\sum_{n=1}^{N} \ln p(x_n|\Theta, \delta_w) + \ln p(\Theta|\alpha)] \ , \tag{19}$$

where

$$\begin{aligned}
\ln p(x_n|\Theta, \delta_w) &\propto [\delta_w x_n U_n^{\mathrm{T}}, -\frac{1}{2}\delta_w \cdot \mathrm{Dvec}^{\mathrm{T}}(U_n \otimes U_n)]t(\beta_\Theta) \\
\ln p(\Theta|\alpha) &\propto [0, -\frac{1}{2}\cdot \mathrm{Dvec}^{\mathrm{T}}(\alpha \mathrm{I})]t(\beta_\Theta)
\end{aligned} \tag{20}$$

where $\mathrm{Dvec}(\cdot)$ is a vector formed by the row vectors of the matrix. $t(\beta_\Theta)$ is the sufficient statistics which is defined as $t(\beta_\Theta) = [\Theta, \mathrm{Dvec}(\Theta \otimes \Theta)]^{\mathrm{T}}$. The noise natural gradient of the lower bound function $L(\beta_\Theta)$, according to (16), is given by

$$\begin{aligned}
\hat{\nabla}L(\beta_\Theta^{k-1}) = [&\frac{N}{S}\sum_{s=1}^{S}[\langle\delta_w\rangle\langle x_s\rangle U_s^{\mathrm{T}}], \\
&\frac{N}{S}\sum_{s=1}^{S}[\frac{\langle\delta_w\rangle}{2}\cdot\mathrm{Dvec}^{\mathrm{T}}(U_s \otimes U_s)] \\
&+ \frac{1}{2}\cdot\mathrm{Dvec}^{\mathrm{T}}(\langle\alpha\rangle\mathrm{I})] - \beta_\Theta^{k-1}
\end{aligned} \tag{21}$$

where $\langle\cdot\rangle$ denotes the expectation operator with respect to $q(\cdot)$. Then, at $k$th iteration, $\beta_\Theta$ is update by

$$\beta_\Theta^k = \beta_\Theta^{k-1} + \rho_k\hat{\nabla}L(\beta_\Theta^{k-1}) \ . \tag{22}$$

Based on the assumption in (3) and the property of the exponential familiy, $q(\Theta)$ is a Gaussian distribution and the mean and variance are given by

$$\begin{aligned}
\langle\Theta\rangle &= \beta_\Theta^k(1:L)\mathrm{Var}(\Theta), \\
\mathrm{Var}(\Theta) &= \mathrm{iDvec}[2\cdot\beta_\Theta^k(L+1:end)]^{-1}
\end{aligned} \tag{23}$$

where iDvec is defined as an operator to convert a vector into a matrix, serving as the inverse operation of Dvec, and $end$ denotes the last index of the vector.

Following the above updating method of $q(\Theta)$, we can similarly derive the update method of other global hidden variables combined with the SVI approach.

## 4   Results

### 4.1   Simulation Studies

In this subsection, we first use a numerical simulation to show the effectiveness of the proposed method. The WH model is described as

$$\begin{aligned}
x_n^0 &= a_0 x_{n-1}^0 + u_{n-1} \\
x_n &= x_n^0 + w_n \\
y_n &= c_0 + c_1 x_n + c_2 x_n^2 + e_n
\end{aligned} \tag{24}$$

where $w_n \sim \mathcal{N}(0,0.1)$ and $e_n \sim \mathcal{N}(0,0.1)$. This model is taken from [9], and four parameters needs to be identified, which are denotes as $\Xi = \{a_0, c_0, c_1, c_2\}$, in which the true values of $a_0, c_0, c_1$ and $c_2$ are $-0.5$, $0$, $1$ and $1$. Setting the forgetting rate $\gamma = 0.3$ and the delay factor $\tau = 5$. The random, uniformly distributed singal is used to excite the process, namely $u_n \sim U[-2,2]$, and 300 samples are generated to identify the model.

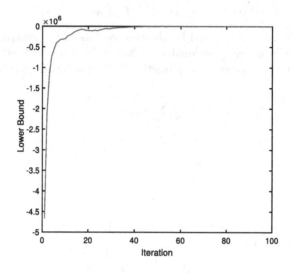

**Fig. 2.** Convergence process of the lower bound.

1, 5%, 10%, 20%, and all sampling points are randomly used to estimate the noise estimation of the natural gradient of the posterior distribution parameters. In each case, 50 Monte Carlo simulations are generated to test the identification, each of which makes the algorithm iterate 100 times to update the variables, and the identified parameter set is listed in Table 1. Figure. 2 is the convergence of the lower bound function.

We can see the effectiveness of the proposed method for the WH model identification considered. When the number of sub-sampling data points increases at each iteration time, the identification of model parameters is more accurate, but the corresponding speed advantage of the algorithm will be reduced. Compared with the VI method, the identification accuracy of the two methods is comparable, but the calculation time of the SVI method is significantly lower than that of the latter, indicating that the proposed method significantly reduces the amount of calculation without reducing the identification accuracy, which provides support for online identification or strong real-time system identification and solves the problem of high computational complexity of Bayesian learning.

**Table 1.** Identification of parameters corresponding to different sub-sampling data points

|             | $a_0$               | $c_0$              | $c_1$              | $c_2$              | RMS    | Time(s) |
|-------------|---------------------|--------------------|--------------------|--------------------|--------|---------|
| True value  | $-0.5$              | 0                  | 1                  | 1                  | -      | -       |
| 1 sample    | $-0.5276 \pm 0.0595$ | $0.1296 \pm 0.1632$ | $0.9796 \pm 0.1611$ | $0.9260 \pm 0.1320$ | 1.0859 | 0.3072  |
| 5% samples  | $-0.4978 \pm 0.0363$ | $0.0528 \pm 0.0779$ | $0.9451 \pm 0.1137$ | $0.9678 \pm 0.1214$ | 1.0178 | 0.9184  |
| 10% samples | $-0.5042 \pm 0.0322$ | $0.0615 \pm 0.0894$ | $0.9117 \pm 0.1157$ | $0.9378 \pm 0.1566$ | 1.0304 | 1.6812  |
| 20% samples | $-0.5014 \pm 0.0247$ | $0.0619 \pm 0.0615$ | $0.9425 \pm 0.0451$ | $0.9607 \pm 0.0664$ | 0.9529 | 3.2019  |
| All samples | $-0.5080 \pm 0.0219$ | $0.0480 \pm 0.0413$ | $0.9318 \pm 0.0401$ | $0.9644 \pm 0.0362$ | 0.9351 | 14.9553 |
| VI method   | $-0.5026 \pm 0.0251$ | $0.0449 \pm 0.0357$ | $0.9388 \pm 0.0338$ | $0.9748 \pm 0.0426$ | 0.9292 | 15.0836 |

To further demonstrate the effectiveness of the SVI method, we consider the following modified model

$$
\begin{aligned}
x_n^0 &= a_0 x_{n-1}^0 + u_{n-1} \\
x_n &= x_n^0 + w_n \\
y_n &= \lambda_0 (c_1 x_n + c_2 x_n^2) + \lambda_1 (c_1 x_{n-1} + c_2 x_{n-1}^2) + e_n
\end{aligned}
\qquad (25)
$$

where $w_n \sim \mathcal{N}(0, 0.1)$ and $e_n \sim \mathcal{N}(0, 0.1)$. $a_0 = -0.5$, $c_1 = c_2 = 1$, $\lambda_0 = 0.8$ and $\lambda_1 = 0.2$. For simplicity, let $d_1 = \lambda_0 c_1$, $d_2 = \lambda_0 c_2$, $d_3 = \lambda_1 c_1$, and $d_4 = \lambda_1 c_2$. Setting the forgetting rate $\gamma = 0.3$ and the delay factor $\tau = 5$.

50 random experiments were conducted, with each experiment iterating the algorithm 100 times, using 5% sampling points to update the variables in each iteration. The means and variances of parameter are listed in Table 2. Figure. 3 is the predicted output obtained by using the SVI method.

**Table 2.** The estimated parameters for model (25)

| Parameters | True value | Estimated value     | RMS    | Time(s) |
|------------|------------|---------------------|--------|---------|
| $a_0$      | $-0.5$     | $-0.5336 \pm 0.0537$ |        |         |
| $d_1$      | 0.8        | $0.8237 \pm 0.0702$  |        |         |
| $d_2$      | 0.8        | $0.7518 \pm 0.0695$  | 0.8485 | 1.1174  |
| $d_3$      | 0.2        | $0.2074 \pm 0.0479$  |        |         |
| $d_4$      | 0.2        | $0.1817 \pm 0.0389$  |        |         |

The results indicate that the proposed method can effectively estimate model parameters, can be used for more complex WH models, and has significant advantages in execution efficiency. In fact, the traditional method is no longer applicable to such a complex WH model. The SVI method can iteratively update the posterior distribution parameters of the hidden variable quickly without obtaining the specific form of the distribution.

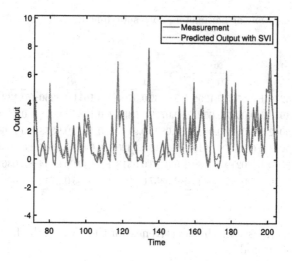

**Fig. 3.** Predicted output for the simulation example.

## 4.2   Benchmark Problem

In this subsection, we use proposed method to identify the WH benchmark problem, which was proposed by Ljung [18] and is the standard model for validating the Wiener-Hammerstein system identification method. The structure of the model is shown in Fig. 1, $G(q)$ of the benchmark is a Chebyshev filter, and $H(q)$ is an inverse Chebyshev filter. The static nonlinear link is composed of a diode circuit. The benchmark process can be described as followed

$$
\begin{aligned}
x_n^0 &= G(q)u_n \\
x_n &= x_n^0 + w_n \\
f(x_n) &= c_0 + c_1 x_n + c_2 x_n^2 , \\
y_n &= \sum_{i=0}^{M} \lambda_i f(x_{n-i}) + e_n
\end{aligned}
\tag{26}
$$

where $w_n \sim \mathcal{N}(0, \delta_w^{-1})$ and $e_n \sim \mathcal{N}(0, \delta_e^{-1})$. In order to show the effectiveness of the proposed SVI method, We use two different structures to describe the model. First, we set $L = 20$ and $M = 0$, so there are 25 parameters needed to be estimated. Then, we set $L = 20$ and $M = 1$, in this case, there are 27 parameters needed to be estimated. In [18], a total of 188000 sets of data points are included. In this paper, two sets of data points at 6000-7999 and 6000-15999 are used to identify the model parameters, and a total of 2000 data points at 150000-151999 are used to verify the validity of the model.

The predicted output is plotted in Fig. 4, The result shows that the identification parameters obtained by the proposed method can accurately predict the output value. The identification results of the SVI and VI method are listed in

**Table 3.** RMS values and time of the different methods

| Samples | Methods | Number of parameters | RMS(V) | Time(s) |
|---|---|---|---|---|
| 2000 | SVI | 25 | 0.0581 | 20.6357 |
| | SVI | 27 | 0.0551 | 29.9847 |
| | VI | 25 | 0.0568 | 200.3195 |
| 10000 | SVI | 25 | 0.0647 | 102.6140 |
| | SVI | 27 | 0.0589 | 116.1317 |
| | VI | 25 | 0.0618 | 1095.6330 |

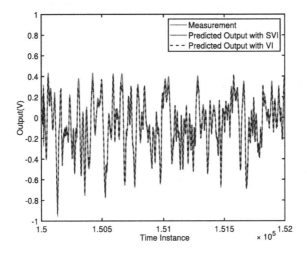

**Fig. 4.** Predicted output of the different methods

Table 3. The root mean square(RMS) value of the predicted error is used to evaluate the accuracy of the model. Obviously, the SVI method not only has slightly higher identification accuracy than the VI method, but the time consumed is significantly lower than the latter. In a word, the above analysis demonstrates the effectiveness of the SVI method for identifying the WH model and its significant advantage in algorithm efficiency.

## 5   Conclusion

In this paper, the problem of WH model identification in the presence of process noise and measurement noise is studied. According to the idea of stochastic optimization, the SVI method is proposed, which calculates the posterior distribution parameters of global hidden variables through the natural gradient descent method to update the model parameters. Compared with the VI, the SVI method only needs part of the intermediate variable information to update the parameters, so as to maximize the likelihood function and significantly reduce the calculation amount of inference, which is of great significance for the identification of large-scale data systems. Two simulation examples are given to illustrate the effectiveness of the proposed method in WH model identification and the advantages of the method in time cost. The application of this method in actual data is verified by a benchmark problem of nonlinear circuit identification, the results show that the proposed method has great advantages in improving identification accuracy and computational efficiency.

# References

1. Noël, J.P., Kerschen, G.: Nonlinear system identification in structural dynamics: 10 more years of progress. Mech. Syst. Signal Process. **83**, 2–35 (2017)
2. Ljung, L.: Perspectives on system identification. Annu. Rev. Control. **34**(1), 1–12 (2010)
3. Schön, T.B., Wills, A., Ninness, B.: System identification of nonlinear state-space models. Automatica **47**(1), 39–49 (2011)
4. Shamma, J.S., Athans, M.: Guaranteed properties of gain scheduled control for linear parameter-varying plants. Automatica **27**(3), 559–564 (1991)
5. Billings, S.A.: Nonlinear System Identification: NARMAX Methods in the Time, Frequency, and Spatio-Temporal Domains. Wiley (2013)
6. Gupta, P., Sinha, N.K.: An improved approach for nonlinear system identification using neural networks. J. Franklin Inst. **336**(4), 721–734 (1999)
7. Schoukens, M., Tiels, K.: Identification of block-oriented nonlinear systems starting from linear approximations: a survey. Automatica **85**, 272–292 (2017)
8. Bershad, N.J., Celka, P., McLaughlin, S.: Analysis of stochastic gradient identification of wiener-hammerstein systems for nonlinearities with hermite polynomial expansions. IEEE Trans. Signal Process. **49**(5), 1060–1072 (2001)
9. Hagenblad, A., Ljung, L., Wills, A.: Maximum likelihood identification of wiener models. Automatica **44**(11), 2697–2705 (2008)
10. Westwick, D.T., Schoukens, J.: Initial estimates of the linear subsystems of wiener-hammerstein models. Automatica **48**(11), 2931–2936 (2012)
11. Liu, Q., Tang, X., Li, J., Zeng, J., Zhang, K., Chai, Y.: Identification of wiener-hammerstein models based on variational Bayesian approach in the presence of process noise. J. Franklin Inst. **358**(10), 5623–5638 (2021)
12. Xie, L., Yang, H., Huang, B.: Fir model identification of multirate processes with random delays using EM algorithm. AIChE J. **59**(11), 4124–4132 (2013)
13. Liu, Q., Lin, W., Jiang, S., Chai, Y., Sun, L.: Robust estimation of wiener models in the presence of outliers using the VB approach. IEEE Trans. Industr. Electron. **68**(11), 11390–11399 (2020)
14. Bishop, C.M. (ed.): Pattern Recognition and Machine Learning. ISS, Springer, New York (2006). https://doi.org/10.1007/978-0-387-45528-0
15. Amari, S.I.: Natural gradient works efficiently in learning. Neural Comput. **10**(2), 251–276 (1998)
16. Hoffman, M.D., Blei, D.M., Wang, C., Paisley, J.: Stochastic variational inference. J. Mach. Learn. Res. 14(2013) 1303–1347 (2013)
17. Robbins, H., Monro, S.: A stochastic approximation method. The annals of mathematical statistics, pp. 400–407 (1951)
18. Schoukens, J., Ljung, L.: Wiener-hammerstein benchmark (2009)

# Design and Control of Continuous Gait for Humanoid Robots: Jumping, Walking, and Running Based on Reinforcement Learning and Adaptive Motion Functions

Zida Zhao[1], Shilong Sun[1,2($\boxtimes$)], Chiyao Li[1], Haodong Huang[1], and Wenfu Xu[1,2]

[1] Harbin Institute of Technology, Shenzhen 518052, China
sunshilong@hit.edu.cn

[2] Guangdong Provincial Key Laboratory of Intelligent Morphing Mechanisms and Adaptive Robots, Shenzhen, China

**Abstract.** Continuous gait design and control enable humanoid robots to smoothly transition and switch between different gaits, adapting to various task requirements, which is crucial for their real-world applications. Traditional gait control methods often rely on predefined rules and models, limiting the flexibility and adaptability of robots. To overcome the above limitations, this study combines adaptive motion functions (AMF) with reinforcement learning (RL) to achieve continuous gait design and control. Firstly, to enable a single policy to achieve different gaits, both the AMF and reward functions are designed as piecewise functions. Secondly, to enhance the flexibility of the AMF, the RL strategy is used to control the motion cycle of the AMF. This allows the robot to learn how to adjust the speed and rhythm of the gaits, achieving smooth gait transitions and switches. Lastly, to fully leverage the advantages of RL, the output of the policy is not directly summed with the AMF as the robot's action command. Instead, the policy output is adjusted and then added to the AMF, with the adjustment factor also being an output of the policy. The method proposed in this paper controls the gait cycle and adjustment factors through policies, improving the flexibility and adaptability of robots and providing insights for the practical application of continuous gaits in humanoid robots.

**Keywords:** Continuous Gait · Adaptive Motion Functions · Reinforcement Learning

## 1 Introduction

Humanoid robots are robotic systems that mimic the appearance and movement capabilities of humans. They are designed to perform tasks and activities similar to those of humans [1]. With the continuous advancement of technology and the development of artificial intelligence, humanoid robots have demonstrated immense potential in various fields such as industry [2], healthcare [3], education [4], and entertainment [5]. Among these, gait design and control are essential components for humanoid robots to accomplish a wide range of tasks.

X. Lan et al. (Eds.): ICIRA 2024, LNAI 15208, pp. 159–173, 2025.
https://doi.org/10.1007/978-981-96-0783-9_12

Research on gait design and control for humanoid robots aims to achieve robot movements that simulate human walking, running, jumping, and other actions while ensuring smooth and efficient motion in different environments and task requirements [6]. Gait design not only focuses on the appearance and aesthetics of the movements but also takes into account the robot's stability, energy efficiency, and adaptability [7].

The continuity of gait transitions and switches is of crucial importance in the design and control of humanoid robot gaits [8]. By achieving continuous gait transitions, robots can better emulate human movement, resulting in smoother and more natural actions. This not only enhances the robot's overall motion quality but also improves its stability and balance [9]. Additionally, continuous gait switching allows robots to adapt to different task requirements by adjusting gait parameters, speed, and force [10]. For example, in a factory production line, robots can adjust their speed and force as needed to ensure safe handling and precise placement of objects. In emergency rescue scenarios, humanoid robots can quickly respond by utilizing continuous gait switches. Moreover, by smoothly transitioning between gaits, robots can avoid unnecessary energy consumption during gait switches, which helps extend the robot's battery life and reduces reliance on energy sources, enabling them to perform tasks for longer durations.

Traditional approaches to gait design and control often rely on predefined rules and models, utilizing mathematical models and kinematic analysis to determine the robot's gait parameters, including cyclic gaits, inverted pendulum gaits, and central pattern gaits, among others [11–13]. However, these methods often struggle with gait transitions and continuity issues since gait transitions typically require manual adjustment and optimization of gait parameters to ensure smooth transitions between different motions. Such adjustments can be time-consuming and labor-intensive and may not adapt quickly to new situations [14, 15]. Additionally, the traditional cyclic gaits are divided into discrete phases, which can result in unpredictable transitions between phases and even lead to unstable states during gait transitions, affecting the walking performance and motion capabilities of the robot [16, 17].

Due to the lack of adaptability and learning capability in traditional methods, they are unable to adjust and improve based on real-time feedback. This limitation results in insufficient adaptability and flexibility when faced with complex environments and task requirements, greatly restricting the application and performance of robots in different environments and tasks. To overcome these issues, researchers have started exploring gait design and control methods based on reinforcement learning (RL) in recent years.

RL is a method that utilizes the feedback mechanism between a robot and its environment to find the optimal strategy through trial and error and optimization [18]. During the training process, the robot interacts with the environment and collects real-time state feedback, evaluating the effectiveness of different actions based on reward signals [19]. Through continuous experimentation and learning, the robot can gradually adjust its gait and behavior to achieve higher rewards [20]. Through RL, robots can autonomously adapt their gaits in complex and dynamic environments to tackle various challenges and tasks. This adaptive gait design and control method provides greater flexibility and adaptability for humanoid robots in different environments and tasks [21, 22].

Nevertheless, RL algorithms encounter various obstacles when applied to gait design and control in humanoid robots. These challenges include the creation of suitable reward functions that effectively guide the learning process, the optimization of motion for stability and efficiency, and enhancing computational efficiency to manage continuous actions and high-dimensional states effectively.[23]. Furthermore, the gaits and actions derived from RL often seem unnatural or less human-like compared to natural human motion. This divergence stems from the fact that RL algorithms primarily learn through trial-and-error and feedback mechanisms. In this process, robots discover efficient action strategies by continuously experimenting and optimizing, which may lead to movements that are effective but lack the fluidity and subtlety of human motion. [24]. During this process, the robot may demonstrate unusual movements, particularly in the early stages of training. These atypical movements can arise from various factors, such as inadequately designed reward functions, inherent randomness in the learning process, or uncertainties within the environment. Moreover, RL algorithms are susceptible to becoming trapped in local optima during their search within the solution space. This entrapment can hinder the robot's ability to discover motions that are more reminiscent of human-like movement [25].

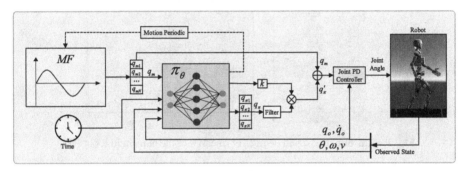

**Fig. 1.** The adaptive motion functions and RL control structure.

To tackle the challenges as mentioned above, this study introduces a novel approach that merges periodic gaits with reinforcement learning for the design and transition of gaits in humanoid robots, as depicted in the accompanying illustration. Initially, we formulate three distinct motion functions to facilitate a variety of gaits. To ensure seamless transitions between these gaits, we implement a policy to regulate the timing of the motion functions. Furthermore, directly applying the policy's output to the motion functions as the robot's action command could lead to erratic robot movements or prolonged training periods. To counter this, we process the policy's output through a straightforward filter and then multiply it by a tuning factor, which is also a component of the policy's output. This strategy effectively eliminates inconsistencies in robot movements and significantly quickens the training process. We utilize this method to achieve continuous gaits for jumping, walking, and running in humanoid robots, as shown in Fig. 1, promoting further advancements in gait design and control.

# 2  Methods

## 2.1  Robot Model

Figure 2 shows the humanoid robot model HIT used in our simulations in this paper. HIT has a total mass of 66.38 kg and a height of 165 cm. It comprises five main parts: body, arms, pelvis, thighs, legs, and feet. A total of 18 degrees of freedom (DOF) were assigned to the robot in the simulation. This includes 2 DOFs for each arm, 2 DOFs for the body, 3 DOFs for each hip joint, 1 DOF for each knee joint, and 2 DOFs for each ankle joint.

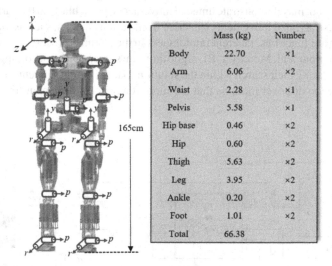

| | Mass (kg) | Number |
|---|---|---|
| Body | 22.70 | ×1 |
| Arm | 6.06 | ×2 |
| Waist | 2.28 | ×1 |
| Pelvis | 5.58 | ×1 |
| Hip base | 0.46 | ×2 |
| Hip | 0.60 | ×2 |
| Thigh | 5.63 | ×2 |
| Leg | 3.95 | ×2 |
| Ankle | 0.20 | ×2 |
| Foot | 1.01 | ×2 |
| Total | 66.38 | |

**Fig. 2.**  Structure, mass, and degrees of freedom of the humanoid robot HIT.

## 2.2  Adaptive Motion Functions

In the field of humanoid robotics, traditional RL control methods overly rely on reward functions and suffer from slow training time and non-human-like training actions. To address these issues, we have designed some guiding gait actions for RL, including three different periodic sinusoidal gaits: jumping, walking, and running. To make the robot's movements and gait transitions more natural, we incorporate the periods of these gaits as part of the RL policy output for real-time updates, thereby achieving an adaptive effect.

To keep the guiding actions as simple as possible, we have designed the angles for a total of 10 joints of the robot, namely the shoulder, elbow, hip, knee, and ankle, as shown in Fig. 3. The angles for the other joints are set to 0. In the jumping gait, the pitch angles for the left and right sides are symmetrical, while in the walking and running gaits, they differ by half a cycle. The periods for each gait are as follows (unit: seconds): jumping 0.58~0.62, walking 0.58~0.62, running 0.38~0.42. Furthermore, it is important to note that the periods of these guiding actions are the midpoints of their respective ranges before the RL process takes place.

Additionally, in the simulation of JWR, the durations of jump, walk, and run were each 5 s, totaling 15 s. In the simulations of the three distinct individual gaits, the total duration for each simulation was 5 s.

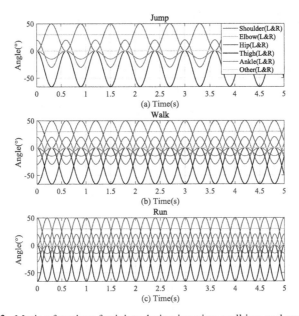

**Fig. 3.** Motion functions for joints during jumping, walking, and running.

## 2.3 Reward Design

The design of the reward function is crucial for the training efficiency of RL, and to achieve more human-like motion effects, the reward function for training humanoid robots is often complex. However, by introducing guiding actions into the control framework, we avoid the need for redundant reward functions. The reward function for JWR is:

$$r = r_a + r_p + r_b + r_v \tag{1}$$

where $r$ is the reward function of JWR, which consists of the following four parts:

$$r_a = 1 \tag{2}$$

$$r_p = 15 - 0.02 \sum_{i=1}^{18} (q_i - q_i^{mf}) \tag{3}$$

$$r_b = -0.05(|\theta_x| + |\theta_y| + |\theta_z|) \tag{4}$$

$$r_v = \begin{cases} r_j = v_z - |v_x| + |v_y| - |p^{footL} - p^{footR}|, & 0 < t < 5s \\ r_w = v_z - |v_x| - |v_y|, & 5s < t < 10s \\ r_r = v_z - |v_x| - |v_y|, & 10s < t < 15s \end{cases} \tag{5}$$

where $r_a$ is the survival reward. If the robot does not terminate the current training episode within the current time step, it receives a reward of 1. This encourages the robot to survive for a longer duration. $r_p$ is the guiding reward and $q$ represents the angles of the joints. This reward encourages the robot's joints to follow the angles of the guiding actions. $r_b$ is the balance reward. $\theta_x$, $\theta_y$, and $\theta_z$ represent the angles of rotation of the body relative to the initial upright position. This reward encourages the robot's body to maintain an upright position during movement. $r_w$, $r_j$ and $r_r$ are the walking reward, jumping reward, and running reward, respectively. $v_x$, $v_y$, and $v_z$ represent the velocities of the body in three directions, while $p^{footL}$ and $p^{footR}$ represent the positions of the feet. This reward is designed for different gaits, and the order of this reward changes depending on the sequence of gait combinations.

Additionally, the training episode automatically ends if the robot's body descends more than 30 cm or if the training step exceeds 7500 steps for JWR and 2500 steps for individual gaits.

## 2.4 Reinforcement Learning

1) Observation

The observations are

$$o_t = [q_m\, t\, q_o\, \dot{q}_o\, \theta\, \omega\, v]^T \tag{6}$$

Among them, $q_m$ it represents the angles of each joint provided by the motion function, which consists of 18 variables. $t$ is the time elapsed since the start of training, consisting of 1 variable. $q_o$ and $\dot{q}_o$ represent the current angles and angular velocities of the robot's body joints, respectively, each consisting of 18 variables. $\theta$ is a quaternion representing the change in body orientation relative to the initial state, consisting of 4 variables. $\omega$ and $v$ represent the angular velocities and linear velocities of the body in three directions, respectively, each consisting of 3 variables. In total, we require 65 variables.

2) Action

From the control framework in Fig. 1, it can be observed that the output of the policy includes the angles $q_\pi$ of each joint, the motion cycle and the adjustment factor $k$. To prevent abrupt changes in $q_\pi$ from causing strange robot movements, we apply a simple filtering to the policy output angles.

$$q_\pi(t) = 0.9 \times q_\pi(t-1) + 0.1 \times q_\pi(t) \tag{7}$$

When we want to send the policy's output actions along with the guiding actions as control commands to the robot, we need to determine the magnitude of $k$. If $k$ is too small, the robot will not be able to explore optimal actions during training, resulting in suboptimal motion performance. On the other hand, if $k$ is too large, the training speed will be reduced, and the guiding actions will not effectively influence the robot's behavior. Therefore, we incorporate $k$ as part of the policy output, known as the adjustment factor, allowing it to be optimized during training. This avoids the need to determine the magnitude of $k$ through continuous trial and error during training. As a result, the final instructions $q(t)$ received by the robot are:

$$q(t) = q_m(t) + k \times q'_\pi(t) \tag{8}$$

3) Proximal Policy Optimization (PPO)

PPO is a well-known RL algorithm that places a strong emphasis on stability and efficient utilization of samples during the training process. By utilizing the gradient update technique of "Proximal Policy Optimization," PPO effectively controls the magnitude of policy updates, preventing learning instability caused by excessively large updates. Furthermore, PPO maximizes the utilization of sampled data under the current policy, leading to improved efficiency in sample usage. These characteristics make PPO especially suitable for tackling complex tasks and high-dimensional state spaces. Thus, we have selected PPO as the RL algorithm for this study, aiming to enhance both the stability and efficiency of the training process. The specific hyperparameters associated with PPO are detailed in Table 1.

**Table 1.** Training parameters of PPO.

| Hyperparameter | Network settings |
|---|---|
| Batch size: 2048 | Normalize: true |
| Buffer size: 20480 | Hidden units: 512 |
| Learning rate: 0.0003 | Num layers: 3 |
| Beta: 0.005 | Vis encode type: simple |
| Epsilon: 0.2 | Memory: null |
| Lambd: 0.95 | Goal conditioning type: hyper |
| Num epoch: 3 | Deterministic: false |

4) Simulation Environment

The RL training is conducted using the ML-Agents package within the Unity software framework, utilizing a fixed time step of 0.002 s. These training tasks are executed on a computer equipped with an Intel i7-12700H processor and NVIDIA RTX A2000 CPU.

# 3 Results

In this section, we will analyze our control framework and the robot's motion process in detail through the reward curve, forward velocity, center of mass position, and actual joint angles. Figure 4 presents the simulation results of continuous motions, including jumping, walking, and running.

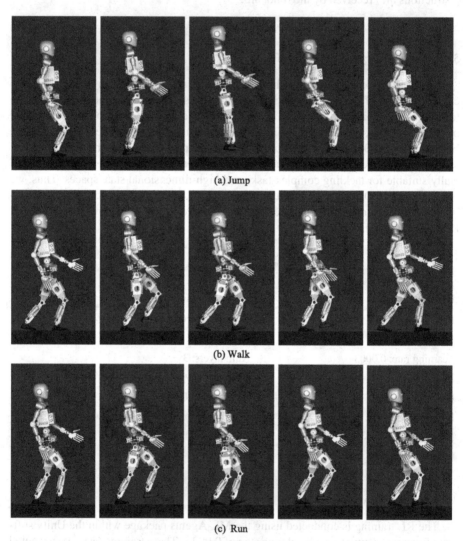

(a) Jump

(b) Walk

(c) Run

**Fig. 4.** The three gaits of the JWR.

### 3.1 Reward Curve and Forward Speed

Figure 5 shows the reward curves for the adjustment factor k = 1 and k = 0~1 in JWR. It can be observed that before 20 million steps, the reward curve for k = 1 grows faster compared to k = 0~1. This is because k, as the output of the policy, undergoes trial and error between 0 and 1 at the beginning of the training, resulting in some actions with lower rewards than k = 1, thus slowing down the reward growth. However, it can be seen from the graph that the difference in rewards is not significant.

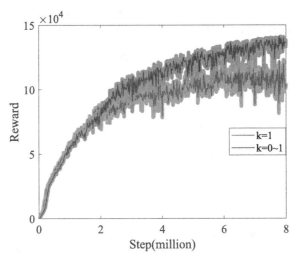

**Fig. 5.** The reward curve of the adjustment factor k = 1 and k = 0~1 of JWR.

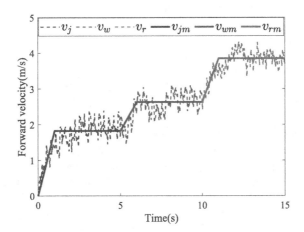

**Fig. 6.** Forward velocity of JWR (k = 0~1).

As the training progresses, the robot gradually learns better strategies and becomes more adept at adjusting the value of the adjustment factor, k. In this process, the robot can more accurately select action strategies based on the requirements of the environment and the task at hand. Consequently, over time, the reward curve starts to grow rapidly in the case of k = 0~1.

Therefore, after 2 million steps, the reward curve for k = 0~1 starts to grow faster compared to k = 1. Moreover, at the 8 millionth step, the maximum reward for k = 1 is 10,800, while for k = 0~1 it is 13,600. This is because after the initial 2 million steps of training, the impact of the value of k on rewards becomes more mature, resulting in higher rewards for k = 0~1 compared to k = 1. This indicates that when the adjustment factor is treated as an output of the policy, the robot achieves better learning results in the end.

Figure 6 shows the forward velocities of JWR for k = 0~1. After the velocities stabilize, the average velocity for jumping is 1.76 m/s, for walking is 2.63 m/s, and for running is 3.85 m/s. In the motion functions described in Fig. 3, we can see that the range of period changes for jumping and walking is the same, but their forward velocities differ significantly. This is because during jumping, the robot not only moves forward but also moves upward, resulting in a lower forward velocity compared to walking. Additionally, the forward velocity of running is 1.46 times greater than walking because the motion function design includes a walking period that is 1.5 times longer than the running period.

## 3.2    Motion Cycle and Adjustment Factor

In the control framework shown in Fig. 1, we know that the motion cycle and adjustment factor are controlled through the policy and are not constant. This approach is taken to make the robot's motion and gait transitions more natural and smooth, thereby enhancing the final training outcome. Figures 7 and 8 depict the time-domain plot and spectrum of JWR's motion function and adjustment factor, respectively.

First, let's analyze the period of JWR's motion function. Figure 7 represents the designed motion function, which fluctuates within the designated range. From Fig. 7(a), we can observe that whether it's jumping, walking, or running, the motion function fluctuates within the designed range and exhibits a certain periodicity. To quantitatively analyze the fluctuation period, we plot the spectrum as shown in Fig. 7(b). From the spectrum, we can identify three peak frequencies: 0.77 Hz, 1.60 Hz, and 2.50 Hz, corresponding to jumping, walking, and running, respectively. However, due to the airborne phase during jumping, its frequency is almost half of the designated frequency. The frequencies of walking and running are similar to the designated frequencies.

Similarly, from Fig. 8(a), we can observe that the adjustment factors for jumping, walking, and running also fluctuate within the designed range and exhibit certain periodicity. Figure 8(b) shows the spectrum, where we can identify three peak frequencies: 0.80 Hz, 1.63 Hz, and 2.50 Hz, corresponding to jumping, walking, and running, respectively.

Furthermore, in Fig. 8(a), it can be observed that when the robot is jumping, the range of the adjustment factor is between 0 and 1. However, when it is in a walking or running state, the range of the adjustment factor varies between 0.3 and 1. We speculate that this difference may be due to the fact that the actual jumping motion performed by the robot is closer to the designed motion function, resulting in a smaller proportion of action being determined by the policy output compared to walking and running.

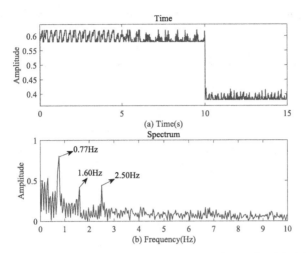

**Fig. 7.** Time-domain plot and spectrum of the motion cycle of the JWR.

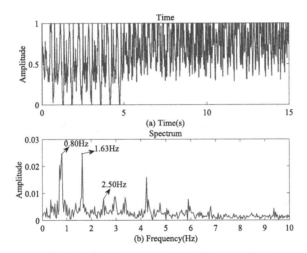

**Fig. 8.** Time-domain plot and spectrum of the adjustment factor of the JWR.

### 3.3 The Center of Mass (CoM)

To further analyze the robot's motion state during movement, we plotted the centroid variation curves as shown in Fig. 9. Firstly, due to different gaits having different forward velocities, there are variations in their forward displacements over the same time period. Specifically, the jumping gait had a forward displacement of 8.63 m, the walking gait had 12.25 m, and the running gait had 18.26 m.

Additionally, we need to pay attention to the height variation of the centroid. From the graph, we can observe that the jumping gait exhibited the highest centroid variation, reaching 25 cm. The walking gait had the second highest variation, with a centroid variation of 16 cm. The running gait had the smallest variation, only reaching 11 cm. The centroid variation range for walking and running gaits indicates that, within the control framework of this study, as the forward velocity of the humanoid robot increases, the centroid height variation decreases, resulting in more stable motion.

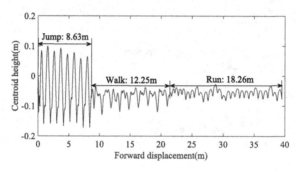

**Fig. 9.**  Change in the height of CoM.

### 3.4  Joint Angle

Figure 10 shows the transformation of the robot joint angles after training is completed. In the previously designed motion functions, only the angles of the ten body joints were included, and the motion functions for the other joints were set to 0. Therefore, we focus on analyzing the angles of these ten joints here. From the graph, it can be observed that during the jumping phase (0–5 s), the angle changes of the corresponding joints on the left and right sides are the same. However, during walking (5–10 s) and running (10–15 s), the angle changes are exactly opposite. This is consistent with the motion functions we designed earlier. Additionally, in order to achieve greater rewards, the final action commands are adjusted based on the motion functions.

When the trained model is applied to an actual robot, there are often differences between the simulation environment and the physical world. It is necessary to increase the robustness of the strategy as much as possible. This requires modifying some simulation parameters and retraining the robot. This process is iterative until a better control strategy is obtained. Undoubtedly, this approach is not efficient. In our control framework, we can treat the trained joint angles as new motion functions and retrain the robot. This can greatly save training time and improve training results. This is also the method we plan to use for future physical transfer.

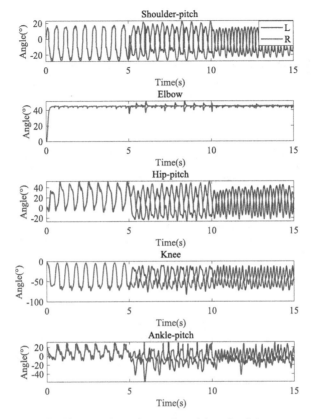

**Fig. 10.** Actual rotation angles of the robot joints.

## 4   Conclusions

To facilitate varied gait transitions in humanoid robots via a RL strategy, this paper introduces a control framework that integrates RL with adaptive motion functions. Within this framework, the motion functions for essential joints are predetermined prior to the training phase. These motion functions, in conjunction with the policy outputs, collaboratively dictate the final action commands executed by the robot during its training. Aiming to render the robot's movements smoother and more lifelike, the policy is employed to learn both the timing of the motion functions and the magnitude of the adjustment factor.

Our analysis revealed that incorporating the adjustment factor into the policy control results in higher rewards, signifying enhanced motion performance. Given the gait's periodic nature, both the motion period and the adjustment factor's variation throughout the motion cycle exhibit periodic patterns, and these two elements are interrelated. Additionally, the actual joint angles obtained can be repurposed as new motion functions in our proposed control framework, substantially boosting the efficiency of policy randomization. This methodology has been validated on a simulated humanoid robot named HIT. The physical counterpart of HIT is currently in the assembly stage, and we plan to apply our methods to the real robot upon its completion.

# References

1. Darvish, K., et al.: Teleoperation of humanoid robots: a survey. IEEE Trans. Robot. (2023)
2. Demir, K.A., Döven, G., Sezen, B.: Industry 5.0 and human-robot co-working. Procedia Comput. Sci. **158**, 688–695 (2019)
3. Saeedvand, S., et al.: A comprehensive survey on humanoid robot development. Knowl. Eng. Rev. **34**, e20 (2019)
4. Du, G., et al.: Online robot teaching with natural human–robot interaction. IEEE Trans. Industr. Electron. **65**(12), 9571–9581 (2018)
5. Kahraman, C., et al.: Fuzzy controlled humanoid robots: a literature review. Robot. Auton. Syst. **134**, 103643 (2020)
6. Fevre, M., Wensing, P.M., Schmiedeler, J.P.: Rapid bipedal gait optimization in CasADi. In: Proceedings of the 2020 IEEE/RSJ International Conference on Intelligent Robots and Systems (IROS). IEEE (2020)
7. Gasparri, G.M., et al.: Efficient walking gait generation via principal component representation of optimal trajectories: application to a planar biped robot with elastic joints. IEEE Robot. Autom. Lett. **3**(3), 2299–2306 (2018)
8. Kumar, M., Gautam, P., Semwal, V.B.: A review of computational model for bipedal robot walking using gait analysis. In: Proceedings of the 2020 International Conference on Emerging Smart Computing and Informatics (ESCI). IEEE (2020)
9. Li, B., Zhu, L., Huang, J.: Stable locomotion of biped robot with gaits of sinusoidal harmonics. IEEE Trans. Control Syst. Technol., 1–13 (2023)
10. Huan, T.T., et al.: Adaptive gait generation for humanoid robot using evolutionary neural model optimized with modified differential evolution technique. Neurocomputing **320**, 112–120 (2018)
11. Hu, C., et al.: An overview on bipedal gait control methods. IET Collaborative Intell. Manuf. **5**(3), e12080 (2023)
12. Xiong, X., Ames, A.: 3-d underactuated bipedal walking via h-lip based gait synthesis and stepping stabilization. IEEE Trans. Rob. **38**(4), 2405–2425 (2022)
13. Guo, Y., et al.: Fast online planning for bipedal locomotion via centroidal model predictive gait synthesis. IEEE Robot. Autom. Lett. **6**(4), 6450–6457 (2021)
14. Haldar, A.I., Pagar, N.D.: Predictive control of zero moment point (ZMP) for terrain robot kinematics. Mater. Today Proc. **80**, 122–127 (2023)
15. Murali, V., Hyun, N.-S.P., Verriest, E.I.: Graceful transitions between periodic walking gaits of fully actuated bipedal robots. In: Proceedings of the 2020 American Control Conference (ACC). IEEE (2020)
16. Xie, Z., Li, L., Luo, X.: Three-dimensional aperiodic biped walking including the double support phase using LIPM and LPM. Robot. Auton. Syst. **143**, 103831 (2021)
17. Safartoobi, M., Dardel, M., Daniali, H.M.: Gait cycles of passive walking biped robot model with flexible legs. Mech. Mach. Theory **159**, 104292 (2021)
18. Rodriguez, D., Behnke, S.: DeepWalk: Omnidirectional bipedal gait by deep reinforcement learning. In: Proceedings of the 2021 IEEE International Conference on Robotics and Automation (ICRA). IEEE (2021)
19. Siekmann, J., et al.: Sim-to-real learning of all common bipedal gaits via periodic reward composition. In: Proceedings of the 2021 IEEE International Conference on Robotics and Automation (ICRA) (2021)
20. Jeon, S.H., et al.: Benchmarking potential based rewards for learning humanoid locomotion. In: Proceedings of the 2023 IEEE International Conference on Robotics and Automation (ICRA), pp. 9204–9210 (2023)

21. Ye, L., et al.: From knowing to doing: learning diverse motor skills through instruction learning. arXiv preprint arXiv:2309.09167 (2023)
22. Castillo, G.A., et al.: Hybrid zero dynamics inspired feedback control policy design for 3D bipedal locomotion using reinforcement learning. In: Proceedings of the 2020 IEEE International Conference on Robotics and Automation (ICRA) (2020)
23. Dulac-Arnold, G., Mankowitz, D., Hester, T.: Challenges of real-world reinforcement learning. arXiv preprint arXiv:1904.12901 (2019)
24. Wang, H.-N., et al.: Deep reinforcement learning: a survey. Front. Inf. Technol. Electron. Eng. 21(12), 1726–1744 (2020)
25. Nguyen, T.T., Nguyen, N.D., Nahavandi, S.: Deep reinforcement learning for multiagent systems: a review of challenges, solutions, and applications. IEEE Trans. Cybern. 50(9), 3826–3839 (2020)

# Deterministic Learning-Based Knowledge Fusion Neural Control for Robot Manipulators with Predefined Performance

Qinchen Yang, Fukai Zhang[✉], Weitian He, and Cong Wang

The School of Control Science and Engineering, Shandong University, Jinan, China
yangqinchen@mail.sdu.edu.cn, {zhangfukai,wangcong}@sdu.edu.cn

**Abstract.** This paper introduces a novel deterministic learning (DL)-based knowledge fusion neural control strategy tailored for unknown robot manipulators with predefined performance. For two different control training scenarios, online fusion and offline fusion control schemes are proposed respectively. In the online knowledge fusion scheme, a collaborative control methodology is embraced, integrating a mechanism for propagating weight update information into the neural network (NN) learning algorithm of DL. This integration facilitates the eventual convergence of system weights across all operational systems toward a shared optimal value. For the offline fusion control scheme, it transforms the fusion problem of multi-trajectory closed-loop dynamics knowledge learned by deterministic learning (DL) into the least squares solution problem of a system of linear equations. Moreover, leveraging the fused dynamic knowledge acquired through the aforementioned approaches, we construct a neural network (NN) learning controller based on integrated knowledge to realize a multi-task intelligent control for robotic manipulators in intricate scenarios. The simulation section provides empirical evidence of the efficacy of the proposed approach.

**Keywords:** Deterministic learning · Knowledge fusion · Neural network · Adaptive neural control

## 1 Introduction

With the advancement of industrial automation today, research on high-performance control of robotic arm systems has received widespread attention due to their significant prospects in various fields of application [1,2]. Simultaneously considering the requirements for tracking performance (PP) in actual control processes, relevant predefined performance methods have also been proposed [3,4].

In recent decades, learning has emerged as a focal point of research within the realm of artificial intelligence. Particularly in intelligent control, notably in adaptive control and system identification, there exists a complex and significant research endeavor centered on achieving autonomous learning capabilities. In this context, learning typically entails the precise identification and approximation of obscure nonlinear dynamics or parameters inherent to the system.

Recently, the deterministic learning (DL) theory, as presented by Wang et al. [5], has unveiled that radial basis function (RBF) regression vectors along periodic or quasi-periodic recurrent trajectories consistently adhere to the condition of persistent excitation (PE). Drawing from this theoretical foundation, adaptive neural network control (ANNC) has been expanded to encompass intelligent learning control applications across diverse arrays of unknown nonlinear systems [6–8].

In the DL-based control scenarios mentioned above, the developed radial basis function neural networks (RBF NNs) excel in precisely identifying unknown nonlinear dynamics along individual recurrent trajectories. However, if the system trajectory strays from the vicinity of the single trajectory, the previously acquired dynamic knowledge may prove inadequate in providing accurate identifications for unknown nonlinear functions. Hence, there arises a need for deeper exploration into closed-loop learning and control issues within a broader approximation domain, as highlighted previously.

Henceforth, we present a novel topic on DL-based knowledge fusion NN control for robot manipulators with PP in this paper. This topic encompasses two distinct strategies: online knowledge fusion and offline knowledge fusion control. The online knowledge fusion control strategy adopts a collaborative learning control approach, wherein a pioneering NN learning control law is devised to converge multiple intelligent robotic systems operating under disparate reference trajectories to a shared optimal value. This facilitates precise closed-loop dynamic identification of unknown dynamics across multiple trajectories. On the other hand, the offline knowledge fusion control method transforms the fusion problem of closed-loop DL outcomes from independent trajectories into an optimal least squares solution problem of linear equation systems, thereby obtaining the fused NN knowledge representation. Subsequently, leveraging the constant value NN derived from fused knowledge, we construct a knowledge fusion learning controller (KFLC), which demonstrated the excellent performance of the robot manipulator systems in complex multi-task learning control scenarios in simulation experiments.

The primary contributions of this paper are as follows: 1) This paper proposes a knowledge fusion NN control method for robotic manipulators based on DL, which achieves a unified closed-loop dynamic NN representation in multi-task scenarios for robotic manipulators. 2) It realizes high-performance control of robotic manipulators under predefined performance, and further enhances the domain of knowledge representation for NNs. 3) By leveraging fused knowledge, an empirical controller is constructed, which further improves control performance.

## 2  Problem Formulation and Preliminaries

### 2.1  Problem Formulation

Consider the following $n$-link uncertain robot manipulator systems:

$$M(q_i)\ddot{q}_i + B(q_i, \dot{q}_i)\dot{q}_i + G(q_i) + F(\dot{q}_i) = \tau_i, \ i \in \{1, 2, \cdots, N\} \tag{1}$$

where $q_i, \dot{q}_i, \ddot{q}_i \in R^n$ represent the joint position, velocity and acceleration vector of the $i$-th robot manipulator; $N$ is the number of multi robot manipulators; $\tau_i \in R^n$ is the input torque vector; $M(q_i) \in R^{n \times n}$ is a known symmetric positive inertia matrix; $B(q_i, \dot{q}_i) \in R^{n \times n}$ denotes the unknown Coriolis matrix; $G(q_i) \in R^n$ is the unknown gravity force vector; and $F(\dot{q}_i) \in R^n$ is an unknown friction vector.

*Property 1.* The inertia matrix $M(q_i)$ is a positive definite and symmetric matrix, and there exist two bounded constants $\lambda_M > \lambda_m > 0$ which satisfy $\lambda_M I > M(q_i) > \lambda_m I$.

Define $X_{i,1} = q_i \in R^n$ and $X_{i,2} = \dot{q}_i \in R^n$ , so the original $n$-link robot manipulators (1) could be transformed into a state-space formulation as follows:

$$\begin{cases} \dot{X}_{i,1} = X_{i,2}, \\ \dot{X}_{i,2} = M^{-1}\tau_i - M^{-1}[F + G + BX_{i,2}] \\ Y = X_{i,1}. \end{cases} \tag{2}$$

Let $A(X_i) = -M^{-1}[F + G + BX_{i,2}]$ as the unknown nonlinear system dynamics, where $X_i = [X_{i,1}^T, X_{i,2}^T]^T \in R^{2n}$.
The system (2) can be rewritten into the following norm form:

$$\begin{cases} \dot{X}_{i,1} = X_{i,2}, \\ \dot{X}_{i,2} = M^{-1}\tau_i + A(X_i) \\ Y = X_{i,1}. \end{cases} \tag{3}$$

The reference systems are given as follows:

$$\begin{cases} \dot{X}_{d_{i1}} = X_{d_{i2}}, \\ \dot{X}_{d_{i2}} = F_d(X_{di}), \\ Y_{di} = X_{d_{i1}}, \end{cases} \tag{4}$$

where $X_{di} = [X_{d_{i1}}^T, X_{d_{i2}}^T]^T \in R^{2n}$; $Y_{di} \in R^n$ denotes the reference output of $i$-th controlled system; and $F_d(X_{di}) \in R^n$ is a known smooth nonlinear function vector. We suppose that $X_{di}$ $(i = 1, \cdots, N)$ are bounded and recurrent signals.

### 2.2  Some Important Lemmas

**Lemma 1.** *(Partial PE condition of RBF NNs) [9]: Given any continuous recurrent trajectory $Z(t)$. We assume that $Z(t)$ is a continuous mapping from*

$[0, \infty)$ to $\mathbb{R}^q$, and it remains within a bounded compact set $\Omega_Z$, where $\Omega_Z \subset \mathbb{R}^q$. For the radial basis function neural network (RBF NN) $W^T S(Z)$, where the centers are distributed on a regular lattice (sufficiently covering the compact set $\Omega_Z$), the regression subvector $S_\zeta(Z)$ is persistently exciting, comprised of RBFs with centers located in close proximity to $Z(t)$.

**Lemma 2.** *(Cooperative PE condition of RBF NNs) [10] Introduce the combined trajectory $Z(t) = \bigcup_{i=1}^{N} Z_i(t) = Z_1(t) \cup Z_2(t) \cup \cdots \cup Z_N(t)$. Assuming that all sub-trajectories $Z_i(t), i = 1, 2, \cdots, N$ are recurrent within a bounded compact set $\Omega_z$. If the neurons of the neural network (NN) are arranged in a regular lattice, covering the region $\Omega_z$ of the joint recurrent trajectory $Z(t)$, then the vector cluster formed by the regression sub-vectors $S_\zeta(Z_i(t)), i = 1, 2, \cdots, N$ along each individual recurrent sub-trajectory $Z_i(t)$ adheres to the cooperative persistent excitation (PE) condition. In other words, there exist two constants $T$ and $\beta$ such that*

$$\int_{t_0}^{t_0+T} \left[ \sum_{i=1}^{N} S_\zeta(Z_i(t)) S_\zeta^T(Z_i(t)) \right] dt \geq \beta I_\zeta, \ \forall t_0 > 0 \tag{5}$$

# 3  Knowledge Fusion Control Schemes via DL

In this section, we will provide two types of knowledge fusion-based neural control schemes for robotics with predefined performance, including online and offline schemes.

## 3.1  Online-Fusion Control Scheme

Define the tracing error of $i$-th robot:

$$E_i = X_{i,1} - X_{d_{i1}} = [e_{i1}, e_{i2}, \cdots, e_{in}]^T \in R^n \tag{6}$$

where $e_{il}$ denotes the tracking error of the $l$-th ($l \in \{1, 2, \cdots, n\}$) joint of the $i$-th robot.

To satisfy predefined performance requirements, it is imperative to ensure that the tracking error of the robotic manipulator remains within a predefined performance function during its operational phase, as follows:

$$- \underline{\delta}_l \beta_l(t) < e_{il} < \bar{\delta}_l \beta_l(t) \tag{7}$$

where $\underline{\delta}_l$, $\bar{\delta}_l$ are positive designed constants, and $\beta_l(t)$ is the predefined performance function which is monotonic and strictly decreasing.

$$\beta_l(t) = (\beta_{l0} - \beta_{l\infty})e^{-\alpha_i t} + \beta_{l\infty} \tag{8}$$

To achieve above process, an equivalent transformation is introduced as follows:

$$e_{il}(t) = \beta_l(t) T_l(z_{il}(t)) \tag{9}$$

where the transformation function $T_l(\cdot)$ should obey the followings properties:

*Property 2.* $\lim\limits_{z_{il} \to -\infty} T_l(z_{il}) = -\underline{\delta}_l$ and $\lim\limits_{z_{il} \to +\infty} T_l(z_{il}) = \bar{\delta}_l$

Therefore, the transformation function $T_l(\cdot)$ can be chosen as:

$$T_l(z_{il}) = \frac{\bar{\delta}_l e^{z_{il}} - \underline{\delta}_l e^{-z_{il}}}{e^{z_{il}} + e^{-z_{il}}} \tag{10}$$

Subsequently, the unconstrained error term $z_{il}$ can be obtained as

$$z_{il} = T^{-1}(e_{il}/\beta_l) = \frac{1}{2}\ln\frac{\underline{\delta}_l + e_{il}/\beta_l}{\bar{\delta}_l - e_{il}/\beta_l} \tag{11}$$

Further, we can obtain the derivative of $z_{il}$ as:

$$\dot{z}_{il} = \gamma_{il}[\dot{e}_{il} - \frac{\dot{\beta}_l}{\beta_l}e_{il}] \tag{12}$$

where $\gamma_{il} = \frac{1}{2\beta_l}[1/(\underline{\delta}_l + e_{il}/\beta_l) + 1/(\bar{\delta}_l - e_{il}/\beta_l)] > 0$.

Moreover, the overall error dynamics of the $i$-th robot can be expressed as:

$$\dot{Z}_i = \Upsilon_i(\dot{E}_i - \rho E_i) \tag{13}$$

where $Z_i = [z_{i1}, \cdots, z_{in}]^T \in R^n$ denotes the $n$-link errors of $i$-th robot after transformation; $\Upsilon_i = diag\{\gamma_{i1}, \gamma_{i2}, \cdots, \gamma_{in}\}$; and $\rho = diag\{\dot{\beta}_1/\beta_1, \cdots, \dot{\beta}_n/\beta_n\}$.

The filtered tracking error $Z_{si} = \Lambda Z_i + \dot{Z}_i$ (where $\Lambda$ is a positive diagonal constant matrix) and its dynamical process can be deduced as:

$$\dot{Z}_{si} = L_i - \Upsilon_i F_d(X_{di}) + \Upsilon_i[A(X_i) + M^{-1}\tau_i] \tag{14}$$

where $L_i = (\Lambda_i \Upsilon_i + \dot{\Upsilon}_i - \Upsilon_i \rho)\dot{E}_i - (\Lambda_i \Upsilon_i \rho + \dot{\Upsilon}_i \rho + \Upsilon_i \dot{\rho})E_i$, and $A(X_i)$ can be regarded as the unknown nonlinear dynamics and approximated by the following RBF NNs:

$$A(X_i) = W^{*T}S(X_i) + \epsilon_i \tag{15}$$

in (15), $\epsilon_i \in R^n$ denotes the approximation error, and $W^* = [W_1^*, \cdots, W_n^*] \in R^{m \times n}$ is the ideal NN weights matrix. The corresponding NN weights estimation error is defined as $\tilde{W}_i = \hat{W}_i - W^*$, where $\hat{W}_i = [\hat{W}_{i1}, \cdots, \hat{W}_{in}]$.

The adaptive NN control law is designed as:

$$u_i = M[-K_i Z_{si} - \hat{W}_i S(X_i) + F_d(X_{di}) - \Upsilon_i^{-1}L_i] \tag{16}$$

The cooperative learning law of $i$-th robot is designed as:

$$\dot{\hat{W}}_i = \Gamma(S(X_i)Z_{si}^T - \sigma_i \hat{W}_i) - \eta \sum_{j=1}^{N} a_{ij}(\hat{W}_i - \hat{W}_j) \tag{17}$$

where $\Gamma$, $\sigma_i$ and $\eta$ are all positive designed constants; $a_{ij} > 0$ denotes the communications equality coefficient between $i$-th and $j$-th robot system.

**Theorem 1.** *(Stability and tracking) Consider the multi-agent systems composed of system plant (1), reference system (4), the PP transformation function (10), the adaptive NN controller (16) and cooperative learning law (17). Starting from the initial conditions $X_i(0)$ residing in a compact set $\Omega_{i0}$ and with $\hat{W}_i(0) = 0$, it can be concluded that all closed-loop signals of each robot system are ultimately uniformly bounded (UUB). Furthermore, the outputs will converge to their respective reference signals within a finite period $T$.*

*Proof:* Consider the following Lyapunov function:

$$V = \frac{1}{2}\sum_{i=1}^{N} Z_{si}^T \Gamma_i^{-1} Z_{si} + \frac{1}{2}\sum_{i=1}^{N} \text{tr}[\tilde{W}_i^T \Gamma^{-1}\tilde{W}_i] \tag{18}$$

Further, we can obtain the derivative of (18)

$$\dot{V} = \sum_{i=1}^{N} Z_{si}^T \Upsilon_i^{-1}\dot{Z}_{si} + \frac{1}{2}\sum_{i=1}^{N} Z_{si}^T \dot{\Upsilon}_i^{-1} Z_{si} + \sum_{i=1}^{N}\text{tr}[\tilde{W}_i^T \Gamma^{-1}\dot{\tilde{W}}_i]$$

$$= \sum_{i=1}^{N}\left[-K_i Z_{si}^T Z_{si} + Z_{si}^T \epsilon_i + \frac{1}{2}Z_{si}^T \dot{\Upsilon}_i^{-1} Z_{si} - \text{tr}(\sigma_i \tilde{W}_i^T \hat{W}_i)\right] - \eta\Gamma^{-1}\text{tr}[\tilde{W}^T(\mathbb{L}\otimes I_m)\tilde{W}] \tag{19}$$

where $\mathbb{L}\in R^{N\times N}$ is symmetric matrix with $\mathbb{L}_{ij} = -a_{ij}(i\neq j)$, $\mathbb{L}_{ii} = \sum_{j=1}^{N} a_{ij}$, and $\tilde{W} = [\tilde{W}_1^T, \tilde{W}_2^T, \cdots, \tilde{W}_N^T]^T \in R^{Nm\times n}$.

In (19), we can observe that:

$$\begin{cases} \text{tr}[\tilde{W}^T(\mathbb{L}\otimes I_m)\tilde{W}] = \sum_{j=1}^{n}\tilde{W}_{\bar{j}}^T(\mathbb{L}\otimes I_m)\tilde{W}_{\bar{j}} > 0 \ (where \ \tilde{W}_{\bar{j}}^T = [\tilde{W}_{1j}^T, \cdots, \tilde{W}_{Nj}^T]) \\[2mm] Z_{si}^T \epsilon_i \leq \dfrac{\|Z_{si}\|^2}{2} + \dfrac{\epsilon^{*2}}{2} \\[2mm] \dfrac{1}{2}Z_{si}^T \dot{\Upsilon}_i Z_{si} \leq \dfrac{\lambda_{max}(\dot{\Upsilon}_i^{-1})}{2}\|Z_{si}\|^2 \\[2mm] \text{tr}[-\sigma_i \tilde{W}_i^T \hat{W}_i] \leq -\dfrac{\sigma_i}{2}\|\tilde{W}_i\|_F^2 + \dfrac{\sigma_i}{2}\|W^*\|_F^2 \end{cases} \tag{20}$$

Substituting (20) into (19), we have

$$\dot{V} \leq \sum_{i=1}^{N}\left[-K_i'\|Z_{si}\|^2 - \frac{\sigma_i}{2}\|\tilde{W}_i\|_F^2 + \frac{1}{2}\epsilon_i^2 + \frac{\sigma_i}{2}\|W^*\|_F^2\right] \tag{21}$$

where $-K_i' = -K_i + \frac{1}{2} + \frac{1}{2}\lambda_{max}(\dot{\Upsilon}_i^{-1})$.

Further, we have

$$\dot{V} \leq -aV + b \Rightarrow V \leq [V(0) - \varrho]e^{-at} + \varrho \tag{22}$$

where $a = \min\left\{-2K_i'/\lambda_{max}(\dot{\Upsilon}_i^{-1}), -\sigma_i/\Gamma^{-1}\right\}$, $b = \sum_{i=1}^{N}(\frac{1}{2}\epsilon_i^2 + \frac{\sigma}{2}\|W^*\|_F^2)$, and $\varrho = b/a$.

From (22), it can be concluded that all closed-loop signals are UUB and tracking errors of each robot keeps within small neighborhoods of zero in a finite time and satisfies the predefined performance boundary function limitation. Here, no further elaboration is necessary.

**Theorem 2.** *Consider the closed-loop system comprised of controlled systems (1), the reference system (4), the adaptive NN controller (16), and the NN weights update law (17). Given the initial conditions $X_i(0)$ and $\hat{W}_i(0)$ similar to Theorem 1, it can be concluded that all adaptive NN $\hat{W}_i$ ($i = 1, \cdots, N$) will converge to their common ideal values $W^*$, which means the fused NN after learning can give an accurate approximation of the unknown dynamics along different trajectories $\varphi(X_{di})$ ($i = 1, \cdots, N$).*

Firstly, consider the closed-loop system of $i$-th robot manipulator:

$$
\begin{cases}
\dot{Z}_{si} = \Upsilon_i(-K_i Z_{si} - \tilde{W}_i^T S(X_i) + \epsilon_i) \\
\dot{\hat{W}}_i = \Gamma(S(X_i)Z_{si}^T - \sigma_i \hat{W}_i) - \eta \sum_{j=1}^{N} a_{ij}(\hat{W}_i - \hat{W}_j)
\end{cases}
\tag{23}
$$

Further, introduce the state transformation $Q_{si} = \Upsilon_i^{-1} Z_{si}$ to eliminate the impact of affine term $\Upsilon_i$, then we have

$$
\begin{cases}
\dot{Q}_{si} = (-K_i + \dot{\Upsilon}_i^{-1})\Upsilon_i Q_{si} - \tilde{W}_{i\zeta}^T S_\zeta(X_i) + \epsilon_{i\zeta} \\
\dot{\hat{W}}_{i\zeta} = \Gamma_\zeta[S_\zeta(X_i)(\Upsilon_i Q_{si}^T - \sigma_i \hat{W}_{i\zeta})] - \eta \sum_{j=1}^{N} a_{ij}(\hat{W}_{i\zeta} - \hat{W}_{j\zeta})
\end{cases}
\tag{24}
$$

the above system (24) can be converted to the following LTV form:

$$
\begin{bmatrix}
\dot{Q}_{si} \\
\hline
\dot{\tilde{W}}_{i1\zeta} \\
\vdots \\
\dot{\tilde{W}}_{in\zeta}
\end{bmatrix}
=
\begin{bmatrix}
A_i(t) & B_i^T(t) \\
-C_i(t) & D_i(t)
\end{bmatrix}
\begin{bmatrix}
Q_{si} \\
\hline
\tilde{W}_{i1\zeta} \\
\vdots \\
\tilde{W}_{in\zeta}
\end{bmatrix}
+
\begin{bmatrix}
\epsilon_{i\zeta} \\
\hline
-\sigma_1 \Gamma_\zeta \hat{W}_{i1\zeta} \\
\vdots \\
-\sigma_n \Gamma_\zeta \hat{W}_{in\zeta}
\end{bmatrix}
\tag{25}
$$

where $A_i(t) = (-K_i + \dot{\Upsilon}_i^{-1})\Upsilon_i \in R^{n \times n}$, $B_i^T(t) = -\text{diag}\{S_\zeta^T, \cdots, S_\zeta^T\} \in R^{n \times m_\zeta n}$, $C_i(t) = -\Gamma_\zeta' S_\zeta' \Upsilon_i \in R^{m_\zeta n \times n}$ (where $\Gamma_\zeta' = \text{diag}\{\Gamma_\zeta, \cdots, \Gamma_\zeta\} \in R^{m_\zeta n \times m_\zeta n}$, $S_\zeta' = \text{diag}\{S_\zeta, \cdots, S_\zeta\} \in R^{m_\zeta n \times n}$), and $D(t) = -\eta \mathbb{L} \otimes I_{m_\zeta n}$.

Consider $N$-number of robot systems, we have

$$
\begin{bmatrix}
\dot{Q}_{s1} \\
\vdots \\
\dot{Q}_{sN} \\
\dot{\tilde{W}}_{11_\zeta} \\
\vdots \\
\dot{\tilde{W}}_{1n_\zeta} \\
\vdots \\
\dot{\tilde{W}}_{N1_\zeta} \\
\vdots \\
\dot{\tilde{W}}_{Nn_\zeta}
\end{bmatrix}
=
\begin{bmatrix}
A(t) & B^T(t) \\
-C(t) & D(t)
\end{bmatrix}
\begin{bmatrix}
Q_{s1} \\
\vdots \\
Q_{sN} \\
\tilde{W}_{11_\zeta} \\
\vdots \\
\tilde{W}_{1n_\zeta} \\
\vdots \\
\tilde{W}_{N1_\zeta} \\
\vdots \\
\tilde{W}_{Nn_\zeta}
\end{bmatrix}
+
\begin{bmatrix}
\epsilon_{1_\zeta} \\
\vdots \\
\epsilon_{N_\zeta} \\
-\sigma_1 \Gamma_\zeta \hat{W}_{11_\zeta} \\
\vdots \\
-\sigma_n \Gamma_\zeta \hat{W}_{1n_\zeta} \\
\vdots \\
-\sigma_1 \Gamma_\zeta \hat{W}_{N1_\zeta} \\
\vdots \\
-\sigma_n \Gamma_\zeta \hat{W}_{Nn_\zeta}
\end{bmatrix}
\tag{26}
$$

where $A(t) = \mathrm{diag}\{(-K_1 + \dot{\Upsilon}_1^{-1})\Upsilon_1, \cdots, (-K_N + \dot{\Upsilon}_N^{-1})\Upsilon_N\} \in R^{Nn \times Nn}$, $B^T(t) = \mathrm{diag}\{B_1^T, \cdots, B_N^T\} \in R^{Nn \times Nm_\zeta n}$, $C(t) = -\mathrm{diag}\{\Gamma_\zeta' S_\zeta' \Upsilon_1, \cdots, \Gamma_\zeta' S_\zeta' \Upsilon_N\} \in R^{Nm_\zeta n \times Nn}$, and $D(t) = -\eta \mathbb{L} \otimes I_{Nm_\zeta n}$.

Then, by choosing $P(t) = \mathrm{diag}\{\Upsilon_1, \cdots, \Upsilon_N\} \in R^{Nn \times Nn} > 0$ which satisfies $P(t)B^T(t) = C^T(t)$, we have

$$
\begin{aligned}
& A(t)^T P(t) + P(t)A(t) + \dot{P}(t) \\
& = \mathrm{diag}\{2(-K_1 \Upsilon_1^2 + \dot{\Upsilon}_1^{-1}\Upsilon_1^2) + \dot{\Upsilon}_1, \cdots, 2(-K_N \Upsilon_N^2 + \dot{\Upsilon}_N^{-1}\Upsilon_N^2) + \dot{\Upsilon}_N\}
\end{aligned}
\tag{27}
$$

Therefore, it can be concluded that if we choose proper control gain matrix $K_1, \cdots, K_n$, the above Eq. (27) can be guaranteed to be negative definite as $A(t)^T P(t) + P(t)A(t) + \dot{P}(t) < 0$.

According to [10], the nominal part of LTV system (26) can be guaranteed exponentially stable if the composite matrix $B(t)$ satisfies cooperative PE condition. This condition is represented as follows:

$$
\int_{t_0}^{t_0+T} B_i(t) B_i^T(t) dt \geq \alpha I_{m_\zeta n \times m_\zeta n}, \ \forall t_0 > 0
\tag{28}
$$

According to Lemma 1, the $S_\zeta(X_i)$ satisfies PE condition. Hence, it not difficult to find that the cooperative PE condition (28) also holds. The perturbation part of (26) can be made enough small by choosing proper $\sigma_i$. Combining the perturbation theory mentioned in [11], we can conclude that closed-loop error LTV system (26) will exponentially converge into small neighborhoods of zero.

Based on above analysis, we can obtain the fused knowledge representation of unknown system dynamics by:

$$
\bar{W}_i = mean_{t \in [t_{ia}, t_{ib}]} \hat{W}_i(t) = \frac{1}{t_{bi} - t_{ai}} \int_{t_{ia}}^{t_{ib}} \hat{W}_i(t)
\tag{29}
$$

in above Eq. (29), since the NN weights of all robots ultimately converge to a common optimal value $W^*$, the constant NN weights saved here can be used as an expression of the fused knowledge. Further, we have

$$A(\varphi_\varsigma) = \bar{W}_{i_\varsigma} S_\varsigma(\varphi_\varsigma) + \epsilon_{i_\varsigma} = \bar{W}_i S(\varphi_\varsigma) + \epsilon_{i'} \tag{30}$$

where $\varphi_\varsigma = \varphi(X_{d1}) \cup \cdots \cup \varphi(X_{dN})$, and $\epsilon_{i_\varsigma}$, $\epsilon_{i'}$ are close to $\epsilon_i$.

Subsequently, we utilize the knowledge obtained by closed-loop online-fusion scheme to constructed a knowledge-fusion learning controller as follows:

$$u_L = M[-K_i Z_{si} - \bar{W}_i S(X_i) + F_d(X_{di}) - \Upsilon_i^{-1} L_i] \tag{31}$$

*Remark 1.* Under the online knowledge fusion controller (31), it can achieve high-performance control with predefined performance for different control tasks (which can be regarded different reference trajectories $\varphi(X_{di})$ $(i = 1, \cdots, N)$). The stability and tracking proofs here are similar to Theorem 1 and are omitted here.

## 3.2   Offline-Fusion Control Scheme

From the previous introduction to the online-fusion control scheme, we can see that it requires multiple robots to run online at the same time, and factors such as information transmission time and reliability need to be considered. When the number of training trajectories increases, the number of neurons and computational resources, as well as runtime, increase accordingly.

In this subsection, an offline-fusion control scheme is proposed. This scheme includes two steps: 1) Single control task training; 2) Offline dynamical knowledge fusion.

Step 1): This step can be achieved with a single robot or multiple robots running in parallel. Here we present one of the methods. Similar to the definition in (3), we construct the same adaptive neural controller with PP as (16). The difference lies in that the NN updating rules and the learning rules in this subsection do not require communication terms:

$$\dot{\tilde{W}}_i = \Gamma(S(X_i) Z_{si}^T - \sigma_i \hat{W}_i) \tag{32}$$

Combining the state transformation $Q_{si} = \Upsilon_i^{-1} Z_{si}$, we can obtain the following LTV system for $i$-th control task:

$$\begin{bmatrix} \dot{Q}_{si} \\ \dot{\tilde{W}}_{i_\varsigma} \end{bmatrix} = \begin{bmatrix} A_i(t) & B_i^T(t) \\ -C_i(t) & 0 \end{bmatrix} \begin{bmatrix} Q_{si} \\ \tilde{W}_{i_\varsigma} \end{bmatrix} + \begin{bmatrix} \epsilon_{i_\varsigma} \\ -\bar{\sigma}\bar{\Gamma}_\varsigma \hat{W}_{i_\varsigma} \end{bmatrix} \tag{33}$$

where $\tilde{W}_{i_\varsigma} = [\tilde{W}_{1_\varsigma}^T, \cdots, \tilde{W}_{n_\varsigma}^T]^T$, $\bar{\sigma} = \mathrm{diag}\{\sigma_1, \cdots, \sigma_n\}$.

Choosing $P(t) = \Upsilon_i$, we have $A_i^T(t)P(t) + P(t)A_i(t) + \dot{P}(t) = 2(-K_i\Upsilon_i^2 + \Upsilon_i^{-1}\Upsilon_i^2) + \Upsilon_i$. Similarly, the above equation holds negative by selecting proper control gain $K_i$. According to [9] and Lemma 1, it can be conclude that LTV system (33) is exponentially stable. Then, we can obtain the dynamical knowledge along single trajectory $\varphi(X_{di})$ $i \in \{1, \cdots, N\}$ as:

$$\bar{W}_i = mean_{t \in [t_{i1}, t_{i2}]} \hat{W}_i(t) = \frac{1}{t_{i2} - t_{i1}} \int_{t_{i1}}^{t_{i2}} \hat{W}_i(t) \tag{34}$$

Then the closed-loop offline knowledge fusion issue can be converted to the following least square (LS) issue to find a optimal fused NN weight $W_f$ value along the union of trajectories $\varphi_\zeta = \varphi_\zeta(X_1) \cup \cdots \cup \varphi_\zeta(X_N)$:

$$\begin{cases} W_{f1}^T S(X_1) = \bar{W}_{11} S(X_1) + \epsilon'_{11} \\ W_{f1}^T S(X_2) = \bar{W}_{21} S(X_2) + \epsilon'_{21} \\ \quad \vdots \\ W_{f1}^T S(X_N) = \bar{W}_{N1} S(X_N) + \epsilon'_{N1} \end{cases}$$

$$\vdots \quad \text{(from 1 to $n$)}$$

$$\begin{cases} W_{fn}^T S(X_1) = \bar{W}_{1n} S(X_1) + \epsilon'_{1n} \\ W_{fn}^T S(X_2) = \bar{W}_{2n} S(X_2) + \epsilon'_{2n} \\ \quad \vdots \\ W_{fn}^T S(X_N) = \bar{W}_{Nn} S(X_N) + \epsilon'_{Nn} \end{cases} \tag{35}$$

If we consider $W_f = [W_{f1}, \cdots, W_{fn}]$ as the unknown variable to be solved, and $U = [U_1, \cdots, U_n] = [\bar{W}_{11} S(X_1), \cdots, \bar{W}_{N1} S(X_N), \cdots, \bar{W}_{1n} S(X_1), \cdots, \bar{W}_{Nn} S(X_N)]$ as the known output of above Eq. set (35). The regression matrix is denoted by $\bar{S} = [S(X_1), \cdots, S(X_N)]^T \in R^{N \times m}$. The offline fused NN weights $W_f$ can be obtain by the following Eq. [12]:

$$W_{fi} \approx \bar{S}^T \bar{S}_\zeta (\bar{S}_\zeta^T \bar{S} \bar{S}^T \bar{S}_\zeta)^{-1} \bar{S}_\zeta^T U_i \tag{36}$$

Subsequently, by utilizing the offline fused knowledge, an offline knowledge fusion controller is established as follows:

$$u_L = M[-K_i Z_{si} - W_f^T S(X_i) + F_d(X_{di}) - \Upsilon_i^{-1} L_i] \tag{37}$$

## 4   Simulation Studies

In this section, we apply the proposed method to a 2-link robot manipulator to validate its effectiveness.

The simulation system is given as follows:

$$M(q_i)\ddot{q}_i + V(q_i, \dot{q}_i)\dot{q}_i + G(q_i) = \tau_i, \tag{38}$$

where

$$M(q_i) = \begin{bmatrix} a + b\cos(q_{i2}) & c + b/2\cos(q_{i2}) \\ c + b/2\cos(q_{i2}) & c \end{bmatrix}$$

$$V(q_i, \dot{q}_i)\dot{q}_i = \begin{bmatrix} -b\sin(q_{i2})(\dot{q}_{i1}\dot{q}_{i2} + 0.5\dot{q}_{i2}^2) \\ 0.5b\sin(q_{i2})\dot{q}_{i1}^2 \end{bmatrix}$$

$$G(q_i) = \begin{bmatrix} d\cos(q_{i1}) + e\cos(q_{i2}) \\ e\cos(q_{i1} + q_{i2}) \end{bmatrix}$$

The vector $q_i = [q_{i1}, q_{i2}]^T$ signifies the positions of the joints in the $i$-th ($i \in \{1, \cdots, N\}$) robotic arm; $\tau_i = [\tau_{i1}, \tau_{i2}]^T$ is used to represent the vector of control inputs. Regarding the system's matrix, we have $a = l_2^2 m_2 + l_1^2(m_1 + m_2)$, $b = 2l_1 l_2 m_2$, $c = l_2^2 m_2$, $d = (m_1 + m_2)l_1 g$, and $e = m_2 l_2 g$. In this formulation, $l_j$ ($j \in \{1, 2\}$) denotes the length of the $j$-th link, $m_j$ ($j \in \{1, 2\}$) refers to the mass of the $j$-th link, and $g$ stands for the acceleration due to gravity. The parameters are chosen as follows: $m_1 = 0.8$ kg, $m_2 = 2.3$ kg, $l_1 = 1$ m, $l_2 = 1$ m, and $g = 9.8 m/s^2$.

The reference tracking model is selected as follows:

$$\begin{cases} \dot{X}_{d_{i1}} = X_{d_{i2}}, \\ \dot{X}_{d_{i2}} = F_{di}(X_{di}), \end{cases} \tag{39}$$

where $Y_{di} = X_{d_{i1}}$ denotes the desired output of $i$-th system. Here, we assume that the reference system (39) produces two different sets of reference trajectories, where $F_{d1} = [0.7\cos(t); 0.9\cos(t)]$, $F_{d2} = [0.8\cos(t); \cos(t)]$. The initial conditions are $X_{d_{11}} = X_{d_{12}} = [0, 0]^T$, and $X_{d_{21}} = X_{d_{22}} = [0, 0]^T$. The tracking errors are assumed to obey the following PP constraints:

$$-\underline{\delta}_l \beta_l(t) < e_{il} < \bar{\delta}_l \beta_l(t), \quad (i \in \{1, 2\}, l \in \{1, 2\}) \tag{40}$$

$$\beta_l(t) = (1.5 - 0.02)\exp^{-t} + 0.02, \quad l \in \{1, 2\} \tag{41}$$

where $\underline{\delta}_1 = 1, \underline{\delta}_2 = 0.8, \bar{\delta}_1 = 0.8, \bar{\delta}_2 = 1$.

The initial values are chosen as $q_1(0) = [0, 0]^T$, $\dot{q}_1(0) = [0, 0]^T$, $q_2(0) = [0, 0]^T$, $\dot{q}_2(0) = [0, 0]^T$, and $[\hat{W}_{11}(0), \hat{W}_{12}(0), \hat{W}_{21}(0), \hat{W}_{22}(0)] = [0, 0, 0, 0]^T$.

We construct the NNs with $N = 720$ nodes evenly distributed on $[-0.2, 1.6] \times [-0.5, 2] \times [-1, 1] \times [-1.5, 1]$, and the width $\eta = 0.5$. The NN weight update law's parameters are selected as $\sigma = 0.01$, $\Gamma = 6$. The control parameters are chosen as $\Lambda_1 = \Lambda_2 = \text{diag}\{2, 2\}$, $K_1 = K_2 = \text{diag}\{8, 10\}$.

The simulation results are shown in Figs. 1, 2, 3 4, 5, 6, 7, 8, 9 and 10. Figure 1 shows the different training reference trajectories for two joints of the robotic arm. Figures 2 and 3 illustrate the tracking errors of two joints of the robotic arm under predefined performance during online fusion control. From Fig. 4, it can be observed that the NNs of the two joints achieve convergence to their common weight. Figures 5 and 6 display the comparative control performance of the knowledge-based controller and the adaptive process after online fusion.

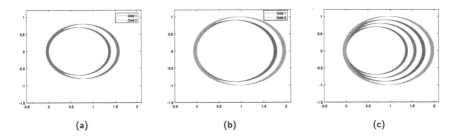

**Fig. 1.** The training reference orbits: (*a*) Joint 1; (*b*) Joint 2

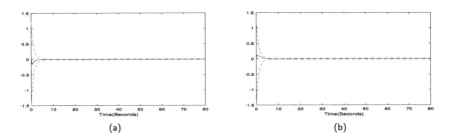

**Fig. 2.** The tracking errors of reference orbit 1: (*a*) Joint 1; (*b*) Joint 2

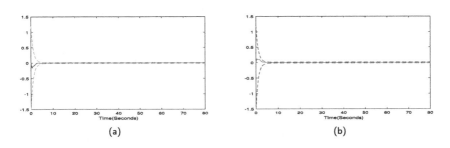

**Fig. 3.** The tracking errors of reference orbit 2: (*a*) Joint 1; (*b*) Joint 2

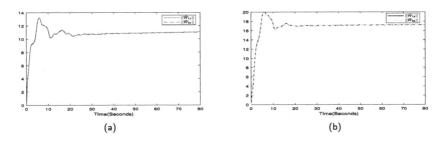

**Fig. 4.** The 2-norm of $||\hat{W}_i||$ along different orbits: (*a*) Joint 1; (*b*) Joint 2

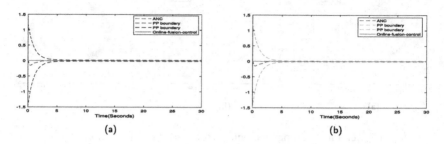

**Fig. 5.** The tracking error (Joint 1) comparison of online-fusion control (*a*) Orbit 1; (*b*) Orbit 2

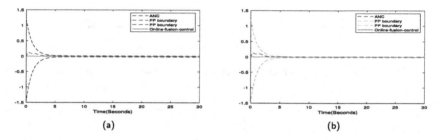

**Fig. 6.** The tracking error (Joint 2) comparison of online-fusion control (*a*) Orbit 1; (*b*) Orbit 2

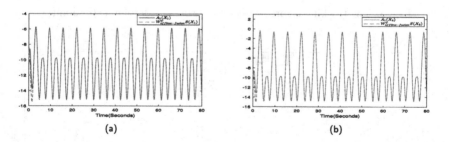

**Fig. 7.** The approximation of Joint 1 unknown function $A_1(\cdot)$ by Offline-fusion NN (*a*) Orbit 1; (*b*) Orbit 2

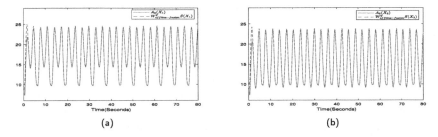

**Fig. 8.** The approximation of Joint 2 unknown function $A_2(\cdot)$ by Offline-fusion NN $(a)$ Orbit 1; $(b)$ Orbit 2

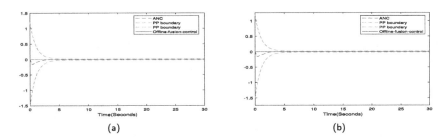

**Fig. 9.** The tracking error (Joint 1) comparison of offline-fusion control $(a)$ Orbit 1; $(b)$ Orbit 2

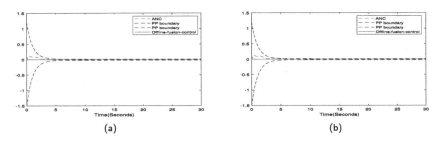

**Fig. 10.** The tracking error (Joint 2) comparison of offline-fusion control $(a)$ Orbit 1; $(b)$ Orbit 2

Compared to the online fusion approach, Figs. 7 and 8 demonstrate that NNs after offline fusion can accurately approximate the dynamics of different training orbits. The control performance of offline fusion knowledge-based controller is shown in Figs. 9 and 10.

## 5   Conclusion

This paper proposes a novel knowledge fusion-based NN control strategy for unknown $n$-link robot manipulators with predefined performance. The strategy encompasses both on-line and off-line knowledge fusion NN control schemes. By expanding the domain of knowledge representation for NNs, the developed knowledge fusion-based learning controller exhibits enhanced control performance in challenging multi-task control scenarios. Simulation results corroborate the efficacy of the proposed approach.

**Funding.** This work was supported by the National Natural Science Foundation of China (62203262.62350083): Natural Science Foundation of Shandong Province (ZR2022QF124).

## References

1. Visioli, A., Legnani, G.: On the trajectory tracking control of industrial SCARA robot manipulators. IEEE Trans. Industr. Electron. **49**(1), 224–232 (2002)
2. Wang, L., Meng, B.: Distributed force/position consensus tracking of networked robotic manipulators. IEEE/CAA J. Automatica Sin. **1**(2), 180–186 (2014)
3. Bechlioulis, C.P., Rovithakis, G.A.: Robust adaptive control of feedback linearizable MIMO nonlinear systems with prescribed performance. IEEE Trans. Autom. Control **53**(9), 2090–2099 (2008)
4. Wang, M., Wang, C., Liu, X.: Dynamic learning from adaptive neural control with predefined performance for a class of nonlinear systems. Inf. Sci. **279**, 874–888 (2014)
5. Wang, C., Hill, D.J.: Learning from neural control. IEEE Trans. Neural Netw. **17**(1), 130–146 (2006). vs. pace0mm
6. Li, D., Han, H., Qiao, J.: Deterministic learning-based adaptive neural control for nonlinear full-state constrained systems. IEEE Trans. Neural Netw. Learn. Syst. **34**(8), 5002–5011 (2021)
7. Guo, Y., Bin, X.: Finite-time deterministic learning command filtered control for hypersonic flight vehicle. IEEE Trans. Aerosp. Electron. Syst. **58**(5), 4214–4225 (2022)
8. Zhao, Z., He, W., Zhang, F., Wang, C., Hong, K.-S.: Deterministic learning from adaptive neural network control for a 2-DOF helicopter system with unknown backlash and model uncertainty. IEEE Trans. Industr. Electron. **70**(9), 9379–9389 (2022)
9. Wang, C., Hill, D.J.: Deterministic Learning Theory for Identification, Recognition, and Control. CRC Press (2009)
10. Chen, W., Hua, S., Zhang, H.: Consensus-based distributed cooperative learning from closed-loop neural control systems. IEEE Trans. Neural Netw. Learn. Syst. **26**(2), 331–345 (2014)
11. Khalil, H.K.: Nonlinear Systems Third Edition (2002)
12. Weiming, W., Jingtao, H., Zhu, Z., Zhang, F., Juanjuan, X., Wang, C.: Deterministic learning-based neural identification and knowledge fusion. Neural Netw. **169**, 165–180 (2024)

# Research on Human Lower Limb Gait Time Series Prediction Method Based on CNN and LSTM

Shuai Fan[1(✉)], Huiyong Luo[1], Yao Xiao[1], Ye Liang[1], Zelin Su[1],
Guangkui Song[2], and Peng Chen[3]

[1] School of Mechanical and Electrical Engineering,
Chengdu University of Technology, Chengdu 610059, China
fansuai12345@163.com
[2] Center for Robotics, University of Electronic Science and Technology of China,
Chengdu 611731, China
[3] College of Engineering, Shantou University, Shantou 515063, China

**Abstract.** In this paper, a human lower limb gait information prediction method based on a fusion of convolutional neural network (CNN) and long short-term memory network (LSTM) is proposed to solve the problem that lower limb rehabilitation exoskeleton cannot smoothly and accurately follow the movement of human lower limbs during the training process. The method first uses CNN to process the spatial features of human gait data, and extracts local features with spatial relationships through convolution and pooling operations. Then, the output of the CNN is passed to the LSTM for temporal dependency processing to capture the sequential pattern and evolutionary law of the motion for the prediction of the next gait state. In the experiments, a CNN-LSTM neural network model was built using Matlab to construct a dataset with the collected lower limb posture data, and the gait categories were used as the output for validation. The experimental results show that the method performs well in gait prediction assessment, and all predicted trajectories are strongly correlated with the measured trajectories with $R^2$ greater than 0.999. Future research could further optimize the structure and parameter settings of the neural network model.

**Keywords:** Rehabilitation exoskeleton · Long short-term memory network · Convolutional neural network · Gait prediction

## 1 Introduction

Lower body trajectory and gait phase prediction are critical for controlling lower extremity exoskeletons that require assistance. Lower extremity rehabilitation exoskeletons are devices that can assist in the rehabilitation of patients with lower extremity dysfunction [1]. In recent years, rehabilitation devices such as lower extremity rehabilitation exoskeletons have developed rapidly as the number of patients with lower extremity disorders caused by aging populations and

X. Lan et al. (Eds.): ICIRA 2024, LNAI 15208, pp. 189–201, 2025.
https://doi.org/10.1007/978-981-96-0783-9_14

strokes has increased [2]. In the rehabilitation process of lower limb rehabilitation exoskeleton, the smoothness of human-computer interaction has always been a major challenge, and the key to solving this challenge is the accurate prediction of human lower limb gait.

Both model-based and machine-learning approaches have been extensively studied in motion trajectory prediction [3], and the method has emerged as a viable approach for gait trajectory prediction because such methods are based on large amounts of data and are independent of biomechanical models and cost functions [4]. Many studies treat gait trajectory data as a time series, in actuality such that the prediction of gait trajectories is essentially time series prediction, where a sequence of future values is predicted based on a sequence of past observations [5–7]. A number of artificial neural network based methods have been developed to estimate the parameters of the gait phase [8–10]. Liu et al. [11] used deep spatio-temporal modelling to assist patients with knee injuries by analysing historical gait trajectories of other joints in healthy subjects and generating knee trajectories one frame in advance on a lower limb exoskeleton device. This approach can provide better support and recovery for patients.Zaroug et al. [12] used an LSTM autoencoder to predict linear acceleration and angular velocity in lower limb kinematic trajectories with a correlation coefficient of 0.98, showing high measurement and prediction accuracy. Liu et al. [13] proposed a neural network model that accurately detects eight gait phases offline. The accuracy of the model ranged from 87.2% to 94.5%, providing an effective tool for gait analysis. Moreira et al. [14] used a long short-term Memory (LSTM) model to generate reference ankle torques for a healthy person walking on a level surface. They achieved a low normalised root mean square error of 4.31% and demonstrated the potential of integrating LSTM into the control of robotic assistive devices. Ren et al. [15] proposed a neural network and LSTM machine learning model for predicting the actual trajectory of human lower limbs. They also designed a wearable joint angle measurement device for gait trajectory prediction and control using a machine learning approach. This method has been validated in the simulation phase, but further research is still needed for accurate gait trajectory prediction with lower limb exoskeleton motion information.

The aim of this paper is to investigate gait features and propose a gait prediction method for lower limb exoskeletons based on fused LSTM and CNN structures to deeply extract spatio-temporal characteristics of gait features. By collecting acceleration, stance angle and angular velocity data of lower limb motion during normal walking, we construct a dataset for training and validation. CNN-LSTM neural network model built on Matlab platform was used to implement gait prediction. The innovation of this study is to combine LSTM and CNN to effectively integrate spatial features and temporal dependencies. With this method, the lower limb exoskeleton can follow the human lower limb movement more smoothly and accurately during rehabilitation training, providing more effective rehabilitation. This is important for improving the control and application of rehabilitation exoskeletons.

## 2    CNN-LSTM Model Design and Optimization

### 2.1    CNN Network Structure

CNN is a feed-forward neural network with convolutional operations and deep structure, commonly used in image processing and natural language processing. Similar to basic neural networks, CNN are biologically inspired by feed-forward artificial neural networks [16]. Each hidden CNN layer consists of a convolutional layer and a pooling layer. The last layer of a CNN is usually a fully connected layer used for data classification.

Figure 1 shows the overall architecture of a CNN, which consists of three types of layers: convolutional, pooling and fully connected. Even numbered layers are used for convolution while odd numbered layers are used for pooling. The output nodes of the convolutional and pooling layers are combined to form a feature graph.

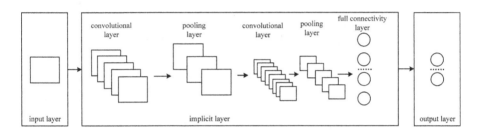

**Fig. 1.** CNN model architecture

### 2.2    LSTM Network Structure

In recent years, LSTM has been widely used in many fields of speech recognition, sentiment analysis, and text analysis [17,18]. LSTM constitutes the lower layer of the model proposed in this paper. This layer stores the temporal information of important attributes of EMG signals. This layer contains memory channels and gate mechanisms, i.e., forget gate, input gate, update gate, and output gate. The LSTM model architecture is shown in Fig. 2.

Cell states($c_{t-1} - c_t$) are the basis of LSTM design. The cell state holds the hidden state information for the current time. The hidden state information includes the hidden state of the previous time step and the temporary hidden state of the current time step. In addition, LSTM includes a unique gate structure for removing or adding information to the cell state.

The first step in LSTM is to decide what information to discard from the cell state. This decision is made by an oblivion gate. The oblivion gate reads the output information from the previous moment and the input information from the current moment and outputs a value between 0 and 1 for each cell state

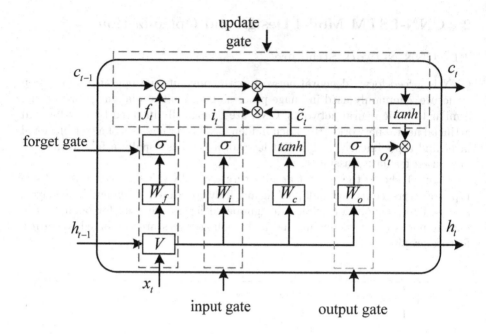

**Fig. 2.** LSTM model architecture

number 1 means completely retained and 0 means completely discarded. The expression is as follows:

$$f_t = \sigma\left(W_f \cdot [h_{t-1}, x_t] + b_f\right) \tag{1}$$

The next step is for the input gate to determine what new information can be added to the cell state. First, a sigmoid layer called the input gate determines the value $i_t$ to be updated. second, each $tanh_h$ layer generates a vector $\tilde{c}_t$ that can be updated instead. These two components are combined to update the cell state.

$$i_t = \sigma(W_i \cdot [h_{t-1}, x_t] + b_i) \tag{2}$$

$$\tilde{c}_t = \tanh(W_i \cdot [h_{t-1}, x_t] + b_g) \tag{3}$$

The function of the update gate is then to convert the old cell data $c_{t-1}$ multiplied by the $f_t$ obtained from the forgetting gate to the new cell data $c_t$. The update gate selects a portion of the old cell information for erasure by the forget gate. The input gate then selects a portion of the candidate cell information to be combined with the new cell information $c_t$. The expression is as follows:

$$c_t = f_t \odot c_{t-1} + i_t \odot \tilde{c}_t \tag{4}$$

Finally, after updating the unit state, the state of the output unit needs to be determined from the input values $h_{t-1}$ and $x_t$. The unit state is transmitted through the t-layer to obtain a vector of values between $[-1,1]$, which are multiplied by the judgment criteria of the output gate to produce the output of the unit.

$$o_t = \sigma \left( W_o \cdot [h_{t-1}, x_t] + b_o \right) \qquad (5)$$

$$h_t = \sigma \left( W_f \cdot [h_{t-1}, x_t] + b_f \right) \qquad (6)$$

where $W_f$, $W_i$, $W_g$, $W_t$ denote cyclic weight matrices, $b_f$, $b_i$, $b_g$, $b_t$ denotes the bias vector, $\sigma$ denotes the Sigmoid activation function, $tan_h$ denotes the hyperbolic tangent activation function, $\odot$ denotes the elementwise multiplication, $x_t$ is the input to the LSTM unit, and $h_t$ is the hidden vector of the time of $t$.

## 2.3 CNN-LSTM Model Optimization Strategy

In this study, by integrating CNN and LSTM, we propose a new deep learning scheme. The feature sequences of the CNN layer are considered as inputs to the LSTM. The CNN-LSTM structure proposed in this paper is shown in Fig. 3. Human lower limb joint angle, acceleration and angular velocity trajectory vectors are used as input vectors to the CNN-LSTM network. The predicted joint motion trajectories are the output vectors of the CNN-LSTM.

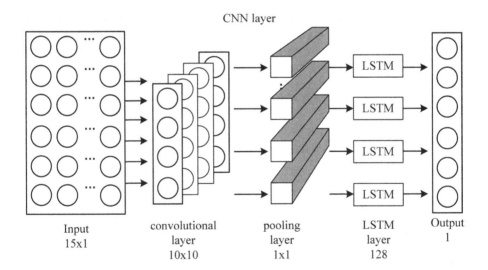

**Fig. 3.** CNN-LSTM model architecture

The hybrid CNN-LSTM prediction model mainly consists of convolutional layer, pooling layer, LSTM layer and fully connected layer. First, the feature data containing human lower limb motion trajectories are formed into a matrix, where each sample forms a row and the feature data are arranged in time series. The time-distributed layer constructed in this way can maintain the dynamic time-order relationship, and CNN deep feature extraction is performed on this basis.

Next, the multi-scale features are fused by operations such as CNN convolution and pooling to remove interference and noise information. The processed time series data are then fed into the LSTM layer. During the training process, the output values and error terms of each LSTM unit are calculated by iteration, and the model parameters are continuously updated until the error converges or the maximum number of iterations is reached. Finally, the prediction results of the human lower limb motion trajectory prediction model are validated using data from a pre-segmented test set and the model performance is evaluated.

## 2.4   Parameter Optimization

The Adaptive Moment Estimation (Adam) algorithm is a commonly used optimization algorithm for training neural networks. It combines gradient descent and momentum methods and adaptively adjusts the learning rate based on the first-order moment estimate and second-order moment estimate of the gradient. Below is the formula and operation of Adam's algorithm.

- Initialize the parameters: $\alpha$ is the learning rate, which is used to control the step size of the parameter update. $m$ is a first-order moment variable (mean gradient), initialized to a zero vector, which is used to store the first-order moment estimate of the gradient. $v$ is a second-order moment variable (square of the mean gradient), initialized to a zero vector, which is used to store the second-order moment estimate of the gradient. $\beta_1$ and $\beta_2$ are the decay rates that control the first-order moments and second-order moments. Assume that the parameter is $W$, the iteration step is $t$, and $f(W)$ is a stochastic objective function with parameter $W$.
- In each training iteration, compute the gradient $g_t$ as follow:

$$g_t = \nabla_W f_t(W_{t-1}) \tag{7}$$

- Update the first-order moment variable $m$ and the second-order moment variable $v$ at the current moment in time:

$$m_t = \beta_1 \cdot m_{t-1} + (1 - \beta_1) \cdot g_t \tag{8}$$

$$v_t = \beta_2 \cdot v_{t-1} + (1 - \beta_2) \cdot g_t^2 \tag{9}$$

- Correcting for bias in the estimation of first-order moment and second-order moment variables:

$$\hat{m}_t = \frac{m_t}{1 - \beta_1^t} \tag{10}$$

$$\hat{v}_t = \frac{v_t}{1 - \beta_2^t} \tag{11}$$

- Updating parameters:

$$W_t = W_{t-1} - \alpha \cdot \frac{\hat{m}_t}{\sqrt{\hat{v}_t} + \varepsilon} \tag{12}$$

where $\varepsilon$ is a very small number for numerical stability.

- Repeat Eq.(7), (8), (9), (10) and (11) until the stopping condition is reached, the maximum number of iterations is reached or the preset error threshold is reached.

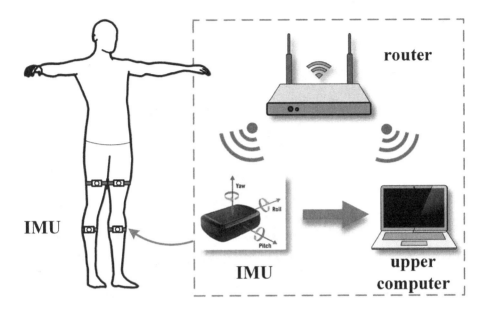

**Fig. 4.** Acquisition Systems

# 3   Experiments and Experimental Results

## 3.1   Data Collection and Processing

Twelve subjects (6 males and 6 females) were recruited from the student population. They were between 20 and 30 years of age and were physically fit. Each subject walked on a flat surface at a pace suitable for them. Data were collected for 20–30 seconds per walking distance for a total of 8–15 gait cycles per person. The order of distances in data collection was randomized. Subjects were equipped with two IMUs (WT901-WIFI), which were secured to the thighs and calves with straps, and gait angle trajectories were acquired directly from the IMU sensors. Data were collected at 2000 Hz and downsampled to 50 Hz to reduce computational load. The IMUs were calibrated before each acquisition. The IMU data came from 2 IMUs and 9 channels of 18 variables, i.e., acceleration, angular velocity, and angle in the three-axis direction. The data acquisition system is shown in Fig. 4.

To improve the convergence process, the data were standardized. First, the mean and standard deviation of the data were calculated and they were used to standardize the data. The Z-score standardization method is used, and the standardized data eliminates the magnitude and scale differences between different features, making them have similar scales.

$$\mu = \frac{1}{n} \sum_{i=1}^{n} x_i \tag{13}$$

$$\sigma = \sqrt{\frac{1}{n} \sum_{i=1}^{n} (x_i - \mu)^2} \tag{14}$$

where $\mu$ denotes the mean, $\sigma$ denotes the standard deviation, $n$ denotes the number of data samples, and $x_i$ denotes the $i$th data sample.

$$x_{norm} = \frac{x - \mu}{\sigma} \tag{15}$$

where $x_{norm}$ denotes the normalized data and $x$ denotes the original data.

Next, a matrix transformation is applied to the normalized data. The matrix transformation serves to recombine the data in the feature space through a linear transformation in order to better capture the relationships between the features. Such a matrix transformation extracts more informative features, which helps to improve the performance and predictive accuracy of the model.

Using the matrix transformed data, one-dimensional column vectors or metrics can be created with a length equal to the size of the lagged training set. Such vectors or metrics preserve the temporal relationships of time-series data, enabling the model to take into account historical information about the data. This form of lagged representation of the data helps the model to better understand the dynamic properties of the data and provide more accurate predictions.

In summary, by normalizing the data and then performing a matrix transformation, a more informative representation of the features can be obtained. Using the matrix-transformed data to create one-dimensional column vectors or metrics that lag the size of the training set preserves the temporal relationships of the data and provides the model with more accurate historical information, which improves the performance of the predictive model and the convergence process.

Based on the samples collected from the above data, we do two types of experiments respectively, one is the experiment of comparing different prediction models, and the other is the validation experiment of comparing different learning rates under the CNN-LSTM prediction model. We use the walking gait data from our own collected database as the data source for analysis and use MATLAB 2022a to construct the CNN-LSTM prediction model.

For the CNN-LSTM model, it is defined as follows. The number of input features and the number of output responses are 1800, and the training solver is set to 500 training rounds. To prevent gradient explosion, we set the gradient trimming threshold to 1. The initial learning rate is 0.005, which is attenuated by multiplying a reduction factor of 0.2 after every 250 rounds of training.

The dataset contains information on the angles, accelerations and angular velocities of the human lower limb joints in the experiment, including the right hip, right knee, left hip and left knee. First of all, the training data must be normalized to a mean value dataset to prevent training dispersion. After pre-processing operation to remove abnormal data from the collected data, the data in the middle section of the traveling process is selected and saved, and a total of 1800 sample data are obtained.

The sample data is divided into two parts, the training set and the test set, in a ratio of 4:1, and the test set is used to evaluate the prediction effect of the CNN-LSTM neural network model. Our goal is to use past human lower limb joint angles, acceleration and angular velocity trajectories to predict each trajectory at the next time step, where we define the prediction time step as 1 sample point.

### 3.2   Experimental Results

We conducted model comparison experiments on the motor gait data of the right leg hip and knee joints of human lower limbs. We used three neural network prediction models, LSTM, CNN and CNN-LSTM, and compared the performance In the experiments, the total number of prediction samples for each prediction model was 1800, of which the training set accounted for 80% and the test set accounted for 20%. We set the maximum number of iterations to 500, and used the Adam gradient descent algorithm with an initial learning rate of 0.005 for model parameter optimization. For evaluation metrics, we chose root mean square error (RMSE), $R^2$(R-squared), maximum and minimum errors, and error rate as the evaluation metrics for model performance. RMSE measures the magnitude of the error between the predicted value and the true value, $R^2$ measures the extent to which the model explains the variability of the observed data, maximum and minimum errors reflect the maximum and minimum deviation of the model in the prediction process, and the error rate is a measure of the difference between the predicted results and the true value, which is used to assess the accuracy or precision of the prediction model. The RMSE calculation formula is as follows:

$$RMSE = \sqrt{\frac{1}{n}\sum_{i=1}^{n}\left(y_{pred} - y_{true}\right)^2} \qquad (16)$$

where $n$ denotes the number of samples, $y_{pred}$ denotes the predicted value, and $y_{true}$ denotes the true value.

The formula for $R^2$ is given below:

$$R^2 = 1 - \frac{\sum_{i=1}^{n}\left(y_{true} - y_{pred}\right)^2}{\sum_{i=1}^{n}\left(y_{true} - \bar{y}_{true}\right)^2} \qquad (17)$$

where $\bar{y}_{true}$ denotes the average of the true values. $R^2$ takes values ranging from 0 to 1, with values closer to 1 indicating a better fit of the model to the data, and values closer to 0 indicating a poorer fit of the model to the data.

The formulae for the maximum and minimum errors are as follows:

$$Minimum\_Error = \min(|y_{true} - y_{pred}|) \qquad (18)$$

$$Maximum\_Error = \max(|y_{true} - y_{pred}|) \qquad (19)$$

The formula for calculating the error rate is as follows:

$$Rate\_Error = \frac{1}{n}\sum_{i=1}^{n}\left|\frac{P^{(i)} - T^{(i)}}{T^{(i)}}\right| \times 100\% \qquad (20)$$

where $n$ denotes the number of samples in the data set, $P^{(i)}$ denotes the predicted value of the $i$th sample, and $T^{(i)}$ denotes the true value of the $i$th sample.

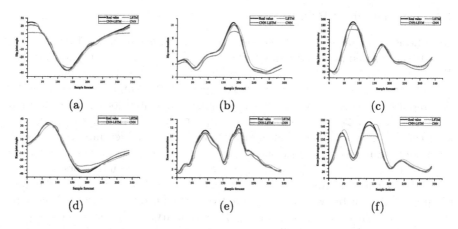

(a)     (b)     (c)

(d)     (e)     (f)

**Fig. 5.** Predictive effectiveness of three neural network prediction models, LSTM, CNN and CNN-LSTM:(a) Hip angle comparison curve (b) Hip acceleration comparison curve (c) Hip joint angular velocity comparison curve (d) Knee angle comparison curve (e) Knee acceleration comparison curve (f) Knee joint angular velocity comparison curve

The prediction results of the three neural network prediction models are shown in Fig. 5. The experimental results show that the method performs well in gait prediction results, and all the predicted trajectories are strongly correlated with the measured trajectories, and the square of the correlation coefficient is greater than 0.99. The network structure integrating CNN and LSTM enables the whole network to better understand and predict the gait information of human lower limbs. By extracting spatial features through CNN and capturing temporal dependencies through LSTM, this method can effectively solve the lower limb exoskeleton following problem and provide a more accurate gait prediction and control method for rehabilitation training.

Learning rate is the most critical parameter in neural networks and has the most obvious impact. In this experiment, we aim to evaluate the performance of the CNN-LSTM algorithm in terms of prediction accuracy by adjusting the learning rate. We set eight different values of learning rate Respectively, $R_1 = 0.4$, $R_2 = 0.3$, $R_3 = 0.2$, $R_4 = 0.1$, $R_5 = 0.05$, $R_6 = 0.005$, $R_7 = 0.0005$, $R_8 = 0.00005$, and recorded the prediction accuracy of the model under each learning rate.

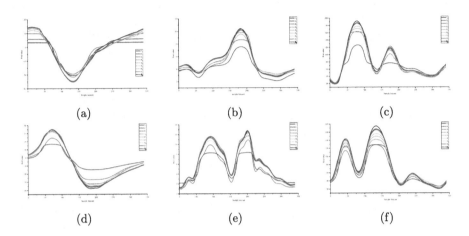

(a)          (b)          (c)

(d)          (e)          (f)

**Fig. 6.** Prediction effect of CNN-LSTM model under different learning rates:(a) Hip angle (b) Hip acceleration (c) Hip joint angular velocity (d) Knee angle (e) Knee acceleration (f) Knee joint angular velocity

As shown in Fig. 6, we find that in most cases, the best prediction is achieved with a learning rate of $R_6 = 0.005$. However, for the hip and knee acceleration metrics, we observed better predictions at a learning rate of than at a learning rate of $R_7 = 0.0005$. This suggests that a lower learning rate better captures the patterns and variations in joint acceleration, thus improving the accuracy of the predictions. However, for the other joint angles and angular velocities as well as the knee angle metrics, we found that the best prediction rate was achieved with a learning rate of $R_6 = 0.005$. This means that in these cases, higher learning rates are more effective in capturing patterns in joint angles and angular velocities, thus improving prediction accuracy.

In this experimental setup, a lower learning rate plays a key role in improving the prediction performance of the model, and a higher learning rate may result in the model not being able to converge sufficiently during the training process, thus affecting the prediction accuracy. On the contrary, a lower learning rate can better control the updating speed of the model parameters to better adapt to the training data, which in turn improves the prediction accuracy of the model. In addition to the learning rate, other factors may also have an impact on the experimental results. For example, the characteristics of the dataset, the choice of model architecture, and the hyper-parameter settings during the training process may have an impact on the performance of the model. Therefore, in further research, we should consider these factors comprehensively and conduct more in-depth analysis and exploration.

## 4    Conclusion

CNN-LSTM neural network realizes the principle prediction of time series before and after relationship through its own excellent regular periodic prediction characteristics, therefore, the prediction of the persistence and stability of the gait planning of the lower limb exoskeleton rehabilitation robot in the gait rehabilitation training of the lower limb is very much in line with its prediction characteristics. According to the time series of walking joint motion angles in one cycle of gait rehabilitation training of the rehabilitation robot, the CNN-LSTM neural network prediction method can be used to accurately predict the time series of joint motion angles in multiple gait cycles. The ability of this CNN-LSTM network to predict future gait trajectories can be applied to the design of an exoskeleton controller that better compensates for system delays to smooth the transition between gait phases.

Future research could further optimize the structure and parameter settings of the neural network model, explore additional gait feature extraction methods, and further validate the method in practical clinical applications. This study will provide useful guidance and insights for the development and application of rehabilitation exoskeletons for human lower limbs.

**Acknowledgments.** The authors gratefully acknowledge the financial support that is provided by the Natural Science Foundation of China (52005082, 52105111), Sichuan Science and Technology Program (2023NSFSC0866), the Basic and Applied Basic Research Foundation of Guangdong Province through Grant 2022A1515010859, the Guangdong Provincial Science and Technology Special Fund Project through Grant STKJ2021171, and the Shantou University (STU) Scientific Research Initiation Grant through Grant NTF21029.

## References

1. Zheng, Y., Ma, C., Wu, Z., Shi, Y., Xiao, M.: Kinematic characteristics analysis of wearable lower limb rehabilitation exoskeleton robot based on ADAMS. Int. J. Mech. Appl. Mech. **2023**(13), 184–192 (2023)
2. Yang, Y., Lu, J.: Effect of lower limb exoskeleton robot on walking function of stroke patients, vol. 14269, pp. 554–563. Hangzhou, China (2023). https://doi.org/10.1007/978-981-99-6489-5_45
3. Su, B., Gutierrez-Farewik, E.M.: Gait trajectory and gait phase prediction based on an LSTM network. Sensors (Switzerland) **20**(24), 1–17 (2020)
4. Huang, Y., An, H., Ma, H., Wei, Q.: Modeling and individualizing continuous joint kinematics using gaussian process enhanced fourier series. IEEE Trans. Neural Syst. Rehabil. Eng. **31**, 779–788 (2023)

5. Huang, Y., Yang, L., Lin, Z.: Gait synergy modeling and joint angle prediction based on LSTM, pp. 166–170. Hybrid, Mianyang, China (2023)

6. Park, T.G., Kim, J.Y.: Real-time prediction of walking state and percent of gait cycle for robotic prosthetic leg using artificial neural network. Intel. Serv. Robot. **15**(4), 527–536 (2022)

7. Saoud, L.S., Hussain, I.: TempoNet: empowering long-term knee joint angle prediction with dynamic temporal attention in exoskeleton control. In: 2023 IEEE-RAS 22nd International Conference on Humanoid Robots (Humanoids), pp. 1–8 (2023)

8. Narayan, J., Abbas, M., Patel, B., Dwivedy, S.K.: Adaptive RBF neural network-computed torque control for a pediatric gait exoskeleton system: an experimental study. Intel. Serv. Robot. **16**(5), 549–564 (2023)

9. Lee, J., Malik, I., Thien, A.C.L., Sivakumar, S.: Lower limb gait estimation using foot motion and neural network. In: 2023 International Conference on Digital Applications, Transformation & Economy (ICDATE), pp. 1–7 (2023)

10. Yu, S., et al.: Artificial neural network-based activities classification, gait phase estimation, and prediction. Ann. Biomed. Eng. **51**(7), 1471–1484 (2023)

11. Liu, D.X., Wu, X., Du, W., Wang, C., Chen, C., Xu, T.: Deep spatial-temporal model for rehabilitation gait: optimal trajectory generation for knee joint of lower-limb exoskeleton. Assem. Autom. **37**(3), 369–378 (2017)

12. Zaroug, A., Lai, D.T.H., Mudie, K., Begg, R.: Lower limb kinematics trajectory prediction using long short-term memory neural networks. Front. Bioeng. Biotechnol. **8**, 362 (2020)

13. Liu, D.X., Wu, X., Du, W., Wang, C., Xu, T.: Gait phase recognition for lower-limb exoskeleton with only joint angular sensors. Sensors **16**(10), 1579 (2016)

14. Moreira, L., Cerqueira, S.M., Figueiredo, J., Vilas-Boas, J., Santos, C.P.: Ai-based reference ankle joint torque trajectory generation for robotic gait assistance: first steps. In: 2020 IEEE International Conference on Autonomous Robot Systems and Competitions (ICARSC), pp. 22–27 (2020)

15. Ren, B., Zhang, Z., Zhang, C., Chen, S.: Motion trajectories prediction of lower limb exoskeleton based on long short-term memory (LSTM) networks. Actuators **11**(3), 73 (2022)

16. Vijayvargiya, A., Khimraj, Kumar, R., Dey, N.: Voting-based 1D CNN model for human lower limb activity recognition using SEMG signal. Phys. Eng. Sci. Med. **44**(4), 1297–1309 (2021)

17. Trisyanto, D.E., Reynard, M., Oey, E., Astuti, W.: Emotion recognition based on voice using combination of long short term memory (LSTM) and recurrent neural network (RNN) for automation music healing application, vol. 1029, pp. 807–818. Sydney, Australia (2023). https://doi.org/10.1007/978-3-031-29078-7_70

18. Mao, J., Qian, Z., Lucas, T.: Sentiment analysis of animated online education texts using long short-term memory networks in the context of the internet of things. IEEE Access **11**, 109121–109130 (2023)

# Adaptive Human-Like Gait Planning for Stair Climbing of Lower Limb Exoskeleton Robots

Chen Yang[1], Xinhao Zhang[1], Chaobin Zou[1(✉)], Wentao Liang[1],
Zonghai Huang[1], Rui Huang[1], Yilin Wang[2], and Hong Cheng[1]

[1] Center for Robotics, School of Automation Engineering, University of Electronic
Science and Technology of China, Chengdu 611731, People's Republic of China
chaobinzou@uestc.edu.cn
[2] Innovation Center of Nursing Research and Nursing Key Laboratory
of Sichuan Province, West China Hospital, Sichuan University,
Chengdu 610041, People's Republic of China

**Abstract.** In recent years, lower limb exoskeletons (LLEs) have attracted considerable interest for the walking assistance of paraplegic patients. As the wearable robots, gait planning is a critical issue for LLEs, especially adaptive gait pattern generation for different terrains such as slopes and stairs. This paper proposes an adaptive human-like gait planning approach (AHGP) for the stair climbing of LLEs, which realizes the generation of adaptive and human-like gait trajectories for varying stair heights. The AHGP divides one step on the stair into five sub-phases, and in each phase, the AHGP employs the artificial potential field to generate the optimal ankle positions to avoid the collision with each step on the stair. To obtain human-like gait patterns, Kernelized Movement Primitives were employed to learn and generate gait trajectories, i.e., the hip and the ankle positions for each leg in the Cartesian space. After learning from the demonstrated trajectories collected from the healthy subjects, the human-like gait trajectories passing through the generated optimal ankle positions can be reproduced to adapt to stairs with different heights. The proposed approach has been tested with the exoskeleton robot simulation model, and the experimental results indicate that the AHGP can generate the appropriate gait trajectories for LLEs to walk over varying stairs.

**Keywords:** Exoskeleton Robots · Gait · Stair · KMP

## 1 Introduction

Robotic Lower Limb Exoskeletons (LLEs) have gained considerable interest in recent years [1], including two types [2], for rehabilitation gait training [3] [4] [5] [6] and walking assistance [7] [8] [9]. Predefined gait trajectories are commonly used to control the LLEs for simple and safe walking on the level ground, such

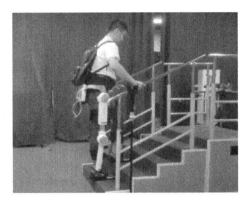

**Fig. 1.** A subject is climbing a stair with the exoskeleton robot AIDER.

as ReWalk [10], eLEGs [11], ATLAS [12], and CUHK-EXO [13]. The predefined gait trajectories are sampled from the healthy subjects by the motion capture system, whose stride lengths are constant with no flexibility. In order to help paraplegic patients walk in their daily lives, gait planning on complex terrains such as slopes and stairs is necessary for LLEs.

As shown in Fig. 1, a subject with gait impairment is walking on the stairs with a lower limb exoskeleton robot named AIDER, how do we generate appropriate gait trajectories for the stairs with different heights? Predefined fixed gait trajectories can be used for a fixed stair but have no flexibility to adapt to stairs with different heights, which may lead to a collision between the foot and the steps on the stair and even result in a fall for the subject with LLEs.

On the other hand, a non-human-like gait pattern may lead to uncomfortable walking postures, and the patients get tired soon. Therefore, for the safe and comfortable walking assistance of LLEs, adaptive human-like gait trajectories are required for stairs with different heights.

Some works have been studied in the past few years. Firstly, keypoint-based trajectory interpolation gait generation approaches have been studied. Zhong *et al.* [14] divided the swing leg of the ascend and descend stairs into three phases, the key landing point of each phase is calculated using a fuzzy logic algorithm based on the sensor data, and then the gait trajectories are generated by cubic spline interpolation. Griffin *et al.* [15] proposed an interpolation algorithm to realize the gait planning for slopes, the basic idea is to specify the location of key points, and then use the minimum shock gait planning method based on a fifth-order polynomial function to generate gait trajectories. However, gait trajectories generated with interpolation are not human-like.

With the development of learning-based approaches, learning gait trajectories from healthy subjects and generating new gait trajectories is a better choice. Zou *et al.* [9] proposed a slope gradient estimator combined with Dynamic Movement Primitives (DMP) to generate gait trajectories for slopes with different gradients. Chen *et al.* [16] proposed a gait planning algorithm based on DMP for ascending

204     C. Yang et al.

stairs, which can learn from the gait trajectories of healthy subjects and then generate new gait trajectories according to the stair dimensions. Xu *et al.* [17] proposed a novel perception approach based on two laser-ranging modules to obtain the terrain parameters, DMP is used to generate the gait trajectories in the terrain. In addition, Siekmann *et al.* [18] proposed a training and control of stair climbing strategy through networks and reinforcement learning. Zhang *et al.* [19] completed the stair climbing by switching mode control between the human and the exoskeleton robot. However, DMP-based approach can only modify the start and end positions of the demonstrated gait trajectory, which is not suitable for obstacles avoidance, *i.e.*, with modifications for some intermediate points on the demonstrated trajectory. Overall, there are two challenges for the adaptive human-like gait patterns generation for different stairs:

1) How to generate appropriate gait trajectories avoiding collisions with each step on the stairs with different heights?
2) How to generate gait trajectories with high similarity to the gait patterns of the healthy subjects?

This paper proposes a novel gait planning approach named AHGP to generate adaptive human-like gait trajectories for walking on stairs with varying heights. Artificial Potential Field (APF) [20] and Kernelized Movement Primitives (KMP) [21] were employed to construct the proposed approach. The main contributions are threefold:

1) The optimal ankle position on each step for stair climbing is generated to avoid the collision with the stairs;
2) Human-like gait trajectories can be generated after learning from the gait patterns collected from the healthy subjects;
3) A comprehensive gait planning algorithm is developed to realize the human-like and smooth walking on stairs with different heights.

The remaining sections are as follows: The detailed design of the proposed AHGP approach is introduced in Sect. 2. The experiments are carried out in Sect. 3, and we conclude the paper in Sect. 4 and suggest future works.

## 2    Adaptive Human-Like Gait Planning Approach

In this section, the design of an adaptive human-like gait planning approach (AHGP) of the stair climbing for lower limb exoskeleton robots is presented. As shown in Fig. 2, the gait planning approach consists of two steps:

1) The **Via-points generator**: one step is divided into five gait phases, and the APF is used to generate the optimal ankle positions that can avoid the collision between the foot and the steps on stairs;
2) The **Gait trajectory generator**: KMP is employed to learn and generate gait trajectories on stairs, and the human-like gait trajectories that pass through the generated via-points can be reproduced.

In the following two subsections, the via-points generator and gait trajectory generator will be introduced in detail.

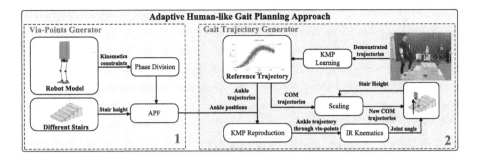

**Fig. 2.** The framework of the AHGP.

## 2.1  Via-Points Generator

As shown in Fig. 3, according to the negative and positive work fluctuations of the Center-of-Mass (COM) rate, one step of the stair climbing can be divided into five sub-phases [22]. In phase A, the foot of the swing leg is completely on the ground. Phase B is the moment that the tiptoe of the swing leg leaves the ground. In phases C and D, the tiptoe of the swing leg is swinging in the air over the stairs. Phase E represents the last phase of a step to touch on the steps, the swing leg will act as the support leg for the next step.

In this paper, the APF algorithm is used to generate the ankle positions of the five sub-phases. This method emulates the concept of a potential field from physics, treating the robot's movement in the environment as a movement within such a field. Here, the target point generates an attractive potential field, which exerts gravitational forces on the robot, thereby pulling it towards the target. Simultaneously, obstacles generate a repulsive potential field, exerting repulsive forces that push the robot away from obstacles. By combining these attractive and repulsive forces, a total potential field is formed, guiding the robot to move along a path with minimal potential energy. The potential function $U$ is used to establish an artificial potential field, which is expressed as the sum of the gravitational and repulsive potentials

$$U(q) = U_{\text{att}}(q) + U_{\text{rep}}(q), \tag{1}$$

where $U(q)$ represents the potential function at point $q$, $U_{\text{att}}(q)$ and $U_{\text{rep}}(q)$ represent the gravitational and repulsive potential functions at point $q$, respectively. The gravitational and repulsive potential functions are expressed as

$$\begin{cases} U_{\text{att}}(q) = \frac{1}{2}\epsilon(d(q))^2 \\ U_{\text{rep}}(q) = \frac{1}{2}\eta(\frac{1}{d(q)})^2, \end{cases} \tag{2}$$

where $\epsilon$ and $\eta$ represent the gravitational gain and repulsive gain, respectively, and $d(q)$ represents the distance between the point q and the obstacle. The distance $d(q)$ varies and is specified for each gait phase. By manipulating these parameters, the degree of collision avoidance can be adjusted for the swing leg.

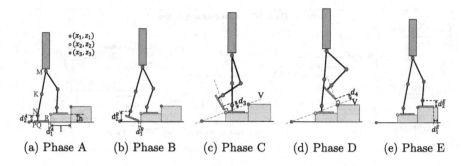

(a) Phase A    (b) Phase B    (c) Phase C    (d) Phase D    (e) Phase E

**Fig. 3.** The artificial potential field setting of the five phases for one step.

As shown in Fig. 3, the gravitational and repulsive potentials are set at each phase to ensure that the swing leg reaches the target position without hitting the stairs. $(x_1, z_1)$, $(x_2, z_2)$ and $(x_3, z_3)$ represent the edge points of the first, second, and third steps, respectively. M, K, and N represent the hip, knee and ankle joints, respectively. P, Q, and R represent the heel, the bottom of the ankle and the tiptoe, respectively. In addition, $h$ and $l$ represent the height and depth of the stair, respectively.

As shown in Fig. 3(a), the foot is completely on the ground in phase A, the gravitational and repulsive potentials can be calculated as

$$\begin{cases} U_{\text{att}}^A = \frac{1}{2}\epsilon_1(d_1^A)^2 + \frac{1}{2}\epsilon_2(d_2^A - d_{NQ})^2, \\ U_{\text{rep}}^A = \frac{1}{2}\eta_1(\frac{1}{d_1^A})^2, \end{cases} \tag{3}$$

the distance between the tiptoe and the bottom end of the first stair $d_1^A$, and the vertical distance between the ankle and the ground $d_2^A$ are expressed as

$$\begin{cases} d_1^A = x_2 - d_{QR} - x_{N_A}, \\ d_2^A = z_{N_A} - z_1, \end{cases} \tag{4}$$

where $d_{QR}$ represents the distance between the point Q and R, $x_{N_A}$ and $z_{N_A}$ represent the coordinates of the swing leg's ankle joint in $x$ and $z$ directions in phase A, respectively. Note that $d_2^A = d_{NQ}$ in phase A, the gravitational potentials can be rewritten as follows

$$U_{\text{att}}^A = \frac{1}{2}\epsilon_1(d_1^A)^2. \tag{5}$$

As shown in Fig. 3(b), phase B is the moment that the tiptoe of the swing leg leaves the ground, $d_1^B$ is the same as phase A, and the gravitational and repulsive potentials can be expressed as

$$\begin{cases} U_{\text{att}}^B = \frac{1}{2}\epsilon_3(d_2^B)^2 \\ U_{\text{rep}}^B = \frac{1}{2}\eta_2(\frac{1}{(d_2^B)})^2, \end{cases} \tag{6}$$

where the vertical distance between the ankle and the ground $d_2^B$ is

$$d_2^B = z_{N_B} - z_1, \tag{7}$$

where $z_{N_B}$ represents the ankle coordinates in the $x$ directions in phase B. As the tiptoe position does not change during phase A to phase B, the constraint satisfies

$$((x_2 - d_1^B) - x_{N_B})^2 + z_{N_B}^2 = d_{N_R}^2. \tag{8}$$

Note that the plantar/flexion of the human ankle is approximately 45°C at most, $d_2$ should be less than $\frac{\sqrt{2}}{2} \cdot (d_{NQ} + d_{QR})$. For phase C, as shown in Fig. 3(c), the virtual plane $v$ through the edge points of the stairs was constructed. Suppose that the tiptoe is on the plumb line of the virtual plane passing through the stair edge point $(x_2, z_2)$, and the calf is perpendicular to the foot

$$(x_{R_C} - x_2) \cdot l + (z_{R_C} - z_2) \cdot h = 0, \tag{9}$$

where $x_{R_C}$ and $z_{R_C}$ represent the ankle coordinates in the $x$ and $z$ directions respectively in phase C. The gravitational and repulsive potentials in phase C can be expressed as follows.

$$\begin{cases} U_{\text{att}}^C = \frac{1}{2}\epsilon_4 d_3^2 \\ U_{\text{rep}}^C = \frac{1}{2}\eta_3 (\frac{1}{d_3})^2, \end{cases} \tag{10}$$

the distance between the tiptoe and the point $(x_2, z_2)$ is calculated as

$$d_3 = d_{R-v} = \frac{|l \cdot x_{R_C} + h \cdot z_{R_C} - l \cdot x_2 - h \cdot z_2|}{\sqrt{l^2 + h^2}}, \tag{11}$$

where $d_R - v$ represent the distance between the tiptoe and the virtual plane $v$. Similarly, as shown in Fig. 3(d), suppose that the tiptoe is on the plumb line of the virtual plane passing through the stair edge point $(x_3, z_3)$, and the calf is perpendicular to the foot

$$(x_{R_D} - x_3) \cdot l + (z_{R_D} - z_3) \cdot h = 0, \tag{12}$$

where $x_{R_D}$ and $z_{R_D}$ represent the ankle coordinates in the $x$ and $z$ directions respectively in phase D. The gravitational and repulsive potentials in phase D can be expressed as follows

$$\begin{cases} U_{\text{att}}^D = \frac{1}{2}\epsilon_5 (d_4)^2, \\ U_{\text{rep}}^D = \frac{1}{2}\eta_4 (\frac{1}{d_4})^2, \end{cases} \tag{13}$$

where the distance between the tiptoe and the point $(x_3, z_3)$ is calculated as follows

$$d_4 = d_{R-v} = \frac{|l \cdot x_{R_D} + h \cdot z_{R_D} - l \cdot x_3 - h \cdot z_3|}{\sqrt{l^2 + h^2}}. \tag{14}$$

As shown in Fig. 3(e), the state of the robot in phase E is the same as the state in phase A, the gravitational and repulsive potentials in phase E are

$$\begin{cases} U_{att}^E = \frac{1}{2}\epsilon_6(d_1^E)^2 + \frac{1}{2}\epsilon_7(d_2^E - d_{NQ})^2, \\ U_{rep}^E = \frac{1}{2}\eta_5(\frac{1}{d_1^E})^2, \end{cases} \tag{15}$$

the distance between the tiptoe and the right vertex of the second stair $d_1^E$, and the vertical distance between the ankle and the ground of the second stair $d_2^E$ are calculated as

$$\begin{cases} d_1^E = (x_3 + l) - d_{QR} - x_{N_E}, \\ d_2^E = z_{N_E} - z_3, \end{cases} \tag{16}$$

where $x_{N_A}$ and $z_{N_A}$ represent the coordinates of the swing leg's ankle in $x$ and $z$ directions in phase E. Then phase E restarts as phase A in the next step.

As mentioned above, assuming that the total potential function of each phase $U_{total} = U_{total_{min}}$, the optimal ankle position of each phase adaptive to stairs with varying heights can be obtained.

## 2.2  Trajectories Generation for the COM

Different COM trajectories are required when walking on stairs with different heights. In this paper, the COM trajectory of a healthy human climbing a fixed-size stair was recorded by X-Sens. Assuming that the COM trajectory of a step is expressed as follows.

$$\begin{cases} x_C = \{x|x_1, x_2, \cdots, x_n\}, \\ z_C = \{z|z_1, z_2, \cdots, z_n\}, \end{cases} \tag{17}$$

where $x_C$ and $z_C$ represent the COM's trajectory in the $x$ and $z$ directions, respectively. $n$ represents the frame number of the COM trajectory, $x_i$ and $z_i$ represent the horizontal and vertical coordinates of the point $i^{th}$, respectively. Suppose that the height of the stair varies, the COM trajectory can be resized as follows

$$\begin{cases} x_C' = \{x|x_1, x_2, \cdots, x_n\}, \\ z_C' = \{z|z_1, z_2 + (z_2 - z_1)\frac{h'}{h}, \cdots, z_n + (z_n - z_1)\frac{h'}{h}\}, \end{cases} \tag{18}$$

where $x_C'$ and $z_C'$ represent the horizontal and vertical COM trajectories on the stair of the new height, respectively. $h$ and $h'$ represent the height of the stairs for the demonstrated gait collection and experiments, respectively. The generated COM's trajectory can be used to ascend stairs with different heights.

## 2.3  Gait Trajectories Generator

As gait trajectories for different stairs are varying with heights, it is impossible to sample all gait trajectories from the healthy subjects. As mentioned above, the APF approach can generate five via-points for the ankle to adapt to changes in stair height. It is better to learn the demonstrated trajectories and generate new trajectories to pass through these five via-points. In this paper, KMP [21] is used to learn the demonstrated trajectories and generate new trajectories with the given via-points. Firstly, let's denote the gait trajectory in one step as

$$\zeta = [x, \dot{x}, z, \dot{z}]^{\top}, \tag{19}$$

a set of demonstrated gait trajectories sampled from healthy subjects climbing stairs can be represented as

$$\left\{ \{t_{n,m}, \zeta_{n,m}\}_{n=1}^{N} \right\}_{m=1}^{M}, \tag{20}$$

where $N$ and $M$ represent the length of each trajectory and the number of demonstrated trajectories, respectively. $t_{n,m}$ is the time of the $n^{th}$ data on the $m^{th}$ demonstrated trajectory. The probability distribution of the demonstrated trajectories is then modelled using the Gaussian Mixture Model (GMM)

$$\begin{bmatrix} t \\ \zeta \end{bmatrix} \sim \sum_{k=1}^{K} \pi_k \mathcal{N} \left( \boldsymbol{\mu}_k, \boldsymbol{\Sigma}_k \right), \tag{21}$$

where $\pi_k$, $\mu k$, and $\Sigma_k$ represent the prior probability, mean, and covariance of the $k^{th}$ Gaussian component, respectively. Subsequently, the probabilistic reference trajectory retrieved according to Gaussian Mixture Regression (GMR) is

$$\hat{\zeta}_n \mid t_n \sim \mathcal{N} \left( \hat{\boldsymbol{\mu}}_n, \hat{\boldsymbol{\Sigma}}_n \right), \tag{22}$$

where each $\hat{\zeta}_n$ and $t_n$ fits a conditional normal distribution respectively with mean $\mu_n$ and covariance $\Sigma_n$.

However, the dynamic adjustment capabilities of the reference trajectory generated from the demonstrated trajectory employing the GMM-GMR method are poor, KMP solves the problem. First, the parametric trajectory consisting of position $\zeta(t)$ and velocity $\dot{\zeta}(t)$ is expressed as follows

$$[\zeta(t), \dot{\zeta}(t)]^{\top} = \Phi(t)^{\top} w, \tag{23}$$

where the matrix $\Phi(t) \in \mathbb{R}^{BO \times 2O}$ is represented as follows

$$\Phi(t) = \begin{bmatrix} \varphi(t) & \mathbf{0} & \cdots & \mathbf{0} & \dot{\varphi}(t) & \mathbf{0} & \cdots & \mathbf{0} \\ \mathbf{0} & \varphi(t) & \cdots & \mathbf{0} & \mathbf{0} & \dot{\varphi}(t) & \cdots & \mathbf{0} \\ \vdots & \vdots & \ddots & \vdots & \vdots & \vdots & \ddots & \vdots \\ \mathbf{0} & \mathbf{0} & \cdots & \varphi(t) & \mathbf{0} & \mathbf{0} & \cdots & \dot{\varphi}(t) \end{bmatrix}, \tag{24}$$

where $O = 1$ represents one dimension of the output, $\varphi(t)$ is a $B$-dimensional basis function, $\dot{\varphi}(t)$ is the first-order derivative of $\varphi(t)$. The specific form of the basis function is not defined and instead uses the kernel method proposed by Huang *et al.* [21]. The weight vector $w \in \mathbb{R}^{B \times 2O}$ is normally distributed as $w \sim \mathcal{N}(\mu_w, \Sigma_w)$. Since the parametric gait trajectory can be expressed as follows

$$\mathcal{P}_p(\zeta \mid t) = \mathcal{N}\left(\zeta \mid \Phi(t)^\top \mu_\omega, \Phi(t)^\top \Sigma_\omega \Phi(t)\right). \qquad (25)$$

To ensure a good match between the parametric gait trajectory and the reference gait trajectory, the Kullback-Leibler divergence (K-L divergence) is utilized to formulate the objective cost function

$$J(\mu_\omega, \Sigma_\omega) = \sum_{n=1}^{N} D_{KL}\left(\mathcal{P}_p(\zeta \mid t_n) \| \mathcal{P}_r(\zeta \mid t_n)\right), \qquad (26)$$

where $D_{KL}(\cdot \| \cdot)$ represents the KL divergence. The parameters $\mu_\omega$ and $\Sigma_\omega$ of the model in equation (25) can be obtained by minimizing the objective function. Suppose the newly introduced trajectory via-points follow a normal distribution

$$\mathcal{P}_d(\zeta \mid t_d) = \mathcal{N}\left(\zeta \mid \Phi(t_d)^\top \mu_d, \Phi(t_d)^\top \Sigma_d \Phi(t_d)\right), \qquad (27)$$

Note that the parameter trajectories must be able to match the probabilistic reference trajectories generated by GMR and pass the given via-points. Thus the parametric trajectory should be optimized to match both $\mathcal{P}_d(\zeta \mid t)$ and $\mathcal{P}_r(\zeta \mid t)$. The reproduced trajectory through via-points can be obtained by minimizing the cost function

$$
\begin{aligned}
J(\mu_\omega, \Sigma_\omega) = &\sum_{n=1}^{N} D_{KL}\left(\mathcal{P}_p(\zeta \mid t_n) \| \mathcal{P}_r(\zeta \mid t_n)\right) \\
&+ \sum_{d=1}^{D} D_{KL}\left(\mathcal{P}_p(\zeta \mid t_d) \| \mathcal{P}_d(\zeta \mid t_d)\right),
\end{aligned} \qquad (28)
$$

where D represents the number of the via-points. However, calculating the minimization of the cost function is complex, so it's a better choice to separately solve for the expectations of the mean and variance of the parameter model. Finally, The expected mean $\mu_w^*$ and covariance $\Sigma_w^*$ of the weight vector $w$ can be calculated as

$$
\begin{cases}
\mu_w^* = \Phi\left(\Phi^\top \Phi + \lambda \Sigma\right)^{-1} \mu \\
\Sigma_w^* = N\left(\Phi \Sigma^{-1} \Phi^\top + \lambda I\right)^{-1},
\end{cases} \qquad (29)
$$

where $\lambda$ is a gain, and

$$
\begin{cases}
\Phi = [\Phi(t_1), \Phi(t_2), \cdots, \Phi(t_{N+D})] \\
\Sigma = \text{blockdiag}\left(\hat{\Sigma}_1, \hat{\Sigma}_2, \cdots, \hat{\Sigma}_{N+D}\right) \\
\mu = [\hat{\mu}_1^\top, \hat{\mu}_2^\top, \cdots, \hat{\mu}_{N+D}^\top]^\top,
\end{cases} \qquad (30)
$$

where $\hat{\mu}_1^\top, \hat{\mu}_2^\top, \cdots, \hat{\mu}_{N+D}^\top$ and $\hat{\Sigma}_1^\top, \hat{\Sigma}_2^\top, \cdots, \hat{\Sigma}_{N+D}^\top$ represent the parameters for the reproduced trajectory.

**Fig. 4.** X-sens.

**Fig. 5.** Gait trajectories collection from the healthy subjects on stairs.

# 3    Experimental Results and Discussion

Two experiments have been conducted to validate the effectiveness of the proposed AHGP approach, the first is the human-like gait trajectories generation with the same height of the stair as the demonstration (Sect. 3.1), and the second is the adaptive gait trajectories for stairs with different heights compared to the first one (Sect. 3.2). Simulations on Matlab were conducted in each experiment to verify the generated gait trajectories and COM trajectories of the AHGP.

## 3.1    Gait Trajectories Learning and Reproduction with KMP

### 3.1.1    Demonstrated Gait Trajectories Collection

As shown in Fig. 4 and Fig. 5, the demonstrated gait trajectories are collected from the healthy subjects by X-sens[1]—a motion capture system. Note that all positions for the marker point with the Inertial Measurement Unit (IMU) are collected for the gait trajectories calculation.

The schematic of the demonstrated trajectories collection is shown in Fig. 6, where the healthy subject is modelled as a legged robot model. The ankle trajectories of the swing leg and COM trajectories are collected for each step ascending the stairs, where the depth and the height of the stairs are 0.3 m and 0.135 m, respectively. In addition, the subject's thigh and calf lengths are 0.45 m and 0.42 m respectively. 100 sets of demonstrated ankle trajectories from $P_{start}$ to

---

[1] www.xsens.com.

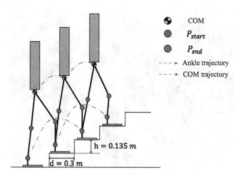

**Fig. 6.** The schematic of gait trajectories on stairs.

$P_{end}$ and COM trajectories were collected for KMP learning to generate the reference trajectories.

Subsequently, the simulation model of the exoskeleton robot is modelled in Matlab. As shown in Fig. 7, the parameters of the simulation model are the same as those of the healthy subject. The thigh and calf lengths of the simulation model are 0.45 m and 0.42 m, respectively. The length of the foot is 0.2 m and the height of the ankle is 0.05 m. In addition, the COM of the human-exoskeleton system has a good correspondence in the sagittal plane with the hip joints [23], therefore the COM of the human-exoskeleton system is set at the center of two hip joints. In the APF algorithm, the dimensions of the stairs are set to be identical to the stair when collecting the demonstrated trajectories. After the simulation model's ankle position of each phase is calculated by APF, the ankle trajectories for stairs climbing were reproduced with the ankle positions and reference trajectories by KMP. Then the ankle trajectory and COM trajectory reproduced by KMP are used for the simulation model to climb the stairs in Matlab-based simulations. Finally, the ankle trajectory reproduced by KMP is compared with the trajectory produced by interpolation.

### 3.1.2   KMP Learning and Reproduction

The first column of Fig. 8(a) and Fig. 9(a) represent the learning process of KMP, the black curves are 100 sets of demonstrated ankle trajectories and COM trajectories, respectively, sampled from the healthy subject, which are split into $x$ and $z$ directions in time domain. The GMM is estimated by the red ellipses representing Gaussian components and then the reference trajectory is generated by GMR. In the second column of Fig. 8(a) and Fig. 9(a), the pink curves KMP 1 are the ankle trajectories and the COM trajectories reproduced by KMP in the time domain, which are close to the reference trajectories. It suggests that the reference trajectory can be effectively reproduced with the KMP-based learning approach. In addition, the reproduced trajectories for ankle and COM in the Cartesian space are shown in Fig. 8(b) and Fig. 9(b).

With the input of stair dimensions and human parameters as mentioned above, the APF algorithm generates the ankle position for each phase, as shown

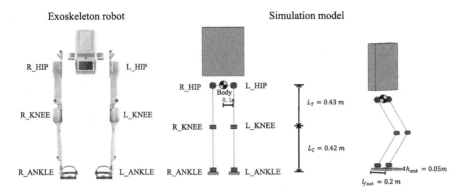

**Fig. 7.** The exoskeleton robot and the corresponding kinematics of the model.

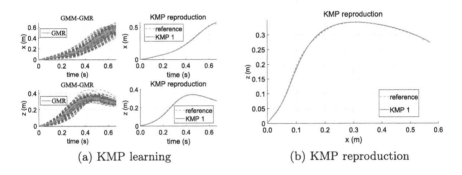

(a) KMP learning                    (b) KMP reproduction

**Fig. 8.** Demonstrated ankle trajectories reproduced by KMP.

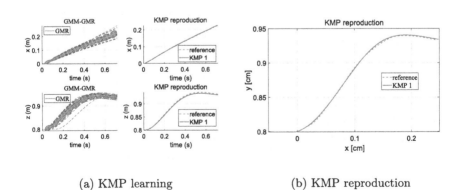

(a) KMP learning                    (b) KMP reproduction

**Fig. 9.** Demonstrated COM trajectories reproduced by KMP.

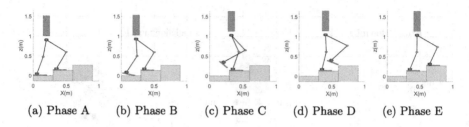

(a) Phase A    (b) Phase B    (c) Phase C    (d) Phase D    (e) Phase E

**Fig. 10.** The generated ankle positions for the five phases.

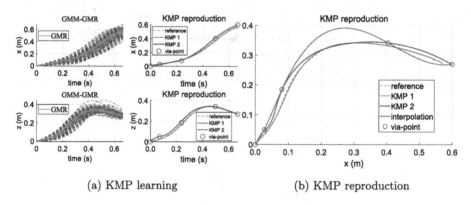

(a) KMP learning    (b) KMP reproduction

**Fig. 11.** Gait trajectories reproduced by the KMP with new via-points.

in Fig. 10. The five phases correspond to the five phases in Fig. 3, respectively. The ankle positions of the swing leg are marked by the red circles. In Phase A, the distance between the swing leg's tiptoe and the second step of the stair is calculated, thus the ankle position is set here to avoid collision with the second step of the stair. Phase B is the moment for lifting the swing leg, the position of the tiptoe is the same as the tiptoe in phase A. Note that constraints are employed to control the height of the ankle's height on stairs. In phases C and phase D, the APF generated ankle positions for the tiptoe to avoid the second and third steps on the stair, respectively. In phase E, the ankle position at the landing phase is calculated. Overall, the generated ankle positions can effectively avoid the collision between the tiptoe and steps on the stair in each phase.

The generated ankle positions are then used to reproduce the reference gait trajectories, which can be used as the via-position constraints for the trajectories' reproduction. As shown in the second column of Fig. 11 (a), first, the pink curves are close to the reference trajectories, which indicates that the KMP learning is effective. The via-points correspond to ankle positions generated by APF, and the blue curves are the ankle trajectories reproduced by KMP in the time domain. It not only passes through via-points but also maintains the shape of the reference trajectory.

In addition, the comparison between the trajectory generated by the interpolation method and the trajectory reproduced by KMP is shown in Fig. 11(b), the

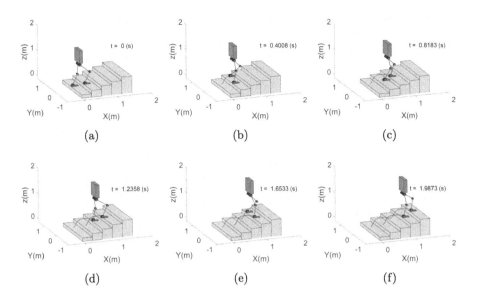

Fig. 12. The stair climbing simulation, where the height of the stair is 13.5 cm.

gait trajectories generated by interpolation and KMP both pass the via-points, but the gait trajectory generated by KMP is closer to the reference gait trajectory. In other words, the gait trajectory generated by KMP is more human-like.

Finally, the ankle trajectories and COM trajectories reproduced by KMP are used for the simulation robot model to ascend the stairs with five steps, the joint angle can be calculated with the ankle trajectory by inverse kinematics. As shown in Fig 12, with the joint angles and COM trajectory reproduced by the AHGP approach, the simulation model realizes the smooth and steady ascending stairs, which indicates that the AHGP approach can generate the appropriate COM trajectory and ankle trajectory as the stair height is kept constant.

### 3.2  Adaptive Gait Trajectories Generation for Different Stairs

In the previous section, it was shown that AHGP can generate the human-like ankle trajectories and COM trajectories on the stairs with a constant height, now we would like to test the adaption of the proposed AHGP approach for stairs with different heights.

### 3.2.1  Experiments Setup

Four experiments were conducted to validate the adaption of the AHGP for different stair heights. According to the national standard, the height of stairs is generally not higher than 20 cm, as shown in Table 1, the stair heights in the four experiments are set as 0.05 m, 0.1 m, 0.15 m, and 0.2 m. Since this paper only considers changes in stair heights, the depth and width of the stairs are

**Table 1.** The stair dimensions of four sets of experiments.

| index | stair height (m) | stair depth (m) | stair width (m) |
|-------|------------------|-----------------|-----------------|
| exp-1 | 0.05 | 0.3 | 1.6 |
| exp-2 | 0.1 | 0.3 | 1.6 |
| exp-3 | 0.15 | 0.3 | 1.6 |
| exp-4 | 0.2 | 0.3 | 1.6 |

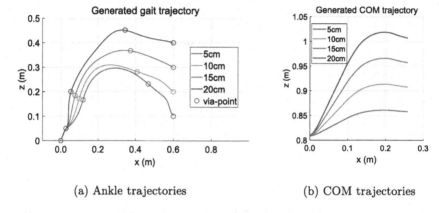

(a) Ankle trajectories                (b) COM trajectories

**Fig. 13.** Trajectories reproduced by the KMP with new via-points.

set as fixed values of 0.3 cm and 1.6 m, respectively. In each experiment, the ankle positions generated by the APF algorithm are validated, and then the ankle trajectory is reproduced with the ankle positions by KMP. In addition, the COM trajectory of each experiment is calculated by the method in Sect. 2.2. Finally, the ankle trajectories and COM trajectories generated by the AHGP approach are used for the simulation model to ascend the stairs with five steps.

### 3.2.2   Experimental Results

As shown in Fig. 13(a), the via-points correspond to the ankle positions generated by APF and the curves represent the ankle trajectories reproduced with the ankle positions by KMP. Note that while the stair heights change, the first and second via-points remain the same. This is because the landing point of the swing leg in phases A and B remains constant when the depth of the stair is constant. For the third and fourth via-points, the higher the height of the stairs, the more the ankle moves backward and upwards to avoid collision with the step on the stair. For the last via-point, the ankle position changes according to the stair heights. The APF algorithm can generate different ankle positions for four experiments based on different stair heights, and the ankle trajectories passing through generated ankle positions are reproduced by KMP. The COM trajectories of the four experiments are shown in Fig. 13(b), which are resized according to the stair heights. After learning the demonstrated COM trajectories, the reference tra-

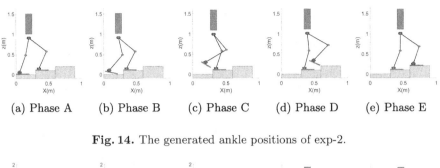

(a) Phase A     (b) Phase B     (c) Phase C     (d) Phase D     (e) Phase E

**Fig. 14.** The generated ankle positions of exp-2.

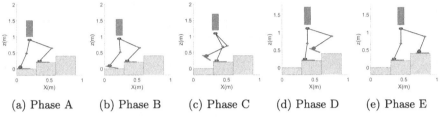

(a) Phase A     (b) Phase B     (c) Phase C     (d) Phase D     (e) Phase E

**Fig. 15.** The generated ankle positions of exp-4.

jectory is reproduced by KMP, and then the COM trajectories for different stair heights can be resized based on the ratio of the stair height to the stair height at the time of demonstrated trajectories collection. Since the depth of the stairs is constant, we only resize the reference COM trajectory in the $z$ direction.

In addition, the ankle positions in each phase are designed to avoid collisions with the steps on stairs with varying heights, to verify the correctness of the generated ankle positions, the generated ankle positions of the exp-2 and exp-4 are depicted in Fig. 14 and Fig. 15, respectively. The swing leg's ankle of the simulation model is marked by the red circle. The simulation model avoids the steps on the stairs in each phase, which indicates that in each phase APF can effectively generate optimal ankle positions to avoid steps on the stairs of different heights. The degree of obstacle avoidance can be adjusted by modifying the parameters of APF; however, the generated ankle positions may not be human-like if only obstacle avoidance is considered.

Finally, the joint angles of the simulation model are obtained by inverse kinematics with the reproduced ankle trajectories. As shown in Fig. 16, with the reproduced ankle trajectories and resized COM trajectories, the simulation model realizes the smooth and stead climbing on stairs with different heights. Overall, APF can generate ankle positions to avoid collisions with each step on the stairs of different heights. After the KMP-based learning of the demonstrated gait trajectories sampled from healthy subjects, the human-like gait trajectories adapting to stairs with different heights can be reproduced by KMP with the generated ankle positions. By combining the APF algorithm and KMP, the proposed approach AHGP is able to generate the adaptive human-like gait trajectories for lower limb exoskeletons stair climbing.

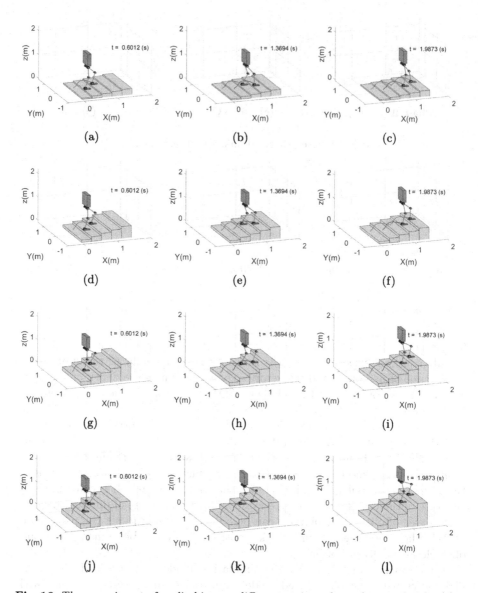

**Fig. 16.** The experiments for climbing on different stairs, where the step height (a) - (c) are 5 cm, (d) - (f) are 10 cm, (g) - (i) are 15 cm, and (j) - (l) are 20 cm.

## 3.3  Discussion

In the first experiment, the ankle trajectories generated by the AHGP approach are very close to the demonstrated trajectories, which indicates that when the stair height is the same as before, human-like gait trajectories can be generated by AHGP. In the second experiment, four experiments with different stair heights were conducted to verify the adaption of AHGP to generate gait trajectories for stairs with varying heights. Experimental results indicate that adaptive human-like gait trajectories can be generated by AHGP, realizing the smooth and human-like walking on stairs with varying heights for lower limb exoskeletons. However, the depth of the step on the stair is not considered in this paper, only steps with different heights are conducted.

# 4  Conclusions and Future Work

In this paper, we proposed a new gait planning approach AHGP during stair movement, based on Artificial Potential Field and Kernelized Movement Primitives, to generate human-like and stair heights adaptive gait trajectories for lower limb exoskeleton. One step on the stairs is divided into five gait phases, and at each phase, the optimal ankle position can be calculated by the Artificial Potential Field algorithm to adapt to the changes in stair height. Demonstrated gait trajectories on stairs are sampled by X-Sens, and then are learned by Kernelized Movement Primitives. After learning from the demonstrated trajectories, with the generated via-points by Artificial Potential Field, stair heights adaptive and human-like gait trajectories can be reproduced. The approach has been tested in Matlab-based simulations, and the simulation results indicate that AHGP can effectively provide adaptive and human-like gait planning under stairs with varying heights for the lower limb exoskeleton.

However, demonstrated gait trajectories are only sampled on stairs with a height of 13.5cm; thus, if the height of the stair is much different from the height of the stair for gait trajectories collecting, generated trajectories may not be smooth enough. Furthermore, in this paper, we only consider the varying in stair height. In the future, more demonstrated gait trajectories should be sampled to improve the smoothness of the generated trajectories. Additionally, gait varying with the step length of the stairs and body parameters will be considered in the future. Finally, AHGP will be expanded and applied to more complex gait planning applications, as well as applied to the real lower limb exoskeleton system.

**Acknowledgments.** This work was supported by the National Natural Science Foundation of China (62203089, 62303092, 62306195, 62103084); in part by the Project funded by China Postdoctoral Science Foundation under Grant 2021M700695, and in part by the Sichuan Science and Technology Program (2022NSFSC0890, 2023YFG0024, 2022YFS0570, 2023YFS0213); in part by the Fundamental Research Funds for the Central Universities (ZYGX2022YGRH003, ZYGX2021YGLH003).

**Disclosure of Interests.** The authors have no competing interests to declare that are relevant to the content of this article.

# References

1. Chen, B., et al.: Recent developments and challenges of lower extremity exoskeletons. J. Orthopaedic Transl. **5**, 26–37 (2016)
2. Cao, J., Xie, S.Q., Das, R., Zhu, G.L.: Control strategies for effective robot assisted gait rehabilitation: the state of art and future prospects. Med. Eng. Phys. **36**(12), 1555–1566 (2014)
3. Kawamoto, H., Lee, S., Kanbe, S., Sankai, Y.: Power assist method for HAL-3 using EMG-based feedback controller. IEEE Int. Conf. Syst. Man Cybern. **2**, 1648–1653 (2003)
4. Mohamad, H., Ozgoli, S.: Online gait generator for lower limb exoskeleton robots: suitable for level ground, slopes, stairs, and obstacle avoidance. Robot. Auton. Syst. **160**, 104319 (2023)
5. Wang, J., Li, J., Zhang, W., Zhou, F.: Research on trajectory tracking of lower limb exoskeleton rehabilitation robot based on sliding mode control. In: Liu, X.-J., Nie, Z., Yu, J., Xie, F., Song, R. (eds.) ICIRA 2021. LNCS (LNAI), vol. 13013, pp. 698–708. Springer, Cham (2021). https://doi.org/10.1007/978-3-030-89095-7_66
6. Zhong, B., et al.: A cable-driven exoskeleton with personalized assistance improves the gait metrics of people in subacute stroke. IEEE Trans. Neural Syst. Rehabil. Eng. **31**, 2560–2569 (2023)
7. Wang, Y., Gao, J., Ma, Z., Li, Y., Zuo, S., Liu, J.: Design and verification of an active lower limb exoskeleton for micro-low gravity simulation training. In: Liu, H., et al. (eds.) International Conference on Intelligent Robotics and Applications: ICIRA 2022, pp. 114–123. Springer, Cham (2022). https://doi.org/10.1007/978-3-031-13844-7_12
8. Miller, L.E., Zimmermann, A.K., Herbert, W.G.: Clinical effectiveness and safety of powered exoskeleton-assisted walking in patients with spinal cord injury: systematic review with meta-analysis. Med. Devices **9**, 455 (2016)
9. Zou, C., Huang, R., Qiu, J., Chen, Q., Cheng, H.: Slope gradient adaptive gait planning for walking assistance lower limb exoskeletons. IEEE Trans. Autom. Sci. Eng. **18**(2), 405–413 (2021)
10. Esquenazi, A., Talaty, M., Packel, A., Saulino, M.: The rewalk powered exoskeleton to restore ambulatory function to individuals with thoracic-level motor-complete spinal cord injury. Am. J. Phys. Med. Rehabil. **91**(11), 911–921 (2012)
11. Strausser, K.A., Kazerooni, H.: The development and testing of a human machine interface for a mobile medical exoskeleton. In: 2011 IEEE/RSJ International Conference on Intelligent Robots and Systems, pp. 4911–4916. IEEE (2011)
12. Sanz-Merodio, D., Cestari, M., Arevalo, J.C., Garcia, E.: Control motion approach of a lower limb orthosis to reduce energy consumption. Int. J. Adv. Robot. Syst. **9**(6), 232 (2012)
13. Chen, B., Zhong, C.-H., Zhao, X., Ma, H., Qin, L., Liao, W.-H.: Reference joint trajectories generation of CUHK-EXO exoskeleton for system balance in walking assistance. IEEE Access **7**, 33809–33821 (2019)
14. Zhong, C.H., Zhao, X., Liang, F.Y., Ma, H., Liao, W.H.: Motion adaption and trajectory generation of stair ascent and descent with a lower limb exoskeleton for paraplegics. In: 2019 IEEE/ASME International Conference on Advanced Intelligent Mechatronics (AIM), pp. 612–617. IEEE (2019)
15. Griffin, R., et al.: Stepping forward with exoskeletons: team IHMC? s design and approach in the 2016 Cybathlon. IEEE Robot. Autom. Mag. **24**(4), 66–74 (2017)

16. Chen, Q., Cheng, H., Huang, R., Qiu, J., Chen, X.: Learning and planning of stair ascent for lower-limb exoskeleton systems. Ind. Robot Int. J. Robot. Res. Appl. **46**(3), 421–430 (2019)

17. Xu, F., et al.: Stair-ascent strategies and performance evaluation for a lower limb exoskeleton. Int. J. Intell. Robot. Appl. **4**(3), 278–293 (2020). https://doi.org/10.1007/s41315-020-00123-6

18. Siekmann, J., Green, K., Warila, J., Fern, A., Hurst, J.: Blind bipedal stair traversal via sim-to-real reinforcement learning. arXiv preprint arXiv:2105.08328 (2021)

19. Zhang, Z.W., et al.: Blending control method of lower limb exoskeleton toward tripping-free stair climbing. ISA Trans. **131**, 610–627 (2022)

20. Warren, C.W.: Global path planning using artificial potential fields. In: 1989 IEEE International Conference on Robotics and Automation, pp. 316–317. IEEE Computer Society (1989)

21. Huang, Y., Rozo, L., Silvério, J., Caldwell, D.G.: Kernelized movement primitives. Int. J. Robot. Res. **38**(7), 833–852 (2019)

22. Ma, T., et al.: Gait phase subdivision and leg stiffness estimation during stair climbing. IEEE Trans. Neural Syst. Rehabil. Eng. **30**, 860–868 (2022)

23. Xi, R., Zhu, Z., Du, F., Yang, M., Wang, X., Wu, Q.: Design concept of the quasi-passive energy-efficient power-assisted lower-limb exoskeleton based on the theory of passive dynamic walking. In: 2016 23rd International Conference on Mechatronics and Machine Vision in Practice (M2VIP), pp. 1–5 (2016)

# Improved Data-Weighted Iterative Parameter Identification Method for Accurate Dynamic Modeling of Collaborative Manipulators

Jie Chen⬤, Wenhui Huang⬤, and Huasong Min$^{(\boxtimes)}$⬤

Institute of Robotics and Intelligent Systems, Wuhan University of Science and Technology,
Wuhan 430081, China
mhuasong@wust.edu.cn

**Abstract.** Collaborative manipulators have become increasingly necessary in industry and human-robot collaboration, and an accurate dynamic model of manipulators serves as an important foundation for applications such as precise position/force control and collision detection. However, data bias, resulting from data sampling errors, and complex non-linear friction significantly reduces the accuracy of identification methods. To address these issues, we propose an improved data-weighted iterative identification method for manipulator dynamic models. The improved data weight function is employed in the inner loop iteration to prevent information loss caused by a fixed weight threshold. Furthermore, a novel friction model considering friction anisotropy and the Stribeck effect is introduced to iterate in the outer loop. Finally, experiments are conducted on three different collaborative manipulator datasets, and we compare the identification accuracy of our proposed method with other state-of-the-art algorithms. The experimental results demonstrate that the accuracy of the proposed method is improved by more than 15% compared to others. The proposed method exhibits excellent torque estimation accuracy and good applicability to different manipulators.

**Keywords:** Collaborative Manipulator · Parameter Identification · Manipulators Dynamic · Nonlinear Friction Model · Data-Weighted Iterative · Information Loss

## 1 Introduction

The collaborative manipulators has been used more and more widely for humans because of its safety, accuracy, flexibility and light-weight [1]. However, accurate dynamic modeling remains an unsolved problem, which is the basis of accurate control, collision detection and flexible operation of collaborative manipulators [2–5]. The precision of dynamic model parameters is low, which is obtained by CAD software [6]. The physical experiment methods are very complicated [7]. Therefore, parameter identification method is usually used to obtain accurate dynamic model parameters.

When the model identification problem is regarded as a linear regression problem, the Ordinary least squares (OLS) and Weighted least squares (WLS) are commonly used

© The Author(s), under exclusive license to Springer Nature Singapore Pte Ltd. 2025
X. Lan et al. (Eds.): ICIRA 2024, LNAI 15208, pp. 222–237, 2025.
https://doi.org/10.1007/978-981-96-0783-9_16

because of their simplicity [8, 9]. The accuracy of dynamic model parameters identified by the least squares method is limited [10–13]. There are many reasons that affect the identification accuracy of the least squares method. Among them, it is inevitable that there will be measurement errors when we collect the motion data of the manipulator, which will make the data biased. In the practical application of the least squares method, the data bias problem significantly reduces the parameters identification accuracy. To eliminate the influence of data bias problem on the identification of least squares method, Han [11] proposed a data weighting method applied to Iteratively Reweighted least squares (IRLS). In this method, data weighting is added to the iterative least squares method as a new iterative period. The data weighting steps is implemented as follows: in the iterative process, the error value of data points is compared with a fixed threshold. When the error is greater than the threshold, the weight value of the data point will be reset to 0, that is, the data point information will be discarded in the identification process. This process forms a three-loop iteration with the iterative combination of error weight and friction model coefficient. This data weighting method can reduce the influence of biased data caused by measurement noise on least square method and improve the accuracy of identification results. Xu [12] improved this method, simplified the three-loop structure into two-loop structure, and applied it to the payload identification of manipulator. On the basis of [10], Deng [13] proposed a new three-loop iterative method and designed a new nonlinear friction model. As mentioned above, in the least squares method, data weighting methods are widely used to reduce the influence of biased data, but there are the following crucial problems: the data weight functions used in these methods need to set a fixed threshold for judgment, and this value can only be adjusted by experience. An inappropriate threshold will seriously reduce the accuracy of identification parameters and obviously increase the difficulty and feasibility of operation. In addition, in the process of data weighting, there are defects in judging biased data points. This method cannot directly prove that the data points that exceed the error threshold are data points affected by measurement noise. In practice, when the threshold is set too low, many valid data points will be mistaken as deviation data points, which will lead to the loss of effective information and have a serious negative impact on the identification accuracy. When the threshold is too large, the data weighting method will lose its effect.

In addition, harmonic drive is widely used in collaborative manipulators because of the accuracy of its torque output, lightweight design and efficiency. To obtain an accurate mathematical model, the nonlinear friction and the characteristics of harmonic drive must be considered when identifying parameters of manipulator dynamics [14]. In the study of joint friction model of manipulator, Coulomb friction effect and viscous friction effect should be considered first, and this classical Coulomb-viscosity has been widely used [12]. In addition, the Stribeck friction model used by Deng [13] considers the Stribeck effect under the low-speed motion of joints, while the LuGre friction model used by Zheng [15] regards the contact of contact surfaces as the contact between elastic bristles, thus describing the nonlinear friction model of manipulators joints more accurately. Madsen [1] improved the generalized Maxwell-Slip friction model into an extended generalized Maxwell-Slip model, and applied it to the dynamic parameter identification of manipulators joints, and achieved good results. However, due to complex factors such as mechanical transmission lag in harmonic drive, the theoretical friction model can not fully represent the actual complex nonlinear friction model. Up to now, the accurate modeling of nonlinear friction model of collaborative manipulators joints has not been completely solved.

To meet the above challenges, we propose an improved data-weighted iterative identification method for accurate parameter identification in dynamic models of collaborative manipulators. The main contributions are as follows: 1) The framework of our proposed iterative identification algorithm is cleverly designed into an inner and outer loop structure. In inner loop, we design a novel data weight function in the inner loop to solve the problem of information loss. It is worth noting that the improved weight function we used in the inner loop design has the ability to control the weight decline rate through two coefficient functions. We can not only set it through experience, but also choose to automatically iterate to the optimal value in the outer loop. This design also makes our method more applicable and convenient in practical application. 2) We consider a more accurate nonlinear friction model in the outer loop of iteration, which contains various friction effects such as Stribeck effect and friction anisotropy, as well as the mechanical hysteresis effect existing in harmonic drive, thus significantly improving the overall accuracy of the dynamic model. This hierarchical design not only improves the robustness of the algorithm, but also ensures the accuracy of the identification results. 3) We have carried out detailed comparative experiments on three different six-degree-of-freedom collaborative manipulators, which not only proves the stability of this method, but also shows that this method has obvious advantages over other advanced methods. At the same time, we prove that the phenomenon of information loss in the process of data weighting plays an important role in the identification effect. This obviously shows that the method proposed in this paper can effectively deal with the influence of complex nonlinear friction model, measurement noise and information loss in the process of data weighting on parameter identification accuracy.

The rest of the article is arranged as follows. Section 2 will outline the basic concepts and related technologies of dynamic parameter identification; Sect. 3 will elaborate the concrete realization and advantages of the proposed improved data-weighted iterative identification method; Sect. 4 will present the results and analysis of experimental verification; Finally, Sect. 5 will summarize the main results of this study and look forward to the future research direction.

## 2  Linear Model of Manipulator Dynamics

Dynamic model is very important for model-based control algorithm, contact force estimation and collision detection. The inverse dynamic model is considered in this paper, which is used to calculate the torque provided by each joint of the manipulators at the target position [12]. The inverse dynamic model of a manipulators with $n$ links represents the joint torque vector $\tau \in R$ as a function of generalized coordinates and their derivatives, as shown below:

$$\tau = M(q) \cdot \ddot{q} + C(q, \dot{q}) \cdot \dot{q} + G(q) + F(\dot{q}) \tag{1}$$

where $M(q) \in R^{n \times n}$ represents inertial torque term, $C(q, \dot{q}) \in R^{n \times n}$ represents Creole force and centrifugal force/torque, and $G(q) \in R^{n \times 1}$ is the gravity term. $F(\dot{q}) \in R^{n \times 1}$ is the friction term, and $q, \dot{q}, \ddot{q} \in R^{n \times 1}$ represents the joint position, joint velocity and joint acceleration. Generally speaking, for the *ith* joint, the friction term can be expressed by the classic Coulomb-Viscous Friction Model as follows:

$$F(\dot{q}_i) = F_{ci}sign(\dot{q}_i)+F_{vi}\dot{q}_i+B_i \tag{2}$$

where $F_{ci}$ represents Coulomb friction coefficient, $F_{vi}$ represents viscous friction coefficient, and $B_i$ represents compensation amount considering motor drive deviation. The mathematical model (1) can be linearized into a regression model about the following standard dynamic parameter sets:

$$\tau = \varnothing_s(q, \dot{q}, \ddot{q}) \, \beta_s \tag{3}$$

where $\varnothing_s(q, \dot{q}, \ddot{q}) \in R^{n\times 14}$ represents the regression matrix and $\beta_s \in R^{14\times 1}$ represents the base parameter set. Based on model (2), each link $i$ has 14 base parameters, which are $\beta_{si}=[M_i, MX_i, MY_i, MZ_i, XX_i, XY_i, XZ_i, YY_i, YZ_i, ZZ_i, I_{ai}, F_{ci}, F_{vi}, B_i, ]^T$, Where $M_i$ is the mass of the link i, $[MX_i, MY_i, MZ_i]$ are the three components of the first moment $MS_i$, $[XX_i, XY_i, XZ_i, YY_i, YZ_i, ZZ_i]$ are six components of inertia tensor $I_i$, and $I_{ai}$ is the inertia component of rotor and gear. $[F_{ci}, F_{vi}, B_i]$ are linear friction coefficients.

Next, we will simplify (3) to a basic parameter set and express it as follows:

$$\tau = \varnothing_b(q, \dot{q}, \ddot{q}) \, \pi \tag{4}$$

where $\varnothing_b(q, \dot{q}, \ddot{q}) \in R^{n\times p}$ is a subset of the regression matrix $\varnothing_s(q, \dot{q}, \ddot{q}) \in R^{n\times 14}$, and $\pi \in R^{p\times 1}$ is the basic parameter set reconstructed based on the standard parameter set $\beta_s \in R^{14\times 1}$. Usually, in the process of continuous excitation of the manipulators system by the excitation trajectory. We assume that $m$ motion data points are measured when the manipulator runs the excitation trajectory, then we extend (4) to the overdetermined equation in the linear regression problem, as shown below:

$$\Gamma = \phi(q, \dot{q}, \ddot{q}) \, \pi+\epsilon \tag{5}$$

where $\Gamma \in R^{mn\times 1}$, $\phi \in R^{mn\times p}$ and $\epsilon \in R^{mn\times l}$are observation vector, observation matrix and error vector respectively, which can be obtained by the following formula:

$$\Gamma = [\tau_1{}^T \, \tau_2{}^T \cdots \tau_m{}^T]^T \tag{6}$$

$$\phi = \begin{bmatrix} \varnothing_{b1}(q_1, \dot{q}_1, \ddot{q}_1) \\ \varnothing_{b2}(q_2, \dot{q}_2, \ddot{q}_2) \\ \vdots \\ \varnothing_{bm}(q_m, \dot{q}_m, \ddot{q}_m) \end{bmatrix} \tag{7}$$

therefore, the base parameter set $\pi \in R^{p\times 1}$ can be fitted by OLS method as follows:

$$\pi = argmin||\Gamma - \phi\beta_b|| \tag{8}$$

the analytical solution of OLS is calculated as follows:

$$\pi = (\phi^T\phi)^{-1}\phi^T \Gamma \tag{9}$$

here we can express the error vector $\epsilon$ as follows:

$$\epsilon = \Gamma - \phi\,\pi$$
(10)

## 3 Improved Data-Weighted Iterative Identification Method

### 3.1 Design of Improved Data Weight Function

Considering the correlation between the measured noise of all joint torques, we think that the above error vector can be reintegrated into the error matrix $C \in R^{mn \times 1}$ as follows:

$$C = \Gamma - \phi\pi$$
(11)

where $C_i$ is the error vector of the $ith$ joint torque, which represents the $ith$ column of matrix $C$. Therefore, the error matrix $C$ is used to calculate the initial covariance matrix $\Lambda \in R^{mn \times mn}$ of the torque error vector, which is expressed as follows:

$$\Lambda = \frac{C \cdot C^T}{m - p}$$
(12)

data weighting method is used here to reduce the influence of biased data on identification accuracy, the data weight matrix [12] $P \in R^{mn \times 1}$ and its extended matrix $P_e \in R^{mn \times p}$ are introduced, where each column is $P$, which can be applied as follows:

$$\begin{cases} \tilde{\phi} = P_e \odot (\Lambda^{\frac{1}{2}}\phi) \\ \tilde{T} = P \odot (\Lambda^{\frac{1}{2}}\Gamma) \end{cases}$$
(13)

where $\odot$ is the matrix element multiplication operator. Then considering the WLS method of data weighting to solve the base parameter set, the solution can be expressed as follows:

$$\pi_{WLS} = (\tilde{\phi}^T \tilde{\phi})^{-1} \tilde{\phi}^T \tilde{T}$$
(14)

when we have calculated the value of $\pi_{WLS}$, the normalized error vector can be calculated as follows:

$$\tilde{R} = \tilde{\Gamma} - \tilde{\phi}\pi_{WLS}$$
(15)

furthermore, the covariance matrix $\Lambda$ of the error matrix vector can be updated with the initial value calculated in (12), as shown below:

$$\Lambda_{new} = \frac{\Lambda^{\frac{1}{2}}\tilde{R} \cdot \tilde{R}^T \Lambda^{\frac{1}{2}}}{m - p}$$
(16)

using the normalized error vector as input, the new data weighted matrix $P_{new}$ can be updated as follows:

$$P_{new} = P_{old} \odot \psi(\tilde{R}, \delta) \tag{17}$$

in this paper, we use a novel data weight function $\psi$ to replace the T class hard redescender function used in references [11–13]. This is because the above method has the following shortcomings in the weighting process of using the T class hard redescender function: Firstly, the error in the error vector $C$ corresponding to $m$ data points is compared with the threshold. When the error value of data point is greater than the threshold, the data point weight will be reset to 0 directly, that is, the data point information will be discarded. The judgment of deviation data here is flawed, as we cannot directly assume that the data point exceeding the set threshold is the deviation data point that should be discarded. In practical work, if we use a small threshold, it will easily lead to the loss of a large number of data points that are not biased data, and the negative impact of this loss on the identification accuracy in the iterative process is irreversible. Moreover, the use of T class hard redescender function needs to be re-debugged to get the appropriate threshold in each use process to achieve the ideal effect, which will consume a lot of computing resources. Therefore, we introduce a new data weight function $\psi$, which is expressed as follows:

$$\psi(\tilde{R}, \delta) = \begin{cases} (B_1)^n \\ (B_2)^n \\ \phantom{x} \cdot \\ \phantom{x} \cdot \\ \phantom{x} \cdot \\ (B_m)^n \end{cases} \tag{18}$$

where $n$ is the number of iterations, the parameter $\delta$ sets the data residual threshold, and $B$ is the parameter of the weight function that controls the speed of weight reduction of each data point. The novel data weight function efficiently facilitates the rapid convergence of the weights associated with nonbiased data points, situated proximate to the established residual threshold, during the iterative process. This method properly reduces the influence of unbiased data points on the final identification results, and this reduction ensures that the data point information will not be completely discarded, but will be partially preserved. At the same time, the data points that are too far away from the residual threshold are considered as deviation data points, and their weights will decrease rapidly with the number of iterations, which means that the information of this data point will have little effect on the final identification effect. It is worth mentioning that the two parameters we need here can not only be set manually according to the empirical values, but also be automatically iterated with the nonlinear friction model in the outer ring to obtain the best results. Here, when initializing two parameters, $\delta$ uses the average value of error vector elements as the initialization threshold, and the value of parameter $B$ to control the weight decrease speed can be set to 0.1–0.9.

## 3.2  Design of Nonlinear Friction Model

To improve the identification accuracy of the dynamic model, a more accurate improved nonlinear model [16] is used here instead of (2). For the *ith* joint, the friction model is calculated as:

$$F(\dot{q}) = \varphi_{i1}(tanh(\varphi_{i2}\dot{q}_i) - tanh(\varphi_{i3})) + \varphi_{i4}tanh(\varphi_{i5}\dot{q}_i) + \varphi_{i6}\dot{q}_i \tag{19}$$

$\varphi_1$, $\varphi_2$ and $\varphi_3$ here are the coefficients of the Stribeck effect term. $\varphi_4$ and $\varphi_5$ are terms simulating Coulomb friction effect, and $\varphi_6$ is a term reflecting viscous friction effect. The influence of friction anisotropy in sliding direction is considered without sacrificing continuously differentiable. The identification of nonlinear friction model parameters can be solved as a nonlinear model parameter optimization problem, and iterated with two parameters $\delta$ and $B$ of the weight function in the outer loop. We define the nonlinear model optimization problem here as:

$$
\begin{aligned}
F_{est} &= \Gamma - \pi_{ip}\phi_{ip} \\
&arg(\varphi_{i1}, \varphi_{i2}, \varphi_{i3}, \varphi_{i4}, \varphi_{i5}, \varphi_{i6})\, min(||F_{est} - F(\dot{q})||_2) \\
i &= 1, 2, 3 \cdots n
\end{aligned}
\tag{20}
$$

here, $\pi_{ip}$ is the linear parameter part of the identified dynamic parameters, that is, the friction-free model parameter part, and $\phi_{ip}$ is the observation matrix of the linear basic parameters of the corresponding part, and the product of which is subtracted from the joint torque $\Gamma$ measured by us to get $F_{est}$. The optimization goal here is that the friction model $F(\dot{q})$ we established needs to be fitted with $F_{est}$ to the greatest extent. It is worth mentioning that we need to rerun the iteration when the outermost loop is iterated.

## 3.3  Improved Data-Weighted Iterative Method Description and Excitation Trajectory Design

We give the pseudo-code description of inner and outer loop iteration in Algorithm 1. This includes all the calculation steps after we take the operation data of the cooperative manipulator under the excitation trajectory as the input of the algorithm.

---

**Algorithm 1: Improved Data-Weighted Iteration Method.**

**Input:** Joint states $(\mathbf{q},\dot{\mathbf{q}},\ddot{\mathbf{q}})$, measured torque $\mathbf{\Gamma}$

**Output:** Identified base parameters $\boldsymbol{\pi}_{\mathbf{WLS}}$

Data weight function parameters $\boldsymbol{\delta}$ and $\mathbf{B}$

Nonlinear friction model parameters $\varphi_{i1}, \varphi_{i2}, \varphi_{i3}, \varphi_{i4}, \varphi_{i5}, \varphi_{i6}$

1.  Initialization of nonlinear parameters optimization function
2.  Initialization of data weight function parameters $\boldsymbol{\delta}$ and $\mathbf{B}$
3.  **While** parameters optimization function done **do**
4.      Initialize P=ones(mn,1)
5.      Initialize $\mathbf{P_e}$= P · ones(1,p)
6.      Solve $\boldsymbol{\pi}_{\mathbf{OLS}}$ by (9)
7.      Solve $\mathcal{R}$ by (11)
8.      Solve $\Lambda$ by (12)
9.      **While P and $\Lambda$ not converge do**
10.         Solve $\tilde{\boldsymbol{\Gamma}}$ and $\tilde{\boldsymbol{\phi}}$ by (13)
11.         Solve $\boldsymbol{\pi}_{\mathbf{WLS}}$ by (14)
12.         Solve $\tilde{\mathcal{R}}$ by (15)
13.         Update $\Lambda$ by (16)
14.         Update P by (17)
15.     **End while**
16.     Solve $\varphi_{i1}, \varphi_{i2}, \varphi_{i3}, \varphi_{i4}, \varphi_{i5}, \varphi_{i6}$ by (19)
17.     Run optimization function by (20)
18.  Update $\varphi_{i1}, \varphi_{i2}, \varphi_{i3}, \varphi_{i4}, \varphi_{i5}, \varphi_{i6}, \boldsymbol{\delta}, \mathbf{B}$
19. **End while**

---

Finally, in order to obtain the approximate analytical solution of the base parameter $\pi$ of the manipulator, we need to design a periodic trajectory to excite the manipulator system. We use the trajectory based on finite Fourier series proposed in reference [17] as the excitation trajectory of the manipulator system. For the *ith* joint, the trajectory can be defined as:

$$q_i(t) = q_{i0} + \sum_{k=1}^{5}\left(\frac{a_k}{\omega_f k}sin\left(\omega_f kt\right) - \frac{b_k}{\omega_f k}cos\left(\omega_f lk\right)\right)$$
$$\ddot{q}_i(t) = \sum_{k=1}^{5}\left(a_k sin\left(\omega_f kt\right) - b_k cos\left(\omega_f lk\right)\right) \qquad (21)$$
$$\ddot{q}_i(t) = \omega_f \sum_{k=1}^{5}\left(-a_k k sin\left(\omega_f kt\right) + b_k k cos\left(\omega_f lk\right)\right)$$

$\omega_f = 0.1\pi$ is the basic angular frequency, $q_{i0}$ is the initial position of the *ith* joint, and $a_k$ and $b_k$ are coefficients. Generally speaking, the excitation trajectory should conform to the constraints including joint angular velocity, velocity and acceleration, and avoid collision with the external environment. In addition to these conditions, we should use the condition number of the regression matrix to design the incentive trajectory, which can be expressed as follows:

$$min\,Cond\left(\phi(q,\dot{q},\ddot{q})\right)$$
$$s.t:\, q_{min} \leq q \leq q_{max}$$
$$\dot{q}_{min} \leq \dot{q} \leq \dot{q}_{max} \qquad (22)$$
$$\ddot{q}_{min} \leq \ddot{q} \leq \ddot{q}_{max}$$

*Cond* represents the condition number, $q_{min}$, $q_{max}$, $\dot{q}_{min}$, $\dot{q}_{max}$, $\ddot{q}_{min}$, $\ddot{q}_{max}$ respectively represent the minimum and maximum values of joint position, joint velocity and joint acceleration.

## 4  Experiment

### 4.1  Experimental Setup

To verify the performance of our proposed method, verification and comparison experiments were carried out on three different collaborative manipulators. We measured and processed the running data of UR5 manipulator under the excitation trajectory for experimental verification. The experimental platform of UR5 is shown in Fig. 1, and the modified DH parameters are shown in Table 1. We also verify our method in the public data set of two different manipulators. The UR10e manipulators data set used in it comes from [5], and the ROCR6 manipulators data set comes from the data set provided by the company Si Valley in China.

**Fig. 1.** Experimental setup of UR5.

We introduced two improved modules in Sect. 3. In order to show and analyze the effects of these two improved modules more intuitively, we designed two experimental groups with different combinations of improved modules, namely MethodA and MethodB, in which MethodA is an IRLS method using only the improved data weight function module, while MethodB is an improved data weighting iterative method combining the improved data weight function and the improved nonlinear friction model. MethodA and MethodB will be compared with the classical methods of OLS and IRLS. At the same time, MethodA and MethodB are compared with the iterative identification method proposed in reference [11] and the improved three-ring iterative method proposed

**Table 1.** Modified DH parameters of UR5

| Link | $\alpha\,(rad)$ | a $(mm)$ | d $(mm)$ | $\theta\,(rad)$ |
| --- | --- | --- | --- | --- |
| 1 | 0 | 0 | 144 | 0 |
| 2 | $\pi/2$ | 0 | 0 | $\pi/2$ |
| 3 | 0 | 264 | 0 | 0 |
| 4 | 0 | 236 | 106 | $\pi/2$ |
| 5 | $\pi/2$ | 0 | 144 | 0 |
| 6 | $-\pi/2$ | 0 | 67 | 0 |

in reference [13], which also adopt the method of data weighting. We apply the nonlinear parameter optimization method to iteration in the outermost layer. Particle Swarm Optimization (PSO) algorithm is selected in the experiment, with a population of 100, ten iterations and a parameter dimension of 38 (Including 36 joint friction parameters and data weight function parameters $\delta$ and $B$ in the inner loop). The UR5 data measured and processed by us, the acceleration is estimated by central difference method, and the noise is denoised by Butterworth lowpass filter. We set the verification set to 2000 sampling points. All the experiments were completed on the platform of MATLAB, and the experimental results were taken as the average of 10 repeated experiments to eliminate random errors and improve the reliability of the results.

## 4.2 Experimental Results and Analysis

The torque estimation curve of the proposed method on the three different collaborative manipulators is shown in Fig. 2, Fig. 3 and Fig. 4. The blue line represents the actually measured torque, and the red line represents the torque predicted based on the proposed method. The black curve shows the deviation between the two. Figure 2, Fig. 3 and Fig. 4 can well prove that our method has good accuracy in identifying the dynamic model of collaborative manipulators, and it can maintain stable identification accuracy on different manipulators data sets and has good adaptability.

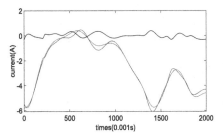 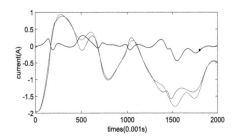

**Fig. 2.** Comparison of the estimated torque and measured torque of axis 2 and axis 3 of UR5 data.

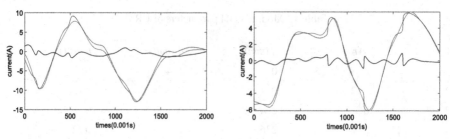

**Fig. 3.** Comparison of the estimated torque and measured torque of axis 2 and axis 3 of UR10e data

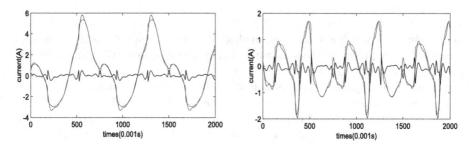

**Fig. 4.** Comparison of the estimated torque and measured torque of axis 2 and axis 3 of ROCR6 data

In order to fully demonstrate the superiority of our proposed method, we carried out detailed comparative experiments on different manipulators. Our MethodA and MethodB are compared with those proposed in OLS, IRLS and [11] and [13] respectively. Among them, OLS, IRLS and [11] all adopt the classical Coulomb-viscous friction model, while [13] adopts different Stribeck nonlinear friction model. Table 2, Table 3 and Table 4 show the RMS (root mean square error) results of the identification model verification using different identification methods on three manipulators respectively.

**Table 2.** RMS of cross-validation residual of UR5

| Method | Link 1 | Link 2 | Link 3 | Link 4 | Link 5 | Link 6 | Average value |
|--------|--------|--------|--------|--------|--------|--------|---------------|
| OLS | 0.1422 | 0.2013 | 0.1436 | 0.1166 | 0.0690 | 0.0474 | 0.1200 |
| IRLS | 0.1421 | 0.2022 | 0.1331 | 0.0833 | 0.0707 | 0.0335 | 0.1108 |
| [11] | 0.1390 | 0.1874 | 0.1268 | 0.0828 | 0.0686 | 0.0326 | 0.1062 |
| MethodA | 0.1354 | 0.1648 | 0.1182 | 0.0756 | 0.0665 | 0.0321 | 0.0988 |
| [13] | 0.1226 | 0.1741 | 0.1289 | 0.0758 | 0.0591 | 0.0315 | 0.0987 |
| MethodB | **0.1012** | **0.1418** | **0.0940** | **0.0505** | **0.0436** | **0.0285** | **0.0766** |

**Table 3.** RMS of cross-validation residual of UR10e

| Method | Link 1 | Link 2 | Link 3 | Link 4 | Link 5 | Link 6 | Average value |
|--------|--------|--------|--------|--------|--------|--------|---------------|
| OLS | 0.6219 | 0.7823 | 0.4643 | 0.1480 | 0.1145 | 0.1547 | 0.3810 |
| IRLS | 0.6194 | 0.7741 | 0.3787 | 0.1974 | 0.1121 | 0.1408 | 0.3704 |
| [11] | 0.6031 | 0.8823 | 0.4093 | 0.1960 | 0.1072 | 0.1447 | 0.3904 |
| MethodA | 0.5699 | 0.7413 | 0.3741 | 0.1901 | 0.1025 | 0.1341 | 0.3520 |
| [13] | 0.4869 | 0.7922 | 0.3662 | 0.1544 | 0.0936 | 0.1067 | 0.3333 |
| MethodB | **0.3755** | **0.6621** | **0.2056** | **0.1452** | **0.0933** | **0.0955** | **0.2629** |

**Table 4.** RMS of cross-validation residual of ROCR6

| Method | Link 1 | Link 2 | Link 3 | Link 4 | Link 5 | Link 6 | Average value |
|--------|--------|--------|--------|--------|--------|--------|---------------|
| OLS | 0.2021 | 0.2270 | 0.1920 | 0.0800 | 0.1220 | 0.0890 | 0.1520 |
| IRLS | 0.2096 | 0.2260 | 0.1890 | 0.0810 | 0.1135 | 0.0750 | 0.1490 |
| [11] | 0.1456 | 0.1854 | 0.1620 | 0.1030 | 0.1012 | 0.0647 | 0.1269 |
| MethodA | 0.1421 | 0.1801 | 0.1422 | 0.0988 | 0.0844 | 0.0652 | 0.1188 |
| [13] | 0.1344 | 0.1821 | 0.1260 | 0.0696 | 0.0768 | 0.0678 | 0.1095 |
| MethodB | **0.1251** | **0.1350** | **0.1209** | **0.0682** | **0.0530** | **0.0581** | **0.0933** |

First of all, comparing the rms error of MethodA with the rms error of [11], we can see that the identification accuracy of MethodA is better than that of [11] on each axis of each manipulator, and the overall identification accuracy is improved by about 10% compared with the result of [11], which proves that the improved data weight function can bring significant accuracy improvement, because the iterative method of improved weight function not only weights the data to reduce the impact of biased data, This also proves that the phenomenon of information loss has a crucial influence on the identification effect of data weighted iteration method.

As can be seen from Table 2, Table 3 and Table 4, MethodB has achieved the best identification effect in the comparative experiments of three manipulators, as shown by the bold data in the table. Compared with OLS and IRLS methods, the root mean square error of MethodB is reduced by about 40%. Compared with [11], the mean square error of each axis of method B is reduced by about 20%, and that of MethodB is reduced by about 15% compared with [13]. This is because MethodB adopts intelligent hierarchical iteration method, which not only uses the improved data weight function in the inner loop, but also uses the improved nonlinear friction model in the outer loop for iteration, thus improving the overall identification accuracy. The comparison results show that this method can really adapt to the complex dynamic characteristics of the collaborative manipulator, thus achieving more accurate parameter identification and more reliable dynamic modeling. In addition, in the above three tables, our MethodB is in the leading position in the recognition effect of different manipulators, which further proves the universality and applicability of our method.

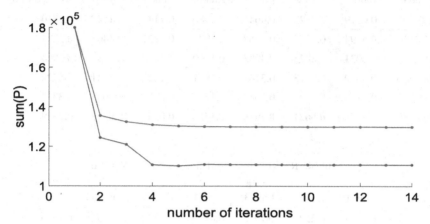

**Fig. 5.** Iterative process of the weight vector sum using improved data weight function $\psi$ (blue) and the T class hard redescender function (orange) (Color figure online)

Figure 5 shows the iterative convergence process of data weights in inner loop iteration. During the execution of the inner loop, we recorded the sum of the weight vectors $P$ with the same threshold. Among them, MethodA uses an improved data weight function $\psi$, which is shown by the blue line in Fig. 5. The T class hard redescender function used in reference [11] is shown by the orange line in Fig. 5. Obviously, it can be observed that both weight functions show good convergence. The difference is that under almost the same number of iterations, the final convergence values of the two functions are obviously different. In Fig. 5, the final convergence value of the blue line is about 15,000 more than that of the orange line. This difference indicates that there is an obvious difference between the two weight functions when dealing with the data points near the threshold, and the extra 15,000 weighted sums represent the suspected biased data points near the threshold, which are polluted by the noise that is considered to be measured by the T class hard redescender function. And the information of these points is discarded. However, the improved weight function $\psi$ we put forward determines that these suspected biased data are valuable, so these points are partially reserved. We regard this difference as the information loss caused by using T class hard redescender function in the data-weighted iteration process. By comparing the identification results in Table 2, Table 3 and Table 4, the accuracy of MethodA is obviously better than that in [11], which proves that better identification accuracy can be achieved while retaining the information of these data points, and also proves that information loss is a phenomenon that cannot be ignored in data weighting methods.

Figure 6 shows the comparison between the improved nonlinear friction model (19) and the classical Coulomb viscous static friction model (2) in fitting friction force $F_{est}$ from (20). In the figure, the black dot represents the residual current value, that is, the fitting target $F_{est}$ of the friction model; The blue dot represents the predicted value of the classical linear model; The purple dot is the predicted value of the improved nonlinear

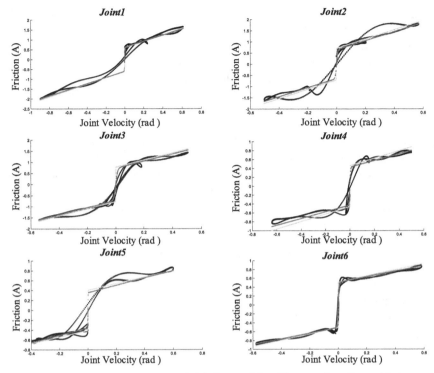

**Fig. 6.** Fitting effect of Coulomb-Viscous friction model and improved nonlinear friction model with $F_{est}$

model. From Fig. 6, we can clearly see that the improved nonlinear friction model we use can better capture the nonlinear characteristics of the friction model in joint motion, mainly because our nonlinear friction model considers Stribeck effect, friction anisotropy at low joint speed and mechanical hysteresis in harmonic transmission, which makes fitting effect of the proposed nonlinear friction model obviously better than Coulomb-viscous friction model. Similarly, from the comparison of MethodB and MethodA in Table 2, Table 3 and Table 4, it can be seen that the identification accuracy is improved by at least 20% after using the improved nonlinear friction model.

## 5  Conclusion

In this paper, we propose an improved data-weighted iterative identification method for dynamic parameters of collaborative manipulators, which solves the problem of information loss in the data-weighted method, and uses an improved nonlinear friction model. The experiments on three different collaborative manipulators show that this method has obvious advantages compared with other advanced methods. This method is divided into inner loop iteration and outer loop iteration. An improved data weight function is introduced into the inner loop, which solves the problem of information loss in the process of data weighting. In the outer loop, the key factors such as Stribeck effect, friction anisotropy and mechanical hysteresis in harmonic drive are considered, and a more accurate nonlinear friction model is used for iteration to improve the accuracy of parameter identification. The experimental results show that the proposed method has the best accuracy in three different manipulator experiments and is improved by more than 15% compared with other methods, showing obvious superiority and applicability. We also prove the improvement effect of the proposed improved module respectively. Among them, the accuracy of the original method can be improved by 10% after using the improved data weight, which proves that the phenomenon of information loss has a vital influence on the iterative weighting method. After using the improved nonlinear friction model, the accuracy of the friction model is improved by 20% compared with the Coulomb-Viscosity model, which also proves that the improved nonlinear friction model can better capture the actual joint friction phenomenon.

Although the method proposed in this paper has achieved ideal results in manipulators dynamic parameter identification, there are still some places worthy of improvement and expansion. This paper does not consider the influence of temperature on harmonic drive, nor does it compare the influence of different optimization methods on weight iteration, which will be the focus of our future work.

**Acknowledgment.** This work is supported by the National Key R&D Program of China (grant No.: 2022YFB4700400), National Natural Science Foundation of China (grant No.: 62073249), Key R&D Program of Hubei Province (grant No.: 2023BBB011).

# References

1. Madsen, E., Rosenlund, O.S., Brandt, D., et al.: Comprehensive modeling and identification of nonlinear joint dynamics for collaborative industrial robot manipulators. Control Eng. Pract. **101**, 104462 (2020)
2. Althoff, M., Giusti, A., Liu, S.B., et al.: Effortless creation of safe robots from modules through self-programming and self-verification. Sci. Robot. **4**(31), eaaw1924 (2019)
3. Ferraguti, F., Talignani, L.C., Sabattini, L., et al.: A variable admittance control strategy for stable physical human–robot interaction. Int. J. Robot. Res. **38**(6), 747–765 (2019)
4. Hong, M., Rozenblit, J.W.: An adaptive force guidance system for computer-guided laparoscopy training. IEEE Trans. Cybern. **52**(8), 8019–8031 (2021)
5. Mamedov, S., Mikhel, S.: Practical aspects of model-based collision detection. Front. Robot. AI **7**, 571574 (2022)
6. Golluccio, G., Gillini, G., Marino, A., et al.: Robot dynamics identification: a reproducible comparison with experiments on the Kinova Jaco. IEEE Robot. Autom. Mag. **28**(3), 128–140 (2020)
7. Benati, M., Gaglio, S., Morasso, P., Tagliasco, V., Zaccaria, R.: Anthropomorphic robots. Biol. Cybern. **38**, 125–140 (1980)
8. Gautier, M.: Dynamic identification of robots with power model. In: Proceedings of International Conference on Robotics and Automation, vol. 3, pp. 1922–1927. IEEE (1997)
9. Gautier, M., Poignet, P.: Extended Kalman filtering and weighted least squares dynamic identification of robot. Control Eng. Pract. **9**(12), 1361–1372 (2001)
10. Leboutet, Q., Roux, J., Janot, A., et al.: Inertial parameter identification in robotics: a survey. Appl. Sci. **11**(9), 4303 (2021)

11. Han, Y., Wu, J., Liu, C., et al.: An iterative approach for accurate dynamic model identification of industrial robots. IEEE Trans. Robot. **36**(5), 1577–1594 (2020)
12. Xu, T., Fan, J., Fang, Q., et al.: An accurate identification method based on double weighting for inertial parameters of robot payloads. Robotica **40**(12), 4358–4374 (2022)
13. Deng, J., Shang, W., Zhang, B., et al.: Dynamic model identification of collaborative robots using a three-loop iterative method. In: 2021 6th IEEE International Conference on Advanced Robotics and Mechatronics (ICARM), pp. 937–942. IEEE (2021)
14. Wang, Q., Wu, H., Cheng, Y., et al.: Friction-identification of harmonic drive joints based on the MCMC method. IEEE Access **10**, 125893–125907 (2022)
15. Zheng, Y.Q.: Parameter identification of LuGre friction model for robot joints. Adv. Mater. Res. **479**, 1084–1090 (2012)
16. Huang, Y., Ke, J., Zhang, X., et al.: Dynamic parameter identification of serial robots using a hybrid approach. IEEE Trans. Robot. **39**(2), 1607–1621 (2022)
17. Swevers, J., Ganseman, C., Tukel, D.B., et al.: Optimal robot excitation and identification. IEEE Trans. Robot. Autom. **13**(5), 730–740 (1997)

# Gaze2Atten: Analyzing Explainable Gaze Dynamics to Monitor Human Attention

Fengjun Mu, Jingting Zhang$^{(\boxtimes)}$, and Chaobin Zou

University of Electronic Science and Technology of China, Chengdu Sichuan, China
zhangjt@uestc.edu.cn

**Abstract.** Attention monitoring is an essential task to evaluate the human cognitive status in human-computer interaction. Prior works either employ an inconvenient invasive method or struggle to provide an explainable mechanism between the original human signal and the attention monitoring results. In this paper, we present Gaze2Atten, a dynamics-based cognitive learning approach for monitoring human attention with the non-invasive gaze signal. Gaze2Atten is constructed based on the dynamic system theory, which makes our mechanism explainable in attention modeling and monitoring. The attention-related gaze dynamics model is first learned based on the cognitive dynamics characteristics of humans. Furthermore, we realize an efficient dynamic pattern-matching method to early detect abnormal attention in the human-computer interaction process. To validate our approach, we designed a serious game to carry out a human-computer interaction behavior, and a parallel gaze data collection of subjects, the analysis shows that Gaze2Atten enables efficient and real-time human attention monitoring.

**Keywords:** Attention Monitoring · Deterministic Learning · Human-Computer Interface

## 1 Introduction

Analyzing users' attention is vital for the decision-making and feedback processes in typical human-computer interaction interactions, such as neurofeedback training [1] and human-machine collaborative driving [2], and robot-assisted training [3]. The attentional state represents the physiological, mental, and behavioral parameters of the human. Many factors such as fatigue, drowsiness, and distraction can influence the user's attention level on the specified tasks, which interferes with the completion of the task. Existing approaches employ invasive or non-invasive ways to obtain the user's physiological and behavioral signals for attention monitoring.

### 1.1 Monitor Attention from Invasive Signals

Invasive physiological signals [4], such as **electrocardiogram (ECG), electroencephalography (EEG), and surface electromyography (sEMG)**,

X. Lan et al. (Eds.): ICIRA 2024, LNAI 15208, pp. 238–256, 2025.
https://doi.org/10.1007/978-981-96-0783-9_17

are rich with information relative to the user's cognitive state, making them valuable for extracting attention-related features. PhyDAA [5] presented a physiological dataset composed of EEG signals and the corresponding score of attention span, and further proposed a machine learning-based framework for assessing attention with EEG, eye-tracker, and head movement signals. Z. Cao. et al. [6] collected the driver behavior and EEG data of a sustained-attention task in an immersive driving simulator, where the attention level is measured with the response time from deviation. V. Delvigne, et al. [7] employ the transformer architecture to exploit the time and frequency information to retrieve the attention state from the EEG signal. In addition, there are many other signal modes that can be used to monitor human attention, such as IMU [8], Interaction Pose [9] [10], and However, the heavy reliance on electrodes that adhere or are worn on the skin results in a cumbersome preparation process, significantly diminishing the method's user-friendliness and restricting the application scenarios for attention monitoring

### 1.2   Monitor Attention from Non-invasive Signals

Non-invasive behavioral signals do not necessitate the installation and configuration of wearable sensors by the user. Instead, they can directly collect attention-related signals from **interaction information or external sensors**. Cutting et al. proposed a novel method for measuring human attention, which involves assessing the attention level by identifying irrelevant distractions that appear around the user interface. Brockmyer et al. collected human responses through a voice-based game participation questionnaire to determine whether subjects were paying attention to the task. However, despite the potential value of these methods, attention monitoring based on interaction information often suffers from high latency and lag issues. This is because interpersonal interaction responses inherently introduce a certain degree of time delay and it is challenging to capture the user's rapid reactions to environmental changes in real-time. Therefore, these approaches are not suitable for scenarios that require highly interactive dynamics. Additionally, some works employ external sensors like cameras to monitor the user's attention. IntelliEye can monitor the learners' focus status with a combination of face, mouse, and web page tracking, which is further used to calculate an attention score. However, simply employing the weighted summary on the behavior boolean variables is only sensitive to the complete deviates from the current task, and it is easy for users to deceive by forging interactive behaviors.

### 1.3   Shortcoming Analysis of Existing Methods

In conclusion, invasive physiological signals can provide rich information but suffer from a cumbersome preparation process due to the reliance on skin-adhering or wearable electrodes, reducing user-friendliness and limiting application scenarios. Non-invasive behavioral signals, on the other hand, avoid the need for sensor installation but often face high latency and lag issues, making them unsuitable for highly interactive dynamics. Additionally, methods that use external sensors like cameras to monitor attention can be easily deceived by users who forge interactive behaviors, as they are typically only sensitive to complete deviations from the task at hand. In conclusion, it's difficult for existing works to detect abnormal attention. This is due to the lack of an explainable model to establish the link between non-intrusive external observation data and attention-related cognitive activities.

### 1.4 Contribution of This Paper

In this paper, we propose a novel approach Gaze2Atten to monitor human attention, which operates exclusively through a non-invasive eye tracker. Gaze2Atten can establish a dynamics model between the user's gaze movements and their attention levels, based on the deterministic learning method [11]. By constructing an explainable predictive model for cognitive gaze data, we can detect and warn of potential lapses in attention before they occur. This feature of early detection is crucial for enhancing the effectiveness of attention-monitoring systems, particularly in environments where sustained focus is essential.

The main contributions of this paper are threefold:

- We propose a dynamics-based Gaze2Atten for monitoring human attention status with the eye-tracker. Based deterministic learning method, we designed an explainable gaze dynamics modeling method for interactive attention analysis.
- Based on the well-learned gaze dynamics model, we realize an efficient dynamic pattern-matching method to detect abnormal attention in the human-computer interaction process. By employing the accurate acquisition and reuse of dynamic knowledge, we can achieve an early and rapid matching of abnormal attention patterns.
- To validate our approach, we designed a serious game to carry out a human-computer interaction behavior, and a parallel gaze data collection of subjects. The experiment is constructed under four different attention levels. Experimental results show the effectiveness of the proposed method.

## 2   Attention Modeling and Monitoring Method

### 2.1   Dynamical System Theory

Dynamical systems are deterministic mathematical structures that describe the behavior of a system as its state changes over time. Dynamic systems theory provides a clear framework for understanding how its state changes over time.

For a dynamic system $< T, S, \phi_t >$ is defined with the time set $T$, a state space $S$, and an evolution operator $\phi_t : x_0 \rightarrow x_t$, where initial state $x_0 \in S$ and the target state $x_t \in S$ is sampled at $t_0 \in T$ and $t \in T$. Since most of the observable variables acquired by the sensor are discrete signals acquired at a fixed frequency $v_{sample}$, the time set $T$ is a discrete set.

R. D. Beer *et al.* [12] analyzed the dynamic characteristics of the human cognitive process by using the theory of dynamic systems on three classic examples. G. Schoner [13] proves that it's possible to understand behavioral pattern generation on different levels(such as kinematic, electromyographic, and neuronal) with stochastic nonlinear dynamics. Therefore, once we can determine the essential cognitive-related macroscopic variables, the dynamics model of human behavior can be derived under different attention statuses, by cooperatively coupling individual microscopic components. A. Frischen et al. [14] proposed that the eye contains rich cognitive information as an essential human perception organ, which can reveal human attention, emotion, and mental states. A. K. Mackenzie et al. [15] proposed the hypothesis that visual attention task and eye movement behavior are highly correlated, and the experiment result proved the assertion.

In summary, existing researches prove that the nonlinear dynamics theory can be used to explain eye movement and monitor human attention states.

The general dynamic equation for the system with the eye movement and the attention status is defined as follows:

$$\dot{x} = N(x, a, \epsilon), \tag{1}$$

where $N$ indicates the nonlinear function of the gaze state vector $x$, the human's attention status $a$, and the $\epsilon$ perception noise from the gaze perception error. Through the human-computer interaction process, attention can be influenced by fatigue, drowsiness, and distraction, which will change the dynamic characteristics of the gaze state $x$ from an external eye-tracker. If we can solve for a concrete representation of $N$, then we can deduce the pattern of attention $a$ corresponding to the temporal dynamic changes of $x$.

## 2.2 Deterministic Learning Method

The biggest challenge in modeling human cognitive behavior is that the definite representation of $N$ cannot be directly obtained with mathematical solutions. The deterministic learning method [11] can identify the nonlinear system's dynamics along periodic and regression trajectories with a locally accurate neural network.

For a nonlinear dynamic system as 1, we considered the following discrete-time system as Eq. 2:

$$x(k+1) = f(x(k)) + v(x(k)) + \phi(x(k)) \tag{2}$$

where $x = [x_1, ..., x_m]^T \in \mathbb{R}^m$ is the system state vector with $m$ channels, $k \in [1, l]$ indicates the index of sample frames within the sequence length $l$, $f(x(k))$ representing the known nominal dynamics, $v(x(k))$ is the unknown dynamics to be accurately identified, $\phi(x(k))$ is the additional disturbances occurs on unexpected fault.

To accurately identify the unknown dynamics, we will employ the RBFNN-based deterministic learning method. In detail, we employ a radial basis function neural network (RBFNN) to approximate the $v(x(k))$ as Eq. 3

$$f_{RBFNN}(x) = \sum_{i=1}^{n} w_i s_i(x) = W^T S(x), \tag{3}$$

where $x = [x_1, ..., x_m]^T \in \mathbb{R}^m$ indicates the input vector of RBFNN, $W = [w_1, ...w_n] \in \mathbb{R}^n$ is the weight vector from the $n$ hidden RBF layer to the output layer, $S(x) = [s_1(||x - \zeta_1||), ..., s_n(||x - \zeta_n||)]$ consists of $n$ RBF function, where $\zeta_i (i \in [1, n])$ is the center of RBF neurons.

Therefore, we determine the expression of the unknown dynamics as Eq. 4.

$$v_i(x(k)) = f_{RBFNN}(x) + \epsilon_i = W_i^T S(x) + \epsilon_i, i = 1, ..., n \tag{4}$$

In Eq. 4, $\epsilon_i$ is the associated ideal estimation error that satisfies $||\epsilon_i|| < \epsilon^*$, where $\epsilon^*$ is a selected constant threshold for the permitted error. Relevant work [] proves that there exists an optimal $W$ matrix $W^*$, which can accurately identify the unknown dynamic system $v(x(k))$. The proposal of deterministic learning gives a method that can make W deterministic converge to the exact value. We propose a dynamics estimator following [17] as Eq. 5

$$\hat{x}_i(k+1) = a_i(\hat{x}_i(k) - x_i(k)) + f_i(x(k), u(k)) + \hat{W}_i^T(k)S(x(k), u(k)), \tag{5}$$

where $\hat{x}(k)$ and $x(k)$ indicate the estimated and the observed state, $a_i$ is a designed positive constant for balancing the error enhancement, $\hat{W}$ is the dynamically updated estimate of the $W^*$.

In Eq. 5, $a_i(\hat{x}_i(k) - x_i(k))$ is the error enhancement term, $f_i(x(k), u(k))$ is the observed system state, $\hat{W}_i^T(k)S(x(k), u(k))$ is the estimated system dynamics between time $k$ and $k+1$. With Eq. 5, we can estimate the system state based on the well-learned dynamics pattern $\bar{W}$.

During the deterministic learning process, we will iterate the sampled states in $x$, and dynamically update $\hat{W}$ with Eq. 6.

$$\hat{W}_i(k+1) = \hat{W}_i(k) - c_i \tilde{x}_i(k+1)S(x(k), u(k)), \tag{6}$$

where $\tilde{x}(k) = \bar{x}(k) - x(k)$ indicates the estimate error of state $x(k)$. With the iteration through all the sampled data in $x$, the well-learned $\bar{W}$ that is close to $W^*$.

## 2.3   Attention-Related Data Acquisition

The raw gaze movement data is divided into the left and right eyes $\check{x}_{left}$ and $\check{x}_{right}$. We first average the $\check{x}_{left}$ and $\check{x}_{right}$ to obtain $\check{x} = [\check{x}_1, ..., \check{x}_n]$, which contains $n$ data frames. Each frame contains the status data $\check{x}_i = \{y_i, z_i, \dot{y}_i, \dot{z}_i\}, (i = 1, ..., n)$ on the $i$, where $(y_i, z_i)$ indicates the gaze point under the pixel coordinate system of the screen, and the gaze point movement speed $(\dot{y}_i, \dot{z}_i)$ indicates the local gaze movement between the $i$ and $i+1$ frames.

**Completion of Partial Missing Fragments.** Since there are system measurement errors from the eye tracker, and the blinking of the subject's eyes during the test can disrupt the continuity of the signal, We need to pad and smooth the original signal $\breve{x}$ in real-time to improve the quality, for better extracting its dynamic characteristics.

Blinking is a short-duration behavior, so the interruption of the eye movement signal caused by blinking can be completed based on the start stage and the end state of the interruption. To avoid the discontinuity of the complete signal, we choose to use the linear interpolation method to pad the missing signal segment. Given a slice of state signal $\breve{x}' = [\breve{x}_1, ..., \breve{x}_n]$, where the signal segment $\breve{x} = [\breve{x}_t, ..., \breve{x}_{t+k-1}]$ in the time interval $[t, t+k)$ is the null value representing the missing signal, the filling process is shown in the Eq. 7.

$$\breve{x}_i = \frac{(i - t + 1)}{k + 1}(\breve{x}'_{t+k} - \breve{x}'_{t-1}) + \breve{x}'_{t-1}, i \in [t, t+k), \tag{7}$$

where $\breve{x}$ is the padded gaze signal. However, there are still plenty of observation noises in $\breve{x}$, which hinders the analysis of essential attention-related eye movement dynamics.

**Attention Related Frequency Band Extraction.** Since the realization principle of the eye tracker is based on the back projection of pupil detection, even if we repair the missing fragments, the signal still contains a lot of observation noise, which will cover up the real attention-related eye movement dynamics characteristics, affecting the learning effect of the deterministic learning method.

The actual motion of the eye in human-computer interaction is of low frequency, which is significantly different from the high-frequency noise of the observation signal. Therefore, we use a low-pass filter to process signal $\breve{x}$ to retain more attention-related eye movement information $x$.

In detail, firstly, we perform a Fourier transform on the signal $\breve{x}$ to convert it from the time domain to the frequency domain as Eq. 8.

$$\breve{x}(f) = \mathcal{F}(\breve{x}), \tag{8}$$

where $\mathcal{F}$ denotes the Fourier transform, $\breve{x}$ is the padded gaze movement signal, and $\breve{x}(f)$ is the representation of the signal in the frequency domain. Based on the frequency domain signal $\breve{x}(f)$, we further apply a low-pass filter to select the low-frequency area for attention-related gaze signal. This process can be represented by boolean selection for removing the high-frequency noise as Eq. 9.

$$\breve{x}_{\text{filtered}}(f) = \breve{x}(f) \cdot H(f) \tag{9}$$

where $H(f)$ is the frequency response function of the filter. Specifically, $H(f)$ is defined as Eq. 10.

$$H(f) = \begin{cases} 1, & \text{if } |f| \leq f_c \\ 0, & \text{if } |f| > f_c \end{cases}, \tag{10}$$

where $f_c$ is the cutoff frequency between the noisy high-frequency and attention-related low-frequency. When the frequency $|f|$ is less than or equal to $f_c$, $H(f)$ will pass through the attention-related signal; when the frequency $|f|$ is greater than $f_c$, $H(f)$ will block the signal to reduce the observation noise.

Finally, we perform an inverse Fourier transform on the filtered signal $\breve{x}_{\text{filtered}}(f)$ to recover from the frequency domain to the time domain:

$$x(t) = \mathcal{F}^{-1}(\breve{x}_{\text{filtered}}(f)) \tag{11}$$

Here, $\mathcal{F}^{-1}$ denotes the inverse Fourier transform, and $x(t)$ is the signal after low-pass filtering, retaining the attention-related eye movement information.

## 2.4   Explainable Cognitive Pattern Deterministic Learning

For modeling the cognitive dynamics with attention-related gaze signals, due to the lack of prior knowledge of the connection between the gaze signal and cognitive status, the known dynamics that cannot be nominated are considered empty items. Based on Eq. 2, the cognitive model is defined as Eq. 2

$$x(k+1) = \begin{cases} v(x(k)) + \epsilon & \text{Normal Mode} \\ v(x(k)) + \phi(x(k)) + \epsilon & \text{Abnormal Mode} \end{cases} \tag{12}$$

where $x = [x_1, ..., x_m]^T \in \mathbb{R}^m$ is the system state vector, $v(x(k))$ is the unknown attention-related gaze dynamics to be accurately identified, $\phi(x(k))$ representing the deviation in gaze dynamics due to the attention aberration with external disturbance or an internal deviation.

The unknown attention-related gaze cognitive dynamics can be modeled based on the processed signal $x$. In detail, we first employ the deterministic learning method as mentioned in Sect. 2.2.

The set of RBF neurons $\zeta$ is generated by a uniform grid in multiple $m$ dimensions. For the processed training trajectory $x$ that contains $m$ channels and the length is $l$, we first iterate over all the sampled trajectories in the training samples, to obtain the reachable region $\{[L_i, U_i] | i \in 1, ..., m\}$ in each dimension. By assigning the grid step interval $\{s_i | i \in 1, ..., m\}$, we can split each reachable region on each dimension for $\{d_i | i \in 1, ..., m\}$ points, and use the intersection points forming the grid as the center of the RBF network. The overall RBF neuron number $n$ can be calculated with Eq. 13.

$$n = \prod_{i=1}^{m} d_i. \tag{13}$$

We have identified the RBF neuron sets $\zeta$, and obtained the RBF function $S(x)$. The RBFNN weight matrix $\bar{W}$ corresponds to the normal pattern can be further learned with the deterministic learning method as Eq. 6. In this learning stage, we donate the gaze movement data collected within the normal human-computer interaction. With the learned $\bar{W}$, we can identify the unknown dynamics $v(x(k))$, and predict the human's gaze movement signal at $k + 1$ time under the normal attention state as Eq. 14.

$$\bar{x}_i(k + 1) = a_i(\bar{x}_i(k) - x_i(k)) + \bar{W}_i^T(k)S(x(k), u(k)). \tag{14}$$

## 2.5   Abnormal Attention Detection

In order to make full use of the interpretability of dynamic features, we first assume that the real-time input human eye movement state is in line with the normal attention pattern. Based on the learned dynamic characteristics W in the normal pattern, we predict the viewpoint state at the next time based on the viewpoint state at each time i. If the input state is contrary to our assumption, that is, the subject's attention is in an abnormal state, then the eye movement prediction based on the dynamic characteristics will have a large error with the real data. Through the judgment of the error, we can achieve early and accurate identification of abnormal attention state.

To quantitatively measure the discrepancy between the predicted state $\bar{x}$ and the actual state $x$, we employ the state residual from [16] as follows:

$$e_i(k) = b_i e_i(k - 1) + \|\bar{W}_i^T S(x_i(k - 1), u(k - 1)) - x_i(k)\|, i = 1, ..., n, \tag{15}$$

where $b_i > 0$ indicates the gain parameter for error, which can determine the contribution of the historical error to the current error, which can affect how the controller responds to past errors, tuning $b_i$ can balance the detection accuracy and recall rate.

As shown in Eq. 12, the gaze dynamics $v(x(k))$ contains a estimation error, which satisfies $\|\epsilon_i\| < \epsilon^*$. Therefore, we have to identify the constant threshold $\epsilon^*$ for the permitted error, which can determine an allowable error range in normal mode.

Based on the well-learned weights $\bar{W}$ and the sampled sequence of state $x$ with length $l$, we set $e_i(0) = 0$ and commence from the initial state $x(0)$, applying Eq. 15 to infer the value of $e_i(k)$ for every $i = 1, ..., n$, and subsequently extract the maximum error $em_i$ encountered during the inference process.

$$em_i = max(e_i(k)), k = 1, ..., l \tag{16}$$

The occurrence of an abnormal attention state can be detected from the deviation between the user's real-time state and the cognitive dynamics prediction, with the learned human cognitive dynamics and the threshold $em_i$. To begin with, we will calculate $e_i(k)$ with the real-time state input as Eq. 15.

In practice, signal interruption will occur due to various unexpected factors, and the completion algorithm is completely irrelevant to the real-time state of the user, that is, the abnormal attention information occurring during the signal interruption cannot be predicted and restored through the completion signal. Therefore, we only employ a low-pass filter on the continuous gaze signal within a sliding window and predict the state $\hat{x}(k)$ of the current time $k$ according to the state $x(k - 1)$ following Eq. 17.

$$\hat{x}_i = \bar{W}_i^T S(x_i(k-1), u(k-1)) \tag{17}$$

$$e_i(k) = \begin{cases} b_i e_i(k-1) + \|\hat{x}_i - x_i(k)\|, x_i(k) \text{ is valid} \\ -1, x_i(k) \text{ is invalid} \end{cases} \tag{18}$$

Then, the rules for classifying normal attention and abnormal attention are as follows:

$$\mathcal{A} = \begin{cases} \text{normal attention}, \|e_i(k)\| < c_i \\ \text{abnormal attention}, \|e_i(k)\| > c_i \\ \text{invalid input}, e_i(k) = -1 \end{cases} \tag{19}$$

## 3   Experimental Validation

In the experimental part, we designed a serious game to verify the process of human interaction, and designed a data collection paradigm that could simulate the cognitive and behavioral activities of users under different attention states. Based on the collected data, we used the method proposed in this paper to construct the interpretable model of human cognitively related attention, and used the abnormal attention detection method to classify and detect cognitive behaviors under different attention states, proving the effectiveness of this method.

### 3.1   A Serious Game for Attention-Related Data Acquisition

In the field of human-computer interaction research, combining advanced sensor technology with interactive game environments provides a new way to study cognitive processes. To obtain human-computer interaction data related to attention and analyze cognitive dynamics to verify the attention-monitoring method proposed in this paper, we use the PyGame framework to implement a serious game based on real-time eye-tracking sensor input. The human-computer interaction system can capture the precise coordinates of the user's visual tracking point on the screen, so as to support the attention analysis of the user.

**Interactive User Interface.** In this game, the main function of the game is to provide users with a reference tracking target point for human-computer interaction, so that they can move according to the preset trajectory and speed curve, so as to control the variables between multiple experimental trials. During the human-computer interaction, the reference point coordinates and the viewpoint tracking point coordinates are recorded in real-time, which are dynamically obtained from the eye-tracking sensor. This synchronous coordinate recording mechanism ensures comparability and data synchronization between different trials and allows a comprehensive analysis of the spatio-temporal characteristics of the user interaction process.

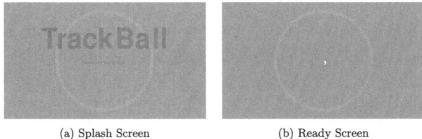

(a) Splash Screen                    (b) Ready Screen

**Fig. 1.** The waiting screen for remaining calm and ready for interaction

As shown in Fig. 1 and Fig. 2, the red ball is the reference target point generated in the game, which moves according to the preset trajectory curve $P_{center}(t) = (x_{center}(t), y_{center}(t))$. The blue ball is a visible representation of the user's gaze point from the eye tracker.

We first calculate the theta value of the reference point in the polar coordinate system. The polar coordinate system takes the center of the picture as the origin, the right side of the picture is the positive direction of the $x$ axis, and the upper side of the picture is the positive direction of the $y$ axis.

$$\theta(t) = \int_0^t \omega(t)dt, \tag{20}$$

where $\omega(t)$ is the curve of the specified speed over time. After that, we convert the reference point to cartesian coordinates to obtain the reference point coordinates. The calculation of $P_{target}(t)$ is Eq. 21.

$$\begin{cases} x_{center}(t) = x_{center} + R \cdot \cos \theta(t) \\ y_{center}(t) = y_{center} + R \cdot \sin \theta(t) \end{cases} \tag{21}$$

With the above data collected, the game becomes a powerful tool to observe the attention shift and cognitive state of the player during the game. The collected data can be used to analyze the user's interaction behavior and response time, establish a human cognitive model, and then analyze the user's non-contact physiological signal characteristics in different cognitive states, providing a data set related to cognitive and physiological signals for academic research.

**Experiment Implement.** In this experiment, the relative position relationship between the eye tracker and the screen was fixed, and the coordinate system between the two was calibrated using the registration process of the eye tracker. The eye tracker adopts Tobii Pro Fusion, the sampling rate is 60 Hz, the low-pass filtering frequency for the $(x, y)$ signal channel is 0.48 Hz, and the low-pass filtering frequency for the $(\dot{x}, \dot{y})$ signal channel is 0.6 Hz. The screen resolution for human-computer interaction is 2880*1920 and the refresh rate is 120 Hz.

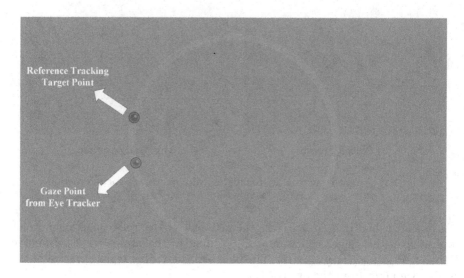

**Fig. 2.** The interaction screen for guiding the user to complete the tasks

## 3.2   Attention Interference Paradigm in Interaction

To obtain the cognitive data of users in different attention states, we need to interfere with the cognitive process of subjects to regulate their attention states. The motivation of this research is to judge the attention state of the subjects based on their eye movement information. Therefore, the interference forms in the experimental paradigm should use visual-related interference forms, such as extra elements in serious games, video watching, and other interference that directly affect the eye movement signals.

Therefore, we chose auditory, tactile, long-short-term memory, and other forms of cognitive interference to avoid directly affecting subjects' eye movements. In this experiment, we designed four different kinds of attention:

- **Without Interference:** Subjects were asked to focus on engaging in a human-computer interaction task in a serious game;
- **Long-Term Memory Interference:** Subjects were asked to complete the long-term information recall task in their brain, the specific form is: the subject silently recites the traditional Chinese long poetry *Mulan Poem*;
- **Complex Interaction Interference:** Specific actively complete complex interactive tasks are as follows: During the interaction, subjects use Google TalkBack to control the mobile phone to complete a series of information search tasks;
- **Short-Term Memory Interference:** The short-term memory task was completed passively under the input of external information(Listen to a segment of crosstalk), and the subjects were asked to briefly retell the listened contents after the experiment (Figs. 3, 4 and 5);

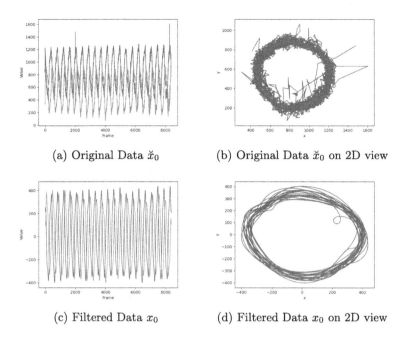

(a) Original Data $\breve{x}_0$

(b) Original Data $\breve{x}_0$ on 2D view

(c) Filtered Data $x_0$

(d) Filtered Data $x_0$ on 2D view

**Fig. 3.** Data collected under the normal attention mode

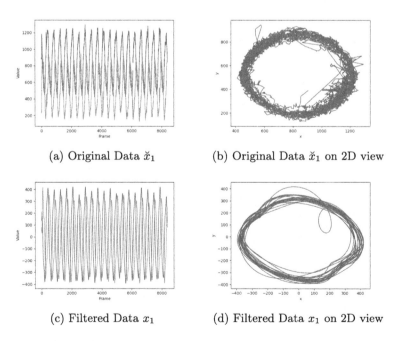

(a) Original Data $\breve{x}_1$

(b) Original Data $\breve{x}_1$ on 2D view

(c) Filtered Data $x_1$

(d) Filtered Data $x_1$ on 2D view

**Fig. 4.** Data collected under the abnormal attention mode I

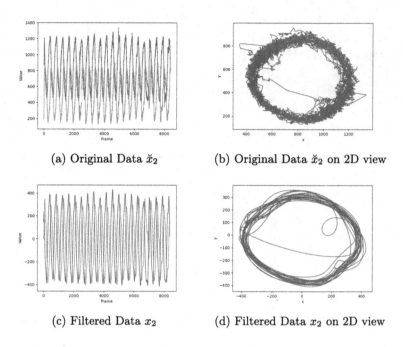

(a) Original Data $\breve{x}_2$                    (b) Original Data $\breve{x}_2$ on 2D view

(c) Filtered Data $x_2$                    (d) Filtered Data $x_2$ on 2D view

**Fig. 5.** Data collected under the abnormal attention mode II

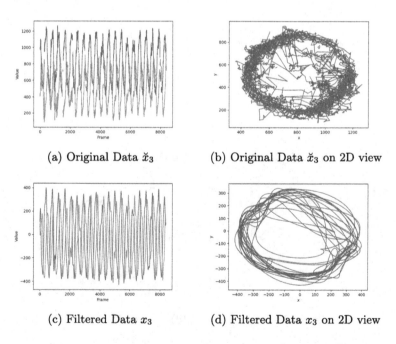

(a) Original Data $\breve{x}_3$                    (b) Original Data $\breve{x}_3$ on 2D view

(c) Filtered Data $x_3$                    (d) Filtered Data $x_3$ on 2D view

**Fig. 6.** Data collected under the abnormal attention mode III

Based on the above four attentional interference modes, we combined them with the velocity function $\omega(t) = 0.5 \cdot \sin 2\theta + 1$ for reference trajectories' generation, each consisting of 10 human-computer interaction cycles.

### 3.3   Construction of Dynamic Cognitive Model

To effectively model the cognitive dynamics of human attention under normal conditions, we employ a deterministic learning approach as mentioned in Sect. 2.2, because of its foundation on the dynamical system theory, which is evidence to support the explainable learned model. Specifically, we utilize the algorithm to conduct a series of optimizations on the weight parameters $\hat{W}$ of the RBF network, denoted by the data shown in Fig. 6. We iterative employ the data for 500 epochs, until $\hat{W}$ only has a minor update as shown in 7, because it's already well-trained.

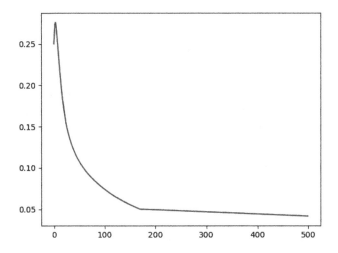

**Fig. 7.** Max Prediction Error *em* through the Training Process

In each iteration, the weights are adjusted to progressively reduce the trajectory tracking errors and enhance the performance of the RBF neural network in simulating cognitive dynamics. Through this rigorous and explainable approach, we aim to refine these weights progressively until they converge to an optimal set approximating $W^*$, denoted by $\bar{W}$. As shown in Fig. This final set of weights represents the culmination of our efforts to closely align the RBF network's output with the empirical data on human attention processes, thereby providing a robust model for understanding and predicting attention dynamics in real-world scenarios (Fig. 8).

As shown in Fig. 9, by using the determination learning to optimize the RBF weights $W$, the max prediction error through the whole data trajectory with $\bar{W}$ is reduced from 0.2761 to 0.0418. In a word, the dynamic system theory

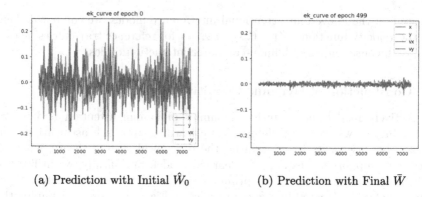

(a) Prediction with Initial $\hat{W}_0$    (b) Prediction with Final $\bar{W}$

**Fig. 8.** Error Curves of Dynamics Prediction by RBF Weights based on the Initial $\hat{W}_0$ and Final $\bar{W}$

can explain the relationship between human eye movement signals and cognitive attention, and the deterministic learning method can effectively build explicable attention models based on cognitive dynamics to achieve accurate tracking of attention-related eye movement signals.

Dynamic system theory can effectively explain the relationship between human eye movement signals and cognitive attention, and deterministic learning method can effectively build explicable attention models based on cognitive dynamics to achieve accurate tracking of attention-related eye movement signals.

### 3.4   Early Abnormal Attention Detection

Based on the learned dynamic feature W, we made subjects conduct human-computer interaction experiments in serious games under different attention interference modes, and conducted detection based on the abnormal attention detection method proposed in this paper. For the cognitive signal sequences $x_0$, $x_1$, $x_2$, and $x_3$, we employ Eq. 18 to calculate the tracking error sequence using $\hat{W}$. The tracking error $e_i(k)$ is shown in Fig. 9.

In Fig. 9b, when predicting the dynamics of data $x_0$ with $\hat{W}$, the maximum global error $max(em_i)$ only reaches 0.0057. Therefore, we selected to set the threshold $c$ as follows:

$$c = \alpha \cdot max(em_i), i = 1, ..., n, \tag{22}$$

After testing under multiple settings, we select to set $\alpha$ to 1.5, which can prevent the wrong detection from being over-sensitive to the small dynamic estimation error in the normal mode.

As shown in Fig. 10, Based on the dynamic W matrix learned from normal mode, the dynamic prediction of eye movement signals is carried out based on physiological signals in an abnormal attention state. The amplitude of the error curve of the abnormal signal is significantly larger than the tracking effect of

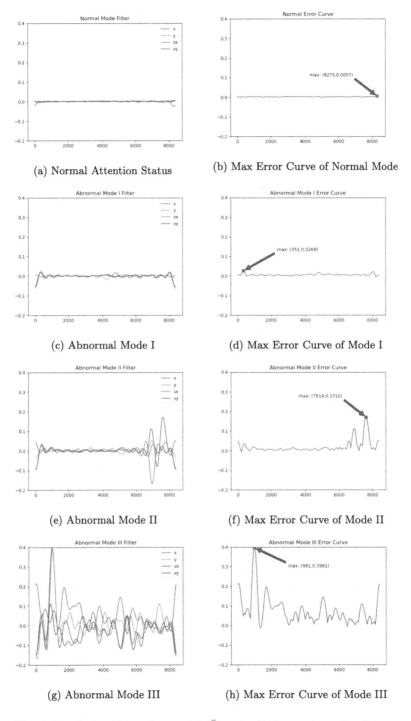

(a) Normal Attention Status

(b) Max Error Curve of Normal Mode

(c) Abnormal Mode I

(d) Max Error Curve of Mode I

(e) Abnormal Mode II

(f) Max Error Curve of Mode II

(g) Abnormal Mode III

(h) Max Error Curve of Mode III

**Fig. 9.** Prediction Error Curve with $\bar{W}$ under Different Attention Status.

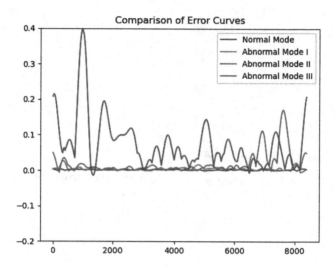

**Fig. 10.** Comparison of the Maximum Dynamic Errors in Various Cognitive States.

the signal in normal mode, and we can detect abnormal attention based on this characteristic. In addition, we found that for different types of abnormal signals, there are also significant differences in their error margins, which to some extent represents the impact of this type of interference on attention.

We also calculated the detection delay from the abnormal attention that happens to the detected time. For abnormal mode I, our method can detect the deviation from the normal attention mode at the $228^{th}$ frame, which means even a minor influence on human attention can be detected in 4.56 s. For major attention deviation of abnormal modes II and III, our method can detect the deviation from the normal attention mode at the $2^{th}$ frame, which means our method can reach an early detection of abnormal attention within 0.04 s.

## 4    Conclusion

In this paper, we introduced a novel dynamics-based approach Gaze2Atten, for monitoring human attention with a non-invasive eye tracker. Based on the dynamic system theory, we first analyze the human's attention-related cognitive signal with a deterministic learning method, which can effectively model the relationship between gaze movements and attention levels. With the well-learned human cognition model, we further employ an abnormal attention detection module for detecting the deviation of attention. Benefits from the employment of dynamic characteristics of attention-related cognition signal, the abnormal attention status can be early detected, which is vital for enhancing the performance of attention-monitoring systems, especially in settings requiring sustained focus. To evaluate the effect of our approach, we built a serious game designed for parallelly human-computer interaction and gaze signal collection and proposed a series of attention interference paradigms to obtain physiological signals under different attention levels. The experimental result validates our cognitive modeling and abnormal attention detection methods.

**Acknowledgments.** This work was supported by the National Natural Science Foundation of China (U1964203, 62203089, 62303092, 62103084), China Postdoctoral Science Foundation under Grant 2021M700695, Sichuan Science and Technology Program (2022NSFSC0890,2022NSFSC0865, 2021YFS0383, 2023YFG0024, 2022YFS0570, 2023YFS0213), and the Fundamental Research Funds for the Central Universities (ZYGX2022YGRH003, ZYGX2021YGLH003)

# References

1. Balani, N., Mulchandani, M.: Integrative approaches for understanding and characterizing ADHD: insights from multimodal data, virtual reality, longitudinal studies, and deep phenotyping. In: Intelligent Solutions for Cognitive Disorders, pp. 99–132 (2024)
2. Kircher, K., Ahlstrom, C.: Evaluation of methods for the assessment of attention while driving. Accid. Anal. Prev. **114**, 40–47 (2018)
3. Zhang, M., Wang, C., Zhang, C., et al.: A unified switching control framework for continuous robot-assisted training IEEE/ASME Trans. Mech. (2023)
4. Jiang, Y., Zheng, C., Ma, R., et al.: Within-session reliability of fNIRS in robot-assisted upper-limb training. IEEE Trans. Neural Syst. Rehabil. Eng. **32**, 1302–1313 (2024)
5. Delvigne, V., Wannous, H., Dutoit, T., et al.: PhyDAA: physiological dataset assessing attention. IEEE Trans. Circuits Syst. Video Technol. **32**(5), 2612–2623 (2021)
6. Cao, Z., Chuang, C., King, J., et al.: Multi-channel EEG recordings during a sustained-attention driving task. Sci. Data **6**(1), 19 (2019)
7. Delvigne, V., Wannous, H., Vandeborre, J.P., et al.: Spatio-temporal analysis of transformer based architecture for attention estimation from EEG. In: Proceeding of International Conference on Pattern Recognition, pp. 1076-1082 (2022)
8. Zhong, W., Zhang, L., Sun, Z., et al.: UI-MoCap: an integrated UWB-IMU circuit enables 3D positioning and enhances IMU data transmission. IEEE Trans. Neural Syst. Rehabil. Eng. **32**, 1034–1044 (2024)
9. Mu, F., Huang, R., Luo, A., et al.: TemporalFusion: temporal motion reasoning with multi-frame fusion for 6D object pose estimation. In: Proceedings of IEEE/RSJ International Conference on Intelligent Robots and Systems, pp. 5930–5936 (2021)
10. Mu, F., Huang, R., Shi, K., et al.: Weak6D: weakly supervised 6D pose estimation with iterative annotation resolver. IEEE Robot. Autom. Lett. **8**(3), 1463–1470 (2022)
11. Zhang, J., Yuan, C., Stegagno, P., et al.: Small fault detection from discrete-time closed-loop control using fault dynamics residuals. Neurocomputing **365**, 239–248 (2019)
12. Beer, R.: Dynamical approaches to cognitive science. Trends Cogn. Sci. **4**(3), 91–99 (2000)
13. Schöner, G., Kelso, J.S.: Dynamic pattern generation in behavioral and neural systems. Science **239**(4847), 1513–1520 (1988)

14. Frischen, A., Bayliss, A.P., Tipper, S.P.: Gaze cueing of attention: visual attention, social cognition, and individual differences. Psychol. Bull. **133**(4), 694 (2007)
15. Mackenzie, A., Harris, J.: A link between attentional function, effective eye movements, and driving ability. J. Exp. Psychol. Hum. Percept. Perform. **43**(2), 381 (2017)
16. Zhang, J., Yuan, C., Stegagno, P., et al.: Small fault detection of discrete-time nonlinear uncertain systems. IEEE Trans. Cybern. **51**(2), 750–764 (2019)
17. Yuan, C., Wang, C.: Design and performance analysis of deterministic learning of sampled-data nonlinear systems. Sci. China Inf. Sci. **57**, 1–18 (2014)

# Dynamical Feature Extraction and Pattern Recognition for Mental Workload Level with FNIRS

Lianchi Zhang, Jingting Zhang$^{(\boxtimes)}$, Fengjun Mu, and Rui Huang

University of Electronic Science and Technology of China, Chengdu 611731, Sichuan, China
zhangjt@uestc.edu.cn

**Abstract.** Mental Workload Level (MWL) is an important indicator reflecting the human's cognitive state in human-computer interaction, such as the applications of vehicle driving and mental state assessment. A useful method of MWL assessment is by utilizing functional near-infrared spectroscopy (fNIRS) to monitor the brain tissue blood oxygen concentration during human's cognitive process. However, existing fNIRS-based MWL classification methods still have limited performance in terms of classification accuracy and interpretability, since they have not precisely extracted the feature describing human's cognitive behavior, e.g., cerebral hemodynamics. To address this issue, this paper proposes a new dynamical feature extraction and pattern recognition method for MWL classification by using Dynamic System Theory (DST) and Deterministic Learning (DL) technique. A so-called dynamical feature is extracted by modeling the cerebral hemodynamics using fNIRS in human's cognitive process, which is mathematically interpretable and specific to the human's MWL according to DST. Dynamical pattern recognition scheme is then proposed by combining DL and Support Vector Machine, aiming to identify high and low levels of MWL with the dynamical feature of fNIRS. Compared to methods such as EEGNet, DeepConvNet, DCNN, SVM, fNIRS-PreT, and Logistic Regression, our method achieved a performance improvement of 2% to 6% for classifying mental workload levels.

**Keywords:** Functional Near-infrared Spectroscopy · Mental Workload Level · Dynamical Pattern Recognition · Deterministic Learning · Dynamic System Theory

## 1 Introduction

Mental Workload Level (MWL) is an important indicator reflecting the cognitive state of humans in human-computer interaction, which plays a crucial role in monitoring human's psychological states and cognitive behaviour [1]. For example, in high-risk tasks of driving vehicles or aircraft, MWL assessment for drivers would avoid potential driving accidents resulted by drivers' increasing cognitive workload and operational errors in processing complex road conditions and vehicle status [2, 3]. In medicine applications, MWL assessment can be used not only to evaluate neurocognitive involvement

© The Author(s), under exclusive license to Springer Nature Singapore Pte Ltd. 2025
X. Lan et al. (Eds.): ICIRA 2024, LNAI 15208, pp. 257–270, 2025.
https://doi.org/10.1007/978-981-96-0783-9_18

in rehabilitation training, for improving the rehabilitation efficacy [4], but also to evaluate cognitive function in patients with depression and other mental illnesses, for providing reliable and accurate illness diagnosis.

In cognitive research, functional near-infrared spectroscopy (fNIRS) is widely used to measure brain workload during mental tasks. It detects frontal cortex activation associated with visual spatial working memory (WM) [5]. Yang et al. [6] demonstrated the classification of MWL using convolutional neural networks (CNNs) based on fNIRS data. Benerradi et al. [7] trained and tested their CNN model on fNIRS data from eight subjects, while Jing et al. [8] employed a Transformer-based classifier across participants using fNIRS data from 68 subjects. However, these deep learning methods require extensive data and lack interpretability. Huang et al. [9] improved data by overlapping windows and applied various machine learning methods. Hasan et al. [10] analyzed the classification performance of various features, including whole-brain and hemispheric states. However, most of existing fNIRS-based MWL classification methods still have limited performance in terms of classification accuracy and interpretability, since they have not precisely extracted the feature describing human's cognitive behavior, e.g., cerebral hemodynamics, lacking medical interpretability for real-world applications.

Dynamical Systems Theory (DST) is a potential tool to extract the feature describing the human's cognition and behaviors, by developing dynamical systems--deterministic mathematical structures--to describe the human behavior as its state changes over time [11]. This theory employs differential and difference equations to model complex systems, and offers modeling tools to capture and quantify human behavior development, as well as explaining observed human patterns mathematically [12]. Some research results based on DST have been gained over the past decades in the cognitive science field [15]. For example, R. D. Beer et al. [16] analyzed the dynamic characteristics of the human cognitive process with DST on three classic examples. G. Schoner et al. [17] proves that it's possible to understand behavioral pattern generation on different levels (such as kinematic, electromyographic, and neuronal) with stochastic nonlinear dynamics. These literatures demonstrate that human's biological functions and tasks are specific to the dynamics (or dynamical pattern) of the human's behavioral variables. This may provide a theoretical tool to characterize human's MWL by using the dynamics of fNIRS from human's cognitive behaviors. However, most of existing literature have provided only theoretical and mathematical models, which is almost-completely unknown and not available for use in real applications.

Dynamical feature exaction of human's behavior variables is a critical step in pattern recognition and classification of human's MWL. In particular, we consider to combine DST and the so-called Deterministic Learning (DL) theory to extract the dynamical feature of cognition-related fNIRS. DL is proposed by Wang et al. [13, 14] and is a novel machine learning scheme tailored for identifying the unknown dynamics of nonlinear dynamical systems. It presents a unified and deterministic framework for effective representation, similarity definition and rapid recognition for dynamical pattern of human's cognition and behavior. Using DL technique to model the dynamics of human's cognition-related fNIRS, a so-called constant Radial Basis Functional Neural Networks (RBF NN) model is obtained to effectively represent the dynamics feature of human's biological functions, i.e., MWL. Such representation is based on the DST, thus is mathematically interpretable and facilitate the desired performance of MWL classification.

In this paper, we will propose a new dynamical feature extraction and dynamical pattern recognition method for MWL classification, by using the combination of DST and DL technique. Specifically, based on DST, a nonlinear dynamical model describing fNIRS signals' regional functional states is first presented, which provide a theoretical mathematical model to describe the human cognitive behavior under different MWL. Then, by using DL technique, dynamical feature of fNIRS is extracted by modeling the cerebral hemodynamics using fNIRS in human's cognitive process, which is mathematically interpretable and specific to the human's MWL according to DST. Dynamical pattern recognition scheme is then proposed by combining DL and Support Vector Machine, aiming to identify high and low levels of MWL with the dynamical feature of fNIRS. Compared to existing methods like EEGNet, DeepConvNet, DCNN, SVM, fNIRS-PreT, and Logistic Regression, the proposed method demonstrates a significant improvement of 2–6% in classifying mental workload levels.

The main contributions of this papers include: (i) proposing a new dynamical feature extraction methods for cognitive-related fNIRS by combining the techniques of DST and DL, which can obtain interpretable features to describe the human's cognitive behavior under different MWL; (ii) developing a novel DL-SVM-based dynamical pattern recognition method for MWL, which can have better performance and applicability in real applications such as driver workload monitoring and cognitive assessment for depression patients.

## 2 FNIRS-Based Cerebral Hemodynamics Modeling and Pattern Recognition Approach Design

### 2.1 Dynamical System Theory

When individuals engage in n-back cognitive tasks of varying difficulty levels, different mental workload levels are reflected in the brain oxygen concentration data collected by FNIRS. In order to accurately assess the real mental workload of individuals based on FNIRS data, we employ a classical theoretical framework called dynamical systems theory. Spencer JP et al. [15] demonstrates that signal dynamics can be described using nonlinear differential equations, which characterize the biological functions of individuals. This method has been widely used in gait analysis, electromyography, and other physiological functions to achieve pattern recognition of individuals at different physiological levels. Therefore, we use dynamical systems theory to mathematically model the mental workload levels of individuals.

FNIRS is a method that measures brain oxygen protein concentration based on the principles of cerebral hemodynamics. To model the mental workload level, we started by understanding the proposed differential equations for elucidating one-dimensional cerebral hemodynamics and oxygen transport models [18]. an equation that describes one-dimensional cerebral hemodynamics model and derive the following dynamic model:

$$\frac{\partial x(z, t)}{\partial t} + u \frac{\partial m}{\partial x} = D_{pl} \frac{\partial^2 m}{\partial x^2} - M(m, x) - F(m, x) \tag{1}$$

where m represents the concentration of free oxygen per unit volume, x represents brain oxygen concentration, $D_{pl}$ is the diffusion coefficient of oxygen in plasma, M refers to the cellular metabolic consumption, which is defined as the oxygen consumption rate per unit volume per unit time, and F denotes the oxygen flux that diffuses from the lumen to the tissue surface per unit time.

The model parameters differ at different mental workload levels. In this paper, as shown in Fig. 1, we consider conducting n = 2 types of experiments with individuals at n mental workload levels. Therefore, the kinetic model parameters D, M, and F take n different values. We can obtain the following equation to model MWL-cerebral hemodynamics, which captures the cognitive processes involved in handling tasks of varying difficulty for professionals like drivers and pilots, as well as the abnormal changes in mental workload levels observed in individuals with depression, particularly in their cognitive behaviors:

$$\dot{x} = f^n(x, m(x)) = D_{pl}^n \frac{\partial^2 m}{\partial x^2} - M^n(m, x) - F^n(m, x) - u^n \frac{\partial m}{\partial x} \qquad (2)$$

Where $f^n$ represents the hemodynamics of individuals at different mental workload levels, which can be used to characterize the biological function (i.e., mental workload levels) of individuals [17]. During human-computer interaction, mental workload is affected by task difficulty, task volume, and interaction duration, which changes the dynamic characteristics of the state vector x of cerebral blood oxygen concentration obtained from the data acquisition device. If we can solve for the specific representation of $f^n$, then we can deduce the mental workload level corresponding to the temporal dynamic changes in x.

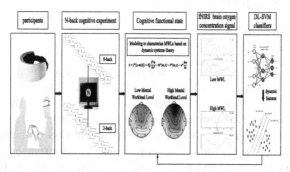

**Fig. 1.** The experimental and model framework proposed in this article. Firstly, the MWL-cerebral hemodynamics is utilized to model the MWL of subjects in two n-back experiments, and then feature extraction and classification are carried out using the DL-SVM method.

## 2.2 Deterministic Learning Theory

However, due to the unavailability of specific parameters, the aforementioned formula $f^n$ in the MWL-cerebral hemodynamics formula cannot be directly obtained with mathematical solutions, making it challenging to directly apply the model for feature extraction and pattern recognition in terms of mental workload levels. Therefore, we employ the integration of dynamical system theory and deterministic learning, which enables us to obtain a mathematical model for mental workload levels.

The deterministic learning method refers to an machine learning algorithm designed for complex dynamic systems and can identify the nonlinear system's dynamics along periodic and regression trajectories with a locally accurate neural network [19]. The methodological workflow is illustrated as shown in the Fig. 2.

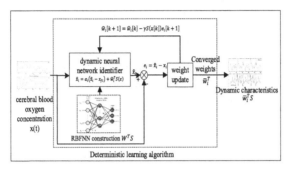

**Fig. 2.** Deterministic learning method framework, using RBF network to learn data and continuously update weights until convergence, ultimately obtaining dynamic features.

For a nonlinear dynamic system as 2, by Euler sampling method, setting sampling rate 5.2 Hz, we can obtain the following discrete time system model to approximate the System 2,:

$$x(k+1) = x(k) + T_s f^n(x(k)) = v_i(x(k)) \qquad (3)$$

where $x$ is the system state vector, m is the different human mental workload levels through the human-computer interaction process, $f^n(x(k))$ representing the known nominal dynamics, $v_1(x(k))$ and $v_2(x(k))$ are the dynamic functions used to represent the human low MWL and high MWL, respectively, both of which are unknown and need to be identified. To precisely determine the unknown dynamics, we'll use the RBFNN based deterministic learning method. In specific, we commence by utilizing a radial basis function neural network (RBFNN) to approximate the $v_i(x(k))(i = 0,1)$ in the Eq. 4

$$f_{nn}(x) = \sum_{i=1}^{N} w_i s_i(x) = W^T S(x) \qquad (4)$$

where $x = [x_1, x_2, \cdots, x_n]^T \epsilon R^n$ represents the input vector for the RBFNN, $W = [W_1, W_2, \cdots, W_m]^T \epsilon R^m$ represents the weight vector from the hidden RBF layer to the output layer, $m > 1$ represents the number of neuron nodes in an RBFNN, $S(x) = [s_1(\|x - \xi_1\|), s_2(\|x - \xi_2\|), \cdots, s_m(\|x - \xi_m\|)]^T$ refers to a regression vector composed of RBF components, $s_i(\cdot)(i = 1, \cdots, m)$ is the nonlinear mapping function of the hidden layer – radial basis function, using a Gaussian function: $s(\|x - \xi_i\|) =$

$exp\left[\frac{-(x-\xi_i)^T(x-\xi_i)}{\eta^2}\right]$, $\xi_i(i = 1, \cdots, m)$ refers to the neuron (node) positions in the network, $\eta$ represents the width of the accept domain.

Therefore, we determine Eq. 5 to construct an RBFNN model to identify the dynamical function of mental workload levels, as follows.

$$\widehat{W}^{nT} S(x) \rightarrow v^n(x(k)) \tag{5}$$

To leverage deterministic learning methods for locally accurate modeling of the intrinsic dynamics $v_i(x(k))$ of cerebral blood oxygenation $x(k)$, by borrowing the DL-based identification scheme in [19], we construct a dynamic neural network identifier based on sampled data as Eq. 6:

$$\hat{x}_i[k + 1] = \alpha_i\left(\hat{x}_i[k] - x_{fi}[k]\right) + \hat{w}_i^T[k]S(X[k]) \tag{6}$$

where $\hat{x}_i$ is represented as the state of a dynamic neural network identifier, $\alpha_i$ is the identifier gain, $x_{fi}[k]$ represents the concatenated data of cerebral blood oxygen saturation, $\hat{w}_i^T[k]S(X[k])$ represents an RBF neural network employed for modeling the dynamical information of the cerebral oxygen system, $\hat{w}_i^T$ represents the weight estimates for RBF Neural Networks. The weight update for the RBF neural network is performed according to the following neural network update rule in the Eq. 7:

$$\hat{w}_i[k + 1] = \hat{w}_i[k] - \gamma S(x[k])e_i[k + 1] \tag{7}$$

Where $e_i[k] = \hat{x}_i[k] - x_i[k]$ represents the tracking error signal for the dynamic neural network identifier, $\gamma$ denotes the learning rate.

After multiple iterations of the deterministic learning algorithm, the well-trained RBF neural network $\overline{w}_i^T S$ embody the unknown dynamics $v_i(x(k))$ of the MWL-cerebral hemodynamics system as Eq. 8.

$$\overline{W}^{nT} S(x) \rightarrow v^n(x(k)) \tag{8}$$

Where $\overline{w}_i^T = mean_{k \in [k_a, k_b]}\hat{w}[k]$, represents the mean neural network weight estimates over a period following the transient process, since the deterministic learning algorithm converges exponentially, the modeled system's intrinsic dynamics can be accurately expressed in the form of a converging constant. Using $\overline{W}^{nT} S$ as a dynamical feature extractor can achieve real-time extraction of FNIRS signal dynamics for subsequent pattern recognition, as shown in Fig. 3.

### 2.3   FNIRS-Based Cerebral Hemodynamics System and Pattern Recognition

Based on the MWL-cerebral hemodynamics model, dynamic characteristics of fNIRS can be obtained, thus enabling the development of an NN model for describing human mental workload levels. In order to further achieve mental workload evaluation, we propose a dynamical pattern recognition scheme combining deterministic learning and SVM.

SVM is a supervised learning algorithm widely used in pattern recognition, image classification, and other fields. It performs classification by finding an optimal hyperplane in the sample space. Specifically, we first construct a training set $T = \left\{ \left( \overline{w}_1^T S, y_1 \right), \left( \overline{w}_2^T S, y_2 \right), \cdots, \left( \overline{w}_n^T S, y_n \right) \right\}$ where $\overline{w}_i^T S$ represents the i-th dynamic feature of cerebral blood oxygenation data, and $y_i$ is the corresponding class label. Then construct a convex quadratic programming problem as Eq. 9.

$$\min_{a} \frac{1}{2} \sum_{i=1}^{N} \sum_{y=1}^{N} \alpha_i \alpha_j y_i y_j \left( \overline{w}_i^T S \cdot \overline{w}_j^T S \right) - \sum_{i=1}^{N} \alpha_i \tag{9}$$

The constraints are $\sum_{i=1}^{N} \alpha_i y_i = 0, 0 \leq \alpha_i \leq C, i = 1, 2, \cdots, N$, where $\alpha_i$ is the Lagrange multiplier. Solving this problem to obtain the optimal solution $\alpha^* = \left( \alpha_1^*, \alpha_2^*, \cdots, \alpha_N^* \right)^T$, calculating the parameter $\omega^* = \sum_{i=1}^{N} \alpha_i^* y_i \overline{w}_i^T S$ and $b^* = y_j - \sum_{i=1}^{N} \alpha_i^* \cdot y_i \left( \overline{w}_i^T S \cdot \overline{w}_j^T S \right)$, can derive the separating hyperplane $\omega^* \cdot \overline{w}^T S + b^* = 0$ and the classification decision function $f \left( \overline{w}^T S \right) = sign \left( w^* \cdot \overline{w}^T S + b^* \right)$. This hyperplane represents the difference in brain oxygen concentration at different mental workload levels. After constructing the DL-SVM classifier, testing data $\overline{w}_x^T S$ can be input into the classifier to classify mental workload levels according to the positive or negative value of $w^* \cdot \overline{w}_x^T S + b^*$, with greater than 0 being high mental workload level and less than 0 being low mental workload level.

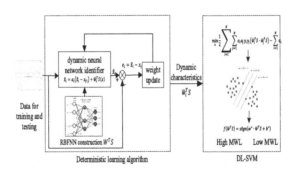

**Fig. 3.** The technical framework of DL-SVM, involves extracting dynamic features using deterministic learning techniques, and then combining SVM technology to obtain the optimal hyperplane capable of distinguishing features of different levels of mental workload.

In the specific implementation, as shown in the technology framework in Fig. 3, we used an fNIRS device to collect brain fNIRS signals from participants performing n-back tasks of varying difficulty. After undergoing several preprocessing steps, we obtained brain oxygenation concentration data representing high and low mental workload levels. This data was then fed into the algorithm framework proposed in Sect. 2.2, resulting in dynamic features $\overline{w}_i^T S (i = 0, 1)$ that characterize different high and low mental workload levels. To fully leverage the interpretability of the dynamic features, we employed support vector machine (SVM) technology, integrating deterministic learning with SVM to construct a pattern classifier model with generalization ability and applicability to small-sample data binary classification.

In DL-SVM classifiers, different patterns $f\left(\overline{w}^T S\right)$ correspond to different levels of mental workload. The extracted dynamic feature $\overline{w}_x^T S$ describes the dynamic changes in brain region oxygenation protein concentration corresponding to the mental workload generated during human cognitive processes. Based on the DL-SVM classifiers, we can ultimately achieve precise observation and evaluation of human mental workload levels using FNIRS signals in the Fig. 1. Moreover, this technology combines dynamical system theory and deterministic learning, therefore possessing medical interpretability.

# 3 Experiments Validation

## 3.1 N-Back Experimental Paradigm for Mental Workload Level Testing

### 3.1.1 Experimental Paradigm

See Fig. 4.

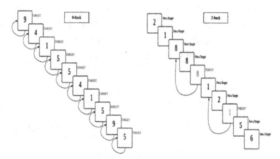

**Fig. 4.** The stimulus presentation order in the n-back experiment: in the 0-back task, the arrows indicate that each letter needs to be judged as whether it is the specified letter; in the 2-back task, the arrows indicate that the current letter needs to be judged as whether it is consistent with the letter pointed to.

### 3.1.2 Dataset and Preprocess

In order to ensure the reliability of the experiment, we use an existing publicly available dataset. Our method was evaluated using the open-access Tufts fNIRS to Mental Workload (fNIRS2MW) dataset [9], which includes data from 68 participants. This dataset contains fNIRS signals recorded while subjects performed different levels of n-back tasks, with the goal of applying brain-computer interfaces (BCIs) to everyday activities. The fNIRS device used in this study consisted of only four pairs of source and detector probes, recording signals from two locations (AB, CD) on the forehead. Each of the eight fNIRS sensors recorded measurements at each timestep.

The instrument recorded data at a sampling frequency of 5.2 Hz. The raw fNIRS signal measurements contained traces of alternating current intensity and phase changes

[20]. The transformed data was then filtered using a third-order zero-phase Butterworth bandpass filter (0.001–0.2 Hz) to remove noise caused by artifacts from respiration, heartbeat, and drift.

### 3.2 FNIRS-Based Brain-Blood Dynamical System Modeling

The dataset provides eight features in total, including different types of hemoglobin strength and phase. Considering the common use of oxygenated hemoglobin concentration as a feature in FNIRS research analysis and the conclusion drawn from paper [10] that oxygenated hemoglobin concentration is the optimal feature for classification, the oxygenated hemoglobin concentrations collected from electrodes AB and CD were selected as the sampled data $x(t)$. . Since the brain oxygen concentration data of different subjects is in different-sized phase space regions, we apply a preprocessing method to normalize the data of all subjects, keeping all the data within the same region $[-1, 1]$ $\times$ $[-1, 1]$. Specifically, we normalize the data of each subject as $x(t) = \frac{x(t)}{x_{max}}$. From the expression, it can be seen that this transformation only performs linear scaling and does not change its dynamical form.

Based on the MWL-cerebral hemodynamics model proposed in Sect. 2, we concatenate the sampled data of each subject 100 times to obtain periodic data $x_{fi}$, , then model it using the deterministic learning algorithm. To identify the normalized dynamic information, a Radial Basis Function (RBF) network with neuron spacing h = 0.1 and acceptance field width $\eta$ = 0.1 is first constructed. The network contains 529 neurons and is systematically overlaid in the $[-1.1, 1.1]$ $\times$ $[-1.1, 1.1]$ region. The specific parameters of the dynamic neural network identifier are shown in the Table 1.

**Table 1.** Parameter setting

| parameter | value |
| --- | --- |
| Neuron spacing | 0.1 |
| Number of neurons | 529 |
| Receptive field width | 0.1 |
| Number of learning repetitions | 100 |
| Learning gain | 5 |
| Ratio of neuron receptive field width | 1 |
| Discriminator gain | 0.2 |
| Penalty coefficient | $1 \times 10^{-6}$ |

After the algorithm converges to obtain the dynamic feature $\overline{w}_i^T S$, $\overline{w}_i^T S$ is input into formula 6 for relearning. During the learning process, the algorithm will gradually predict the values of the original signal. This will yield a dynamic signal that fits the original signal, as shown in the Fig. 5 and Fig. 6. For brain oxygen protein concentration data in dimensions AB and CD, the dynamic signals match well with the original signals, indicating that the algorithm has effectively learned the dynamic features of brain oxygen protein concentration data in all dimensions. The local dynamics along the state trajectory can be well learned by the network, which proves the interpretability of using the dynamic characteristics in DL-SVM for classification.

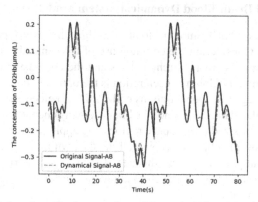

**Fig. 5.** Deterministic learning effectiveness chart of electrodes AB, comparing the original signals collected by electrodes AB with the dynamic signals obtained from their respective dynamic features. A better fit between the two signals in the chart indicates that the algorithm has extracted effective dynamic features of the signals from electrodes AB.

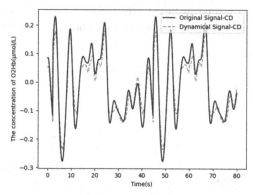

**Fig. 6.** Deterministic learning effectiveness chart of electrodes CD, with a description similar to Fig. 5.

## 3.3   Dynamical Feature Extraction and Pattern Recognition

Based on the DL-SVM classifier proposed in Sect. 2, experiments were conducted to classify cross-subject mental workload levels using the dynamic features obtained in Sect. 3.2. Specifically, the blood oxygen protein concentration data under 0-back and 2-back conditions were respectively considered as low mental workload level and high mental workload level for deterministic learning to extract dynamic features

$\overline{w}_i^T S(i = 0,1)$. . To test the effectiveness of dynamic features in mental workload levels classification, we subdivided the training and testing sets finely, and then iterated through 10 different test set ratios in the interval [0.05, 0.50] with a step size of 0.05. By combining random seed techniques, we obtained multiple sets of classification results accuracy for different subject data random combinations. To visually compare the classification performance of the DL-SVM classifier and the linear SVM classifier, a box plot of the obtained 20 sets of data is shown in the Fig. 7. From the Fig. 7, it can be seen that with a higher training set ratio, the DL-SVM classifier shows a significant improvement in classification performance. With a lower training set ratio, the two classifiers achieve similar classification performance. Therefore, it can be concluded that dynamic features effectively enhance the SVM classifier's classification performance for mental workload levels.

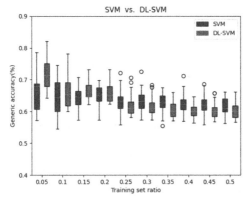

**Fig. 7.** Comparison of classification performance between SVM and DL-SVM. Blue represents SVM, green represents DL-SVM, and the training set ratio denotes the proportion of the training data set to all data. Our method achieved better results when the ratio was low, while the two algorithms showed similar performance when the ratio was high.

Then, to thoroughly test the DL-SVM classifier's performance on cross-subject data, the training and testing sets were split in ratios of 4:4, 16:4, and 64:4, with random seeds used to ensure randomness. The numbers in the ratio represent the number of participants selected out of a total of 68 participants. The training set was input into the DL-SVM classifier for training to obtain hyperplanes and decision functions, while the classifier did not have access to the testing data during training. Finally, the classifier was used to classify high and low mental workload levels based on the training set, and the classification results were compared with those of a standalone linear SVM and some common machine learning and deep learning algorithms. As shown in Table 2 and Fig. 8, the DL-SVM classifier achieved the highest average classification accuracy in all ratios, outperforming other machine learning and deep learning algorithms in each ratio. This indicates that the dynamic features extracted as a novel feature of FNIRS signals can characterize mental workload levels, and the proposed DL-SVM classifier demonstrates excellent performance in classifying mental workload levels, with potential applications in detecting mental workload levels of drivers and pilots. The interpretability of the dynamic features provides a new method for diagnosing changes in mental workload levels, such as in patients with depression, in clinical settings.

**Table 2.** Logistic Regression, EEGNet, DCNN, fNIRS-PreT, DeepConvNet, SVM and DL-SVM Classifiers' average binary classification accuracy (%) for Detecting Low vs. High MWL. 4:4, 16:4, 64:4 represent the number of participant data used for training and testing.

| Methods | Generic Accuracy (%) | | | Mean (%) |
|---|---|---|---|---|
| | 4:4 | 16:4 | 64:4 | |
| Logistic Regression | 59.82 | 65.77 | 67.15 | 64.25 |
| | (54.73, 64.88) | (60.86, 70.44) | (62.15, 71.75) | |
| DeepConvNet | 59.74 | 66.57 | 67.62 | 64.64 |
| | (51.59, 61.75) | (62.14, 70.81) | (63.47, 71.8) | |
| EEGNet | 54.8 | 61.74 | 68.81 | 61.78 |
| | (50.58, 59.51) | (57.08, 66.41) | (64.38, 73.06) | |
| DCNN | 59.73 | 65.21 | 67.89 | 64.28 |
| | (55.02, 64.53) | (60.62, 69.72) | (63.37, 72.14) | |
| fNIRS-PreT | 57.34 | 60.83 | 67.67 | 61.95 |
| | (52.87, 61.53) | (56.71, 64.90) | (63.73, 71.36) | |
| SVM | **61.47** | **64.74** | **66.48** | **64.23** |
| | **(56.25, 66.18)** | **(57.32, 70.73)** | **(59.76, 78.57)** | |
| DL-SVM | **60.02** | **66.11** | **70.54** | **65.56** |
| | **(56.62, 66.18)** | **(62.20, 73.17)** | **(64.29, 82.14)** | |

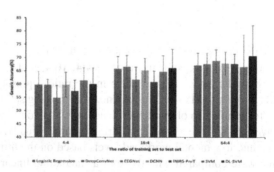

**Fig. 8.** Bar graph with error bars, used to represent classification accuracy of different classifiers for detecting high and low MWL at three different ratios. Our method (purple color) achieved the best classification results. (Color figure online)

# 4 Conclusions

This paper has proposed a new dynamical feature extraction and pattern recognition method for MWL classification by using the techniques of DST and DL. A dynamical feature extraction method has been proposed by using DL to model the cerebral hemodynamics using fNIRS in human's cognitive process, which is mathematically interpretable and specific to the human's MWL according to DST. Then, dynamical pattern recognition scheme has been designed by combining DL and Support Vector Machine, aiming to identify high and low levels of MWL with the dynamical feature of fNIRS. The experimental results have been provided and demonstrated that the proposed method can achieve better classification performance compared to conventional machine learning methods. This study could provide a promising brain-computer interface (BCI) method for monitoring MWL in areas such as vehicle driving and psychological state assessment.

# References

1. Wickens, C.D.: Multiple resources and performance prediction. Theor. Issues Ergon. Sci. **3**(2), 159–177 (2002)
2. Zhang, Q., Yang, K., Qu, X., Tao, D.: Evaluation of drivers' mental workload based on multi-modal physiological signals. J. Shenzhen Univ. Sci. Eng. **39**(3), 278–286 (2022)
3. National Safety Council: Understanding the distracted brain: why driving while using hands-free cell phones is risky behavior. National Safety Council, Spring Lake (2012)
4. Ghani, U., Signal, N., Niazi, I.K., Taylor, D.: Efficacy of a single-task ERP measure to evaluate cognitive workload during a novel exergame. Front. Hum. Neurosci. 519 (2021)
5. Witmer J.S., Aeschlimann E.A., Metz A.J., Troche S.J., Rammsayer T.H.: Functional near-infrared spectroscopy recordings of visuospatial working memory processes. Part II: a replication study in children on sensitivity and mental-ability-induced differences in functional activation. Brain Sci., 152 (2018)
6. Yang, D., et al.: Detection of mild cognitive impairment using convolutional neural network: temporal-feature maps of functional near-infrared spectroscopy. Front. Aging Neurosci. (2020)
7. Benerradi, J., Maior, H.A., Marinescu, A., Clos, J., Wilson, M.L.: Exploring machine learning approaches for classifying mental workload using fNIRS data from HCI tasks. In: Proceedings of the Halfway to the Future Symposium 2019, pp. 1–11 (2019)
8. Jing, Y., et al.: Transformer based cross-subject mental workload classification using FNIRS for real-world application. In: 2023 45th Annual International Conference of the IEEE Engineering in Medicine & Biology Society (EMBC), Sydney, Australia, pp. 1–5 (2023)
9. Huang, Z., et al.: The tufts fNIRS mental workload dataset & benchmark for brain-computer interfaces that generalize. In: Thirty-fifth Conference on Neural Information Processing Systems Datasets and Benchmarks Track (Round 2) (2021)
10. Hasan, M., Mahmud, M., Poudel, S., Donthula, K., Poudel, K.: Mental workload classification from fNIRS signals by leveraging machine learning. In: 2023 IEEE Signal Processing in Medicine and Biology Symposium (SPMB), Philadelphia, PA, USA, pp. 1–6 (2023)
11. Spencer, J.P., Austin, A., Schutte, A.R.: Contributions of dynamic systems theory to cognitive development. Cogn. Dev., 401–418 (2012)
12. Molenaar, P.C.M., Newell, K.M. (eds.): Individual Pathways of Change: Statistical Models for Analyzing Learning and Development. American Psychological Association, Washington, DC (2010)

13. Wang, C., Hill, D.J.: Learning from neural control. IEEE Trans. Neural Netw., 130–146 (2006)
14. Wang, C., Hill, D.J.: Deterministic learning and rapid dynamical pattern recognition. IEEE Trans. Neural Netw., 617–630 (2007)
15. Spencer, J.P., Perone, S., Buss, A.T.: Twenty years and going strong: a dynamic systems revolution in motor and cognitive development. Child Dev. Perspect., 260–266 (2011)
16. Beer, R.D.: Dynamical approaches to cognitive science. Trends Cogn. Sci., 91–99 (2000)
17. Schöner, G., Kelso, J.A.: Dynamic pattern generation in behavioral and neural systems. Science, 1513–1520 (1988)
18. Ji, C., He, Y.: A modeling study of blood flow and oxygen transport in the circle of Willis. Chin. J. Theor. Appl. Mech., 591–599 (2012)
19. Zhang, J., Yuan, C., Stegagno, P., He, H., Wang, C.: Small fault detection of discrete-time nonlinear uncertain systems. IEEE Trans. Cybern. 51(2), 750–764 (2021)
20. Blaney, G., Sassaroli, A., Pham, T., Fernandez, C., Fantini, S.: Phase dual-slopes in frequency-domain near-infrared spectroscopy for enhanced sensitivity to brain tissue: first applications to human subjects. J. Biophotonics 13(1), e201960018 (2020)

# A Novel Framework of Motor-Cognitive Human-Robot Interaction Game Design with Skill Level Recognition

Chen Chen, Fengjun Mu, Zhinan Peng, and Rui Huang[✉]

University of Electronic Science and Technology of China, Chengdu Sichuan, China
ruihuang@uestc.edu.cn

**Abstract.** Stroke patients commonly suffer from motor impairments, leading to a heightened interest in the application of rehabilitation robots and serious games for motor re-learning therapies. A wealth of research has established that the integration of motor and cognitive training modalities can substantially enhance the rehabilitation process. Nevertheless, accurately assessing patients' motor and cognitive statuses remains a significant challenge for current methodologies, thereby impeding real-time monitoring and adaptive adjustments to the rehabilitation regimen. In this work, we introduce a personalized motor-cognitive training framework anchored in serious gaming. Leveraging dynamic system theory, our framework is capable of extracting interpretable dynamic characteristics from the human-robot interaction, enabling a precise evaluation of subjects' motor skill abilities. The training parameters can be dynamically tuned with the assessed skill levels, which supports multidimensional personalized rehabilitation. Building upon this approach, we have engineered an innovative motor-cognitive rehabilitation platform that synergizes serious games with robotic movement interaction. We have conducted experiments to validate the platform's efficacy, demonstrating its potential to advance the field of post-stroke rehabilitation.

**Keywords:** Motor Re-Learning · Dynamical Systems Theory · Deterministic Learning · Human-Robot Interaction

## 1 Introduction

Stroke remains a major global health issue, affecting up to 80% of survivors with motor impairments [1]. Effective functional rehabilitation training is crucial for mitigating the impact on motor and cognitive functions from post-stroke, which can significantly improve the patient's quality of life. Early studies typically treated motor and cognitive training as distinct disciplines, designing rehabilitation methods to enhance one specific aspect of human function. Recent evidence underscores a considerable overlap between motor and cognitive functions, suggesting that integrating these rehabilitation efforts post-stroke is crucial for effective neural recovery [2]. Consequently, the design and implementation of a robotic system for combined motor-cognitive rehabilitation training in stroke patients emerge as a significant research focus.

Existing work in the field of motor rehabilitation has predominantly focused on developing adaptive controllers to assist patients in completing movement tasks [3–5]. Podubecka et al. [6] introduced a robotic system for passive training, and Agarwal et al. [7] discussed assistive controllers for motor rehabilitation. However, these approaches solely address motor training without cognitive involvement, resulting in patient disengagement during rehabilitation and suboptimal outcomes. To solve this problem, some studies integrate motor rehabilitation with cognitive training. For instance, Frisoli et al. [8] proposed an exoskeleton for upper limb rehabilitation combined with virtual reality, integrating motor and cognitive aspects to enhance rehabilitation, but lacked personalized assessment of patient motor function. Liu et al. [9] designed a virtual tracking task with haptic feedback combining movement and cognition, and proposed a method to establish a standardized reference index based on the quantitative performance in the task process to evaluate the wrist fine motor function, but the assessment was not accurate and personalized enough. However, they only consider the static feature to classify the patient's status, ignoring the dynamic process through the human-robot interaction. The insufficient modeling of patient motion and cognition dynamics leads to suboptimal rehabilitation outcomes, and the lack of personalized assessment of patient engagement in motor learning rehabilitation.

To achieve personalized and efficient motor-cognitive rehabilitation training, the key is to assess the patient's motor and cognitive status. Patient's motor cognitive status in training can be measured by skill level. The skill level represents the performance level of subjects in motor relearning tasks. It is a measure of motor cognition synthesis. Existing work [10] incorporates a force sensor on the rehabilitation robot to identify user movement intention for therapeutic exercises, while work [11] proposes an algorithm that uses multi-axis force sensor data to enhance human-robot interaction transparency. Furthermore, there are studies [12–14] focused on detecting exercise intention through human movement data detected by inertial measurement unit(IMU) and physiological signals such as electrocardiogram (ECG), electromyography (EMG), and galvanic skin response (GSR). However, these works only utilize motion-related data to evaluate the patient's motor status, neglecting essential cognitive-related information. On the other hand, research [15] combines robot-assisted therapy with EEG-based brain-computer interface (BCI) to detect patients' motor intentions in order to evaluate and investigate the effect of rehabilitation training. Work [16] investigated the within-session reliability of fNIRS measure in robot-assisted training. Nevertheless, these methods solely rely on cognitive-related signal. Lastly, studies by [17,18] propose a multimodal adaptive rehabilitation framework aimed at optimizing motor learning effects by modeling training tasks and evaluating subjects' skill levels through demonstration learning methods. However, these approaches lack medical interpretability thus limiting their application in medical rehabilitation.

To address these challenges, we introduce a personalized rehabilitation training platform for post-stroke patients, based on real-time evaluations of motor-cognitive function levels. The proposed platform encompasses a multi-modal training program, a module for recognizing patterns in skill levels, and an adaptive module for task parameter regulation. It captures multi-modal data on patient motor-cognitive functions through both a gaming platform and a 6-axis force sensor system integrated into the robot's end-effector. By applying dynamical system theory and deterministic learning techniques, our innovative pattern recognition technology facilitates the real-time assessment of patients' motor-cognitive function levels during gaming activities. Furthermore, the platform features a dynamic mechanism for adjusting game modes based on evaluation outcomes, enabling the customization of motor-cognitive training programs to optimize training efficacy.

The main contributions of our study are:

1) We propose an innovative rehabilitation framework, that employs the dynamical system theory to explain motor and cognitive behavior. Based on the deterministic learning techniques, this framework can evaluate the patients' explainable motor function levels.
2) The training programs for motor-cognitive rehabilitation across multiple dimensions can personally adjust the task parameters, based on the patient's motion and cognition status. This method achieves multidimensional functional rehabilitation for motor-cognitive functions, enhancing rehabilitation outcomes.
3) Based on the proposed evaluation and personalization method, we construct an innovative rehabilitation platform with cognitive serious games for robot-assisted motor training. The experiment validates the effectiveness.

## 2  Framework of Motor-Cognitive Human-Robot Training

We propose a personalized motor-cognitive training framework anchored in human-robot interaction game. The framework can individually adjust the training difficulty through real-time assessment of the subject's skill level to maximize the patient's training effectiveness (Fig. 1). The motor-cognitive framework consists of three parts:

1) Multi-modal training program, which combines the cognitive-related object tracking game with the motor-related human-robot interaction, can realize the comprehensive improvement of the subjects' motor-cognitive ability;
2) A skill level pattern recognition module, which can evaluate subjects' skill level in real time;
3) An adaptive module for task parameter regulation, which can personalize the difficulty of motor-cognitive training based on the subject's skill level.

Based on this setting, the motor-cognitive training framework realizes the motor relearning mechanism, which can rehabilitate and improve the motor cognitive ability of patients after stroke [19].

## 2.1   The Motor-Cognitive Multi-mode Training Program

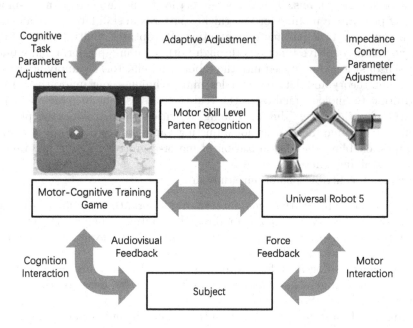

**Fig. 1.** A human-computer interactive game framework for motor-cognitive training.

The motor-cognitive multi-modal training program consists of a motor-cognitive interactive game based on object tracking task and motor interaction training based on Universal Robot 5 (UR5). The motor-cognitive interactive game uses the position of the robot's end-effector as input. Subjects are required to control the white cursor in the game through motor interaction(pulling and pushing) with the end-effector of UR5. The position of the white cursor should follow the movement of the red rectangular target to keep it within the range of the red rectangle as much as possible. The red rectangular target will move periodically according to the setting parameters. During motor-cognitive interaction training, the subject engages in simultaneous cognitive and motor interactions with both the game and the robot. They receive audio-visual feedback from the motor-cognitive game and force feedback from the robot.

The motor-cognitive interactive game is based on the Unity game engine. The game consists of two main game objects(a white cursor and a red rectangular object) and two visual feedback bars(a pink speed visual feedback bar and a purple force visual feedback bar). The white cursor is the object controlled by the subject, and the red rectangle is a target object moving on a fixed trajectory. The Speed and Force visual feedback bar displays the speed and force of the subject as they interact with the end of the robot in real-time on the screen. The game interface visualizes the force and speed of the subject's participation in the interaction process, offering visual feedback to enhance transparency in human-computer interaction and improve the training effect for the subject [20].

For patients who still have some autonomous propulsion ability, their affected arm strength is weaker and may not be sufficient to drive the robot movement. Based on the above reasons, we design a motor interaction mode based on an admittance controller. The motor interaction mode enables patients to maintain as much independent control as possible while reducing the resistance of human-robot motor interaction. The end-effector of the robot is equipped with a 6D force sensor produced by OnRobot. It can detect the external force $F_{ext}$, which represents the force exerted by the patient on the robot system. The expected movement of the robot end-effector can be calculated by $F_{ext}$ according to the following formula:

$$M\ddot{x}_d + D\dot{x} + Kx = F_{ext}. \tag{1}$$

where $M, D$ and $K$ are the inertia coefficient, damping coefficient, and stiffness coefficient respectively, $x_d$ represents the control variable over the position of the end-effector. According to the data detected by the force sensor, the robot adjusts the position of the end-effector and the change of the interaction force during the interaction between the patient and the robot through the admittance control strategy.

When subjects participate in the training process, the position information of the cursor in the game can characterize the subject's cognitive level to a certain extent [21]. This data, combined with force and velocity data from the subject's interaction with the robot, can reflect the subject's motor and cognitive abilities. Game interaction position data, along with the robot's end-effector force and speed data, are input into the skill level pattern recognition module for further ability assessment.

## 2.2   Skill Level Recognition with Motor-Cognitive Measurement

In order to achieve personalized and efficient motor-cognitive rehabilitation training, we propose a skill level pattern recognition algorithm based on motor cognitive multimodal measurement. This method utilizes Dynamical System Theory modeling and extracts features using Deterministic Learning Technology. Skill Level refers to the subject's proficiency in the task [17], which is a comprehensive assessment of the subject's motor and cognitive abilities. Based on the skill level when the subject participates, the task adaptive control module dynamically adjusts the game task parameters and robot control parameters to maximize the subject's adaptability during human-computer interaction and optimize the training effect.

**Dynamical System Theoretical Modeling of Human-Robot Interaction.** Dynamical systems are deterministic mathematical structures that describe the behavior of a system as its state changes over time. Dynamical systems theory provides a clear mathematical description for understanding how their states change over time. In the field of clinical medicine, it is often used to construct differential equations to study the subject's cognitive, motor, or physiological behavior patterns, such as gait, electromyography, etc. [22,23].

In order to evaluate the motor function level in real time based on the patient's human-robot interaction behavior in the above game framework, based on researches [2,24], we know that the patient's movement and cognition are closely related during the motor re-leaning process, and cognitive signals and multimodal fusion of motor signals can be used to assess the patient's skill level. Therefore, based on the dynamical system modeling method of [23], we propose the following differential equation based on multi-modal measurement of human motion and cognition, which can characterize human skill level:

$$\dot{x} = f(x, u, \varepsilon) \tag{2}$$

where $x$ represents the multi-mode state vector including interaction position in game, force of the end of robot and speed of the end; $u$ represents the patient's skill level; $\varepsilon$ represents the sampling error.

During human-computer interaction, skill levels are affected by individual patient differences, task difficulty, task volume, and interaction duration, thereby changing the dynamic characteristics of the motor-cognitive Multi-mode state vector $x$. If we are able to solve for a specific representation of $f$, then we can derive the skill level that corresponds to the temporal dynamics in $x$.

**Skill Level Recognition Based on Deterministic Learning.** However, in the above differential equation that represents the level of motor skills, the specific parameters of f are unknown, and the dynamic model is difficult to be directly used for feature extraction and pattern recognition. Therefore, we use the combined application of dynamical system theory and deterministic learning [25] to fit the dynamical model of skill level through deterministic learning technology.

We consider the discrete form of the above dynamic model as shown in Eq. 2:

$$x(k+1) = f(x(k)) + v_i(x(k)). \tag{3}$$

where $f(x(k))$ represents the known nominal dynamics; $v_i(x(k))$ represents the unknown dynamics to be learned.

The $v_i(x(k))$ above is fitted using the Radial Basis Function Neural Network (RBFNN) expressed in Eq. 3.

$$f_{nn}(x) = \sum_{i=1}^{m} w_i s_i(x) = W^\mathsf{T} S(x) \tag{4}$$

where $x$ represents the input of RBFNN, which is the above-mentioned motor-cognitive multi-modal data state vector, and $W$ represents the weight matrix of RBFNN. $S(\cdot)$ represents the radial basis function of the hidden layer, and the Gaussian function is used in this article.

The weights updating for the RBFNN is performed according to the following rule in the Eq. 4:

$$\hat{w}_i[k+1] = \hat{w}_i[k] - \gamma S(x[k])e_i[k+1] \qquad (5)$$

where

$$e_i[k] = \hat{x}_i[k] - x_i[k]$$

represents the tracking error signal for the dynamic neural network identifier; $\gamma$ denotes the learning rate.

The RBFNN trained based on the above steps can effectively fit the above dynamic model representing the level of motor skills. Its average output x over a period of time can be regarded as the dynamic characteristics of the dynamic model characterizing the skill level.

$$\text{Skill Level} = \begin{cases} \text{Low,} & \arg\min_i |\hat{x}_i - x| = 0 \\ \text{Medium,} & \arg\min_i |\hat{x}_i - x| = 1 \\ \text{High,} & \arg\min_i |\hat{x}_i - x| = 2 \end{cases} \qquad (6)$$

Based on the above theory, we propose an innovative motor function pattern recognition algorithm based on multi-modal measurement of motion and cognition. This algorithm is based on dynamical system theory and deterministic Learning technology, and can realize pattern recognition of human movement cognitive behavior. The pattern recognition results can realize the evaluation of human motor function status to dynamically adjust the game mode and achieve personalized training. Dynamic features actually describe the dynamic changes in the patient's cognitive and motor abilities during human-computer interaction. Their interpretability is guaranteed based on the dynamical system theory. The skill level pattern recognition based on this has practical significance in medical rehabilitation.

## 2.3   Task Parameter Adaptive Regulation

The adaptive module for task parameter regulation is designed to personalize the difficulty of motor-cognitive training based on the subject's skill level. This module dynamically adjusts training parameters, ensuring that each individual receives an appropriate level of challenge. By continuously monitoring and adapting to the user's performance, it aims to optimize the training effectiveness and facilitate better training effect.

In the object tracking game, the settable parameters of the red rectangular target include the size of the rectangular target, the movement speed of the rectangular target, and the movement trajectory of the rectangular target. These set parameters are controlled by the game task adaptive regulation module to change the task difficulty of the motor cognitive interactive game.

In addition, The impedance control parameters of the robot are managed by the task parameter regulation module. By adjusting the inertia, damping, and stiffness parameters of the impedance control, the resistance in the interaction between the subject and the robot is modified to tailor the level of difficulty in motor interaction.

We tentatively divide training difficulty into three modes, which respectively represent Low, medium and high difficulty: 1) For low skill level, the framework will reduce the difficulty of training to maintain patient participation; 2) For medium skill level, the framework will be more inclined to maintain the difficulty of training; 3) With high skill levels, the frame is more likely to increase the difficulty to enhance the patient's training effect. Task parameter adaptive regulation module is set as follows:

$$\text{MODE} = \begin{cases} \text{Low Diffculty,} & \text{Skill Level} = \text{Low} \\ \text{Medium Diffculty,} & \text{Skill Level} = \text{Medium} \\ \text{High Diffculty,} & \text{Skill Level} = \text{High} \end{cases} \qquad (7)$$

When the subject's skill level changes and the accumulated time exceeds a certain threshold, the game mode is changed to the corresponding task difficulty.

## 3    Design and Experiment of Motor-Cognitive Human-Robot Interaction Game

In this study, interactive data was collected from a healthy male subject.In order to simulate the above three different skill levels, the subject interacted with motor-cognitive game at three different load levels. The subject was asked to pull the end of the robot to control the position of the white cursor in the game to follow the position of the pink rectangular target.(Fig. 2)

**Fig. 2.** The experimental platform is composed of computer and UR5 robot equipped with force sensor, The robot communicates with the computer by socket.

We used the six-dimensional force sensor at the end of UR5 to collect the change of force during the movement interaction between the subject and the robot, used the UR5 communication service to obtain the change of the end speed of the robot, and used the unity game engine to obtain the change of the cursor position in the game, so as to complete the multi-modal measurement of cognitive movement of the subject.

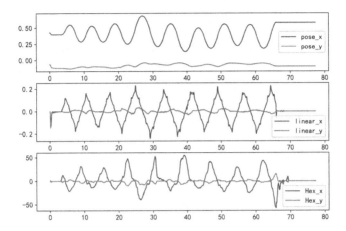

**Fig. 3.** A piece of raw data for a motion interaction, including in-game object position, robot end speed, and robot end force.

Based on the collected data(Fig. 3), we have completed the modeling of unknown dynamics in the human-computer interaction system according to the aforementioned theory. We construct a radial basis function neural network uniformly distributed in the range $[-1.1, 1.1] \times [-1.1, 1.1] \times [-1.1, 1.1]$ with nodes intervals of 0.1(Fig. 4). The RBF neural network has been utilized to learn the corresponding parameters $\bar{w}_i$ for the collected data(Fig. 5), where $i = 0, 1, 2$, representing three distinct levels of motor skill. Based on the established dynamical model, the precise prediction of the skill level in the subject's motor cognitive process is realized by comparing the errors between $\hat{x}_i$ and $x_i$(Fig. 6).

According to the aforementioned skill levels, we have established three training modes, each representing a different level of training task difficulty. The specific parameter settings are detailed in Table 1. Mode 1 corresponds to relatively simple task difficulty, with the target rectangle moving speed set at 0.8 times the normal speed and the target size set at 1.2 times the normal difficulty. The robot admittance control parameters are $M = 0.1$, $D = 5$, and $K = 0.2$ respectively. This allows for easy interaction between the patient and the robot while following the task goal. Mode 2 represents medium task difficulty with normal moving speed for the target rectangle and initial size for the target, along with robot admittance control parameters of $M = 0.2$, $D = 6$, and $K = 0.2$ respectively. Mode 3 is designed for difficult tasks with a faster moving speed for the target rectangle (set at 1.2 times of normal) and a smaller target size (set at 0.8 times of initial). The robot admittance control parameters are $M = 0.5$,

Trajectory and neural centers

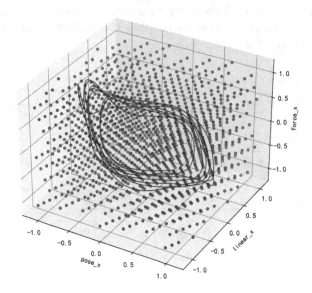

**Fig. 4.** The 3D trajectory of the pre-processed interactive data (take the in-game position in the X-axis direction, the robot end speed, and the robot end force), and the "o" mark in the figure represents the partial node position of the radial basis function neural network.

$D = 8$, and $K = 0.2$, respectively. The motion interaction intensity between patient and robot is increased in this mode requiring higher cognitive ability from patients.

Different modes impose varying requirements on patients' skill levels as well as training intensity. Real-time monitoring of individuals' motor skill states enables personalized adjustment of game modes leading to improved training effects. It should be noted that these parameters can be further personalized and effective according to clinician guidance.

Finally, by combining the above motor function level recognition module and game task adaptive adjustment module, we can individually adjust the difficulty of motor cognitive training, and finally build a multimodal training framework of cognitive game and human-robot motor interaction to realize the comprehensive improvement of human motor cognitive function.

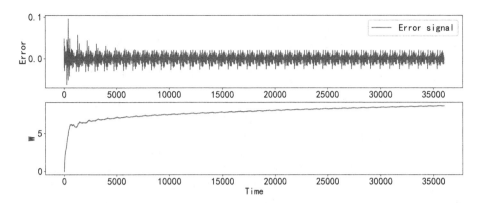

**Fig. 5.** $e_i[k]$ and $\hat{w}[k]$ converge gradually with the increase of training iterations, and the radial basis function neural network begins to fit the above motor cognitive dynamic model. The average value of $\hat{w}[k]$ over a period of time after convergence is $\bar{w}$.

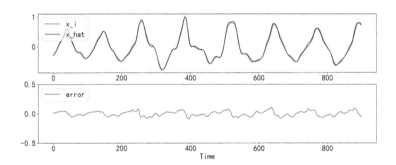

**Fig. 6.** In the figure above, The red curve in the figure above represents the change of one dimension of $x_i$ (the force at the end-effector of the robot in the X-axis direction) with time, and the blue curve represents the output $\hat{x}(Color figure online)_i$ of the RBF neural network with parameter $\bar{w}_i$ under input $x$; The following figure shows the error between $x_i$ and $\hat{x}_i$.

**Table 1.** Game and control parameter table for three game modes. In the table, TMS represents the moving speed of the target rectangle in the game, TRS represents the size of the target rectangle in the game, and M, D and K are the admittance control parameters of the robot: inertia coefficient, damping coefficient and stiffness coefficient

| Parameters | Training Mode 1 | Training Mode 2 | Training Mode 3 |
|---|---|---|---|
| TMS | 0.8 | 1 | 1.2 |
| TRS | 1.2 | 1 | 0.8 |
| M | 0.1 | 0.2 | 0.5 |
| D | 5 | 6 | 8 |
| K | 0.2 | 0.2 | 0.2 |

## 4  Conclusion

We presented a framework for personalized motor-cognitive training. The framework can adjust the training difficulty individually based on people's skill level, and realize multi-dimensional rehabilitation of motor-cognitive integration. As part of the framework development, we propose a skill level recognition algorithm. The algorithm modeled the training task based on the dynamical system theory and fitted the model based on the deterministic Learning method, so as to realize the real-time assessment of the skill level of patients. Finally, we conducted an experimental study on a subject, and the results show that the skill level recognition algorithm based on dynamic system theory and deterministic Learning method can effectively learn the subject's interactive training model and complete the accurate assessment of the subject's skill level.

In the future, we plan to improve the assessment algorithm based on the existing framework to achieve a more refined identification of subjects' skill level. In addition, we also plan to utilize fuzzy inference algorithm to optimize our mission difficulty adjustment strategy to make it smoother.

## References

1. Langhorne, P., Coupar, F., Pollock, A.: Motor recovery after stroke: a systematic review. Lancet Neurol. **8**(8), 741–754 (2009). https://doi.org/10.1016/S1474-4422(09)70150-4
2. Mullick, A.A., Subramanian, S.K., Levin, M.F.: Emerging evidence of the association between cognitive deficits and arm motor recovery after stroke: a meta-analysis. Restor. Neurol. Neurosci. **33**(3), 389–403 (2015). https://doi.org/10.3233/RNN-150510
3. Mao, Y., Agrawal, S.K.: Design of a cable-driven arm exoskeleton (CAREX) for neural rehabilitation. IEEE Trans. Rob. **28**(4), 922–931 (2012). https://doi.org/10.1109/TRO.2012.2189496
4. Wang, C., Peng, L., Hou, Z.G.: A control framework for adaptation of training task and robotic assistance for promoting motor learning with an upper limb rehabilitation robot. IEEE Trans. Syst. Man Cybern. Syst. **52**(12), 7737–7747 (2022). https://doi.org/10.1109/TSMC.2022.3163916
5. Zhang, M., Wang, C., Zhang, C., Li, P., Liu, L.: A unified switching control framework for continuous robot-assisted training. IEEE/ASME Trans. Mechatron., 1–13 (2023). https://doi.org/10.1109/TMECH.2023.3330875
6. Podubecka, J., Scheer, S., Theilig, S., Wiederer, R., Oberhoffer, R., Nowak, D.: Zyklisches apparatives Bewegungstraining versus konventionelles Gangtraining in der Rehabilitation des hemiparetischen Ganges nach Schlaganfall: Eine Pilotstudie. Fortschritte der Neurologie · Psychiatrie **79**(07), 411–418 (2011). https://doi.org/10.1055/s-0031-1273338
7. Agarwal, P., Deshpande, A.D.: Subject-specific assist-as-needed controllers for a hand exoskeleton for rehabilitation. IEEE Robot. Autom. Lett. **3**(1), 508–515 (2018). https://doi.org/10.1109/LRA.2017.2768124
8. Frisoli, A., et al.: Arm rehabilitation with a robotic exoskeleleton in virtual reality. In: 2007 IEEE 10th International Conference on Rehabilitation Robotics, pp. 631–642. IEEE, Noordwijk, Netherlands (2007). https://doi.org/10.1109/ICORR.2007.4428491

9. Liu, X., et al.: Design of virtual guiding tasks with haptic feedback for assessing the wrist motor function of patients with upper motor neuron lesions. IEEE Trans. Neural Syst. Rehabil. Eng. **27**(5), 984–994 (2019). https://doi.org/10.1109/TNSRE.2019.2909287

10. Xing, L., Wang, X., Wang, J.: A motion intention-based upper limb rehabilitation training system to stimulate motor nerve through virtual reality. Int. J. Adv. Rob. Syst. **14**, 172988141774328 (2017). https://doi.org/10.1177/1729881417743283

11. Lee, K.H., Baek, S.G., Lee, H.J., Choi, H.R., Moon, H., Koo, J.C.: Enhanced transparency for physical human-robot interaction using human hand impedance compensation. IEEE/ASME Trans. Mechatron. **23**(6), 2662–2670 (2018). https://doi.org/10.1109/TMECH.2018.2875690

12. Marchal-Crespo, L., et al.: Motor execution detection based on autonomic nervous system responses. Physiol. Meas. **34**(1), 35–51 (2013). https://doi.org/10.1088/0967-3334/34/1/35

13. Gopura, R.A.R.C., Kiguchi, K.: EMG-based control of an exoskeleton robot for human forearm and wrist motion assist. In: 2008 IEEE International Conference on Robotics and Automation, pp. 731–736 (2008). https://doi.org/10.1109/ROBOT.2008.4543292

14. Zhong, W., Zhang, L., Sun, Z., Dong, M., Zhang, M.: UI-MoCap: an integrated UWB-IMU circuit enables 3D positioning and enhances IMU data transmission. IEEE Trans. Neural Syst. Rehabil. Eng. **32**, 1034–1044 (2024). https://doi.org/10.1109/TNSRE.2024.3369647

15. Park, W., Kwon, G.H., Kim, D.H., Kim, Y.H., Kim, S.P., Kim, L.: Assessment of cognitive engagement in stroke patients from single-trial EEG during motor rehabilitation. IEEE Trans. Neural Syst. Rehabil. Eng. **23**(3), 351–362 (2015). https://doi.org/10.1109/TNSRE.2014.2356472

16. Jiang, Y.C., et al.: Within-session reliability of fNIRS in robot-assisted upper-limb training. IEEE Trans. Neural Syst. Rehabil. Eng. **32**, 1302–1313 (2024). https://doi.org/10.1109/TNSRE.2024.3378467

17. Agarwal, P., Deshpande, A.D.: A framework for adaptation of training task, assistance and feedback for optimizing motor (Re)-learning with a robotic exoskeleton. IEEE Robot. Autom. Lett. **4**(2), 808–815 (2019). https://doi.org/10.1109/LRA.2019.2891431

18. Agarwal, P., Deshpande, A.D.: A novel framework for optimizing motor (Re)-learning with a robotic exoskeleton. In: 2017 IEEE International Conference on Robotics and Automation (ICRA), pp. 490–497. IEEE, Singapore, Singapore (2017). https://doi.org/10.1109/ICRA.2017.7989061

19. Moreau, D., Morrison, A.B., Conway, A.R.A.: An ecological approach to cognitive enhancement: complex motor training. Acta Physiol. (Oxf) **157**, 44–55 (2015). https://doi.org/10.1016/j.actpsy.2015.02.007

20. Hasegawa, N., Takeda, K., Sakuma, M., Mani, H., Maejima, H., Asaka, T.: Learning effects of dynamic postural control by auditory biofeedback versus visual biofeedback training. Gait & Posture **58**, 188–193 (2017). https://doi.org/10.1016/j.gaitpost.2017.08.001

21. Heuer, H., Lüttgen, J.: Robot assistance of motor learning: a neuro-cognitive perspective. Neurosci. Biobehav. Rev. **56**, 222–240 (2015). https://doi.org/10.1016/j.neubiorev.2015.07.005

22. Perc, M.: The dynamics of human gait. Eur. J. Phys. **26**, 525–534 (2005). https://doi.org/10.1088/0143-0807/26/3/017

23. Schöner, G., Kelso, J.A.S.: Dynamic pattern generation in behavioral and neural systems. Science **239**(4847), 1513–1520 (1988). https://doi.org/10.1126/science. 3281253
24. Lin, D.J., et al.: Cognitive demands influence upper extremity motor performance during recovery from acute stroke. Neurology **96**(21) (2021). https://doi.org/10. 1212/WNL.0000000000011992
25. Wang, C., Hill, D.: Deterministic learning theory for identification, recognition, and control (2009). https://doi.org/10.1201/9781420007763

# AI-Driven Smart Industrial Systems

# Pose Calibration and Trajectory Adjustment of Robot Based on Monocular Vision

Yang Zhang[1,2], Xingwei Zhao[1,3(✉)], and Bo Tao[1]

[1] The State Key Laboratory of Intelligent Manufacturing Equipment and Technology, Huazhong University of Science and Technology, Wuhan 430074, China
zhaoxingwei@hust.edu.cn

[2] Wuhan United Imaging Healthcare Surgical Technology Company Ltd., Wuhan 430074, China

[3] Huazhong University of Science and Technology Wuxi Research Institute, Wuhan, China

**Abstract.** In some industries, such as auto fast repair industry, work pieces are fixture-free, which will lead to the pose error and bring down the quality of the product. In this paper, a pose calibration and trajectory adjustment of robot (PCTAR) based on monocular vision method is put forward. This PCTAR method uses a camera to take pictures of the work piece in the ideal pose and the actual pose. Based on the essential matrix between these two images and some additional information, the pose error of the work piece can be calculated. Then, according to the transformation relation between coordinate systems, the trajectory of robot can be calibrated. This PCTAR method uses only one camera, which means the cost is low, and the calibration process is simple and easy to operate. The results of simulations and experiments have shown that this PCTAR method achieves satisfactory performance.

**Keywords:** Robot · Pose Calibration · Trajectory Adjustment · Monocular Vision

## 1 Introduction

With the development of robot technology, robots are increasingly used in manufacturing process. Compared with the time-consuming and tedious traditional teaching method [1], automatic off-line trajectory generation method [2–5] has a great advantage. Thus, off-line trajectory is widely used in surface manufacturing, such as spray painting, spray forming and polishing. However, in the actual conditions, the pose (Pose stands for both position and orientation.) of the work piece is often inconsistent with the ideal pose, which is shown in Fig. 1. And the pose error will lead to a decline in the quality of the work piece. Therefore, for robots with off-line planning trajectories, calibration of the work piece is indispensable. At present, special fixtures are often used to eliminate the pose error. However, in some industries, such as auto fast repair industry and furniture manufacturing, fixtures cannot be used. A pose calibration method for fixture-free work pieces is needed.

X. Lan et al. (Eds.): ICIRA 2024, LNAI 15208, pp. 287–299, 2025.
https://doi.org/10.1007/978-981-96-0783-9_20

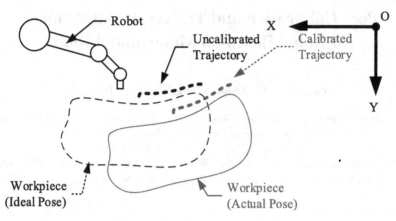

**Fig. 1.** Pose error of a work piece

Pose Calibration is widely studied. Du *et al.* [6] proposed a method for robot automatic calibration and tool pose estimation. In this method, both an inertial measurement unit (IMU) and a position marker, detected by two cameras, are installed on the robot execution end, which means this method needs at least two kinds of sensors. Sun Y *et al.* [7] used LVDT (Linear Voltage Displacement Transducer) to detect the relative deviation of the actual work piece surface from the zero reference paths, and they used the measured deviation to calculate the transfer matrix from the actual work piece to the CAD model. Li X *et al.* [8] used triggers (contact sensors or laser distance sensors) to contact a number of points on three planes of the workpiece to compute the normal vectors of the three planes. Then these three vectors were used to construct the workpiece coordinates, and the workpiece calibration was completed. These two methods that use contact sensors are costly and time consuming. Collet *et al.* [9] proposed a method for estimating the total pose of a target from a single image, which needed multiple images of the target in advance to train the target recognition and localization system and formed a model of the target. The training of this method takes a long time. Assa *et al.* [10] proposed a vision-based multi-sensor fusion method that used one or more pairs of Eye-in-Hand and Eye-to-Hand cameras as inputs. And extended Kalman filtering was used to process the acquired data so as to obtain the target pose. This method requires multiple cameras at a high cost. Above methods require the use of multiple sensors or cameras, which brings about high costs. Multi-sensor information fusion is complex, and the calibration between cameras is time-consuming.

In this paper, a pose calibration and trajectory adjustment of robot (PCTAR) based on monocular vision method is proposed. This method only uses one camera to achieve the pose calibration of the workpiece. According to the transformation relation between coordinate systems, the trajectory of robot is calibrated. At the end of the article, the car painting is taken as an example to validate this method. The pose calibration experiment is carried out with the right door of the car, and the calibration of the trajectory is simulated with Matlab robotic toolbox [11]. Simulation and experimental results show that this method can meet the requirements.

## 2  Principle of PCTAR Method

It is known that the pose information of a workpiece can be obtained directly by binocular vision. However, methods based on binocular vision require a cumbersome calibration of two cameras. The PCTAR method in this paper can obtain the pose information of a workpiece via monocular vision, which is not only low cost but also fast.

The PCTAR method uses only one camera. Set up the camera in the place where the workpiece can be clearly observed by it. This camera is called the real camera. Use the real camera to take a picture of the ideal workpiece (the workpiece in the ideal pose), and the obtained image is called the reference image. Figure 2 shows the ideal pose schematic diagram. Since there are no fixtures, the pose of the actual workpiece (the workpiece in the actual pose) is inconsistent with the ideal pose. Use the real camera to take a picture of the actual workpiece, and the obtained image is called the target image. Figure 3 shows the actual pose schematic diagram.

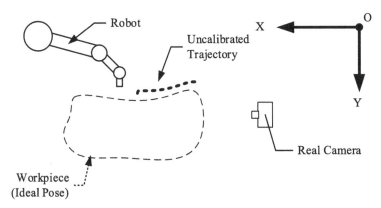

**Fig. 2.** Ideal pose schematic diagram

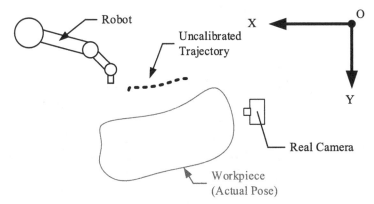

**Fig. 3.** Actual pose schematic diagram

The pose error of the workpiece is obtained as follows. Firstly, suppose there is a virtual camera whose parameters are the same as the real camera. And the virtual camera coincides with the pose of the real camera. Secondly, attach the virtual camera to the ideal workpiece, and then their relative pose remains the same. Thirdly, if the ideal workpiece is moved to coincide with the actual workpiece by a certain rotation and translation, the real camera will also be moved to another position by the same rotation and translation. Figure 4 shows the pose relationship between the virtual camera and the real camera. Obviously, the relative pose between the virtual camera and the real camera describes the pose error of the actual work piece. Finally, suppose the virtual camera can take pictures. Use the virtual camera to take a picture of the actual workpiece, and the obtained image is called the virtual image. If the background of images is ignored, the virtual image is the same as the reference image. Therefore, only the reference image and the target image are needed. The PCTAR method uses these two images to calculate the relative pose between the virtual camera and the real camera, so as to realize the pose calibration of the workpiece and the adjustment of the robot trajectory. The calculation process of pose calibration and trajectory adjustment is introduced in Sect. 3.

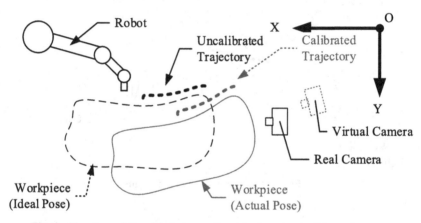

**Fig. 4.** The pose relationship between the virtual camera and the real camera

## 3  Pose Calibration and Trajectory Adjustment

### 3.1  Pose Calibration

A reference image and a target image are obtained in Sect. 2. In order to identify the workpiece in the two images, it is necessary to perform feature detection on the images. In this paper, the SURF (Speeded up Robust Features) algorithm [12–14] is used to extract and match the features of the images, and the RANSAC (Random Sample Consensus) algorithm [15] is used to remove wrong matching results. The final matching results can be used to calculate the pose error.

The pose error of a workpiece can be decomposed into two parts, namely the rotation error and the translation error. The rotation error can be represented by a rotation matrix, and the translation error can be represented by a translation vector. According to the principle of the epipolar geometry, the essential matrix between the two images describes the relative pose of the actual camera and the virtual camera. Decompose the essential matrix, and the rotation matrix and the translation vector can be gotten. The calculation process of the rotation matrix and the translation vector is introduced in the following two subsections.

**Solution of the Rotation Matrix.** Theorem 1 [16]: A $3 \times 3$ matrix $E$ is an essential matrix if and only if two of its singular values are equal, and the third is zero.

Assume that the three singular values of the essential matrix are a, b, and c, respectively. And $a \geq b \geq c.$. However, the result of singular value decomposition is not ideal in actual calculation. The first two singular values ($a$ and $b$) are not equal and the last singular value is not equal to zero. In this case, it is necessary to appropriately process the essential matrix. The essential matrix $E$ is decomposed as follows.

$$E = U \begin{bmatrix} (a+b)/2 & & \\ & (a+b)/2 & \\ & & 0 \end{bmatrix} V^T$$

Theorem 2 [16]: Suppose that the SVD (Singular Value Decomposition) of $E$ is $U diag(1, 1, 0) V^T$. There are (ignoring signs) two possible factorizations $E = SR$ as follows:

$$S = UZU^T \quad R_a = UWV^T \quad or \quad R_b = UW^T V^T \tag{1}$$

Theorem 2 shows that the rotation matrix is $R_a$ or $R_b$. And the translation vector is also available.

$$t_n = U \begin{bmatrix} 0 \\ 0 \\ 1 \end{bmatrix} \quad t = \alpha t_n \tag{2}$$

The translation vector is notated as $t$, and $\alpha$ is a factor which is not equal to zero. Considering the sign, there are four possible solutions as shown below.

$$\begin{Bmatrix} R = R_a \\ t = \alpha t_n \end{Bmatrix} \quad \begin{Bmatrix} R = R_b \\ t = \alpha t_n \end{Bmatrix} \quad \begin{Bmatrix} R = R_a \\ t = -\alpha t_n \end{Bmatrix} \quad \begin{Bmatrix} R = R_b \\ t = -\alpha t_n \end{Bmatrix} \tag{3}$$

Figure 5 shows the four possible solutions [16]. Obviously, only one solution satisfies the real working conditions. A method will be proposed in the next subsection for eliminating ineligible solutions.

**Solution of the Translation Vector.** In the previous subsection, we also obtain the expression of the translation vector while solving the rotation matrix. In theory, it is only need to solve the scaling factor, and the translation vector can be obtained. However, the ambiguity of the projection determines that the depth information of the object cannot

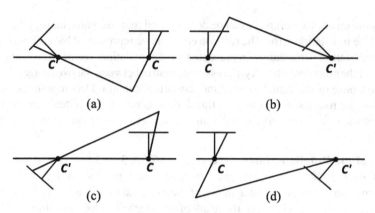

**Fig. 5.** Four possible solutions

be recovered from the simple image information without additional information. Even if the binocular vision measurement can obtain the depth information, it needs to calibrate the left and right cameras in order to realize the complete restoration of the three-dimensional spatial information. Therefore, a method of adding external information is used to solve the translation vector instead of directly solving the scaling factor. The additional information here refers to the relative position of the two points in the world coordinate system.

Two points $X_1 = \begin{bmatrix} X_1 & Y_1 & Z_1 \end{bmatrix}^T$ and $X_2 = \begin{bmatrix} X_2 & Y_2 & Z_2 \end{bmatrix}^T$ in the space are projected onto the reference image and the target image, respectively. And four projection points are $x_1 = \begin{bmatrix} u_1 & v_1 & 1 \end{bmatrix}^T$, $x_2 = \begin{bmatrix} u_2 & v_2 & 1 \end{bmatrix}^T$, $x'_1 = \begin{bmatrix} u'_1 & v'_1 & 1 \end{bmatrix}^T$, and $x'_2 = \begin{bmatrix} u'_2 & v'_2 & 1 \end{bmatrix}^T$. Figure 6 shows the projection relationship.

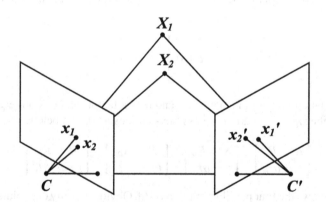

**Fig. 6.** Projection relationship

For convenience, it is assumed that the virtual camera coordinate system and the world coordinate system coincide. Then the virtual camera parameters are $P = K[I|0]$, and the real camera parameters are $P' = K[R|t]$. The matrix $K$ is the camera intrinsic parameter matrix, and the matrix $[R|t]$ is the camera external parameter matrix.

According to the pinhole camera model, the following equation [16] can be obtained.

$$\lambda x = KRX + Kt \tag{4}$$

$\lambda$ is the homogeneous scaling factor. For the reference image and the target image, the following equations are obtained.

$$\begin{aligned}
\lambda_1 x_1 &= KR_1 X_1 + Kt_1 = KX_1 \\
\lambda_2 x_2 &= KR_1 X_2 + Kt_1 = KX_2
\end{aligned} \tag{5}$$

$$\begin{aligned}
\lambda_1' x'_1 &= KR_2 X_1 + Kt_2 = KRX_1 + Kt \\
\lambda_2' x'_2 &= KR_2 X_2 + Kt_2 = KRX_2 + Kt
\end{aligned} \tag{6}$$

The relative positions of $X_1$ and $X_2$ are known. Notate it as $\Delta$.

$$\Delta = X_1 - X_2 = \begin{bmatrix} X_1 - X_2 \\ Y_1 - Y_2 \\ Z_1 - Z_2 \end{bmatrix} \tag{7}$$

The two equations in (5) are subtracted.

$$\lambda_1 x_1 - \lambda_2 x_2 = KX_1 - KX_2 = K(X_1 - X_2) = K\Delta \tag{8}$$

$\lambda_1$ and $\lambda_2$ are obtained by solving the Eq. (8). Then $X_1$ and $X_2$ are obtained by substituting $\lambda_1$ and $\lambda_2$ into the Eq. (5).

$$\begin{aligned}
X_1 &= K^{-1} \lambda_1 x_1 \\
X_2 &= K^{-1} \lambda_2 x_2
\end{aligned} \tag{9}$$

Similarly, the two equations in (6) are subtracted.

$$\lambda_1' x'_1 - \lambda_2' x'_2 = KRX_1 + Kt - (KRX_2 + Kt) = KR\Delta \tag{10}$$

Since there are two possible solutions of matrix $R$, two sets of possible homogeneous scaling factors are obtained.

$$\begin{cases} \lambda_1' = \lambda_{a1}' \\ \lambda_2' = \lambda_{a2}' \end{cases} \text{(when } R = R_a) \quad \begin{cases} \lambda_1' = \lambda_{b1}' \\ \lambda_2' = \lambda_{b2}' \end{cases} \text{(when } R = R_b) \tag{11}$$

Therefore, two sets of possible translation vectors are obtained.

$$\begin{aligned}
&\begin{cases} t_{a1} = K^{-1}(KR_a X_1 - \lambda_{a1}' x'_1) \\ t_{a2} = K^{-1}(KR_a X_2 - \lambda_{a2}' x'_2) \end{cases} \text{(when } R = R_a) \\
&\begin{cases} t_{b1} = K^{-1}(KR_b X_1 - \lambda_{b1}' x'_1) \\ t_{b2} = K^{-1}(KR_b X_2 - \lambda_{b2}' x'_2) \end{cases} \text{(when } R = R_b)
\end{aligned} \tag{12}$$

Since the pose of the virtual camera and the real camera in the world coordinate system are fixed, the real camera external parameters remain unchanged. Only one set of solutions in the Eqs. (12) can satisfy the Eq. (13).

$$t = \alpha t_n = \alpha U \begin{bmatrix} 0 \\ 0 \\ 1 \end{bmatrix} \tag{13}$$

At the beginning of this subsection, it is assumed that the world coordinate system coincides with the virtual camera coordinate system. However, the reality is that these two coordinate systems often do not coincide, so the above derivation needs to be amended. The relative position of the two points in the virtual camera coordinate system can not be measured, but the relative position of the two points in the world coordinate system can be measured. The Eq. (14) is the conversion formula.

$$\Delta = R_w^T \Delta_w \tag{14}$$

where $\Delta_w$ represents the relative position of the two feature points in the world coordinate system. $R_w$ and $t_w$ are the calibration results of the real camera. Figure 7 shows the two points and the pose relationship when the workpiece is in the actual pose.

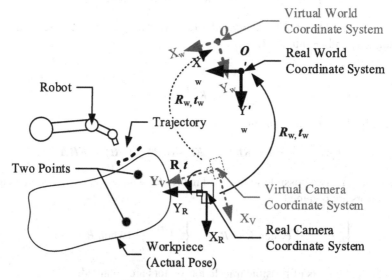

Fig. 7. Coordinates relationship

## 3.2 Trajectory Adjustment of Robot

According to the relative pose between the virtual camera and the real camera, the relationship among the virtual camera coordinate system, the virtual world coordinate system, the real camera coordinate system and the real world coordinate system can be summarized, which is shown in the Fig. 7.

The uncalibrated trajectory is described relative to the virtual world coordinate system, but the desired calibrated trajectory needs to be described relative to the real world coordinate system. Therefore, descriptions of the trajectory need to be changed from the virtual world coordinate system to the real world coordinate system, which takes three steps as follows [17].

1) Change the description of the uncalibrated trajectory from the virtual world coordinate system to the virtual camera coordinate system. The relationship between the virtual camera coordinate system and the virtual world coordinate system is as follows.

$$X = T_1 x = \left[ \begin{array}{c|c} R_w & t_w \\ \hline 0 & 1 \end{array} \right] x \tag{15}$$

where $X$ describes unclibrated trajectory points relative to the virtual world coordinate system, and $x$ describes trajectory points relative to the virtual camera coordinate system. The inverse transformation of the Eq. (15) is used to obtain the trajectory points relative to the virtual camera coordinate system.

$$x = T_1^{-1} X = \left[ \begin{array}{c|c} R_w^T & -R_w^T t_w \\ \hline 0 & 1 \end{array} \right] X \tag{16}$$

2) Change the description of the trajectory from the virtual camera coordinate system to the real camera coordinate system. The relationship between the virtual camera coordinate system and the real camera coordinate system is as follows.

$$x' = T_2 x = \left[ \begin{array}{c|c} R & t \\ \hline 0 & 1 \end{array} \right] x \tag{17}$$

where $x$ describes trajectory points relative to the virtual camera coordinate system, and $x'$ describes trajectory points relative to the real camera coordinate system.

3) Change the description of the trajectory from the real camera coordinate system to the real world coordinate system, and the desired calibrated trajectory is obtained.

$$X' = T_3 x' = \left[ \begin{array}{c|c} R_w & t_w \\ \hline 0 & 1 \end{array} \right] x' \tag{18}$$

where $X'$ describes trajectory points relative to the real world coordinate system, and $x'$ describes trajectory points relative to the real camera coordinate system.

According to Eqs. (16), (17) and (18), the calibrated trajectory expression can be obtained.

$$X' = T_3 T_2 T_1^{-1} X = \left[ \begin{array}{c|c} R_w R R_w^T & -R_w R R_w^T t_w + R_w t + t_w \\ \hline 0 & 1 \end{array} \right] X \tag{19}$$

## 4   Experimental Verification

In this paper, in order to test the correctness and feasibility of the method, the spraying process of car fast repair is chosen as the verification object. And a car door is chosen as the experimental object. The workflow of the pose calibration and trajectory adjustment method based on monocular vision is shown in Fig. 8.

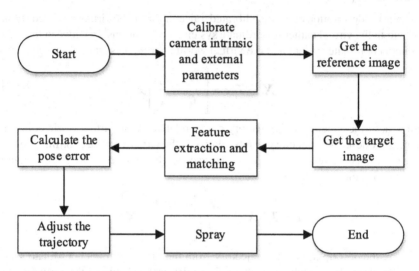

**Fig. 8.** The workflow of the pose calibration and trajectory adjustment method

A Basler acA1300-60gc industrial camera and an ordinary PC are used to form the image acquisition and processing system [18, 19]. The real camera parameters are calibrated and calculated by Zhang calibration method [20]. In order to facilitate the identification of the two points, two circular points whose diameters are 20 mm are chosen. The two points are attached to a relatively flat position of the door, their relative position in the world coordinate system is $\boldsymbol{\Delta}_w = \begin{bmatrix} 150\ 0\ 0 \end{bmatrix}^T$. Figure 9 shows the car door and two circular points.

After the preparation work is completed, use the real camera to take the reference image and the target image of the car door. The pose error of the car door and the calibration results are shown in Table 1. The results in Table 1 show that the accuracy of the PCTAR method is high enough. Furthermore, a lot of pose calibration experiments are done to test the method. Experimental results show that the translation absolute error is within 3cm, and the rotation absolute error is within 1°, when the rotation angle of the workpiece is within 25°.

After calibration of the workpiece, it is necessary to adjust the spraying trajectory of the robot. Matlab robotic toolbox is used to simulate the calibrated trajectory. The uncalibrated trajectory and the calibrated trajectory of the car door are shown in the Fig. 10.

**Fig. 9.** The car door and two circular points

**Table 1.** Calibration result

| Experimental results | X(mm) | Y(mm) | $\theta(\circ)$ |
|---|---|---|---|
| Pose error | 200 | −100 | −25 |
| Calibrated result | 184 | −106.6 | −25.1 |
| Absolute error | 16 | 6.6 | 0.1 |

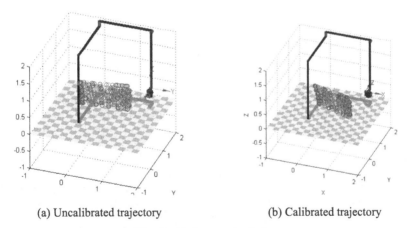

(a) Uncalibrated trajectory                    (b) Calibrated trajectory

**Fig. 10.** Trajectory simulation

The results of the simulation show that the PCTAR method can effectively eliminate the effect of pose error. Figure 11 shows the spray performance of the uncalibrated trajectory and calibrated trajectory. Apparently, the spray performance of the calibrated trajectory is better than the uncalibrated trajectory.

(a) Uncalibrated trajectory                    (b) Calibrated trajectory

**Fig. 11.**  Spray performance

## 5   Conclusion

Aiming at the problem of the pose error of the workpiece during process, a pose calibration and trajectory adjustment method based on monocular vision is proposed. This
method can be used to calibrate the pose of the fixture-free workpiece. Then, according to
the calibration result, the trajectory can be adjusted. Simulations and experiments show
that this method can get good results. This method can be used in many applications
where robots are used.

## References

1. Lee, W., Bang, Y.-B., Lee, K.-M., Shin, B.-H., Paik, J.K., Kim, I.-S.: Motion teaching method
   for complex robot links using motor current. Int. J. Control Autom. Syst. **8**, 1072–1081 (2010)
2. Chen, H., Xi, N.: Automated robot tool trajectory connection for spray forming process. J.
   Manuf. Sci. Eng. **134**, 021017 (2012)
3. Chen, W., Li, X., Ge, H., Wang, L., Zhang, Y.: Trajectory planning for spray painting robot
   based on point cloud slicing technique. Electronics **9**(6), 908 (2020)
4. Chen, W., Liu, J., Tang, Y., Ge, H.: Automatic spray trajectory optimization on Bézier surface.
   Electronics **8**(2), 168 (2019)
5. Nieto Bastida, S., Lin, C.-Y.: Autonomous trajectory planning for spray painting on complex
   surfaces based on a point cloud model. Sensors **23**(24), 9634 (2023)
6. Du, G., Liang, Y., Li, C., Liu, P.X., Li, D.: Online robot kinematic calibration using hybrid
   filter with multiple sensors. IEEE Trans. Instrum. Measur. **69**(9), 7092–7107(2020)
7. Sun, Y., Giblin David, J., Kazem, K.: Accurate robotic belt grinding of workpieces with
   complex geometries using relative calibration techniques. Rob. Comput.-Integr. Manuf. **25**,
   204–210 (2009)
8. Li, X., Fuhlbrigge Thomas, A., Sang, C., Biao, Z.: Automatic offline program calibration in
   robotic cells. In: 2014 IEEE 4th Annual International Conference on Cyber Technology in
   Automation, Control, and Intelligent Systems (CYBER), pp. 585–590. IEEE (2014)
9. Alvaro, C., Dmitry, B., Srinivasa Siddhartha, S., Dave, F.: Object recognition and full pose
   registration from a single image for robotic manipulation. In: IEEE International Conference
   on Robotics and Automation, ICRA 2009, pp. 48–55. IEEE (2009)
10. Akbar, A., Farrokh, J.-S.: A robust vision-based sensor fusion approach for real-time pose
    estimation. IEEE Trans. Cybern. **44**, 217–227 (2014)

11. Corke, P.I.: A robotics toolbox for MATLAB. IEEE Robot. Autom. Mag. **3**, 24–32 (1996)
12. Lowe David, G.: Object recognition from local scale-invariant features. In: Computer Vision 1999. The Proceedings of the Seventh IEEE International Conference, pp. 1150–1157 (1999)
13. Lowe David, G.: Distinctive image features from scale-invariant keypoints. Int. J. Comput. Vis. **60**, 91–110 (2004)
14. Herbert, B., Andreas, E., Tinne, T., Van Luc, G.: Speeded-up robust features (SURF). Comput. Vision Image Understand. **110**, 346–359 (2008)
15. Fischler Martin, A., Bolles, R.C.: Random sample consensus: a paradigm for model fitting with applications to image analysis and automated cartography. Commun. ACM **24**, 381–395 (1981)
16. Richard, H., Andrew, Z.: Multiple View Geometry in Computer Vision. Cambridge University Press (2003)
17. Craig John, J.: Introduction to Robotics: Mechanics and Control. Pearson Prentice Hall, Upper Saddle River (2005)
18. Jean-Yves, B.: Camera Calibration Toolbox for Matlab (2004)
19. Gary, B., Adrian, K.: Learning OpenCV: Computer Vision with the OpenCV Library. O'Reilly Media, Inc. (2008)
20. Zhang, Z.: A flexible new technique for camera calibration. IEEE Trans. Pattern Anal. Mach. Intell. **22**, 1330–1334 (2000)

# A Hybrid Elasto-Geometrical Calibration Method for Industrial Robot Using Only Position Measurement

Zhongkai Zhang⬤, Yan Lu⬤, Hongbo Hu⬤, Zhikai Shen,
and Chungang Zhuang$^{(\boxtimes)}$⬤

School of Mechanical Engineering, Shanghai Jiao Tong University, Shanghai 200240, China
cgzhuang@sjtu.edu.cn

**Abstract.** In scenarios of manufacturing and high-precision operations, achieving high positioning accuracy of industrial robots is crucial. Kinematic calibration plays a vital role in reducing positioning errors. Considering both the geometric errors introduced by the machining and assembly processes and the joint compliance errors stemming from gearboxes, this paper establishes an elasto-geometrical error model based on the robot MDH model and the joint compliance model, and only position errors are required for calibration. The established model enables the identification of kinematic parameters, transformation frame parameters, and all joint stiffness under external loads. Furthermore, a hybrid calibration algorithm is proposed by combining least squares and heuristic algorithms, and redundancy is then analyzed and eliminated to further improve accuracy. By designing the hybrid algorithm, the proposed method can converge to the optimal solution quickly while maintaining sufficient global search capabilities. Finally, a simulation is conducted and the absolute positioning error decreases from 2.8658 mm to 0.1682 mm, validating the effectiveness of the proposed model and algorithm.

**Keywords:** Elasto-geometrical calibration · Joint stiffness · Redundancy analysis · Heuristic algorithm

## 1 Introduction

Nowadays, industrial robots have been playing an important role in manufacturing and other high-precision demanded scenarios for decades. Excellent absolute positioning accuracy undoubtedly ensures the performance of robots in various tasks. However, affected by inevitable errors from robot manufacturing and assembling, the nominal kinematic parameters provided by manufacturers usually differ from the actual. Meanwhile, the harmonic gearboxes installed in robot joints will deflect when external loads are applied, which leads to a deviation between the motor position collected from its decoder and the actual link position. Therefore, it is necessary to calibrate the kinematic model and identify the joint compliance at the same time.

Kinematic calibration of industrial robots usually contains four steps: modeling, measuring, identification and compensation. An accurate and complete model for calibration is essential. The conventional Denavit-Hartenberg (DH) model [1] was first applied in kinematic calibration. To further tackle the singularity of parallel joints in calibration, Hayati proposed a new model by adding the fifth parameter, namely the modified Denavit-Hartenberg (MDH) model [2]. The stiffness modeling mainly includes joints and links, yet in industrial occasions, the deformation of links is negligible because such impact on the robot end-effector position is small [3]. Focusing on joint stiffness, many scholars have made efforts in its modeling and identification [4], which enable the possibility of integrating robot kinematic and stiffness calibration into a single framework [5]. In previous studies, joint stiffness identification was mostly performed in a full-pose fashion [4, 6], which made the modeling and identification more complex. When lack of orientation in position measurements in elasto-geometrical calibration, the compliance of joint 6 cannot be identified directly since it does not affect the end-effector position. Additional works need to be done to realize a position-only calibration with all joint stiffness identifiable.

Identification of established elasto-geometrical model parameters is similar to kinematic calibration methods, in which many nonlinear least-square techniques were implemented to obtain precise results. The Levenberg-Marquardt (LM) method [7] is one of the most prevalent ways of calculating the nonlinear kinematic calibration, yet it tends to fall into local minimal in practice. Therefore, some heuristic algorithms were implemented into calibration to improve the global searching ability, such as Beetle Swarm Optimization (BSO) [8], Simulated Annealing (SA) algorithm [9], Differential Evolution (DE) algorithm [10], etc. Redundant parameters in the kinematic model [11, 12] are another concern that will influence the identification result, and identification algorithms should eliminate those parameters to ensure the accuracy of calibration results. In the process of elasto-geometrical calibration, the redundancy of compliance and kinematics and their coupling have made the existing identification methods difficult to find a global solution and slow to converge. Therefore, it is convenient to take advantage of redundancy elimination and different identification algorithms to further improve the absolute positioning accuracy.

In this paper, the elasto-geometrical model of robots is first established. Consequently, the spherically mounted retroflector (SMR) is installed with offset to the center point of the end-effector, thus the rotation of the last joint could be reflected in the translation of SMR for measuring. External loads are applied additionally concerning another offset point to produce deflections in the first and last joint, making all joint compliances identifiable. After the modeling and linearization, a hybrid identification method composed of least-square and heuristic algorithms is proposed, and their redundancy is analyzed and eliminated numerically by the advantages of the methods utilized in dynamics base parameters [13]. The proposed method ensures the minimality of the elasto-geometrical model and improves both calibration accuracy and efficiency. To validate the proposed method, simulations were conducted using ROKAE XB7S, showing effectiveness and advancement in calibration results.

The main contributions of this paper are as follows:

- An elasto-geometrical model using only position measurement is established. From adjusting the measuring point of the end-effector, the model is able to identify kinematic and all joint compliance parameters when external forces are applied.

- A hybrid identification method composing least-squares and heuristic algorithms is proposed. Redundant parameters are analyzed and eliminated in identification and the strategy for integrating different algorithms is fully described.

The remainder of this paper is organized as follows. Section 2 established a linearized calibration model including joint compliance and kinematic errors using only position measurements. A hybrid identification method based on the least square method and the heuristic algorithm was developed in Sect. 3. Section 4 presents the experimental setup, data processing and analysis, corresponding results are also discussed. Finally, conclusions were drawn in Sect. 5.

## 2 Robot Elasto-Geometrical Model

### 2.1 Kinematic Model

In this paper, the 6 degrees of freedom (DoF) industrial robot ROKAE XB7S is modeled to evaluate the following approaches. Due to the parallel between joint 2 and joint 3, the MDH formulation [2] is adopted to avoid the singularity and evaluate the parallelism. Based on the definition, the transformation between two adjacent frames $\{i - 1\}$ and $\{i\}$ can be formulated as:

$$T_{i-1,i} = R(x_{i-1}, \alpha_{i-1})T(x_{i-1}, a_{i-1})R(z_i, \theta_i)T(z_i, d_i)R(y_i, \beta_i) \tag{1}$$

where $a_{i-1}$ is the link length, $\alpha_{i-1}$ is the twist angle, $\theta_i$ is the joint angle, $d_i$ is the link offset and $\beta_i$ is the extra twist angle around the y-axis. Operator $R(\bullet)$ and $T(\bullet)$ represent rotation and translation matrix according to specific axis and parameter, respectively. Therefore, the coordinate system of ROKAE XB7S is established as shown in Fig. 1, and corresponding MDH parameters are listed in Table 1.

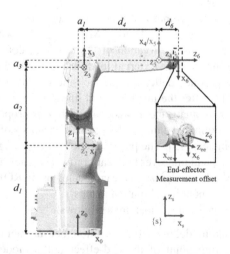

**Fig. 1.** The MDH coordinate frames of ROKAE XB7S robot

**Table 1.** The nominal MDH parameters of ROKAE XB7S robot

| Joint | $a_{i-1}$(mm) | $\alpha_{i-1}$(rad) | $d_i$(mm) | $\theta_i$(rad) | $\beta_i$(rad) |
|---|---|---|---|---|---|
| 1 | 0 | 0 | 380 | 0 | 0 |
| 2 | 30 | $-\pi/2$ | 0 | $-\pi/2$ | 0 |
| 3 | 340 | 0 | 0 | 0 | 0 |
| 4 | 35 | $-\pi/2$ | 335 | 0 | 0 |
| 5 | 0 | $\pi/2$ | 0 | 0 | 0 |
| 6 | 0 | $-\pi/2$ | 83 | $\pi$ | 0 |

However, it is noteworthy that the frame {0} and {6} cannot be used directly in calibration, since the displacement of frame {0} w.r.t. the laser tracker world frame {s} is unknown, either the SMR reference frame {r} w.r.t. to frame {6}. To complete the coordinates in calibration, extra transformation matrices are defined as:

$$T_{s0} = R(x_s, \alpha_s)R(y_s, \beta_s)R(x_s, \gamma_s)T(x_s, x_s)T(y_s, y_s)T(z_s, z_s) \qquad (2)$$

$$T_{6r} = R(x_6, \alpha_r)R(y_6, \beta_r)R(x_6, \gamma_r)T(x_6, x_r)T(y_6, y_r)T(z_6, z_r) \qquad (3)$$

where $(\alpha_s, \beta_s, \gamma_s)$ is the XYZ fixed Euler angle and $(x_s, y_s, z_s)$ is the translation, both expressed in world frame {s}. Similarly, $(\alpha_r, \beta_r, \gamma_r)$ and $(x_r, y_r, z_r)$ are orientation and translation, respectively, of the SMR frame w.r.t. the frame {6}.

Hence, the forward kinematic model of XB7S could be derived as:

$$T_{sr} = T_{s0}(\prod_{i=1}^{6} T_{i-1,i})T_{6r} \qquad (4)$$

The selection matrix is then applied to obtain the position measurement:

$$p = \left[I_3\ 0_{3\times1}\right]T_{sr}(q)\left[0_{1\times3}\ 1\right]^T \qquad (5)$$

in which $p \in \mathbb{R}^3$ represents the SMR position expressed in the laser tracker reference frame {s}, and $q$ is the vector of input joint angles.

## 2.2 Stiffness Model

According to the previous works in stiffness identification, the joint considering compliance was usually regarded as a torsional spring [14]. The linear model of joint deflection and torque can be described as:

$$\theta_c = C\tau \qquad (6)$$

where $\theta_c$ is the vector of joint deflections, $\tau$ is the vector of joint torques caused by gravity and external loads. Since each joint deflection is only related to the torque provided itself, $C \in \mathbb{R}^{6\times6}$ is a diagonal matrix composed of 6 compliance coefficients.

After having Eq. (6), the joint deflection can be mapped to the end-effector position using the kinematic Jacobian matrix $J \in \mathbb{R}^{6 \times 6}$. Assuming the deflections caused by joints and the corresponding error in cartesian space are infinitesimally small, the error caused by deflections could be calculated as:

$$p_c = J_v C \tau \tag{7}$$

where $J_v \in \mathbb{R}^{3 \times 6}$ is the truncated jacobian keeping only translation part.

Generally, the kinematic Jacobian is defined w.r.t. the robot frame {0} and {6}, so that the calculated position error of frame {6} is expressed in the robot base frame {0}. Nevertheless, to combine the elastic position error with the kinematic, it is necessary to transform the Jacobian matrix to the desired frame {s} and {r} since their expression should be uniform. To begin with, the basic jacobian is denoted as $J_6^0$, and the desired jacobian is denoted as $J_r^s$. Two types of transformation are involved in this process. For the first step, the velocity in different coordinates could be transformed using a rotation matrix as $v_6^0 = R_{06} v_6^6$, , hence the jacobian in frame {6} is calculated as:

$$\begin{aligned} J_6^6 &= \begin{bmatrix} R_{06} & O \\ O & R_{06} \end{bmatrix}^{-1} J_6^0 \\ &= (I_2 \otimes R_{06})^{-1} J_6^0 \end{aligned} \tag{8}$$

in which $R_{06}$ is the rotation matrix between frame {0} and {6}. For simplicity, here the Kronecker product $\otimes$ is used for shortening the matrix notation. Consequently, the jacobian in frame {6} could be transformed to the SMR frame {r}. Due to both the expression frame and point having changed, the translation term was complemented to satisfy such a situation. Thus, the jacobian in frame {r} is calculated as:

$$\begin{aligned} J_r^r &= \begin{bmatrix} R_{6r} & O \\ \hat{p}_{6r} R_{6r} & R_{6r} \end{bmatrix}^{-1} J_6^6 \\ &= [Ad_{T_{6r}}]^{-1} J_6^6 \end{aligned} \tag{9}$$

in which $T_{6r}$ is the transformation matrix between frame {6} and {r}, $R_{6r}$ and $p_{6r}$ are the rotation matrix and translation vector of $T_{6r}$ respectively, the operator $\wedge$ represents the mapping from vector to 3 dimension anti-symmetric matrix, $[Ad_{T_{6r}}] \in \mathbb{R}^{6 \times 6}$ is the symbol of adjoint matrix [15] corresponding to $T_{6r}$. Finally, the desired jacobian $J_r^s$ could be calculated similarly to the first step:

$$J_r^s = (I_2 \otimes R_{sr}) J_r^r \tag{10}$$

in which $R_{sr}$ is the rotation matrix between frame {s} and {r}. According to the above equations, (10) could be reformulated as:

$$J_r^s = (I_2 \otimes R_{sr})[Ad_{T_{6r}}]^{-1}(I_2 \otimes R_{06})^{-1} J_6^0 \tag{11}$$

As a result, the deflections $p_c$ can be calculated in (7) since the truncated Jacobian $J_v$ is equal to the last three rows of $J_r^s$.

### 2.3 Elasto-Geometrical Error Model and Linearization

To estimate the model parameters error through measured end-effector position, $N$ points with their Cartesian position were collected for a least-square problem. For $N$ measured points, the error optimization problem can be described as follows:

$$\min_{x,\sigma,c} \sum_{N}^{i=1} \|p_{i,act} - p_i\| \tag{12}$$

where $x \in \mathbb{R}^{30}$ is the estimated MDH parameters expressed in a single column vector, $\sigma \in \mathbb{R}^{12}$ is the vector form of frame parameters in (2) and (3), $c \in \mathbb{R}^6$ is the vector form of compliance matrix $C$, $p_{i,act}$ and $p_i$ is the actual and nominal position of the $i$-th point.

The actual MDH parameters and joint compliance are calculated by solving the problem (12). Here, linearization techniques are used to solve least-square problems. Based on the kinematic and stiffness model, the composed elasto-geometrical error model could be established through their first-order analysis:

$$\delta p = \frac{\partial p}{\partial x}\delta x + \frac{\partial p}{\partial \sigma}\delta \sigma + \frac{\partial p}{\partial c}\delta c \tag{13}$$

Therefore, the linearized error model for a single point can be expressed as:

$$\Delta p_i = \left[ J_x\ J_\sigma\ J_v \mathrm{diag}(\tau) \right]_i \left[ \Delta x\ \Delta \sigma\ \Delta c \right]^T$$
$$= Y_i \pi \tag{14}$$

where $\Delta p_i \in \mathbb{R}^3$ is the $i$-th position error between the actual position and estimated, $\mathrm{diag}(\tau)$ denotes the diagonal form of torque vector, $J_x$ and $J_\sigma$ are the jacobian matrices of $x$ and $\sigma$, $Y_i \in \mathbb{R}^{3\times48}$ is the $i$-th linearized regression matrix, and $\pi \in \mathbb{R}^{48}$ is the parameter error between actual and nominal value. Finally, stacking $N$ measured points together, the complete elasto-geometrical model can be denoted as:

$$\Delta P = \tilde{Y}\pi \tag{15}$$

where $\Delta P \in \mathbb{R}^{48N}$ is the $N$ stacked point positions expressed in vector form, and $\tilde{Y} \in \mathbb{R}^{3N\times48}$ is the $N$ stacked regressor. The calibration is then processed by iterative solving (15) until $\pi$ converges to zero.

Notably, all joint compliances are supposed to be identified in the abovementioned model. External forces should be applied to the end-effector to ensure the torques of joints 1 and 6 are not zero so that the deflections from them are able to be embodied in measured end-effector positions. By installing the tip SMR with offset, the rotation of joint 6 is capable of affecting collected SMR positions, thereby the positions could be converted into parameter errors using modified Jacobian in the last section.

## 3 Parameter Identification

### 3.1 Least Square Identification Based on Base Parameters

In the linearized Eq. (15) derived in the previous section, the regression matrix $\tilde{Y}$ experiences a rank deficiency in practice, rendering it incapable of direct least square calculation. To address this issue, previous works employed methods such as the LM algorithm [7], or truncating the regression matrix [14] to obtain accurate solutions.

However, the kinematic and frame parameters in elasto-geometrical model exhibit coupling in identification. The rank of regressor $\tilde{Y}$ and linear relationships between its columns also vary during iterations. By examining the structure of regressor, it is found that the parameters of $T_{6r}$ and $\beta_6$, the parameters of $T_{s0}$ itself are linear dependent, and the linear correlation of $d_2$ and $d_3$ changed after the first computation. Also, the parameter $\beta_i, i = 1, 3 \sim 5$ is usually set to 0 in typical kinematic calibration since they do not exist in actual robot configurations. These lead to an inconsistency between the redundant parameters identified through analytical methods and the ones that should actually be removed. Furthermore, the elasto-geometrical model should be updated based on the latest results during least square calculation, yet the base parameter set obtained from least square cannot be directly utilized to establish new model.

Referred to the base parameter mapping [13], similar techniques are employed to tackle these issues. Firstly, the Gauss-Jordan elimination is implemented to identify redundant parameters. By defining the permutation matrix $P = [P_b \ P_d]$, the independent and correlated parts are separated as:

$$\tilde{Y}P = [\tilde{Y}_b \ \tilde{Y}_d] \tag{16}$$

where $\tilde{Y}_b$ and $\tilde{Y}_d$ are the independent and correlated parts of the regressor, respectively. After that, the base parameters could be calculated as:

$$\varphi = (\tilde{Y}_b^T \tilde{Y}_b)^{-1} \tilde{Y}_b^T \Delta P \tag{17}$$

where $\varphi$ is the base parameters differ from the independent ones. Thus, the relationship between the base and full parameter set is described as:

$$\pi = P \begin{bmatrix} 1 & -K_d \\ 0 & 1 \end{bmatrix} \begin{bmatrix} \varphi \\ \pi_d \end{bmatrix} \tag{18}$$

where $\pi_d$ is the correlated parameter set directly derived from $\pi$, and $K_d$ is the coefficient matrix obtained from Gauss-Jordan elimination. Since the nominal model is treated as no error at all, the correlated set $\pi_d$ is assumed to be a zero vector. Therefore, the linear correlation features in the model are ignored, and the mapping relationship for establishing an updated model during each iteration could also be automatically calculated. The redundancy elimination in nonlinear calibration is then conveniently achieved without complicated analytical derivation.

## 3.2 Least Square and Heuristic Based Hybrid Identification Method

In practice, influenced by model nonlinearity and noise, using least squares alone often fails to yield satisfactory identification results. To further enhance calibration accuracy, this paper first aims to utilize the GAPSO method [16], which combines genetic algorithm (GA) with particle swarm optimization (PSO). In the previous studies, the GA has shown weak local search capabilities while the PSO has good local convergence but insufficient global performance. The GAPSO combined the advantages of both and improved the accuracy of kinematic calibration.

The GAPSO also confronts the issue of redundancy in implementation. In comparison to the base parameter least squares (LSmin) techniques discussed in the last section, the GAPSO without eliminating redundancy requires manual setting of partial $\beta$ and coordinate system parameters to zero [8], and the searching range is then restricted in a truncated $\mathbb{R}^{40}$ space. Such approach overlooks the coupling relationships between parameters and only eliminates partial redundancy, resulting in lower search efficiency and worse computational accuracy for the GAPSO. To further improve the performance of GAPSO, similar techniques are utilized to concatenate the original searching space from $\pi \in \mathbb{R}^{48}$ to smaller $\varphi \in \mathbb{R}^{34}$, based on the Jacobian information provided in the previous section. By computing the permutation matrix $P$ at the beginning of each GAPSO iteration, each individual in GAPSO can be mapped back to the original space by calculating (18). The GAPSO combined with base parameter processing is denoted as GAPSOmin in the following context.

Following the optimization boundary and population selection rules, the GAPSOmin conducts GA and PSO computations sequentially after completing random population initialization of base parameters. In a single iteration, the GAPSOmin first selects individuals to perform crossover and mutation, the new population is then filtered to remove inferior redundant individuals. Consequently, the data of GA individuals from the current generation are recorded into PSO particles. The optimal cost of each individual and the overall optimal cost of all individuals correspond to the best position of a single particle and the global best position of all particles in PSO, denoted as $\varphi_{i,\text{pbest}}^k$ and $\varphi_{\text{gbest}}^k$ for the $i$-th particle and $k$-th iteration respectively. Hence, the velocity update rule for particle $i$ in the $k$-th iteration is described as:

$$\Delta\varphi_i^{k+1} = \omega(k)\Delta\varphi_i^k + c_1 r_1(\varphi_{i,\text{pbest}}^k - \varphi_i^k) + c_2 r_2(\varphi_{\text{gbest}}^k - \varphi_i^k) \qquad (19)$$

where $\varphi_i^k$ and $\Delta\varphi_i^k$ are the particle position and velocity, $c_1$ and $c_2$ are individual and group learning factors and were set to 1.5, $r_1$ and $r_2$ are random vectors generated between 0 and 1. Here, the weight coefficient $\omega(k)$ is used to speed up the convergence and varies with iterations:

$$\omega(k) = (\lambda_{\text{damp}})^k (\omega_{\min} + (\omega_{\max} - \omega_{\min})\frac{k_{\max} - k}{k}) \qquad (20)$$

where $\omega_{\max}$ and $\omega_{\min}$ are the maximum and minimum of $\omega(k)$ and were set to 0.9 and 0.4, $k_{\max}$ and $k$ is the max iterations and current iteration number, $\lambda_{\text{damp}}$ is the extra damping coefficient and was set to 0.99. Finally, the particle position is updated using the velocity calculated from (19) as:

$$\varphi_i^{k+1} = \varphi_i^k + \Delta\varphi_i^k \qquad (21)$$

where $\varphi_i^{k+1}$ is the base parameters of particle $i$ in the $k + 1$ iteration. After computing the GAPSO $k_{\max}$ iterations, it is considered that the algorithm has converged to a stable value. The final solution of GAPSOmin is then obtained by mapping the global best base parameters $\varphi$ back to the original $\pi \in \mathbb{R}^{48}$ space.

Compared to heuristic algorithms, LSmin typically exhibits faster convergence in implementation. Inspired by another hybrid algorithm [10], the least squares techniques can be combined with heuristic algorithms to further enhance identification performance. Based on the previous analysis, it could be observed that a single iteration of LSmin is similar to a complete calculation of GAPSOmin, as both involve base parameter mapping before and after computation to obtain new elasto-geometrical model. This reveals some equivalence in LSmin and GAPSOmin, thereby constituting a single iteration of the hybrid algorithm. The hybrid algorithm established by alternating LSmin and GAPSOmin first seeks optimal parameters within manually defined global constraints and then performs an LSmin calculation on the model updated from the GAPSOmin iteration. The updated model from LSmin can serve as the centroid for initializing the population of the next GAPSOmin iteration. Subsequentially, constraining GAPSOmin to search within a smaller range around the solution from the previous iteration accelerates the convergence of the hybrid algorithm. The initialization of the population of GAPSOmin after $m$ iterations follows the equation:

$$\boldsymbol{\varphi}_i^0 = a(m)(\boldsymbol{\varphi}_{lb} + (\boldsymbol{\varphi}_{ub} - \boldsymbol{\varphi}_{lb}))\boldsymbol{r} \tag{22}$$

where $\boldsymbol{\varphi}_{lb}$ and $\boldsymbol{\varphi}_{ub}$ are the lower and upper limits of base parameter, $\boldsymbol{r}$ is a uniformly generated random vector between 0 and 1, $a(m)$ is the constraint scaling factor and decreases continuously as the number of iterations increases. The relationship between the scaling factor $a(m)$ and the iteration number $m$ is defined as:

$$a(m) = \begin{cases} 3^{-\frac{m-1}{2}}, m < 6 \\ 3^{-3}, m \geq 6 \end{cases} \tag{23}$$

Here, the boundaries of full parameter set $\pi$ are represented in Table 2. Since the limits of $\pi$ could not be directly applied in GAPSOmin, similar mappings were used to obtain the boundaries of base parameters $\boldsymbol{\varphi}$.

Table 2. The full parameter set limits for GAPSOmin

| Parameter | $\Delta a_{i-1}$(mm) $\Delta d_i$(mm) | $\Delta \alpha_{i-1}$(rad) $\Delta \theta_i$(rad) | $\Delta \beta_i$(rad) | $\Delta \sigma_{trans}$(rad) | $\Delta \sigma_{rot}$(rad) |
|---|---|---|---|---|---|
| Limits | [−1, 1] | [−0.01, 0.01] | [−0.01, 0.01] | [−0.05, 0.05] | [−0.5, 0.5] |

Thus, the hybrid calibration method (GAPSO-LSmin) based on the least square and heuristic algorithm proposed in this paper is depicted in Fig. 2. The GAPSOmin and LSmin proceed at odd-iteration and even-iteration, respectively. Considering the balance between computational cost and accuracy, the max iteration number of GAPSOmin $k_{max}$ was set to 250 and the population size was 50. Due to the model stabilizing in the final few iterations, the max iteration number for GAPSO-LSmin is then set to 10.

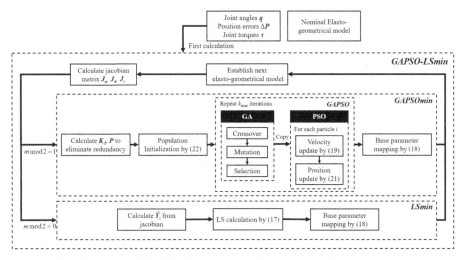

**Fig. 2.** Proposed GAPSO-LSmin method in elasto-geometrical calibration

# 4 Simulation

## 4.1 Simulation Setup

To validate the previously proposed elasto-geometrical model and calibration algorithm, this paper employs MATLAB and Simulink module to generate data and positioning error. In the simulation, by artificially setting joint stiffness models and contaminated kinematic model, along with the robot model containing only nominal kinematic parameters, it is possible to provide different poses and collect the positioning errors of the SMR for elasto-geometrical calibration. If only a single SMR mounted with offset is used for calibration, three types of data, joint angles, actual SMR positions, and joint torques, are needed to calibrate both the kinematic parameters and all joint stiffnesses under applied external forces.

In practice, the selection of the external wrench direction and magnitude affects the final calibration accuracy of the algorithm [14]. To simplify, it is assumed that the robot can directly measure its joint torques and ignore the influence of wrench selection. By randomly generating wrenches, the simulation ensures that the deformation caused by external forces on joints 1 and 6 can be reflected in the positioning changes of the SMR, thereby facilitating the subsequent validation.

Despite this, the selection of calibration configurations also affects the final accuracy. Since there are no nonlinear effects in the simulation, 100 poses are randomly generated and the first 50 were used for the calibration, while the remaining 50 are used for cross-validation. The spatial distribution of these poses is shown in Fig. 3.

Consequently, a contaminated kinematic model and joint compliances are set to generate error data, as shown in Table 3 and 4. Here, the transformation frame parameters are ignored and will be set as actual values in the following calibration. The offset of SMR is already set in the translation part of end-effector frame parameters to ensure stiffness identification. Additionally, the normal distributed error $N(0, 0.01)$ is added

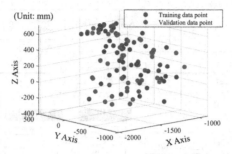

**Fig. 3.** Spatial distribution of generated end-effector points for calibration and validation

to the data to simulate the measurement errors. Combining the collected data with the nominal kinematic model, the proposed calibration method could be utilized to identify independent parameters, followed by validation of absolute positioning accuracy based on the obtained results.

**Table 3.** The preset contaminated MDH parameters

| Joint | $a_{i-1}$(mm) | $\alpha_{i-1}$(rad) | $d_i$(mm) | $\theta_i$(rad) | $\beta_i$(rad) |
|---|---|---|---|---|---|
| 1 | 0.500000 | 0.000200 | 380.500000 | 0.000300 | 0 |
| 2 | 30.200000 | −1.570300 | 0.380000 | −1.570300 | 0.000200 |
| 3 | 340.600000 | 0.000700 | 0.230000 | 0.000300 | 0 |
| 4 | 35.400000 | −1.570500 | 335.780000 | 0.000800 | 0 |
| 5 | 0.500000 | 1.571200 | 0.560000 | 0.000700 | 0 |
| 6 | 0.200000 | −1.570900 | 83.450000 | 3.142200 | 0 |

**Table 4.** The preset joint compliances ($10^{(-5)}$ rad/Nm)

| Joint | 1 | 2 | 3 | 4 | 5 | 6 |
|---|---|---|---|---|---|---|
| Compliance | 0.2000 | 1.0000 | 2.0000 | 3.0000 | 4.0000 | 5.0000 |

### 4.2 Result Analysis

Finally, in this subsection, validation is conducted based on the LM [10], the PSO [17], the GAPSO [16], the GAPSOmin, and the proposed GAPSO-LSmin method. Using nominal kinematic parameters, preset world and end-effector frame parameters, and zero joint compliances as initial values, the calibration results obtained using the proposed GAPSO-LSmin method are presented in Tables 5 and 6. Due to the existence of parallel between joints 2 and 3, the parameters $d_2$ and $d_3$ are redundant in the identification results, and all $\beta$ parameters except $\beta_2$ and $\beta_6$ are 0. Thus, these parameters are set to zero in the tables.

**Table 5.** The identified MDH parameters using GAPSO-LSmin calibration

| Joint | $a_{i-1}$ (mm) | $\alpha_{i-1}$ (rad) | $d_i$ (mm) | $\theta_i$ (rad) | $\beta_i$ (rad) |
|---|---|---|---|---|---|
| 1 | 0.556932 | 0.000201 | 380.531756 | 0.000406 | 0 |
| 2 | 30.190862 | -1.570412 | -11.230957 | -1.570213 | 0.000376 |
| 3 | 340.621760 | 0.000159 | 11.886729 | -0.000858 | 0 |
| 4 | 34.831968 | -1.570216 | 335.798368 | 0.000860 | 0 |
| 5 | 0.635924 | 1.573093 | 0.261545 | 0.002950 | 0 |
| 6 | 0.367765 | -1.570314 | 83.449739 | 3.141716 | -0.000165 |

**Table 6.** The identified joint compliances using GAPSO-LSmin ($10^{(-5)}$ rad/Nm)

| Joint | 1 | 2 | 3 | 4 | 5 | 6 |
|---|---|---|---|---|---|---|
| Compliance | 1.5850 | 0.8279 | 1.8222 | 10.3820 | 10.4281 | -2.3009 |

By modifying the nominal elasto-geometrical model using identified values, the spatial distance before and after calibration at each measurement point can be calculated as the positioning error. Four metrics, mean, variance, maximum value and minimum value are used for evaluating all selected calibration methods, the results are shown in Table 7. Using the previously cross-validation data points, the proposed method outperformed others and its average error decreased from 2.8658 mm to 0.1682 mm after calibration, compared to the 0.1333 mm of actual model after adding noise. This indicates that the hybrid algorithm could enhance the absolute positioning accuracy of the robot. Figure 4 illustrates the improvement in positioning accuracy before and after calibration for selected data points.

As shown in Table 6, the compliance of all robot joints can be identified using only positioning information of the derived elasto-geometrical model compared to the kinematic calibration or elasto-geometrical calibration considering only joints 2 to 5 [16]. Furthermore, an analysis of the iterative processes of the aforementioned identification methods was conducted. For comparison, the PSO, GAPSO, and GAPSOmin are all iterated with for 250 iterations with 50 individuals, as shown in Fig. 5.

It can be observed that due to the incorporation of GA in GAPSO, its local convergence performance is poorer, resulting in a higher positioning error of 0.6056 mm compared to the 0.4966 mm of PSO on the training data. In contrast, GAPSOmin shows a significant improvement in accuracy by leveraging the first-order Jacobian. Its final positioning error on the training data is only 0.4173 mm, validating that mapping the GAPSO to the base parameters space can enhance the identification accuracy and convergence speed of heuristic algorithms.

**Table 7.** The positioning accuracy cross-validation results of different methods

|  | Mean(mm) | Std(mm) | Min(mm) | Max(mm) |
|---|---|---|---|---|
| Before calibration | 2.8658 | 0.3097 | 1.9233 | 3.4698 |
| LM | 0.1695 | 0.0905 | 0.0302 | 0.4034 |
| PSO | 0.6811 | 0.4979 | 0.0677 | 2.4335 |
| GAPSO | 0.7350 | 0.4085 | 0.0915 | 2.0903 |
| GAPSOmin | 0.4206 | 0.2454 | 0.0890 | 1.1983 |
| **GAPSO-LSmin** | 0.1682 | 0.0902 | 0.0309 | 0.3972 |
| Preset model | 0.1333 | 0.0946 | 0.0019 | 0.4121 |

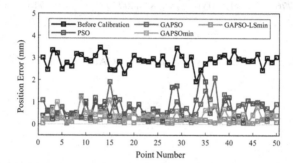

**Fig. 4.** Positioning error of cross-validation data after compensation (50 points)

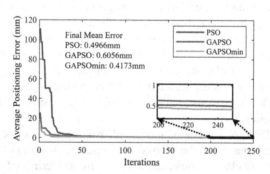

**Fig. 5.** The identification iterative process of PSO, GAPSO, GAPSOmin

The GAPSO-LSmin combines the advantages of both least squares and GAPSOmin. Its training accuracy stabilizes at 0.1137 mm after 10 iterations, as depicted in Fig. 6. As the number of iterations of the hybrid algorithm increases, GAPSOmin gradually converges near the optimal value. It is noteworthy that the final converged solution of the hybrid algorithm exhibits overfitting on the training data, leading to some parameters violating physical constraints as shown in Table 6. Nevertheless, the simulation results indicate that the GAPSO-LSmin method could solve the calibration problem and obtain a better global solution compared to other selected methods.

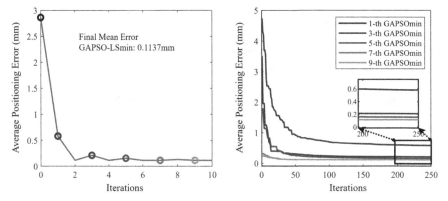

**Fig. 6.** The identification iterations of GAPSO-LSmin

In the Table 7, it is noteworthy that cross-validation result of the LM method resembles the GAPSO-LSmin. Here, the LM method employs a damping coefficient to tackle the rank deficiency in the regressor without analyze and eliminate the model redundancy. Due to the fast convergence of the LM, it is performed 20 times empirically and stabilizes at 0.1134 mm using training data, which is better compared to the GAPSO-LSmin. Nevertheless, the cross accuracy of the LM is 0.1695 mm and slightly below the proposed approach since its global search performance is worse. The phenomenon of the result proximity indicates that the GAPSO-LSmin tends to converge to a solution which is adjacent to the LM does. This is because the nonlinearity of joint compliance and other factors are not considered in the simulation, resulting in the similar performance of the GAPSO-LSmin and the LM under such circumstance. Therefore, further experiment is indispensable to validate the performance of different algorithms.

## 5   Conclusion

In this paper, an elasto-geometrical model using only position measurement was established and calibrated using the proposed hybrid identification method. The GAPSO-LSmin method eliminated redundancy in the model and identified the elasto-geometrical model through alternating between least squares and heuristic algorithm computations. Simulation results indicated that under appropriate external forces applied to joints 1 and 6, the resulting deformation in position is sufficient for their stiffness identification. This provided a feasible approach for identifying all joint stiffness and kinematic parameters experimentally by installing the single SMR in an offset position. After handling redundant parameters, the GAPSO-LSmin method obtained the global optimum with a rapid convergence speed. Its identification accuracy is significantly improved compared to other algorithms, demonstrating the effectiveness of the hybrid algorithm in the calibration of elasto-geometrical model.

For future work, the model and algorithm proposed in this paper can be further validated through experimentation. The selection of calibration configurations and the external wrenches to optimize the calibration can be further considered. Moreover, the proposed linearized model ignored the link elasticity and orientation error which may lead to the reduced calibration accuracy. The nonlinearity of joint compliance caused by the external forces at different configurations is also neglected. Therefore, it is possible to further develop the elasto-geometrical model and investigate the effect of joint nonlinearity to improve the calibration accuracy.

**Acknowledgement.** This work was supported in part by the National Key Research and Development Program of China under Grant 2022YFB4700300 and the NSFC-Shenzhen Robot Basic Research Center project under Grant U2013204.

# References

1. Denavit, J., Hartenberg, R.S.: A kinematic notation for lower-pair mechanisms based on matrices. Trans. ASME J. Appl. Mech. **22**, 215–221 (1955)
2. Hayati, S.A.: Robot arm geometric link parameter estimation. In: IEEE Conference on Decision and Control, San Antonio, TX, USA, pp. 1477–1483 (1983)
3. Chen, X., Zhang, Q., Zhang, Y.: Non-kinematic calibration of industrial robots using a rigid–elasto coupling error model and a full pose measurement method. Robot. Comput. Integr. Manuf. **57**, 46–58 (2019)
4. Dumas, C., Caro, S., Garnier, S., Furet, B.: Joint stiffness identification of six revolute industrial serial robots. Rob. Comput.-Integr. Manuf. **27**(4), 881–888 (2011)
5. Kamali, K., Joubair, A., Bonev, I.A., Bigras, P.: Elasto-geometrical calibration of an industrial robot under multidirectional external loads using a laser tracker. In: IEEE International Conference on Robotics and Automation (ICRA), Stockholm, Sweden, pp. 4320–4327 (2016)
6. Guérin, D., Caro, S., Garnier, S., Girin, A.: Optimal measurement pose selection for joint stiffness identification of an industrial robot mounted on a rail. In: IEEE/ASME International Conference on Advanced Intelligent Mechatronics, Besacon, France, pp. 1722–1727 (2014)
7. Zhao, H., Yu, L., Jia, H., Li, W., Sun, J.: A new kinematic model of portable articulated coordinate measuring machine. Appl. Sci.-Basel **6**(7), 181 (2016)
8. Chen, X., Zhan, Q.: The kinematic calibration of an industrial robot with an improved beetle swarm optimization algorithm. IEEE Rob. Autom. Lett. **7**(2), 4694–4701 (2022)
9. Messay, T., Ordonez, R., Marcil, E.: Computationally efficient and robust kinematic calibration methodologies and their application to industrial robots. Robot. Comput. Integr. Manuf. **37**, 33–48 (2016)
10. Luo, G., Zou, L., Wang, Z., Lv, C., Ou, J., Huang, Y.: A novel kinematic parameters calibration method for industrial robot based on Levenberg-Marquardt and Differential Evolution hybrid algorithm. Rob. Comput.-Integr. Manufact. **71**, 102165 (2021)
11. Meggiolaro, M.A., Dubowsky, S.: An analytical method to eliminate the redundant parameters in robot calibration. In: IEEE International Conference on Robotics and Automation (ICRA), San Francisco, CA, USA, pp. 3609–3615 (2000)
12. Miao, L., Zhang, L., Song, Z., Guo, Y., Zhu, W., Ke, Y.: A two-step method for kinematic parameters calibration based on complete pose measurement—verification on a heavy-duty robot. Rob. Comput.-Integr. Manuf. **83**, 102550 (2023)
13. Sousa, C.D., Cortesão, R.: Physical feasibility of robot base inertial parameter identification: a linear matrix inequality approach. Int. J. Rob. Res. **33**(6), 931–944 (2014)

14. Kamali, K., Bonev, I.A.: Optimal experiment design for elasto-geometrical calibration of industrial robots. IEEE/ASME Trans. Mechatron. **24**(6), 2733–2744 (2019)
15. Lynch, K.M., Park, F.C.: Modern Robotics: Mechanics, Planning, and Control, 1st edn. Cambridge University Press, USA (2017)
16. Deng, K., Gao, D., Ma, S., Zhao, C., Lu, Y.: Elasto-geometrical error and gravity model calibration of an industrial robot using the same optimized configuration set. Rob. Comput.-Integr. Manuf. **83**, 102558 (2023)
17. Alıcı, G., Jagielski, R., Sekercioglu, Y.A., et al.: Prediction of geometric errors of robot manipulators with Particle Swarm Optimisation method. Rob. Auton. Syst. **54**(12), 956–966 (2006)

# Industrial Robot Joint Electromechanical Coupling Modeling and SPMSM Electrical Parameters Identification

Pengxin Zha, Yan Lu, Hongbo Hu, Zhikai Shen, and Chungang Zhuang$^{(\boxtimes)}$

Robotics Institute, School of Mechanical Engineering, Shanghai Jiao Tong University, Shanghai 200240, China
cgzhuang@sjtu.edu.cn

**Abstract.** This article proposes an approach for modeling the electromechanical coupling in industrial robot joints and an approach for identifying the electrical parameters of surface-mounted permanent magnet synchronous motors (SPMSMs) used in robot joints. First, a more accurate joint modeling method is presented that considers both PMSM friction and gear reducer friction, with the PMSM rotor friction modeled using an improved Coulomb-viscous model and the gear reducer friction represented using a simple method that ensures better accuracy for parameter identification. Second, a method is proposed for separately identifying the SPMSM inductance in the $d-q$ frame and the resistance and flux linkage in the $\alpha-\beta$ frame using a Recursive Least Squares (RLS) algorithm, addressing the rank deficiency issues that arise when using the q-axis voltage equation alone to identify multiple parameters. The proposed approaches enable more precise modeling of industrial robot electromechanical coupling and more accurate identification of SPMSM electrical parameters, which establish the foundation for further research on the electromechanical coupling phenomenon of industrial robot joints.

**Keywords:** Industrial Robot Joint · Parameter Estimation · Permanent Magnet Synchronous Motors (PMSMs)

## 1 Introduction

With the rise of advanced technology, robots have become increasingly widespread and versatile. From robotic arms to medical and industrial robots, their applications are expanding rapidly [1–3]. The joint servo transmission system is the core part of the robot, and its working performance directly affects the safety and service life of the robot [4]. Robot joints are mainly composed of servo motors, reducers, couplings, loads, and their control systems, which is a typical electromechanical coupling system [5]. Permanent magnet synchronous motors (PMSMs) are the most widely used motors in robotics. because of their high efficiency, power factor and power density. In non-steady operating conditions, the joint system of industrial robots exhibits electromechanical coupling

© The Author(s), under exclusive license to Springer Nature Singapore Pte Ltd. 2025
X. Lan et al. (Eds.): ICIRA 2024, LNAI 15208, pp. 316–331, 2025.
https://doi.org/10.1007/978-981-96-0783-9_22

due to the interaction between the mechanical parameters of the transmission system and the electrical parameters of the motor. This electromechanical coupling can significantly impact the operational safety and dynamic performance of industrial robots. To explore this impact, it is imperative to undertake a comprehensive study of the motion state of industrial robots under the influence of electromechanical coupling.

Firstly, Modeling studies should be conducted on the joint systems of industrial robots to uncover the mechanisms by which electromechanical coupling affects these systems. Previous studies have often not explored joint modeling in-depth, typically using the Coulomb-viscous friction model or the Stribeck friction model to represent the overall friction in the joints [6,7]. For industrial robots, the joint modules often incorporate harmonic drives or RV reducers. These components ensure high transmission precision and allow for a smaller size and higher transmission ratios. However, they also introduce more complex sources of friction and issues of joint flexibility. The methods used in previous studies do not accurately reflect the internal friction in joints equipped with harmonic drives or RV reducers. It is necessary to refine the modeling of robot joints to consider the contributions of components like reducers to the dynamics model. Therefore, for serial robots, represented by industrial robots, it is essential to refine their joint models to improve the precision of the robot overall model.

Secondly, as the most widely used motors in robotics, PMSMs require accurate knowledge of motor parameters to explore the impact of electromechanical coupling on industrial robot joints and perform high-performance control design for PMSMs [8], such as direct d-axis inductance, quadrature q-axis inductance, magnet flux linkage, stator resistance. Parameter estimation techniques can be categorized into offline and online methods. The offline estimation methods rely on the offline measurements of motor parameters [9,10]. In contrast, online methods are capable of determining all parameters in real time, with many studies concentrating on real-time parameter identification. In [11], the identification of resistance and inductance was conducted by maintaining the flux at a nominal level. In [12], resistance and flux were identified for the first time using a d-axis current injection technique.

Most electrical parameters online identification methods of PMSM are conducted in the $d-q$ frame. On one hand, for the simplified d-axis voltage equation due to id=0, the rank of the observation matrix is 1 in the steady state, which is equal to the number of parameter (stator resistance) to be identified. Therefore, theoretically, the stator inductance can be accurately identified. On the other hand, for the simplified q-axis voltage equation due to id=0, the rank of the observation matrix is also 1 in the steady state, which is less than the number of parameters (flux linkage and stator resistance) to be identified, which means that these two parameters cannot be accurately identified theoretically. Approaches are presented to overcome the problem of rank deficiency in the $d-q$ frame, in [13,14], the researchers proposed that injecting a signal into the d-axis current could address the issue of rank deficiency when identifying multiple parameters, but this approach resulted in noticeable disturbances in the torque. Additionally, other strategies detailed in [15,16] employed sinusoidal injections into the d-axis current, based on dynamic equations, which caused fluctuations in torque during the identification phase. In addition to injecting signals, other methods have also been proposed to solve the problem of rank deficiency. In [17], the author addressed the rank deficiency issue by creating two steady states in the $d - q$ frame of PMSMs. However, the analysis of the adaptability and robustness of the identification algorithm under various operating conditions needs further exploration. In [17], In contrast to the electrical parameter identification of PMSMs in the $d - q$ frame, a new method has been proposed to identify the full parameter of PMSMs using a Recursive Least Squares (RLS) algorithm in the $\alpha$-$\beta$ frame [18], but it needs to have higher identification accuracy when the motor is rated speed and rated torque.

Considering the various challenges discussed above related to electromechanical coupling modeling of industrial robot joints and the identification of electrical parameters in PMSMs, a more precise modeling approach for robot joints and advanced techniques for parameter identification in PMSMs using both $d - q$ and $\alpha$-$\beta$ frame have been proposed.

(1) A more accurate joint modeling method that considers both PMSM friction and gear reducer friction has been proposed. The friction of the PMSM rotor is modeled using an improved Coulomb-viscous model to prevent abrupt changes during joint rotation. The friction of the gear reducer is represented with an improved approach that not only accurately describes the reducer's friction but also ensures a smaller condition number for the observation matrix when identifying the dynamic parameters of the joint using the least squares method, resulting in better accuracy for parameter identification.

(2) A method has been proposed for identifying the electrical parameters of surface-mounted permanent magnet synchronous motors (SPMSM) separately in the $d - q$ and $\alpha$-$\beta$ coordinate systems. Considering that the simplified d-axis voltage equation is of full rank, RLS is used to identify the inductance. To solve the problem of poor identification results arising from the rank deficiency of the observation matrix when using the q-axis voltage equation to identify the resistance and flux linkage of sPMSM, the remaining two parameters are identified using RLS in the $\alpha$-$\beta$ stationary frame.

## 2    Electromechanical Coupling Modeling of Industrial Robot Joint

### 2.1    PMSM Dynamic Modeling

The servo transmission system in industrial robot joints uses permanent magnet synchronous servo motors, which significantly improve performance and offer enhanced stability and reduced vibrations compared to traditional electrically excited motors. For PMSM, its dynamic equations can be described as follows:

$$\tau_e = J_m \ddot{q}_m + \tau_{mf} + \tau_{r1} \tag{1}$$

where $\tau_e$ is the electromagnetic torque of PMSM, $J_m$ is the moment of inertia of the rotor, $q_m$ is the angle of rotor, $\tau_{mf}$ is the equivalent friction of PMSM, and $\tau_{r1}$ is the output torque of PMSM.

For the electromagnetic torque of PMSM, it can be obtained as follows:

$$\tau_e = \frac{3}{2}n_p(\psi_f i_q + (L_d - L_q)i_d i_q) \tag{2}$$

where $n_p$ is the number of pole pairs in the motor, $\psi_f$ is the flux linkage, $L_d$ and $L_q$ are the d-axis stator inductance, and q-axis stator inductance, and $i_d$ and $i_q$ are the currents in the $d - q$ frame. For surface-mounted permanent magnet synchronous motor (SPMSM), where $L_d = L_q$. Therefore (2) can be simplified as follows:

$$\tau_e = \frac{3}{2}n_p \psi_f i_q = K i_q \tag{3}$$

where $K$ is the motor electromagnetic torque constant.

In general, the friction $\tau_{mf}$ can be described as:

$$\tau_{mf} = f_{mc}\text{sign}(\dot{q}_m) + f_{mv}\dot{q}_m + f_b \tag{4}$$

where $f_{mc}$ is the Coulomb friction coefficient of the motor, $f_{mv}$ is the viscous friction coefficient of the motor, $f_b$ is the offset generated by the motor current offset, and sign($\cdot$) is a sign function.

In practice, to avoid a step in Coulomb friction when the speed is zero, an improved Coulomb friction model is used, so (4) is usually equivalent to the following form:

$$\tau_{mf} = f_{mc}\left(\frac{2}{1 + e^{-100\dot{q}_m}} - 1\right) + f_{mv}\dot{q}_m + f_b \tag{5}$$

## 2.2  Robot Joint Dynamic Modeling

Industrial robot joints mainly consist of PMSM, reducer, and position encoder. To identify the complete joint dynamics parameters, a torque sensor needs to be installed at the end of the joint. The simplified diagram of an industrial robot joint considering flexibility is shown in Fig. 1. The meanings of the symbols appearing in Fig. 1 are shown in Table 1.

Combined with the PMSM dynamic equation proposed above, the dynamic equation of the joint can be described as follows:

$$\tau_e = J_m \ddot{q}_m + \tau_{mf} + \tau_{r1} \tag{6}$$

$$\tau_{r2} = \eta\tau_{r1} - \tau_{rf} \tag{7}$$

$$\Delta q = \frac{q_m}{\eta} - q_l = K\tau_{r2} \tag{8}$$

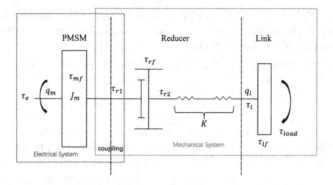

**Fig. 1.** Simplified diagram of robot joint

**Table 1.** Meaning of the symbols in Fig. 1.

| Symbols | Meanings |
| --- | --- |
| $\tau_e$ | PMSM electromagnetic torque |
| $\tau_{mf}$ | PMSM friction torque |
| $J_m$ | Moment of inertia of PMSM rotor |
| $q_m$ | Angle of PMSM rotor |
| $\tau_{r1}$ | Output torque of PMSM |
| $\tau_{rf}$ | Friction torque of reducer |
| $\tau_{r2}$ | Output torque of reducer |
| $K$ | Flexibility of reducer |
| $q_l$ | Angle of link |
| $\tau_l$ | Input torque of link |
| $\tau_{lf}$ | Friction torque of link |
| $\tau_{load}$ | Load torque of link |

Generally, the friction torque of the reducer is described by the Coulomb-viscous friction model. In this case, when using the least-squares method to identify the joint dynamics parameters, the observation matrix simultaneously contains the Coulomb friction and viscous friction terms of both the motor and the reducer, which makes the observation matrix nearly rank-deficient, leading to inaccurate identification of the joint dynamics parameters. Therefore, to solve this problem, the friction torque of the reducer is assumed to be proportional to the input torque of the reducer and can be described as:

$$\tau_{rf} = \zeta \eta \tau_{r1} \tag{9}$$

where $\zeta$ is the friction torque coefficient of the reducer. Since the input torque of the reducer cannot be directly measured, and considering that the PMSM rotor inertia $J_m$ and the PMSM friction torque $\tau_{mf}$ are relatively small, the

PMSM electromagnetic torque $\tau_e$ can be used to estimate the friction torque of the reducer, which can be described as:

$$\tau_{rf} = \zeta\eta\tau_{r1} \approx \zeta\eta\tau_e \tag{10}$$

Refer to (6), (7), and (10), the torque difference $\Delta\tau$ obtained by subtracting the PMSM electromagnetic torque $\tau_e$ collected by the motor driver and the reducer output torque $\tau_{r2}$ collected by the joint end torque sensor can be described as:

$$\Delta\tau = \eta\tau_e - \tau_{r2} = \eta J_m\ddot{q}_m + \eta\tau_{mf} + \tau_{rf} \tag{11}$$

where $\Delta\tau$ is the difference in torque at both ends of the joint, which is considered to be the overall torque loss of the robot joint.

Refer to (5) and (10), $\Delta\tau$ can be calculated as:

$$\Delta\tau = \eta\left(J_m\ddot{q}_m + f_{mc}\left(\frac{2}{1+e^{-100\dot{q}_m}} - 1\right) + f_{mv}\dot{q}_m + f_b + \zeta\tau_e\right) \tag{12}$$

Then, the regression model can be obtained by linearizing (10):

$$\Delta\tau = \eta\tau_e - \tau_{r2} = \left[\ddot{q}_m \left(\frac{2}{1+e^{-100\dot{q}_m}} - 1\right) \dot{q}_m 1 \tau_e\right]\begin{bmatrix} \eta J_m \\ \eta f_{mc} \\ \eta f_{mv} \\ \eta f_b \\ \eta\zeta \end{bmatrix} \tag{13}$$

$$\boldsymbol{\Delta\tau} = \boldsymbol{\Phi_t}\left(\mathbf{q_m},\dot{\mathbf{q}}_\mathbf{m},\ddot{\mathbf{q}}_\mathbf{m}\right)\theta_t \tag{14}$$

where $\boldsymbol{\Phi_t}\left(\mathbf{q_m},\dot{\mathbf{q}}_\mathbf{m},\ddot{\mathbf{q}}_\mathbf{m}\right) \in \Re^{n\times 5}$ is the observation matrix, $\theta_t \in \Re^{5\times n}$ is the dynamic parameter set of the joint, $n$ is the number of sampling points.

For the flexibility of robot joint $K$, it can be obtained from (8):

$$\boldsymbol{\Delta q} = \tau_{\mathbf{r2}}\mathbf{K} \tag{15}$$

where $\tau_{\mathbf{r2}} \in \Re^{n\times 1}$ is the observation matrix, $\mathbf{K} \in \Re^{1\times 1}$ is the flexibility of the robot joint.

Therefore, after collecting and filtering the actual data $\tau_e$, $\tau_{r2}$, $\mathbf{q_m}$, $\dot{\mathbf{q}}_\mathbf{m}$, $q_l$ of the robot joint, the least squares method is used to identify the dynamic parameters and flexibility of the robot joint based on (14) and (15).

# 3   SPMSM Electrical Parameters Identification

## 3.1   RLS Algorithm

Referred to [18], the RLS (Recursive Least Squares) algorithm is an effective and widely used method for online parameter estimation. The core idea of the RLS algorithm is to update the parameter estimates in a recursive manner, which makes it suitable for real-time systems [19,20]. Assuming a system with N input variables, the relationship between the system output $y(i)$ and the input $\varphi(i)$ can be expressed as a linear model:

$$y(i) = \theta_1(i)\,\varphi_1(i) + \theta_2(i)\,\varphi_2(i) + \cdots + \theta_N(i)\,\varphi_N(i)$$
$$= \Theta(i)^T \Phi(i) \tag{16}$$

where $i$ represents the $i$th iteration, $y$ is the output of the system, and $\varphi_j$ denotes the $j$th input, which cannot be zero or close to zero, as this would prevent the accurate identification of the corresponding weight coefficients $\theta_j$. Generally, the weight coefficients $\theta_j$ are unknown and need to be identified. To facilitate this identification, an instrumental variable $x(i)$ is introduced, which is also a linear combination of the input variables, similar to the system output $y$:

$$x(i) = \hat{\theta}_1(i)\,\varphi_1(i) + \hat{\theta}_2(i)\,\varphi_2(i) + \cdots + \hat{\theta}_N(i)\,\varphi_N(i)$$
$$= \hat{\Theta}(i)^T \Phi(i) \tag{17}$$

where $\hat{\theta}_j$ represents the identified coefficient for the $j$th input. The difference between the actual system output $y(i)$ and the instrumental variable $x(i)$ is defined as the residual error term $e(i) = y(i) - x(i)$. However, the residual error can be positive or negative which is not suitable to be used as an evaluation criterion directly, so a cost function is introduced as:

$$J(i) = \frac{1}{2}[y(i) - x(i)]^2 \tag{18}$$

The RLS is to minimize the cost function $J(i)$, and estimated weight coefficients can be updated through the principle of gradient descent:

$$\hat{\theta}(i) = \hat{\theta}(i-1) + \mathbf{K}(i)\left[y(i) - \hat{\theta}(i-1)^T \varphi(i)\right]$$
$$\mathbf{K}(i) = \frac{\mathbf{P}(i-1)\,\varphi(i)}{\lambda + \varphi(i)^T \mathbf{P}(i-1)\,\varphi(i)} \tag{19}$$
$$\mathbf{P}(i) = \frac{1}{\lambda}\left[\mathbf{I} - \mathbf{K}(i)\,\varphi(i)^T\right]\mathbf{P}(i-1)$$

where $\lambda$ is the forgetting factor, which enables the algorithm to adaptively emphasize recent data, thereby improving its ability to track time-varying parameters, $\lambda$ is always set between 0.9 and 1.

The RLS algorithm cannot be applied to estimate weight coefficients for all forms of the system. In the $d - q$ frame, the value of voltage and current are constant, but in the $\alpha - \beta$ frame, the voltage and current are sinusoidal. For a single input single output system:

$$y = ux \tag{20}$$

where $x$ is the single input of the system, $y$ is the single output of the system and $u$ is the weight coefficient. When both $x$ and $y$ are constant values, the weight coefficient $u$ can be identified with only one real value. For a system with two inputs and one output, which can be expressed as:

$$y = ux_1 + vx_2 \tag{21}$$

where $x_1$ and $x_2$ are two inputs of the system, $y$ is the output of the system and $u$ and $v$ are the weight coefficients. When $x_1$ and $x_2$ and $y$ are still constant values, the weight coefficients cannot be identified certainly, which could exist countless solutions of $u$ and $v$ such as $(u_1, v_1)$, $(u_2, v_2)$, $(u_3, v_3)$, and so on. However, the situation is totally different if there is a fixed phase difference (not $0°$ and $180°$) between $x_1$ and $x_2$, $u$ and $v$ can be identified with only one value according to the mathematical triangle theorem [20]. When there are three inputs with a fixed phase difference, which can be described as:

$$y = ux_1 + vx_2 + wx_3 \tag{22}$$

where $x_3$ is the third input and $w$ is the corresponding coefficient. Likewise, there could also exist countless solutions of $u$, $v$ and $w$ such as $(u_1, v_1, w_1)$, $(u_2, v_2, w_2)$, $(u_3, v_3, w_3)$, and so on.

Therefore, it can be concluded that when there is one input and one output of voltage function in the $d - q$ frame or two inputs and one output of voltage function in $\alpha - \beta$ frame, the weight coefficient can be estimated.

## 3.2 Identification of the SPMSM Inductance $L_s$ in the $d - q$ Frame

The electrical dynamics of SPMSM in the synchronously rotating $d - q$ reference frame can be derived as the following differential equations:

$$\begin{aligned} u_d &= R_s i_d - \omega_e L_q i_q + L_d \frac{di_d}{dt} \\ u_q &= R_s i_q + \omega_e L_d i_d + \omega_e \psi_f + L_q \frac{di_q}{dt} \end{aligned} \tag{23}$$

where $u_d$ and $u_q$ are the voltages in the $d - q$ frame, $i_d$ and $i_q$ are the currents in the $d - q$ frame, $R_s$, $L_d$, and $L_q$ represent the stator resistance, d-axis stator inductance, and q-axis stator inductance, respectively, $\omega_e$ is the electrical angular velocity, and $\varphi_f$ is the flux linkage. For surface-mounted permanent magnet synchronous motors (SPMSM):

$$L_d = L_q = L_s \tag{24}$$

The vector control of SPMSM often adopts the $id = 0$ control strategy [21, 22] and in steady state (20) can be simplified to:

$$\begin{aligned} u_d &= -\omega_e L_s i_q \\ u_q &= R_s i_q + \omega_e \psi_f \end{aligned} \tag{25}$$

For the voltage function in the $d$ axis, there is one input $-\omega_e i_q$ and one output $u_d$, so the weight coefficient $L_s$ can be estimated accurately. However, for the voltage function in the $q$ axis with two constant inputs and one constant output, the weight coefficients $R_s$ and $\varphi_f$ can not be estimated according to (21). So, the inductance $L_s$ of SPMSM can be estimated using the RLS algorithm and the pseudocode is presented in Algorithm 2.

---

**Algorithm 1: SPMSM $L_s$ identification in $d-q$ frame**

---

**Input**: Filtered data: $u_d, i_q, \omega_e$

**Output**: SPMSM estimated inductance: $\hat{L}_s$

1  Initializing: $\lambda = \lambda_{init}, P = P_{init}, \hat{L}_s = L_{init}$

2  while $\hat{L}_s \mapsto$ do

3    | calculate gain matrix $K \leftarrow$ Eq. (19)

4    | calculate estimated inductance $\hat{L}_s \leftarrow$ Eq. (19)

5    | calculate covariance matrix $P \leftarrow$ Eq. (19)

6  end

7  Return $\hat{L}_s$

---

Fig. 2. The pseudocode of alogrithm 1

## 3.3   Identification of the Resistance $R_s$ and Flux $\varphi_f$ in the $\alpha - \beta$ Frame

According to [18], the voltage functions in the $\alpha - \beta$ frame can be described as:

$$u_\alpha - \left[\hat{L}_d\ \hat{\psi}_f\right] X_{\alpha 2} = \left[\hat{R}_s\ \hat{L}_d\right] X_{\alpha 1}$$
$$u_\beta - \left[\hat{R}_s\ \hat{L}_d\right] X_{\beta 2} = \left[\hat{L}_d\ \hat{\psi}_f\right] X_{\beta 1} \tag{26}$$

where

$$X_{\alpha 1} = \begin{bmatrix} i_\alpha \\ \frac{1}{2}\frac{di_\alpha}{dt} + \left(\frac{1}{2}\frac{di_\beta}{dt} - \omega_e i_\alpha\right)\sin 2\theta_e + \left(\frac{1}{2}\frac{di_\alpha}{dt} + \omega_e i_\beta\right)\cos 2\theta_e \end{bmatrix}$$

$$X_{\alpha 2} = \begin{bmatrix} \frac{1}{2}\frac{di_\alpha}{dt} - \left(\frac{1}{2}\frac{di_\beta}{dt} - \omega_e i_\alpha\right)\sin 2\theta_e - \left(\frac{1}{2}\frac{di_\alpha}{dt} + \omega_e i_\beta\right)\cos 2\theta_e \\ -\omega_e \sin\theta_e \end{bmatrix}$$

$$X_{\beta 1} = \begin{bmatrix} \frac{1}{2}\frac{di_\beta}{dt} + \left(\frac{1}{2}\frac{di_\beta}{dt} - \omega_e i_\alpha\right)\cos 2\theta_e - \left(\frac{1}{2}\frac{di_\alpha}{dt} + \omega_e i_\beta\right)\sin 2\theta_e \\ \omega_e \cos\theta_e \end{bmatrix} \tag{27}$$

$$X_{\beta 2} = \begin{bmatrix} i_\beta \\ \frac{1}{2}\frac{di_\beta}{dt} - \left(\frac{1}{2}\frac{di_\beta}{dt} - \omega_e i_\alpha\right)\cos 2\theta_e + \left(\frac{1}{2}\frac{di_\alpha}{dt} + \omega_e i_\beta\right)\sin 2\theta_e \end{bmatrix}$$

It should be noted that the current and voltage of PMSM in $\alpha - \beta$ frame cannot be obtained directly from PMSM generally. In this paper, the currents in $\alpha - \beta$ frame are calculated from three-phase current through Clark transformation:

$$\begin{bmatrix} i_\alpha \\ i_\beta \end{bmatrix} = \frac{2}{3} \begin{bmatrix} 1 & -0.5 & -0.5 \\ 0 & \frac{\sqrt{3}}{2} & -\frac{\sqrt{3}}{2} \end{bmatrix} \begin{bmatrix} i_A \\ i_B \\ i_C \end{bmatrix} \tag{28}$$

But in order to obtain the voltage in $\alpha - \beta$ frame, first, the relationship between the current in $\alpha - \beta$ frame that we obtained through (28) and the current in $d - q$ frame is used to obtain the sine and cosine value of the electrical angle $\theta_e$:

$$\cos \theta_e = \frac{i_\alpha i_d + i_\beta i_q}{i_d^2 + i_q^2}$$
$$\sin \theta_e = \frac{i_\beta i_d - i_\alpha i_q}{i_d^2 + i_q^2} \tag{29}$$

Then, the voltage in the $\alpha - \beta$ frame can be calculated from voltages in the $d - q$ frame through Park transformation:

$$\begin{bmatrix} u_\alpha \\ u_\beta \end{bmatrix} = \begin{bmatrix} \cos \theta_e & -\sin \theta_e \\ \sin \theta_e & \cos \theta_e \end{bmatrix} \begin{bmatrix} u_d \\ u_q \end{bmatrix}. \tag{30}$$

According to (26) and (27), the resistance $\hat{R}_s$ and flux $\hat{\psi}_f$ identification process can be divided into two steps: Firstly, the voltage function in $\alpha$ frame is

---

**Algorithm 2: SPMSM $R_s, \psi_f$ identification in $\alpha - \beta$ frame**

**Input**: Filtered data: $i_A, i_B, i_C, i_d, i_q, u_d, u_q, \omega_e$

**Output**: SPMSM estimated resistance and flux linkage: $\hat{R}_s, \hat{\psi}_f$

1  Initializing: $\lambda_1 = \lambda_{1init}, \lambda_2 = \lambda_{2init}, P_1 = P_{1init}, P_2 = P_{2init}$
    $\hat{R}_s = R_{init}, \hat{\psi}_f = \psi_{init}$
2  calculate $\cos \theta_e, \sin \theta_e \leftarrow$ Eq.(29)
3  calculate $i_\alpha, i_\beta, u_\alpha, u_\beta \leftarrow$ Eq.(28),(30)
4  while $\left( \hat{R}_s \ \&\& \ \hat{\psi}_f \right) \mapsto$ do
5   calculate current differential $di_\alpha / dt, di_\beta / dt$
6   calculate matrix $X_{\alpha 1}, X_{\alpha 2}, X_{\beta 1}, X_{\beta 2} \leftarrow$ Eq.(27)
7   update $\hat{W}_{\alpha 2}, \hat{W}_{\beta 1}$ with estimated $\hat{L}_q, \hat{\psi}_f \leftarrow$ Eq.(26)
8   calculate gain matrix $K_\alpha \leftarrow$ Eq.(19)
9   calculate estimated $\hat{R}_s, \hat{L}_d \leftarrow$ Eq.(19)
10  calculate covariance matrix $P_\alpha \leftarrow$ Eq.(19)
11  update $\hat{W}_{\alpha 1}, \hat{W}_{\beta 2}$ with estimated $\hat{R}_s, \hat{L}_d \leftarrow$ Eq.(26)
12  calculate gain matrix $K_\beta \leftarrow$ Eq.(19)
13  calculate estimated $\hat{L}_q, \hat{\psi}_f \leftarrow$ Eq.(19)
14  calculate covariance matrix $P_\beta \leftarrow$ Eq.(19)
16 end
17 Return $\hat{R}_s, \hat{\psi}_f$

---

**Fig. 3.** The pseudocode of alogrithm 2

used to identify $\hat{R}_s$, while the voltage function in $\beta$ frame is used for identify $\hat{\psi}_f$. For the voltage equation in the $\alpha$ frame, the estimated value of $\hat{W}_{\alpha 2}$ is required to calculate the RLS algorithm input $u_\alpha - \hat{W}_{\alpha 2}X_{\alpha 2}$, and the value of $\hat{W}_{\alpha 2}$ comes from the estimated result of the voltage equation in $\beta$ frame. Secondly, for the voltage equation in $\beta$ frame, the value of $\hat{W}_{\beta 2}$ is needed to calculate the RLS algorithm input, and this value comes from the estimated result of the voltage function in $\alpha$ frame. In summary, two RLS algorithms are required to complete one round of parameters identification. The pseudocode is presented in Algorithm 3.

## 4  Experiment

In this section, the second joint of the SIASUN SR10C robot is built to conduct industrial robot joint dynamic parameter identification and SPMSM electrical parameter identification experiments to verify the effectiveness of the proposed methods, as shown in Fig. 4.

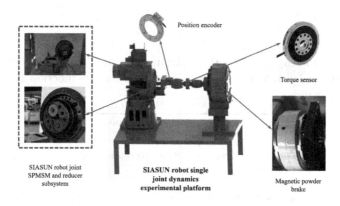

**Fig. 4.** SIASUN robot single joint dynamics experimental platform

In order to complete the joint dynamics parameter identification experiment, PMSM operates at the angular velocity shown in Fig. 3, the motor is accelerated from standstill to 50 r/min and runs at a constant speed for a while, and then the motor is accelerated in reverse to −50/min, and keep running at this speed for a while, and finally slow down to a stop. During this operation, TwinCAT software is used to collect various data of the robot joint at a frequency of 100 hz. The experimental data to be collected mainly includes motor electromagnetic torque $\tau_e$, motor rotor angle $q_m$, angular velocity $\dot{q}_m$, link end position $q_l$, and reducer output torque $\tau_{r2}$. For the acquisition of the motor rotor angular acceleration $\ddot{q}_m$, the rotor angular velocity collected by the motor encoder is differentially processed, and the butterworth low-pass filter function in Matlab is used to

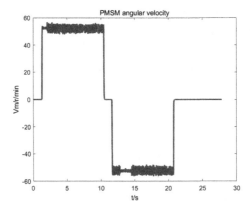

**Fig. 5.** Angular velocity of the SPMSM in experiment

process the data to eliminate the high-frequency noise caused by the differential calculation.

After collecting and processing the data, the joint dynamics model parameters can be identified. After identification, the joint dynamic model parameters are shown in Table 2:

**Table 2.** The joint dynamic model parameters

| $J_m$ | $f_{mc}$ | $f_{mv}$ | $f_b$ | $\xi$ | $K$ |
|---|---|---|---|---|---|
| $2.1 \times 10^{-3}$ | $6.2 \times 10^{-3}$ | $2.3 \times 10^{-3}$ | $-1.65 \times 10^{-2}$ | $3.242 \times 10^{-1}$ | $5.11 \times 10^{-4}$ |

Based on the above identification results, the predicted value of torque loss of the joint dynamics model $\Delta\tau_{pre}$ can be calculated as:

$$\Delta\tau_{\text{pre}} = \eta \left( J_m^{\text{pre}} \ddot{q}_m + f_{\text{mc}}^{\text{pre}} \left( \frac{2}{1 + e^{-100\dot{q}_m}} - 1 \right) + f_{\text{mv}}^{\text{pre}} \dot{q}_m + f_b^{\text{pre}} + \xi^{\text{pre}} \tau_e \right) \quad (31)$$

The curves of the predicted value and actual value of torque loss are shown in Fig. 6. The evaluation criterion for evaluating whether the predicted torque loss matches the actual torque loss is the relative RMS, denoted as $\varepsilon_{RMS}$:

$$\varepsilon_{RMS} = 100 \frac{\sqrt{\frac{1}{K} \sum_{j=1}^{K} \left( \Delta\tau^j - \Delta\tau_{pre}^j \right)^2}}{\max(\tau_m)} = 9.293\% \quad (32)$$

where $\Delta\tau^j$, $\Delta\tau_{pre}^j$ are the $j$th actual torque loss and predicted torque loss of the joint respectively, and $K$ are the number of sampling points.

In order to use Algorithm 2 to identify the inductance $L_S$ of the SPMSM in the $d - q$ frame, let the motor rotate at a rated speed of 2000 r/min, and use

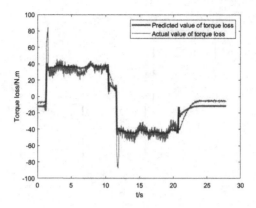

**Fig. 6.** Predicted value and actual value of torque loss

TSINO DYNATRON motor drive software DriveMaster to measure the current and voltage in $d - q$ frame and motor angular velocity at a frequency of 320 hz. The collected data are processed by first-order low-pass filtering, and the identification result of the inductance using the RLS in the $d - q$ frame is shown in Fig. 7. It can be seen that the identification value of the inductance quickly converges to the nominal value in Table 3.

**Table 3.** Nominal Parameters of the Experimental PMSM

| Parameter | Value |
|---|---|
| Type | SPMSM |
| $R_s(\Omega)$ | 0.46 |
| $L_s(mH)$ | 4.90 |
| $\psi_f(Wb)$ | None |
| Rated Speed (rpm) | 2000 |
| Rated Torque (Nm) | 7.16 |

In order to use Algorithm 3 to identify the resistance $R_s$ and flux linkage $\psi_f$ of the SPMSM in the $\alpha - \beta$ frame, TSINO DYNATRON motor drive software DriveMaster is also used to measure the current $i_d$, $i_q$, voltage $u_d$, $u_q$, three-phase current $i_A$, $i_B$, $i_C$ and motor angular velocity $\omega_m$ at a frequency of 320hz and perform first-order low-pass filtering on the collected data. The identification results of $R_s$ and $\psi_f$ using RLS in the $\alpha - \beta$ frame are shown in Fig. 7.

It can be seen that the identification results of $R_s$ and $\psi_f$ also quickly converge to the nominal values in Table 3. The errors between the identification value and the nominal value of electrical parameters are shown in Table 4.

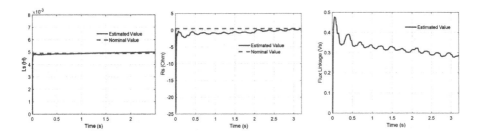

**Fig. 7.** Identified results of $L_s$, $R_s$ and $\psi_f$

**Table 4.** Error between SPMSM Electrical Parameter Identification and Nominal Values

| Parameter | Nominal Value | Identified Value | Error (%) |
|---|---|---|---|
| Inductance ($\mu$H) | 4.9 | 4.997 | 1.98 |
| Resistance ($\Omega$) | 0.46 | 0.4698 | 2.13 |
| Flux Linkage (Wb) | None | 0.288 | None |

## 5   Conclusion

This article proposes an approach for modeling the electromechanical coupling in industrial robot joints and an approach for identifying the electrical parameters of surface-mounted permanent magnet synchronous motors (SPMSMs) used in robot joints. Firstly, a more accurate joint modeling method is proposed that takes into account both the PMSM friction and the gear reducer friction. By using an improved Coulomb-viscous model for the PMSM rotor friction and a simple yet effective representation of the reducer friction, better accuracy can be achieved in identifying the joint's dynamic parameters. This refined joint modeling is crucial, as industrial robot joints often incorporate complex components like harmonic drives and RV reducers, which introduce additional sources of friction and flexibility that need to be properly characterized. Secondly, a method has been developed to separately identify the SPMSM inductance in the $d - q$ frame and the resistance and flux linkage in the $\alpha$-$\beta$ frame, using a Recursive Least Squares (RLS) algorithm. This approach addresses the rank deficiency issues that arise when relying solely on the q-axis voltage equation to identify multiple parameters. By tackling this challenge, more accurate estimates of the key SPMSM electrical parameters can be obtained.

**Acknowledgement.** This work was supported in part by the National Key Research and Development Program of China under Grant 2022YFB4700300 and the NSFC-Shenzhen Robot Basic Research Center project under Grant U2013204. (Corresponding author: Chungang Zhuang)

# References

1. Lee, H.: The study of mechanical arm and intelligent robot. IEEE Access **8**, 119624–119634 (2020)
2. Dupont, P.E., et al.: A decade retrospective of medical robotics research from 2010 to 2020. Sci. Robot. **6**(60), eabi8017 (2021)
3. Wallén, J.: The History of the Industrial Robot. Linköping University Electronic Press (2008)
4. Brogårdh, T.: Present and future robot control development-An industrial perspective. Annu. Rev. Control. **31**(1), 69–79 (2007)
5. Hu, J., Wang, Z., Liu, Y., et al.: Vibration characteristics of industrial robot joint servo transmission system based on electromechanical coupling. Meas. Sci. Technol. **34**(12), 125147 (2023)
6. Ding, Y., Chen, B., Wu, H.: An identification method of industrial robot's dynamic parameters. J. South China Univ. Technol. (Nat. Sci. Edn.) **43**(3), 49–56 (2015)
7. Lu, Y., Shen, Z., Hu, H., et al.: A unified framework of in-situ calibration and synchronous identification for industrial robots using composite sensing. IEEE Trans. Autom. Sci. Eng., 1–20 (2024)
8. Inoue, T., Inoue, Y., Morimoto, S., et al.: Maximum torque per ampere control of a direct torque-controlled PMSM in a stator flux linkage synchronous frame. IEEE Trans. Ind. Appl. **52**(3), 2360–2367 (2016)
9. Liu, K., Zhu, Z.: Online estimation of the rotor flux linkage and voltage-source inverter nonlinearity in permanent magnet synchronous machine drives. IEEE Trans. Power Electron. **29**(1), 418–427 (2013)
10. Hwang, C., Cho, Y.: Effects of leakage flux on magnetic fields of interior permanent magnet synchronous motors. IEEE Trans. Magn. **37**(4), 3021–3024 (2001)
11. Ichikawa, S., Tomita, M., Doki, S., et al.: Sensorless control of permanent-magnet synchronous motors using online parameter identification based on system identification theory. IEEE Trans. Industr. Electron. **53**(2), 363–372 (2006)
12. Lee, K., Jung, D., Ha, I.: An online identification method for both stator resistance and back-EMF coefficient of PMSMs without rotational transducers. IEEE Trans. Industr. Electron. **51**(2), 507–510 (2004)
13. Liu, K., et al.: Online multiparameter estimation of nonsalient-pole PM synchronous machines with temperature variation tracking. IEEE Trans. Ind. Electron. **58**(5), 1776–1788 (2010)
14. Feng, G., Lai, C., Kar, N.: A novel current injection-based online parameter estimation method for PMSMs considering magnetic saturation. IEEE Trans. Magn. **52**(7), 1–4 (2016)
15. Lai, C., et al.: Torque ripple minimization for interior PMSM with consideration of magnetic saturation incorporating on-line parameter identification. In: 2016 IEEE Conference on Electromagnetic Field Computation (CEFC), p. 1 (2016)
16. Liu, Q., Hameyer, K.: A fast online full parameter estimation of a PMSM with sinusoidal signal injection. In: 2015 IEEE Energy Conversion Congress and Exposition (ECCE), pp. 4091–4096 (2015)
17. Zhou, M., Jiang, L., Wang, C.: Real-time multiparameter identification of a salient-pole PMSM based on two steady states. Energies **13**(22), 6109 (2020)
18. YU, Y., et al.: Full parameter estimation for permanent magnet synchronous motors. IEEE Trans. Ind. Electron. **69**(5), 4376–4386 (2021)
19. Rafaq, M., Mwasilu, F., Kim, J., et al.: Online parameter identification for model-based sensorless control of interior permanent magnet synchronous machine. IEEE Trans. Power Electron. **32**(6), 4631–4643 (2016)

20. Lu, H., Wang, Y., Yuan, Y., et al.: Online identification for permanent magnet synchronous motor based on recursive fixed memory least square method under steady state. In: 2017 36th Chinese Control Conference (CCC), pp. 4824–4829 (2017)
21. Wu, C., Jiang, S., Bian, C.: Online parameter identification of SPMSM based on improved artificial bee colony algorithm. Arch. Electr. Eng. **70**(4), 777–790 (2021)
22. Huang, X., Yu, Y., Li, Z., et al.: Online identification of inductance and flux linkage for inverter-fed SPMSMs using switching state functions. IEEE Trans. Power Electron. **38**(1), 917–930 (2022)

# Electroluminescence Image-Based Automated Defect Detection for Solar Photovoltaic Cells

Yufei Zhang, Xu Zhang, and Dawei Tu[✉]

School of Mechatronic Engineering and Automation, Shanghai University, Shanghai, China
tdw@shu.edu.cn

**Abstract.** Solar photovoltaic (PV) cells are the primary elements of the PV power generation process, and their quality directly influences the overall efficiency and reliability of the power generation. Visual inspection of PV electroluminescence (EL) images in the factory is a classical method for defect detection, but it is a time-consuming and labor-intensive process. Therefore, an improved YOLOv8 model YOLOv8-DGN was proposed for EL images. In this paper, we introduced depthwise separable convolution (DWConv) and GhostConv into YOLOv8n to reduce the number of parameters and computational complexity. To improve the model's detection performance on small-size defects, the Normalized Gaussian Wasserstein distance (NWD) was employed to replace the original loss function of YOLOv8. The experimental results showed that the proposed model YOLOv8-DGN was superior to the baseline model YOLOv8, with a mAP50 of 91.68% while parameters, FLOPs and weights decreased by 0.46M, 0.8G and 0.9MB, respectively. Compared to other SOTA models, YOLOv8-DGN also achieves superior detection results and is more suitable for some industrial hardware-constrained environments. .

**Keywords:** Electroluminescence image · Solar photovoltaic cells · Defect detection · Deep learning

## 1 Introduction

The acceleration of scientific and technological advancement coupled with the persistent expansion of the global population, has led to a sustained surge in energy demand. The depletion of non-renewable energy sources has prompted a growing interest in solar energy, which is both renewable and non-polluting [1]. The appropriate utilization of solar energy is a viable solution for global energy scarcity and climate change [2]. As the installed capacity of PV systems increases, the quality of solar PV cells—the primary components of PV power generation—affects the efficiency of power generation directly. Therefore, the defect detection technology of PV cells is crucial [3].

EL imaging is an effective method for detecting internal defects in PV cells and can provide high-resolution EL images of PV cells [4]. Furthermore, with the rapid development of computer technology, deep learning-based object detection models are widely accepted by society due to their excellent learning ability. Therefore, the utilization of

© The Author(s), under exclusive license to Springer Nature Singapore Pte Ltd. 2025
X. Lan et al. (Eds.): ICIRA 2024, LNAI 15208, pp. 332–343, 2025.
https://doi.org/10.1007/978-981-96-0783-9_23

deep learning-based object detection models for defect detection in PV cell EL images is an efficient method. Compared to the two-stage algorithms, the single-stage object detection algorithms represented by the YOLO series, exhibit superior detection speed and maintain a high level of detection accuracy. Xu [5] et al. integrated the attention modules CBAM and ECA into the YOLOv5s model to enhance the model focusing on PV cell defects, resulting in a 3.3% increase in mAP. Zhang [6] et al. proposed an improved YOLOv5 algorithm by introducing deformable convolution, attention module ECA and tiny defect detection head, thus more accurate solar cell defect detection was realized. Although the above methods effectively improve the model's detection performance, they inevitably cause the size of the model to increase, resulting in the model being unable to be ported to mobile devices for real-time monitoring of solar PV cells.

Therefore, an improved YOLOv8 [7] model YOLOv8-DGN was proposed in this paper, which can maintain good detection performance while significantly reducing the computational complexity and the number of parameters of the model. The experimental results demonstrate the effectiveness of the improvements and the superior performance of the proposed model. Specific improvements are as follows:

(1) Replacing part of the conventional convolution in the backbone network with the DWConv, whose channel-by-channel convolution achieves an effective reduction in the number of model parameters and computation.
(2) Introducing the GhostConv to the head network for low-cost linear processing of redundant features.
(3) Replacing the original loss function with the NWD to enhance the performance of the model for detecting small-size defects.

## 2 Improved YOLOv8 Network Structure

YOLOv8 is a single-stage object detection algorithm that provides good detection accuracy and speed. Among the YOLOv8 series, YOLOv8n has the lowest number of parameters and computations, while maintaining excellent detection performance. Therefore, we proposed an improved YOLOv8 network structure YOLOv8-DGN based on YOLOv8n.

To reduce the computational cost of the convolution, we replaced part of the conventional convolution in the backbone and neck network with the DWConv [8] and GhostConv [9], respectively. In addition, the NWD [10] loss function was introduced to improve the model's feature extraction capability for small-sized defects in PV cells. Figure 1 shows the YOLOv8-DGN network structure. The dashed boxes in the Fig. 1 show the exact location of the improvements.

### 2.1 Depthwise Separable Convolution

In the conventional convolution operation, each convolution kernel convolves all input channels simultaneously and the number of convolution kernel channels equals the number of input channels. While the number of convolution kernels in the DWConv equals the number of input channels, each convolution kernel convolves only one channel at a time. The DWConv obtains the same number of outputs as the number of input channels

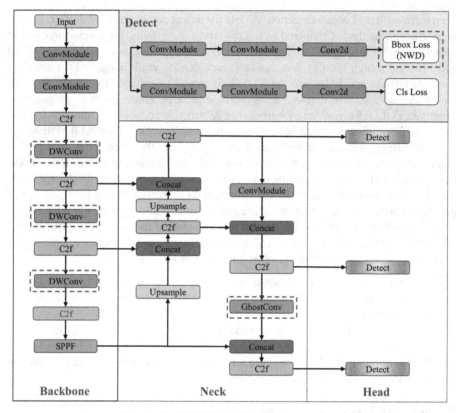

**Fig. 1.** The YOLOv8-DGN network structure

by stacking the feature maps obtained from the convolution of each channel. By stacking the feature maps obtained by convolution of each channel, the DWConv can obtain the same number of outputs as the input channels. Therefore, the DWConv maintains detection performance and reduces the computational cost of the model by efficiently integrating channel information. The DWConv structure is shown in Fig. 2.

The computational cost of conventional convolution and the DWConv are shown in Eqs. (1) and (2), respectively, and the number of the parameters are shown in Eqs. (3) and (4), respectively:

$$C_{Conv} = K \times K \times N \times C \times H \times W \tag{1}$$

$$C_{DW-Conv} = K \times K \times C \times H \times W + N \times C \times H \times W \tag{2}$$

$$P_{Conv} = K \times K \times N \times C \tag{3}$$

$$P_{DW-Conv} = K \times K \times C + N \times C \tag{4}$$

Where $H \times W \times C$ represents the size of the input feature map; $K \times K$ is the size of the kernel; N denotes the number of the kernels.

3 Channel input                    Filter * 3                    Map * 3

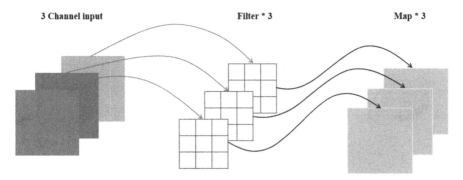

**Fig. 2.** The DWConv structure

Therefore, the ratio of the computational cost and the number of parameters for the conventional convolution and the DWConv are shown in Eqs. (5) and (6), respectively.

$$\frac{C_{Conv}}{C_{DW-Conv}} = \frac{K \times K \times N \times C \times H \times W}{K \times K \times C \times H \times W + N \times C \times H \times W} = N + K^2 \quad (5)$$

$$\frac{P_{Conv}}{P_{DW-Conv}} = \frac{K \times K \times N \times C}{K \times K \times C + N \times C} = N + K^2 \quad (6)$$

Equations (5) and (6) show that the computational cost and the number of parameters of traditional convolution are $N+K^2$ times higher than that of the DWConv. The backbone is an important part of the YOLOv8 for extracting image features. Therefore, we replaced part of the conventional convolution in the backbone with the DWConv, which can effectively realize the light weight of the model.

## 2.2 GhostConv

Conventional convolution has many similar and superfluous features, increasing the model complexity. The GhostConv first employs a conventional convolution to extract features, subsequently reducing the number of channels. Then, linear operations are applied to the feature maps extracted by the conventional convolution, followed by the concatenation of the two sets of feature maps. The GhostConv employs linear operations to generate the majority of the feature maps, thus reducing the number of convolutional kernels and channels required. This effectively reduces the complexity of the model. Therefore, we replaced the conventional conv in the head with the GhostConv. Figure 3 shows the structure of the GhostConv.

## 2.3 Normalized Gaussian Wasserstein Distance

The YOLOv8 calculates how well the Ground Truth (GT) box matches the prediction box by the IoU. However, a small change in bounding box position can cause a large change in IoU for small-size objects, which may cause the positive and negative samples to be similar in features. Therefore, the positive samples will be misclassified as negative

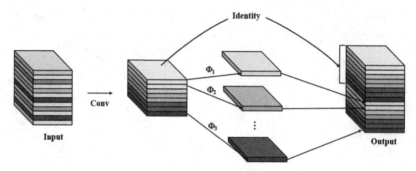

**Fig. 3.** The structure of the GhostConv

samples thus affecting the detection accuracy and convergence of the model. Figure 4 shows the sensitivity analysis of IoU on tiny and normal-scale objects. Given the presence of small-size defects in PV cells, we utilized the NWD as the model loss function to improve the model's small-size defects detection performance. The NWD models the bounding box as the Gaussian distribution and then applies the Wasserstein distance metric to quantify the discrepancy between the GT box and the prediction box.

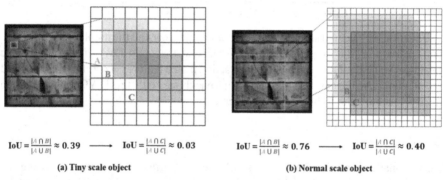

$IoU = \frac{|A \cap B|}{|A \cup B|} \approx 0.39 \longrightarrow IoU = \frac{|A \cap C|}{|A \cup C|} \approx 0.03$     $IoU = \frac{|A \cap B|}{|A \cup B|} \approx 0.76 \longrightarrow IoU = \frac{|A \cap C|}{|A \cup C|} \approx 0.40$

(a) Tiny scale object                                     (b) Normal scale object

**Fig. 4.** Sensitivity analysis of IoU on tiny and normal scale objects. Note: Each grid represents a pixel, box A denotes the GT box, box B and box C denote the prediction box with 1 pixel and 3 pixels diagonal deviation, respectively.

The target is typically situated at the center of the bounding box, while the background is located at the edge. Therefore, we set the center pixel's weight to the highest value and gradually decreased it to the edge of the bounding box. Specifically, the bounding box can be represented as follows:

$$R = (c_x, c_y, w, h) \tag{7}$$

where $(c_x, c_y)$ is the center coordinate of the bounding box; w and h denote the width and height of the bounding box, respectively.

The bounding box R can be fitted to the Gaussian distribution, with x and y being the mean and covariance matrices of the Gaussian distribution, respectively. They are shown in Eq. (8):

$$\mu = \begin{bmatrix} c_x \\ c_y \end{bmatrix}, \sum = \begin{bmatrix} \frac{w^2}{4} & 0 \\ 0 & \frac{h^2}{4} \end{bmatrix} \tag{8}$$

Next, the Wasserstein distance is employed to compute the distance between the two-dimensional Gaussian distribution x and y. The Wasserstein distance is calculated as follows:

$$W_2^2(\mu_1, \mu_2) = m_1 - m_{22}^2 + \text{Tr}(\Sigma_1 + \Sigma_2 - 2(\Sigma_2^{1/2}\Sigma_1\Sigma_2^{1/2})^{1/2}) \tag{9}$$

Equation (9) can be simplified as follows:

$$W_2^2(\mu_1, \mu_2) = \|m_1 - m_2\|_2^2 + \|\Sigma_1^{\frac{1}{2}} - \Sigma_2^{\frac{1}{2}}\|_F^2 \tag{10}$$

Therefore, the Wasserstein distance between the Gaussian distributions Np and Ng for the prediction box Bp = (cxp, yp, wp, hp) and the GT box Bg = (cxg, yg, wg, hg) can be calculated by Eq. (11):

$$W_2^2(N_p, N_g) = \left( \left[ c_{x_p}, c_{y_p}, \frac{w_p}{2}, \frac{h_p}{2} \right]^T, \left[ c_{x_g}, c_{y_g}, \frac{w_g}{2}, \frac{h_g}{2} \right]^T \right)_2^2 \tag{11}$$

The range of the bounding box similarity metric should range in (0, 1), thus we normalized the Wasserstein distance to obtain the NWD. The NWD can be calculate as shown in Eq. (12).

$$NWD(N_p, N_g) = exp\left( -\frac{\sqrt{W_2^2(N_p, N_g)}}{C} \right) \tag{12}$$

Where C is a constant associated with the dataset.

Therefore, the loss function based on NWD is shown in Eq. (13).

$$L_{\text{NWD}} = 1 - NWD(N_p, N_g) \tag{13}$$

## 3 Experiments

### 3.1 PVEL-AD Dataset

PVEL-AD [11] dataset is an open dataset containing a total of 12 types of defect images for the evaluation of PV cell defect detection algorithms, which was jointly released by the Hebei University of Technology and the BeiHang University. In this paper, six classes with a high number of images in the PVEL-AD dataset were retained, which are crack, finger, black_core, quick_line, horizontal_dislocation and shortcut_circuit, totaling 4325 images. Figure 5 shows the six classes of defects.

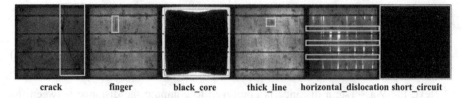

crack          finger          black_core          thick_line     horizontal_dislocation short_circuit

**Fig. 5.** Six classes of defects

## 3.2 Data Preprocessing

We used 90% of the data in the dataset to train and 10% to validate, i.e. the number of images in the training and validation datasets is 3892 and 433. To increase sample diversity and improve model robustness, mosaic data augmentation was used for training the model. Mosaic augmentation randomly crops and merges four images into one, thus enriching the background information and increasing the probability that each image contains a small object. Furthermore, gamut change, panning, vertical flipping, and scaling are applied to these four images. Train batches are shown in Fig. 6.

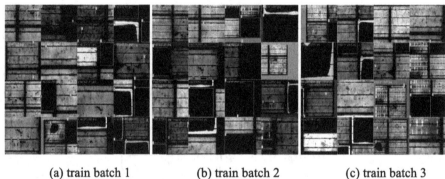

(a) train batch 1               (b) train batch 2               (c) train batch 3

**Fig. 6.** Train batches

## 3.3 Experimental Environment

The hardware environment as follows:

(1) CPU: 13th Gen Intel(R) Core (TM) i5-13400
(2) GPU: NVIDIA GeForce RTX 3060 with 12 GB

The software environment as follows:

(1) Operating system: Windows 11 64-bit
(2) Library files: Python 3.8.18, PyTorch 1.12.0, and CUDA 11.6.

## 3.4 Training Parameters

In this paper, the experiments were all conducted with the same training parameters, as shown in Table 1.

**Table 1.** The specification of training parameters

| Parameters | Values |
|---|---|
| Batch size | 16 |
| Learning rate | 0.001 |
| Epochs | 100 |
| Weight decay coefficient | 0.937 |
| Momentum decay coefficient | 0.0005 |
| Optimizer | SGD |

### 3.5 Evaluation Metrics

The detection performance of the model was evaluated by using Precision (P), Recall (R), mAP50 and mAP50-95. Furthermore, computational cost (FLOPs) and parameters (Params) were utilized to evaluate the number of computations and parameters of the model, respectively.

### 3.6 Ablation Experiments

To verify the effectiveness of each improved module, ablation experiments were performed. Table 2 shows the results of the ablation experiments, where the improved modules are denoted by $\sqrt{}$. The low-cost linear operations of the GhostConv on redundant features with similar features reduce the Params and FLOPs from 3.01M and 8.1 G to 2.93M and 8 G, respectively. Moreover, the P and mAP50 are also slightly improved. NWD's Gaussian bounding box modeling effectively reduces the model's sensitivity to small changes in bounding box position and improves the P by 3.7% without increasing the complexity of the model. Due to the special treatment of redundant features by the DWConv, the model achieved optimal mAP50, Param, and Flops values of 91.63%, 2.55M, and 7.3G, respectively. The DWConv has a positive effect on the light weight of the model. Although the DWConv reduces the P of the model, it is still 2.2% higher than the baseline, which is an acceptable result. The above analysis shows that each improvement module positively affects the model. Therefore, the validity of each improvement module was verified.

### 3.7 Comparison Experiments

To evaluate the performance of the proposed model, we conducted comparison experiments between the proposed model and other SOTA models. Table 3 shows the comparison results. YOLOv6n performs the worst with a mAP50 of only 73.89% due to its precision cliff dropping during training, as shown in Fig. 7. YOLOv8-DGN achieves optimal results on R and mAP50, reaching 0.868 and 91.68%. Compared to the baseline, although YOLOv8-DGN's mAP50-95 decreased, the remaining metrics were still better than the baseline. Specifically, Params, Flops, and Weights decrease by 0.46M, 0.8G,

**Table 2.** The results of the ablation experiments

| Baseline | GhostConv | NWD | DW Conv | P | mAP50/% | Params/M | Flops/G |
|---|---|---|---|---|---|---|---|
| YOLOv8n | | | | 0.853 | 90.70% | 3.01 | 8.1 |
| | ✓ | | | 0.854 | 90.88% | 2.93 | 8.0 |
| | ✓ | ✓ | | 0.890 | 90.96% | 2.93 | 8.0 |
| | ✓ | ✓ | ✓ | 0.875 | 91.63% | 2.55 | 7.3 |

**Table 3.** The results of the comparison experiments

| Model | P | R | mAP50 | mAP50-95 | Param/M | Flops/G | Weights/MB |
|---|---|---|---|---|---|---|---|
| YOLOv3-tiny [12] | 0.767 | 0.788 | 86.35% | 56.29% | 12.1 | 18.9 | 24.4 |
| YOLOv5u [13] | 0.829 | 0.864 | 90.26% | 65.13% | 2.5 | 7.1 | 5.3 |
| YOLOv6n [14] | 0.717 | 0.709 | 73.89% | 55.42% | 4.23 | 11.8 | 8.7 |
| YOLOv8n | 0.853 | 0.859 | 90.70% | 66.91% | 3.01 | 8.1 | 6.3 |
| YOLOv8-DGN | 0.875 | 0.868 | 91.68% | 66.69% | 2.55 | 7.3 | 5.4 |

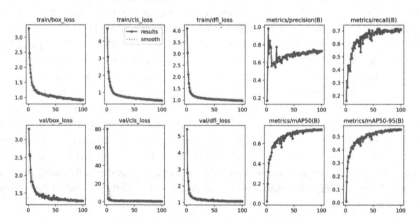

**Fig. 7.** YOLOv6 Training Visualization

and 0.9MB, respectively, indicating that the YOLOv8-DGN is more hardware-friendly. YOLOv5u is nearly identical to YOLOv8-DGN in terms of Params, Flops and Weights, but YOLOv8-DGN has a better detection performance. The above analysis shows that YOLOv8-DGN somewhat outperforms other SOTA models in detection performance and has an excellent lightweight, making it suitable for some industrial scenarios with limited computing resources.

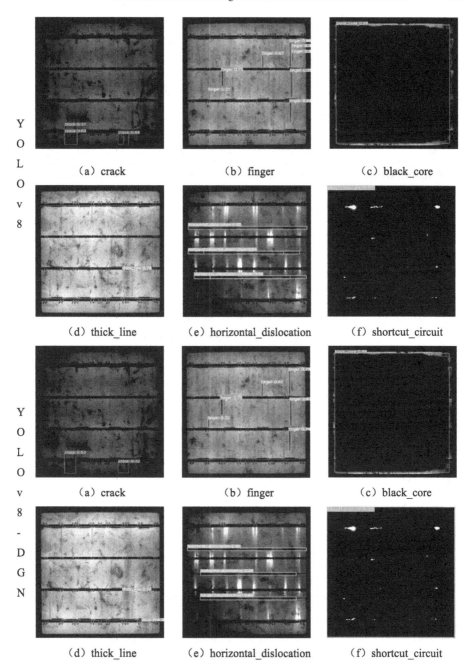

**Fig. 8.** Comparison results between baseline and proposed model

Figure 8 shows that YOLOv8-DGN has fewer missed detections than baseline when detecting small-size defects such as crack, finger, and thick_line, and generally provides a high level of confidence. Although the confidence level of the YOLOv8-DGN in detecting short_circuit is relatively low compared to baseline, it can accurately distinguish between black_core and short_circuit with similar features, so this is acceptable. Furthermore, YOLOv8 provides more redundant prediction boxes when detecting horizontal_displacement, whereas YOLOv8-DGN can detect defects more efficiently. In summary, the YOLOv8-DGN has excellent detection performance.

## 4 Conclusion

In this paper, an improved YOLOv8 defect detection model YOLOv8-DGN was proposed for solar PV cell EL images. Specifically, the DWConv and GhostConv were introduced to lightweight the model, and NWD replaced the original loss function for small-size defects. To evaluate the effectiveness of the improved modules and the detection performance of the proposed model, we carried out the ablation and comparison experiments using the public dataset PVEL-AD. The experiment results showed that the proposed model maintains high detection accuracy while being competitive in terms of the number of parameters and computation. Compared to the baseline, the proposed model achieves mAP50 of 91.68%with a reduction in Params and Flops to 2.55M and 7.3G, respectively. Furthermore, the proposed model also gives excellent results compared to other SOTA models. This research provides a solution for the industrial system of PV cell defect detection.

**Acknowledgements.** This research was supported by the National Natural Science Foundation of China (Nos. 62176149 and 61673252).

## References

1. Dincer, I.: Renewable energy and sustainable development: a crucial review. Renew. Sustain. Energy Rev. **4**, 157–175 (2000)
2. Naveen, S., et al.: A review on solar energy intensified biomass valorization and value-added products production: practicability, challenges, techno economic and lifecycle assessment. J. Clean. Prod. **405**, 137028 (2023)
3. Li, L., Wang, Z., Zhang, T.: GBH-YOLOv5: ghost convolution with BottleneckCSP and tiny target prediction head incorporating YOLOv5 for PV panel defect detection. Electronics **12** (2023)
4. Tang, W., Yang, Q., Yan, W.: Deep learning based model for defect detection of monocrystalline-Si solar PV module cells in electroluminescence images using data augmentation. In: 2019 IEEE PES Asia-Pacific Power and Energy Engineering Conference (APPEEC), pp. 1–5 (2019)
5. Xu, S., Qian, H., Shen, W., Wang, F., Liu, X., Xu, Z.: Defect detection for PV modules based on the improved YOLOv5s. In: 2022 China Automation Congress (CAC), pp. 1431–1436 (2022)
6. Zhang, M., Yin, L.: Solar cell surface defect detection based on improved YOLO v5. IEEE Access **10**, 80804–80815 (2022)

7. Jocher, G., Chaurasia, A., Qiu, J.: Ultralytics YOLOv8. https://github.com/ultralytics/ultral ytics
8. Chollet, F.: Xception: deep learning with depthwise separable convolutions. In: 2017 IEEE Conference on Computer Vision and Pattern Recognition (CVPR), pp. 1800–1807 (2017)
9. Han, K., Wang, Y., Tian, Q., Guo, J., Xu, C., Xu, C.: GhostNet: more features from cheap operations. In: 2020 IEEE/CVF Conference on Computer Vision and Pattern Recognition (CVPR), pp. 1577–1586 (2020)
10. Xu, C., Wang, J., Yang, W., Yu, H., Yu, L., Xia, G.-S.: Detecting tiny objects in aerial images: a normalized Wasserstein distance and a new benchmark. ISPRS J. Photogramm. Remote Sens. **190**, 79–93 (2022)
11. Su, B., Zhou, Z., Chen, H.: PVEL-AD: a large-scale open-world dataset for photovoltaic cell anomaly detection. IEEE Trans. Ind. Inf. **19**, 404–413 (2023)
12. Redmon, J., Farhadi, A.: YOLOv3: an incremental improvement. arXiv preprint arXiv:1804. 02767 (2018)
13. Jocher, G.: Ultralytics YOLOv5. https://github.com/ultralytics/yolov5
14. Li, C., et al.: YOLOv6: a single-stage object detection framework for industrial applications. arXiv preprint arXiv:2209.02976 (2022)

# ExpertAP: Leveraging Multi-unit Operational Patterns for Advanced Turbine Anomaly Prediction

Yuanxian Liang, Xiaodong Zheng$^{(\boxtimes)}$, Dongjun Pang, Wenhao Zhu,
Maoyuan Liu, Shuangsi Xue, and Hui Cao

School of Electrical Engineering, Xi'an Jiaotong University, Xi'an 710049, China
zxd_xjtu@stu.xjtu.edu.cn

**Abstract.** Analysing historical data from turbines can identify faults
and even predict potential failures. However, most articles focus solely
on one single unit, overlooking the historical operational patterns of turbines from other units, which serve as important references for human
experts. We propose ExpertAP, an approach that first learns the running
patterns of turbines from historical data of different units and then performs anomaly prediction for the target turbine. This approach faces two
key challenges: The scarcity of high-quality anomaly labels and the difficulty in using historical anomaly labels. Regarding the first challenge,
we thus introduce a semi-supervised backbone which is pre-trained with
the task of sequence reconstruction using data from multiple units and
fine-tuned with the task of anomaly prediction using data from the target unit. We also propose a novel two-dimensional selection strategy:
Filtering out anomaly labels in the dimension of the variable during pre-
training and filtering out redundant normal time-series sequences in the
dimension of time during fine-tuning. Regarding the second challenge,
the anomaly labels are modelled as binary time series, which significantly differ from the sensor data generated from continuous sampling.
Therefore, we design different embedding layers for the anomaly labels
and sensor data. These layers are trained during fine-tuning to align the
two types of input data in the latent space, allowing us to utilize historical anomaly labels as a basis for anomaly prediction. The proposed
framework was tested on real data collected from the Turbine Supervision Instrumentation (TSI) system, showing promising test results.

**Keywords:** Turbine anomaly prediction · Deep Learning ·
Semi-supervised learning

## 1 Introduction

Thermal power plants provide the world with a large and stable electricity supply. As an important component of thermal power plants [3], the turbine's failure
can lead to the overall shutdown of the power plant, resulting in significant economic losses and safety issues [1]. If the operation of the unit could be manually

X. Lan et al. (Eds.): ICIRA 2024, LNAI 15208, pp. 344–359, 2025.
https://doi.org/10.1007/978-981-96-0783-9_24

suspended before the failure occurs, and equipment defects could be investigated, this would greatly reduce the losses caused by unexpected shutdown accidents [2].

Condition monitoring (CM) has become an essential tool in industrial production for this very reason [1,2]. By analyzing real-time status parameters of equipment to identify anomalies and provide early warnings, CM helps prevent unexpected failures. In the context of turbines, which convert thermal energy into mechanical energy through steam-driven blade rotation [4], indicators such as pressure, temperature, and vibration can reflect the operating conditions of the turbine. To enhance the effectiveness of condition monitoring for turbines, engineers have developed the Turbine Supervisory Instrumentation (TSI) system [5]. This system measures and records a range of state parameters during turbine operation, significantly improving the ability to monitor and maintain turbine health.

Currently, the main method for detecting anomalies in steam turbines or wind turbines is to build a normal behaviour model(NBM) [6] and calculate the difference between real state parameters and their expected values to determine if the turbine has malfunctioned. Chen et al. [5] built NBM under different working conditions using Gaussian process, and detecting anomalies by setting the threshold of the deviation. Chen et al. [7–9] utilized LSTM, RNN, and other deep neural networks to build NBMs and demonstrated good performance in longer historical windows. To avoid the inflexibility of manually setting a threshold, Zhang et al. [10] implemented a dynamic threshold by adding a trainable classifier on top of NBM.

With the increasing digitization and informatization of power plants, we now have access to historical operating data spanning months or even years from different power plants and units. This enables experienced engineers to discover the operational risks of a turbine by comparing the operating states over longer time windows and across different units. People therefore are no longer satisfied with existing anomaly detection models based on short-term information from a single unit. Instead, anomaly prediction models which can realize analysis over multi-unit, long-term, and multivariate TSI data are eagerly awaited.

However, building anomaly prediction models based on big data faces two challenges: One major challenge is the scarcity of high-quality anomaly labels. Anomalous operations in thermal power generation are rare, and not all abnormal data can be accurately detected and labelled, as anomaly labels are often derived from actual accidents or expert judgments. Another challenge arises from the difficulty in utilizing historical anomaly labels. For human experts, both anomaly labels and sensor data within a historical time window can serve as bases for predicting future faults. However, machines face a different scenario: The significant differences in data characteristics between continuously sampled sensor data and binary anomaly labels, make it challenging to integrate both types of data. Using the same encoding method for both would result in poor performance, as the binary nature of anomaly labels does not align well with the continuous nature of sensor data, complicating accurate interpretation and prediction.

For the first challenge, we introduce semi-supervised learning into the anomaly prediction task: We pre-train the model using raw sensor data from multiple turbine units, with the task of filling in partially missing time series. This enables the model to learn representations of turbine operational patterns. In the fine-tuning phase, we utilize turbine data from a single unit with anomaly labels to train the model to predict future anomalies within a certain time window. This equips the model with the capability to predict anomalies for the target turbine. For the second challenge, we design an embedding layer for anomaly labels that are different from those for other variables. These embedding layers are trained to align the two types of input data in the latent space, allowing us to utilize historical anomaly labels as the basis for fault prediction. Additionally, we propose a two-dimensional selection strategy to complement the semi-supervised training. During pre-training, we filter the data variable-wise by removing all anomaly labels, preventing the model from being influenced by missing or erroneous labels in multi-unit data. During the fine-tuning phase, we perform time-wise filtering of the data, removing a large number of low-value normal sequences, and alleviating the tendency for fault-free predictions caused by label imbalance.

The main contributions of our work are as follows:

1. We introduce the transformer structure and semi-supervised learning into the anomaly prediction task for the turbine, demonstrating the enhanced representation learning ability of the model through pre-training using data from multiple units.

2. We propose a two-dimensional selection strategy complementing the semi-supervised learning setting: Filtering based on the dimension of the variable reduces the impact of incorrect and missing labels on the model's representation learning task while filtering based on dimensions of time mitigates the tendency for fault-free predictions caused by label imbalance.

3. We design separate embedding layers for anomaly labels and other sensor data, thereby reducing the gap between the features of anomaly labels and other sensor data during fine-tuning. This enables the model to simultaneously utilize historical anomaly label data and sensor data as the basis for anomaly prediction.

The structure of the upcoming chapters is as follows: In Sect. 2, we first introduce the anomaly prediction task for time-series data and related time-series mining tasks. In Sect. 3, we explain how we model the turbine anomaly prediction task as a multivariate time-series anomaly prediction problem. In Sect. 4, we present our proposed ExpertAP approach, and in Sect. 5, we show our test results on real turbine data. Finally, in Sect. 6, we summarize our work and outline plans for future research.

# 2   Time-Series Anomaly Prediction and Related Tasks

Before the introduction of time-series anomaly prediction, we first introduce two closely related time-series mining tasks: Time-series forecasting and time-series anomaly detection.

**Time-Series Forecasting** (TSF) involves predicting future values from historical data [11]. Recent studies extensively employ deep learning for this task. CNN-based models, originally designed for image datasets, utilize multiple layers of causal convolution [12–14]. Many RNN-based models have been developed for temporal forecasting, building on their historical use in sequence modelling [15–17]. Transformer-based models [18], known for modelling long-range dependencies in sequential data, are making significant advances in TSF [19–21]. Yun et al. [33] theoretically established that transformer-based models are universal approximators of sequence-to-sequence functions. Notably, models like PatchTST [22] not only excelled in public TSF problems but also reduced data requirements via semi-supervised learning and channel independence, enabling large-scale pre-training.

**Time-Series Anomaly Detection**(TSAD) involves identifying unexpected patterns in data, including point anomalies, contextual anomalies, or discords [23]. Various solutions exist for TSAD. Clustering models [24] detect anomalies by projecting data into a multidimensional space, clustering it, and calculating the likelihood of new data fitting into predefined clusters. Predictive models like ARIMA [25] and DeepANT [26] forecasted future states based on past data, identifying anomalies from the discrepancy between predicted and actual values. The advancement of deep learning has introduced models such as CNN [23], GNN [31], and Transformer [32] for anomaly detection.

**Time-Series Anomaly Prediction**(TSAP) involves predicting potential anomalies. It is worth noting that if we define a state variable "anomaly" that indicates whether the system is anomalous or not at a certain moment, then the TSAP is transformed into forecasting this state variable. However, this transformation does not mean that we can directly apply TSP algorithms to TSAP due to two main reasons: Firstly, most TSAP lack complete and valuable anomaly labels, often resulting in missing or incomplete "anomaly" variables. Secondly, unlike continuous input variables in TSF, the "anomaly" variable (either 0 or 1) lacks continuity. These differences highlight the specificity and predictive nature of TSAP, distinguishing it from general TSF and TSAD. Nowadays, most TSAP solutions focus on early classification, categorizing time series data as "Abnormal" or "Normal" [27,28]. Some works [29,30] addressed abnormal prediction for continuous monitoring of abnormal evolution paths, typically using statistical or traditional machine learning methods. Compared to the extensive use of deep learning in TSF and TSAD, existing TSAP solutions lack adaptability and flexibility. Our work employs semi-supervised learning and a transformer-based model, representing a novel approach to TSAP.

# 3  Modelling of Turbine Anomaly Prediction

As described above, our data primarily consists of two types: Sensor data from the TSI system and anomaly labels from historical fault records or expert diagnoses. The TSI system uses a series of sensors to collect data such as turbine speed, bearing temperature, and bearing vibration, all of which are stored as time-series data. Anomaly labels, indicated by 1 or 0, show whether the turbine is in an abnormal state at a given time. We sample uniformly along the timeline and fill in missing anomaly data with 0, creating binary time-series data. Fault events are rare, so most anomaly labels are 0. By aligning the time steps, we integrate the sensor data and anomaly labels into multivariate time-series data. In this combined data, sensor data show continuous trends, while anomaly labels switch between 0 and 1.

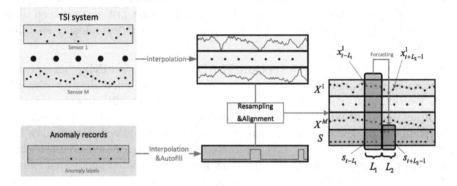

**Fig. 1.** Modelling of turbine anomaly prediction

We can therefore model the turbine anomaly prediction problem as follows: Given a complete and uniformly sampled multivariate time-series dataset $\{X^1, ..., X^M, S\}$. Among this, $\{X^i | i \in \{1, ..., M\}\}$ represents time-series data generated from sensor data, which we can refer to as "monitoring variables", $S$ represents time-series data steam from anomaly labels, which we can refer to as "state variable". We assume that $L_1$ and $L_2$ are respectively the length of the window of past and future. For time step $t_k$, we define a window of past $X_{L_1}$ and window of future $X_{L_2}$ as:

$$X_{L_1} = \{X_{L_1}^1, X_{L_1}^2, ..., X_{L_1}^M, S_{L_1}\} \tag{1}$$

$$X_{L_2} = \{X_{L_2}^1, X_{L_2}^2, ..., X_{L_2}^M, S_{L_2}\} \tag{2}$$

where for $i \in \{1, ..., M\}$:

$$X_{L_1}^i = \{x_{t_k-L_1}^i, x_{t_k-L_1+1}^i, ..., x_{t_k-1}^i\}$$
$$X_{L_2}^i = \{x_{t_k}^i, x_{t_k+1}^i, ..., x_{t_k+L_2-1}^i\}$$
$$S_{L_1} = \{s_{t_k-L_1}, s_{t_k-L_1+1}, ..., s_{t_k-1}\}$$
$$S_{L_2} = \{s_{t_k}, s_{t_k+1}, ..., s_{t_k+L_2-1}\}$$

By analyzing the window of past $X_{L_1}$, our task is to determine the likelihood of the turbine experiencing faults at time step $t$ within the windows of future $X_{L_2}$, which can be expressed as Eq. 3. The overall modelling process is shown in Fig. 1.

$$\mathbb{P}(s_t = 1 \mid t \in \{t_k, ..., t_k + L_2 - 1\}) \tag{3}$$

## 4   Method

In this section, we will showcase our Expert4AP method. In 4.1, we will provide an overview of the pre-training and fine-tuning processes. In 4.2, we will detail our transformer-based backbone design and data selection strategy.

### 4.1   Two-Step Training Process

**Pre-training Step.** In this step, following the notation mentioned in Eq. 1, we perform variable-dimensional selection on our data: We only select monitoring variables $X^i$, where $i \in \{1, ..., M\}$, as input series.

At each iteration $k$, given time step $t_k$ and the sampling window $X_{L_1}$, we select monitoring variables $X_{L_1}^i$ from multi-variable series $X_{L_1}$ and feed them independently into backbone of ExpertAP. Through instance normalization and patching, we segment $X_{L_1}^i$ into multiple smaller patches $X_P^i$. Similar to the mask mechanism used in MLM (Masked Language Model [34]), these patches are randomly set to zero. Embedding layers $E_X$ and $E_{pos}$ respectively encode the numerical and positional information of the input patches. After being encoded by the transformer encoder, the output of embedding layers is reconstructed into patches through a reconstruction head. Through patch assembling, we expect the model to reconstruct the original input sequences and thus define the loss function based on the difference between input and output sequences as Eq. 4. The overall pre-training process is shown in Fig. 2.

$$L_{\text{Pre}}(X_{L_1}, \hat{X}_{L_1}) = \sum_{i=1}^{M} \sum_{t=t_k-L_1}^{t_k-1} \left(x_t^i - \hat{x}_t^i\right)^2 \tag{4}$$

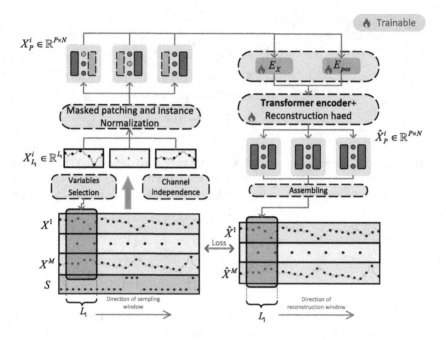

**Fig. 2.** Pre-training step for ExpertAP

**Fine-Tuning Step** In this step, following the notation mentioned in Eq. 1&2, we perform time-dimensional selection on our data: We only input the window $X_{L_1}$ if and only if there is at least one positive abnormal label[1] in $X_{L_1}$ or $X_{L_2}$, which thus can be expressed as

$$\left\{ X_{L_1} \ \middle| \ \sum_{t=t_k-L_1}^{t_k+L_2-1} s_t \geq 1 \right\}$$

At each iteration $k$, given selected sampling window $X_{L_1}$, following the instance normalization and patching, the patches derived from the series $X_{L_1}^i$ and $S_{L_1}$ are transformed by different embedding matrixes $E_X$ and $E_S$. The output of embedding layers is joined together and then fed into the transformer-based encoder and then a regressive head. The final output $\hat{S}_{L_2}$ are expected to fit the window of real state time series $S_{L_2}$ from label window $X_{L_2}$. We thus define the loss function as Eq. 5. The overall fine-tuning process is shown in Fig. 3.

$$L_{\text{Fin}}(S_{L_1}, \hat{S}_{L_1}) = \sum_{t=t_k}^{t_k+L_2-1} (s_t - \hat{s}_t)^2 \tag{5}$$

---

[1] In practice, to avoid the model tending to classify all sequences as potentially anomalous, we perform time-dimensional selection over each batch of windows instead of each window. We only dismiss the batch with low anomalies rate and thus allow windows without anomalies as input.

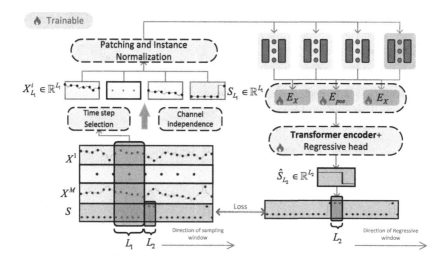

**Fig. 3.** Fine-tuning step for ExpertAP

## 4.2  Details in Architecture

**Two-Dimensional Selection and Separate Embedding Design.** Two-dimensional selection aims to address the issues of erroneous and missing anomaly labels. In the pre-training step, with variable-dimensional selection, all time steps will be considered regardless of whether there is a valid state variable. By eliminating the dependence on anomaly labels across the entire period, the model is expected to learn patterns only from the monitoring variables. In the fine-tuning step, with time-dimensional selection, only windows with valid state variables are selected, which mitigates the tendency for fault-free predictions caused by label imbalance.

Inspired by the channel independence in PatchTST [22], we treat multivariable time-series data as multiple univariable time-series data. However, since the nature of the state variable and monitoring variable differ significantly, instead of transforming all patched variables basing one single embedding layer $W_X$, we initialize an embedding layer $W_S$ for state variable. These embeddings are trainable and will align the output of monitoring and state variable in the prediction task.

**Patching and Instance Normalization.** Patching time-series data is just like tokenization in the NLP task, which helps adapt time-series data for our transformer-based model. Here we follow the scenario used in PatchTST [22], which simply normalizes each time-series instance $X^i$ with zero means and unit standard deviation before patching. Then windows of time-series data $X_L^i \in \mathbb{R}^L$ are selected from $X^i$, and patched into a sequence of patch $X_p^i \in \mathbb{R}^{P \times N}$, where $N$ is the number of patches.

# 5     Experimemt

## 5.1     Dataset

We used real data from the TSI systems of two turbine units, designated as Unit A and Unit B. We collected historical operational records and abnormal event records from two specific years to create our dataset.

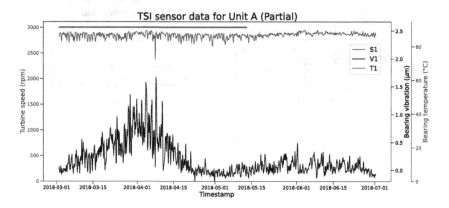

**Fig. 4.** Subset of historical data from Unit A, where anomaly labels are omitted as there are no valid anomalies present.

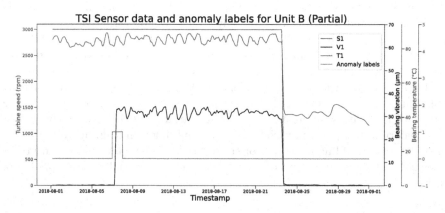

**Fig. 5.** Subset of historical data from Unit B, which includes one clearly defined instance of abnormal event.

The monitoring variables (i.e., sensor data, see Sect. 3) include data from three bearing vibration sensors, three bearing temperature sensors, and two turbine speed sensors, focusing on bearing abnormal vibration faults. The state variables (i.e., abnormal labels, see Sect. 3) are derived from abnormal operation records. Unit A, having operated stably, has no effective anomaly labels. In contrast, the turbine bearings of Unit B have a clear history of abnormal operations, from which we obtained effective abnormal labels for Unit B.

The summary of raw data is shown in Tab. 1. To address inconsistent data collection intervals, we aligned the time steps of all variables using methods described in Sect. 3, resulting in a multivariate time series of length 376991.

For demonstration, we selected a portion of historical data from Unit A (see Fig. 4). The data shows a stable turbine speed at 3000 rpm and bearing vibrations below 20 μm, with no significant changes in any variables. In contrast, data from Unit B (see Fig. 5) shows a significant spike in bearing vibration despite a stable turbine speed, indicating a typical turbine fault.

All the models were trained/tested on a single Nvidia RTX 4090 GPU (24GB).

**Table 1.** Summary of variables and their sources

| Variable name | Number of sampling points | Source of variables |
| --- | --- | --- |
| V1 | 1766846 | Vibration of bearing (sensor 1) |
| V2 | 1887488 | Vibration of bearing (sensor 2) |
| V3 | 1516917 | Vibration of bearing (sensor 3) |
| T1 | 485600 | Temperature of bearing (sensor 1) |
| T2 | 499337 | Temperature of bearing (sensor 2) |
| T3 | 165483 | Temperature of bearing (sensor 3) |
| S1 | 1537535 | Turbine speed (Sensor 1) |
| S2 | 1537513 | Turbine speed (Sensor 2) |
| Anomaly labels | 598 | Abnormal operation records |

## 5.2  Pattern Learning via Pre-Training

In our paper, we aim to achieve the learning of turbine operation patterns through pre-training task. Specifically, in the pre-training task, we focus on sequence reconstruction: The closer the reconstructed values are to the actual values, the better the model's learning. We abbreviate the Two-Dimensional Selection strategy as **TDS**, the Multi-Unit pre-training dataset as **MU**, and the Single-Unit pre-training dataset as **SU**. For example, the scenario of pre-training with the multi-unit dataset and TDS strategy is denoted as **MU&TDS**. We measured the reconstruction effects of eight monitoring variables using Mean Absolute Error (MAE), averaging variables of the same type as shown in Tab. 2. Additionally, we presented the model's reconstruction performance of V1 (Fig. 6&7), T1 (Fig. 8&9), and S1 (Fig. 10&11) within time-step windows of length 512 and 256.

**Table 2.** Averaged MAE value of reconstruction for three types of monitoring variables

| Nub. of time steps | Variables | | | | | | | | |
|---|---|---|---|---|---|---|---|---|---|
| | $V_{Avg}$ | | | $T_{Avg}$ | | | $S_{Avg}$ | | |
| | SU | MU | MU&TDS | SU | MU | MU&TDS | SU | MU | MU&TDS |
| 512 | 0.2361 | 0.2170 | 0.2075 | 0.2425 | 0.2324 | 0.2174 | 0.1567 | 0.1364 | 0.1024 |
| 256 | 0.2983 | 0.2336 | 0.2169 | 0.2734 | 0.2386 | 0.2212 | 0.2343 | 0.1641 | 0.1576 |

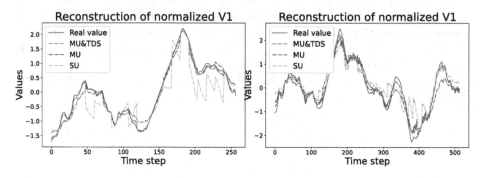

**Fig. 6.** Reconstruction of V1 (Length of window = 256)    **Fig. 7.** Reconstruction of V1 (Length of window = 512)

It is evident that, among the three types of monitoring variables, the models trained with the multi-unit training dataset (MU) consistently outperform those trained with the single-unit dataset (SU) in terms of variable reconstruction. This observation also suggests Two-dimensional Selection Strategy (TDS) significantly enhances data reconstruction capabilities when employed with MU datasets.

## 5.3 Anomaly Prediction via Fine-Tuning

During the fine-tuning phase, our goal is to predict anomalies for the target unit by forecasting the future state variable based on historical data. The closer the prediction is to the actual values, the better the model's anomaly prediction capability. Since the state variable is binary, this task can be regarded as both a regression and binary classification problem, which can be evaluated by both MAE and F1 scores.

We first examined the impact of window length on anomaly prediction performance using heatmaps (see Fig. 13&12). We found that the model performs better with longer historical windows and shorter prediction windows, which aligns with our intuitions. Due to space constraints, we present the model's optimal performance (Window of Future = 24) in subsequent comparative experiments. Similar conclusions were observed with other window lengths.

Next, we tested the model's prediction performance using MU and SU as training sets under different settings. For brevity, we denote the Separated

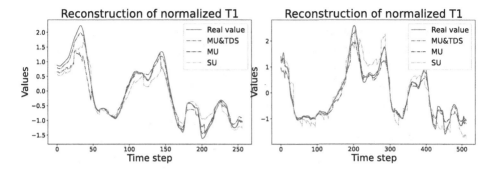

**Fig. 8.** Reconstruction of T1 (Length of window = 256)

**Fig. 9.** Reconstruction of T1 (Length of window = 512)

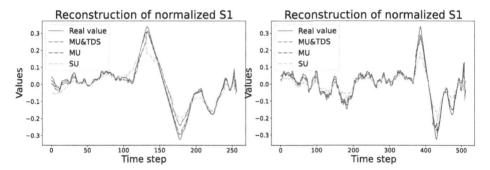

**Fig. 10.** Reconstruction of S1 (Length of window = 256)

**Fig. 11.** Reconstruction of S1 (Length of window = 512)

Embedding Design as **SED**. Similar to the notation used in Subsect. 5.2, the scenario using multi-unit pre-training dataset along with SED and TDS is denoted as **MU&SED&TDS**. For comparison purposes, we presented both MU and SU as control groups in all figures (Fig 14&15 show MAE scores, Fig. 16&17 show F1 scores).

It can be observed that both TDS and SED effectively enhance the model's anomaly prediction capability, with the effect being more pronounced when MU is used as the pre-training dataset. We also found that F1 scores highlight this trend more clearly than MAE scores. Considering the scarcity of anomaly labels, the MAE values are very low, meaning that even if the model tends towards predicting no anomalies, it won't significantly affect the MAE score. Therefore, we consider the F1 score to be a more valuable metric for evaluation.

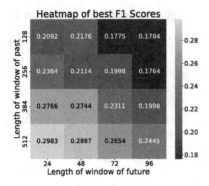

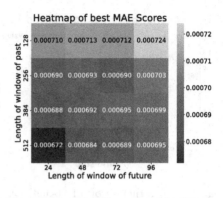

**Fig. 12.** Best F1 score with different window-length settings

**Fig. 13.** Best MAE score with different window-length settings

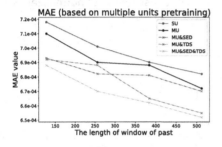

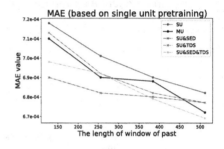

**Fig. 14.** Best MAE score (MU based)

**Fig. 15.** Best MAE score (SU based)

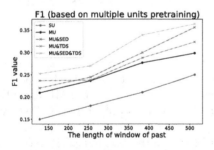

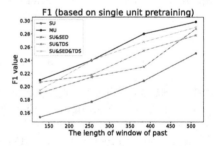

**Fig. 16.** Best F1 score (MU based)

**Fig. 17.** Best F1 score (SU based)

# 6    Conclusion

In this study, we propose the ExpertAP method, which emulates human experts by first learning general turbine operation patterns from multi-unit data and then focusing on predicting faults in the target turbine. ExpertAP also leverages the two-dimensional selection strategy in a semi-supervised learning setting to address the scarcity of high-quality anomaly labels. It also incorporates the separate embedding design to use historical anomaly labels effectively for prediction.

We validated ExpertAP using real TSI data from two thermal power plant units. For learning turbine operation patterns, we tested the reconstruction capability with window lengths of 512 and 256. Results showed that multi-unit pre-training with the two-dimensional selection strategy reduced the model's reconstruction error (MAE) by 15.41% (window length = 512) and 27.94% (window length = 256) compared to the baseline, indicating stronger pattern learning. For anomaly prediction, we evaluated the model's anomaly prediction ability after pre-training on single-unit and multi-unit data. Results showed that with the same pre-training data, the two-dimensional selection strategy and separate embedding design increased the F1 score by 23.21% and decreased MAE by 2.54% compared to the baseline, demonstrating enhanced anomaly prediction capability.

ExpertAP is data-driven and can perform anomaly prediction on devices with similar data and anomaly characteristics to turbines. In the future, we plan to test the real-time performance of our method and extend anomaly prediction tasks to other equipment in thermal power plants to contribute to safe energy generation.

## References

1. Qu, F., Liu, J., Zhu, H., et al.: Wind turbine condition monitoring based on assembled multidimensional membership functions using fuzzy inference system[J]. IEEE Trans. Industr. Inf. **16**(6), 4028–4037 (2019)
2. Gu, H., Si, F., Cui, Y., et al.: Information entropy theory for steam turbine system monitoring study. Eng. Rep. **2**(11), e12261 (2020)
3. Zhao, X., Ru, D., Wang, P., et al.: Fatigue life prediction of a supercritical steam turbine rotor based on neural networks. Eng. Fail. Anal. **127**, 105435 (2021)
4. Quintanar-Gago, D.A., Nelson, P.F., Díaz-Sánchez, Á., et al.: Assessment of steam turbine blade failure and damage mechanisms using a Bayesian network. Reliabil. Eng. Syst. Saf. **207**, 107329 (2021)
5. Chen, Z., Zhou, D., Zio, E., et al.: Adaptive transfer learning for multimode process monitoring and unsupervised anomaly detection in steam turbines. Reliabil. Eng. Syst. Saf. **234**, 109162 (2023)
6. Schlechtingen M, Santos I F, Achiche S. Wind turbine condition monitoring based on SCADA data using normal behavior models. Part 1: System description[J]. Applied Soft Computing, 2013, 13(1): 259-270
7. Chen, J., Li, J., Chen, W., et al.: Anomaly detection for wind turbines based on the reconstruction of condition parameters using stacked denoising autoencoders[J]. Renewable Energy **147**, 1469–1480 (2020)
8. Renström, N., Bangalore, P., Highcock, E.: System-wide anomaly detection in wind turbines using deep autoencoders[J]. Renewable Energy **157**, 647–659 (2020)
9. Chen, H., Liu, H., Chu, X., et al.: Anomaly detection and critical SCADA parameters identification for wind turbines based on LSTM-AE neural network[J]. Renewable Energy **172**, 829–840 (2021)

10. Zhang, C., Hu, D., Yang, T.: Anomaly detection and diagnosis for wind tur-
    bines using long short-term memory-based stacked denoising autoencoders and
    XGBoost[J]. Reliability Engineering & System Safety **222**, 108445 (2022)
11. Mahalakshmi G, Sridevi S, Rajaram S. A survey on forecasting of time series
    data[C]//2016 international conference on computing technologies and intelligent
    data engineering (ICCTIDE'16). IEEE, 2016: 1-8
12. Van Den Oord A, Dieleman S, Zen H, et al. Wavenet: A generative model for raw
    audio[J]. arXiv preprint arXiv:1609.03499, 2016, 12
13. Bai S, Kolter J Z, Koltun V. An empirical evaluation of generic convolutional and
    recurrent networks for sequence modeling[J]. arXiv preprint arXiv:1803.01271, 2018
14. Borovykh A, Bohte S, Oosterlee C W. Conditional time series forecasting with
    convolutional neural networks[J]. arXiv preprint arXiv:1703.04691, 2017
15. Salinas, D., Flunkert, V., Gasthaus, J., et al.: DeepAR: Probabilistic forecasting
    with autoregressive recurrent networks[J]. Int. J. Forecast. **36**(3), 1181–1191 (2020)
16. Rangapuram S S, Seeger M W, Gasthaus J, et al. Deep state space models for time
    series forecasting[J]. Advances in neural information processing systems, 2018, 31
17. Lim B, Zohren S, Roberts S. Recurrent neural filters: Learning independent
    bayesian filtering steps for time series prediction[C]//2020 International Joint Con-
    ference on Neural Networks (IJCNN). IEEE, 2020: 1-8
18. Vaswani A, Shazeer N, Parmar N, et al. Attention is all you need[J]. Advances in
    neural information processing systems, 2017, 30
19. Zhou H, Zhang S, Peng J, et al. Informer: Beyond efficient transformer for long
    sequence time-series forecasting[C]//Proceedings of the AAAI conference on arti-
    ficial intelligence. 2021, 35(12): 11106-11115
20. Wu, H., Xu, J., Wang, J., et al.: Autoformer: Decomposition transformers with
    auto-correlation for long-term series forecasting[J]. Adv. Neural. Inf. Process. Syst.
    **34**, 22419–22430 (2021)
21. Liu S, Yu H, Liao C, et al. Pyraformer: Low-complexity pyramidal attention for
    long-range time series modeling and forecasting[C]//International conference on
    learning representations. 2021
22. Nie, Y., Nguyen, N.H., Sinthong, P., et al.: A time series is worth 64 words: long-
    term forecasting with transformers. arXiv preprint arXiv:2211.14730 (2022)
23. Choi, K., Yi, J., Park, C., et al.: Deep learning for anomaly detection in time-series
    data: review, analysis, and guidelines. IEEE Access **9**, 120043–120065 (2021)
24. Manevitz, L.M., Yousef, M.: One-class SVMs for document classification. J. Mach.
    Learn. Res. **2**(Dec), 139–154 (2001)
25. Box, G.E.P., Pierce, D.A.: Distribution of residual autocorrelations in
    autoregressive-integrated moving average time series models. J. Am. Stat. Assoc.
    **65**(332), 1509–1526 (1970)
26. Munir, M., Siddiqui, S.A., Dengel, A., et al.: DeepAnT: a deep learning approach
    for unsupervised anomaly detection in time series. IEEE Access **7**, 1991–2005
    (2018)
27. Xing, Z., Pei, J., Dong, G., et al.: Mining sequence classifiers for early prediction. In:
    Proceedings of the 2008 SIAM International Conference on Data Mining. Society
    for Industrial and Applied Mathematics, pp. 644–655 (2008)
28. Xing, Z., Pei, J., Philip, S.Y.: Early prediction on time series: a nearest neighbor
    approach. In: IJCAI, pp. 1297–1302 (2009)
29. Ulanova, L., Yan, T., Chen, H., et al.: Efficient long-term degradation profiling
    in time series for complex physical systems. In: Proceedings of the 21th ACM
    SIGKDD International Conference on Knowledge Discovery and Data Mining, pp.
    2167–2176 (2015)

30. Yin, X.X., Miao, Y., Zhang, Y.: Time series based data explorer and stream analysis for anomaly prediction. Wireless Commun. Mob. Comput. **2022**, 5885904 (2022)
31. Ning, Z., Jiang, Z., Miao, H., et al.: MST-GNN: a multi-scale temporal-enhanced graph neural network for anomaly detection in multivariate time series. In: Li, B., Yue, L., Tao, C., Han, X., Calvanese, D., Amagasa, T. (ed.s) Asia-Pacific Web (APWeb) and Web-Age Information Management (WAIM) Joint International Conference on Web and Big Data, pp. 382–390. Springer Nature Switzerland, Cham (2022). https://doi.org/10.1007/978-3-031-25158-0_29
32. Xu, J., Wu, H., Wang, J., et al.: Anomaly transformer: Time series anomaly detection with association discrepancy. arXiv preprint arXiv:2110.02642 (2021)
33. Yun, C., Bhojanapalli, S., Rawat, A.S., et al.: Are transformers universal approximators of sequence-to-sequence functions?. arXiv preprint arXiv:1912.10077 (2019)
34. Devlin, J., Chang, M.W., Lee, K., et al.: BERT: pre-training of deep bidirectional transformers for language understanding. arXiv preprint arXiv:1810.04805 (2018)

# Positioning Error Compensation for Fully-Gear-Driven Robotic Manipulator Based on Visual Calculation

Zhi Liu[1], Jituo Li[1(✉)], Wentang Chen[1], Tingxi Xue[1], Pei Yuan[2], Dingcan Jin[2], Jiefeng Jin[2], and Yifeng Zhang[2]

[1] School of Mechanical Engineering, Zhejiang University, Hangzhou 310027, China
jituo_li@zju.edu.cn
[2] Hangzhou Boomy Intelligent Technology Co., Ltd., Hangzhou 310052, China

**Abstract.** In response to the problem of excessive positioning errors in Fully-Gear-Driven Robotic Manipulator(FGDRM) that hinders automated operations, this paper proposes a positioning error compensation technique for FGDRM based on visual calculation. A visual measurement system is established, in which methods of multi-cameras arrangement optimization and FGDRM pose calculation are proposed. Additionally, an online positioning error compensation approach based on a fuzzy neural network PID algorithm is proposed. Experimental results demonstrate that the positioning accuracy for point-to-point, straight-line, and arc trajectories is improved by over 93%, with the mean positioning error reduced from 73.39 mm to 2.93 mm. This technique provides a support for the automation of FGDRM operations.

**Keywords:** Fully-gear-driven robotic manipulator · visual pose calculation · multi-cameras arrangement · fuzzy neural network PID

## 1 Introduction

How to empower a robot having the ability of autonomously operating in deep-sea, deep space, and nuclear radiation environments is a problem of significant scientific and practical importance. Factors such as high pressure and erosion in deep-sea environments, high radiation and temperature differentials in deep space, and high radioactivity in nuclear environments [1] can easily cause electronic components operating in these environments to fail [2]. Therefore, conventional industrial robots with embedded electronic drivers and controllers on joints are usually not suitable for such physical environments. The rapid failure of the robots deployed for rescue operations at the Fukushima nuclear disaster site is a typical example. Consequently, gear-driven or wire-driven robots are commonly used in these environments. In applications, their electronic components and power devices are shielded in a safe environment, and pure mechanical transmission methods are employed to transfer power to the robot's end effectors.

X. Lan et al. (Eds.): ICIRA 2024, LNAI 15208, pp. 360–375, 2025.
https://doi.org/10.1007/978-981-96-0783-9_25

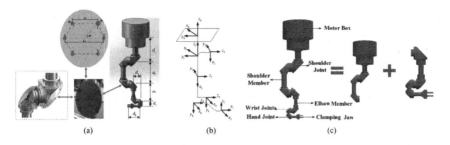

**Fig. 1.** (a) structure of FGDRM (b) joint coordinate system (c) divide-and-conquer illustration of FGDRM

This paper focuses on a Fully-Gear-Driven Robotic Manipulator(FGDRM), as shown in Fig. 1. Each joint of FGDRM is controlled by a gear transmission chain consisting of multiple bevel gears, as shown the left bottom image in Fig. 1(a), leading to cumulative positioning errors on the end effector, making it difficult to meet automatic operations. Therefore, in practical working scenarios, a master-slave teleoperation approach is often adopted, where the pose of FGDRM is manually controlled [3]. This paper proposes a method for computing and compensating the pose of FGDRM based on vision to provide a foundation for automated operations. To reduce the number of cameras, a monocular vision-based approach is employed to estimate FGDRM pose. Given the potential issues of the end effector exceeding the camera's view cone and self-occlusion of FGDRM during operation, multiple cameras are utilized, and the arrangement of the cameras is optimized to maximize the coverage of FGDRM workspace by the cameras'view cones.

The main contributions of this paper are as follows:

- A real-time vision-based pose computation method is proposed for fully-gear-driven robotic manipulator.
- A method of optimistically arranging cameras is proposed to improve the visibility and pose estimation accuracy of robotic manipulator end effector.
- A FNN-PID (Fuzzy Neural Network-Proportional Integral Derivative) based online error compensation method is proposed to significantly improve the positioning accuracy of the robotic manipulator.

## 2    Related Work

Technically, methods of robot error compensation can be classified into three categories: offline compensation, joint compensation, and online compensation.

Offline compensation, involves offline measurement of the robot's errors in different poses using devices such as laser trackers. Such data is then used to construct an error prediction model. During online application, this model compensates errors by adjusting the robot's control parameters. Offline compensation can be further divided into model-based and non-model-based.

Model-based error compensation relies on the robot's kinematic model, such as the D-H model [4], MD-H (Modified DH) [5], or local POE error model

[6] whose kinematic geometric parameters are usually identified by using optimization methods like least squares [7,8], Levenberg-Marquardt algorithm [9], Extended Kalman Filtering (EKF) [10], or manta ray foraging optimization algorithm [11].

Non-model-based error compensation is proposed to address the complexity and coupling of various factors that affect robot positioning errors. In this case, the robot is treated as a "black box", and methods such as curve fitting [12], spatial interpolation [13], and neural networks [14,15] are used to predict and compensate for errors under different robot inputs.

Joint compensation is used to eliminate joint errors in robots. It involves estimating the rotary joint axes [16] and measuring the actual joint angles [17,18] and providing feedback to the controller for corrective compensation. While joint compensation can eliminate joint errors, it does not address the influence of kinematic parameter errors and other factors on positioning errors.

Online compensation measures robot's end-effector pose, and feedback to the controller to compensate the pose error in a closed-loop. Laser trackers offer high measurement accuracy [19,20], but they are expensive. Optical cameras have emerged as a new research direction. Such as using optical measurement instrument together with 3D-piezo-actuator to achieve online compensation [21, 22], or using stereo vision to guide the pose adjustment in a closed-loop manner [23]. Different filters were used to reduce the pose measurement error [3,24], due to image noise, vibrations etc.

However, due to the structural differences between FGDRM and conventional industrial robots, existing methods for conventional industrial robots are unable to achieve good results for FGDRM. The main reason is that the sources of positioning error of FGDRM are complex and coupled with each other, the constantly accumulated gear transmission error and the error of flexibility factors with large fluctuations make it difficult to establish an accurate error model.

Online compensation does not care about the complex sources of error and error models of the manipulator. The positioning accuracy after compensation is relevant to the accuracy of the position and posture measuring device, but irrelevant to the original positioning accuracy of the manipulator. This matches the error characteristics of FGDRM. However there is still a lack of online error compensation for FGDRM. We propose an online compensation method based on visual calculation for FGDRM in this paper.

## 3 Methodology

### 3.1 Overview

In our approach, we perform vison-based online error compensation (close-loop) after identifying the dynamic parameters of FGDRM and performing kinematic compensation of FGDRM (open-loop). Our vision-based close-loop method measures and corrects the actual posture of FGDRM. It mainly composes of three modules as shown the blue grey filled text boxes in Fig. 2, with their functions briefly described as follows.

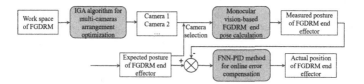

**Fig. 2.** Overall framework of our approach

Firstly, we propose a monocular vision-based method to calculate the positions of red-colored screws on FGDRM, and based on which we calculate the posture of FGDRM. Other than monocular method, binocular or multicular methods might be used. However, the extreme physical application environments can easily interfere with vision camera and lens components, affecting image quality and even damaging camera components. The cameras need to be reinforced to withstand radiation. But the price of such camera can still reach tens of thousands of dollars. Considering economic factors, we propose a monocular vison-based method to monitor the posture of FGDRM. It will be detailed in Sect. 3.2.

Secondly, considering the issues existing in actual measurement, such as the end of the robotic arm leaving the camera's field of view or being obscured by the main body of the robotic arm itself. We adopt multiple cameras and optimize their layout with improved genetic algorithm (IGA) to make their visual cones cover the work space of FGDRM as well as possible. It will be detailed in Sect. 3.3.

Thirdly, we propose a fuzzy neural network PID (PNN-PID) method that takes the measured FGDRM posture as feedback to correct the actual posture of FGDRM to approach the expected posture, as will be detailed in Sect. 3.4.

## 3.2    Monocular Based Pose Calculation for FGDRM End Effector

Taking advantage of linking screws on the joint end caps, we stick red circular markers on the top of these screws, as shown in Fig. 1(a), and calculate the spatial pose of these markers by using monocular-based computer vision approach. To improve the calculation accuracy of FGDRM's end effector pose, based on the FGDRM's serial structures and theoretical pose error analysis, we incorporate the pose result of the third joint into the end effector pose calculation. Kalman filter is used to smooth the end effector pose estimation.

**Preliminary Calculation of FGDRM's End Effector Pose.** As shown the D-H model of FGDRM in Fig. 1(b), the transformation between adjacent coordinate systems on joints is represented by the transformation matrix $_i^{i-1}T$, the transformation matrix of the end effector coordinate system 6 relative to the base coordinate system 0 is calculated as

$$_6^0T = T\left(\theta_1, \theta_2, \theta_3, \theta_4, \theta_5, \theta_6\right) = {}_1^0T\,{}_2^1T\,{}_3^2T\,{}_4^3T\,{}_5^4T\,{}_6^5T \tag{1}$$

To calculate the pose of end effector, firstly the centers of red markers are detected from the image; secondly, by considering the actual spatial relative arrangement between these red markers, the EPnP algorithm [25] is employed to calculate the pose of the end effector.

To evaluate the pose calculation accuracy of the aforementioned method, a simulation environment was set up in software of Unity. The motion of a virtual FGDRM was controlled programmatically, and the pose of FGDRM's end effector was calculated in real-time from images captured by a virtual camera. The measurement error is shown in Fig. 3(a). The average positional measurement error was 1.68 mm, and could be calculated within 0.05 s. However, the error exhibited big fluctuations within a range of 0.1 to 3.86 mm, mainly due to the noise in images and instability in the pose calculation, which will be optimized as follows.

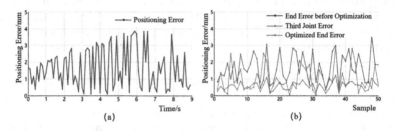

(a)                                                        (b)

**Fig. 3.** Virtually evaluate robotic arm position measurement errors. (a) Preliminary positioning error in calculating end effector pose. (b) Positioning error after using the divide-and-conquer method

**Optimization of End Effector Pose Calculation Based on Divide-and-Conquer Method.** Due to the serial structure of the FGDRM, the positional errors of the upper joints(such as the 1st, 2nd, 3rd joint) are expected to be smaller than those of the lower joints(i.e. the 4th, 5th and 6th joint). On the other hand, for a mechanical manipulator with fewer than 6 joints, its inverse kinematic solution of the end effector poses exhibits redundant parameters. Therefore, as shown in Fig. 1(c), we split the 6-joint FGDRM into two 3-joint mechanical arms using the third joint as a boundary. The pose analysis is first performed separately for the two arms, avoiding the use of pose terms with larger errors. Subsequently, the two arms are combined to obtain a more accurate end effector pose. The specific procedure is as follows:

Step 1: Obtain the transformation matrices of the end effector and the third joint against the camera, ${}^{cam}_{6}T$, ${}^{cam}_{3}T$, using the method. The conversion matrices from the stationary camera to the base coordinate system of the manipulator, denoted as ${}^{0}_{cam}T$, can be obtained through hand-eye calibration. Then, we have:

$$
{}^{0}_{3}T = {}^{0}_{cam}T {}^{cam}_{3}T \tag{2}
$$

$$\begin{matrix} 0 \\ 6 \end{matrix} T = \begin{matrix} 0 \\ cam \end{matrix} T \begin{matrix} cam \\ 6 \end{matrix} T \qquad (3)$$

Step 2: The FGDRM is divided into two 3-axis parts with their end effector poses being as $\begin{smallmatrix}0\\3\end{smallmatrix}T$, $\begin{smallmatrix}3\\6\end{smallmatrix}T = \begin{smallmatrix}0\\6\end{smallmatrix}T (\begin{smallmatrix}0\\3\end{smallmatrix}T)^{-1}$, respectively;

Step 3: Based on the error analysis as will be discussed in Sect. 3.3, select the more accurate data with relatively small error from $\begin{smallmatrix}0\\3\end{smallmatrix}T$ and $\begin{smallmatrix}3\\6\end{smallmatrix}T$, to calculate the pose of the two 3-axis arms are inversely calculated. Denoting the the joint angles for the two arms as $\theta_1$, $\theta_2$ and $\theta_3$ and $\theta_4$, $\theta_5$ and $\theta_6$, respectively. Then the end effector pose of the 6-axis FGDRM is computed as:

$$T = T(\theta_1, \theta_2, \theta_3, \theta_4, \theta_5, \theta_6) \qquad (4)$$

With the above method, the optimization of end effector pose calculation was performed on 50 samples of the robotic arm positions. The positioning errors before and after the divide-and-conquer optimization are shown in Fig. 3(b). After optimization, the mean visual positioning error decreased from 1.682 mm to 0.591 mm, and the standard deviation reduced from 1.13 mm to 0.256 mm.

**Smooth Optimization Based on Kalman Filtering.** During the motion of a FGDRM, factors such as end-effector vibration, imaging noise, and motion blur can disturb the pose measurement. We employ a Kalman filter to smooth the results, resulting in Fig. 4(a). The mean position measurement error is reduced from 1.682 mm to 0.873 mm. The comprehensive evaluation of the divide-and-conquer based optimization and filtering smoothing results in Fig. 4(b). The mean position measurement error is reduced from 0.591 mm to 0.378 mm.

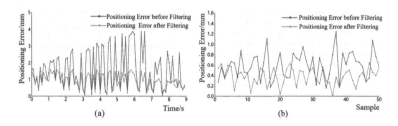

(a)                                (b)

**Fig. 4.** Virtually estimate position measurement errors of end-effector before and after filtering: (a) filtering and smoothing optimization effects (b) effects the combination of divide-and-conquer computation and filtering smoothing

### 3.3   Cameras Arrangement Optimization Based on IGA

We enhance the visibility coverage and pose measurement accuracy of the FGDRM's end-effector by optimizing the arrangement of cameras.

**Analysis of End-Effector Pose Measurement Error and End-Effector Visibility.** Taking the perspective projection model as the camera imaging model, as shown in Fig. 5(b), the projection involves the transformation among four coordinate systems: pixel coordinate system, $O - uv$, image coordinate system, $O - xy$, camera coordinate system, $O_C - X_C Y_C Z_C$, and world coordinate system, $O_W - X_W Y_W Z_W$. Based on the projection model and the analysis of the red markers arrangement, we set the theoretical error model of the visual pose estimation as

$$\begin{cases} \partial d = -\mu d^2 \partial n / (l_0 f) \\ \partial l_0 = d\mu \partial n / f \\ \partial \gamma = 2\Delta \partial n / \sqrt{2l_0^2 - \Delta^2 n^2} \\ \partial \alpha = \partial n \Delta_A \end{cases} \tag{5}$$

where $\partial d$ represents the positional error in the $Zc$ axis direction; $\partial l_0$ denotes the positional error in the $Xc/Yc$ axis direction; $\partial \gamma$ represents the attitude error in roll angle around the $Zc$ axis; $\partial \alpha$ corresponds to the attitude error in yaw/pitch angles around the $Xc/Yc$ axes; $\mu$ is the pixel size; d is the distance from the target object to plane $O_C - X_C Y_C$; $f$ is the focal length; $n$ is the number of pixels between adjacent marker points in the image; the pixel resolution is denoted as $\Delta = \mu d / f$; $l_0$ is the distance between adjacent markers; $\partial n$ represents the localization accuracy of the marker points in the image, and $\Delta_A$ denotes the partial derivative of $\alpha$ with respect to $n$.

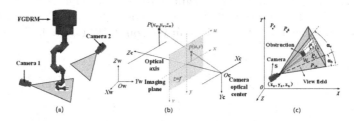

**Fig. 5.** Pose measurement of FGDRM end effector: (a) measurement system (b) camera model (c) visibility model of camera

According to the real experimental environment, we have $\mu = 2.4\mu m, f = 12mm, l_0 = 50mm$, the theoretical measurement errors for each component of the pose can be obtained, as shown in Table 1.

From equation (5) and Table 1, the following four points can be drawn. (a) The position error in the Zc-axis direction is greater than that in the Xc/Yc-axis direction, and the yaw angle error is larger than the roll angle error. (b) the measurement error is inverse to the distance between adjacent markers. (c) Cameras with longer focal lengths, smaller pixel sizes, and lower distortion have lower measurement errors. (d) the relative position between robot end and the camera also affects the measurement error.

The visibility model of the camera is illustrated in Fig. 5(c). Whether an object is being imaged by the camera depends on two factors. One is whether the object is within the camera's viewing frustum. The other is whether there are any occlusions between the object and the camera. Each occluding object creates a invisible region, as the white regions in Fig. 5(c).

**Table 1.** Position Measurement Errors Pre- and Post-Optimization

| distance $d$/mm | Positioning Errors | | Orientation Errors | |
|---|---|---|---|---|
| | $Z$ $\partial d$/mm | $X/Y$ $\partial l_0$/mm | $\partial \gamma/°$ | $\partial \alpha/°$ |
| 500 | 0.429 | 0.394 | 0.098 | 0.201 |
| 1000 | 0.715 | 0.689 | 0.197 | 0.395 |
| 1500 | 1.859 | 1.283 | 0.295 | 0.591 |
| 2000 | 3.861 | 2.377 | 0.393 | 0.788 |

**IGA Algorithm for Cameras Arrangement Optimization.** Camera arrangement optimization considers both the accuracy of end effector's pose measurement and the visibility of red markers on joints. Given that genetic algorithms have shown promising results in solving problems with large and complex search spaces, they can be utilized for optimizing cameras arrangement. However, genetic algorithms often suffer from limitations such as strong global search capabilities but weak local search capabilities, premature convergence, and the potential disruption of excellent genes by random crossover strategies. In this regard, we propose an Improved Genetic Algorithm (IGA), as shown in Fig. 6.

To addresses the issue of "destruction of excellent genes" in classical genetic algorithms, we propose an "elitism" strategy. Specifically, if the fitness of all individuals in the new generation is lower than that of the best individual in the previous generation, the best individual from the previous generation is retained in the new colony. The lowest fitness individual in the new colony is eliminated to maintain the stability of the colony size. This ensures that the best individual is not compromised. Moreover, to address the problem of "poor local search capability" in classical genetic algorithms, we leverage the strong local search capability of nonlinear optimization to obtain the global optimal solution. Specifically, in the new colony, we use each individual as an initial value and apply a sequential least squares programming algorithm for nonlinear optimization. The optimized individuals form the final new generation colony.

In IGA, taking the number of cameras and their positions as the parameters to be optimized, a scoring system serviced as fitness function is designed based on the analysis of pose measurement errors and markers' visibility. The scoring items include camera field of view, target relative distance, target relative position, and target relative orientation. The total score of the $i$-th camera for the $j$-th robotic arm state of FGDRM, $S_{ij}$, is calculated as

$$S_{ij} = s_1 + s_2 + s_3 + s_4 \quad i = 1, 2 \cdots n \; j = 1, 2 \cdots m \tag{6}$$

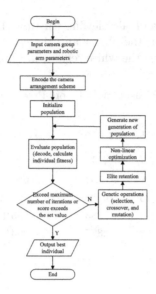

**Fig. 6.** IGA Algorithm Flowchart

where $s_1, s_2, s_3$, and $s_4$ denote the scores for the four individual item.

The evaluation score, $S_j$, for the camera group with respect to the $j$-th FGDRM state is determined by taking the highest score among all cameras as

$$S_j = \max(S_{1j}, S_{2j}...S_{nj}) \tag{7}$$

The final score represented by the fitness value $S$, is calculated as the average score across all FGDRM states ($m$ in total):

$$S = (\sum_{1}^{m} S_j)/m \tag{8}$$

The optimization process is performed by sequentially setting the number of cameras to 1, 2, 3, and 4, respectively. The changes in colony fitness during the iteration process is illustrated in Fig. 7.

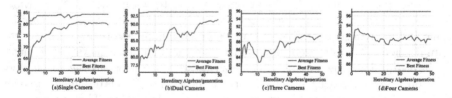

**Fig. 7.** Optimizing camera arrangement with different numbers of cameras

To verify the effectiveness of our approach, we compare the parameters obtained from the pre-optimized scheme, based on manual expertise, with those obtained from the IGA algorithm, representing the post-optimized scheme. The results listed in Table 2 indicate a significant improvement in coverage rate for the optimized camera arrangement. Simultaneously, the mean measurement error has decreased. From the experimental data, it can be observed a two-camera configuration already yields relatively low mean measurement errors.

**Table 2.** Coverage Rate and Mean Measurement Error Before and After Camera Placement Optimization

| Metrics | | 1 camera | 2 cameras | 3 cameras | 4 cameras |
|---|---|---|---|---|---|
| Before optimized | Visibility Coverage Rate | 73.33 | 83.33 | 90 | 93.33 |
| | Mean Measurement Error /mm | 2.07 | 1.84 | 1.52 | 1.36 |
| After optimized | Visibility coverage rate /% | 93.33 | 100 | 100 | 100 |
| | Mean measurement error /mm | 1.03 | 0.92 | 0.88 | 0.73 |

### 3.4   Online Error Compensation of FGDRM with FNN-PID

After visually computing the end-effector pose, we send the pose error between the calculated result and the desired value to the online compensation controller, which drives the motors to control the joint motion of the FGDRM.

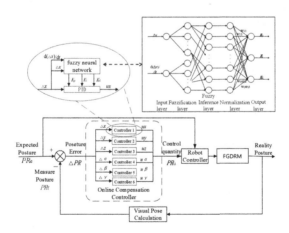

**Fig. 8.** FNN-PID based online error compensation controller

We adopt the widely proven PID method for compensating posture error of FGDRM. However, the classical PID has a weakness that once the control coefficients are determined, they cannot be changed during the control process. It affects the system's adaptive and anti-interference capabilities. In this paper, we propose Fuzzy Neural Network PID (FNN-PID) control algorithm to adaptively adjust the parameters of PID in real-time. As shown in Fig. 8, the pose error is represented by six independent parameters, each corresponds to an individual FNN-PID controller. Taking Controller 1 for example, the inputs are the error $\Delta x$ in the $x$ direction and its rate of change $d(\Delta x)/dt$; they are first fed into the fuzzy neural network to generate three PID control coefficients: $K_p$, $K_i$ and $K_d$. These coefficients are used to adjust the PID controller, which then outputs the control signal $ux$, thus the error of $x$ is adaptively compensated. The fuzzy neural network consists of five layers: the input layer, fuzzification layer, fuzzy inference layer, normalization layer, and output layer. The calculation process for each layer is as follows:

- **Input layer** consists of two nodes representing the input variables. The input values $In_m^{(1)} = x_m$, and the output values $Out_{mn}^{(1)} = x_{mn} = x_m$, where $x_m$ represents the $m$-th input variable. In this case, they are $\Delta x$ and $d(\Delta x)/dt$. The variable $x_{mn}$ is the $m$-th input variable value on the $n$-th fuzzy subset of 7 in total.
- **Fuzzification layer** consists of 14 nodes that serve as membership functions in fuzzy control. The inputs to this layer are the outputs of the input layer: $In_{mn}^{(2)} = Out_{mn}^{(1)}$. The outputs represents the membership degrees and are denoted as $A_m^n(x_m)$ with their calculation as follows:

$$Out_{mn}^{(2)} = \exp\left\{-(x_m - c_{mn})^2 / (\sigma_{mn})^2\right\} = A_m^n(x_m) \qquad (9)$$

where $c_{mn}$ and $\sigma_{mn}$ represent the center and width of the membership function for the $m$-th input value on the $n$-th variable, respectively.
- **Fuzzy inference layer** consists of 49 nodes. Each represents a fuzzy rule, its inputs are given by $In_m^{(3)} = Out_{mn}^{(2)}$. The outputs are obtained by

$$Out_l^{(3)} = A_1^{n_1}(x_1) \times A_2^{n_2}(x_2) \qquad (10)$$

where $A_1^{n_1}(x_1)$ represents the membership degree of the first input variable in the $n_1$ fuzzy subset, and $A_2^{n_2}(x_2)$ represents the membership degree of the second input variable in the $A_2^{n_2}(x_2)$ fuzzy subset.
- **Normalization Layer**: It has 49 nodes. Its input is $In_l^{(4)} = Out_l^{(3)}$, and its outputs are

$$Out_l^{(4)} = Out_l^{(3)} / \sum_{i=1}^{49} Out_l^{(3)} \qquad (11)$$

- **Output Layer**: It contains 3 nodes and performs defuzzification operations. Its input is $In_l^{(5)} = Out_l^{(4)}$, and its outputs $K_p$, $K_i$ and $K_d$ are calculated as:

$$Out_k^{(5)} = \sum_{l=1}^{49} w_{lk} Out_l^{(4)} \qquad (12)$$

where $w_{lk}$ represents the network weights in the output layer. Thus we have:

$$K_p = Out_1^{(5)}, K_i = Out_2^{(5)}, K_d = Out_3^{(5)} \qquad (13)$$

We evaluated the effectiveness of FNN-PID-based online compensation algorithm through simulation experiments. A 5-seconds FGDRM motion simulation sequence data were constructed, and the simulation step size was set to 0.1 s based on the manipulator motion speed. Radom errors on D-H parameters and joint angles were added in creating the sequence data. The online compensation result of FNN-PID-based method is shown in Fig. 9. For comparison, online compensation results by using BP-PID (Back Propogation PID) and FPID(Fuzzy PID) were also provided in Fig. 9. Compared with the other two methods, FNN-PID has better convergence performance and speed.

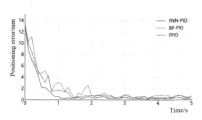

**Fig. 9.** Evaluating effectiveness of FNN-PID

# 4   Experiments

## 4.1   Experimental Platform

As shown in Fig. 10, the experiment platform consists of a FGDRM and its controller, a host computer, a camera system, and a laser tracker. Two cameras are utilized. A Faro Vantage E6 Max laser tracker is used to track the shperical maker attached on the end effector of FGDRM to get the ground truth pose.

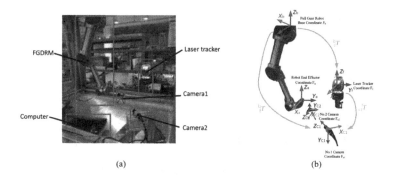

(a)                                                    (b)

**Fig. 10.** (a) The experiment platform (b) The system for the experiment

## 4.2   Measurement Experiments

Experiments were carried out to validate the effectiveness of our pose measurement and the optimization of camera arrangement for FGDRM. The experimental procedure was as follows:

Two cameras are arranged with the method in Sect. 3. In the experiment, 125 sampling points that well cover the working space of the robotic manipulator are selected by either adjusting the joint angles or adjusting the end effector position. Their spatial distributions are shown in Fig. 11(a) and Fig. 11(b), respectively. The results are listed in Table 3, as well as visualized by coloring the sampling points in Fig. 11. It can be drawn from the experimental data that first, the mean measurement error in the real-world experiments was 1.58 mm in joint space and 1.83 mm in Cartesian space, confirming the effectiveness of our measurement algorithm.

**Table 3.** Analysis of position measurement errors

| Spatial types | Min/mm | Max/mm | Mean/mm | Standard Deviation/mm |
|---|---|---|---|---|
| Joint space | 0.74 | 2.54 | 1.58 | 0.401 |
| Cartesian space | 1.12 | 2.61 | 1.83 | 0.359 |

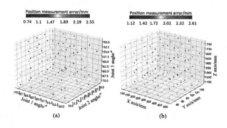

(a)                                    (b)

**Fig. 11.** Distribution of position measurement errors

## 4.3   Online Compensation Experiment

To validate the practical effectiveness of the online error compensation system, comparison of end effector errors with and without error compensation steps were experimented.

**Table 4.** Positioning Error Before and After Error Compensation

|  | Min/mm | Max/mm | Mean/mm | Standard Deviation/mm | Accuracy Improvement/% |
|---|---|---|---|---|---|
| Before compensation | 39.63 | 96.78 | 73.39 | 12.14 | - |
| After compensation | 0.09 | 5.82 | 2.93 | 1.31 | 96.01 |

**Point-To-Point Error.** The desired pose is sent to the controller, which drives the FGDRM to perform point-to-point movement under the online compensation state. After $0.5\,\text{s}$ of online compensation, the real position of the end effector, $P_f$, is obtained by using the laser tracker. With the expected position being $P_b$, the positioning error $\Delta P'$ is calculated as $\Delta P' = \|P_b - P_f\|$.

A total of 100 FGDRM poses were randomly selected from the 125 sampling points as the experimental samples. The variation of positioning errors is shown in Fig. 12(a) and Table 4. The experimental data demonstrate a significant improvement in the error metrics after online compensation. The mean positioning error decreased from $73.39\,\text{mm}$ to $2.93\,\text{mm}$, resulting in a 96.01% improvement.

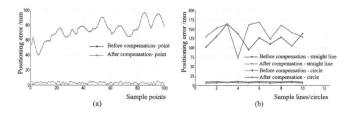

**Fig. 12.** Positioning errors before and after compensation

**Linear Motion Error.** The desired straight-line trajectory is sent to the controller, which drives the FGDRM to perform straight-line motion under online compensation state. At $m$ evenly spaced intervals, the laser tracker records the real position of the FGDRM's end effector. Each desired straight-line trajectory needs to be run $n$ times. The position trajectory error $AT$ is defined as the maximum deviation between $m$ positions on the desired trajectory and the centroid of the corresponding measured point set.

Ten linear trajectories were selected as experimental samples, and the errors are shown in Fig. 12(b). The error mean decreased from $123.72\,\text{mm}$ to $6.99\,\text{mm}$, resulting in a 94.35% reduction in errors.

**Circular Motion Error.** The FGDRM is controlled to perform multiple circular motions. Similar to the error measurement in linear motion, ten arc trajectories were selected as experimental samples, and the results are shown in

Fig. 12(b). The mean error decreased from 140.40 mm to 9.66 mm, resulting in a 93.11% reduction in errors.

As proved by the experimental results, our method effectively improves the motion accuracy of FGDRM, which takes an important step towards the automatic manipulation of FGDRM.

## 5    Conclusions

This paper addresses the issue of excessive positioning errors in fully-gear-driven robotic manipulators(FGDRM), which hinders their automation capabilities. A vision-based error compensation technique for FGDRM has been proposed. It utilizes real-time calculation of the robotic manipulators's end effector pose using monocular vision as feedback. The technique includes an improved genetic algorithm-based camera arrangement optimization method to enhance camera visibility for FGDRM. Additionally, it establishes a closed-loop system for online error compensation using a fuzzy neural network-based PID controller, ensuring stable and efficient error compensation.

Experimental results demonstrate significant improvements in positioning accuracy after applying the proposed error compensation technique to FGDRM. The accuracy of point-to-point positioning increased by 96.01%, linear trajectory precision improved by 94.35%, and arc trajectory precision increased by 93.11%. Our method potentially provides a solid foundation for FGDRM automation tasks.

**Acknowledgement.** This work was supported in part by "Leading Goose" R&D Program of Zhejiang Province, China (No.2022C01054, No.2023C01067).

## References

1. Field, K.G., Remec, I., Le Pape, Y.: Radiation effects in concrete for nuclear power plants-part I: quantification of radiation exposure and radiation effects. Nucl. Eng. Des. **282**, 126–143 (2015)
2. Schwank, J.R., et al.: Radiation effects in MOS oxides. IEEE Trans. Nucl. Sci. **55**(4), 1833–1853 (2008)
3. Geffard, F., et al.: Tao 2000 v2 computer-assisted force feedback telemanipulators used as maintenance and production tools at the areva nc-la hague fuel recycling plant. J. Field Robot. **29**(1), 161–174 (2012)
4. Denavit, J., Hartenberg, R.: A kinematic notation for lower-pair mechanisms based on matrices. J. Appl. Mech. **22**(2), 215–221 (1955)
5. Zhu, W., Mei, B., Ke, Y.: Kinematic modeling and parameter identification of a new circumferential drilling machine for aircraft assembly. Int. J. Adv. Manuf. Technol. **72**, 1143–1158 (2014)
6. Zhang, X., Song, Y., Yang, Y., Pan, H.: Stereo vision based autonomous robot calibration. Robot. Auton. Syst. **93**, 43–51 (2017)
7. Zhuang, H., Roth, Z.S., Wang, K.: Robot calibration by mobile camera systems. J. Robot. Syst. **11**(3), 155–167 (1994)

8. Zak, G., Benhabib, B., Fenton, R., Saban, I.: Application of the weighted least squares parameter estimation method to the robot calibration. J. Mech. Des. **116**(3), 890–893 (1994)

9. Lightcap, C., Hamner, S., Schmitz, T., Banks, S.: Improved positioning accuracy of the PA10-6CE robot with geometric and flexibility calibration. IEEE Trans. Rob. **24**(2), 452–456 (2008)

10. Omodei, A., Legnani, G., Adamini, R.: Three methodologies for the calibration of industrial manipulators: experimental results on a scara robot. J. Robot. Syst. **17**(6), 291–307 (2000)

11. Xu, X., et al.: A novel calibration method for robot kinematic parameters based on improved manta ray foraging optimization algorithm. IEEE Trans. Instrum. Meas. **72**(7501611), 1–11 (2023)

12. Alici, G., Shirinzadeh, B.: A systematic technique to estimate positioning errors for robot accuracy improvement using laser interferometry based sensing. Mech. Mach. Theory **40**(8), 879–906 (2005)

13. Bai, Y.: On the comparison of model-based and modeless robotic calibration based on a fuzzy interpolation method. Int. J. Adv. Manuf. Technol. **31**, 1243–1250 (2007)

14. Angelidis, A., Vosniakos, G.C.: Prediction and compensation of relative position error along industrial robot end-effector paths. Int. J. Precis. Eng. Manuf. **15**, 63–73 (2014)

15. Nguyen, H.X., Cao, H.Q., Nguyen, T.T., Tran, T.N.C., Tran, H.N., Jeon, J.W.: Improving robot precision positioning using a neural network based on levenBERG Marquardt-Apso algorithm. IEEE Access **9**, 75415–75425 (2021)

16. Boldsaikhan, E.: Measuring and estimating rotary joint axes of an articulated robot. IEEE Trans. Instrum. Meas. **69**(10), 8279–8287 (2020)

17. DeVlieg, R., Szallay, T.: Improved accuracy of unguided articulated robots. SAE Int. J. Aerosp. **2**(2009-01-3108), 40–45 (2009)

18. Saund, B., DeVlieg, R.: High accuracy articulated robots with CNC control systems. SAE Int. J. Aerospace **6**(2013-01-2292), 780–784 (2013)

19. Yang, J., Wang, D., Fan, B., Dong, D., Zhou, W.: Online absolute pose compensation and steering control of industrial robot based on six degrees of freedom laser measurement. Opt. Eng. **56**(3), 034111–034111 (2017)

20. Moeller, C., et al.: Real time pose control of an industrial robotic system for machining of large scale components in aerospace industry using laser tracker system. SAE Int. J. Aerosp. **10**(2), 100–108 (2017)

21. Lehmann, C., Pellicciari, M., Drust, M., Gunnink, J.W.: Machining with industrial robots: the COMET project approach. In: Neto, P., Moreira, A.P. (eds.) WRSM 2013. CCIS, vol. 371, pp. 27–36. Springer, Heidelberg (2013). https://doi.org/10.1007/978-3-642-39223-8_3

22. Schneider, U., So, O., Drust, M., Robertsson, A., Hägele, M., Johansson, R., et al.: Integrated approach to robotic machining with macro/micro-actuation. Robot. Comput. Integr. Manuf. **30**(6), 636–647 (2014)

23. Gharaaty, S., Shu, T., Xie, W.F., Joubair, A., Bonev, I.A.: Accuracy enhancement of industrial robots by on-line pose correction. In: 2017 2nd Asia-Pacific Conference on Intelligent Robot Systems (ACIRS), pp. 214–220. IEEE (2017)

24. Shu, T., Gharaaty, S., Xie, W., Joubair, A., Bonev, I.A.: Dynamic path tracking of industrial robots with high accuracy using photogrammetry sensor. IEEE/ASME Trans. Mechatron. **23**(3), 1159–1170 (2018)

25. Lepetit, V., Moreno-Noguer, F., Fua, P.: Epnp: an accurate o(n) solution to the pnp problem. Int. J. Comput. Vision **81**, 155–166 (2009). https://doi.org/10.1007/s11263-008-0152-6

# A Deformation Error Prediction Method for Industrial Robots Based on Error Superposition

Zhenya He[1,2(✉)], Haolun Yuan[1], and Xianmin Zhang[1,2]

[1] Guangdong Provincial Key Laboratory of Precision Equipment and Manufacturing Technology, South China University of Technology, Guangzhou 510640, China
mezhyhe@scut.edu.cn

[2] School of Mechanical and Automotive Engineering, South China University of Technology, Guangzhou 510640, China

**Abstract.** To improve the precision of robot machining, a deformation error prediction method for industrial robots based on error superposition, Deformation Error Prediction Fusion Model (DEPFM), is proposed in this paper. Based on the approximate linear relationship between the external force and the deformation error of the robot, the superposition principle of the deformation error is derived. Based on the Extreme Learning Machine (ELM), a Deformation Error Prediction sub-Model (DEPsM) is established, which is suitable for special external force. Finally, DEPsM is fused to get DEPFM for any external force according to the superposition principle of deformation errors. After verifying its effectiveness through simulation, the deformation error prediction experiment is carried out on an industrial robot, and the DEPFM is compared with the traditional stiffness model. The experimental results show that DEPFM can accurately predict the deformation error of the robot with the average prediction error of 30 $\mu$m and the prediction accuracy of 93.7%. Compared with the traditional stiffness model, the average prediction error is reduced by 63.8%.

**Keywords:** Industrial Robots · Deformation Error · Error Superposition

## 1 Introduction

With the reduction of manufacturing cost and improvement of precision, robots have been widely used in various fields of society [1, 2]. Because of its high flexibility and versatility, the robot has taken the place of CNC machine tools in some industrial processing fields [3, 4]. But the special open-chain serial structure results in the weak stiffness of the robot, the deformation error will occur when the load is large, which limits its further development in the field of milling [5, 6]. Many scholars have studied the deformation error of the robot, and proposed many solutions, mainly by optimizing the structure of the robot itself to reduce the deformation error, on-line measurement and compensation of deformation error and off-line optimization based on stiffness model [7]. Because the first two schemes are expensive and difficult to implement, off-line optimization based on stiffness model is the main solution.

X. Lan et al. (Eds.): ICIRA 2024, LNAI 15208, pp. 376–391, 2025.
https://doi.org/10.1007/978-981-96-0783-9_26

Abele et al. [8] first putted forward the traditional joint stiffness model of the robot, and many scholars have carried out research based on it. Chen et al. [9] proposed the Normal Stiffness Performance Index (NSPI) to evaluate the stiffness performance of a robot in a given pose and optimized the pose of a 6-dof industrial robot in milling applications by maximizing the NSPI. NSPI is also used to obtain the optimal cutting tool feed direction. Zargabashi et al. [10] used Jacobian condition number as an index to improve the joint velocity distribution to optimize the processing performance of the robot. Li et al. [11] proposed a joint stiffness identification algorithm and deformation error compensation algorithm for serial robots. Klimchik et al. [12] incorporated gravity and end load into the stiffness modeling process and verified the accuracy of the stiffness model by experiments. Yang et al. [13] proposed an identification method based on servo motor current and corresponding position displacement, which can obtain joint stiffness more accurately.

The traditional joint stiffness model is only suitable for robots with strong link stiffness because it ignores the influence of link stiffness. If a machine learning algorithm is used instead of the joint stiffness model to predict deformation error, it will theoretically have higher prediction accuracy and wider applicability with sufficient data, because the machine learning algorithm does not rely on any assumptions and its prediction effect is only related to the quality of the error data. However, due to the difficulty of collecting data (especially force) and the large amount of data needed, there are few researches on using machine learning algorithm to predict deformation error. The method proposed in this paper uses machine learning algorithm to predict deformation error of robot, which has higher prediction accuracy and wider applicability than traditional methods, the training process of the model is optimized by the superposition principle of deformation error, and the difficulty of data collection is reduced.

To improve the precision of robot machining, a deformation error prediction method for industrial robots based on error superposition, Deformation Error Prediction Fusion Model (DEPFM), is proposed in this paper. In Sect. 2, the superposition principle of deformation error is derived based on the approximate linear relationship between the external force and deformation error. In Sect. 3, a deformation error prediction model, DEPsM, is proposed, which is suitable for special external force. Based on the superposition principle of deformation error and the DEPsM, the DEPFM is proposed. To verify its effectiveness, simulation experiment is carried out in Sect. 4. In Sect. 5, the deformation error prediction experiment is carried out on the industrial robot, and the DEPFM is compared with the traditional stiffness model.

# 2 Superposition Principle of Deformation Error

## 2.1 Traditional Robot Joint Stiffness Model

Industrial robots consist of links and joints. Because links and joints are non-rigid objects, when under load, elastic deformation of the robot will happen, forming deformation error. Because the stiffness of the links is much larger than that of the joint, the traditional stiffness model regards the links as rigid body, neglecting the deformation of the links, that is, the deformation error of the robot is caused by the torsion of the joints.

Robot positive kinematics based on exponential product equation

$$g_{st}(\boldsymbol{\theta}) = e^{\hat{\xi}_1\theta_1} e^{\hat{\xi}_2\theta_2} \cdots e^{\hat{\xi}_n\theta_n} g_{st}(0) \tag{1}$$

Where $\boldsymbol{\xi}_i$ is the joint movement screw.

According to the principle of virtual work, the relationship between joint torque and external force can be obtained

$$\boldsymbol{\tau} = \boldsymbol{J}^T \boldsymbol{F}_s = \boldsymbol{J}^T \begin{bmatrix} \boldsymbol{p}_f \times \boldsymbol{f} \\ \boldsymbol{f} \end{bmatrix} \tag{2}$$

Where $\boldsymbol{\tau}$ is the robot joint torque, $\boldsymbol{J}$ is the robot Jacobian matrix, $\boldsymbol{F}_s$ is the force screw, $\boldsymbol{p}_f$ is the robot force point coordinates, $\boldsymbol{f}$ is the external force vector.

The relationship between the end-point velocity and the joint angular velocity of the robot

$$\delta \boldsymbol{p} = [-\hat{\boldsymbol{p}}, I]\boldsymbol{J}\delta\boldsymbol{\theta} \tag{3}$$

Where $\delta \boldsymbol{p}$ is the velocity of the end point, which can be regarded as the tiny displacement of the end point. $\delta\boldsymbol{\theta}$ is the angular velocity of the robot joint, which can be regarded as the tiny angular displacement of the joint. $\hat{\boldsymbol{p}}$ is the skew-symmetric matrix of $\boldsymbol{p}$.

The relationship between joint stiffness and joint torque

$$\boldsymbol{\tau} = \boldsymbol{K}_\theta \delta\boldsymbol{\theta} \tag{4}$$

Where $\boldsymbol{K}_\theta$ is the Joint stiffness diagonal matrix.

By combining Eq. (2), (3), and (4), it can be concluded

$$\delta \boldsymbol{p} = [-\hat{\boldsymbol{p}}, I]\boldsymbol{J}\boldsymbol{K}_\theta^{-1}\boldsymbol{J}^T \begin{bmatrix} \boldsymbol{p}_f \times \boldsymbol{f} \\ \boldsymbol{f} \end{bmatrix} \tag{5}$$

Equation (5) is the relationship between deformation error and external force under the traditional stiffness model.

## 2.2  Deformation Error Analysis

Let $\boldsymbol{K} = [-\hat{\boldsymbol{p}}, I]\boldsymbol{J}\boldsymbol{K}_\theta^{-1}\boldsymbol{J}^T = [k_1, k_2]$, it can be concluded from Eq. (5)

$$\delta \boldsymbol{p} = [k_1, k_2]\begin{bmatrix} \boldsymbol{p}_f \times \boldsymbol{f} \\ \boldsymbol{f} \end{bmatrix} = k_1\hat{\boldsymbol{p}}_f\boldsymbol{f} + k_2\boldsymbol{f} = (k_1\hat{\boldsymbol{p}}_f + k_2)\boldsymbol{f} = \boldsymbol{K}_f\boldsymbol{f} \tag{6}$$

Where $\boldsymbol{K}_f$ is the displacement stiffness matrix, $\boldsymbol{K}_f = k_1\hat{\boldsymbol{p}}_f + k_2$.

According to Eq. (6), under the same pose, the force displacement at the end of the robot is linearly related to the external force applied. Even considering other factors that cause deformation errors, in fact, there is still an approximate linear relationship between robot deformation error and external forces applied, that is

$$x = \boldsymbol{K}'_f\boldsymbol{f} \tag{7}$$

Where $x$ is deformation error, $K'_f$ is the actual displacement stiffness matrix.

In a certain pose of the robot, assuming that there are external forces $f_1, f_2$ and $f_3$, which are linearly independent, and its corresponding deformation errors $x_1, x_2$ and $x_3$, then there exists $a$, $b$, and $c$, which make any external force vector be

$$f = af_1 + bf_2 + cf_3 = [f_1, f_2, f_3]\begin{bmatrix} a \\ b \\ c \end{bmatrix} = f_\lambda \lambda \tag{8}$$

Where $f_\lambda = [f_1, f_2, f_3]$, called the basis of force. $\lambda = [a, b, c]^{\mathrm{T}} = f_\lambda^{-1} f$, called force weight.

From Eq. (7), it can be concluded that $x_1 = K'_f f_1$, $x_2 = K'_f f_2$, $x_3 = K'_f f_3$, combined with Eq. (8), there is

$$x = K'_f f = K'_f [f_1, f_2, f_3]\begin{bmatrix} a \\ b \\ c \end{bmatrix} = [x_1, x_2, x_3]\lambda \tag{9}$$

Where $x$ is the deformation error corresponding to external force $f$.

From the above analysis, it can be seen that under the same pose, the deformation error caused by any external force can be transformed into the superposition of deformation errors $x_1, x_2$ and $x_3$ caused by any three linearly independent external forces $f_1, f_2$ and $f_3$, without calculating the actual joint stiffness.

## 3 Deformation Error Prediction Fusion Model

The deformation error is determined by the robot joint angle, external force and force point position. When using machine learning algorithms to fit deformation error, it is necessary to change the robot joint angle, external force and force point position to obtain a large amount of deformation error data. However, in the experiment, it is difficult to change and accurately record the external force, and adding external force vectors as input for training will significantly increase the training set size required for model training and increase the difficulty of model training. This paper proposes a special deformation error prediction model, DEPsM, that only takes joint angles as input. Combining the superposition principle of deformation error and DEPsM, DEPFM is obtained to solve the difficulties caused by external force mentioned above.

### 3.1 Principle of Extreme Learning Machine

ELM is a machine learning algorithm used to train a single-hidden layer feedforward neural network. Different from the traditional neural network training algorithm based on gradient descent, the input layer weight and hidden layer bias of ELM are randomly determined at the beginning, while the output layer weight is obtained by minimizing the loss function, which is composed of the error term and the regular term of the output layer weight norm. The ELM network structure is shown in Fig. 1.

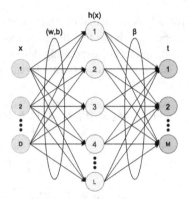

**Fig. 1.** Structural diagram of ELM network.

Let the training set be $\{x_i, t_i | x_i \in R^D, t_i \in R^m, i = 1, 2, 3, \cdots, N\}$, where $x_i = [x_{i1}, x_{i2}, \cdots, x_{iD}]^T$ and $t_i = [t_{i1}, t_{i2}, \cdots, t_{im}]^T$. Let the number of nodes in the hidden layer be $L$ and let the output of the hidden layer be $H(x)$,

$$H(x) = [h_1(x), h_2(x), \cdots, h_L(x)] \tag{10}$$

Where $h_j(x) = g(w_j, b_j, x) = g(w_jx + b_j)$ and $g(w_jx + b_j)$ is the activation function. The sigmoid function is used as the activation function,

$$g(w_jx + b_j) = \frac{1}{1 + e^{-(w_jx+b_j)}} \tag{11}$$

The output of the network can be obtained from the above formula and diagram,

$$f_m(x) = \sum_{i=1}^{L} \beta_i h_i(x) = H(x)\beta \tag{12}$$

Where $\beta = [\beta_1, \beta_2, \cdots, \beta_L]^T$.

When training begins, the input layer weight and hidden layer bias $(w, b)$ are randomly determined, and the feedforward network output can be obtained through Eq. (11) and (12). The variance of the feedforward network output and the output of the training samples $T$ are used to form the loss function

$$\min_{\beta} \|H\beta - T\|^2 \tag{13}$$

where $H$ is the hidden layer output, $\beta$ is the weight of the hidden layer to the output layer, and $T$ is the sample label value. To improve the generalization ability of the ELM model, the regularization of the model is introduced by the regular term $L^2$. The loss function becomes

$$\min_{\beta} \|H\beta - T\|^2 + \frac{c}{2}\|\beta\|^2 \tag{14}$$

When the number of nodes of the hidden layer is less than the number of training samples, the solution is obtained according to ridge regression

$$\beta = (H^T H + cI)^{-1} H^T T \tag{15}$$

## 3.2 Deformation Error Prediction Sub-model

The input of the DEPsM is only the robot joint angle. The DEPsM is trained with deformation error data caused by special force. In general, the force point coincides or is relatively stationary with the end point of the robot, that is, the position of the force point is determined by the joint angles. Assuming that the magnitude of the external force is constant and the external force always points towards a fixed point or its direction is fixed,

$$f = M \left( p_c - p_f \right) \tag{16}$$

or

$$f = M \omega \tag{17}$$

Where $M$ is the magnitude of the external force, $p_c$ is the fixed point pointed by the external force and $\omega$ is the unit direction vector of the external force. The schematic diagram of the above special external force is shown in Fig. 2 and 3.

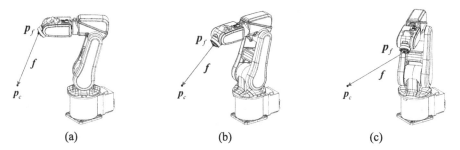

(a)                    (b)                    (c)

**Fig. 2.** The external force pointing towards a fixed point.

At this point, the external force changes from an independent variable to a dependent variable determined by the joint angle, or constant value. The deformation error changes from being determined by the robot joint angle, external force and force point to being determined solely by the robot joint angle. Collect deformation error data under this special situation and use ELM to train with the nominal joint angle of the robot as input and deformation error as output, and finally obtain the DEPsM. When the external force points to different fixed points or directions, the relationship between deformation error and joint angle will also change. Therefore, there are different DEPsM corresponding to different fixed points or force directions.

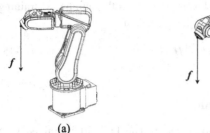  

(a)                              (b)                              (c)

**Fig. 3.** The external force at a fixed direction.

### 3.3 Establishment of DEPFM

By combining the DEPsM and the superposition principle of deformation errors, the model fusion process can be obtained:

(1) Use three different DEPsM to obtain the deformation errors $x_1$, $x_2$ and $x_3$ caused by three linearly independent external forces $f_1, f_2$ and $f_3$ of the robot in a certain pose.
(2) Using robot forward kinematics, calculate the external force $f_1, f_2$ and $f_3$ according to Eq. (16) and (17) and the force weight $\lambda$ according to Eq. (8).
(3) According to Eq. (9), the deformation error $x$ caused by external force $f$ is finally obtained.

The schematic diagram of deformation error superposition is shown in Fig. 4. The process of establishing DEPFM is shown in Fig. 5.

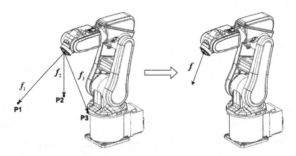

**Fig. 4.** Deformation error superposition.

## 4    Simulation and Analysis

### 4.1    Simulation Deformation Error Data

This paper used the kinematic parameters of the IRB120 robot, assuming appropriate joint stiffness coefficients, to obtain deformation errors based on the traditional robot stiffness model. Add random error with a range of $[-20, 20]$ μm to simulate measurement noise in experiments, ultimately obtaining simulation deformation error data. The

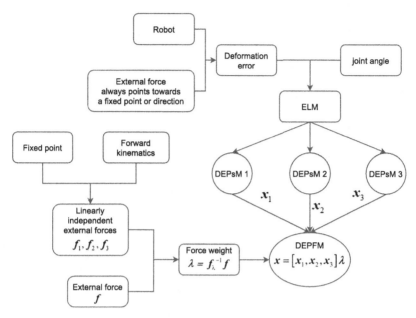

**Fig. 5.** The process of establishing DEPFM.

kinematic parameters of the IRB120 robot are shown in Table 1, and the simulation joints stiffness coefficients are shown in Table 2.

**Table 1.** Kinematic parameters of IRB120 robot

| Joint number | Screw parameter |
|---|---|
| 1 | $[0, 0, 1, 0, 0, 0]^{\mathrm{T}}$ |
| 2 | $[0, 1, 0, -290, 0, 0]^{\mathrm{T}}$ |
| 3 | $[0, 1, 0, -560, 0, 0]^{\mathrm{T}}$ |
| 4 | $[1, 0, 0, 0, 630, 0]^{\mathrm{T}}$ |
| 5 | $[0, 1, 0, -630, 0, 302]^{\mathrm{T}}$ |
| 6 | $[1, 0, 0, 0, 630, 0]^{\mathrm{T}}$ |
| $g_{st}(0)$ | $[0, 1.5708, 0, -210.06, 0, 788.53]^{\mathrm{T}}$ |

Select the commonly used workspace of the robot as the measurement space. When collecting training set data, the space is uniformly divided based on the number of measurement positions to form multiple grids, and the grid vertices are used as measurement positions for deformation errors, which is beneficial for improving the generalization performance of the prediction model in the entire measurement space. The measurement positions of the test set are randomly distributed, which can better evaluate the prediction

**Table 2.** Simulation joint stiffness coefficient (N · mm/rad).

| Joint number | 1 | 2 | 3 | 4 | 5 | 6 |
|---|---|---|---|---|---|---|
| Stiffness coefficient | $1.35 \times 10^7$ | $2.15 \times 10^7$ | $2.76 \times 10^8$ | $1.31 \times 10^6$ | $2.35 \times 10^6$ | $3.75 \times 10^5$ |

performance of the model. The measurement position of deformation error is shown in Fig. 6.

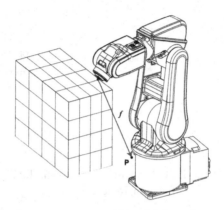

**Fig. 6.** Measurement position of deformation error.

### 4.2  Simulation Results

In the simulation experiment, the external force acting on the robot is 30 N. Using the robot base coordinate system as the reference coordinate system, collect deformation error data when external forces point to fixed points $P_1(800, -750, 150)$ and $P_2(800, 750, 150)$, to train the DEPsM A and B using ELM respectively. Collect deformation error data when the direction of the external force is fixed at $(0, 0, 1)$, to train the DEPsM C using ELM. Using the above model A, B and C, ultimately fused to obtain the DEPFM. Calculate the prediction error of the three DEPsM and the DEPFM using the test set data to verify the prediction performance of the model. When collecting the test set data of DEPFM, the external force is fixed at $(20, 0, -20)$N, which is different from the external force robot in training set, to verify the fusion effect of the models. Prediction error

$$e_p = |E - E_p| = \sqrt{(\Delta x - \Delta x_p)^2 + (\Delta y - \Delta y_p)^2 + (\Delta z - \Delta z_p)^2} \qquad (18)$$

Where $E$ is the actual deformation error and $E_p$ is the deformation error predicted by the model. Model A, B and C has a training set volume of 150. By using the traversal method, a suitable number of hidden layer nodes for ELM is 70, with a regularization coefficient of $10^{-5}$. The prediction results of DEPFM are shown in Fig. 7 and Table 3. The prediction performance of the deformation error fusion model is shown in Fig. 8 and Table 4.

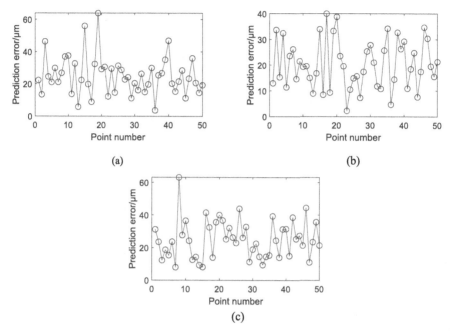

(a)

(b)

(c)

**Fig. 7.** Prediction error of DEPsM: (a) model A, (b) model B, and (c) model C.

**Table 3.** Prediction error evaluation of DEPsM ($\mu$m).

| Model | Average | Max | Min | Standard deviation | Accuracy |
|-------|---------|-----|-----|--------------------|----------|
| A | 25 | 64 | 4 | 12 | 95.2% |
| B | 25 | 63 | 8 | 11 | 94.8% |
| C | 20 | 40 | 2 | 9 | 94.7% |

From the above results, it can be seen that the DEPsM can accurately and stably predict the deformation error of robots under special forces based on joint angles. The average prediction error is less than 25 $\mu$m, and the prediction accuracy is over 94%, which verifies the effectiveness of DEPsM.

Due to the fusion of three DEPsM, the prediction performance of the DEPFM depends on the prediction performance of DEPsM. From the above results, it can be seen that the DEPFM can also accurately and stably predict the deformation error, with an average prediction deviation of 24 $\mu$m and an accuracy of 86%. The reason for the decrease in accuracy is that the deformation error under the external force $(20, 0, -20)$N

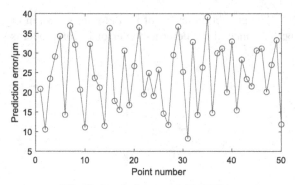

**Fig. 8.** Prediction error of DEPFM.

**Table 4.** Prediction error evaluation of DEPFM (μm).

| Average | Max | Min | Standard deviation | Accuracy |
|---------|-----|-----|--------------------|----------|
| 24      | 39  | 8   | 8                  | 86%      |

is smaller, but the average prediction error is almost the same as the DEPsM. The above results verify the effectiveness of DEPFM.

## 5  Experiment and Results

### 5.1  Experimental Setup

The robot used in this experiment is the IRB120 industrial robot, with an effective load of 3 kg and a repeated positioning accuracy of 0.01 mm. The measurement equipment is a laser tracker, and its accuracy is $10\,\mu m + 5\,\mu m/m$ when the measurement range is $2.5\,m \times 5\,m \times 10\,m$. The experimental system is shown in Fig. 9.

The experiment measurement space is a $200\,mm \times 400\,mm \times 400\,mm$ rectangular prism, and the external force acting on the robot is always 3 kg. The deformation error of the robot is obtained by subtracting the coordinates of the end effector when the robot is under force from the coordinates of the end effector when no force is applied.

Similar to simulation experiments, the number of training set data for each DEPsM is 150, and its position distribution is based on 4.1. The training set of DEPsM A and B is the deformation error data when the external force always point to the fixed points $P_1(881.35, 384.97, 99.42)$ mm and $P_2(813.87, -767.08, 184.50)$ mm, while the training set of DEPsM C is the deformation error data when the direction of the external force is fixed at $[0, 0, -1]$.

Randomly select 25 measurement positions in the measurement space and collect deformation error data when external forces always point to the fixed points $P_1$, $P_2$ and $P_3$ $(1070.55, -14.22, 97.40)$ mm, and a fixed external force direction of $(0, 0, -1)$. A total of 100 deformation error data under different forces are used as the test set to verify the effectiveness of DEPFM.

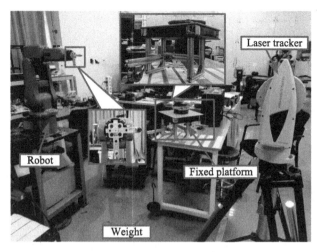

**Fig. 9.** Experimental system.

## 5.2 Prediction Performance of DEPFM

When training the DEPsM, the number of hidden layer nodes in ELM is 150, and the regularization coefficient is $10^{-5}$. The prediction performance of DEPFM is shown in Fig. 10, Fig. 11, and Table 5.

From the above results, it can be seen that DEPFM can accurately and stably predict the deformation error, with an average prediction deviation of 30 μm and an accuracy of 93.7%, verifying the effectiveness and accuracy of DEPFM.

## 5.3 Method Comparison

To demonstrate the accuracy and superiority of the prediction method proposed in this paper, a comparison was done between the traditional stiffness model and DEPFM, using the same deformation error data. The comparison results of the two methods are shown in Fig. 12 and Table 6.

From the above results, it can be seen that compared with traditional stiffness model, DEPFM has significantly improved prediction accuracy, with an average prediction deviation reduced from 81 μm to 30 μm, a decrease of 63.8%. The maximum value also decreased from 231 μm to 78 μm, a decrease of 66.2%.

Comparing with the traditional model which just considers the stiffness of the joints and ignores the stiffness of the links, the DEPFM is not limited by the stiffness of robot's links, due to the establishment of DEPFM is based on the ELM. It is a synthetic model with higher accuracy and robustness, considering the joint stiffness, link stiffness, and other component.

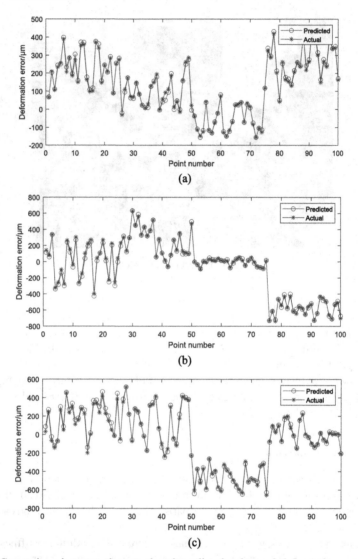

**Fig. 10.** Comparison between the actual and predicted values of deformation errors: (a) X direction, (b) Y direction, and (c) Z direction.

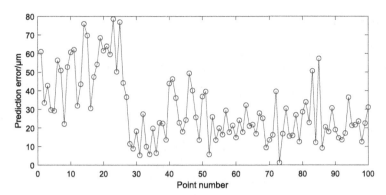

**Fig. 11.** Prediction error of DEPFM

**Table 5.** Prediction error evaluation of DEPFM (μm).

| Average | Max | Min | Standard deviation | Accuracy |
|---------|-----|-----|--------------------|----------|
| 30 | 78 | 1 | 18 | 93.7% |

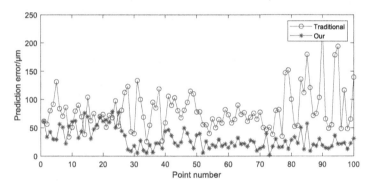

**Fig. 12.** Comparison of prediction error between two methods.

**Table 6.** Comparison of prediction error between two methods (μm).

| Model | Average | Max | Min | Standard deviation | Accuracy |
|-------|---------|-----|-----|--------------------|----------|
| Traditional | 81 | 231 | 25 | 36 | 83.3% |
| DEPFM | 30 | 78 | 1 | 18 | 93.7% |

# 6  Conclusion

To improve the machining accuracy of robots, this paper proposes a deformation error prediction method based on error superposition. First, based on the approximate linear relationship between the external force and the deformation error, the superposition principle of deformation error is derived. Then, a deformation error prediction model based on ELM, called DEPsM, which is suitable for special external force, is proposed. Finally, combining DEPsM and the superposition principle of deformation errors, a deformation error prediction model suitable for any external force, called DEPFM, is proposed. After verifying its effectiveness in simulation, deformation error prediction experiments were conducted on an industrial robot. According to the experiment results, the following conclusions can be drawn:

(1) DEPFM can accurately predict deformation error. The experiment results show that the average prediction error of DEPFM is 30 μm, with a prediction accuracy of 93.7%. Compared with the traditional stiffness model, the prediction error is reduced by 63.8%.
(2) DEPFM is simple and practical, which can be widely applicable to most industrial robots. The establishment of DEPFM is not limited by link stiffness. Moreover, it does not require complex calculations like the traditional stiffness model. The collection process of deformation error data is simple and does not require complex and expensive force measurement equipment.

**Acknowledgements.** This work was supported by the Science and Technology Project of Guangzhou (No. 202201010072), the National Natural Science Foundation of China (No. 51805172), and the Guangdong Basic and Applied Basic Research Foundation (No. 2019A1515011515).

# References

1. Ji, W., Wang, L.: Industrial robotic machining: a review. Int. J. Adv. Manuf. Technol. **103**(1–4), 1239–1255 (2019). https://doi.org/10.1007/s00170-019-03403-z
2. Kim, S.H., et al.: Robotic machining: a review of recent progress. Int. J. Precis. Eng. Manuf. **20**(9), 1629–1642 (2019). https://doi.org/10.1007/s12541-019-00187-w
3. Kainrath, M., Aburaia, M., Stuja, K., Lackner, M., Markl, E.: Accuracy improvement and process flow adaption for robot machining. In: Durakbasa, N.M., Gençyılmaz, M.G. (eds.) ISPR 2020, pp. 189–200. LNME. Springer, Cham (2021). https://doi.org/10.1007/978-3-030-62784-3_16
4. Tao, B., Zhao, X., Ding, H.: Mobile-robotic machining for large complex components: a review study. Science China Technol. Sci. **62**(8), 1388–1400 (2019). https://doi.org/10.1007/s11431-019-9510-1
5. Nam Huynh, H., et al.: Modelling the dynamics of industrial robots for milling operations. Robot. Comput. Integr. Manuf. **61**, Article no. 101852 (2020)
6. Zhenya, H., et al.: A new prediction method of displacement errors caused by low stiffness for industrial robot. Sensors **22**(16), Article no. 5963 (2022)
7. Kai, W., et al.: Review of industrial robot stiffness identification and modelling. Appl. Sci. **12**(17), Article no. 8719 (2022)

8. Abele, E., et al.: Modeling and identification of an industrial robot for machining applications. CIRP Ann. Manuf. Technol. **56**(1), 387–390 (2007)

9. Chen, C., et al.: Stiffness performance index based posture and feed orientation optimization in robotic milling process. Robot. Comput. Integr. Manuf. **55**, 29–40 (2019)

10. Zargarbashi, S.H.H., et al.: The Jacobian condition number as a dexterity index in 6R machining robots. Robot. Comput. Integr. Manuf. **28**(6), 694–699 (2012)

11. Guozhi, L.Z., et al.: Joint stiffness identification and deformation compensation of serial robots based on dual quaternion algebra. Appl. Sci. **9**(1), Article no. 65 (2019)

12. Klimchik, A., et al.: Identification of geometrical and elastostatic parameters of heavy industrial robots. In: IEEE International Conference on Robotics and Automation (ICRA), Karlsruhe, Germany, pp. 3707–3714. IEEE (2013)

13. Kun, Y., et al.: A new methodology for joint stiffness identification of heavy duty industrial robots with the counterbalancing system. Robot. Comput. Integr. Manuf. **53**, 58–71 (2018)

# Visual Weld Seam Tracking Through Feature-Fused Kernelized Correlation Filters and Generative Adversarial Networks

Yongsheng Dong⬡, Haotian Zhou⬡, Junxian Zhou⬡, and Huasong Min$^{(\boxtimes)}$⬡

Institute of Robotics and Intelligent Systems, Wuhan University of Science and Technology, Wuhan 430081, China
mhuasong@wust.edu.cn

**Abstract.** Vision-based seam tracking is a crucial technology widely used in robotic welding. However, during the welding process, intense noise from the arc and spatter leads to large welding seam tracking errors. To solve this problem, this paper proposes a seam tracking method that integrates a feature-fused Kernelized Correlation Filters (FF-KCF) with a Generative Adversarial Network. Firstly, FF-KCF fuses histogram of oriented gradients (HOG) and scale invariant local ternary pattern (SILTP) features to overcome the limitations of individual features and capture a comprehensive feature representation of the weld seam. Secondly, a feature-supervised Conditional Generative Adversarial network is introduced to repair laser stripe images affected by intense noise, addressing model drift issues in noisy environments and long sequence tracking. Model parameter updates and image repair frequencies are controlled by the Peak-to-Sidelobe Ratio (PSR) to enhance tracking efficiency. Finally, a direction clustering least squares fitting algorithm (DC-LS) is proposed to identify feature points in the initial frame image, solving the problem of manually specifying the tracking object in the initial frame required by the FF-KCF. The proposed methodology is validated on the collected dataset. The experimental results show that the tracking speed can reach up to 17.3 FPS, and the average error is kept within 2.2 pixels. Compared to state-of-the-art methods, the proposed method demonstrates superior performance in terms of accuracy and stability, meeting the requirements for precision and real-time seam tracking.

**Keywords:** Robotic welding · Laser vision sensor · Seam tracking · Kernelized correlation filters · Conditional generation adversarial network

## 1 Introduction

Robotic welding has been widely adopted in the manufacturing industry. However, most welding robots still operate in a "teach-playback" mode. Their intelligence level is relatively low, which makes it difficult to address welding path deviations caused by welding thermal deformation and assembly errors. Enhancing the intelligence of welding robots to ensure welding quality is imperative.

© The Author(s), under exclusive license to Springer Nature Singapore Pte Ltd. 2025
X. Lan et al. (Eds.): ICIRA 2024, LNAI 15208, pp. 392–408, 2025.
https://doi.org/10.1007/978-981-96-0783-9_27

The essence of weld seam tracking based on laser vision sensors is quickly and accurately extracting weld seam feature points from laser stripe images [1]. This can be categorized into traditional image processing, object detection, and object tracking methods. Conventional image processing methods typically first filter out noise from the seam images, then extract the laser stripe skeleton, and finally detect the seam feature points [2]. Zeng et al. [3] used contour and corner detection to extract seam feature points. Wu et al. [4] employed median filtering and Otsu's method for preprocessing welding images and proposed a modified Hough transform to extract feature points. However, these image processing methods lack generalization, applying only to specific types of seams. Additionally, pixel-structure-based processing methods may lead to erroneous results in welding images with noise such as arcs.

Due to the limitations of image processing methods, many studies have turned to object detection techniques. Ma et al. [5] proposed a feature point extraction method called Shuffle-YOLO, which uses the feature extraction module of ShuffleNet-V2 to reduce the model parameters of YOLOv5, solving the inefficiency issues of YOLO in seam tracking. However, welding is a continuous and dynamic process, and their method uses only single-frame information, neglecting the temporal context information of consecutive images. This leads to detection algorithm failures in the presence of significant noise in the images. Zou et al. [6] used RNN to consider the temporal context information of consecutive images and implemented weld seam tracking under noise interference using the SSD model. However, the object detection method cannot effectively extract feature points when encountering extreme noise. Meanwhile, object detection methods require diverse datasets. The dataset's quality directly affects the model's performance, and collecting images in actual welding processes can consume many workpieces.

In recent years, to meet the requirements for both real-time performance and accuracy, many studies have introduced object tracking algorithms to track feature points. Jia et al. [7] achieved the tracking of intersecting seams by enhancing the Spatio-Temporal Context (STC) tracker with an extending and adopting Kalman Filter. Fan et al. [8] verified the excellent applicability of Efficient Convolution Operators (ECO) improved by the Particle Filter across various welding types. Zou et al. [9] employed Convolutional Long Short-Term Memory (ConvLSTM) networks to establish the temporal correlation of welding sequences, reducing noise contamination in the sample set. They also periodically corrected the tracking results and reinitialized model parameters based on the confidence of a Faster R-CNN network. Although this method effectively handles feature point recognition under strong noise, it suffers from low computational efficiency due to the model's complexity.

Generally, these tracker-based methods leverage the similarity between adjacent frames for tracking, making them independent of weld seam types and suitable for seam tracking. However, these methods still have limitations. On one hand, most trackers, such as STC, use a single feature to find the most similar position through correlation filtering. However, a single feature is often insufficient to distinguish between stripes and welding noise. On the other hand, model drift can occur under strong noise interference and long welding sequence tracking. Quoc-Chi Nguyen et al. [10] proposed a method for locating weld seam feature points by combining a convolutional filter tracker with deep reinforcement learning, effectively solving the problem of model drift. First, the feature points are roughly located using the filter tracker, and then the tracking points are fine-tuned using a Deep Q-network. However, fine-tuning the tracking points becomes challenging difficult in scenarios where strong interference makes tracking difficult for the tracker. One possible solution is to introduce an image inpainting network into the tracker. By effectively repairing the images, clean samples can be provided for the tracker to track.

This paper proposes a seam tracking method that combines a feature-fused kernelized correlation filter (FF-KCF) with a feature-supervised generative adversarial network (FS-GAN) to achieve better tracking performance under complex welding conditions. The contributions of this paper can be summarized as follows:

- A feature point identification algorithm, DC-LS, is proposed to address the issue of the FF-KCF requiring manual specification of the tracking object in the initial frame.
- Integrating SILTP and HOG to represent the object features addresses the issue of information loss in HOG features under interference.
- A feature-supervised CGAN network is proposed to repair welding images disrupted by strong noise, addressing model drift and inaccurate localization caused by multiple interference factors in complex environments.

## 2   Methodology

Weld seam tracking is an essential component of intelligent welding. However, image processing-based methods have disadvantages in terms of flexibility and robustness. Object tracking technology is utilized to address this challenge. Since the KCF [11] method offers good real-time performance, it is used for tracking in welding.

### 2.1   Problem Description

During the welding process, the seam images captured by the vision sensor can be contaminated by noise. Depending on the noise intensity, it can be classified into no contamination, mild contamination, and severe contamination. Figure 1 shows seam images under different noise intensities and their corresponding filter response maps. As shown in Fig. 1(a), the response map exhibits a unimodal distribution with a relatively stable peak due to the absence of noise interference. In Fig. 1(b), the laser stripe area experiences slight interference, resulting in additional small peaks and fluctuations near the main peak in the response map. As shown in Fig. 1(c), when subjected to severe noise interference, the laser stripe area becomes blurred, significantly increasing the difficulty of identifying the seam center. Consequently, the peak value in the response map drops sharply, and the response values of the object area are not prominent compared to the background area.

### 2.2   Overall Framework

Based on the above analysis, we introduce the PSR to describe the noise intensity in seam images. The expression for PSR is given by

$$P_{sr} = \frac{f_{\max} - \mu_f}{\sigma_f} \tag{1}$$

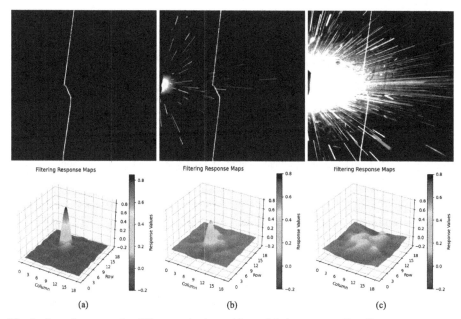

**Fig. 1.** Seam images under different noise intensities and their corresponding filter response maps. (a) No contamination, (b) Mild contamination, and (c) Severe contamination.

Where $f_x$ is the peak value of the filter response, and $\mu_f$ and $\sigma_f$ are the mean and standard deviation of the filter response map. Typically, kernelized correlation filters update the object template in each frame. However, when the object template is updated with serious noise interference or tracking deviation, the introduced noise information can easily pollute the weld object template, thus affecting tracking accuracy. Additionally, repairing images frame by frame can be time-consuming. Therefore, we use PSR to control the model parameter updates and the frequency of image inpainting. The overall flowchart of the proposed tracking method is shown in Fig. 2. Firstly, the tracking object is marked using DC-LS in the initial welding stage, and the tracker template is initialized. Then, the object is tracked in consecutive frame images. After obtaining the response map for each frame, the PSR value of the current response map is calculated according to Eq. 1. When the PSR value is less than the threshold $T$, it indicates insufficient confidence in the tracking result. At this point, the original image is input into the FS-GAN network for repair. The repaired image is then re-input into the FF-KCF for localization. When the PSR is greater than the threshold, the tracking feature point is output, and the model is updated simultaneously. Multiple comparative tests demonstrated that setting $T$ to 10 yields good results.

## 2.3 Feature-Fused Kernelized Correlation Filters

KCF is a framework proposed by João F. et al. that utilizes the correlation between the features of the object region to achieve object tracking. This algorithm effectively increases the number of negative samples through the augmentation of the circulant

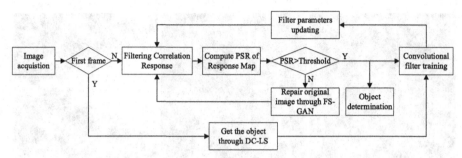

**Fig. 2.** Flowchart of the object location and seam feature point acquisition.

matrix, thereby enhancing the tracker's performance. This sample set's construction conveniently utilizes the properties of the Fast Fourier Transform (FFT) and Fourier Diagonalization to improve computational efficiency.

Although KCF using HOG features has achieved excellent results in object tracking, the welding process is often accompanied by arc light and spatter, causing inconsistent image brightness. In particular, spatter noise frequently obscures the laser stripe. If only HOG features are used as sample inputs for tracking, the gradient information may be disrupted, leading to inaccurate feature extraction.

The Local Binary Pattern (LBP) texture feature has the ability to resist local occlusion and is robust to grayscale changes caused by rotation and illumination. However, LBP lacks stability when neighboring pixels are similar. The SILTP feature [12] is more robust because it introduces a smaller tolerance range. By integrating HOG and SILTP features, the tracking method can overcome the limitations of individual features and capture a complete representation of the object. The extraction effect of SILTP features is shown in Fig. 3.

**Fig. 3.** SILTP Features. (a) Original image, and (b) Extracted image.

By combining HOG and SILTP features, they are fused at the feature level to form a new feature representation. Let the HOG feature vector be $\alpha$, and the SILTP feature vector be $\beta$; The fused feature vector $\gamma$ is then given by,

$$\gamma = (\lambda\alpha, (1 - \lambda)\beta) \tag{2}$$

where $\gamma$ is the weight coefficient. The experiment shows that the effect is better when $\gamma$ is 0.6.

## 2.4  Initial Frame Feature Point Detection

FF-KCF relies on manually selecting the tracking object in the initial frame image. This can be challenging for operators lacking welding experience, and the selection accuracy is also limited. Considering that arc interference is minimal at the initial welding stage, we proposed the DC-LS method to address this issue. By identifying the feature points in the initial frame image, the simplicity of the algorithm is improved.

Initially, the grayscale centroid method is used to extract the set of center points $\{P\}$ of the laser stripe. Approximate every $m$ consecutive points in the set $\{P\}$ as a straight line segment. Assuming the points in the set $\{P\}$ are divided into $n$ line segments, it can be represented as the set $\{L\} = \{L_1, L_2,..., L_n\}$. Apply least squares fitting to these $n$ line segments to obtain the equations of the segments. The direction cosines between adjacent line segments are then calculated

$$\cos(\theta) = \frac{u_1 \cdot u_2 + v_1 \cdot v_2}{\sqrt{(u_1^2 + v_1^2) \times (u_2^2 + v_2^2)}} \tag{3}$$

Where $[u_1, v_1]$ and $[u_2, v_2]$ are the directional vectors of adjacent line segments $L_i$ and $L_{i+1}$, respectively. If $\cos(\theta)$ is greater than the threshold $\cos(\theta_t)$, it indicates that the two line segments have the same direction and form a single line, so the points of the fitted line segments $L_i$ and $L_{i+1}$ are added to the subset $\{G\}$. Conversely, if $\cos(\theta)$ is less than the threshold, it suggests that the two line segments have different directions, and the points of the fitted line segment are added to a new subset $\{G_{i+1}\}$. Thus, we obtain a set of segments with different directions $\{G\} = \{G_1, G_2,..., G_j\}$, where $\{G_i\}$ consists of pixel points of segments with the same direction. However, the sets of points for lines in different directions contain many noise points, which affect the fitting of the segmented lines, resulting in inaccurate identification of feature points.

We judge whether there are excessive noise points in the current fitted line by using the distance range $D$ from the points to the line and the fitting degree $R$ of the line. Calculate the $R$ of straight lines with different directions in $\{G\}$

$$R = 1 - \frac{M}{D^2} \tag{4}$$

Where $M$ is the mean squared distance between the points involved in the fitting and the fitted line. If $R$ is less than $R_t$, it indicates the presence of noise points in the fitted line; in this case, remove the point farthest from the fitted line. Otherwise, it indicates that the optimal line has been found. Calculate the intersection points between adjacent optimal lines to obtain feature points. Experimental comparisons led to the selection of $D$ as 2, $R_t$ as 0.92, and $\cos(\theta_t)$ as 0.9. The results of the DC-LS extraction are shown in Fig. 4.

## 2.5  Feature-Supervised Conditional Generative Adversarial Network

CGAN is a method proposed by Mirza [13] for training generative models. CGAN consists of two parts: a generator and a discriminator. The generator captures the data

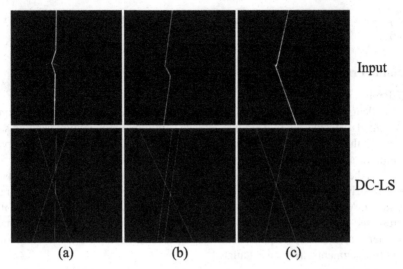

Input

DC-LS

(a)                    (b)                    (c)

**Fig. 4.** DC-LS feature point extraction. (a) V-groove, (b) lap, and (c) fillet joint.

distribution, while the discriminator estimates the probability that a sample comes from real data rather than generated samples. By incorporating conditional information $y$, it guides image generation and reduces the uncertainty in GAN [14] results. Its objective function is as follows:

$$\min_{G} \max_{D} V(D, G) = \mathbb{E}_{x \sim y}[\log D(x|y)] + \mathbb{E}_{x}[\log(1 - D(G(x)))] \tag{5}$$

Besides CGAN, recent Diffusion Models generate samples by gradually adding noise and learning the reverse process, demonstrating good sample quality and theoretical foundations. However, the generation process of Diffusion Models involves computations over multiple time steps, resulting in low computational efficiency [15], which limits their application in weld seam tracking. Based on the principle of CGAN, the contaminated welding image is taken as condition y and input to the generator and the discriminator simultaneously, which can cause the generator to synthesize the corresponding restored image from the noisy image.

**Network Structure.** Figure 5 shows the overall architecture of the FS-GAN. It aims to obtain an excellent generator through adversarial training. The corrupted image is fed into the generator, which uses convolutional and deconvolutional layers to construct a clean laser stripe image.

The network structure of the generator is shown in Fig. 6(a). Our generator employs a fully convolutional neural network to map the corrupted image to a clean laser stripe image. We use a 4 × 4 convolution operation with a stride of two for downsampling to avoid the instability in training caused by sparse gradients. In the generator, except for the last convolutional layer, which is directly followed by a Tanh activation function to prevent mode collapse, all convolutional and deconvolutional layers are followed by Batchnorm units and Leaky-ReLU activation functions. Additionally, to address the

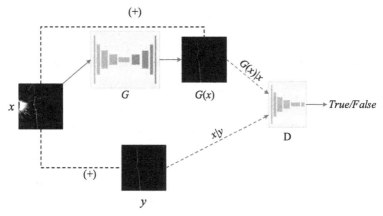

**Fig. 5.** The overall architecture of FS-GAN. The symbol (+) indicates the concatenation of two images.

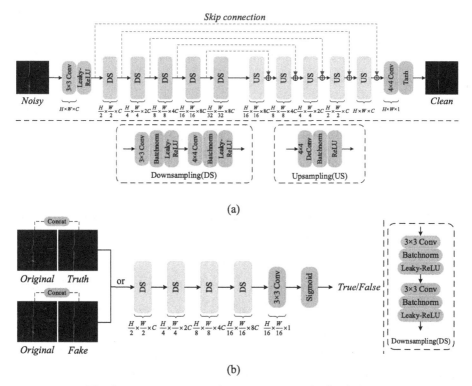

**Fig. 6.** Network structure of (a) generator and (b) discriminator.

information loss caused by feature downsampling, skip connections are used to integrate the abstract semantic information of the decoder with the low-level detail information of the encoder.

Inspired by [16], we designed a weight-sharing dual downsampling encoder as a feature extraction supervision module. During training, we input the clean image into the module and use the encoder for feature extraction. Then, by employing perceptual loss, we enforce the extraction of features from the corrupted image that are similar to those of the target image.

The discriminator has a similar structure to that of the generator, as shown in Fig. 6(b). The last layer of the discriminator uses sigmoid activation function to output the probability of discriminating generated samples and ground truth samples.

**Loss Function.** The training of GANs can be unstable and may result in the generator producing incomplete results. Perceptual loss guides the generator's training by comparing the differences between the generated and target images in feature space. By introducing perceptual loss, the generator is compelled to produce feature representations that are more similar to the real images, thus improving the quality of the generated images. We combine adversarial loss, perceptual loss, and target pixel distance loss by weighting them to form a new loss function, defined as follows:

$$\mathcal{L}_{Total} = \mathcal{L}_A + \lambda_1 \mathcal{L}_E + \lambda_2 \mathcal{L}_{layer} \tag{6}$$

Where $\mathcal{L}_A$ is the adversarial loss, $\mathcal{L}_E$ is the per-pixel loss function, and $\mathcal{L}_{layer}$ is the perceptual loss. The weight coefficients are $\lambda_1 = 100$ and $\lambda_2 = 0.0002$.

The adversarial loss is defined as:

$$\mathcal{L}_A = \mathbb{E}_{x,y}[\log D(x|y)] + \mathbb{E}_x[\log(1 - D(G(x)))] \tag{7}$$

The pixel distance loss calculates the pixel-level differences between the generated laser stripe image and the real target stripe image. $\mathcal{L}_E$ regularization is added to avoid the issue of blurriness in the output image. The loss function is defined as follows:

$$\mathcal{L}_E = \mathbb{E}_{x,y}[\|y - G(x)\|_1] \tag{8}$$

Perceptual loss aims to enhance the similarity of extracted features from low-dimensional to high-dimensional representations. The perceptual loss is calculated as follows:

$$\mathcal{L}_{layer} = \sum_{l=1}^{L} \eta_l \mathbb{E}_{x,y}[\|G_l(y) - G_l(x)\|_1] \tag{9}$$

Where $x$ and $y$ are the paired noisy and clean images, respectively; $\eta_l$ is the predefined weight for the loss of the $l^{th}$ Conv layer, and we set $\eta_l = \log(l)$.

## 3 Experimental Results and Discussion

In this section, we first present the experimental results of FS-GAN on the test set. Then, we compare FS-GAN with several other methods and provide a quantitative analysis. Next, the integral tracking method is verified by experiments on three types of welds. Finally, we perform comparative experiments between the integral tracking method and several other methods to demonstrate the effectiveness of our approach.

## 3.1  Implementation Details

**Dataset.** We used a line laser vision sensor to collect over 1600 weld images, including 605 lap weld images, 584 butt weld images, and 488 fillet weld images, to train our network. The feature points of these three types of weld seams are defined as shown in Fig. 7. Since using actual welding to collect data would result in significant workpiece loss, we conducted welding experiments to collect images by referencing the approach used in the rain removal image training set [17]. We collected noise interference images without laser stripes during actual welding. Additionally, clean laser stripe images were collected under different robot postures. The image data was augmented to prevent overfitting and improve the model's generalization ability. First, some clean laser stripe images were randomly rotated and shifted to increase image diversity. Second, some images underwent random contrast adjustment to simulate illumination changes caused by arc light during welding. Then, the processed laser stripe images were superimposed with the actual noise images. Finally, the two parts were concatenated to form image pairs as the final dataset. The images were divided into training, validation, and test sets in a ratio of 8:1:1.

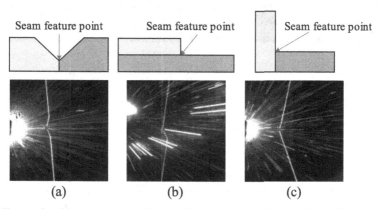

**Fig. 7.** Types of weld seams and their laser stripe images: (a) V-groove joint, (b) Lap joint, and (c) Fillet joint.

**Training Setup.** The experimental environment for training the FS-GAN network includes the Ubuntu 16 operating system and an NVIDIA GeForce GTX 2080 GPU. The deep learning framework used is TensorFlow 1.13, equipped with CUDA 10.0. During training, FS-GAN uses the Adam optimizer for model parameter updates. The learning rate is 0.0002, the first momentum term is 0.5, and the batch size is 1.

## 3.2  Image Inpainting Experiment

**Image Inpainting Result.** The repair experiment was conducted on the test dataset images to verify the effectiveness of image inpainting. The welding images of three types of joints were input into the trained inpainting network for repair. Some inpainting results are shown in Fig. 8, with an average processing time of 40.32 ms. By comparing the output images with the target images, it can be seen that the network has excellent inpainting performance on welding images. Despite the laser stripes being obscured by noise, the network can still restore relatively complete laser stripes. The processing speed for test images is 24.8 FPS, meeting the real-time requirements of the welding process.

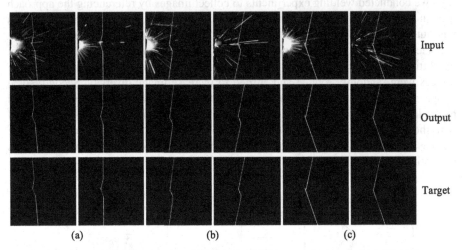

**Fig. 8.** Image inpainting results of FS-GAN. (a) V-groove, (b) lap, and (c) fillet joint.

**Comparison Experiment of Image Inpainting.** Comparative experiments with other generative model-based image inpainting methods were conducted to further demonstrate the effectiveness of our FS-GAN. First, we trained a CGAN [13] network with the same network structure to verify the effectiveness of feature supervision. Second, we introduced a conditional variational autoencoder (CVAE [18]), another generative model, to demonstrate the robustness of adversarial training against welding noise. Figure 9 shows some visual results of image inpainting. As can be seen, although CVAE removed most of the welding noise, it also removed parts of the laser stripes, causing them to appear broken. Due to the lack of feature supervision, the CGAN network exhibited more detail loss and produced blurred results and artifacts around the laser stripes. In contrast, FS-GAN retained more details, resulting in more realistic images.

To accurately evaluate the performance of different image inpainting models, this study introduces the Universal Quality Index (UQI), Structural Similarity Index (SSIM), and Peak Signal-to-Noise Ratio (PSNR) as evaluation metrics. Table 1 presents the average UQI, SSIM, and PSNR for 128 test images. The results show that FS-GAN outperforms CGAN and CVAE in all three quantitative tests. Through analysis, it is observed that CVAE focuses on learning the latent representation of the data, but due to the diversity of welding noise, this representation might not effectively capture the noise characteristics. It prefers to learn the smoothed version of the denoised image, which ignores some details. CGAN, through adversarial training, encourages the generator to produce more realistic images, which more effectively capture the noise characteristics and generate results closer to real images.

| Input | FS-GAN(ours) | CGAN | CVAE | Target |

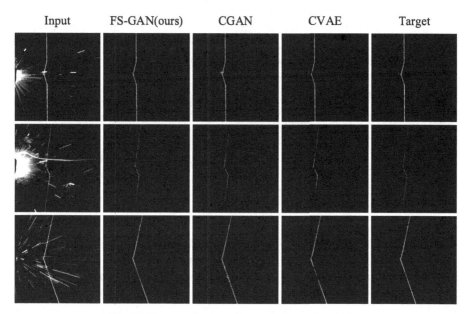

**Fig. 9.** Comparative experiments on image inpainting

**Table 1.** FS-GAN is quantitatively compared with other methods for image inpainting.

| Methods | Avg. UQI | Avg. SSIM | Avg. PSNR |
|---|---|---|---|
| FS-GAN (ours) | 0.925 | 0.907 | 36.862 |
| CGAN | 0.893 | 0.885 | 35.653 |
| CVAE | 0.872 | 0.857 | 33.284 |

### 3.3 Weld Seam Tracking Experiment

**Method Performance Verification.** To verify the performance of the proposed method in acquiring weld seam feature points, three widely used types of seams were used: V-groove butt joint, lap joint, and fillet joint. A series of laser stripe images were recorded during the welding process, and feature points on these images were manually marked as references. The Euclidean distance between the extracted points $\hat{p}$ and the reference points $p$ is considered as the extraction error.

$$E(\hat{p}, p) = \|\hat{p} - p\|_2 \tag{10}$$

The results are shown in Fig. 10. It can be seen that the extraction error of lap weld is less than 5 pixels under the interference of welding noise. Additionally, we further calculated the mean and variance of the errors to more accurately quantify the tracking performance. The results are shown in Table 2. The mean and variance of the tracking errors for lap welds are approximately 1.7 and 0.53 pixels, respectively, which demonstrates that our method maintains satisfactory tracking stability even under welding noise interference. The tracking error graphs for the other two seam types are shown in Fig. 11 and Fig. 12.

**Table 2.** The mean and variance of tracking errors for our method on different types of weld seams.

| Joint Types | V-groove Joint | Lap Joint | Fillet Joint |
|---|---|---|---|
| Mean (pixel) | 2.5 | 1.7 | 2.2 |
| Variance (pixel) | 0.64 | 0.53 | 0.52 |

It can be seen that our method is suitable for different types of weld seams and can maintain satisfactory accuracy. The average error can be kept within 3 pixels, indicating that the method has excellent resistance to welding noise. Additionally, the method also remains stable without significant model drift during long sequence tracking. This stability is due to the tracking template being updated only when the tracking confidence is high, resulting in a lower probability of the object template being contaminated.

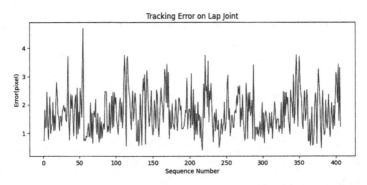

**Fig. 10.** Tracking error on lap joint under welding noise interference

The tracking results are compared with those of KCF without the inpainting network to validate the effectiveness of FS-GAN. The comparison results of the tracking process are shown in Fig. 13. The red box represents the tracking result, while the green box represents the ground truth. From the tracking results in Fig. 13(a), it can be seen that some welding images without FS-GAN repair experience severe tracking drift due to interference. Therefore, as the update process proceeds, subsequent tracking objects may drift further from the true object. In contrast, our method reduces interference by restoring images, achieving better tracking.

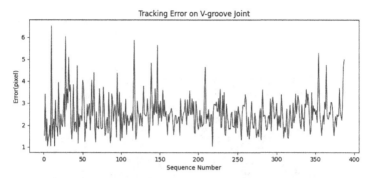

**Fig. 11.** Tracking error on V-groove joint under welding noise interference

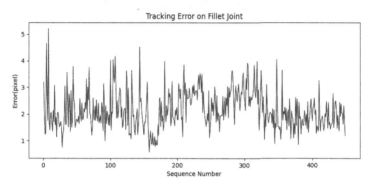

**Fig. 12.** Tracking error on fillet joint under welding noise interference

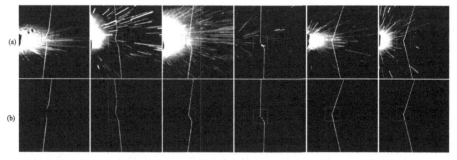

**Fig. 13.** Impact of the FS-GAN on tracking results. (a) Result without the FS-GAN and (b) result with the FS-GAN (Color figure online)

**Comparative Experiments.** The proposed method was evaluated through comparative experiments. First, it was compared with the traditional geometric feature-based method [3], and the results are shown in Fig. 14. Method [3] uses contour and corner detection to extract weld seam feature points. As shown in Fig. 14(a), it may fail in scenarios with welding noise because the welding noise is similar to the laser stripes. In contrast, our method can handle various welding noises and exhibits reliable stability, as shown in Fig. 14(b).

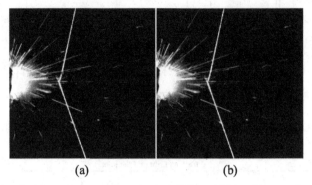

(a)                                    (b)

**Fig. 14.** Red dots in (a) are the extraction results of [3] and (b) tracking results of our method. (Color figure online)

Additionally, we compared our method with STC and ECO to further evaluate its performance. The mean tracking error (Mte) was used to assess the static accuracy of the method, and variance (Var) was used to determine the stability of the method.

$$Mte = \frac{1}{n} \sum_{i=1}^{n} E(\hat{p}_i, p_i) \tag{11}$$

As shown in the tracking performance comparison in Table 3, the STC tracker tends to exhibit larger errors in the presence of some welding noise. This is because the HOG features used by STC are insufficient to maintain tracking stability. The ECO-based method has smaller tracking errors. It enhances tracking stability by introducing decomposed convolution operators to select optimized features. Additionally, it incorporates an efficient model update strategy, which improves both tracking speed and robustness.

In comparison, our method demonstrates good accuracy and stability. Furthermore, the proposed DC-LS extraction method is suitable for various types of weld seams, further expanding the scope of its application. To validate the effectiveness of SILTP, we used features extracted by VGGNet and SILTP to enhance KCF. The results showed that VGGNet-extracted features more effectively reduced KCF tracking errors, but its processing speed was lower than that of SILTP. After careful consideration, we chose SILTP to ensure the overall framework's real-time performance. Even under the interference of welding noise, our method achieves satisfactory tracking performance on different weld seams.

**Table 3.** Tracking performance comparison

| Methods | Mte (pixel) | Var (pixel) | Speed (FPS) |
|---|---|---|---|
| STC [7] | 9.8 | 3.74 | 29.3 |
| ECO [8] | 5.2 | 0.96 | 108.7 |
| KCF+VGGNet [19] | 9.5 | 4.43 | 78.7 |
| KCF+SILTP | 10.7 | 3.61 | 82.3 |
| Ours | 2.2 | 0.58 | 17.3 |

# 4 Conclusion

This paper meets the challenge of difficult weld seam tracking in complex environments by proposing a weld seam tracking method that combines feature-fused Kernelized Correlation Filters and feature-supervised Conditional Generative Adversarial Networks. Firstly, the FF-KCF is proposed by enhancing HOG features with SILTP features. Secondly, FS-GAN is designed to repair welding images to address the issue of model drift. FS-GAN incorporates perceptual loss and pixel distance loss to guide the generation of repaired images. Additionally, PSR is used to control the frequency of model parameter updates and image repairs to improve tracking efficiency. Lastly, a Directional Clustering Least Squares analysis algorithm is proposed to specify tracking objects to enhance the simplicity of the method. Experimental results demonstrate that the proposed method keeps the error within 2.2 pixels, showing significant advantages in handling weld seam tracking in complex environments and effectively improving model tracking accuracy. Moreover, its average variance is 0.58 pixels, resolving the model drift issue in KCF methods during long sequence tracking.

Weld seam tracking involves real-time correction of the welding path and real-time optimization of welding parameters. Building on the application of our method, we will continue to explore welding parameter optimization methods based on machine learning and multi-sensor fusion. In the future, we hope to integrate welding path correction with welding parameter optimization to develop an adaptive welding system that can accommodate changes in welding conditions.

**Acknowledgment.** This work is supported by the National Key R&D Program of China (grant No.: 2022YFB4700400), National Natural Science Foundation of China (grant No.: 62073249), Key R&D Program of Hubei Province (grant No.: 2023BBB011).

# References

1. Eren, B., Demir, M.H., Mistikoglu, S.: Recent developments in computer vision and artificial intelligence aided intelligent robotic welding applications. Int. J. Adv. Manuf. Technol. **126**(11), 4763–4809 (2023)
2. Guo, Q., Yang, Z., Xu, J., et al.: Progress, challenges and trends on vision sensing technologies in automatic/intelligent robotic welding: state-of-the-art review. Robot. Comput. Integr. Manuf. **89**, 102767 (2024)

3. Zeng, J., Cao, G., Li, W., et al.: Feature point extraction based on contour detection and corner detection for weld seam. In: Journal of Physics: Conference Series, p. 012161. IOP Publishing, Hangzhou (2018)
4. Wu, Q.Q., Lee, J.P., Park, M.H., et al.: A study on the modified Hough algorithm for image processing in weld seam tracking. J. Mech. Sci. Technol. **29**, 4859–4865 (2015)
5. Ma, Y., Fan, J., Yang, H., et al.: An efficient and robust complex weld seam feature point extraction method for seam tracking and posture adjustment. IEEE Trans. Ind. Inf. **19**(11), 10704–10715 (2023)
6. Zou, Y., Zhu, M., Chen, X.: A robust detector for automated welding seam tracking system. J. Dyn. Syst. Meas. Control **143**(7), 071001 (2021)
7. Jia, Z., Wang, T., He, J., et al.: Real-time spatial intersecting seam tracking based on laser vision stereo sensor. Measurement **149**, 106987 (2020)
8. Fan, J., Deng, S., Ma, Y., et al.: Seam feature point acquisition based on efficient convolution operator and particle filter in GMAW. IEEE Trans. Ind. Inf. **17**(2), 1220–1230 (2021)
9. Zou, Y., Lan, R., Wei, X., et al.: Robust seam tracking via a deep learning framework combining tracking and detection. Appl. Opt. **59**(14), 4321–4331 (2020)
10. Nguyen, Q.C., Hua, H.Q.B., Pham, P.T.: Development of a vision system integrated with industrial robots for online weld seam tracking. J. Manuf. Process. **119**, 414–424 (2024)
11. Henriques, J.F., Caseiro, R., Martins, P., et al.: High-speed tracking with kernelized correlation filters. IEEE Trans. Pattern Anal. Mach. Intell. **37**(3), 583–596 (2014)
12. Liao, S., Zhao, G., Kellokumpu, V., et al.: Modeling pixel process with scale invariant local patterns for background subtraction in complex scenes. In: 2010 IEEE Computer Society Conference on Computer Vision and Pattern Recognition, San Francisco, pp. 1301–1306. IEEE (2010)
13. Mirza, M., Osindero, S.: Conditional generative adversarial nets. arXiv e-prints, arXiv:1411.1784 (2014)
14. Goodfellow, I., Pouget-Abadie, J., Mirza, M., et al.: Generative adversarial nets. In: Advances in Neural Information Processing Systems, vol. 27 (2014)
15. Croitoru, F.A., Hondru, V., Ionescu, R.T., et al.: Diffusion models in vision: a survey. IEEE Trans. Pattern Anal. Mach. Intell. **45**(9), 10850–10869 (2023)
16. Xiang, P., Wang, L., Wu, F., et al.: Single-image de-raining with feature-supervised generative adversarial network. IEEE Signal Process. Lett. **26**(5), 650–654 (2019)
17. Zhang, H., Sindagi, V., Patel, V.M.: Image de-raining using a conditional generative adversarial network. IEEE Trans. Circuits Syst. Video Technol. **30**(11), 3943–3956 (2019)
18. Sohn, K., Lee, H., Yan, X.: Learning structured output representation using deep conditional generative models. In: Advances in Neural Information Processing Systems, vol. 28 (2015)
19. Maharani, D.A., Machbub, C., Yulianti, L., et al.: Deep features fusion for KCF-based moving object tracking. J. Big Data **10**(1), 136 (2023)

# Natural Interaction and Coordinated Collaboration of Robots in Dynamic Unstructured Environments

# Coordinated Control for Graceful Motion of a Mobile Manipulator

Fujie Yu[1], Dianrui Wang[1], Chengxu Yang[1], and Qining Wang[1,2(✉)]

[1] Department of Rehabilitation Science and Engineering, University of Health and Rehabilitation Sciences, Qingdao 66071, China
`yufujie@uor.edu.cn`
[2] Department of Advanced Manufacturing and Robotics, College of Engineering, and the Institute for Artificial Intelligence, Peking University, Beijing 100871, China
`qiningwang@pku.edu.cn`

**Abstract.** The mobile manipulator holds potential for executing multi-scene operational tasks through the collaborative movement of both the mobile base and manipulator. However, the conventional sequential base-manipulator control method for mobile manipulator is restricted in speed and gracefulness by the need for the mobile base to stop moving before the manipulator starts moving. In contrast, humans effortlessly handle such tasks while walking or running, simultaneously managing secondary tasks such as avoiding obstacles, optimizing posture, and monitoring the environment. Regrettably, mobile manipulators lack this agile finesse displayed by humans. To address this shortfall, this paper introduces a coordinated motion planning method that considers the manipulator and mobile base as a whole structure based on the task-priority redundancy resolution and considers the optimal mobile base placement in navigation. The simulation results demonstrate that the suggested method significantly improves the speed, reliably, and task completion efficiency of the mobile manipulator.

**Keywords:** Autonomous robots · Control strategies · Motion planning

## 1  Introduction

Mobile manipulators can complete a wide range of operation tasks in a better posture, and have become the key equipment for realizing the intelligence of industrial production [1]. As the core of mobile manipulators, the base-manipulator motion control directly determines its motion behavior and application performance [2]. Most of the existing control structures of mobile manipulators regard the mobile base and the manipulator as two independent subsystems and perform tasks in the order that the mobile base first moves to a position near the target to stop, and the manipulator then operates [3,5]. With the expansion of mobile manipulators to a wider range of application scenarios, this sequential base-manipulator control architecture is difficult to meet the practical applications due to the rigid and single motion expression and unnatural motion behavior [6].

X. Lan et al. (Eds.): ICIRA 2024, LNAI 15208, pp. 411–423, 2025.
https://doi.org/10.1007/978-981-96-0783-9_28

Why does a mobile manipulator stop when operating something? We humans are perfectly capable of performing such operational tasks while walking or even running, and further motor subtasks such as avoiding obstacles, optimizing body posture, or observing the surrounding environment can be handled in parallel during mobile manipulation. However, this sense of sporty elegance displayed by our humans is still lacking in mobile manipulators. Different from the sequential base-manipulator control, coordinated motion planning techniques have demonstrated the feasibility of creating the necessary constraints for the integrated and graceful motion behavior of mobile manipulators by exploiting the system's redundant degrees of freedom (DoFs). By merging and processing multiple motion constraint tasks such as base-manipulator motion allocation, manipulator joint limits, singular configuration avoidance, collision avoidance, etc., more elegant motion behavior of the mobile manipulator can be achieved [7,9].

However, attaining the graceful motion of a mobile manipulator through coordinated control encounters several challenges: 1) The redundancy caused by the combination of the mobile base and the manipulator greatly increases the complexity and difficulty of the motion planning, which requires the coordinated motion planning method can reasonably allocate the system degrees of freedom to comprehensively consider the constraints of the end-effector tracking, the obstacle avoidance, and the joint limitations; 2) The mobile base with a slower dynamic response will affect the overall dynamic response control of the mobile manipulator, resulting in the inability to achieve high response speed in system joint space motion planning; 3) In multi-step operation tasks, the principle of base placement directly determines whether the mobile manipulator can choose the best body movement trajectory to efficiently perform the hand operation task, but traditional coordinated control methods have not investigated how to incorporate and deal with the optimal placement constraints of the mobile base in coordinated motion planning; 4) Most of the current coordinated control methods are based on open-loop execution of planned trajectories, and their success depends critically on the initial system state provided and the accuracy with which the robot follows the plan, rather than on improving the robustness of the system by fusing the system closed-loop sensory information.

To address these challenges, a new coordinated motion control approach for the mobile manipulator is developed in this paper to complete the necessary motion constraints related to graceful movement operation with full-body motion behavior. In this approach, the parallel task-priority redundancy resolution scheme is adopted to manage multiple tasks while enhancing system response speed. Additionally, an optimal bas-placement task based on the minimum cost goal is constructed to achieve the time-saving robot placement. A comparative analysis is conducted between the proposed approach and the sequential base-manipulator control method, focusing on speed, reliability, and elegance. The results demonstrate significant enhancements in speed and fluidity with our proposed approach.

## 2    Kinematics

An omnidirectional mobile manipulator with pertinent frames attached is shown in Fig. 1. Through the widely recognized forward kinematics [10], the system configuration can be given by vector

$$\boldsymbol{\xi} = \begin{bmatrix} \boldsymbol{\eta}_1^{\mathrm{T}} & \boldsymbol{\eta}_2^{\mathrm{T}} & \boldsymbol{q}^{\mathrm{T}} \end{bmatrix}^{\mathrm{T}}, \tag{1}$$

where $\boldsymbol{\eta}_1 = [x\ y]^{\mathrm{T}}$ is the positions of the mobile base; $\boldsymbol{\eta}_2 = [\psi]^{\mathrm{T}}$ is the Euler angles of the mobile base; $\boldsymbol{q}$ is vectors of joint positions.

Let define vector $\boldsymbol{v} = \begin{bmatrix} \boldsymbol{v}_1^{\mathrm{T}} & \boldsymbol{v}_2^{\mathrm{T}} \end{bmatrix}^{\mathrm{T}}$ as the base's velocity in a base-fixed frame $\boldsymbol{\Sigma}_b$, where $\boldsymbol{v}_1 = [u\ v]^{\mathrm{T}}$ and $\boldsymbol{v}_2 = [r]^{\mathrm{T}}$ are the angular velocities of the mobile base with respect to the inertial frame $\boldsymbol{\Sigma}_o$, respectively. The vector $\boldsymbol{v}$ meets the following equations:

$$\boldsymbol{v}_1 = \boldsymbol{R}_I^B \dot{\boldsymbol{\eta}}_1, \tag{2}$$

$$\boldsymbol{v}_2 = \dot{\boldsymbol{\eta}}_2, \tag{3}$$

where $\boldsymbol{R}_I^B$ indicates the rotation matrix of the frame $\boldsymbol{\Sigma}_o$ with respect to the frame $\boldsymbol{\Sigma}_b$.

By introducing vector $\boldsymbol{\zeta} = \begin{bmatrix} \boldsymbol{v}_1^{\mathrm{T}} & \boldsymbol{v}_2^{\mathrm{T}} & \dot{\boldsymbol{q}}^{\mathrm{T}} \end{bmatrix}^{\mathrm{T}}$, the relationship between the aforementioned velocities can be given as:

$$\boldsymbol{\zeta} = \begin{bmatrix} \boldsymbol{R}_I^B & \boldsymbol{O}_{3*3} & \boldsymbol{O}_{3*n} \\ \boldsymbol{O}_{3*3} & \boldsymbol{I}_3 & \boldsymbol{O}_{3*n} \\ \boldsymbol{O}_{n*3} & \boldsymbol{O}_{n*3} & \boldsymbol{I}_n \end{bmatrix} \dot{\boldsymbol{\xi}}, \tag{4}$$

Let us define $\boldsymbol{\eta}_{ee1} \in \mathbf{IR}^3$ and $\boldsymbol{\eta}_{ee2} \in \mathbf{IR}^3$ as the position and orientation of the end-effector in the frame $\boldsymbol{\Sigma}_o$, respectively. The configuration of a mobile manipulator can now be expressed using the following equation:

$$\boldsymbol{\eta}_{ee} = \begin{bmatrix} \boldsymbol{\eta}_{ee1} \\ \boldsymbol{\eta}_{ee2} \end{bmatrix} = {}_I^E\mathrm{T}\left(\boldsymbol{\eta}, \boldsymbol{q}\right). \tag{5}$$

The following Jacobian matrix provides the end-effector's linear and angular velocities with respect to the frame $\boldsymbol{\Sigma}_o$:

The end-effector's linear and angular velocities with respect to the frame $\boldsymbol{\Sigma}_o$ are provided by the following Jacobian matrix:

$$\dot{\boldsymbol{x}}_E = \begin{bmatrix} \dot{\boldsymbol{\eta}}_{ee1} \\ \dot{\boldsymbol{\eta}}_{ee2} \end{bmatrix} = \begin{bmatrix} \boldsymbol{J}_{pos} \\ \boldsymbol{J}_{ori} \end{bmatrix} \boldsymbol{\zeta} = \boldsymbol{J}_{\mathrm{MM}} \boldsymbol{\zeta}, \tag{6}$$

where $\boldsymbol{J}_{\mathrm{MM}}$ contains $\boldsymbol{J}_{pos}$ and $\boldsymbol{J}_{ori}$. $\boldsymbol{J}_{pos}$ denotes the relationship between the system velocity expressed in $\boldsymbol{\Sigma}_b$ and the end-effector's linear velocity expressed in $\boldsymbol{\Sigma}_o$; $\boldsymbol{J}_{ori}$ describes the relationship between the system velocity expressed in $\boldsymbol{\Sigma}_b$ and the end-effector's angular velocity expressed in $\boldsymbol{\Sigma}_o$ [11]. $\boldsymbol{J}_{pos}$ and $\boldsymbol{J}_{ori}$ are given as follows:

$$J_{pos} = \left[ R_B^I \ - \left( S\left(R_B^I r_{B0}^B\right) + S\left(R_0^I \eta_{0,en}^0\right)\right) R_B^I \ J_{pos,man} \right], \tag{7}$$

$$J_{ori}\left(R_B^I, q\right) = \left[ O_{3*3} \ R_B^I \ J_{ori,man} \right], \tag{8}$$

where $R_B^I$ represents the rotation matrix mapping the frame $\Sigma_b$ to the frame $\Sigma_o$; $r_{B0}^B$ is the vector connecting the frame $\Sigma_b$ and the arm-base frame as observed from the frame $\Sigma_b$; $R_0^I$ represents the rotation matrix of the arm-base frame with respect to the frame $\Sigma_b$; and $S$ is the skew-symmetric matrix.

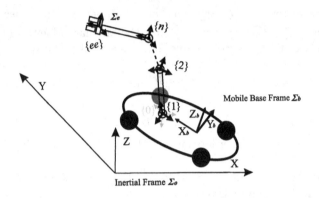

**Fig. 1.** Sketch of the mobile manipulator with relevant frames attached.

## 3    Mobile Manipulation with Arm-Vehicle Coordination Scheme

We demonstrate a system that can perform reactive manipulation tasks by reaching out and driving past a target. The system creates motion that seamlessly joins the subtasks by taking into account both the current and future objectives of a high-level task. This is made possible by a generic architecture that splits control up into multiple modules to allow for reactive manipulation while on the go. The only requirements for the architecture outlined are that the robot provides joint angle and odometry sensing and a velocity control interface. Other than that, the architecture can be applied to a broad variety of robot designs. While pick and place activities are the main emphasis of this study, the same architecture can be used to accomplish other jobs that can be accomplished using end-effector velocity control. Such tasks include pressing a button, flicking a switch, or turning a handle (Fig. 2).

**Parallel task-priority redundancy resolution controller:** Let us define the controlled task variable as

$$\sigma = f\left(\xi(t)\right) \in \mathbf{IR}^m, \tag{9}$$

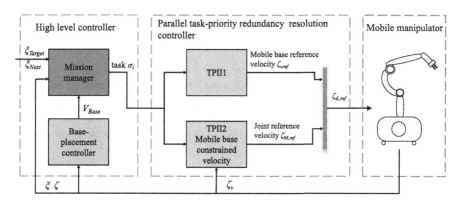

**Fig. 2.** Proposed architecture for graceful manipulation.

with the corresponding time derivative relationship:

$$\dot{\boldsymbol{\sigma}}(t) = \frac{\partial f\left(\boldsymbol{\xi}(t)\right)}{\partial \boldsymbol{\xi}}\dot{\boldsymbol{\xi}} = \boldsymbol{J}\left(\boldsymbol{\xi}(t)\right)\dot{\boldsymbol{\xi}}(t), \tag{10}$$

where $\boldsymbol{f}\left(\boldsymbol{\xi}(t)\right)$ is the forward kinematics function; $\boldsymbol{J}\left(\boldsymbol{\xi}(t)\right) \in \mathrm{IR}^{m*n}$ is the Jacobian matrix of the mobile manipulator; and $\boldsymbol{\xi} \in \mathrm{IR}^{n}$ is the vector of the mobile manipulator state.

For redundant systems, the inverse solution is not unique due to the kinematic redundancy [12]. The general inverse solution of Eq. (11) is to use the pseudoinverse of the Jacobian matrix:

$$\dot{\boldsymbol{\zeta}}_d = \boldsymbol{J}^{\dagger}\left(\dot{\boldsymbol{\sigma}}_d + \boldsymbol{\Lambda}\tilde{\boldsymbol{\sigma}}\right) = \boldsymbol{J}^{\dagger}\dot{\boldsymbol{\sigma}}_{ref}, \tag{11}$$

where $\boldsymbol{J}^{\dagger}$ is the Moore-Penrose pseudoinverse of the Jacobian matrix $\boldsymbol{J}$ satisfying $\boldsymbol{J}^{\dagger} = \boldsymbol{J}^T\left(\boldsymbol{J}\boldsymbol{J}^T\right)^{-1}$; $\tilde{\boldsymbol{\sigma}} \in \mathrm{IR}^m$ is the task error defined as $\tilde{\boldsymbol{\sigma}} = \boldsymbol{\sigma}_d - \boldsymbol{\sigma}$; and $\boldsymbol{\Lambda} \in \mathrm{IR}^{m*m}$ is a positive-definite matrix of gains. For highly redundant systems, it is usually necessary to execute multiple tasks simultaneously. Task priority redundancy resolution algorithm is suitable as it can prioritize multiple tasks to avoid inter-task conflicts [13,15]. For manoeuvres composed of $k$ tasks, the task-priority redundancy resolution algorithm is express as

$$\dot{\boldsymbol{\zeta}}_d = \underbrace{\boldsymbol{J}_1^{\dagger}\dot{\boldsymbol{\sigma}}_{1,ref}}_{\dot{q}_{1,des}} + \boldsymbol{N}_1\underbrace{\boldsymbol{J}_2^{\dagger}\dot{\boldsymbol{\sigma}}_{2,ref}}_{\dot{q}_{2,des}} + ... + \boldsymbol{N}_{12...(k-1)}^A\underbrace{\boldsymbol{J}_k^{\dagger}\dot{\boldsymbol{\sigma}}_{k,ref}}_{\dot{q}_{k,des}}, \tag{12}$$

where $\boldsymbol{N}_{12...(k-1)}^A$ is the null space of the augmented Jacobian matrix, which is given by

$$\boldsymbol{J}_{12...(k-1)}^A = \begin{bmatrix} \boldsymbol{J}_1 & \boldsymbol{J}_2 & ... & \boldsymbol{J}_{k-1} \end{bmatrix}^{\mathrm{T}}. \tag{13}$$

The task-priority redundancy resolution algorithm's control aim was created for equality tasks, which supply a single desired value for a set of given robot states. Nonetheless, some objectives, such avoiding joint limitations, might be managed in accordance with the intended range of values. These objectives are classified as inequality tasks, and they become active when the goal value falls outside of their range. One workable solution for handling inequality tasks is to think of them as equality-based activities that become active or inactive dependent on their present value. The activation thresholds for each inequality task must be specified, in particular, by $\boldsymbol{\sigma} \in D = [\boldsymbol{\sigma}_{a,l}, \boldsymbol{\sigma}_{a,u}]$. Whether the task is to be activated as a new equality-based task is determined by the tangent cone of the set $D$, which is provided by

$$T_D\left(\boldsymbol{\sigma}\right) = \begin{cases} [0,\ \infty) & \sigma \leq \sigma_{a,l} \\ R & \sigma = (\sigma_{a,l},\ \sigma_{a,u}) \\ (-\infty,\ 0] & \sigma \geq \sigma_{a,u} \end{cases} . \tag{14}$$

Note that if $\dot{\boldsymbol{\sigma}}\left(t\right) \in T_D\left(\boldsymbol{\sigma}\right)\ \forall t > t_0$, then this implies that $\boldsymbol{\sigma}\left(t\right) \in D\ \forall t > t_0$. If $\boldsymbol{\sigma}$ is in the interior of $D$, the derivative is always in the tangent cone, as this is defined as $R$. If $\boldsymbol{\sigma} = \boldsymbol{\sigma}_{a,l}$, the task is at the lower border of the set. In this case, if $\dot{\boldsymbol{\sigma}}\left(t\right) \in [0,\ \infty)$, then $\boldsymbol{\sigma}$ will either stay on the border or move into the interior of the set. Similarly, if $\boldsymbol{\sigma} = \boldsymbol{\sigma}_{a,u}$ and $\dot{\boldsymbol{\sigma}}\left(t\right) \in (-\infty,\ 0]$, $\boldsymbol{\sigma}$ will not leave $D$.

To improve system responsiveness, we developed a parallel task-priority redundancy scheme with a higher-level block TPII. TPII contains the same control task with the same hierarchy developed up till the previous exercise. The strategy allows us to optimize the outputs based on two different sub-blocks: TPII 1 and TPII 2.

TPII 1: In this instance, we are computing the joint and mobile base's velocities simultaneously. Following this process, we save the mobile base's velocity ($v$) and discard the joint velocities. The $v$ value will be the input of the dynamic control layer.

TPII 2: we utilize TPII again to separate the velocities between the manipulator and the mobile base. Assuming total non-controllability of the mobile base, we carry out a second optimization. To emulate that, we use the $nr$ task in this manner: we set the genuine velocity of the robot's base as the reference value and we set $nr$ activation to true. This allows us to re-optimize the manipulator's velocities by constraining the mobile base velocities to be equal to the actual velocities (so the one with disturbances). Thus, the solution of joint velocities $\dot{q}$ given by TPII 2 tries to reach the goal for the end-effector frame, while compensating for disturbances in the mobile base's velocities.

Finally, the reference velocity provided as input to the dynamic control layer is given by:

$$\dot{\bar{\boldsymbol{y}}} = \begin{bmatrix} \dot{\bar{q}} \ \text{TPII 2} \\ \bar{\nu} \ \text{TPII 1} \end{bmatrix} \tag{15}$$

Because TPII 2 can be updated at the higher manipulator control rate and TPII 1 can be executed at the mobile base control frequency, it should be noted that this parallel technique for coordinated control between the mobile and manipulator is also appropriate for implementing multi-rate control of the two subsystems.

**Base-Placement Controller:** Navigation and manipulation capabilities must work together seamlessly for mobile manipulation tasks. The key to finishing these kinds of operations rapidly is figuring out where robots can pick up and position stuff most effectively. Inadequate robot positioning results in unfeasible solutions or necessitates more extensive mobile base repositioning to access target items, hence lengthening the task completion time. In this work, we describe a unique control approach that automatically finds the best base placements in a collision-free way given a set of objects.

By calculating the path cost from the present robot posture to potential base placements and from the candidates to the drop site, the best base placement is chosen from a discretized set. On a circle with radius $R_c$, candidates are positioned uniformly around the target item in $\omega$ deg increments, yielding a total of $360/\omega$ potential base positions. There are two possible orientations allocated to each position; the robot's forward vector can face either clockwise or counterclockwise, tangential to the circle, yielding a total of $720/\omega$ options. Every colored sphere in Fig. 3 is a contender; those in the top ring face clockwise, while those in the bottom ring face counter-clockwise.

The robot is maneuvered into a closest approach posture by the base controller, which links the current pose to the next objective and puts the robot within the target's manipulation range. The method for computing $Cost$ given the current base posture, the manipulation target, the next target, and the closest approach radius ($r_C$) is shown geometrically in Fig. 3. Path cost is calculated by the following equation:

$$Cost = \begin{cases} \rho + L - p * cos(h_{cw}, a) & clockwise \\ \rho + L - p * cos(h_{ccw}, a) & counterclockwise \end{cases} \tag{16}$$

where $\rho$ is the distance between the current position of the robot and the particle; $L$ is the vector from the particle to the next target; $a$ is the vector that connects the current target with the next target; $p$ is the weight gain; $h_{cw}$ and $h_{ccw}$ are the clockwise and counterclockwise vectors of the particle along the tangent to the circle, respectively. When the angle of the pinch is greater it means that the cost will be greater, but the cosine value is decreasing in the range 0 to $\pi/2$, so the resulting cosine value is added with a minus sign and calculated with the other two parts.

The global planner from the base control system is used to calculate the path cost for each candidate. After calculating the cost value corresponding to each of the clockwise and counterclockwise directions, the direction corresponding to the smallest value is selected as the basis for the next movement of the mobile base. The navigation aim is the posture with the highest ranking among the candidate set. The end result is a system that effectively connects the present robot pose with the drop pose by choosing a candidate base placement that is within the target's manipulation range. The chosen base stance prompts the robot to circle the object counter-clockwise while it moves in the direction of the drop point to finish the grip. Real-time updates to this computation are made in response to perceived state modifications. If the manipulability of the object is greater than a threshold of 0.08 when the robot reaches the target, we consider it to be within manipulation range. This translates to an approximate 0.6 m manipulation range for the targets in our trials. Although the system is not susceptible to the manipulability threshold, it is advisable to refrain from using the robot's maximum reach in order to keep it from achieving a singularity.

The ideal base placement should be adjusted continuously based on the robot's present condition in order to facilitate failure recovery. The system can then reassess the ideal base stance, which is within the object's manipulation range but as close to the drop point as feasible, if extra time is needed to recover from a failed grip. To achieve failure recovery, when the end of the manipulator reaches a given position, it is considered a successful grasp, it exits the loop around the particle and drives to the next target. If the grasping fails, after the pedestal enters from the optimal entry point, the pedestal's speed slows down a little bit for every particle it passes through, creating more time to achieve a higher success rate for successful grasping. The controlled speed of the pedestal is shown in the following equation:

$$w_{ang,i} = (1 - kp_l)w_{ang,i-1} \qquad (17)$$

$$v_{lin,i} = (1 - kp_l)v_{lin,i-1} \qquad (18)$$

where $p_l$ is the number of particles the mobile base passes through, $k$ is the control gain of the mobile base's speed.

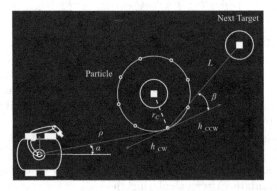

**Fig. 3.** Illustration of sampled base placement results for a pick-and-place task. Each particle represents a candidate base placement around the target object.

## 4   Implementation to Mobile Manipulator

We present an example implementation for performing pick and place tasks with a mobile manipulator that consists of a 6°C-of-freedom UR5e manipulator mounted to a KUKA mecanum-drive mobile base. The pick-and-place task consists of four operational steps, and the arrival of the end-effector at the desired position of the operational target is the default success of the task to focus the study on the control architecture. Performance is evaluated based on metrics such as fast (cost time), safe (joint limits, etc.), and reliable (success rate) related to the robot's motion behavior, demonstrating the mapping of motion behavior to motion elegance for a mobile manipulator. To demonstrate crucial behaviors appropriate for the mobile manipulator, the parallel task-priority redundancy resolution technique also incorporates the end-effector position task and joint limits task in addition to the base-placement task.

Since the goal of the simulations is to demonstrate the efficacy of the coordinated control strategy, only the kinematic loop performance is displayed in this article to maintain clarity. A greater inaccuracy will impact the actual base/joint position because the tracking error must also be taken into account. Notably, this tracking error is bounded if the law-level dynamic controller is appropriately built. Furthermore, the performance of the kinematic loop is unaffected.

The following parameters are chosen: $r_c = 0.55$, $r_m = 0.1$, $\omega = 36$. The mobile manipulator starts from the initial configuration $\eta_{init} = [0\ 0\ 0]^T$ m, deg and $q_{init} = [0\ 0\ 0\ 0\ 0\ 0]^T$ deg that corresponds to the end-effector position $\eta_{ee1} = [0.53\ 0.11 0.1]^T$m and orientation $\eta_{ee2} = [-125\ 0\ -90]^T$ deg. The simulation time is 50 s. The following joint limits are considered: $q_{\min} = [-\pi\ -0.94\pi\ -0.83\pi\ -\pi\ -0.89\pi\ -\pi]^T$rad and $q_{\max} = [\pi\ 0\ 0.83\pi\ \pi\ 0.89\pi\ \pi]^T$rad. The goal position of the mobile manipulator is $[-1.15\ 1.85\ 0]^T$ m. The positions of the four selected targets are $point1 = [0.675; -2.825; 1.0]^T$ m, $point2 = [-0.872; -8.296; 1.0]^T$ m, $point3 = [3.478; -7.171; 1.0]^T$ m, and $point4 = [3.88; -3.2; 1.0]^T]$ m, respectively.

# 5   Results and Discussion

The simulation results are shown in Figs. 4 and 5 and Table 1. From Figs. 4 and 5 we can conclude that the proposed coordinated control scheme can not only ensure the desired trajectory tracking of the end-effector by coordinating the manipulator and the mobile base but also handle other secondary motion constraints related to safety, optimization, etc. For example, the joint limits task is activated to prevent joint 2 from exceeding its thresholds.

Figure 4 intuitively illustrates that the mobile manipulator starts from the initial position and arrives at a preset desired position at around 12, 21, 26 and 32 s respectively, which corresponds to the position error and the activation of the mobile base in Fig. 5. Then, the mobile base returns to the goal position. The result also shows that the end-effector of the manipulator successfully accomplished the multi-operation task with the cooperation of the mobile base and the manipulator. For simplicity, we did not set up a complex operation trajectory in this simulation, and the operation is considered successful as long as the end-effector reaches the preset target point.

Table 1 presents a comparison of simulation results between our method and the sequential base-manipulator control method. Sequential control approach 1

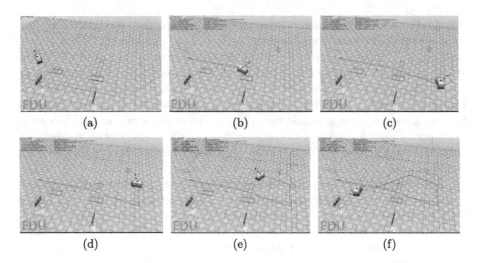

(a)                    (b)                    (c)

(d)                    (e)                    (f)

**Fig. 4.** The posture transformation of the mobile manipulator during the simulation.

represents conventional control methods, and due to the lack of publicly available performance data, the results of this method are estimated from experience. To further investigate the graceful impact of coordinated control on mobile manipulators, the sequential control method (Sequential control approach 2) was used to repeat the simulation. However, the task time is fixed, so the average speed and acceleration of the mobile robot arm have changed. Compared with the sequential base-manipulator control method, our method can achieve the same reliability while reducing execution time by up to 48%. The sequential base-manipulator control method stops the base when grabbing objects, which increases the task time. The efficient task execution of the mobile manipulator is characterized by the following two aspects: 1) utilizing the task-priority redundancy solution algorithm to complete the motion allocation between the mobile base and the manipulator realizes that the mobile manipulator gracefully executes the motion operations with uniform motion behaviors and greatly improves the speed and smoothness of motion behaviors; 2) providing optimal base placement for mobile manipulators will further improve their efficiency in executing operational tasks, which is particularly important in multi-step operations.

Generally speaking, tracking trajectories with high speeds or significant accelerations is undesirable for the mobile manipulator. Maximum acceleration (Max $|\vec{a}|$) has been introduced as a measure of gracefulness. We also demonstrate the mobile base mean velocity magnitude (Mean $|\vec{v}|$). The outcome shows that compared to the sequential control approach, the suggested approach has a lower maximum acceleration for the mobile manipulator. Compared to the sequential control approach, our approach tasks in a similar time but reduces acceleration metrics by over 50%. In addition, the sequential base-manipulator control method cannot respond to imprecise perception and robot control, which can easily lead to several instances of base grasping loss. Due to setting up a failure

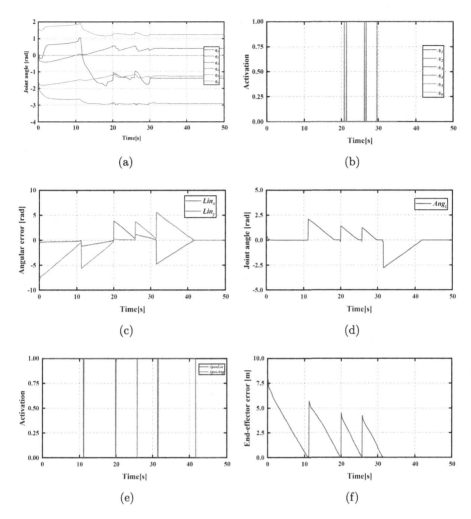

**Fig. 5.** Proposed approach. (a) Joint positions. (b) Activation for joint limits. (c) Mobile base position error. (d) Mobile base attitude error. (e) Activation for Mobile base. (f) End-effector tracking error.

recovery task, our method can also demonstrate high reliability at higher speeds. The sequential base-manipulator control method provides slow task execution and significantly higher acceleration than our method at similar speeds.

In summary, the proposed method considers both the navigation cost between operational tasks and the operational cost of reducing the time required to complete tasks, enabling time-saving base placement in multi-step mobile manipulation tasks. Especially in dynamic environments, the proposed method can integrate sensor data online, dynamically update navigation and operation-related costs, and provide real-time optimal base placement for the current robot state.

**Table 1.** Pick and place results.

| Control strategies | Time(s) | Mean $|\vec{v}|$ (ms$^{-1}$) | Max $|\vec{a}|$) (ms$^{-2}$) |
|---|---|---|---|
| Sequential control approach 1 | 65 | 0.32 | 0.31 |
| Sequential control approach 2 | 50 | 0.48 | 0.50 |
| Proposed approach | 50 | 0.42 | 0.25 |

## 6  Conclusion

This paper presents an architecture for mobile manipulation that demonstrates task execution similar to independently controlled mobile approaches, but more elegant, time-saving, and robust. In addition, the framework demonstrates the feasibility of handling faults in mobile operation tasks. While our simulation models grasp simple objects in a tidy environment, the control module can be realized by combining it with the dynamic windowing approach to perform other tasks in complex dynamic environments, such as pressing buttons, flicking switches, or opening doors while moving. Besides, the control logic of the base-placement controller is still relatively simple, and the robot does not know how long it may take to recover from a malfunction; these issues provide an opportunity for further development of mobile operating systems that can operate effectively in complex environments and adapt to uncertainty and malfunctions.

## References

1. Yuan, W., Liu, Y., Su, C., Zhao, F.: Whole-body control of an autonomous mobile manipulator using model predictive control and adaptive fuzzy technique. IEEE Trans. Fuzzy Syst. **31**(3), 799–809 (2023)
2. Heshmati-Alamdari, S., Karras, G.C., Kyriakopoulos, K.J.: A predictive control approach for cooperative transportation by multiple underwater vehicle manipulator systems. IEEE Trans. Control Syst. Technol. **30**(3), 917–930 (2022)
3. Tan, N., Zhong, Z., Yu, P., Li, Z., Ni, F.: A discrete model-free scheme for fault-tolerant tracking control of redundant manipulators. IEEE Trans. Industr. Inf. **18**(12), 8595–8606 (2022)
4. Dai, G., Liu, Y.: Distributed coordination and cooperation control for networked mobile manipulators. IEEE Trans. Industr. Electron. **64**(6), 5065–5074 (2017)
5. Liu, Y., Li, Z., Su, H., Su, C.-Y.: Whole-body control of an autonomous mobile manipulator using series elastic actuators. IEEE/ASME Trans. Mechatron. **26**(2), 657–667 (2021)
6. Janson, L., Pavone, M.: Fast marching trees: a fast marching sampling-based method for optimal motion planning in many dimensions. Int. J. Robot. Res. **34**(7), 883–921 (2015)
7. Xing, H., Ding, L., Gao, H., Li, W., Tavakoli, M.: Dual-user haptic teleoperation of complementary motions of a redundant wheeled mobile manipulator considering task priority. IEEE Trans. Syst. Man Cybern. Syst. **52**(10), 6283–6295 (2022)

8. Zhang, Y., Li, S., Gui, J., Luo, X.: Velocity-level control with compliance to acceleration-level constraints: a novel scheme for manipulator redundancy resolution. IEEE Trans. Industr. Inf. **14**(3), 921–930 (2018)
9. Qi, R., Khajepour, A., Melek, W.W.: Redundancy resolution and disturbance rejection via torque optimization in hybrid cable-driven robots. IEEE Trans. Syst. Man Cybern. Syst. **52**(7), 4069–4079 (2022)
10. Falco, P., Natale, C.: On the stability of closed-loop inverse kinematics algorithms for redundant robots. IEEE Trans. Rob. **27**(4), 780–784 (2011)
11. Ma, Y., Gong, Y., Xiao, C., Gao, Y., Zhang, J.: Path planning for autonomous underwater vehicles: an ant colony algorithm incorporating alarm pheromone. IEEE Trans. Veh. Technol. **68**(1), 141–154 (2019)
12. Pan, J., et al.: A self-aligning upper-limb exoskeleton preserving natural shoulder movements: kinematic compatibility analysis. IEEE Trans. Neural Syst. Rehabil. Eng. **31**, 4954–4964 (2023)
13. Chen, D., Li, S., Wu, Q., Luo, X.: New disturbance rejection constraint for redundant robot manipulators: an optimization perspective. IEEE Trans. Industr. Inf. **16**(4), 2221–2232 (2020)
14. Sharifi, M., Azimi, V., Mushahwar, V.K., Tavakoli, M.: Impedance learning-based adaptive control for human-robot interaction. IEEE Trans. Control Syst. Technol. **30**(4), 1345–1358 (2022)
15. Shen, J., Wang, Y., Azizkhani, M., Qiu, D., Chen, Y.: Concentric tube robot redundancy resolution via velocity/compliance manipulability optimization. IEEE Robot. Autom. Lett. **8**(11), 7495–7502 (2023)

# Active Target Location and Grasping Based on Language-Vision-Action

Xinxin Zhu, Jin Liu, Jialong Xie, Chaoqun Wang, and Fengyu Zhou[✉]

Center for Robotics, School of Control Science and Engineering, Shandong
University, No. 17923, Jingshi Road, Jinan 250061, China
zhoufengyu@sdu.edu.cn

**Abstract.** This paper investigates a challenging scene in robot daily
grasping services, where the target exists obstruction and visual ambiguity. Specifically, the fine-grained visual information of the target object
is obstructed, e.g., text information. Besides, there are multiple objects
similar to the appearance of the target object in the scene. To tackle
this issue, this paper proposes an active target location and grasping
framework based on joint language-vision-action. Firstly, we take the
textual label information of the target object as a clue to guide the robot
to explore objects. Then, to obtain more fine-grained text information
about the objects in the scene, we enable the robot actively to pick up the
object for observation like humans. Consequently, the robot can acquire
the target object with detailed context from multiple objects and eliminate visual ambiguity. Finally, extensive experiments are conducted in
both simulation and real-world scenes to verify the effectiveness of the
proposed active target location and grasping system.

**Keywords:** obstruction · visual ambiguity · fine-grained visual
information · active target location

## 1 Introduction

With the development of robot technology and the expansion of application
fields, robots need more intelligence and autonomy to interact with humans
more efficiently. It typically involves complex techniques, such as language-
conditioned grasping detection, motion planning and control [1]. Importantly,
language-conditioned grasping detection [2–5] is attracting more attention
because it provides powerful support for the development of human-computer
interaction. However, existing works mainly relied on the coarse-grained visual
attributes [4,5] to locate and grasp the target object. For example, if the robot
is asked the following question: "The blue cup next to the computer." and "The
bottle on the counter.", where the target object to be obtained only has category information (i.e., "cup" and "bottle"). There may be ambiguity in the robot
acquiring the target object once multiple objects with similar visual attributes
are in this scene. To tackle this problem, several studies proposed to utilize

the text information on an object, which is also regarded as the natural ID, to locate the target to eliminate the visual ambiguity [6,7]. However, these works mainly solve the language-conditioned grasping detection problem when the target object is visible. When the target object is obstructed, the robot may struggle to locate and grasp the target object.

Recently, a novel task called Remote Embodied Visual Referencing Expression in Real Industrial Environments (REVERIE) [8] has been proposed in the field of robot navigation. In such a setting, the target object might not be in sight at first, and the robot needs to explore the environment to identify the target object given natural language instruction. It is a more challenging task as it requires a combination of language, vision, and action to enable the robot to actively explore objects in the environment. Although REVERIE is a new task derived from the field of robot navigation, many researchers in the field of robot manipulation have done many works on this topic [9–12,15], because this is universal in people's life scenes. In some unstructured environments, when the target object is placed behind or below other objects [11], inside a container, on an elevated platform, etc., the robot cannot locate it directly. The robot needs to actively perceive the environment, obtain more information about the object and its surrounding environment [9,13,16], and make some actions [11,14] based on the current environment to try to display the target object in the current field of view of the robot, and then complete target location and grasping [12]. [15] proposed a new robot manipulation framework for visual-auditory referential expression. The robot actively manipulates the bottle to generate sound signals and inputs them into the audio recognition module to determine what object is inside the bottle.

The above works do not consider a more common scenario in daily life that combines REVERIE and target disambiguation [17,18] (REVERIE-Disambiguation-Robot-Grasping-Task). For example, when the natural language instruction is "Pass me Vitamin C Tablets on the table.", the reference object is the object name "Vitamin C Tablets". There are three pill bottles on the table, and their visual attributes are similar, one of which is the target object. The robot cannot see the target object which has the text name "Vitamin C Tablets" on the bottle in the current field of view, so the robot is difficult to complete the visual location. When humans deal with this scene, they will pick up three pill bottles in turn and then observe the text information on the surface of the pill bottle to determine which pill bottle refers to the target object, "Vitamin C Tablets". Inspired by this behavior, in this paper, we propose an active target location and grasping framework based on joint language, vision, and action. We first use LLM and the knowledge base to parse the natural language instruction, transforming the target object name into global visual attributes of the object, including fine-grained category, color, and shape. e.g., the target object name "Vitamin C Tablets" corresponds to "Fine-grained category: pill bottle; Color: white; Shape: cylinder". The robot matches each object in the scene based on these three visual attributes to obtain matching scores for all objects. Then the robot actively explores the text information on the surface of the objects in the scene through actions, and finally determines the target object "Vitamin C Tablets". The main contributions of the paper are summarized as follows:

- We propose a REVERIE-Disambiguation-Robot-Grasping-Task, which enables the robot to find the target object under the natural language instruction more effectively.
- We propose an active target location and grasping system based on joint language-vision-action, which enables the robot to actively explore fine-grained text information on objects and complete the location and grasping of the target object from multiple similar-looking objects in the scene.

The remainder of the paper is organized as follows. In Sect. 2, the problem formulation is described. And Sect. 3 describes the implementation details of the proposed method. Then, the experimental results are analyzed in Sect. 4. Finally, we conclude the paper in Sect. 5.

## 2  Problem Formulation

For REVERIE-Disambiguation-Robot-Grasping-Task, formally, the input includes the RGB-D image $I$ and the user's instruction $Q$ with the text label information of the target object. The text label information of the target object in the user's instruction $Q$ is unique, but there are multiple objects with similar visual attributes in the scene, e.g., medicine bottles for treating different diseases. In addition, the fine-grained text information of the target object is obstructed. Therefore, the information provided by user instruction is not enough to distinguish the ground-truth target $x_*$ from other objects $\{x_i\}_{i=1}^{N}$ in the input image $I$. For this, we take the fine-grained text information on the target object in the user's instruction as a clue, enabling the robot to actively pick up the object for seeing the fine-grained text information on objects like humans, thereby finding the target object from multiple similar-looking objects in the scene. As it is a new task, we make the following assumptions: (1) There is only one target object in the scene; (2) The text label information in the natural language instruction exists on the target object.

## 3  Methods

As shown in Fig. 1, the proposed framework is composed of a natural language instruction parsing module, a scene understanding module, object grounding, and Act-to-See, which enables the robot to actively explore the fine-grained text information of the object in the scene and find the target object. 1) the natural language instruction parsing module parses the natural language instruction into fine-grained category, color, and shape. 2) The scene understanding module is used to understand the fine-grained categories and the main visual attribute information, including the color and shape of each object in the input image $I$.

3) Based on the results of the instruction parsing module and scene understanding module, object grounding obtains the matching score between each object detected in the input image $I$ and the user's instruction $Q$. 4) Finally, the robot will actively explore the fine-grained text information of the object in the scene through actions in order from high to low matching scores until the target object is found.

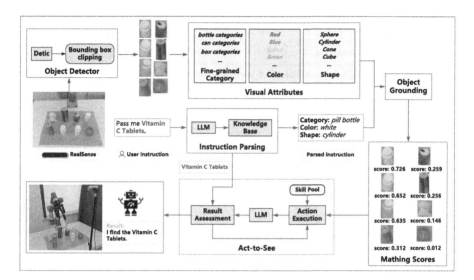

**Fig. 1.** Active target location and grasping framework based on joint language-vision-action.

## 3.1   Instruction Parsing

Due to the issue of information inconsistency between the visual information in the input image and the fine-grained text information in the user's instruction, it is difficult to locate the target object directly. For this, we design an instruction parsing module. Instruction parsing is mainly divided into two stages. The first stage uses the large language model to extract the reference object from the user's instruction. The second stage is to use the constructed knowledge base to infer the visual attributes of the reference object, including fine-grained category, color, and shape.

**1) Reference Object Extraction:** To improve the generalization and accuracy of instruction parsing, we use large language pre-training models (e.g., GPT-3 [19], GLM-4 [20], etc. ) to extract the reference object from the user's instruction. They are trained through massive data on the Internet, which can more accurately understand the complex instructions, and effectively improve the accuracy of instruction parsing. Our instruction types are shown in Table 1. Specifically, the few-shots prompt method is used to extract the reference object from the instruction. In contrast to the zero-shot prompt method, it can achieve context learning by leveraging the learning ability of the large language model, and results in better performance on our instruction parsing tasks.

**Table 1.** User Instruction Types

| Instruction Types | OBJECT_TEXT_LABEL |
|---|---|
| Pass me OBJECT_TEXT_LABEL | nurofen, Strawberry jelly, etc. |
| Find OBJECT_TEXT_LABEL and give it to me | nurofen, Strawberry jelly, etc. |

**2) Visual Attributes Reasoning:** To address the issue of information inconsistency between the visual information and the fine-grained text information, we constructed a visual attributes knowledge base corresponding to fine-grained text information using a knowledge graph, including fine-grained categories $\left\{ Attr_{x_i}^{category} \right\}_{i=1}^{N}$, colors $\left\{ Attr_{x_i}^{color} \right\}_{i=1}^{N}$, and shapes $\left\{ Attr_{x_i}^{shape} \right\}_{i=1}^{N}$, which correspond to the visual attributes extracted by the scene understanding module.

## 3.2   Scene Understanding

The scene understanding module is used to extract three types of visual attributes, including fine-grained category, color, and shape of each object in the scene. The fusion of these three types of visual feature can locate the reference object in the global vision.

**1) Object Detection:** To detect open-set objects, we apply the most recently proposed open-vocabulary object detector, Detic [21], which can use open vocabulary to locate and classify unknown objects. Then, we crop the detected objects, and the cropped objects will be used in all subsequent steps of the visual attributes extraction.

**2) Visual Attributes Extraction:** We use CLIP [22] for zero-shot classification of the previously cropped objects. Specifically, we first pre-define possible fine-grained categories, colors, and shapes, as shown in Table 2, which can effectively describe the global visual attributes of objects. Then, the pre-trained CLIP is used to classify and recognize the three types of visual attributes respectively to obtain the target fine-grained category probability $p_{x_i}^{category}$, target color probability $p_{x_i}^{color}$, and target shape probability $p_{x_i}^{shape}$ of the $i$-th object $x_i$ in the scene.

**Table 2.** Predefined Visual Attributes

| Fine-grained categories | Colors | Shapes |
|---|---|---|
| bottle, pill bottle, soda bottle, water bottle, etc. | Red, Orange, Yellow, Green, | Sphere, Cylinder, |
| can, soda can, beer can, etc. | Blue, Purple, White, Gray, | Cone, Cube, |
| box, cereal box, packing box, cigar box, etc. | Black, Brown, etc. | Disk, etc. |

### 3.3 Object Grounding

We adopt the modular design to match the three visual attributes of each object in the scene and the target visual attributes obtained from the instruction parsing module. Specifically, we use the weighted average of the three visual attribute probabilities to calculate the matching score of each object in the scene:

$$S\left(x_i | Attr_{x_*}\right) = \sum_{j \in \{category, color, shape\}} w^j p^j_{x_i} \qquad (1)$$

where $S(x_i)$ is the target matching score of the object $x_i$, $w^j$ represents the weight and $p^j_{x_i}$ denotes the probability of the $j$-th target fine-grained visual feature of the object $x_i$ as determined by the visual attributes extraction module. $j$ represents the fine-grained category, color, and shape, respectively. The average weighted method is used to calculate the target matching score, $w^j = 1/3$.

### 3.4 Act-To-See

Our system allows the robot to actively explore objects in the scene through actions and find the target object through Act-to-See, as shown in Algorithm 1. Specifically, we first place the RealSense camera in a definite position as the eye of the robot. The robot plans a grasp pose [23] for grasping the object of the highest matching score in sence and moves it into the vision of the robot's eye. Then, the robot rotates the object at a certain angle each time. For cubic objects, the robot can rotate 90 degrees each time, while for cylindrical objects, the robot can rotate 30 degrees at a time to avoid missing important text information on objects [7]. In the vision of the robot's eye for the first time and after each rotation, the robot recognizes the fine-grained text information on the object being grasped by calling the large language pre-training models, matching it with the target object name in the input instruction. If the name of the target object is not detected, the robot will proceed to grasp the object with the second-highest matching score in the scene and execute the same action sequence above. This process will be repeated until the target object is successfully found. In algorithm 1, $M$ represents the maximum number of rotations, which is set to either 3 or 9. This corresponds to box-category objects that rotate 90 degrees per iteration and cylindrical objects that rotate 30 degrees per iteration. The reason for this configuration is that rotating each object by 270 degrees ensures that all text information on its surface becomes visible, thereby eliminating the issue of missing fine-grained text information on the object's surface.

---

**Algorithm 1. Robotic Active Target Location and Grasping System**

Input: RGB-D image $I$ and User Instruction $Q$

1.  $OBJECT\_TEXT\_LABEL_{x_i} \leftarrow LLM(Q)$
2.  $\{Attr_{x_*}^j\} \leftarrow Knowledge\_Base(OBJECT\_TEXT\_LABEL_{x_i})$
3.  $\{x_i\} \leftarrow Object\_Detector(I)$
4.  $\{S_i\} \leftarrow Object\_Grounding(\{x_i\}, \{Attr_{x_*}^j\}), j \in \{category, color, shape\}$
5.  for $grasp\_i \leftarrow 0$ to $N$ do
6.      $Grasp(x_i) \leftarrow max(S_i)$
7.      $Move(x_i)$
8.      $rotate\_angle \leftarrow angle\_cla(Attr_{x_i}^{shape})$
9.      for $rotate\_i \leftarrow 0$ to $M$ do
10.         $Rotate(x_i, rotate\_angle)$
11.         $OBJECT\_TEXT\_LABEL_{x_i} \leftarrow LLM(I)$
12.         if $Result\_Assessment(OBJECT\_TEXT\_LABEL_{x_i}, OBJECT\_TEXT\_LABEL_{x_*})$
13.             break
14.         end if
15.     end for
16. end for

---

# 4 Experiments

We constructed a service robot grasping experiment in a home scene to evaluate the overall performance of our system in REVERIE-Disambiguation-Robot-Grasping-Task. In experiments, the user sends an instruction with fine-grained text information about the target object to the robot. Then, we enable the robot to actively explore the text information on objects in the scene and finally find and grasp the target object.

## 4.1 Experimental Settings

**1) Platform:** We conducted experiments using UR3e in both Pybullet simulation and real-world environment, with a Geforce GTX 3090 GPU. Input images are from a RealSense camera with 640×480 resolution. We place the RealSense camera above the front of UR3e as its eye. Figure 2 (a) shows the real experimental platform.

**2) Experimental Objects:** Due to the specific task requirements of this paper, we are unable to find a publicly available dataset that meets our needs. Therefore, we selected 42 objects from the real-world scene, including pill bottles, soda cans, beer cans, canned food, medicine boxes, and boxed food. Figure 2 (b) shows some of the experimental objects.

**3) Metrics:** To comprehensively evaluate the performance of our system, we set up 2 different metrics: (1) Success Rate (**SR**) for the percentage of successfully finding and grasping the target object; (2) Inspired by [18], the number of active explorations (#**Explorations**) for locating and grasping the target object can effectively measure the timeliness of the proposed method. This metric represents the process of performing an "Act-to-See" on the grasped object, that is, after each active exploration, it can be determined whether the grasped object is the target. Fewer active explorations correlate with shorter task completion times, thereby indicating higher task execution efficiency, whereas a greater number of explorations suggest the opposite. Therefore, the number of active explorations can be considered a reliable indicator of the task execution efficiency of the proposed method.

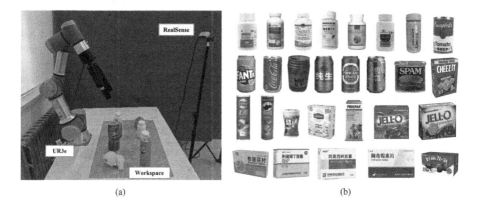

(a)                                         (b)

**Fig. 2.** Real experimental platform (a) and Partial experimental objects (b)

## 4.2 Simulation Experiments

To make simulate object interactions as similar to the real world as possible, we modify the texture information and physical coefficients of these experimental objects. In experiments, we use ChatGLM for parsing instructions and recognizing the fine-grained text information on objects. To comprehensively evaluate our method, we set up a total of 8 objects in each experimental scene, with 2, 3, 4, 5, or 6 objects with similar visual attributes, and the target object is one of them. In the experiment, the objects are placed in 8 predetermined positions, but the angles are indeterminate to ensure that the initial states of these objects in the scene are random.

**1) System Evaluation Results:** After evaluation, as shown in Table 3, our system achieved an average task success rate of 92.5% in experiments. It can be seen that when the number of similar objects (#**Objects**) in the scene increases, the average number of active explorations (#**Explorations_aver**) also increases, but the ratio is smaller than the former, indicating that our model is efficient. We also analyze the experimental results when the target object belongs to different categories, as shown in Fig. 3. Our system has the highest task success rate on bottle objects, while the task success rate is relatively low on box objects. The reason is that some of the fine-grained text information of the box object is above the object. When the robot grasps the box object, the gripper may block the text information on the object, causing the problem of losing some of the fine-grained text information in the character recognition process, failing in the task. Therefore, this may be an issue that we can further study in the future. In addition, if there are multiple target objects in a scene, our system can only grasp one target object for the user based on the highest matching score among them, because the natural language instructions only contain information about the name of the target object and do not contain information such as orientation relationship, and size that can eliminate ambiguity among multiple targets. Finally, to better observe the grasping process in the simulated environment, we demonstrate the process of the robot actively exploring and grasping the object "Vitamin C Tablets" in Fig. 4.

**Table 3.** The main results of our system in different scenarios

| #Objects | SR | #Explorations_aver |
|---|---|---|
| 2 | 89.6% | 1.61 |
| 3 | 91.8% | 2.02 |
| 4 | 93.3% | 2.25 |
| 5 | 90.0% | 2.81 |
| 6 | 98.0% | 2.95 |

**2) Active Exploration Mechanism Evaluation Results:** To verify the effectiveness of our proposed active exploration mechanism, we conduct 387 experiments in the same experimental scenario as above for our model and the model with no active exploration mechanism. In Table 4, the model that removes the active exploration mechanism has only a 40.1% task success rate, and our model can achieve a 91.5% task success rate, which is improved by 51.4%, indicating the effectiveness of the active exploration mechanism in our model. It shows that active exploration is important and makes robots adapt to different scenes and complete complex tasks.

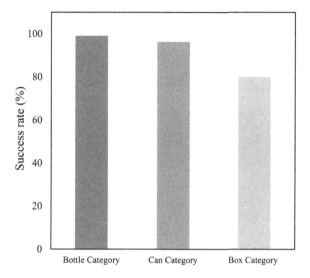

**Fig. 3.** The task success rate of the system for different categories of objects

**Fig. 4.** The process of actively locating and grasping "Vitamin C Tablets"

**Table 4.** The evaluation results of active exploration mechanism

| Models | SR |
| --- | --- |
| No exploration | 40.1% |
| Our full model | 91.5% |

## 4.3   Real-Robot Experiments

We use UR3e with robtiq140 gripper to evaluate the performance of our system in real-world environments. In experiments, we set the same experimental scenario as the simulation experiment, and only conduct experimental scenarios with 2 and 3 similar objects. The quantitative results are shown in Table 5. Our model can achieve a task success rate of over 91%, indicating its effectiveness in real-world environments. The results can validate the foresight and correctness of our active location and grasping framework and demonstrate its potential in robot daily grasping services. The qualitative results are shown in Fig. 5.

**Table 5.** The main results of our system in real-world experiments

| #Objects | SR | #Explorations_aver |
|---|---|---|
| 2 | 91.1% | 1.78 |
| 3 | 93.2% | 2.62 |

| (a) | (b) | (c) | (d) | (e) | (f) |

**Fig. 5.** The process of grasping in response to the query "Pass me the Vitamin C Tablets". a) setting the initial pose of the robot arm and executing target matching, b) executing the grasp movement, c) move the object to the vision of the robot's eye d) recognizing the text information on the grasped object, e) executing the rotate movement and recognizing the text information, and f) successfully finding and grasping the Vitamin C Tablets.

## 5  Conclusion

In this work, we investigate a novel challenging task in robot daily grasping services that combines REVERIE and target disambiguation. For this task, we propose an active target location and grasping system based on joint language-vision-action, which enables the robot to actively pick up objects for observation like humans to obtain more fine-grained text information about the objects in the scene and find the target object from multiple objects with coarse-grained visual ambiguity. The extensive experiments conducted in both simulated and real-world environments have demonstrated the effectiveness of our system, with the task success rates exceeding 91%. In future work, we aim to enhance the efficiency of active exploration by leveraging the advanced reasoning and decision-making capabilities of large-scale language models. Besides, we would like to design algorithms to endow robots with the ability to understand more complex natural language instructions, such as "Pass me the large bottle of vitamin C tablets on the far left.", making robots locate the target object that the user wants from multiple target objects in a scene. This is a problem worth further research.

**Acknowledgments.** This work was supported in part by the Key R & D Project of Shandong Province under Grant 2023TZXD018, the Central Government Guiding Local Science and Technology Development Foundation of Shandong Province under Grant YDZX2023122. Besides, this research was supported by Meituan Academy of Robotics Shenzhen.

# References

1. Zhou, Z., Li, S.: Self-sustained and coordinated rhythmic deformations with SMA for controller-free locomotion. In: Advanced Intelligent Systems, p. 2300667 (2024)
2. Wang, S., Zhou, Z., Li, B., Li, Z., Kan, Z.: Multi-modal interaction with transformers: bridging robots and human with natural language. Robotica **42**(2), 415–434 (2024)
3. Korekata, R., et al.: Switching head-tail funnel uniter for dual referring expression comprehension with fetch-and-Carry tasks. In: 2023 IEEE/RSJ International Conference on Intelligent Robots and Systems (IROS), pp. 3865–3872. IEEE (2023)
4. Cheang, C., Lin, H., Fu, Y., Xue, X.: Learning 6-DOF object poses to grasp category-level objects by language instructions. In: 2022 International Conference on Robotics and Automation (ICRA), pp. 8476–8482. IEEE (2022)
5. Sun, Q., Lin, H., Fu, Y., Fu, Y., Xue, X.: Language guided robotic grasping with fine-grained instructions. In: 2023 IEEE/RSJ International Conference on Intelligent Robots and Systems (IROS), pp. 1319–1326. IEEE (2023)
6. Sun, Y., Bo, L., Fox, D.: Attribute based object identification. In: 2013 IEEE International Conference on Robotics and Automation, pp. 2096–2103. IEEE (2013)
7. Liu, Z., Ding, K., Xu, Q., Song, Y., Yuan, X., Li, Y.: Scene images and text information-based object location of robot grasping. IET Cyber Syst. Robot. **4**(2), 116–130 (2022)
8. Qi, Y., et al.: Reverie: Remote embodied visual referring expression in real indoor environments. In: Proceedings of the IEEE/CVF Conference on Computer Vision and Pattern Recognition, pp. 9982–9991 (2020)
9. Kahn, G., et al.: Active exploration using trajectory optimization for robotic grasping in the presence of occlusions. In: 2015 IEEE International Conference on Robotics and Automation (ICRA), pp. 4783–4790. IEEE (2015)
10. Shridhar, M., Mittal, D., Hsu, D.: Ingress: interactive visual grounding of referring expressions. Int. J. Robot.Res. **39**(2–3), 217–232 (2020)
11. Yu, H., Lou, X., Yang, Y., Choi, C.: IOSG: image-driven object searching and grasping. In: 2023 IEEE/RSJ International Conference on Intelligent Robots and Systems (IROS), pp. 3145–3152. IEEE (2023)
12. Fu, L., et al.: Legs: Learning efficient grasp sets for exploratory grasping. In: 2022 International Conference on Robotics and Automation (ICRA), pp. 8259–8265. IEEE (2022)
13. Xu, K., et al.: A joint modeling of vision-language-action for target-oriented grasping in clutter. In: 2023 IEEE International Conference on Robotics and Automation (ICRA), pp. 11597–11604. IEEE (2023)
14. Jiang, Y., Jia, Y., Li, X.: Contact-aware non-prehensile manipulation for object retrieval in cluttered environments. In: 2023 IEEE/RSJ International Conference on Intelligent Robots and Systems (IROS), pp. 10604–10611. IEEE (2023)
15. Wang, Y., Wang, K., Wang, Y., Guo, D., Liu, H., Sun, F.: Audio-visual grounding referring expression for robotic manipulation. In: 2022 International Conference on Robotics and Automation (ICRA), pp. 9258–9264. IEEE (2022)
16. Behrens, J.K., Nazarczuk, M., Stepanova, K., Hoffmann, M., Demiris, Y., Mikolajczyk, K.: Embodied reasoning for discovering object properties via manipulation. In: 2021 IEEE International Conference on Robotics and Automation (ICRA), pp. 10139–10145. IEEE (2021)
17. Yang, Y., Lou, X., Choi, C.: Interactive robotic grasping with attribute-guided disambiguation. In: 2022 International Conference on Robotics and Automation (ICRA), pp. 8914–8920. IEEE (2022)

18. Mo, Y., Zhang, H., Kong, T.: Towards open-world interactive disambiguation for robotic grasping. In: 2023 IEEE International Conference on Robotics and Automation (ICRA), pp. 8061–8067. IEEE (2023)
19. Brown, T., et al.: Language models are few-shot learners. Adv. Neural. Inf. Process. Syst. **33**, 1877–1901 (2020)
20. Du, Z., et al: GLM: general language model pretraining with autoregressive blank infilling. arXiv preprint arXiv:2103.10360 (2021)
21. Zhou, X., Girdhar, R., Joulin, A., Krähenbühl, P., Misra, I.: Detecting twenty-thousand classes using image-level supervision. In: European Conference on Computer Vision. pp. 350–368. Springer (2022). https://doi.org/10.1007/978-3-031-20077-9_21
22. Radford, A., et al.: Learning transferable visual models from natural language supervision. In: International Conference on Machine Learning, pp. 8748–8763. PMLR (2021)
23. Vuong, A.D., et al.: Grasp-anything: large-scale grasp dataset from foundation models. arXiv preprint arXiv:2309.09818 (2023)

# Stereo Visual SLAM System with Road Constrained Based on Graph Optimization

Yuan Zhu, Hao An, Huaide Wang, Ruidong Xu, and Ke Lu[✉]

School of Automotive Studies, Tongji University, Shanghai 201800, China
luke@tongji.edu.cn

**Abstract.** In visual SLAM systems for autonomous vehicles, the influence of feature distribution leads to fewer vertical constraints, resulting in significant vertical drift and affecting the long-term localization performance of the system. This paper proposes a graph optimization-based stereo visual SLAM system with road constraints, which enhances vertical constraints by extracting more features from the road and establishing explicit constraints between the vehicle and the road plane. First, a stereo matching method for road feature points is proposed to compensate for the disparity-induced road feature offset between the left and right images, improving the system's ability to extract road features and enhancing feature distribution. Then, the local road plane is used to represent the road, and explicit constraints between the road and the vehicle are established to further increase vertical constraints on the system. Finally, the local road plane, vehicle pose, and map points are optimized jointly as nodes in a nonlinear optimization. Validation through the KITTI dataset and real vehicle experiments shows that the proposed system reduces vertical drift and achieves more accurate localization results.

**Keywords:** Visual SLAM · Graph optimization · Road constrainted

## 1 Introduction

With the rapid development of autonomous driving technology, the demand for precision in vehicle environment perception and localization has also increased. Among various localization and navigation technologies, stereo visual SLAM (Simultaneous Localization and Mapping) has garnered widespread attention due to its unique advantages. Stereo visual SLAM can achieve precise localization and mapping without relying on GPS signals, thereby assisting vehicles in navigating complex urban environments accurately [1]. Compared to LiDAR SLAM, stereo cameras are often more cost-effective and can capture richer visual and texture information, enhancing the reliability and environmental adaptability of autonomous driving systems [2].

Supported by the Perspective Study Funding of Nanchang Automotive Institute of Intelligence and New Energy, Tongji University (Grant Number: TPD-TC202211-07).

However, the application of stereo visual SLAM in vehicle localization faces challenges of limited vertical constraints and significant accumulated errors, primarily due to two reasons: First, in road scenes, the sky, which occupies a large portion of the vertical field of view, contains no features, while the road below, due to its self-similarity and low texture characteristics, makes feature extraction difficult [3]. As a result, the feature distribution in the vertical direction is more concentrated, leading to a significantly lower number of effective features compared to the horizontal and longitudinal directions. Second, vehicles are constrained by environmental and kinematic factors, requiring them to adhere to the road while driving, which limits their vertical motion. SLAM systems typically assume the camera moves in a six-degree-of-freedom space, and its motion is estimated according to SE(3). With insufficient constraints, vertical motion estimation is prone to errors, causing pose drift too [4].

There are two solutions to the above issues. The first method is to integrate visual sensors with IMU, utilizing the inertial information provided by the IMU to introduce additional constraints on the vehicle pose, thereby improving the accuracy of vehicle pose estimation. Methods that integrate IMU include VINS-MONO [5], ORB-SLAM3 [6], and others. These methods can improve system localization accuracy in drones or handheld devices. However, for ground vehicles, which often operate in straight-line or uniformly accelerated motion, the stimulation to the IMU is minimal, resulting in reduced observability and decreased overall system localization performance [7]. The second method is to introduce constraints between the road and the vehicle into the SLAM system, ensuring that the vehicle adheres to the road while driving. This method first requires establishing an appropriate road model and then using this model to impose constraints from the road onto the vehicle.

Currently, there are two main approaches to road modeling. The first approach treats the road as an approximate plane, considering non-planar motion perturbations as noise, and uses this plane to constrain the vehicle. Wu et al. [7] proposed the concept of constraining vehicles to move on an approximate plane, explicitly introducing planar motion constraints in the estimation algorithm to reduce localization errors. Zheng et al. [4] restricted ground vehicle motion to an approximate plane, applying SE(2) constraints on top of SE(3), effectively handling the planar motion characteristics of ground vehicles. The same author [8] later proposed another method that parameterized the vehicle pose directly in SE(2) while accounting for non-SE(2) motion perturbations. These methods effectively use the road to constrain vehicle motion characteristics and improve localization and map construction accuracy in structured indoor or industrial environments. However, in road scenes with significant undulations, single-plane constraints no longer match the real road shape, and the inconsistency between the incorrect plane assumptions and reality introduces additional errors into the system [9]. The second approach uses surface models [10,11] and discrete planes [9,12,13] to establish road models. Zhang et al. [10] proposed using quadratic polynomial approximations to describe the motion manifold of ground robots. This approximation method allows the system to consider ground robot motion constraints during pose estimation. The subsequent work [11] further developed the use and integration of road manifolds. However, using quadratic polynomials to represent road models has a significant drawback: the large number of parameters leads to slow convergence during model initialization and when the model changes significantly. Zhou et al. [9] first proposed a method to represent roads using discrete plane models with vehicle motion constrained by the corresponding local plane model. DPC-SLAM [12] also used discrete planes to represent the road model and further considered the initialization of discrete planes and the fusion of overlapping planes. RC-SLAM [13] accounted for the depth uncertainty of road feature points, using homography constraints to construct discrete planes. Although discrete plane-based road modeling methods accurately represent the real road conditions, they require a sufficient number and information-rich road feature points. Road feature points are difficult to extract due to low texture and self-similarity, and the depth gradient of the ground during stereo matching reduces the similarity of the same feature patch in the left and right images, making effective matching challenging [3]. These factors make it difficult to extract accurate road models from sparse ground feature points.

To address vehicle vertical constraints, this paper proposes a stereo visual SLAM system with road constraints. To solve feature offset issues in road feature points caused by stereo disparity, a stereo matching method is introduced. This method uses depth information from the camera and local road geometry to correct row feature offset, enhancing similarity in left and right image patches, thereby extracting more road feature points and optimizing the system's vertical feature distribution. Additionally, a method to represent local roads using discrete planes is designed, extracting high-dimensional road plane features from low-dimensional road point features and establishing explicit constraints between the local road and the vehicle to increase vertical constraints. Finally, the local road model, vehicle pose, and map points are used as optimization nodes in a graph optimization model for joint nonlinear optimization. This approach reduces vertical drift and improves localization accuracy and robustness by fully extracting road features and adding local road constraints. The main contributions of this paper are as follows:

- A road feature extraction and stereo matching method is proposed. This method corrects the row feature offset caused by stereo disparity row by row using depth from the camera-local road geometry, enhancing the ability to extract road features, and further optimizing vertical feature distribution.
- A tightly coupled road-constrained graph optimization framework is proposed, treating the self-vehicle pose, map points, and local road model as joint optimization nodes. Without adding additional sensors, the system reduces vertical drift and improves localization accuracy.
- A complete visual SLAM system for autonomous driving is proposed by fully considering environmental constraints. Validation through datasets and real vehicle experiments shows that the proposed system outperforms state-of-the-art VSLAM systems in vehicle localization performance.

The structure of the paper is as follows: An overview of the proposed system and notations are presented in Sect. 2. Section 3 introduces details of the proposed system. Section 4 covers the experimental setup and results, along with the analysis of results. In Sect. 5, the conclusion is finally given.

## 2   Overview

### 2.1   Notations

In this paper, $(\cdot)^w$ represents the world coordinate system, $(\cdot)^c$ represents the camera coordinate system, $(\cdot)^w_c$ represents the transformation from the camera coordinate system to the world coordinate system. The transformation matrix $T \in \mathrm{SE}(3)$ is used to express the pose transformation, with $T$ consisting of the rotation matrix $R \in \mathrm{SO}(3)$ and the translation vector $\mathbf{t} \in {}^3$. The transformation matrix $T^w_c$ can be used to convert feature points $P^w$ from world to $k^{\mathrm{th}}$ camera coordinate system:

$$P^{c_k} = \left(T^{c_k}_w P^{w\prime}\right)_{[1:3]} = R^{c_k}_w P^w + t^{c_k}_w, \tag{1}$$

where $P^{w\prime}$ is the homogeneous form of $P^w$.

For local road plane $\pi$, the Hesse Form (HF) is used for representation: $\pi = \begin{bmatrix} n^{\mathrm{T}} & d \end{bmatrix}^{\mathrm{T}}$, where $n$ is the identity matrix, representing the normal direction of the plane $\pi$, and $d$ is the distance from the plane $\pi$ to the origin of the coordinate system. For feature points $P^{road}$ located on the plane, $n^{\mathrm{T}} P - d = 0$ should be satisfied. The transformation matrix $L^c_w$ can be used to convert the plane from the world coordinate system to the camera coordinate system:

$$\begin{bmatrix} n^c \\ d^c \end{bmatrix} = L^c_w \begin{bmatrix} n^w \\ d^w \end{bmatrix} = \begin{bmatrix} R^c_w & 0 \\ (-t^w_c)^{\mathrm{T}} & 1 \end{bmatrix} \begin{bmatrix} n^w \\ d^w \end{bmatrix}, \tag{2}$$

where $R^w_c$ and $t^w_c$ represent the rotation matrix and translation vector from the world coordinate system to the camera coordinate system, respectively. Since the Hesse Form uses four parameters to represent a plane, making it an over-parameterized representation, the plane $\Pi$ is represented using the Closest Point (CP) [16] during optimization. The conversion relationship between CP and HF is given as follows:

$$\Pi = nd, \tag{3}$$

$$\begin{bmatrix} n \\ d \end{bmatrix} = \begin{bmatrix} \Pi / \|\Pi\| \\ \|\Pi\| \end{bmatrix}. \tag{4}$$

### 2.2   System Overview

The pipeline of the proposed system is shown in Fig. 1. The input of the entire system consists of stereo images and the semantic mask of the road area obtained from the left image through a semantic segmentation network [14]. The output of the system is the optimized vehicle trajectory and map, which includes feature points and local road planes. The entire system comprises three parts: the front-end, local road fitting, and back-end.

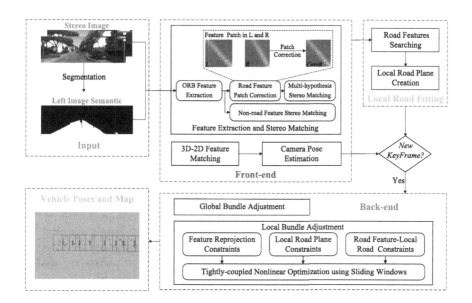

**Fig. 1.** The pipeline of the proposed stereo visual SLAM system.

In the front-end, the ORB feature points [15] are classified into road feature points and non-road feature points based on the semantic segmentation results of the road. Non-road feature points use the conventional stereo matching method, while road feature points use the proposed stereo matching for depth recovery of ground features. All feature points are then matched between frames to estimate the inter-frame pose changes of the camera.

The local road fitting module uses the results from the map to fit the local road plane under the vehicle. First, road feature points in the front-end are searched based on preset orientations. These road feature points are then used to initialize the parameters of the local road plane, obtaining an initial local road model.

In the back-end, loop closure detection is performed. If a loop closure is detected, global bundle adjustment (BA) is executed to optimize the global poses within the loop. In local BA, reprojection constraints of feature points, constraints between the vehicle and the road plane, and constraints between the road plane and ground feature points are established. These three types of constraints are used for joint optimization of feature points, vehicle poses, and local road planes. After executing global BA and local BA, the back-end outputs the vehicle pose and a map that includes feature points and local road planes.

# 3   Proposed System

## 3.1   Front-End

The front-end of the proposed system is similar to systems [15] based on ORB feature points. Feature points on the image are first extracted, then features are matched between the left and right images to recover the depth. Feature matching is also performed between consecutive frames, and finally, the camera pose is estimated using bundle adjustment based on the feature matching results. The difference from the aforementioned process is that the proposed system divides feature points into road feature points and non-road feature points based on the results of road semantic segmentation, and a targeted road feature extraction and stereo matching method is proposed.

About the vertical distribution, the upper part is mainly the sky area, where features are at an infinite distance from the vehicle and need to be discarded. The lower part is the road surface. Although the road surface itself has low texture and repetitive characteristics, it contains many corner points in road lines and traffic signs. Effectively utilizing these features can greatly improve the vertical distribution of features. Current methods based on feature points and descriptors can individually extract these corner points from the road surface in the left or right image, but during stereo matching, these corner points are difficult to match successfully. Even if matched successfully, they might be considered outliers and deleted. As shown in Fig. 2. (a) and Fig. 2. (b), the patches of ground feature points have significant differences in appearance between the left and right images. This is because the ground is almost parallel to the camera axis, resulting in a large depth gradient between pixel rows in the ground area on the imaging plane. This leads to a progressively increasing pixel shift between rows in the left and right images due to disparity, causing noticeable differences in the appearance of feature patches. It is worth noting that this appearance difference is more pronounced in stereo cameras with a long baseline.

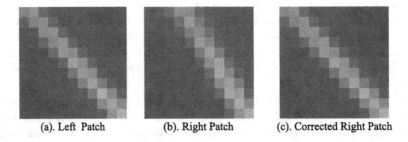

(a). Left Patch            (b). Right Patch            (c). Corrected Right Patch

**Fig. 2.** The patch of the same feature point in the left and right images.

To address the above issues, a feature offset correction method for stereo matching of road feature points is proposed. As shown in Fig. 3, the camera-road plane geometry can be used to calculate the depth $D$ of the feature points:

$$D = \frac{\tan \theta * f_y * H}{f_y + \tan \theta * (v - c_y)}, \tag{5}$$

where $f_y$ and $c_y$ are the camera's intrinsic parameters, $v$ is the row coordinate of the feature point in the pixel coordinate system, $H$ is the height of the camera from the ground, and $\theta$ is the angle between the vertical axis of the camera and the ground. Since the road is relatively smooth locally, $H$ and $\theta$ can be approximated using the parameters between the camera and the road plane from the previous frame. Given the known depth of the feature point, the disparity of this feature between the stereo images can be calculated based on this depth as follows:

$$d = \frac{f_x * b}{\tan \theta * f_y * H} (f_y + \tan \theta * (v - c_y)), \tag{6}$$

where $b$ is the baseline of stereo camera, $f_x$ is the camera's intrinsic parameters. According to Eq. 6, the stereo disparity for each column in the pixel coordinate system can be calculated.

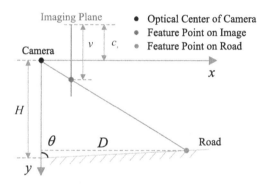

**Fig. 3.** Camera-local road plane geometry.

Algorithm 1 presents the process of stereo matching for road feature points. It iterates over the features located on the road in the left image and finds the best matching features in the right image. In lines 3–4, based on the features in the left image, the appropriate search range in the right image is determined using epipolar constraints and the depth provided by the camera-plane geometry. In lines 5–9, a feature patch in the right image is constructed within the search range, and then the feature patch's offset is corrected row by row using Eq. 6, as shown in Fig. 2. (c). The similarity between the corrected right feature patch and the left feature patch is then calculated using Normalized Cross Correlation (NCC). In lines 10–14, the similarity scores of all feature patches in the right image are sorted. If the score difference between the top three patches is significant, the highest-scoring patch is considered the best match, and sub-pixel matching is performed. Finally, in lines 16–22, the similarity scores of all matched features are processed, with lower-scoring features being filtered out as outliers. Based on these matching results, the spatial positions of the road feature points can be recovered.

---

**Algorithm 1:** Calculation of stereo disparity search range

**Input:** Stereo images $L$ and $R$, left semantic image $SL$, camera intrinsic matrix $K$, $\theta$, $H$.

**Output:** Matched stereo features $F_L$, $F_R$.

1   $F_L \leftarrow$ feature_extraction $(L, SL)$ // Road features extraction.

    // Searching the best matched features in $R$:

2   **for** $i = 1$ to $|F_L|$ **do**

3     $P_{L,i} \leftarrow$ patch_construction $(F_{L,i})$ // Constructing 11*11 patch around feature $F_{L,i}$.

4     $S_{R,i} \leftarrow$ search_area $(P_{L,i}, K, \theta, H)$ // Determining the search area of $P_{L,i}$ in $R$.

5     **for** $j = 1$ to $|S_{R,i}|$ **do**

6       $P_{R,j} \leftarrow$ patch_construction $(F_{R,j})$

7       $P_{R,j}^* \leftarrow$ patch_correction $(P_{R,j}, K, \theta, H)$

8       $patch\_scores \leftarrow$ patch_ncc $(P_{L,i}, P_{R,j}^*)$

9     **end**

10     $sorted\_patch\_scores =$ score_sort$(patch\_scores)$

11     **if** $sorted\_patch\_scores\,[1:3]$ are different **then**

12       $F_R^* \leftarrow$ patch_refined $(sorted\_patch\_scores\,[1])$

13       $patch\_scores^* \leftarrow patch\_scores\,(F_R^*)$

14     **end**

15 **end**

    // Remove outliers with the worst scores:

16 **for** $k = 1$ to $|F_R^*|$ **do**

17     **if** $patch\_scores_k^* > 0.7*$mean(sum$(patch\_scores^*))$ **then**

18       $F_R \leftarrow F_{R,k}^*$

19       $patch\_scores^* \leftarrow patch\_scores\,(F_R^*)$

20     **else**

21       $F_L \leftarrow$ remove$(F_L, F_{L,k})$

22     **end**

23 **end**

24 **return** $F_L$, $F_R$

---

### 3.2 Local Road Fitting

When a new keyframe is generated from the front-end, the local road fitting module generates the local road plane for the position of that keyframe. Before fitting the plane using road feature points, it is necessary to determine the search range for local road feature points. The estimated keyframe pose from the front-end is used as the search center, and a circle with a radius of 5 m is designed to search for all road feature points that fall within this area in the map.

After determining the search range for feature points, all feature points are used to fit a local plane using the least squares method from the observed road points. After obtaining the initial parameters of this local plane, further evaluation of the local road plane is required based on the number of feature points and the average distance of feature points to the plane. If any condition is not met, the plane is discarded. If the error is smaller than the average threshold and the number of points exceeds the threshold, the plane is further optimized using the road points within the local plane area, and a robust kernel function is used to reduce the weight of outliers. Compared to directly fitting the plane using road points, this method reduces the discrepancies between the fitted plane and the actual road surface due to errors in plane segmentation results. As shown in Fig. 4, the cost function for optimization is defined as the distance from the road points to the plane, as shown in the following:

$$e\left(\boldsymbol{\Pi}, \boldsymbol{P}\right) = \|\boldsymbol{\Pi}\| - \frac{\boldsymbol{\Pi}^{\mathrm{T}} \boldsymbol{P}}{\|\boldsymbol{\Pi}\|}, \tag{7}$$

where $\boldsymbol{\Pi}$ is the plane, $\boldsymbol{P}$ is a road point within the plane, and $e$ represents the distance from the road point to the plane, i.e., the error. When fitting the local plane, only the plane is optimized, not the road points. Therefore, it is only necessary to compute the Jacobian of the error function $e\left(\boldsymbol{\Pi}, \boldsymbol{P}\right)$ with respect to the plane parameters $\boldsymbol{\Pi}$, as shown below:

$$J\left(\boldsymbol{\Pi}^{\mathrm{T}}\right) = \frac{\boldsymbol{\Pi}^{\mathrm{T}}}{\|\boldsymbol{\Pi}\|} + \frac{\boldsymbol{P}^{\mathrm{T}} \boldsymbol{\Pi} \boldsymbol{\Pi}^{\mathrm{T}}}{\|\boldsymbol{\Pi}\|^{3}} - \frac{\boldsymbol{P}^{\mathrm{T}}}{\|\boldsymbol{\Pi}\|}. \tag{8}$$

### 3.3   Back-End

In the back-end, loop detection is first performed for keyframes detected by the front-end. If no loop is detected, a local bundle adjustment (BA) is performed. If a loop is detected, a global BA is performed, adding loop constraints on top of the local BA. The back-end optimization adopts a tightly coupled approach to optimize the camera pose, map points, and parameters of the discrete planes.

Figure 5 shows the factor graph of the proposed system, where circles represent the optimization variables and squares represent the constraints between the optimization variables. The constraints include the reprojection constraints from road feature points and non-road feature points, the constraints from the local road plane to the vehicle, and the constraints between the road plane and the road feature points. Based on these three types of constraints, respective error functions are constructed and jointly optimized. The overall loss function is as follows:

$$E\left(\{\boldsymbol{T}_{w}^{c_i}, \boldsymbol{P}_j, \boldsymbol{\Pi}_k\}\right) = \sum_{i,j} \left\|e_1^{i,j}\right\|_{\Sigma_{i,j}^{-1}} + \sum_{i,k} \left\|e_2^{i,k}\right\|_{\Sigma_{i,k}^{-1}} + \sum_{k,j} \left\|e_3^{k,j}\right\|_{\Sigma_{k,j}^{-1}}, \tag{9}$$

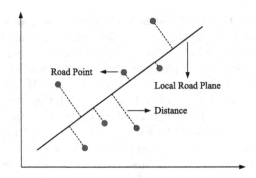

**Fig. 4.** The relationship between road points and the local road plane.

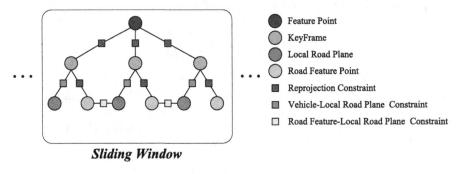

**Fig. 5.** The factor graph of the proposed Local Bundle Adjustment.

where $e_1$ is the reprojection error of feature points, $e_2$ is the error between vehicle and local plane, $e_2$ is the error between the local plane and road feature points. $\Sigma^{-1}$ is the information matrix, representing the uncertainty of the estimations.

The reprojection error projects 3D space points onto a 2D image and adjusts the camera pose and the positions of the map points to minimize the error between the projected position and the matched position, as shown below:

$$e_1^{i,j} = e\left(T_w^{c_i}, P_j\right) = u_j - \frac{1}{s_j} K T_w^{c_i} P_j', \tag{10}$$

where $u_j$ represents the pixel coordinates of the feature associated with the feature point $P_j$ and $s_j$ represents the depth of the feature point $P_j$.

The error between vehicle and local plane is calculated using the distance between the four wheels of the vehicle and the local road plane. When the distance between the wheels and the plane is zero, it indicates that the vehicle is in close contact with the plane, adhering to the environmental constraint that the vehicle is attached to the road surface. The distance from the wheels to the associated plane is used to represent the camera pose-plane error, as shown below:

$$e_2^{i,k} = e\left(T_w^{c_i}, \Pi_k\right) = \|\Pi_k\| - \frac{\Pi_k^T\left((T_w^{c_i})^{-1}W_m\right)}{\|\Pi_k\|}, \tag{11}$$

where $W_m$ is the translation of the wheel contact point relative to the camera, and $\Pi_k$ represents the $k^{th}$ local road plane, which is associated with the $i^{th}$ keyframe. The left-multiplicative perturbation model is used to derive the error $e_2^{i,k}$ with respect to the camera pose. The Jacobian of the error with respect to the camera pose and the plane is shown below:

$$J\left(T_w^{c_i}\right) = -\frac{\Pi_k^T\left[R^T\widehat{W}_m \ -R^T\right]}{\|\Pi_k\|}, \tag{12}$$

$$J\left(\Pi_k^T\right) = \frac{\Pi_k^T}{\|\Pi_k\|} + \frac{\left((T_w^{c_i})^{-1}W_m\right)^T\Pi_k\Pi_k^T}{\|\Pi_k\|^3} - \frac{\left((T_w^{c_i})^{-1}W_m\right)^T}{\|\Pi_k\|}, \tag{13}$$

where $\widehat{W}$ is the skew-symmetric matrix.

The error between the local plane and road feature points is represented by the distance from the road points to the plane. The smaller the distance from the road points to the plane, the closer the road points are to the plane, indicating that the local plane better fits the actual road surface. The error is expressed as:

$$e_3^{k,j} = e\left(\Pi_k, P_j\right) = \|\Pi_k\| - \frac{\Pi_k^T P_j}{\|\Pi_k\|}, \tag{14}$$

where $P_j$ is the $j^{th}$ road feature point. The Jacobian of the error function with respect to the plane and the road points can be expressed as:

$$J\left(\Pi_k^T\right) = \frac{\Pi_k^T}{\|\Pi_k\|} + \frac{P_j^T\Pi_k\Pi_k^T}{\|\Pi_k\|^3} - \frac{P_j^T}{\|\Pi_k\|}, \tag{15}$$

$$J\left(P_j\right) = -\frac{\Pi_k^T}{\|\Pi_k\|}. \tag{16}$$

## 4    Experiments

In experiments, two different metrics were used to evaluate the localization accuracy of the SLAM system: Absolute Trajectory Error (ATE) [17] and Relative Pose Error (RPE) [18]. To objectively verify the performance of the proposed system, this paper compares it with other state-of-the-art stereo VSLAM systems, including ORB-SLAM2 (Stereo) [15], ORB-SLAM3 (Stereo) [6], and OV²-SLAM (Stereo) [19]. To ensure the validity of the tests, all the selected comparison algorithms are open-source and were run on the same computer, with the results saved for comparative analysis. To reduce the impact of randomness on the algorithms, each algorithm was run 10 times consecutively, and the average value was taken as the final result.

## 4.1  KITTI Dataset

The KITTI Visual Odometry dataset [18] provides various sensor data, including IMU, LiDAR, stereo RGB camera, stereo grayscale camera, and ground truth of vehicle pose. Stereo RGB images and ground truth of vehicle pose were used to evaluate all the systems. This paper selected sequences 01, 03, 04, and 10 to evaluate the proposed system. The reason for selecting these four sequences is that they represent significantly different road scenes and do not contain loop closures, allowing for a more straightforward comparison of the systems' localization accuracy.

Table 1 shows the comparison results of the proposed system and the comparison systems on four sequences from the KITTI dataset. In sequences 01 and 04, the proposed system's ATE is significantly better than that of the other systems. The characteristics of these two sequences are relatively straight roads with continuous road regions in the field of view, allowing the system to better extract feature points from the road. Additionally, the local road planes fitted using these feature points can more effectively establish constraints with the vehicle, thereby improving localization accuracy. the relative translational error and relative rotational error results show that the proposed system exhibits the best performance across all sequences. The improvement indicates that the constraints of the discrete planes have a significant effect on constraining vehicle motion within a local range. This makes the vehicle's motion trajectory more closely follow the actual road shape, meaning that the proposed system can significantly reduce drift and provide more accurate scale estimation within local regions.

**Table 1.** Experimental evaluation on KITTI dataset $[t_{ate}\,(\mathrm{m})\,, t_{rel}\,(\%)\,, r_{rel}\,(°/100\mathrm{m})]$.

| Seq. | Proposed System | | | ORB-SLAM2 | | | ORB-SLAM3 | | | OV²-SLAM | | |
|---|---|---|---|---|---|---|---|---|---|---|---|---|
| | $t_{ate}$ | $t_{rel}$ | $r_{rel}$ | $t_{ate}$ | $t_{rel}$ | $r_{rel}$ | $t_{ate}$ | $t_{rel}$ | $r_{rel}$ | $t_{ate}$ | $t_{rel}$ | $r_{rel}$ |
| 01 | **10.63** | **1.99** | **0.30** | 15.64 | 2.54 | **0.30** | 14.74 | 2.00 | 0.34 | 19.25 | 5.27 | 0.33 |
| 03 | 5.55 | **2.46** | **0.30** | 5.95 | 2.64 | 0.43 | **5.35** | 2.94 | 0.41 | 6.33 | 3.24 | 0.31 |
| 04 | **1.79** | **0.41** | **0.11** | 2.47 | **0.41** | 0.19 | 3.13 | 0.51 | 0.15 | 4.19 | 0.82 | 0.27 |
| 10 | 3.05 | **0.92** | **0.36** | **3.00** | 1.07 | 0.47 | 3.20 | 1.04 | 0.51 | 3.57 | 1.16 | 0.39 |

* The best results are shown in bold.

To further compare the systems, Fig 6 and Fig. 7 present the overhead views of the trajectories of the proposed system and the comparison systems in sequences 01 and 04 of the KITTI dataset. It can be seen that the trajectory of the proposed system is significantly closer to the ground truth. This result indicates that although the primary aim of the proposed system is to improve accuracy in the vertical direction, the system extracts more features from the ground, enhancing the global distribution of features and significantly aiding pose estimation.

Additionally, the constraints from the local road to the vehicle also play an important role in enhancing inter-frame constraint capabilities, thereby improving the system's global consistency and reducing drift. Specifically, Fig. 8 and Fig. 9 further show the pose estimation results of the proposed system and the comparison systems in vertical directions in sequences 01 and 04 of the KITTI dataset. It can be seen that the proposed system's error in the vertical direction has been significantly improved. These figures visually demonstrate that the proposed system effectively reduces vertical errors and drift in the vertical direction. This improvement is evident not only in the accuracy of the global trajectory but also in the errors in each specific direction. In the vertical direction, the proposed system's error is significantly reduced, showcasing the system's superior performance in handling vertical displacement. Overall, by enhancing ground feature extraction and local road constraints, the proposed system demonstrates outstanding performance on the KITTI dataset, significantly improving localization accuracy.

### 4.2    Real-World Dataset

To further validate the effectiveness of the proposed system in real-world scenarios, two sequences were collected on campus using the data collection vehicle shown in Fig. 10. The vehicle was equipped with sensors including a stereo camera with a 0.2-meter baseline, an XENS MT-30 IMU, an 80-line LiDAR, a GNSS, and a Bynav X1 GNSS/INS navigation system used as ground truth. All data were recorded by a Data Logger.

Table 2 shows the results of the proposed system and the comparison systems on two sequences from the real-world dataset. It can be seen that the proposed system also outperforms the comparison systems in terms of ATE, consistent with the test results on the KITTI dataset. Figure 11 shows the comparison of

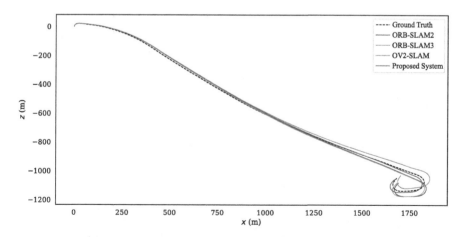

**Fig. 6.** The trajectories of the proposed system and the comparison systems with ground truth in KITTI sequence 01.

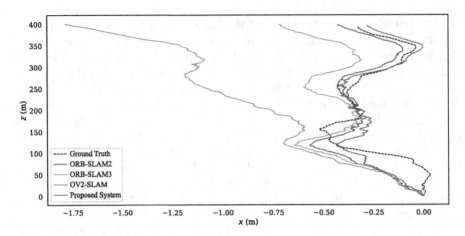

**Fig. 7.** The trajectories of the proposed system and the comparison systems with ground truth in KITTI sequence 04.

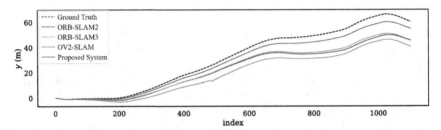

**Fig. 8.** The proposed system and the comparison systems in vertical directions in KITTI sequences 01.

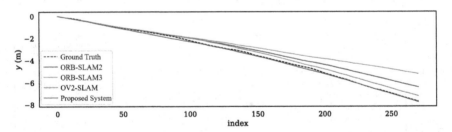

**Fig. 9.** The proposed system and the comparison systems in vertical directions in KITTI sequences 04.

the trajectories of all systems with the ground truth on sequence 01, the proposed system's trajectory is closer to the ground truth, further proving that the proposed system can effectively improve localization accuracy. Since the stereo camera on the data collection vehicle has a small baseline, the road feature offset is not severe. Other systems can also extract a certain number of features from

**Fig. 10.** The data collection vehicle and equipped sensors.

**Table 2.** Experimental evaluation on Real-world $[t_{ate}\,(\mathrm{m})\,,t_{rel}\,(\%)\,,r_{rel}\,(°/100\mathrm{m})]$.

| Seq. | Proposed System | | | ORB-SLAM2 | | | ORB-SLAM3 | | | OV²-SLAM | | |
|---|---|---|---|---|---|---|---|---|---|---|---|---|
| | $t_{ate}$ | $t_{rel}$ | $r_{rel}$ | $t_{ate}$ | $t_{rel}$ | $r_{rel}$ | $t_{ate}$ | $t_{rel}$ | $r_{rel}$ | $t_{ate}$ | $t_{rel}$ | $r_{rel}$ |
| 00 | **4.23** | **0.96** | **0.28** | 4.96 | 1.01 | 0.28 | 5.10 | 1.03 | **0.28** | 5.72 | 1.25 | 0.34 |
| 01 | **3.05** | **0.92** | 0.40 | 4.52 | 1.21 | **0.39** | 4.67 | 1.25 | 0.42 | 5.90 | 1.47 | 0.45 |

*The best results are shown in bold.

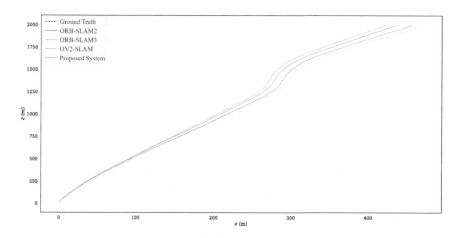

**Fig. 11.** The trajectories of the proposed system and the comparison systems with ground truth in Real-world sequence 01.

the ground, so the proposed system does not show a significant improvement in feature distribution. However, the proposed method includes explicit constraints between the road and the vehicle, which leads to the proposed system achieving the best results in relative translational error across both sequences.

# 5   Conclusion

In this paper, a graph optimization-based stereo visual SLAM system for autonomous vehicles has been introduced to mitigate the issue of vertical drift by enhancing vertical constraints. The approach focuses on improving feature extraction from the road features and establishing constraints between vehicle and road. The proposed stereo matching method leads to improved feature distribution and extraction capabilities. The road is represented by a local road plane, and explicit constraints are established to significantly enhance the vertical constraints on the vehicle's pose estimation. The local road plane, vehicle pose, and map points are jointly optimized within a nonlinear framework to ensure a robust and accurate localization process. Experimental validation on the KITTI and real-world dataset has demonstrated that the proposed method effectively reduces vertical drift and provides more accurate localization results.

**Acknowledgments.** This study was funded by the Perspective Study Funding of Nanchang Automotive Institute of Intelligence and New Energy, Tongji University (grant number TPD-TC202211-07).

**Disclosure of Interests.** The authors have no competing interests to declare that are relevant to the content of this article.

# References

1. Cheng, J., Zhang, L., Chen, Q., Hu, X., Cai, J.: A review of visual SLAM methods for autonomous driving vehicles. Eng. Appl. Artif. Intell. **114**, 104992 (2022)
2. Cadena, C., Carlone, L., Carrillo, H., Latif, Y., Scaramuzza, D., Neira, J., Reid, I., Leonard, J.J.: Past, Present, and Future of Simultaneous Localization and Mapping: Toward the Robust-Perception Age. IEEE Trans. Rob. **32**, 1309–1332 (2016)
3. Cvišić, I., Marković, I., Petrović, I.: SOFT2: Stereo Visual Odometry for Road Vehicles Based on a Point-to-Epipolar-Line Metric. IEEE Transactions on Robotics. 1–16 (2022)
4. Zheng, F., Tang, H., Liu, Y.-H.: Odometry-Vision-Based Ground Vehicle Motion Estimation With SE(2)-Constrained SE(3) Poses. IEEE Transactions on Cybernetics. **49**, 2652–2663 (2019)
5. Qin, T., Li, P., Shen, S.: VINS-Mono: A Robust and Versatile Monocular Visual-Inertial State Estimator. IEEE Trans. Rob. **34**, 1004–1020 (2018)
6. Campos, C., Elvira, R., Rodríguez, J.J.G., M. Montiel, J.M., D. Tardós, J.: ORB-SLAM3: An Accurate Open-Source Library for Visual, Visual–Inertial, and Multimap SLAM. IEEE Transactions on Robotics. 1–17 (2021)
7. Wu, K.J., Guo, C.X., Georgiou, G., Roumeliotis, S.I.: VINS on wheels. In: 2017 IEEE International Conference on Robotics and Automation (ICRA), pp. 5155–5162 (2017)
8. Zheng, F., Liu, Y.-H.: Visual-odometric localization and mapping for ground vehicles using SE(2)-XYZ Constraints. In: 2019 International Conference on Robotics and Automation (ICRA), pp. 3556–3562 (2019)

9. Zhou, P., Liu, Y., Gu, P., Liu, J., Meng, Z.: Visual localization and mapping leveraging the constraints of local ground manifolds. IEEE Robot. Autom. Lett. **7**, 4196–4203 (2022)

10. Zhang, M., Chen, Y., Li, M.: Vision-Aided Localization For Ground Robots. In: 2019 IEEE/RSJ International Conference on Intelligent Robots and Systems (IROS), pp. 2455–2461 (2019)

11. Zhang, M., Zuo, X., Chen, Y., Liu, Y., Li, M.: Pose Estimation for Ground Robots: on manifold representation, integration, reparameterization, and optimization. IEEE Trans. Rob. **37**, 1081–1099 (2021)

12. Wu, Z., Wang, H., An, H., Zhu, Y., Xu, R., Lu, K.: DPC-SLAM: discrete Plane Constrained VSLAM for Intelligent Vehicle in Road Environment. In: 2023 IEEE 26th International Conference on Intelligent Transportation Systems (ITSC), pp. 1555–1562 (2023)

13. Zhu, Y., An, H., Wang, H., Xu, R., Wu, M., Lu, K.: RC-SLAM: road constrained stereo visual SLAM system based on graph optimization. Sensors. **24**, 536 (2024)

14. Chen, L.-C., Zhu, Y., Papandreou, G., Schroff, F., Adam, H.: Encoder-decoder with Atrous separable convolution for semantic image segmentation. In: Ferrari, V., Hebert, M., Sminchisescu, C., Weiss, Y. (eds.) ECCV 2018. LNCS, vol. 11211, pp. 833–851. Springer, Cham (2018). https://doi.org/10.1007/978-3-030-01234-2_49

15. Mur-Artal, R., Tardós, J.D.: ORB-SLAM2: an open-source SLAM system for monocular, stereo, and RGB-D Cameras. IEEE Trans. Rob. **33**, 1255–1262 (2017)

16. Geneva, P., Eckenhoff, K., Yang, Y., Huang, G.: LIPS: LiDAR-Inertial 3D Plane SLAM. In: 2018 IEEE/RSJ International Conference on Intelligent Robots and Systems (IROS), pp. 123–130 (2018)

17. Sturm, J., Engelhard, N., Endres, F., Burgard, W., Cremers, D.: A benchmark for the evaluation of RGB-D SLAM systems. In: 2012 IEEE/RSJ International Conference on Intelligent Robots and Systems, pp. 573–580 (2012)

18. Geiger, A., Lenz, P., Stiller, C., Urtasun, R.: Vision meets robotics: the KITTI dataset. Int. J. Robot. Res. **32**, 1231–1237 (2013)

19. Ferrera, M., Eudes, A., Moras, J., Sanfourche, M., Le Besnerais, G.: OV2SLAM: a fully online and versatile visual SLAM for real-time applications. IEEE Robot. Autom. Lett. **6**, 1399–1406 (2021)

# An MPC-Based Control Scheme for an Aircraft Towing and Taxiing System Under Uncertainties

Weining Huang[1] , Pengjie Xu[1], Tianrui Zhao[1], Wei Zhang[2], and Yanzheng Zhao [1(✉)]

[1] School of Mechanical Engineering, Shanghai Jiao Tong University, Shanghai 200240, China
{waderhuang,xupengjie194105,zhaotianrui,yzh-zhao}@sjtu.edu.cn
[2] School of Aeronautical Engineering, Civil Aviation University of China, Tianjin 300300, China
weizhang@cauc.edu.cn

**Abstract.** The market of the civil aviation industry has witnessed great growth in recent years and it is estimated to continue to boom in the future. However, at the same time, environmental issues are emerging. To mitigate the conflict, in this paper, a control system based on adaptive MPC and extended Kalman filter is designed for the aircraft towing and taxiing (ATT) system in the application of an autonomous tractor in the airport. First, the kinematics model of the ATT system is established, and then, the model is linearized and discretized for the design of the adaptive MPC controller. Afterward, the cost function is designed considering the trajectory tracking accuracy and passenger comfort simultaneously under safe operation conditions. Several constraints including hitch angle constraints and constraints on control inputs and their relative variables are designed to meet the system requirements. The extended Kalman filter is utilized in the control system for counteracting the potential uncertainties. Finally, simulations in two scenarios are conducted to verify the ability of the designed control system to track the reference trajectory and control inputs while resisting uncertainties. The results demonstrate the robustness and effectiveness in operation under uncertainties.

**Keywords:** Adaptive MPC · Extended Kalman Filter · Constraints · Uncertainties

## 1 Introduction

The market of the civil aviation industry has experienced rapid growth in recent years and it will continue to expand significantly in the next decades [1]. However, the prosperity of the industry also leads to massive carbon and other kinds of emissions [2–4], and in fact, large amounts of emissions occur during the landing and take-off cycle, including the taxiing operations on the ground [5,6]. Furthermore, challenges such as airport congestion, excessive time expenditure, and low efficiency have also been identified in aircraft towing and taxiing [7].

Nowadays, to mitigate carbon and other emissions, enhance the operational efficiency and safety of airports, and reduce fuel consumption, some researchers are actively pursuing studies in the field of autonomous aircraft towing and taxiing (ATT)

systems [7–10]. The TU Darmstadt and the TU Braunschweig have jointly launched a project called Zero Emission Taxi Operations, ultimately aiming at developing autonomous tugs for aircraft. An Israeli company, IAD has developed a semi-robotic aircraft tractor called TaxiBot, which is envisioned to realize complete automation in 2030 [9]. Li et al. [10] developed a towing and taxiing system based on pilot mode to overcome the ongoing difficulty of interaction between pilot and tractor driver. As a result, the tractor of the system can operate autonomously in response to the signals from the pilot. Yu et al. [11] studied a double-layer cooperative control strategy combined with autonomous trajectory planning on the towbarless traction system for carrier-based aircraft, and it was validated that the system can improve the overall operating efficiency on deck.

Indeed, research on autonomous towing and taxiing for aircraft exhibits numerous similarities with that of tractor-trailer wheeled robot (TTWR) systems, whose control strategies can be effectively applied to the ATT system. Both TTWR and ATT are underactuated, highly nonlinear systems subject to non-holonomic constraints, making it a challenging problem to control them. Khalaji et al. [12] combined the Lyapunov kinematic control law with a robust adaptive feedback linearizing dynamic controller using the upper-bound estimation of the uncertainties and disturbances, and the obtained results demonstrated the robustness and effectiveness of the proposed control framework. Alipour et al. [13] considered the lateral and longitudinal slip in the dynamics model of the TTWR system, and then applied a sliding mode based robust controller to the system. Jin et al. [14] introduced the concepts of light-of-sight distance and angle, and proposed the universal barrier function according to them. The simulation results demonstrated the exponential convergence nature of the tracking error. In addition to the aforementioned methods, numerous other control techniques like $H_\infty$ control, adaptive sliding mode control, reinforcement learning, and so on also hold significant inspirations for the design of TTWR system control [15–18].

From above, it can be concluded that most studies concentrate on the accuracy of trajectory tracking. However, few of them considered passenger comfort, which is important in the application of the civil aviation industry. Another issue to be addressed is the safety risks resulting from excessive hitch angles, which may give rise to the jack-knife phenomenon and then lead to accidents [19].

MPC is a control strategy based on optimization methods, and it has been widely applied in the field of autonomous control and driving, including systems like TTWR [20–22]. MPC utilizes the system model to predict the upcoming outputs of the system, and then minimize the tracking error within the prediction horizon in every optimization step, therefore its robustness and accuracy of trajectory tracking are ensured. Furthermore, MPC effectively manages system constraints, including system states and inputs, making it an ideal candidate for controller design in the ATT system. Based on the application scenario of the ATT system, namely the nonlinear system and linear constraints, in this paper, adaptive MPC is used for efficient and accurate trajectory tracking. At the same time, by constraining system inputs and hitch angles, passenger comfort and safety are ensured. Besides, to counteract the system uncertainties caused by inaccuracy of sensor measurements and system modeling, the extended Kalman filter is applied to the designed control system.

The main contributions of this paper are as follows: (1) Apply the TTWR modeling method to the ATT system and then the kinematics model of it is derived. (2) Linearize the derived model and then design the adaptive MPC for it, considering several system constraints including control inputs and hitch angles. (3) An MPC-based control framework is constructed with the application of the extended Kalman filter, and then the simulations are carried out under uncertainties.

The remainder of the paper is organized as follows: In Sec.2, the kinematics model of the ATT system is constructed. In Sec.3, the structure of the control system is established and the MPC-based controller is designed. In Sec.4, the simulation experiments show the robustness and effectiveness of the proposed control scheme, and then in Sec.5, the work is summarized.

## 2  System Description

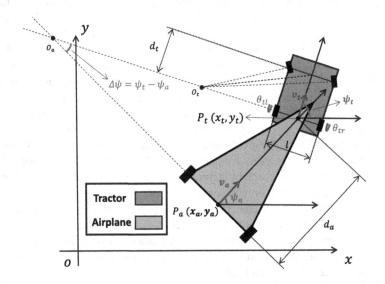

**Fig. 1.** Schematic diagram of the ATT system

The schematic diagram of the aircraft ATT system is demonstrated in Fig. 1, including the tractor, which provides system power, and the aircraft being towed without a power source. Here, it is assumed that the system is operating at a relatively low speed and subject to non-slip conditions, and therefore, the kinematics model can represent the system well [23].

The tractor is considered to follow 100% Ackerman steering geometry, so The steering center of all wheels is located at $O_t$ on the extension of the tractor's rear axle. The aircraft itself is simply considered a tricycle model, whose steering center is $O_a$. $P_t$ is the middle point of the tractor's rear axle and it is also where the aircraft and the tractor are connected. $P_a$ is the middle point of the aircraft's rear landing gear, and the distance between $P_t$ and $P_a$ is represented as $d_a$.

## 2.1 Kinematics Model

The system kinematic equations can be derived as

$$\begin{cases} \dot{x}_a = v_t \cos(\psi_t - \psi_a)\cos\psi_a \\ \dot{y}_a = v_t \cos(\psi_t - \psi_a)\sin\psi_a \\ \dot{\psi}_t = \omega_t \\ \dot{\psi}_a = \frac{v_t}{d_a}\sin(\psi_t - \psi_a) \end{cases} \tag{1}$$

where $(x_a, y_a) \in R^2$ is the coordinate of point $P_a$ in the inertia frame, $\psi_t$ and $\psi_a$ are respectively the orientation of the tractor and the aircraft. $v_t$ and $\omega_t$ are taken as system input, representing the linear and angular velocity of the tractor. In a compact form, the kinematics model can be written as follows

$$\dot{\zeta} = S(\zeta)u = \begin{bmatrix} \cos(\psi_t - \psi_a)\cos\psi_a & 0 \\ \cos(\psi_t - \psi_a)\sin\psi_a & 0 \\ 0 & 1 \\ \frac{\sin(\psi_t - \psi_a)}{d_a} & 0 \end{bmatrix} \begin{bmatrix} v_t \\ \omega_t \end{bmatrix} \tag{2}$$

Here, we consider $\zeta(t) = [x_a, y_a, \psi_t, \psi_a]^T \in R^4$ as the system state vector, while $u(t) = [v_t, \omega_t]^T \in R^2$ as the system input vector. More specifically, the system inputs can be calculated as follows

$$\begin{cases} u_1 = v_t = \frac{r}{2}(\dot{\theta}_{tr} + \dot{\theta}_{tl}) \\ u_2 = \dot{\psi}_t = \omega_t = \frac{r}{l}(\dot{\theta}_{tr} - \dot{\theta}_{tl}) \end{cases} \tag{3}$$

where $\theta_{tl}$ and $\theta_{tr}$ are each the angular velocity of the left and right wheel of the tractor. $r$ is the radius of the tractor's wheels and $l$ represents the tractor's width as shown in Fig. 1.

Moreover, $(x_t, y_t) \in R^2$ is the coordinate of $P_t$ in the inertia frame, it can be easily obtained that

$$\begin{cases} x_t = x_a + d_a\cos\psi_a \\ y_t = y_a + d_a\sin\psi_a \end{cases} \tag{4}$$

# 3  MPC-Based Control System Design

The core control objective is to track a given reference trajectory for point $P_a$, and then, to ensure trajectory tracking accuracy, passenger comfort, and safety under the system uncertainties, the control system is designed as shown in Fig. 2.

## 3.1 Model Linearization

The linearized model and linear constraints are typically utilized in the design of an adaptive MPC controller. So the nonlinear model (2) can be linearized using first-order Taylor expansion as follows

$$\dot{\zeta} = f(\zeta, u) = f(\zeta_r, u_r) + \frac{\partial f}{\partial \zeta}\bigg|_{\zeta_r, u_r} (\zeta - \zeta_r) + \frac{\partial f}{\partial u}\bigg|_{\zeta_r, u_r} (u - u_r) \tag{5}$$

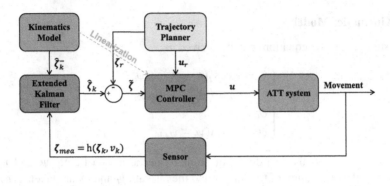

Fig. 2. Block diagram of the control system

where $\boldsymbol{\zeta}_r = [x_{ar}, y_{ar}, \psi_{tr}, \psi_{ar}]^T \in R^4$ and $\boldsymbol{u}_r = [v_{tr}, \omega_{tr}]^T \in R^2$ represent the given ideal state and input of the system, and they should satisfy the system kinematics equations, namely $\dot{\boldsymbol{\zeta}}_r = \boldsymbol{f}(\boldsymbol{\zeta}_r, \boldsymbol{u}_r)$. Define $\tilde{\boldsymbol{\zeta}} = \boldsymbol{\zeta} - \boldsymbol{\zeta}_r$ as the state error vector and $\tilde{\boldsymbol{u}} = \boldsymbol{u} - \boldsymbol{u}_r$ as the input error vector respectively, (5) can be written as

$$\dot{\tilde{\boldsymbol{\zeta}}} = \dot{\boldsymbol{\zeta}} - \dot{\boldsymbol{\zeta}}_r = \left. \frac{\partial \boldsymbol{f}}{\partial \boldsymbol{\zeta}} \right|_{\boldsymbol{\zeta}_r, \boldsymbol{u}_r} \tilde{\boldsymbol{\zeta}} + \left. \frac{\partial \boldsymbol{f}}{\partial \boldsymbol{u}} \right|_{\boldsymbol{\zeta}_r, \boldsymbol{u}_r} \tilde{\boldsymbol{u}} \tag{6}$$

After calculating the partial derivatives about $\zeta$ and $u$, the linearized kinematics model of the system can be derived that

$$\dot{\tilde{\boldsymbol{\zeta}}} = \boldsymbol{A}_0(\boldsymbol{\zeta}_r, \boldsymbol{u}_r)\tilde{\boldsymbol{\zeta}} + \boldsymbol{B}_0(\boldsymbol{\zeta}_r, \boldsymbol{u}_r)\tilde{\boldsymbol{u}} \tag{7}$$

where $\boldsymbol{A}_0(\boldsymbol{\zeta}_r, \boldsymbol{u}_r)$ given in (8) and $\boldsymbol{B}_0(\boldsymbol{\zeta}_r, \boldsymbol{u}_r)$ in (9) are time-variant Jacobian matrices of the kinematics model.

$$\boldsymbol{A}_0(\boldsymbol{\zeta}_r, \boldsymbol{u}_r) = \begin{bmatrix} 0 & 0 & -\bar{v}_{tr}\cos(\psi_{ar}) & v_{tr}\sin(\psi_{tr} - 2\psi_{ar}) \\ 0 & 0 & -\bar{v}_{tr}\sin(\psi_{ar}) & v_{tr}\cos(\psi_{tr} - 2\psi_{ar}) \\ 0 & 0 & 0 & 0 \\ 0 & 0 & \frac{v_{tr}\cos(\psi_{tr} - \psi_{ar})}{d_a} & \frac{-v_{tr}\cos(\psi_{tr} - \psi_{ar})}{d_a} \end{bmatrix} \tag{8}$$

where $\bar{v}_{tr} = v_{tr}\sin(\psi_{tr} - \psi_{ar})$

$$\boldsymbol{B}_0(\boldsymbol{\zeta}_r, \boldsymbol{u}_r) = \begin{bmatrix} \cos(\psi_{tr} - \psi_{ar})\cos(\psi_{ar}) & 0 \\ \cos(\psi_{tr} - \psi_{ar})\sin(\psi_{ar}) & 0 \\ 0 & 1 \\ \frac{\sin(\psi_{tr} - \psi_{ar})}{d_a} & 0 \end{bmatrix} \tag{9}$$

Furthermore, in practical use, the model should be discretized for the design of the adaptive MPC controller as follows

$$\tilde{\boldsymbol{\zeta}}(k+1) = \boldsymbol{A}_{k,t}\tilde{\boldsymbol{\zeta}}(k) + \boldsymbol{B}_{k,t}\tilde{\boldsymbol{u}}(k) \tag{10}$$

where $\boldsymbol{A}_{k,t} = \boldsymbol{A}_0 T_s + \boldsymbol{I}$ and $\boldsymbol{B}_{k,t} = \boldsymbol{B}_0 T_s$, representing the system matrices at the sampling instant $k$, with $T_s$ being system discretization sampling time.

## 3.2 Prediction Equation

The controller is designed for high-accuracy trajectory tracking and smooth control simultaneously. To realize this, a new system state is established as follows.

$$\boldsymbol{\chi}(k+1|t) = \begin{bmatrix} \tilde{\boldsymbol{\zeta}}(k+1|t) \\ \tilde{\boldsymbol{u}}(k|t) \end{bmatrix} \tag{11}$$

where $\tilde{\boldsymbol{\zeta}}(k+1|t)$ represents the state error prediction for time instant $k+1$ at time $t$, and $\tilde{\boldsymbol{u}}(k|t)$ represents the control input error that the system should be applying at time instant k to achieve the best performance.

So accordingly, the new state space equations are established as follows

$$\begin{cases} \boldsymbol{\chi}(k+1|t) = \tilde{\boldsymbol{A}}_{k,t}\boldsymbol{\chi}(k|t) + \tilde{\boldsymbol{B}}_{k,t}\Delta\boldsymbol{u}(k|t) \\ \boldsymbol{\eta}(k+1|t) = \tilde{\boldsymbol{C}}_{k,t}\boldsymbol{\chi}(k+1|t) \end{cases} \tag{12}$$

where $\tilde{\boldsymbol{A}}_{k,t} = \begin{bmatrix} \boldsymbol{A}_{k,t} & \boldsymbol{B}_{k,t} \\ \boldsymbol{0}_{m\times n} & \boldsymbol{I}_m \end{bmatrix}$, $\tilde{\boldsymbol{B}}_{k,t} = \begin{bmatrix} \boldsymbol{B}_{k,t} \\ \boldsymbol{I}_m \end{bmatrix}$. Here, $m = 4$, which represents the dimension of the system's kinematic model, and $n = 2$, which represents the dimension of the control input. Besides, $\Delta\boldsymbol{u}(k|t) = \tilde{\boldsymbol{u}}(k|t) - \tilde{\boldsymbol{u}}(k-1|t)$, is the control error increment.

To simplify the calculation, it is assumed that system matrices remain constant at all time instants during the prediction procedure. That is to say, $\tilde{\boldsymbol{A}}_{k,t} = \tilde{\boldsymbol{A}}_{t,t}$ and $\tilde{\boldsymbol{B}}_{k,t} = \tilde{\boldsymbol{B}}_{t,t}$, $k = t+1, t+2, \ldots, t+N_p-1$. So the prediction equation can be derived as follows

$$\boldsymbol{Y}(t) = \boldsymbol{\Phi}_t\boldsymbol{\chi}(t|t) + \boldsymbol{\Theta}_t\Delta\boldsymbol{U}(t) \tag{13}$$

where $\boldsymbol{Y}(t) = \begin{bmatrix} \boldsymbol{\eta}(t+1|t)^{\mathrm{T}}, \boldsymbol{\eta}(t+2|t)^{\mathrm{T}}, \ldots, \boldsymbol{\eta}(t+N_c|t)^{\mathrm{T}}, \ldots, \boldsymbol{\eta}(t+N_p|t)^{\mathrm{T}} \end{bmatrix}^{\mathrm{T}}$ represents the state prediction vector and $\Delta\boldsymbol{U}(t) = \begin{bmatrix} \Delta\boldsymbol{u}(t|t)^{\mathrm{T}}, \Delta\boldsymbol{u}(t+1|t)^{\mathrm{T}}, \ldots, \Delta\boldsymbol{u}(t+N_c|t)^{\mathrm{T}} \end{bmatrix}^{\mathrm{T}}$ represents computed control vector respectively. $N_p$ is the prediction horizon and $N_c$ is the control horizon. $\boldsymbol{\Phi}_t$ and $\boldsymbol{\Theta}_t$ are given in (14) and (15).

$$\boldsymbol{\Phi}_t = \begin{bmatrix} (\tilde{\boldsymbol{C}}_{t,t}\tilde{\boldsymbol{A}}_{t,t})^{\mathrm{T}}, (\tilde{\boldsymbol{C}}_{t,t}\tilde{\boldsymbol{A}}_{t,t}^2)^{\mathrm{T}}, \ldots, (\tilde{\boldsymbol{C}}_{t,t}\tilde{\boldsymbol{A}}_{t,t}^{N_c})^{\mathrm{T}}, \ldots, (\tilde{\boldsymbol{C}}_{t,t}\tilde{\boldsymbol{A}}_{t,t}^{N_p})^{\mathrm{T}} \end{bmatrix}^{\mathrm{T}} \tag{14}$$

$$\boldsymbol{\Theta}_t = \begin{bmatrix} \tilde{\boldsymbol{C}}_{t,t}\tilde{\boldsymbol{B}}_{t,t} & 0 & 0 & 0 \\ \tilde{\boldsymbol{C}}_{t,t}\tilde{\boldsymbol{A}}_{t,t}\tilde{\boldsymbol{B}}_{t,t} & \tilde{\boldsymbol{C}}_{t,t}\tilde{\boldsymbol{B}}_{t,t} & 0 & 0 \\ \cdots & \cdots & \ddots & \cdots \\ \tilde{\boldsymbol{C}}_{t,t}\tilde{\boldsymbol{A}}_{t,t}^{N_c}\tilde{\boldsymbol{B}}_{t,t} & \tilde{\boldsymbol{C}}_{t,t}\tilde{\boldsymbol{A}}_{t,t}^{N_c-1}\tilde{\boldsymbol{B}}_{t,t} & \cdots & \tilde{\boldsymbol{C}}_{t,t}\tilde{\boldsymbol{B}}_{t,t} \\ \tilde{\boldsymbol{C}}_{t,t}\tilde{\boldsymbol{A}}_{t,t}^{N_c+1}\tilde{\boldsymbol{B}}_{t,t} & \tilde{\boldsymbol{C}}_{t,t}\tilde{\boldsymbol{A}}_{t,t}^{N_c}\tilde{\boldsymbol{B}}_{t,t} & \cdots & \tilde{\boldsymbol{C}}_{t,t}\tilde{\boldsymbol{A}}_{t,t}\tilde{\boldsymbol{B}}_{t,t} \\ \vdots & \vdots & \ddots & \vdots \\ \tilde{\boldsymbol{C}}_{t,t}\tilde{\boldsymbol{A}}_{t,t}^{N_p-1}\tilde{\boldsymbol{B}}_{t,t} & \tilde{\boldsymbol{C}}_{t,t}\tilde{\boldsymbol{A}}_{t,t}^{N_p-2}\tilde{\boldsymbol{B}}_{t,t} & \cdots & \tilde{\boldsymbol{C}}_{t,t}\tilde{\boldsymbol{A}}_{t,t}^{N_p-N_c-1}\tilde{\boldsymbol{B}}_{t,t} \end{bmatrix} \tag{15}$$

### 3.3   Design of Cost Function

To simultaneously guarantee the accuracy of system trajectory tracking and the comfort of passengers on board the aircraft, the cost function for the MPC controller is designed as follows

$$J(t) = \sum_{i=1}^{N_p} \|\boldsymbol{\eta}(t+i|t) - \boldsymbol{\eta}_r(t+i|t)\|_Q^2$$
$$+ \sum_{i=0}^{N_c} \|\Delta \boldsymbol{u}(t+i|t)\|_R^2 + \rho \varepsilon^2 \tag{16}$$

where $\boldsymbol{\eta}_r(k+i|t)$ represents the ideal new state of the system, $\boldsymbol{Q}$ and $\boldsymbol{R}$ are the weight matrices to be designed. $\varepsilon$ is the slack factor designed for ease of computation, and $\rho$ is the corresponding weight. Substitute (13) into (16), it can be derived that

$$J(t) = \|\boldsymbol{Y}(t) - \boldsymbol{Y}_r(t)\|^{\mathrm{T}} \tilde{\boldsymbol{Q}} \|\boldsymbol{Y}(t) - \boldsymbol{Y}_r(t)\|$$
$$+ \|\Delta \boldsymbol{U}(t)\|^{\mathrm{T}} \tilde{\boldsymbol{Q}} \|\Delta \boldsymbol{U}(t)\| + \rho \varepsilon^2 \tag{17}$$

where $\tilde{\boldsymbol{Q}} = \boldsymbol{I}_{N_p} \otimes \boldsymbol{Q}$ and $\tilde{\boldsymbol{Q}} = \boldsymbol{I}_{N_c+1} \otimes \boldsymbol{Q}$, when $\otimes$ stands for Kronecker product. $\boldsymbol{Y}_r(t)$ consists of the ideal new states within the prediction horizon, and obviously $\boldsymbol{Y}_r(t) = 0$. Using (13) again in (17), it can be derived that

$$J(t) = \Delta \bar{\boldsymbol{U}}^{\mathrm{T}} \boldsymbol{H}_t \Delta \bar{\boldsymbol{U}} + \boldsymbol{G}_t \Delta \bar{\boldsymbol{U}} + \boldsymbol{E}_t^{\mathrm{T}} \tilde{\boldsymbol{Q}} \boldsymbol{E}_t \tag{18}$$

where $\Delta \bar{\boldsymbol{U}} = [\Delta \boldsymbol{U}^{\mathrm{T}}(t), \varepsilon]^{\mathrm{T}}$ is the target variable to be optimized, and $\boldsymbol{E}_t = \boldsymbol{\Phi}_t \boldsymbol{\chi}(t|t)$, is the defined system tracking error during the prediction horizon. In practical calculation, the last term is eliminated, which is unrelated to the target variable, and it can be converted to a standard quadratic programming problem. $H_t$ and $G_t$ are given detailed below.

$$\boldsymbol{H}_t = \begin{bmatrix} \boldsymbol{\Theta}_t^{\mathrm{T}} \tilde{\boldsymbol{Q}} \boldsymbol{\Theta}_t + \check{\boldsymbol{R}} & 0 \\ 0 & \rho \end{bmatrix} \quad \boldsymbol{G}_t = [2\boldsymbol{E}_t^{\mathrm{T}} \tilde{\boldsymbol{Q}} \boldsymbol{\Theta}_t, 0] \tag{19}$$

### 3.4   Design of System Constraints

**Hitch Angle Constraints.** To meet the system design requirements, the constraints on the adaptive MPC controller must be meticulously designed. First, the constraints on the hitch angle must be considered due to safety concerns. Define hitch angle as $\Delta \psi = \psi_t - \psi_r$, and the prediction equation of which can be derived as follows

$$\Delta \boldsymbol{\Psi}(t) = [\Delta \psi(t+1|t), \Delta \psi(t+2|t), \dots, \Delta \psi(t+N_p|t)]^{\mathrm{T}}$$
$$= \boldsymbol{D} \boldsymbol{\Omega}_t^{-1} (\boldsymbol{E}_t + \boldsymbol{\Theta}_t \Delta \boldsymbol{U}(t)) \tag{20}$$

where $\boldsymbol{D} = \begin{bmatrix} \boldsymbol{d}^{\mathrm{T}} & 0 & 0 & 0 \\ 0 & \boldsymbol{d}^{\mathrm{T}} & 0 & 0 \\ \vdots & \vdots & \ddots & \vdots \\ 0 & 0 & \dots & \boldsymbol{d}^{\mathrm{T}} \end{bmatrix}$, $\boldsymbol{d} = [0,0,1,-1,0,0]^{\mathrm{T}}$, and $\boldsymbol{\Omega}_t = \boldsymbol{I}_{N_p} \otimes \tilde{\boldsymbol{C}}_{t,t}$.

The constraints on hitch angles during the prediction horizon can be written as

$$\Delta\boldsymbol{\Psi}_{\min} \leq \Delta\boldsymbol{\Psi}(t) \leq \Delta\boldsymbol{\Psi}_{\max} \tag{21}$$

Besides, constraints on the control inputs and their associated variables are taken into account. Here, two scenarios are considered: whether the system is far from its ideal state, and it is judged as follows

$$\begin{cases} \|\boldsymbol{\chi}(t)\| \leq v & \text{Close to Ideal State (CTIS)} \\ \|\boldsymbol{\chi}(t)\| > v & \text{Far from Ideal State (FFIS)} \end{cases} \tag{22}$$

where $\boldsymbol{\chi}(t) = [\tilde{\boldsymbol{\zeta}}(t), \tilde{\boldsymbol{u}}(t)]^{\mathrm{T}} \in R^{m+n}$ as is described previously, and $v$ is the designed threshold.

**FFIS Constraints.** To quickly bring the system back to the trajectory close to the ideal, a moderate deviation from the ideal control input is permitted, so the constraints are designed as follows

$$\begin{cases} \Delta\boldsymbol{u}_{\min} \leq \Delta\boldsymbol{u}(t+i|t) \leq \Delta\boldsymbol{u}_{\max} \\ \boldsymbol{u}_{\min} \leq \boldsymbol{u}(t+i|t) \leq \boldsymbol{u}_{\max} \quad i = 0, 1, \ldots, N_c \end{cases} \tag{23}$$

Here, the value of the input vector itself, $\boldsymbol{u}(t+i|t)$ is constrained to satisfy the actuator constraints, while $\Delta\boldsymbol{u}(t+i|t)$ is bounded to constraint the system acceleration. Also, it can be concluded that

$$\tilde{\boldsymbol{u}}(t+k|t) = \sum_{i=0}^{k} \Delta\boldsymbol{u}(t+i|t) + \tilde{\boldsymbol{u}}(t-1) \quad k = 0, 1, \ldots, N_c \tag{24}$$

Assume $\boldsymbol{u}_r(t+k|t) \approx \boldsymbol{u}_r(t-1)$, it can be derived that

$$\boldsymbol{u}(t+k|t) = \sum_{i=0}^{k} \Delta\boldsymbol{u}(t+i|t) + \boldsymbol{u}(t-1) \quad k = 0, 1, \ldots, N_c \tag{25}$$

Using (25) in (23), and then adding hitch angle constraints (21), the optimization problem can be written as follows

$$\min J(t) = \Delta\bar{\boldsymbol{U}}^{\mathrm{T}} \boldsymbol{H}_t \Delta\bar{\boldsymbol{U}} + \boldsymbol{G}_t \Delta\bar{\boldsymbol{U}}$$

$$s.t, \begin{cases} \Delta\boldsymbol{U}_{\min} \leq \Delta\boldsymbol{U}(t) \leq \Delta\boldsymbol{U}_{\max} \\ \boldsymbol{U}_{\min} \leq \bar{\boldsymbol{L}}_{N_c}\Delta\boldsymbol{U}(t) + \boldsymbol{U}(t-1) \leq \boldsymbol{U}_{\max} \\ \Delta\boldsymbol{\Psi}_{\min} \leq \boldsymbol{D}\boldsymbol{\Omega}_t^{-1}(\boldsymbol{E}_t + \boldsymbol{\Theta}_t\Delta\boldsymbol{U}(t)) \leq \Delta\boldsymbol{\Psi}_{\max} \end{cases} \tag{26}$$

where $\bar{\boldsymbol{L}}_{N_c} = \begin{bmatrix} \boldsymbol{L}_{N_c+1} \otimes \boldsymbol{I}_m & 0 \\ 0 & 1 \end{bmatrix}$, $\boldsymbol{U}(t-1) = \begin{bmatrix} 1_{N_c+1} \otimes \boldsymbol{u}(t-1) \\ 0 \end{bmatrix}$, $\boldsymbol{L}_{N_c+1}$ is a lower triangular matrix of dimension with all elements equal to 1, and $1_{N_c+1}$ is a $N_c + 1$ dimension column vector with all elements equal to 1.

**CTIS Constraints.** Otherwise, when the system is near the ideal states, the deviation from the ideal control input should be constrained, so the constraints are designed below

$$\begin{cases} \Delta u_{\min} \leq \Delta u(t+i|t) \leq \Delta u_{\max} \\ \tilde{u}_{\min} \leq \tilde{u}(t+i|t) \leq \tilde{u}_{\max} \quad i = 0,1,\ldots,N_c \end{cases} \tag{27}$$

The restriction of $\tilde{u}(t+i|t)$ can lead to a smoother trajectory, thereby ensuring passenger comfort. Using (24) in (27), similar to (26), when minimizing the same cost function, the constraints can be written as

$$\begin{cases} \Delta U_{\min} \leq \Delta U(t) \leq \Delta U_{\max} \\ \tilde{U}_{\min} \leq \bar{L}_{N_c} \Delta U(t) + \tilde{U}(t-1) \leq \tilde{U}_{\max} \\ \Delta \Psi_{\min} \leq D\Omega_t^{-1}(E_t + \Theta_t \Delta U(t)) \leq \Delta \Psi_{\max} \end{cases} \tag{28}$$

where $\tilde{U}(t-1) = \begin{bmatrix} 1_{N_c+1} \otimes \tilde{u}(t-1) \\ 0 \end{bmatrix}$.

After solving the optimization problem, a series of control error increments are obtained, namely $\Delta U^*(t) = [\Delta u^*(t|t)^{\mathrm{T}}, \Delta u^*(t+1|t)^{\mathrm{T}}, \ldots, \Delta u^*(t+N_c|t)^{\mathrm{T}}]^{\mathrm{T}}$. However, only the first element is applied to the system, and the actual control input is derived as follows

$$u(t) = \Delta u^*(t|t) + \tilde{u}(t-1) + u_r(t) \tag{29}$$

### 3.5   Application of Extended Kalman Filter

As is shown in Fig. 2, the extended Kalman filter integrates the information from both sensors and the system model, the prior estimation $\hat{\zeta}_k^-$ and the posterior estimation $\hat{\zeta}_k$ of which in instant k is obtained as follows

$$\begin{cases} \hat{\zeta}_k^- = f(\hat{\zeta}_{k-1}, u_{k-1}, 0) \\ \hat{\zeta}_k = \hat{\zeta}_k^- + K_k(z_k - h(\hat{\zeta}_k^-, 0)) \end{cases} \tag{30}$$

where $z_k$ is the measurement value of it. h represents the measurement function and $K_k$ is the Kalman gain matrix given in (31). In practical scenarios, $\hat{\zeta}_k$ is regarded as the observed state of the system and is applied in the adaptive MPC controller.

$$K_k = P_k^- H_k^{\mathrm{T}} (H_k P_k^- H_k^{\mathrm{T}} + V_k R_{\mathrm{mea}} V_k^{\mathrm{T}})^{-1} \tag{31}$$

where $H_k = \frac{\partial h}{\partial \zeta}\big|_{\hat{\zeta}_k^-, v_k=0}$ and $V_k = \frac{\partial h}{\partial v}\big|_{\hat{\zeta}_k^-, v_k=0}$, $R_{\mathrm{mea}}$ is the covariance matrix of the measurement errors. $P_k^-$ given in (32) represents the covariance matrix of the prior estimation.

$$P_k^- = A_k P_{k-1} A_k^{\mathrm{T}} + W_k Q_{\mathrm{pro}} W_k^{\mathrm{T}} \tag{32}$$

where $A_k = \frac{\partial f}{\partial \zeta}\big|_{\hat{\zeta}_{k-1}, u_{k-1}}$ is the Jacobian matrix used in the estimation process, $W_k = \frac{\partial h}{\partial w}\big|_{\hat{\zeta}_{k-1}, u_{k-1}}$ and $Q_{\mathrm{pro}}$ is the covariance matrix of the process errors. $P_k$ given below is the covariance matrix of the posterior estimate.

$$P_k = (I - K_k H) P_k^- \tag{33}$$

# 4  Simulation and Analysis

## 4.1  Simulation Preparation

To validate the effectiveness and reliability of the designed control system, MATLAB simulations are conducted in two scenarios for comparison. The first scenario is the ideal one, assuming that the ATT system operates in a fully deterministic state without any uncertainties. Another scenario is the one where the system works under uncertainties from the sensor, model, and so on, which is much more realistic. In the simulation, the aircraft is a 1:25 scale model of B737 and the tractor is proportionally sized. For both simulation scenarios, the ATT system is to track an 8-shaped reference trajectory, which is obtained as follows

$$\begin{cases} x_r(t) = 5\sin(0.1t) \\ y_r(t) = 5\sin(0.1t)\cos(0.1t) \end{cases} \tag{34}$$

According to the safety regulations of the civil aviation rules, and considering the passenger comfort, the constraints for the adaptive MPC controller are given in Table 1. The parameters for the adaptive MPC controller and extended Kalman filter are given in Table 2.

**Table 1.** Constraints for adaptive MPC controller

| Constraints | Upper Bound | Lower Bound |
|---|---|---|
| $\Delta \boldsymbol{u}(t+i|t)$ | $[0.035(\text{m/s}), 0.20(\text{rad/s})]^\text{T}$ | $[-0.035(\text{m/s}), -0.20(\text{rad/s})]^\text{T}$ |
| $\boldsymbol{u}(t+i|t)$ | $[0.85(\text{m/s}), 0.5(\text{rad/s})]^\text{T}$ | $[0.15(\text{m/s}), -0.5(\text{rad/s})]^\text{T}$ |
| $\tilde{\boldsymbol{u}}(t+i|t)$ | $[0.035(\text{m/s}), 0.02(\text{rad/s})]^\text{T}$ | $[-0.035(\text{m/s}), -0.02(\text{rad/s})]^\text{T}$ |
| $\Delta \psi(t+i|t)$ | $40°$ | $-40°$ |

**Table 2.** Parameters for adaptive MPC controller and extended Kalman filter

| Parameters | Value | Parameters | Value |
|---|---|---|---|
| $N_p$ | 35 | $\rho$ | 5 |
| $N_c$ | 30 | $v$ | 0.1 |
| $\boldsymbol{Q}$ | $\begin{bmatrix} 10*\boldsymbol{I}_{2\times2} & 0 \\ 0 & \boldsymbol{I}_{4\times4} \end{bmatrix}$ | Process Noise Variance | $[0.01, 0.01, \frac{\pi}{1800}, \frac{\pi}{1800}]^\text{T}$ |
| $\boldsymbol{R}$ | $\begin{bmatrix} 1 & 0 \\ 0 & 1 \end{bmatrix}$ | Sensor Noise Variance | $[0.05, 0.05, \frac{\pi}{3600}, \frac{\pi}{3600}]^\text{T}$ |

## 4.2    Simulation Results

**Simulation in the Ideal Scenario.** When the system operates without uncertainties, the simulation results are demonstrated in Figs. 3, 4 and 5, showing the ability of the controller to track the given trajectory. In Fig. 3, the red and blue lines represent the actual paths of $P_a$ attached to the aircraft and $P_t$ mounted on the tractor respectively. The target path, namely the red line highly coincides with the reference path though an initial deviation is imposed on the system, indicating the effectiveness of the controller.

The trajectory errors of 4 state variables are shown in Fig. 4, it is clear that the tracking errors are relatively large in the beginning due to the given initial error, and then, all system state errors tend to converge to 0, proving the robustness and stability of the system. Figure 5 demonstrates the trajectory of control inputs $v_t$ and $\omega_t$, and we can tell from the figure that both control inputs converge to their reference curves after handling with a relatively large error in the beginning, and then, the trajectories both align with the ideal reference ones. And obviously, the control inputs are all within the constrained range, so the operating safety is ensured.

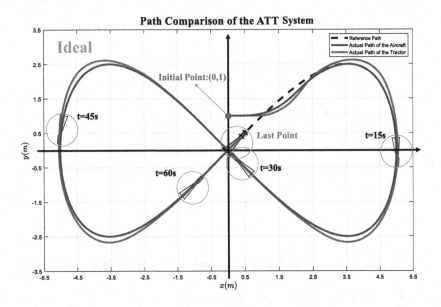

**Fig. 3.** Path tracking results(Ideal)

**Simulation Considering System Uncertainties.** The simulation under uncertainties and interference is more close to reality and of referential value. Figures 6, 7 and 8 demonstrates the obtained results when the system is suffering from uncertainties, which are simulated through random noise. The variance of the noise can be seen in Table 2. It can be observed from Fig. 6 that compared to the ideal situation, the actual path of the aircraft is rather rough due to the random noise, but they still converge to

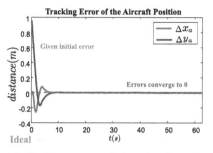

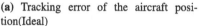

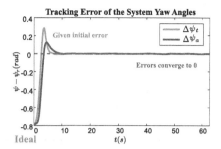

**(a)** Tracking error of the aircraft position(Ideal)

**(b)** Tracking error of the system yaw angles(Ideal)

**Fig. 4.** Tracking error of the system states(Ideal)

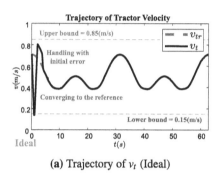

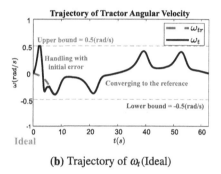

**(a)** Trajectory of $v_t$ (Ideal)

**(b)** Trajectory of $\omega_t$(Ideal)

**Fig. 5.** Trajectory of control inputs(Ideal)

the reference one after the stage of counteracting the initial errors, and the tracking error fluctuates within a certain margin of error, indicating the efficacy and robustness of the control system. Figure 7 shows that the state errors can converge to an acceptable neighborhood of 0 under uncertainties, which further proves the ability of the designed control system to withstand interference.

It can be seen from Fig. 8 that compared to the ideal situation, when the system is compensating for the uncertainties, the trajectory of control inputs will be relatively jagged. However, when the constrained range is satisfied, the control inputs are mostly smooth and in the neighborhood of the reference one. When the system states are far from the ideal ones, the control inputs will strive to return the system to the reference trajectory, after which, the control trajectory will be smooth and accurate, and the system can iterate in this manner while counteracting uncertainties.

### 4.3   Results Comparison Study

Some of the key metrics of the system performance are listed in Table 3 for comparison. First, to verify and quantify the tracking ability of the system, the RMSE for the trajectory is listed. The RMSE in the second scenario is a little higher than the first

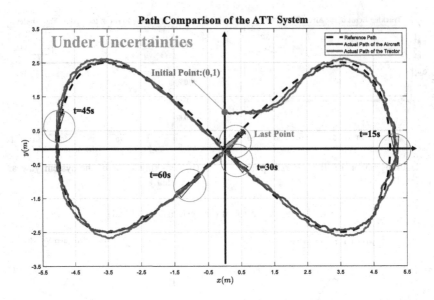

**Fig. 6.** Path tracking results(Under Uncertainties)

**(a)** Tracking error of the aircraft position(Under uncertainties)

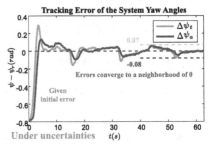

**(b)** Tracking error of the system yaw angles(Under uncertainties)

**Fig. 7.** Tracking error of the system states(Under uncertainties)

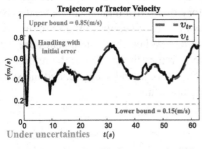

**(a)** Trajectory of $v_t$ (Under uncertainties)

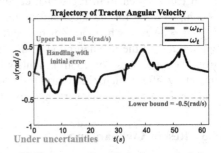

**(b)** Trajectory of $\omega_t$(Under uncertainties)

**Fig. 8.** Trajectory of control inputs(Under uncertainties)

one, however it is still acceptable for the application in the airports. For both simulation scenarios, the hitch angles are always constrained right under the safety threshold. To study the passenger comfort during the operation of the system, the average acceleration and angular acceleration are calculated. In the ideal situation, both the acceleration and angular acceleration are too small to feel. Furthermore, in the second scenario, the average angular acceleration remains the same, and the acceleration is also small enough, indicating that passenger comfort can be ensured. So it can be inferred that the designed system can operate well in reality, when tracking the reference trajectory with a tolerable deviation, and the passenger comfort is guaranteed under safe operations.

**Table 3.** Results comparison

| Parameters | Ideal | Under Uncertainties |
|---|---|---|
| RMSE of Trajectory | 0.1108(m) | 0.1384(m) |
| Max Hitch Angle | $30.96°$ | $31.37°$ |
| Average Acceleration | $0.0510\,(m^2/s))$ | $0.0884\,(m^2/s)$ |
| Average Angular Acceleration | $0.0652\,(rad^2/s)$ | $0.1025\,(rad^2/s)$ |

## 5 Conclusion

The paper designed a control system for the aircraft towing and taxiing (ATT) system in the kinematics level based on adaptive MPC and extended Kalman filter. The cost function is designed for accurate trajectory tracking and a smooth control input trajectory as possible. The hitch angle constraints are designed under safety concerns. The 'Close to Ideal State'(CLIS) constraints and the 'Far from Ideal State'(FFIS) constraints are designed and applied depending on whether the system is far from the ideal state.

Simulations on the ideal scenario and under uncertainties are conducted, and the results verify that the system can track the trajectory effectively with a relatively smooth control input. Although under uncertainties, the system can counter the interference well and the tracking error is within an acceptable range, indicating the robustness and effectiveness of the designed control system.

## References

1. Maksymov, V., Yurchenko, O.: Forecast of demand for aviation maintenance and air navigation specialists for the next 20 years. In: 2018 IEEE 5th International Conference on Methods and Systems of Navigation and Motion Control (MSNMC), pp. 267–270. IEEE (2018)
2. Xiong, X., Song, X., Kaygorodova, A., Ding, X., Guo, L., Huang, J.: Aviation and carbon emissions: evidence from airport operations. J. Air Transp. Manag. **109**, 102383 (2023)
3. Kuzu, S.L.: Estimation and dispersion modeling of landing and take-off (LTO) cycle emissions from atatürk international airport. Air Quality, Atmos. Health **11**, 153–161 (2018)

4.  Soltani, M., Ahmadi, S., Akgunduz, A., Bhuiyan, N.: An eco-friendly aircraft taxiing app-roach with collision and conflict avoidance. Transp. Res. Part C: Emerg. Technol. **121**, 102872 (2020)
5.  Zoutendijk, M., Mitici, M., Hoekstra, J.: An investigation of operational management solu-tions and challenges for electric taxiing of aircraft. Res. Transport. Bus. Manag. **49**, 101019 (2023)
6.  Salihu, A.L., Lloyd, S.M., Akgunduz, A.: Electrification of airport taxiway operations: a sim-ulation framework for analyzing congestion and cost. Transp. Res. Part D: Transp. Environ. **97**, 102962 (2021)
7.  Khammash, L., Mantecchini, L., Reis, V.: Micro-simulation of airport taxiing procedures to improve operation sustainability: application of semi-robotic towing tractor. In: 2017 5th IEEE International Conference on Models and Technologies for Intelligent Transportation Systems (MT-ITS), pp. 616–621. IEEE (2017)
8.  Zoutendijk, M.: Sustainable and data-driven airport operations: Optimisation models and machine learning approaches (2024)
9.  Frank, S., Schachtebeck, P.M., Hecker, P.: Sensor concept for highly-automated airport tugs for reduced emisson taxi operations. In: ICAS. 30th Congress of the International Council of the Aeronautical Sciences. Bonn: ICAS, pp. 1–9 (2016)
10. Li, B., Liu, J., Zhao, Y., Zhang, P., Zhang, W.: An aircraft towing and taxiing system based on pilot control mode. In: 2022 China Automation Congress (CAC), pp. 6206–6211. IEEE (2022)
11. Yu, M., Gong, X., Fan, G., Zhang, Y.: Trajectory planning and tracking for carrier aircraft-tractor system based on autonomous and cooperative movement. Math. Probl. Eng. **2020**, 1–24 (2020)
12. Khalaji, A.K., Moosavian, S.A.A.: Robust adaptive controller for a tractor-trailer mobile robot. IEEE/ASME Trans. Mechatron. **19**(3), 943–953 (2013)
13. Alipour, K., Robat, A.B., Tarvirdizadeh, B.: Dynamics modeling and sliding mode control of tractor-trailer wheeled mobile robots subject to wheels slip. Mech. Mach. Theory **138**, 16–37 (2019)
14. Jin, X., Dai, S.L., Liang, J., Guo, D., Tan, H.: Constrained line-of-sight tracking control of a tractor-trailer mobile robot system with multiple constraints. In: 2021 American Control Conference (ACC), pp. 1046–1051. IEEE (2021)
15. Yao, Q., Tian, Y., Wang, Q., Wang, S.: Control strategies on path tracking for autonomous vehicle: state of the art and future challenges. IEEE Access **8**, 161211–161222 (2020)
16. Ghadiri, H., Emami, M., Khodadadi, H.: Adaptive super-twisting non-singular terminal slid-ing mode control for tracking of quadrotor with bounded disturbances. Aerosp. Sci. Technol. **112**, 106616 (2021)
17. Kassaeiyan, P., Alipour, K., Tarvirdizadeh, B.: A full-state trajectory tracking controller for tractor-trailer wheeled mobile robots. Mech. Mach. Theory **150**, 103872 (2020)
18. Xu, P., Cui, Y., Shen, Y., Zhu, W., Zhang, Y., Wang, B., Tang, Q.: Reinforcement learning compensated coordination control of multiple mobile manipulators for tight cooperation. Eng. Appl. Artif. Intell. **123**, 106281 (2023)
19. Beglini, M., Belvedere, T., Lanari, L., Oriolo, G.: An intrinsically stable MPC approach for anti-jackknifing control of tractor-trailer vehicles. IEEE/ASME Trans. Mechatron. **27**(6), 4417–4428 (2022)
20. Kassaeiyan, P., Tarvirdizadeh, B., Alipour, K.: Control of tractor-trailer wheeled robots con-sidering self-collision effect and actuator saturation limitations. Mech. Syst. Signal Process. **127**, 388–411 (2019)
21. Hewing, L., Kabzan, J., Zeilinger, M.N.: Cautious model predictive control using gaussian process regression. IEEE Trans. Control Syst. Technol. **28**(6), 2736–2743 (2019)

22. Dekkata, S.C.: Model predictive control for unmanned ground vehicles using robot operating system. Ph.D. thesis, North Carolina Agricultural and Technical State University (2021)
23. Karkee, M., Steward, B.L.: Study of the open and closed loop characteristics of a tractor and a single axle towed implement system. J. Terrramech. **47**(6), 379–393 (2010)

# Author Index

Printed in the United States
by Baker & Taylor Publisher Services